Medical Negligence Case Law

by Rodney Nelson-Jones M.A. (Oxon),
Partner in Field Fisher Waterhouse, Solicitors
and Frank Burton B.A., Ph.D., Barrister-at-law

London
Fourmat Publishing
1990

ISBN 1 85190 087 X

First published 1990

© 1990 Rodney Nelson-Jones and Frank Burton
Published by Fourmat Publishing,
133 Upper Street, Islington, London N1 1QP

Printed in Great Britain by
Billing & Sons Ltd, Worcester

Medical Negligence Case Law

Fourmat Publishing

To Nurse Ita Burton
and Dr A Nelson-Jones
Our medical parents

Preface

The 1980s have seen a rapid growth in medical malpractice cases. For example, approximately 185 were awaiting trial in 1988 compared with approximately 35 a quarter of a century earlier. Yet, until recently no modern book has been devoted to medical malpractice; and the various case reports have been scattered far and wide.

Few statutes impinge on the subject. It has mainly developed through its case law, so that is how the authors have sought to explain it. Part I outlines the principles of the law of medical malpractice, by which is meant not only medical negligence but also medical trespass to the person (assault and battery). Part II consists of reports of 320 medical malpractice cases, collated from numerous disparate sources, combining to form the largest published collection of its kind. The Appendix contains the statutory materials.

Part I and Part II have been designed to dovetail into one another. When a medical malpractice case is mentioned in Part I, the page number of the report in Part II is given. Conversely, at the end of each report in Part II is to be found the number of any page in Part I in which the case is mentioned. Ease of reference is also assisted by the case subject index in Part II. Use of this index should direct the reader to all cases involving, for instance, general practitioners or *res ipsa loquitur*, so that anyone with a particular medical or legal concern can study the comparable cases. The overwhelming majority of cases concern the United Kingdom, but a few of the most important foreign cases have also been included.

The authors hope that the book combines human interest and legal enlightenment. Naturally it is intended to be read by lawyers and law students. However, it is hoped that its emphasis on cases and examples will also render it accessible to those in the medical profession who have to deal with medical malpractice cases. The book's aim is to provide all its readers with a statement of general principles of the law supplemented by numerous examples of their practical application.

The authors wish to express their gratitude to Ronald Walker QC, John Finch, Dr Robin Rudd and Dr A Nelson-Jones for reading the draft manuscript and perceptively advising; Mark Antingham, Sonia Khera, Yoshio Kitaarai, Wakar Kalhoro and Dr Dina Dhorajiwala for their diligent and extensive research; Chris Martin and Breige Murphy for invaluable checking and compiling; Nahnah Tettey for her typing; and last but not least to our wives, Caroline Reid and Kusum Nelson-Jones, for their intellectual and other assistance. For any errors that remain, despite such support, the authors are of course solely responsible.

The law is stated as at 1 January 1990.

Rodney Nelson-Jones   Frank Burton
Field Fisher Waterhouse   12 King's Bench Walk

Contents

List of cases in Part I only

page

List of cases in Part II

page

Case report glossary

AC	Appeal cases
All ER	All England Law Reports
BMJ	British Medical Journal
Bing N Cas	Bingham's New Cases
Bulst	Bulstrode's King's Bench Reports
CCLT	Canadian Cases on the Law of Torts
CLY	Current Law Yearbook
C&P	Carrington & Payne's Nisi Prius Reports
Ch	Law Reports, Chancery
DLR	Dominion Law Reports
ER	English Reports
East	East's Term Reports, King's Bench
F	Fraser, Session Cases
F 2d	Federal Reporter – 2nd Series
FCR	Family Court Reporter
F&F	Foster & Finlayson's Nisi Prius Reports
HLR	Housing Law Reports
H Bl	H. Blackstone's Common Pleas Reports
H & C	Hurlston & Coltman's Exchequer Reports
ICR	Industrial Court Reports
IR	Irish Reports (Eire)
The Independent	The Independent
KB	King's Bench (Law Reports)
Kemp & Kemp	"The Quantum of Damages", by Kemp & Kemp
LGR	Local Government Reports
LJKB	Law Journal Reports, King's Bench
LR Ex	Law Reports, Exchequer
LS Gaz	Law Society's Gazette
LTJ	Law Times Journal
Lloyds Rep	Lloyds List Report
MLJ	Medico-Legal Journal
MLR	Modern Law Review
NE	North Eastern Reporter
NI	Northern Ireland Law Reports
NLJ	New Law Journal
P 2d	Pacific Reporter, 2nd Series
PMILL	The Personal and Medical Injuries' Law Letter
Pa	Pennsylvania Supreme Court Reports
Price	Price's Exchequer Reports
QB	Queen's Bench (Law Reports)
SASR	South Australian State Reports
SC	Session Cases
Sc LR	Scottish Law Reporter

SJ	Solicitors' Journal
SLT	Scots Law Times
TLR	Times Law Reports
The Times	The Times
WLR	Weekly Law Reports
WN	Weekly Notes (Law Reports)
WWR	Western Weekly Reports
Wils KB	Wilson's Kings Bench Reports

PART I

General principles of law

Section A: Causes of action

Chapter I

Liability in tort

An act of medical malpractice may give rise to two common law actions in tort. The first, that of trespass to the person, or battery, is of limited significance. The second, that of negligence, forms the basis of most malpractice claims and is the foundation of the modern law determining a medical practitioner's liability to a patient.

1. Battery

A battery is an intentional or reckless unlawful application of force to another person and is a crime as well as a tort at common law. The attempt to apply what is frequently thought of as a criminal doctrine to the act of a physician in the course of treatment of a patient has been strongly criticised by the judiciary. Theoretically many procedures which a doctor performs might be batteries such as injections, surgery, or manipulations, if done without the consent of the patients. The touching of a person in this manner without consent violates an individual's right of self determination of his or her own body and possibly would constitute an act of trespass to the person. The attraction for a litigant to sue in battery is that liability for this tort is strict, and accordingly the difficulties of establishing negligence would be circumvented. Moreover, proof of damage is not an essential part of the cause of action, and liability can be established in those cases where a patient either suffers no physical harm or suffers harm which is not a direct cause of the tort. For example, a woman may consent to relatively minor gynaecological surgery and during the course of the operation the surgeon may find a disease or complication which requires major surgery and may result in sterilisation. The subsequent sterilisation may in fact result in the woman regaining health. She would, however, be able to sue for battery if she could demonstrate that she gave no consent to the sterilisation.

The question of what constitutes consent has accordingly been inextricably connected with the tort of battery. Where litigants have sought to argue that their consent for an operation or a mode of treatment was given on the basis of inadequate information either of the risks of the treatment or of the extent of the treatment, they have sought to sue in battery (cf *Chatterton* v *Gerson*

(1980) (*page 178*); *Sidaway* v *Board of Governors of Bethlem Royal Hospital and the Maudsley Hospital* (1984) (*page 314*); *Hills* v *Potter* (1984) (*page 233*)). The courts, however, have been intolerant of this approach which has been seen as a device to side-step the difficulties in sustaining an action for negligence based on failures to communicate proper information.

In *Hills* v *Potter* (above) the plaintiff sued in negligence and in battery following the failure of an operation to relieve symptoms caused by a deformity of her neck known as spasmodic torticollis. The operation, although performed with skill and competence, resulted in a severe deterioration so that the plaintiff became paralysed from the neck downwards. The plaintiff alleged that she had not been properly informed about the risks inherent in the surgery and that her consent was therefore vitiated by lack of information that paralysis could result. Hirst J found in relation to the action in battery:

> "As to the claim for assault and battery, the plaintiff's undoubted consent to the operation which was in fact performed negatives any possibility of liability under this head, see *Chatterton* v *Gerson*. I should add that I respectfully agree with Bristow J in deploring reliance on these torts in medical cases of this kind, the proper cause of action, if any, is negligence" ([1984] 1 WLR at 653d/e).

In *Chatterton* v *Gerson* (ibid) Bristow J had acknowledged that:

> "It is clear law that in any context in which consent of the injured party is a defence to what would otherwise be a crime or civil wrong the consent must be real" ([1980] 3 WLR at 1012d).

However, consent was judged to be real as long as the patient was informed in "broad terms" of the nature of the intended procedure and no action for trespass to the person would lie. Alternatively, where information was withheld in bad faith the consent could be vitiated by fraud and a cause of action could be sustained. Bristow J also gave a further example in the course of his judgment concerning an unreported case in which a boy was admitted for a tonsillectomy and was in fact circumcised. The judge indicated that in such circumstances an action in trespass would be appropriate. He went on, however, to say:

> "But in my judgement it would be very much against the interests of justice if actions which are really based on a failure of a doctor to perform his duty adequately to inform were pleaded in trespass" ([1980] 3 WLR at 1013b/c).

The Master of the Rolls in *Sidaway* v *Board of Governors of Bethlem Royal Hospital and the Maudsley Hospital* (ibid) adopted a similar position on consent when he expressed the view:

> "I am wholly satisfied that as a matter of English law a consent is not vitiated by a failure on the part of a doctor to give a patient sufficient information before the consent is given. It is only if the consent is obtained by a fraud or by a misrepresentation of the nature of what is to be done that it can be said that an apparent consent is not a true consent. This is the position in the criminal law (*R* v *Clarence* (1888)) and the cause of action based upon trespass to the person is closely analogous" ([1984] 2 WLR at 790a/b).

Similarly, Lord Scarman in the House of Lords in *Sidaway* v *Board of*

Governors of Bethlem Royal Hospital (above) concurred with the general disdain in relying on the tort of battery although he was in a minority in seeking to extend the principles of informed consent and the law of negligence:

> "The doctrine (of informed consent) is new ground insofar as English law is concerned. Apart from the judgment of Bristow J in *Chatterton* v *Gerson*, I know of only one case prior to the present appeal to which an English court has discussed it. In *Hills* v *Potter* Hirst J followed Skinner J in this case, adding a comment with which I respectfully agree, that it would be deplorable to base the law in medical cases of this kind on the tort of assault and battery" ([1985] 2 WLR at 489d/e).

Lord Diplock also remarked in the same case:

> "That as long ago as 1767 in *Slater* v *Baker* (2 WILS 359) (*page 317*) a suggestion where injury was caused by surgery a form of action lay in trespass *vi et armis* was rejected with scant sympathy by the Court of King's Bench" (at 497h).

Those cases alleging improper disclosure of risks inherent in modes of treatment are accordingly discussed in further detail in Chapter 8 which is concerned with actions for negligence or breach of contract in failing to inform a patient of the possible consequences of medical decisions and choices.

It would therefore appear that the tort of battery is limited firstly to those cases where consent is vitiated by fraud or misrepresentation, and secondly to those cases where although there is no misrepresentation there is no consent at all. For example, in *Cull* v *Butler* (1932) (*page 192*) the defendant was held liable for a trespass to the person in circumstances where the plaintiff's specific refusal to consent to a hysterectomy was ignored. Liability was admitted in the cases of *Hamilton* v *Birmingham Regional Hospital Board* (1969) (*page 226*) and *Devi* v *West Midlands Regional Health Authority* (1981) (*page 198*), where sterilisations were undertaken without the consent of the patients. There is no requirement for the touching in question to be hostile as was indicated by the Court of Appeal in *Wilson* v *Pringle* (1987). Lord Donaldson, the Master of the Rolls, applied Lord Justice Goff's reasoning in *Collins* v *Wilcock* (1984) when he stated in *F* v *West Berkshire Health Authority* (1989) (*page 207*):

> "In the absence of consent all, or almost all, medical treatment and all surgical treatment of an adult is unlawful however beneficial such treatment might be. This is incontestable" ([1989] 2 WLR at 1034 g/h).

Lord Goff further indicated in the House of Lords in the same case that:

> "It has recently been said that the touching must be 'hostile' — see *Wilson* v *Pringle* (1987). I respectfully doubt whether this is correct. A prank that gets out of hand, an over-friendly slap on the back, surgical treatment by a surgeon who mistakenly thinks that the patient has consented to it — all these things may transcend the bounds of lawfulness without being characterised as hostile" (at 1083c/d).

Accordingly, whether the touching is hostile (as in *Barbara* v *Home Office* (1984) (*page 156*)) or, as is much more likely to be the case, the medical intervention is done in the supposed interests of the patient the absence of consent will found a cause of action in battery. (See also the transatlantic examples of *Marshall* v *Curry* (1933) (*page 270*) and *Allan* v *Mount Sinai Hospital* (1980) (*page 152*). The most dramatic example is, however, to be found in the case of *Malette* v *Shulman* (1988) (*page 267*) where a doctor was found to have committed a battery upon a Jehovah's Witness by transfusing her blood in circumstances where her consent was not given and it was clear she would have objected if able to do so.)

Particular difficulties may arise in those cases where a patient is unable to consent because of his or her particular physical or mental condition. The law has therefore evolved certain specific principles with reference to consent in the cases of minors, mental patients, and those persons rendered unconscious and requiring emergency treatment. Children have a statutory right to consent to medical treatment when they are aged between sixteen and eighteen years, pursuant to s 8(1) Family Law Reform Act 1969. In *Gillick* v *West Norfolk and Wisbech Area Health Authority* (1986) (*page 217*), the House of Lords ruled that a minor under sixteen did not merely by virtue of age alone lack the legal capacity to consent to medical advice and treatment. Provided that a person under sixteen was capable of understanding the proposed treatment and of expressing his own wishes, a valid consent could be given notwithstanding parental opposition. This particular case concerned the lawfulness of giving contraceptive advice, but the general principle applies to all forms of medical treatment. Each case would therefore turn upon the specific capacity of the child's comprehension. Where a minor is a ward of court there is statutory provision for the court to order medical treatment if it is in the child's best interests. Accordingly in *Re P (a minor)* (1981) (*page 281*), a fifteen year old unmarried mother who was pregnant was allowed to undergo a termination of her second pregnancy notwithstanding her father's opposition to the abortion. Similar principles were laid down in the case of *Re B (a minor)* (1988) (*page 154*) where a mentally handicapped girl under the age of majority, and who was incapable of giving consent, underwent a lawful sterilisation.

In cases of adults who are incompetent within the meaning of the Mental Health Act 1983, there is no statutory power through which the court can give or withhold consent to medical treatment. However, in *F* v *West Berkshire Health Authority* (1989) (*page 207*) the House of Lords determined that the court had a common law power to declare the lawfulness of any proposed operation on a mentally incompetent adult. This case concerned a thirty-six year old in-patient of a mental hospital who was incapable of giving consent because she had a mental age of approximately four and a verbal capacity of a two year old. Those caring for her determined that it would be in her best interests if she underwent a sterilisation because it was most likely that she was having sexual relations and she was not able to co-operate with any form of contraception. The House of Lords concurred with both the first instance judge and the Court of Appeal that the sterilisation in question would not be unlawful if it was necessary in the patient's best interests. The legal justification for determining that such medical treatment without consent on a person who was mentally incompetent did not constitute an assault was argued by analogy with the emergency cases. Where a patient is presented to a medical practitioner in a state of unconsciousness and is accordingly unable to give consent to any medical treatment, the courts have recognized that the care given to the unconscious patient would not constitute an assault. This justification was previously deemed to have been based on a notion of implied

6

consent or because it fell into a category of a generally acceptable form of touching of everyday life (see *Collins* v *Wilcock* (1984)). The true basis was, however, determined in *F* v *West Berkshire Health Authority* (above) to be a mixture of necessity and public interest. The doctor is immune from prosecution for trespass in emergency circumstances because he is acting in the best interests of patients in attempting to save their lives or to ensure improvement or prevent deterioration in their physical or mental well-being. ([1989] 2 WLR at 1067 d-e per Lord Brandon.)

The House of Lords deemed there to be no difference in principle between those cases concerning emergency treatment and those cases arising out of mental incapacity, provided that the medical practitioners were acting in the best interests of the patient (per Lord Goff at 1086a-h). It is, however, likely that in respect of emergency cases the treatment has to be orientated towards the specific emergency. If a medical practitioner deems that there ought to be a further treatment for long-term future well-being, then he will be under a duty to seek consent when the patient is able to provide it. The House of Lords affirmed that the test as to what was in the best interests of the patient was to be the same test in respect of whether any particular form of treatment was or was not negligent, namely whether the doctor acted in accordance with the properly held views of a responsible and competent body of practitioners in the field in question (the so-called *Bolam* test established in *Bolam* v *Friern Hospital Management Committee* (1957) (*page 166*)). Lord Bridge gave the following reason for the same test being applied:

> "Moreover, it seems to me of first importance that the common law should be readily intelligible to and applicable by all those who undertake the care of persons lacking the capacity to consent to treatment. It would be intolerable for members of the medical, nursing and other professions devoted to the care of the sick that, in caring for those lacking the capacity to consent to treatment they should be put in the dilemma that, if they administer the treatment which they believe to be in the patient's best interest, acting with due skill and care, they run the risk of being held guilty of trespass to the person, but if they withhold that treatment they may be in breach of a duty of care owed to the patient. If those who undertake responsibility for the care of incompetent or unconscious patients administer curative or prophylactic treatment which they believe to be appropriate to the patient's existing condition of disease, injury or bodily malfunction or susceptibility to such condition in the future, the lawfulness of that treatment should be judged by one standard not two. It follows that if the professionals in question have acted with due skill and care judged by the well known test laid down in *Bolam* v *Friern Hospital Management Committee* (1957), they should be immune from liability and trespass, just as they are immune from liability in negligence" ([1989] 2 WLR 1064c-f).

2. Negligence

Negligence is the breach of a legal duty of care owed by a defendant to a plaintiff which results in damage caused by the defendant to the plaintiff. That such a legal duty of care is owed by a medical practitioner to the patient has long been recognized in common law (cf *Pippin* v *Sheppard* (1822) (*page 289*), *Pimm* v *Roper* (1862) (*page 289*), *Edgar* v *Lamont* (1914) (*page 203*), *Gladwell* v *Steggall* (1839) (*page 218*)).

This duty attaches to all those who hold themselves out as skilled in medical, nursing and paramedical matters and arises independently of any contractual relationship. A litigant may therefore sue concurrently in contract and in tort. The duty of care is imposed even when a practitioner acts gratuitously in a voluntary capacity (cf the Australian case of *Goode* v *Nash* (1979) (*page 220*)).

The internal structure of the tort of negligence is simple and has proved to be a pragmatic cause of action which has had a flexibility in adapting to changing social circumstances. Its internal component parts require a plaintiff to show first that a legal duty of care was owed to him by the defendant. This normally imposes little difficulty in medical malpractice cases where duties are clearly owed by doctors, nurses, dentists, psychiatrists, radiologists, pharmacists *et al* directly to the patient. In addition there may be owed duties to third parties who are of a sufficient proximity to the patient that a foreseeable risk of detriment to them arises. There is, however, no absolute legal duty for a doctor to volunteer his services to a non-patient stranger, no matter how grave the need for treatment is. The practitioner has no duty in law to act as a good Samaritan. The duty of care is also frequently owed by the treating institution such as a hospital. Institutional liability can arise through a failure in respect of a direct duty owed, such as failing to provide a sufficient number of staff, or failing to exercise care in selecting staff or monitoring the quality of the staff or in supervising the staff, or failing to provide a safe system of health care, or providing dangerous equipment or premises. The institution's duty of care may also be direct in the sense of being a non-delegable primary duty assumed by the hospital when a patient is admitted for treatment. Furthermore, an employing health authority or hospital may be vicariously liable for the negligent acts of its servants and agents (cf *Cassidy* v *Ministry of Health* (1951) (*page 176*) and *Roe* v *Minister of Health* (1954) (*page 301*)).

Secondly, after establishing a duty of care a plaintiff must then demonstrate a breach of that duty. Breach of duty is analysed by examining whether the defendant has fallen below the standard of care deemed appropriate by the courts. Such carelessness has consistently been evaluated by the courts in medical malpractice actions as that which departs from the standard practised and accepted by a responsible body of medical persons skilled in the particular area of medicine in question. The court will be concerned to decide as a matter of fact whether a practitioner has fallen below the ordinary skill of an ordinary competent practitioner exercising and professing to have the particular skill in issue (*Bolam* v *Friern Hospital Management Committee* (1957) (*page 166*)). This criterion is determined in most cases by the courts hearing the expert opinion of medical witnesses giving their views on current modes of accepted practice and the particular level of skill exercised by the practitioner in question. This approach is adopted irrespective of whether the alleged lack of care concerns diagnosis and treatment, failure to furnish sufficient information in respect of various forms of treatment, negligent advice, or failure to establish proper communication between practitioners and between the patient and practitioner. Whether there has been a breach of the standard of care is a matter of fact which requires careful analysis in each case.

Thirdly, the plaintiff must prove that he has suffered damage which was caused by the defendant's negligence. If no damage is proved, there is no cause of action because this is an essential part of the tort. Cases appearing to indicate gross failures on the part of practitioners, such as failing to attend to a patient despite requests can often fail at this hurdle (see the striking facts in *Barnett* v *Chelsea & Kensington Hospital Management Committee* (1969) (*page 158*)). Similarly, it will not avail a patient to prove that a diagnosis made would not have been made by any competent practitioner or that the treatment received was manifestly sub-standard unless the patient can go on to prove that his health deteriorated, or that he suffered some other damage directly caused by the negligence. Often a patient will be faced with evidence that the progress of his disease would have occurred even if the diagnosis and treatment had been competent. In consent cases the patient also has to establish that, if the warning of the risk had been made clear, the operation or treatment would not have been agreed to. These elements of duty and standard of care, breach, proof and causation give rise to their own particular body of principles and will be analysed separately in the following chapters.

3. Vicarious liability

Vicarious liability arises when the law holds one person or institution responsible for the tortious actions of another even though there is no misconduct or blame on that person or institution. The prime example of vicarious liability is that of an employer being held liable for the torts of an employee. In very limited circumstances, the courts will hold employers liable for the torts of independent contractors and agents employed by them. However, the predominant principle is that an employer is not to be held liable for the acts of an independent contractor. A practitioner is obviously responsible in law for his own actions and will be liable personally if found to have caused damage by negligence. From the viewpoint of a plaintiff there are advantages in suing an employing authority. In the case of a hospital, a patient may be unable precisely to define which member of the medical team was in fact responsible for the particular negligent act or acts. In suing the employer who is responsible for the acts of all the team, this difficulty no longer arises. Moreover, although hospital doctors are required by the terms of their contract to be insured and are insured with either the Medical Defence Union or the Medical Protection Society, many paramedical practitioners in hospitals and most nurses are not required to be insured. There is also nothing to stop a plaintiff suing more than one party such as the health authority and any named doctor, although there is no clear benefit in doing this. It can be beneficial in some circumstances to sue two parties who are both good for the damages as this can increase the prospects of a settlement. However, naming the doctor in the action can possibly increase his determination to defend what he is likely to perceive as an assault on his reputation. One employee is not vicariously liable for the acts of another and accordingly a consultant is not vicariously liable for the acts of his registrars (cf *Rosen* v *Edgar* (1986) (*page 302*)).

With regard to general practitioners, there is little scope for bringing in another party because the general practitioner is not the employee of the Family Practitioner Committee. The G.P. is deemed to be employed on a contract for services, not a contract of service, and no vicarious liability arises in this situation. The general practitioner is an independent contractor to this extent. If, however, a doctor practises in partnership, his partners will also be liable for the torts of a fellow partner (s 10 Partnership Act 1890). The liability of each partner for the other's negligence also extends to the negligence of the partnership's staff. A general practitioner and his partners will therefore be liable for the acts of their employees, such as receptionists and other members of staff who provide auxiliary services. It is unlikely that a general practitioner would be held liable for the negligent acts of a locum general practitioner unless it could be demonstrated that there was negligence in appointing the locum or in failing to provide him with proper information. In such a case the liability would be primary not vicarious.

Initially the courts sought to refrain from imposing liability on hospitals for negligent acts done by skilled personnel, which included nursing and medical staff, during the course of their employment. The hospitals were successful in putting forward an argument that they themselves did not undertake to perform the treatment but only to put the patient into the hands of employees with particular skills. Surgeons and other skilled personnel were deemed to exercise their calling independent of any control by any hospital and were accordingly employed on a contract for services but not of services (cf *Strangways-Lesmere* v *Clayton* (1936) (*page 323*), *Davis* v *LCC* (1914) (*page 196*), *Evans* v *Liverpool Corporation* (1906), *Marshall* v *County Council of Lindsey, Lincolnshire* (1937) (*page 269*)).

In 1942 the courts began to accept the principle of vicarious liability more readily in the area of health care. In *Gold* v *Essex County Council* (1942) (*page 218*), an infant plaintiff, represented by A.D. Denning KC (later Master of the Rolls), brought an action for damages arising out of a facial injury due to the negligence of a radiographer in failing to screen the child properly. At first instance the judge held that the authority was not liable for the radiographer who fell into the same category as nurses who exercised their skills independently of the direct control of the hospital. The Court of Appeal accepted the arguments of counsel for the plaintiff that the radiographers and nurses were in fact acting under contracts of service, and the employing health authority was held liable.

With the nationalisation and reorganisation of health care in 1948 came an extension of the vicarious liability of a hospital and health authority to cover that of doctors and surgeons. In *Cassidy* v *Ministry of Health* (1951) (*page 176*), a hospital employing two doctors on contracts of service was found vicariously liable for their negligent care which led to a severe deterioration in the plaintiff's condition of Dupuytren's contracture. Lord Justice Denning traced the judicial reluctance to impose liability on hospital authorities and explained it partly as an attempt to prevent charities being burdened with liabilities they could not afford. He went on to express these views:

". . . When hospital authorities undertake to treat a patient and themselves select and appoint and employ the professional men and women who are to give the treatment they are responsible for the negligence of those persons in failing to give proper treatment, no matter whether they are doctors, surgeons, nurses or anyone else. Once hospital authorities are held responsible for the nurses and radiographers, as they had been in *Gold's* case (1942) (*page 218*), I can see no possible reason why they should not also be responsible for the house surgeons and resident medical officers on their permanent staff. It has been said, however, by no less an authority than Goddard LJ in *Gold's* case, that the liability for doctors on the permanent staff depends 'on whether there is a contract of service and that must depend on the facts of any particular case'. I venture to take a different view. I think it depends on this: who employs the doctors or surgeons, is it the patient or hospital authorities? If the patient himself selects and employs the doctor or surgeon as in *Hillyer's* case (1909) the hospital authorities are of course not liable for his negligence because he was not employed by them. Where however the doctor or surgeon, be he a consultant or not, is employed and paid not by the patient but by the hospital authorities, I am of the opinion that the hospital authorities are liable for his negligence in treating the patient. It does not depend on whether the contract under which he is employed is a contract of service or a contract for services. This is a fine distinction which is sometimes of importance but not in cases such as the present where the hospital authorities are themselves under a duty to use care in treating the patient" ([1951] 1 All ER 586d-h).

The basis of this responsibility was explained as partly being determined by the law of agency in the case of *Roe* v *Minister of Health* (1954) (*page 301*). This case concerned consolidated actions by two plaintiffs who had both been rendered paraplegic as a consequence of a spinal anaesthetic administered by a visiting anaesthetist for minor operations on 13 October 1947. No negligence was established in this case but the Court of Appeal held that in principle there was a relationship giving rise to vicarious liability. Denning LJ said:

". . . I think that the hospital authorities are responsible for the whole of their staff, not only for the nurses and doctors, but also for the anaesthetists and the surgeons. It does not matter whether they are permanent or temporary, resident or visiting, whole time or part time. The hospital authorities are responsible for all of them. The reason is because, even if they are not servants, they are the agents of the hospital to give the treatment. The only exception is the case of consultants or anaesthetists selected and employed by the patient himself" ([1954] 2 QB at 82).

It might well be that the doctrine of vicarious liability through the law of agency may be of greater significance in cases of negligent private hospital treatment but perhaps also in respect of the privatisation of aspects of National Health Service care.

It is, however, possible to see in the judgments of Lord Justice Denning a clear attempt to impose a direct non-delegable duty of care on the hospital or health authority which is personal to them and not dependent upon the doctrine of vicarious liability. In *Cassidy* v *Ministry of Health* (1951) (*page 176*) the argument was by analogy with the duty owed by the general practitioner:

"If a man goes to a doctor because he is ill, no one doubts that the doctor must exercise reasonable care and skill in his treatment of him and that is so whether the doctor is paid for his services or not. If, however, the doctor is unable to treat the man himself and sends him to hospital, are not the hospital authorities under a duty of care in their treatment of him? I think they are. Clearly, if he is a paying patient, paying them directly for their treatment of him they must take reasonable care of him and why should it make any difference if he does not pay them directly, but only indirectly through the rates which he pays to the local authority or through insurance contributions which he makes in order to get the treatment? I see no difference at all. Even if he is so poor that he can pay nothing, and the hospital treats him out of charity, still the hospital authority is under a duty to take reasonable care of him just as the doctor is who treats him without asking a fee. In my opinion, authorities who run a hospital, be they local authorities, government boards, or any other corporation, are in law under the self same duty as the humblest doctor. Whenever they accept a patient for treatment, they must use reasonable care and skill to cure him of his ailment. Hospital authorities cannot, of course, do it by themselves. They have no ears to listen through the stethoscope, no hands to hold the knives. They must do it by the staff which they employ, and, if their staff are negligent in giving the treatment, they are just as liable for that negligence as anyone else who employs others to do his duties for him. What possible difference in law, I ask, can there be between hospital authorities who accept a patient for treatment and railway or shipping authorities who accept a passenger for carriage? None whatever. Once they undertake the task, they are under a duty to use care in the doing of it and that is so whether they do it for reward or not. It is no answer for them to say that their staff are professional men and women who do not tolerate any interference by their lay masters in the way they do their work. The doctor who treats a patient in a Walton hospital can say, equally with a ship's captain who sails his ship from Liverpool and with a crane driver who works his crane at the docks: 'I take no orders from anybody'. That 'sturdy answer' as Lord Simmonds described it in *Mersey Docks and Harbour Board* v *Coggins and Griffiths (Liverpool) Limited* (1946), only means in each case that he is a skilled man who knows his work and will carry it out in his own way. It does not mean that the authorities who employ him are not liable for his negligence. The reason why the employers are liable in such cases is not because they can control the way in which the work is done — they often have not sufficient knowledge to do so — but because they employed the staff and had chosen them for the task and have in their hands the ultimate sanction of good conduct — the power of dismissal" ([1951] 1 All ER at 584h, 585a-f).

If this analysis were to be accepted, there are grounds for applying it back to the general practitioner situation. By accepting a patient on to the general practitioner's list, the general practitioner may be deemed to have agreed to provide the patient with treatment and it would be no answer for the G.P. to say that he employed a locum to undertake the tasks.

The argument that the hospital authority has a personal non-delegable duty of care coupled with the doctrine of vicarious liability for servants and agents has been instrumental in establishing the main action in medical malpractice as an action in negligence. Even where there is a direct contractual relationship, as with a private hospital, it is most likely that the hospital will be liable for the actions not only of its employed staff but also for those independent contractors whom it selects and chooses. As indicated, apart from the contention that the hospital will owe this personal duty of care, the hospital clearly owes a direct duty of care concerning such matters as patient surveillance (*Selfe* v *Ilford and District Hospital Management Committee* (1970) (*page 313*), *Thorne* v *Northern Group Hospital Management Committee* (1964) (*page 328*)), dangers from infection (*Evans* v *Liverpool Corporation* (1906), *Heafield* v *Crane* (1937) (*page 231*)), and the provision of proper and safe equipment (*Clarke* v *Adams* (1950) (*page 181*)). In *Wilsher* v *Essex Area Health Authority* (1987) (*page 344*) the Court of Appeal also expressed the view that a health authority which conducted a hospital so that it failed to provide doctors of sufficient skill and experience to give treatment offered at the hospital could be directly liable in negligence to the patient. There was no reason why in principle the health authority should not be liable if its organisation is at fault. Lord Justice Mustill ([1987] 2 WLR at 437) indicated that such liability might arise where junior doctors without sufficient skill or experience were wrongly appointed and were not given sufficient training to be able to comprehend the significance of a monitor giving misleading and dangerous results. The Vice-Chancellor, Sir Nicholas Browne-Wilkinson, said this:

"In my judgement, a health authority which so conducts its hospital that it fails to provide doctors of sufficient skill and experience to give the treatment offered at the hospital may be directly liable in negligence to the patient. Although we were told in argument that no case has ever been decided on this ground and it is not the practice to formulate claims in this way, I can see no reason why, in principle, the health authority should not be so liable if its organisation is at fault: see *McDermid* v *Nash Dredging and Reclamation Company Limited* [1986] QB 965 especially at pp 978–979" ([1987] 2 WLR 465e-g).

It may accordingly be expected that actions based upon a personal non-delegable duty similar to that owed by an employer to his employee and premised upon failures analogous to failing to provide a safe system of work may feature in future proceedings.

Chapter 2

Liability in contract

Actions for medical malpractice are primarily actions based on the tort of negligence. This is firstly because for the majority of patients there is only a weak factual basis for suing in contract. Most patients receive treatment under the National Health Service scheme and there is probably no direct contract entered into between the National Health Service patient and his general practitioner, his treating hospital or his dispensing pharmacist. It is arguable that a general practitioner enters into a contract with a patient when the doctor accepts the patient on to the practitioner's list and the practice sees an increase in remuneration. However, the consideration moves indirectly because it is not paid for by the patient except through taxation (see *Appleby* v *Sleep* (1968) (*page 152*)). The contract of a general practitioner is in fact with the Family Practitioner Committee in his area and is defined and controlled by the NHS General Medical and Pharmaceutical Services Regulations 1974. These regulations do not define the contractual terms between a doctor and a patient but they do have significance in determining the general practitioner's duties towards his patient. In *Hotson* v *East Berkshire Health Authority* (1987) (*page 240*) the Court of Appeal's discussion on the differences between suing in contract and in tort appears to have accepted that there is no contract between a patient and the National Health Service or its staff. This particular action, however, was not initiated in contract.

Secondly, any private patient is entitled to sue concurrently in tort and in contract, and usually will. Often a private patient has not entered into a strictly defined contract with expressly written terms governing the agreement for medical care. The courts have therefore had to construe what the implied obligations were in any given private agreement. In fact the courts have construed the implied contractual duty of care as identical to the duty of care owed in tort. Accordingly, the true nature of medical malpractice actions can realistically be described as medical negligence cases.

There are, however, and will continue to be, differences between the two causes of action. If a doctor expressly agrees to undertake an operation or a course of treatment in a particular way and departs from this agreement then an action for breach of contract on the express term will arise. The litigant will not then be required to prove that the doctor departed from the implied obligation to use reasonable care and skill. However, for a court to find that a doctor did agree to guarantee a result or to refrain from a specific procedure, the term of the contract must be explicit and unequivocal. So an operation performed privately for sterilisation will not be construed in the absence of any express agreement as a contract to render the patient infertile. In *Thake* v

Maurice (1986) (*page 327*) the plaintiff sued for breach of contract, collateral warranty and misrepresentation seeking damages for the fathering of a child after having a vasectomy. The surgeon in counselling the plaintiff had emphasised the irreversible nature of the operation but had neglected to warn the plaintiff that there was a small risk of the operation being naturally reversed. The judge at first instance (Peter Pain J) had held that the agreement was to render the plaintiff irreversibly sterile. The Court of Appeal reversed this finding. The operation, which had been competently performed, was not based upon a guarantee to make the plaintiff infertile but was an agreement to perform a vasectomy using reasonable skill and care (Kerr LJ dissenting). Neill LJ inclined to the view that:

> "I do not consider that a reasonable person would have expected a responsible medical man to be intending to give a guarantee. Medicine, though a highly skilled profession, is not, and is not generally regarded as being, an exact science. The reasonable man would have expected the defendant to exercise all the proper skill and care of a surgeon in that speciality; he would not in my view have expected the defendant to give a guarantee of 100 per cent success." ([1986] 2 WLR at 354 d.)

Similarly, Nourse LJ found that to imply such an agreement effectively cuts across the universal warranty normally implied in such cases, that of using reasonable skill and care, and quoted with approval Slade LJ in *Eyre* v *Measday* (1986) (*page 207*), an action concerning an unsuccessful sterilisation on a female:

> ". . . but in my opinion, in the absence of any express warranty, the court should be slow to imply against a medical man an unqualified warranty as to the results of intended operations, for the very simple reason that, objectively speaking, it is most unlikely that a responsible medical man will intend to give a warranty of this nature." ([1986] 2 WLR at 355 f.)

There is therefore no question of any contractual presumption that because an accident happened in the course of treatment, or a misdiagnosis was made, or a person's expectation from an operation had been dashed by poor results, that any breach of contract has occurred. A litigant must demonstrate a breach of an express term or else it is most likely that the court would imply the normal obligation common to the breach of duty in tort and in contract in medical malpractice actions (cf *Worster* v *City and Hackney Health Authority* (1987) (*page 348*)). Lord Templeman in *Sidaway* v *Board of Governors of the Bethlem Royal Hospital and the Maudsley Hospital* (1985) (*page 314*) has expressed the view that this obligation was originally contractual:

> "The relationship between doctor and patient is contractual in origin, the doctor performing services in consideration for fees payable by the patient. The doctor, obedient to the high standards set by the medical profession impliedly contracts to act at all times in the best interest of the patient . . . At the end of the day, the doctor bearing in mind the best interests of the patient and bearing in mind the patient's right of information which will enable the patient to make a balanced judgement must decide what information should be given to the patient and in what terms that information should be couched." ([1985] 2 WLR at 508e, 509d.)

Whether the implied contractual terms between a doctor and patient are expressed as acting in the best interest of the patient or not, in fact they amount to no more than that which is now implied by statute under the provisions of s 13 Supply of Goods and Services Act 1982. This section provides that in a contract for the supply of goods and service where the supplier is acting in the course of a business, it is an implied term that the supplier will carry out his service with reasonable care and skill. This is in effect a position which has long been recognized at common law (see *Morris* v *Winsbury-White* (1937) (*page 275*), *Shiells & Thorne* v *Blackburne* (1789)). From the doctor's perspective it is not possible to contract out of such a duty where personal injury has been caused by the doctor's negligence; see s 2 Unfair Contract Terms Act 1977.

Where, however, a product is supplied and used in the course of private medical treatment, stricter duties of care may be implied. A term will be implied by s 4(5) Supply of Goods and Services Act 1982 that goods (in medical treatment cases, perhaps such goods as valves, artificial limbs, even possibly blood) supplied under the contract are fit for the purpose for which they are supplied. This area of law is discussed later in connection with the application of the Consumer Protection Act 1987 to health care.

Occasionally an action in contract may have a significance because it does not require, as an action in negligence does, proof of damage as an essential ingredient in its cause of action. However, although this could be crucial in, say, the question of costs at the end of an action, as the Master of the Rolls indicated in *Hotson* v *East Berkshire Health Authority* (1987) (*page 240*):

> "Even in contract, if more than a bare right of action is to be established, the plaintiff must prove a loss of substance and once again, this must be proved on the balance of probabilities" ([1987] 2 WLR at 295 d).

Similarly, the Master of the Rolls indicated that the distinction may give rise to practical importance in the time limitation imposed by law in bringing certain actions. In some cases a cause of action arising in tort, when damage occurs, can arise significantly later than the cause of action in contract which arises immediately on breach.

In *Hotson* v *East Berkshire Health Authority* the Court of Appeal (see Dillon LJ [1987] 2 WLR at 298 g) dismissed the contention that the loss of a chance (in that case the chance of avoiding avascular necrosis) which was capable of being valued should not sound in damages in tort just as much as it could in contract. The Court of Appeal accordingly rejected the argument that there was any significant distinction between the two causes of action in this respect.

In *Lee* v *South West Thames Regional Health Authority* (1985) (*page 257*) the Master of the Rolls, Lord Donaldson, expressed the view, albeit *obiter*, that a patient has an implied contractual right to ascertain what treatment he did in fact receive and accordingly may bring an action for specific performance of that implied term as a way of circumventing discovery and possibly the problems that arise when a defendant claims privilege in respect of certain documents. The case of *Lee* concerned an application for a report which probably indicated that a mishap had occurred during an ambulance trip which resulted in serious injury to an infant plaintiff. The Court of Appeal held that in the particular facts of that case the document was privileged, but the Master of the Rolls went on to say this:

> "We reach this conclusion with undisguised reluctance, because we think

that there is something seriously wrong with the law if Marlon's mother cannot find out what exactly caused this brain damage. It should never be forgotten that we are here concerned with a hospital-patient relationship. The recent decision of the House of Lords in *Sidaway* v *Board of Governors of the Bethlem Royal Hospital and the Maudsley Hospital* (1985) affirms that a doctor is under a duty to answer his patient's questions as to the treatment proposed. We see no reason why this should not be a similar duty in relation to hospital staff. This duty is subject to the exercise of clinical judgement as to the terms in which the information is given and extent to which in the patients' interest, information should be withheld. Why, we ask ourselves, is the position any different if the patient asks what treatment he has in fact had? . . . If the duty is the same, then if the patient is refused information to which he is entitled, it must be for consideration whether he could not bring an action for breach of contract claiming specific performance of the duty to inform. In other words, whether the patient could not bring an action for discovery, albeit upon a novel basis" ([1985] 1 WLR at 850g–851c).

However, in *Naylor* v *Preston Area Health Authority* (1987) (*page 278*) the Master of the Rolls sought to explain that this was not a specific right limited to contract:

"In this context I was disturbed to be told during the argument of the present appeals that the view was held in some quarters that whilst the duty of candid disclosure, to which we there referred, might give rise to a contractual implied term and so benefit private fee-paying patients, it did not translate into a legal or equitable right for the benefit of N.H.S. patients. This I would entirely repudiate. In my judgement, still admittedly and regretfully *obiter*, it is but one aspect of the general duty of care, arising out of the patient-medical practitioner or hospital authority relationship and gives rise to rights both in contract and in tort." ([1987] 1 WLR at 967g-h).

In summary, except in rare cases where a contract to effect a cure or guarantee an outcome or to follow or refrain from a certain method of treatment can be expressly construed, a breach of a contractual duty of care will amount to a breach of a tortious duty of care (cf *Gordon* v *Goldberg* (1920) (*page 221*), *Ruddock* v *Lowe* (1865) (*page 305*), *Walton* v *Lief* (1933) (*page 336*), *Shallard* v *Arline* (1939) (*page 313*), *Hodson* v *Mellor* (1911) (*page 235*)). Given that there may be technical benefits deriving from a contractual cause of action, it will continue to be prudent to sue, if possible, concurrently in contract and tort. Contractual relationships between parties other than the actual patient can, of course, give rise to specific duties of care affecting that patient. Such duties will arise, however, in tort not in contract because the patient is not a party to the contractual arrangement. If, therefore, a doctor agrees to write a medical reference to a prospective or actual employer or to furnish a report for insurance purposes, the doctor will owe the subject of that report a duty of care in tort. (See also the Access to Medical Reports Act 1988.)

Chapter 3

Statutory liability

Certain limited inroads on the fault principle inherent within actions for damages based on negligence and breach of contract have arisen out of the Consumer Protection Act 1987 and the Vaccine Damage Payments Act 1979. Both these Acts have dispensed with the necessity of proving negligence in specific cases of injury and have instigated two statutory causes of action.

1. The Consumer Protection Act 1987

Part I of the Consumer Protection Act 1987 represents the British interpretation of the EC Product Liability Directive (85/374/EEC) and is predominantly the culmination of pressure largely arising out of the extensive legal difficulties that the victims of the thalidomide disaster had in sustaining actions against the pharmaceutical manufacturers of the drug. The often insuperable problems for plaintiffs in establishing the tort of negligence in matters of defective products have long been recognized and particularly with reference to drugs (see the Law Commission (Liability for Defective Products) 1977 Law Com NO 82 CMND 6831, and the Pearson Report, the Royal Commission on Civil Liability and Compensation for Personal Inury 1978 CMND 7054). These reports recommended that a manufacturer's liability for injury caused by defective products should be strict, that is not dependent upon proof of any fault (whether breach of contract or negligence). The implementation of strict liability would obviate the complex, lengthy and expensive enquiries into whether the product in question was foreseeably hazardous, whether the damage that resulted could reasonably have been discovered, whether adequate testing and monitoring had been undertaken, whether the incidence of the defects either in design or in manufacturing would be impracticable or too expensive to alter, and whether there should be different criteria if a litigant sued in contract or in tort. Some of these difficulties have probably been minimised by the provisions of s 1 Consumer Protection Act 1987 which came into force on 1 March 1988 (SI 1987/1680). Section 1 of the Act (reprinted in the Appendix) defines what a product is and includes standard consumer goods as well as raw materials; the definition includes many products encountered in medical treatment processes, whether they be surgical instruments, intra-uterine devices, or drugs. Blood and blood-based materials are probably included in the definition of a product, because by s 1(2)(b) a producer in relation to a product is defined as:

"In the case of a substance which has not been manufactured but has been won or abstracted, the person who won or abstracted it".

18

Moreover, by s 45 of the Act, a substance is defined as meaning any natural or artificial substance, whether in solid, liquid or gaseous form or in the form of a vapour, and includes substances that are comprised in or mixed with other goods. It is therefore arguable that blood and blood-based materials are abstracted products for which, if they are defective (for example, if the blood is contaminated and causes acquired immune deficiency syndrome (Aids) the producer or supplier might be strictly liable. This would have significant importance for haemophiliacs and their spouses who contract Aids following transfusions of infected blood. Legislation in the United States of America has determined that blood should be a service rather than a product and accordingly outside American strict liability legislation. The Pearson Commission (above) did, however, recommend that human blood and organs should be treated as products and the distributors should be liable as the producers (see paragraph 1276).

Section 2 imposes strict liability against the producers of this product and also certain suppliers. Section 2(1) states:

"Subject to the following provisions of this Part, where any damage is caused wholly or partly by a defect in a product every person to whom sub-section (2) below applies shall be liable for the damage".

A plaintiff therefore has to prove that the particular product in question had a defect, that the plaintiff suffered damage, and that that damage was caused by the defect. Accordingly, those particularly difficult questions of causation which can arise when a plaintiff is attempting to prove that he is the victim of the side effects of drugs will still occur. Such drug-affected plaintiffs will have to prove that it was the drug that caused the injury or the exacerbation and not the constitutional disease. An infant plaintiff suing for damage occasioned to it as a foetus will also have to prove that it was the drug rather than a congenital defect which has caused the abnormality (cf *Kay* v *Ayrshire and Arran Health Board* (1987) (*page 251*)). However, on the wording of the Act, it does not appear to be required that the damage was reasonably foreseeable. Also, given the wording of the Act, there would appear to be no impediment to the reasoning of *McGhee* v *National Coal Board* (1973) being applied to the extent that if the product's defect, on the balance of probability, materially contributed to or materially increased the risk of injury, causation will be proved in the absence of clear proof as to what did cause the disease or abnormalities.

Section 2(3) imposes a strict liability upon the supplier of a product in those circumstances where the injured person requests the supplier to identify who the producer of the product was and the supplier is unable to do so within a reasonable time. This liability is not a vicarious liability and, therefore, if the supplier can name the producer, the supplier will escape liability even if the producer is a company in liquidation, or a person who is dead or bankrupt or cannot be traced. This provision can have serious consequences for pharmacists, doctors, nurses and other practitioners who are often the last chain in the link of supply of medicines, drugs and medical aids to the patient. In the case of a hospital, the supplier will be deemed to be the health authority and not the particular member of staff. However, general practitioners and dentists and pharmacists may be directly liable. A pharmacist who mixes his own medicines or drugs before he supplies them would be liable if he could not name the manufacturer of the component parts. A general practitioner who gives a drug to a patient to help alleviate symptoms before the patient can get to a chemist would again be liable for any defect in the product if he could not name the manufacturer or his suppliers. This particular provision of the Act will therefore impose considerable burdens on practitioners to keep very detailed records over a wide range of products. Practitioners will not only need to be able to identify drugs and medicines but also a whole gamut of medical equipment such as needles, syringes, catheters, catgut, dacron grafts, screws, plates, surgical instruments, cardiac pacemakers and even the cement used for artificial joint replacement. Such records will need to indicate the name of the manufacturers and/or the practitioners' suppliers, the date of manufacture and/or supply, the batch number of each item and the date received and dispensed or used.

Section 3(1) of the Act defines a defect and does so in terms of safety:

"Subject to the following provisions of this section, there is a defect in a product for the purposes of this Part if the safety of the product is not such as persons generally are entitled to expect; and for those purposes 'safety', in relation to a product, shall include safety with respect to products comprised in that product and safety in the context of risks of damage to property, as well as in the context of risks of death or personal injury".

The Department of Trade and Industry, in an explanatory note, has indicated in this respect that:

"The safety which a person is entitled to expect raises particularly complex issues in respect of medicinal products and adverse reactions to them. Establishing the existence of a defect in a medicine administered to a patient is complicated by the fact that not only is the human body a highly complex organism but at the time of treatment is already subject to an adverse pathological condition. In order to avoid an adverse reaction a medicine will have to be able to cope successfully with already faulty organs, disease and almost infinite variations in individual susceptibility to the effect of medicines from person to person. The more active the medicine, and the greater its beneficial potential, the more extensive its effects are likely to be, and therefore the greater the chances of an adverse effect. A medicine used to treat a life threatening condition is likely to be much more powerful than a medicine used in the treatment of a less serious condition, and the safety that one is reasonably entitled to expect of such a medicine may therefore be correspondingly lower". (*Implementation of E.C. Directive on Product Liability: An Explanatory and Consultative Note* by the Department of Trade and Industry, 1985.)

It can therefore be reasonably anticipated that what constitutes a defect is likely to be a matter for complex litigation. A drug designed to combat cancer with a known serious side effect in ten per cent of cases might be safe, whereas, a similar incidence of adverse reaction would be unsafe in a drug designed for minor pain relief. Clearly a drug that is harmful only to a foetus would not be defective if proper and adequate warning was given so that no pregnant woman would ever take it. Again a warning might be adequate to make a drug safe in circumstances where it was known that a small percentage of users would have an allergic reaction (see also s 3(2) Consumer Protection Act 1987 and *Product Liability* (Fourmat, revised edition, 1988) by Rodney Nelson-Jones and Peter Stewart, pages 48–52).

A great deal of the effect of strict liability has, however, been removed by the inclusion within s 4(1)(e) of the so-called "development risks" defence:

"In any civil proceedings by virtue of this Part against any person . . . in respect of a defect in a product it shall be a defence for him to show

. . . (e) that the state of scientific and technical knowledge at the relevant time was not such that a producer of products of the same description as the product in question might be expected to have discovered the defect if it had existed in his products while they were under his control".

The relevant time (defined in s 4(2)) is when the product was supplied and not when it was manufactured, so that a producer has a duty to act on knowledge that becomes available in the interim. Obviously the product has to be under the defendant's control. The incorporation of this development risks defence, against the advice of the Pearson Commission and contrary to the position in a number of EC countries, probably means that plaintiffs damaged by pharmaceutical products are not in a much better position than the plaintiffs in the thalidomide, opren or debendox litigation. What the Act does do, however, is to reverse the burden of proof and imposes on the defendant the task of making out the defence. This may well be a benefit, as it requires the defendants to make the running in proving the state of knowledge and research and that the defect was undiscoverable at the time in question. Furthermore, if the defect was in fact discoverable it will be no defence that the cost of discovery would have been disproportionate:

"So far as discovery of a defect is concerned, s 4(1)(e) effectively preserves the principles of negligence law. Only the onus of proof is different. Once a defect is or might be expected to have been discovered, however, the strict liability of s 2(1) applies. The producer cannot plead how difficult or expensive it would have been to have eliminated the defect. If he ought to have discovered it, it will not assist him to show that he manufactured the product to an accepted national or international safety standard. Nor can he rely on traditional practice by others in his industry." (*Product Liability* (Fourmat, revised edition, 1988) by Nelson-Jones and Stewart, page 68.)

Nevertheless one major difficulty that plaintiffs may have under this Act with respect to pharmaceutical products is that the Medicines Act 1968 entrusts the licensing of drugs to the Minister of Health (ss 7 and 35 Medicines Act 1968) who acts on advice given by the Medicines Commission. The Commission has a particular committee known as the Commission on the Safety of Medicines which is specifically concerned with the licensing of new drugs. All licensed drugs will therefore have the authority of approval of the Commission on the Safety of Medicines for their licence which may well be an important criterion in determining the development risks state of knowledge defence.

By s 4(1)(d), a manufacturer or supplier is afforded a defence based upon the fact that the defect did not exist within the product when manufactured or supplied. Defects can, of course, arise out of the mis-handling or storing of products, and hospitals and practitioners may be vulnerable in this respect particularly in connection with, for example, blood and blood-based products. The Act concerns products supplied after 1 March 1988 only (s 50(7)).

By s 6(3), the Consumer Protection Act 1987 applies to the provisions of the Congenital Disabilities (Civil Liability) Act 1976 and therefore affords protection to the unborn child. The Act limits a product's liability to a ten year period from the relevant time of supply. Any injured person must sue within three years of the accrual of the cause of action or from the date of knowledge that he had a cause of action, subject to the court exercising its discretion within s 33 Limitation Act 1980 (see Chapter 13).

2. The Vaccine Damage Payments Act 1979

Although vaccination is not compulsory, the health ministries throughout the United Kingdom have long advocated that children should be vaccinated against certain diseases, particularly tetanus, whooping cough, diphtheria, poliomyelitis, measles, tuberculosis and, in the case of females, rubella. The Department of Health has frequently offered detailed advice to general practitioners with respect to the vaccination programme. In the early 1970s serious concern arose about the safety of the whooping cough (pertussis) vaccine, both from general practitioners and from a group of parents who formed the Association of Vaccine-Damaged Children. Evidence was then emerging that serious and permanent brain damage could follow vaccination and may have been caused by it. As a result of this publicity, the number of children vaccinated for whooping cough fell from 79% to 38% in 1976. The Pearson Commission (above) considered the question of vaccine-damaged children and emphasised the almost hopeless position a victim was in if he attempted to sue in tort. The general practitioner would have a good defence that he was acting in accordance with Government advice and, of course, within the orthodox accepted normal practice of the overwhelming majority of general practitioners. Similarly suing the manufacturers in negligence involved dislodging the argument that the vast majority of children and, accordingly, the whole of society derived benefit. Suing the Department of Health is equally fraught with difficulty. In *Loveday* v *Renton* (1988) (*page 262*) an infant plaintiff who suffered from permanent brain damage after a whooping cough vaccination sued her general practitioner, and on a preliminary hearing on the question of causation failed to establish that the vaccine could cause permanent brain damage in young children. Stuart-Smith LJ found that all four of the suggested biological mechanisms by which the plaintiff sought to explain the link between the vaccine and the brain damage were improbable. The trial judge also went on to indicate that even if there had been a finding of causation in the plaintiff's favour, she would face insuperable difficulties in proving negligence on the part of the doctor or nurse who administered the vaccine. In *Department of Health and Social Security* v *Kinnear* (1984) (*page 198*), Stuart-Smith J indicated that no cause of action could arise out of a policy adopted in good faith on the part of the department, pursuant to the provisions of s 26 National Health Service Act 1946, to make arrangements regarding the immunisation of people against diseases. This action was, however, allowed to proceed on the basis that there were further allegations of an operational nature concerning the Department of Health and Social Security's giving negligent and misleading advice as to the manner and circumstances in which the immunisations were to be performed. When this matter came on for trial, the plaintiff's case collapsed because legal aid was withdrawn following certain advice given to the Law Society.

The Pearson Report (above) had recognized the difficulty that plaintiffs would have in establishing causation, namely whether the febrile convulsions occurred naturally or as a result of the vaccine. The Report recommended that where vaccine damage can be proved to have followed from medical procedures advocated by the Government, then the child should have the right to bring an action in tort on the basis of strict liability against the Government. The Vaccine Damage Payments Act 1979 was a compromise which provided for a lump sum payment of £10,000 to be paid to any person who the Secretary of State was satisfied had suffered severe disablement as a result of vaccine damage. The claimant must have suffered at least eighty per cent disablement from the nominated vaccines contained in s 1 of the Act and must have been injected after 5 July 1948 (when the Health Service came into existence). The claimant must have been vaccinated when he or she was under eighteen except in the cases of rubella or poliomyelitis. The Act also applies to protect an unborn child whose mother had been so vaccinated. The claimant must, however, satisfy the Secretary of State on the balance of probabilities that the damage was caused by the vaccine, and difficult problems of causation can arise. If a claimant is turned down, he has the right to have the case heard by an independent tribunal. The £10,000 limit was increased to £20,000 in July 1985. The obvious criticism of this Act is that such damages bear little comparison to those which would be awarded at common law for an eighty per cent disablement case. The reasoning behind this small incursion into the principle of fault liability was justified on the basis that this particular group of disabled people had acted mainly through their parents on advice from the State in respect of a benefit which was intended for the whole of society. It was thought appropriate, therefore, that the State should be the bearer of the consequences of the risks involved.

Just how difficult the problem of causation can be, even within a no-negligence system of strict liability, is illustrated in the difficulty of the infant plaintiff in *Loveday* v *Renton* (above) with her earlier application for compensation under the Vaccine Damage Payments Act. The child's first application was refused, and on appeal the tribunal did not accept that on the balance of probabilities the vaccination was the cause of her brain damage. The tribunal's decision, however, was quashed by the High Court who ordered a differently constituted tribunal to re-hear the application on the grounds that the tribunal had not given proper reasons and had not considered the possibility that any pre-existing brain damage the infant applicant suffered from may have been aggravated by the PTP vaccine. The second tribunal also refused an award. The High Court again quashed this decision on the grounds of certain evidential and procedural irregularities, but refused to make an order that the tribunal be directed to find a causative link between the vaccine and the damage. The Court of Appeal concurred with this refusal, indicating that there was not sufficient evidence for the court to conclude that the child's condition resulted inevitably from vaccination. The court, however, did express the view that it would not rule out the possibility of directing a tribunal on causation in different cases (*R* v *Vaccine Damage Tribunal* (1985) (*page 295*)).

Conversely, in the Scottish case of *Bonthrone* v *Millan* (1985) (*page 168*) a child was awarded compensation for damage that the vaccine tribunal found was caused by the second dose of a PTP vaccine. The applicant subsequently brought an action in negligence alleging a want of care on the part of the doctor and health visitor in failing to appreciate the adverse reactions of the child following the first PTP vaccination. Lord Jauncey dismissed the action in negligence and in addition indicated that there was no proved causal link between the damage that had occurred and the pertussis vaccine.

Section B: Medical malpractice: general principles

Chapter 4

The duty of care

1. Negligence and contract

Whether a litigant sues in contract or in tort or in both concurrently for damages arising out of alleged medical malpractice, the duty of care imposed by the law of tort will be identical to that implied, in the absence of express terms, in the law of contract. This duty of care adheres to any person who holds himself out as a medical practitioner and is owed not only to patients but also to certain classes of third parties recognized by the law as being so closely and directly affected by treatment or advice that the doctor or other practitioner ought to have had them in mind. In medical malpractice actions, such third parties may be the offspring of women who, while they were pregnant, received treatment which resulted in the so-called wrongful birth of the child, such as in cases of failed sterilisation. In some such cases the child may also be born with disabilities. Where a child suffers a disability due to a tortious act committed on his parents, the common law duty of care has been replaced by a statutory duty of care contained in the Congenital Disabilities (Civil Liability) Act 1976. These duties of care will be examined separately.

It is hardly surprising that a duty of care independent of contract has long been recognized as owed by a medical practitioner to his patient. In *Pippin* v *Sheppard* (1822) (*page 289*) Baron Garrow had no reservation in finding that a wife whose husband had employed a surgeon to treat her had in law a cause of action against the doctor directly:

"To hold to the contrary, would be to leave such persons in a remedyless state. In cases of the most brutal inattention and neglect, patients would be precluded frequently from seeking damages by course of law, if it were necessary, to enable them to recover, that there should have been a previous retainer, on their part, of the person professing to be able to cure them. In all cases of surgeons retained by any of the public establishments, it would happen that the patient would be without redress, for it could hardly be expected that the Governors of an infirmary should bring an action against the surgeon, employed by them to attend the child of poor

parents who may have suffered from his negligence and inattention."
([1822] 11 Price at 409.)

A similar duty was accepted as owed to a ten year old girl whose mother had
contracted with a clergyman, who also practised medicine, to attend upon her
daughter's injured knee (*Gladwell* v *Steggall* (1839) (*page 218*)). In *Edgar* v
Lamont (1914) (*page 203*), Lord Salvesen recognized a similar duty in
Scottish law when he held:

> "It seems to me that the clear ground of action is that a doctor owes a duty
> to the patient, whoever has called him in and whoever is liable for his bill,
> and it is for breach of that duty that he is liable, in other words, that it is for
> negligence arising in the course of the employment, and not in respect of
> the breach of contract with the employer" ([1914] SC at 279–80).

A woman was accordingly allowed to sue in respect of the loss of her finger
allegedly due to the defendant's negligence while treating her under a
contract made with her husband.

The modern law of negligence has extended this duty to all categories of
medical practitioners. It is not necessary for a plaintiff to show that his
case falls into an already proven category of successful actions. All the
plaintiff need establish is that there is a sufficient degree of proximity between
the medical practitioner and the injured or affected person that the
practitioner ought reasonably to have foreseen the risk of that injury or
damage to that person. Such a duty of care will arise to all those who are
treated. Reported cases cover a wide range of medical services: casualty
officers (*Barnett* v *Chelsea and Kensington Hospital Management Committee*
(1969) (*page 158*)); nurses (*Cassidy* v *Ministry of Health* (1951) (*page 176*),
Selfe v *Ilford and District Hospital Management Committee* (1970) (*page 313*),
Sutton v *Population Services Family Planning Programme Limited* (1981)
(*page 324*)); physiotherapists (*Clarke* v *Adams* (1950) (*page 181*)); pharmacists (*Collins* v *Hertfordshire County Council* (1947) (*page 182*)); radiographers
(*Gold* v *Essex County Council* (1942) (*page 218*)); psychiatrists (*Bolam* v
Friern Hospital Management Committee (1954) (*page 166*)); *Landau* v *Werner*
(1961) (*page 254*)); pathologists (*Crivon* v *Barnet Group Hospital Management Committee* (1958) (*page 189*)); gynaecologists (*Clark* v *MacLennan*
(1983) (*page 180*)); dentists (*Fish* v *Kapur* (1948) (*page 210*), *Edwards* v
Mallan (1908) (*page 204*)); anaesthetists (*Jones* v *Manchester Corporation*
(1982) (*page 247*)); general practitioners (*Chapman* v *Rix* (1960) (*page 177*),
Coles v *Reading and District Hospital Management Committee* (1963) (*page
182*)); and surgeons (*Collins* v *Hertfordshire County Council* (1947) (*page
182*), *Ashcroft* v *Mersey Regional Health Authority* (1983) (*page 153*)).

In addition, hospital authorities owe certain duties of care directly to patients
in respect of supervising them so that they do not come to harm (*Hyde* v
Tameside Area Health Authority (1981) (*page 244*), *Gravestock* v *Lewisham
Group Hospital Management Committee* (1955) (*page 221*), *Gauntlett* v
Northampton Health Authority (1985) (*page 216*)).

The hospital authority must also properly supervise its own staff (*Jones* v
Manchester Corporation (1952) (*page 247*), *Wilsher* v *Essex Area Health
Authority* (1988) (page 344)). It must also provide a proper system of
organisation and co-ordination of skilled staff and a proper system of medical
care (*Wilsher* (above), *Cox* v *Carshalton Group Hospital Management
Committee* (1955) (*page 188*)).

Further duties of care are owed to patients to protect them from the risk of infection while in an institution (*Heafield* v *Crane* (1937) (*page 231*)). A general duty is also owed to the public at large as well as to the inmates of prisons in respect of potentially violent patients, to ensure that they are properly segregated or supervised (*Holgate* v *Lancashire Mental Hospitals Board* (1937) (*page 236*), *Ellis* v *Home Office* (1953) (*page 205*)).

The duty of care that is owed obtains throughout all stages of advice and treatment and for certain types of practitioners, such as general practitioners and casualty officers, frequently includes a duty to take on a patient. Giesen (*International Medical Malpractice Law*, Mohr and Martinus Nijhoff, 1988) summarises the medical practitioner's duty of care in the following manner:

"Thus a person who is a medical professional, or holds himself out as ready to give medical advice or treatment, impliedly undertakes that he is possessed of skill and knowledge for the purpose, and when consulted by a patient will owe him a duty of care, namely in deciding whether to undertake the case, in taking a proper case history, in making a careful diagnosis, in properly informing his patient about any proposed treatment or operation and inherent risks of treatment and no treatment, in obtaining the patient's consent to such treatment and in his administration of that treatment or performance of that operation and, at all stages, in answering questions where he knows or ought to know that the patient intends to rely on his answer" (page 81, paragraph 118).

It is also most likely that a practitioner owes a patient a duty to inform him of what treatment he actually did receive as opposed to the treatment he expected to receive (*Lee* v *South West Thames Regional Health Authority* (1985) (*page 257*), *Naylor* v *Preston Area Health Authority* (1987) (*page 278*)). In both these cases the Master of the Rolls, Sir John Donaldson, indicated that a patient probably had an actionable right to find out what actually did occur during any mishap. Certainly part of the duty of care will be to inform a patient if there has been any product left in the patient such as a needle (*Gerber* v *Pines* (1935) (*page 216*)), or where part of a tooth was inhaled by an unconscious patient during dental treatment (*Cooper* v *Miron* (1927) (*page 185*)).

In addition to patients, the practitioner will also owe a duty of care to all those persons who come within the so-called "neighbour principle" espoused in the famous dictum of Lord Atkin in *Donoghue* v *Stevenson* (1932):

"The rule that you are to love your neighbour becomes in law, you must not injure your neighbour; and the lawyers question, who is my neighbour? receives a restricted reply. You must take reasonable care to avoid acts or omissions which you can reasonably foresee would be likely to injure your neighbour. Who then in law is my neighbour? The answer seems to be — persons who are so closely and directly affected by my act that I ought reasonably to have them in contemplation as being so affected when I am directing my mind to the acts or omissions which are called in question" ([1932] AC at 580).

Such a duty will be owed to a paid volunteer who takes part in medical trials (*Halushka* v *University of Saskatchewan* (1965) (*page 225*)). The duty was also conceded in *G* v *North Tees Health Authority* (1989) (*page 214*) as owed to the mother of a child in circumstances where the child had been processed as a victim of sexual abuse because of the negligent contamination of the child's vaginal swab with an adult's. This had led to the child suffering distress and disturbance and also to a nervous reaction in the mother. (See also the non-medical negligence case of *McLoughlin* v *O'Brian* (1983).)

The subject of a medical reference commissioned by a third party such as a prospective employer or an insurer will also be owed a duty of care by the practitioner in the compilation of the report. (cf the Access to Medical Reports Act 1988 which provides a right for the subject of such reports to have access to them.) If a report is commissioned for the legal purposes of assessing damages in a personal injury action, then the doctor who compiles the report will owe the subject a duty of care (*McGrath* v *Kiely and Powell* (1965) (*page 264*)). The position is less clear where a patient is seen in a therapeutic context and is given certain advice which he then acts upon, and under-settles a claim against a third party for damages. In *Stevens* v *Bermondsey and Southwark Group Hospital Management Committee* (1963) (*page 322*), Paull J held that in such circumstances, unless there were special reasons, a doctor was not required to contemplate or foresee any question connected with a third party's liability to his patient.

In the Canadian case of *Urbanski* v *Patel* (1978) (*page 330*), a duty of care was found to be owed to a father who donated one of his own kidneys to his daughter who had had her only kidney negligently removed instead of an ovarian cyst. The father was allowed to recover in respect of his own losses on the basis that it was reasonably foreseeable that he or some other rescuer would come to the assistance of the patient who had suffered on account of the practitioner's negligence. In *Tarasoff* v *The Regents of the University of California* (1976) (*page 325*), a duty of care was imposed upon psycho-therapists with respect to the potential victim of one of their patients. The court determined that in circumstances where the patient had told the psychotherapists of his intention to kill an unnamed girl, who was in fact easily identifiable, then a duty of care was owed to warn the potential victim of the threat. The patient did in fact murder the girl. The psychotherapist's defence that to inform the victim would cut across their duty of confidentiality to the patient was rejected by the court. It was held that the protective function of the privilege of confidentiality ended where the public peril began. In *Gillick* v *West Norfolk and Wisbech Area Health Authority* (1986) (*page 217*), the House of Lords recognized the duty of confidentiality imposed upon a medical practitioner not to disclose information about the patient without consent. There are, however, a number of statutory inroads into this principle whereby practitioners are required by law to give varying degrees of information concerning infectious diseases, drug dependency, abortion, drivers involved in accidents, and persons believed to be engaged in terrorism (see the Public Health (Control of Disease) Act 1984, AIDS Control Act 1987, the Abortion Act 1967, the Misuse of Drugs Act 1971, the Road Traffic Act 1972, and the Prevention of Terrorism (Temporary Provisions) Act 1984).

A medical practitioner is not under a duty to act gratuitously or voluntarily, and accordingly is not required by law to come to the aid of an injured person who is not his patient or who is not presented to a hospital. If, however, a doctor does freely give his services a duty of care will be imposed upon him, as happened in the Australian case of *Goode* v *Nash* (1979) (*page 220*) where a doctor engaged in charity work was required to pay damages for negligent treatment. Conversely, non-qualified persons who hold themselves out as qualified, or claim to have a particular medical or healing skill, owe a duty of care to the person they treat (*Ruddock* v *Lowe* (1865) (*page 305*), *Markham* v *Abrahams* (1911) (*page 269*), *Brogan* v *Bennett* (1955) (*page 170*) and *Sones* v *Foster* (1937) (*page 321*)).

Financial and health policy decisions made by the Secretary of State and the health authorities impose in effect a limit on the duty of care by determining priorities which may affect, for example, the length of waiting lists for operations. The courts have held that although in principle the decisions of the National Health Service authorities are amenable to judicial review, the remedy would only be rarely available. Accordingly, in *R* v *Secretary of State for Social Services and Others, ex parte Hincks* (1979) (*page 295*) orthopaedic patients sought a declaration against the Secretary of State and the hospital authorities that they were in breach of their duties under s 1 National Health Service Act 1977 to promote a comprehensive health service designed to secure improvement in health and to prevent illness because they had been obliged to wait for periods longer than was medically advisable for operations. The court held that it would not interfere with the Secretary of State's duty under the National Health Service Act 1977 unless he had acted in a manner which no reasonable minister would have done. Again, in *R* v *Central Birmingham Health Authority, ex parte Walker* (1987) (*page 293*), an applicant whose child needed an operation was refused leave to judicially review the allocation of resources within the health authority's area because there was no prima-facie basis for saying that the authority had acted irrationally within the meaning of *Associated Provincial Picture Houses* v *Wednesbury Corporation* (1948). The Court of Appeal expressed similar views in *R* v *Central Birmingham Health Authority, ex parte Collier* (1988) (*page 293*), where the father of a child sought leave to judicially review the health authority's failure to operate on his son who was desperately ill and needed surgery. The child was in fact at the top of the waiting list but due to shortage of intensive care beds and nurses he was left for months without an operation. The court emphasised that it had no power to allocate financial resources and there had been no breach of public duty on the part of the authority.

2. The Congenital Disabilities (Civil Liability) Act 1976

This Act implements the recommendations of the Law Commission Report (Cmnd 5709 August 1974) on Injuries to Unborn Children and was intended to clarify the position whether at common law a child had a cause of action for personal injuries sustained to it before its birth. Before the implementation of this Act there was no direct English authority which had extended the duty of care owed by a medical practitioner or other person to a pregnant woman directly to her unborn child. In the thalidomide litigation, such a cause of action was assumed in the case of *Distillers Co (Biochemicals) Limited* v *Thompson* (1971) (*page 199*). However, in the substantive litigation concerning allegations that severe deformities were occasioned to children as a result of their mothers being prescribed thalidomide while pregnant, the issue was not resolved, as a forty per cent settlement between the parties was reached (see *S* v *Distillers Co (Biochemicals) Limited* (1970) (*page 305*)).

In *Williams* v *Luff* (1978) liability was conceded at common law with respect to a child, aged six at the date of the trial, who sustained injuries whilst *en ventre sa mère* when his mother was involved in a car accident. Similarly, in *McKay* v *Essex Area Health Authority* (1982) (*page 265*), the duty owed to the unborn child was conceded.

Section 1 of the 1976 Act, which came into force on 22 July 1976, establishes the right of a disabled child to claim compensation from a person responsible for his disabilities which were caused via a tortious act perpetrated on the child's parent or parents. The tortious act of the mother herself is explicitly excluded by s 1(1) except that a mother is liable to her own disabled child in cases where she committed a tort while driving a motor car (s 2).

The Act applies to all births after 22 July 1976 and the cause of action arises only when the child was born alive. The child, suing by his next friend, must prove that the disability he suffers from, whether a disease, deformity, or abnormality, which may be in the nature of a future predisposition, resulted from what is defined as an "occurrence" as defined in the Act. This occurrence is effectively a tortious act which:

(a)   affected the capacity of the child's mother or father to produce a healthy child; or

(b)   affected the mother's capacity whilst pregnant to produce a healthy child; or

(c)   affected either the mother or the child during birth itself.

The Act retains the fault principle, and therefore the occurrence causing the disability must have been produced by a tortious act against the parent or parents. Such an act could be the negligent prescription of a drug unsuitable for a woman whilst pregnant or, in the case of a father, negligent exposure to substances that caused mutations in the father's sperm. The tort against the parent is to be considered without reference to time limitations imposed by the Limitation Acts, and there is no requirement that the parent suffered any actionable injury. The child's cause of action is extinguished if either or both parents knew in cases where the tort occurs before conception that there was a pre-conception risk of any child conceived being born with disabilities. If, however, the father is the defendant and only he knew of the risk of pre-conception disablement, the cause of action does survive for the child. Therefore a couple knowingly taking a risk of conceiving and bearing a handicapped child as a result of a third party's tort exclude the possibility of their offspring suing the tortfeasor. However, in circumstances which are reasonably difficult to envisage, where the father is the tortfeasor and he alone knows of the risk and does not tell the mother, the child is able to sue the father.

Section 1(5) gives statutory approval to the common law standard of care in ordinary medical negligence actions by providing for a statutory defence, in effect for the medical practitioner, who may have treated the parents:

"The defendant is not answerable to the child, for anything he did or omitted to do when responsible in a professional capacity for treating or advising the parent, if he took reasonable care having due regard to then received professional opinion applicable to the particular class of case, but this does not mean that he is unanswerable only because he departed from received opinion".

This is almost precisely the test laid down in *Bolam* v *Friern Hospital*

Management Committee (1957) (*page 166*) as the proper criterion for the standard of care in medical malpractice actions.

Section 1(6) is now probably otiose in that it provided for liability to the child being excluded or limited by a contract made with the parent. This provision falls foul of s 2 Unfair Contract Terms Act 1977 which precludes any person excluding or restricting liability for death or personal injury resulting from negligence in contractual relationships. Section 1(7) provides a further partial or complete defence equivalent to contributory negligence by allowing a child's award to be reduced to such an extent as the court thinks just and equitable having regard to any share the parents have in the responsibility for their child being born disabled.

It is settled law that just as a mother may sue at common law for damage sustained to her in respect of negligence causing damage to her child as a developing foetus, so too may the living child sue for damages under the statutory cause of action in the 1976 Act in respect of his disabilities. A child's claim, however, for so-called "wrongful life" would not be allowed either at common law or under the Act. In *McKay* v *Essex Area Health Authority* (1982) (*page 265*), a mother and her daughter sued the area health authority's laboratory and a doctor in respect of their joint responsibility which led to the mother being wrongfully informed that she had not been infected with German measles during her pregnancy. The infant plaintiff was born disabled before the Congenital Disabilities (Civil Liability) Act 1976 was passed and the matter was considered at common law although the Court of Appeal expressed their views on the likely effect of the Act with respect to the cause of action in issue. The case concerns only that part of the infant's claim for damages based on the allegation that but for the defendant's negligence she would not have been born at all. This claim was premised on the likelihood that had Mrs McKay been properly tested and properly informed that she had contracted rubella she would have had an abortion. The court struck out that part of the infant plaintiff's claim for damages based upon the fact that she had been born. The child's allegations in this respect were held to be essentially that although she had been born with deformities caused by rubella the defendants were negligent in allowing her to be born alive at all. The Court of Appeal held that although it was lawful for a doctor to help and to advise a pregnant woman with respect to having an abortion in these circumstances, there was no legal duty to the foetus to terminate its life. Such a claim was thought to be contrary to public policy as being an affront to the sanctity of life. It was also thought to pose insuperable problems in quantifying damages as it required the court to indulge in a metaphysic of establishing the value of non-existence over existence. Stephenson LJ said this about the 1976 Act:

> "That enactment has the effect explained by Ackner LJ of depriving any child born after its passing on July 22 1976 of this cause of action. Section 1(2)(b) repeats the same clause of the draft bill annexed as an appendix to the Law Commission Report on injuries to unborn children 1974 (law com. no. 60) (Cmnd 5709), and was intended to give the child no right of action for 'wrongful life' and to import the assumption that but for the occurrence giving rise to a disabled birth, the child would have been born normal and healthy, not that it would not have been born at all: see pages 46 and 47 of the report. I reject Mr Willmer's submission that it did not carry out that intention, which in my judgement, the language of the paragraph plainly

expresses. But the Act went further than the draft bill in replacing, by section 4(5) 'any law in force before its passing, whereby a person could be liable to a child in respect of disabilities with which it might be born'" ([1982] 1 QB at 1178 a-c).

Section 1(2) requires the tortious occurrence to have the effect "so that the child is born with disabilities which would not have otherwise been present" and this, as Ackner LJ indicated, rules out any future claim based upon any right not to be born at all (at pages 1186 h–1187 c). In *C v S* (1987) (*page 174*) and in *Paton* v *British Pregnancy Advisory Service Trustees* (1979) (*page 285*), the court held in a different context that a foetus could not be party to an action as no right of its own could arise until it was born and had a separate existence from its mother. In both these cases the prospective fathers who sought to restrain in one case a girlfriend and in the other a wife from having an abortion were not permitted to bring such an application in the name of the foetus. In addition, the application brought directly on behalf of the prospective fathers was dismissed. In *C v S* the prospective father sought an order restraining his ex-girlfriend from having an abortion on the basis that the pregnancy would constitute a criminal offence. This was dismissed. In *Paton* the court held that the Abortion Act 1967 gave no right to a father to be consulted in respect of a termination of a pregnancy.

The court's denial of a cause of action based upon a duty owed to the foetus of a right not to be born follows the predominant tendency in other jurisdictions to prohibit such a cause of action (cf Giesen at page 104, paragraph 120). The striking out of this cause of action left to be determined the infant plaintiff's claim in *McKay* for damages based upon the pleaded allegations that her injuries would in fact have been less severe had the general practitioner injected the mother with globulins to arrest the damage that had already, and irreversibly, been caused by the rubella. It also left for determination the mother's claim based upon her having to rear a child burdened with serious disabilities. These causes of action and heads of damage for so-called wrongful *birth*, often arising from failed sterilisations, are recognized in law and are considered in the chapters on causation (Chapter 6) and on damages (Chapter 12) (cf *Emeh* v *Kensington and Chelsea and Westminster Area Health Authority* (1985) (*page 205*), *Sciuraga* v *Powell* (1980) (*page 312*), *Udale* v *Bloomsbury Area Health Authority* (1983) (*page 329*), *Thake* v *Maurice* (1986) (*page 327*)).

Chapter 5

The standard of skill and care

1. Introduction

To prosecute successfully an action for medical malpractice either in tort or in contract, a litigant must establish that the practitioner was in breach of his duty of care (that is, he fell below the standard required of him in law). The setting of this standard by the courts has been one of the most crucial legal determinants in deciding the likely prospects of plaintiffs succeeding in proving that the conduct in question amounted to negligence. The courts have set what is essentially a pragmatic standard of care which is flexible to the extent that it mirrors developments within medical knowledge and caters for alterations in modes of acceptable practice. It is also a standard which recognizes that medical treatment is consubstantial with risk, that beneficial guaranteed outcomes cannot be provided, and that the practitioner is not an insurer of success. The judicial formulation and refinement of the standard of care has openly conceded that there are public policy limitations insinuated into the criterion of acceptable practice set by the courts. The natural sympathy to find for a plaintiff who may be seriously disabled and who is most frequently an innocent victim is held in check by the requirement to demonstrate fault to the degree of culpability required. Any substantial inroads upon the fault principle have been seen as requiring legislative and not judicial decisions, creating, as they would, marked effects on the structure of the finance of the insurance markets and the health authorities' budgets. Judicial reservations have also articulated that a raising of the standard of care required would possibly inhibit research and produce modes of treatment which were orientated towards minimising litigation risks rather than being in the true best therapeutic interests of the patient and the community at large. The courts have further frequently recognized the low margin for error in many aspects of medical care where the delicacy and complexity of treatment may mean that even minor lapses can produce calamitous consequences incapable of rectification. It is also likely that there are other unarticulated factors which have had an effect in determining the particular criterion of care required by the courts. Commentators have detected on occasions a certain judicial reluctance to cast aspersions on the high esteem of the medical profession acknowledging the adverse consequences that a finding of negligence may have on a medical career. A more realistic approach may be found in the words of the current Master of the Rolls when, as Donaldson LJ in *Whitehouse* v *Jordan* (1980) (*page 341*), he said:

> "There are very few professional men who will assert that they have never fallen below the high standards rightly expected of them. That they have

never been negligent. If they do, it is unlikely that they should be believed. This is as true of lawyers as of medical men. If the judge's conclusion is right, what distinguishes Mr Jordan from his professional colleagues is not that on one isolated occasion his acknowledged skill partially deserted him, but that damage resulted. Whether or not damage results from a negligent act is almost always a matter of chance and it ill-becomes anyone to adopt an attitude of superiority" ([1980] 1 All ER at 666).

2. Normal orthodox practice

The standard of care that has been the basis of the modern law of medical malpractice was formulated by McNair J in *Bolam* v *Friern Hospital Management Committee* (1957) (*page 166*) in a judgment which continues to be relevant a generation later. The case concerned ECT treatment given to a patient suffering from depression, and the action raised allegations that the doctor had failed to administer a relaxant drug before the electric shock treatment was given, had failed to control the plaintiff's bodily movements during the administering of the shocks and had failed to warn the plaintiff of the risks inherent in the process. The plaintiff suffered fractures as a result of spasms caused by his body. Evidence was adduced at the trial that different doctors adopted different methods and techniques in administering the treatment; some would use a variety of restraining sheets, some would use manual controls and some would use relaxant drugs. The risk of a fracture occurring was perhaps in the order of one in ten thousand. The jury found for the defendants after McNair J had directed them on negligence in the following way:

"The test is the standard of the ordinary skilled man exercising and professing to have that special skill. A man need not possess the highest expert skill; it is well established law that it is sufficient if he exercises the ordinary skill of an ordinary competent man exercising that particular art . . . negligence means failure to act in accordance with the standards of reasonably competent medical men at the time . . . there may be one or more perfectly proper standards; and if he conforms with one of these standards, then he is not negligent . . . he is not guilty of negligence if he has acted in accordance with the practice accepted as proper by a responsible body of medical men skilled in that particular art . . . putting it the other way round, a man is not negligent, if he is acting in accordance with such a practice, merely because there is a body of opinion who would take a contrary view . . . it is not essential for you to decide which of two practices is the better practice, as long as you accept that what the defendants did was in accordance with a practice accepted by responsible persons" ([1957] 1 WLR 586–7).

The House of Lords has affirmed this approach in a number of leading cases, whether they concern questions of treatment (*Whitehouse* v *Jordan* (1981) (*page 341*), *Wilsher* v *Essex Area Health Authority* (1988) (*page 344*)); diagnosis (*Maynard* v *West Midlands Regional Health Authority* (1984) (*page 271*)); disclosure of information and consent (*Sidaway* v *Governors of Bethlem Royal Hospital and the Maudsley Hospital* (1985) (*page 314*)); or in determining the best medical interests of the patient where a person is mentally incompetent to consent (*F* v *West Berkshire Health Authority* (1989) (*page 207*)).

The accepted legal criterion is the average yardstick of the ordinary skilful and competent practitioner conforming to a practice accepted as proper by a responsible body of medical opinion skilled in the relevant areas of patient care in issue. A practitioner is not to be found negligent merely because there is a body of competent professional opinion who would adopt a different approach. An important consequence of this standard is that the court will not be concerned in adjudicating upon conflicts of medical opinion in respect of accepted modes of practice. Moreover, except in very plain cases, it will be for medical experts to give evidence to determine whether a practitioner acted within any one of such accepted modes.

McNair J was justified in indicating to the jury in *Bolam's* case (*page 166*) that the degree of skill in issue had been well established as that of the average ordinary professional and not that of the highest specialist. In *Seare* v *Prentice* (1807) (*page 312*), Lord Ellenborough CJ held that:

> "An ordinary degree of skill is necessary for a surgeon who undertakes to perform surgical operations, which is proved in the case of Wilson, and indeed by all analogous authorities; in the same manner as it is necessary for every other man to have it in the course of his employment" ((1807) 8 East at 352).

In *Lanphier* v *Phipos* (1838) (*page 255*), Tindal CJ expressed the matter particularly cogently when he stated to the jury:

> "What you will have to say is this, whether you are satisfied that the injury sustained is attributable to the want of reasonable and proper degree of care and skill in the defendant's treatment. Every person who enters into a learned profession undertakes to bring to the exercise of it a reasonable degree of care and skill. He does not undertake, if he is an attorney, that at all events you shall gain your case, nor does he undertake to use the highest possible degree of skill. There may be persons who have a higher education and greater advantages than he has, but he undertakes to bring a fair, reasonable and competent degree of skill, and you will say whether in this case the injury was occasioned by the want of such skill in the defendant." ([1838] 8 C & P at 479.)

The historical evolution of this standard of care is also to be found in the cases of *Hancke* v *Hooper* (1835) (*page 226*) and *Rich* v *Pierpont* (1862) (*page 298*). (See also *Professional Negligence* (Sweet & Maxwell, 2nd edition, 1987) by Jackson and Powell at page 291 and *Medical Negligence* (Butterworth, 1957) by Nathan and Barrowclough.)

McNair J in *Bolam* quoted with approval the opinion of the Lord President, Lord Clyde, in *Hunter* v *Hanley* (1955) (*page 243*):

> "In the realm of diagnosis and treatment there is ample scope for genuine differences of opinion and one man clearly is not negligent merely because his conclusion differs from that of other professional men, nor because he has displayed less skill or knowledge than others would have shown. The true test is whether he has been proved to be guilty of such failure as no doctor of ordinary skill would be guilty if acting with ordinary care . . . the standard seems to be the same in England". ([1955] SC at 204–5.)

(See also *R* v *Bateman* (1925) (*page 292*); *Akerele* v *R* (1943) (*page 151*).)

Finally, *Bolam* is instructive for the further direction which McNair J gave to the jury quoting Lord Denning in *Roe* v *Minister of Health* (1954) (*page 301*). The Court of Appeal in *Roe* had affirmed the first instance decision of McNair J. In *Bolam*, McNair J warned the jury that finding for the plaintiff out of sympathy without fault on the part of the practitioner could lead to defensive medicine, by introducing to them Lord Denning's view:

"One final word. These two men have suffered such terrible consequences that there is a natural feeling that they should be compensated. But we should be doing a disservice to the community at large if we were to impose liability on hospitals and doctors for everything that happens to go wrong. Doctors would be led to think more of their own safety than of the good of their patients. Initiative would be stifled and confidence shaken . . . we must insist on due care for the patient at every point, but we must not condemn as negligence that which is only misadventure". ([1957] 1 WLR at 595 in *Bolam*, and [1954] 2 QB at 85–86 in *Roe*.)

It was not, therefore, perhaps surprising that it was Lord Denning in *Whitehouse* v *Jordan* (1980) (*page 341*) who came to emphasise that an error of clinical judgement by a medical practitioner did not of itself amount to negligence. The then Master of the Rolls insisted that the law allowed for errors of judgement which of themselves did not amount to negligence in medical malpractice cases. He warned that there were dangers in imposing too high a standard on doctors, such as juries did in America, causing insurance premiums to soar to meet colossal damages resulting in increased premium fees for doctors and the deterring of persons entering certain branches of the profession:

"In the interest of all we must avoid such consequences in England. Not only must we avoid excessive damages. We must say, and say firmly, that in a professional man, an error of judgement is not negligent. To test it, I would suggest that if you ask the average competent and careful practitioner: 'Is this the sort of mistake that you yourself might have made?' If he says 'Yes, even doing the best I could, it might have happened to me', then it is not negligent. In saying this, I am only reaffirming what I said in *Hatcher* v *Black* (1954) (*page 229*) (a case I tried myself), *Roe* v *Minister of Health* (1954) (*page 301*) and *Hucks* v *Cole* (1968) (*page 241*)" ([1980] 1 All ER at 658 d-e).

The House of Lords, though affirming the Court of Appeal in allowing the defendants' appeal, disapproved of the interpretation made by the Master of the Rolls on the standard of care, and reaffirmed the *Bolam* test. Lords Edmund-Davies, Fraser and Russell expressed the view that to say a surgeon committed an error of judgement was ambiguous and did not indicate whether the surgeon had been negligent or not because some errors were consistent with the due exercise of professional skill while others were so glaringly below proper standards they made a finding of negligence inevitable. The proper test was whether a surgeon had failed to measure up in any respect, in clinical judgement or otherwise, to the standard of the ordinary skilled surgeon exercising and professing to have the special skill of a surgeon. Lord Edmund-Davies was particularly emphatic in his rejection of the "error of judgement" test:

"The principal questions calling for decision are:
(a) In what manner did Mr Jordan use the forceps? and

(b) Was that manner consistent with the degree of skill which a member of his profession is required by law to exercise?

Surprising though it is at this late stage in the development of the law of negligence, counsel for Mr Jordan persisted in submitting that his client should be completely exculpated were the answer to question (b), 'Well, at the worst he was guilty of an error of clinical judgement'. My Lords, it is high time that the unacceptability of such an answer be finally exposed. To say that a surgeon committed an error of clinical judgement is wholly ambiguous, for, whilst some such errors may be completely consistent with the due exercise of professional skill, other acts or omissions in the course of exercising 'clinical judgement' may be so glaringly below proper standards as to make a finding of negligence inevitable . . . doctors and surgeons fall into no special category, and to avoid any future disputation of a similar kind, I would have it accepted that the doctrine was enunciated, and by no means for the first time, by McNair J in *Bolam* . . . in the following words, which were applied by the Privy Council in *Chin Keow* v *Government of Malaysia* (1967) (*page 180*):

'. . where you get a situation which involves the use of some special skill or competence, then the test as to whether there has been negligence or not is not the test of a man on the top of the Clapham omnibus because he has not got this special skill. The test is the standard of the ordinary skilled man exercising and professing to have that special skill'." ([1981] 1 All ER at 276g–277b.)

The degree of skill of a practitioner is to be judged objectively and it is not therefore pertinent that because of lack of experience, ability or knowledge the standard could not in fact have been reached by any particular practitioner (*Jones* v *Manchester Corporation* (1952) (*page 247*)). A novice must recognize his limitations, and seek instructions or refuse to undertake work he is not competent to do. In certain cases it may well be negligent not to obtain a second opinion (*Payne* v *St Helier Group Hospital Management Committee* (1952) (*page 287*)).

The Vice-Chancellor, Sir Nicholas Browne-Wilkinson, in *Wilsher* v *Essex Area Health Authority* (1987) (*page 344*) expressed a different view suggesting that in certain circumstances the standard ought to be subjective. The Vice-Chancellor maintained that a houseman, for example, in his first year after qualifying did not have the skill and experience that he was seeking to learn and gain. Lack of experience could lead to mistakes which could not properly be described as arising out of personal fault but arose out of simply being a novice. The Vice-Chancellor thought that it was a requirement within the law of negligence that there had been some personal fault. This view was *obiter* and a minority opinion. The subjective view has the obvious disadvantage of limiting the rights of a patient to the particular experience of a dcotor. Moreover the court would be faced with the difficulty in establishing any one practitioner's particular degree of skill. It is submitted that any failure to live up to an objective standard should not be premised upon any personal fault or moral blameworthiness. To put it otherwise would make the law of medical negligence capriciously dependent on the subjective skills of any one practitioner and cuts across the principle of objective standards clearly settled in other areas of the law of negligence (cf *Nettleship* v *Weston* (1971), *Roberts* v *Ramsbottom* (1980)).

An objective standard, therefore, makes no allowance for any particular practitioner being either physically or mentally ill (*Crompton* v *General Medical Council No. 2* (1985); *Nickolls* v *Ministry of Health* (1955) (*page 280*)). The standard of care is to be construed in the light of the status of the position held and not the personality holding it. It is therefore reasonable to invoke a higher standard for a specialist over and above a general practitioner and for a consultant over a house surgeon (*Junor* v *McNicol* (1959) (*page 248*), *Langley* v *Campbell* (1975) (*page 255*)). A specialist is to be judged by the standards of that speciality (*Maynard* v *West Midlands Regional Health Authority* (1984) (*page 271*), *Sidaway* v *Board of Governors of the Bethlem Royal Hospital and the Maudsley Hospital* (1985) (*page 314*)). The more skilled a position that a person holds, the more that will be demanded of him (*Ashcroft* v *Mersey Regional Health Authority* [1983] 2 All ER at 247 c-e) (*page 153*)).

The standard invoked at the trial is the standard that is obtained at the time of the consultation or treatment and therefore is without consideration of developments in practice and knowledge during the interim between the incident and the trial. Denning LJ in *Roe* v *Minister of Health* (1954) (*page 301*) expressed the view that:

> "We must not look at the 1947 accident with 1954 spectacles" ([1954] 2 QB at 84).

Similar principles governed the finding of negligence in *Hopley* v *British Transport Commission* (1960) (*page 238*) and the finding of no negligence in *Gale* v *Cowie* (1965) (*page 215*). It will be incumbent upon a practitioner to keep abreast of advances in knowledge and technique within his area of expertise as they become disseminated through the medical journals. The standard of care would not however require him to be cognisant with every such article and it is likely that a reasonable time would be allowed for the dissemination and acceptance of knowledge and techniques (*Crawford* v *Board of Governors of Charing Cross Hospital* (1953) (*page 188*)).

It is therefore most unlikely that adherence to an orthodox mode of practice would ever result in a practitioner being found to have been negligent. The courts have indicated that in principle the orthodox practice must be a proper practice but in fact there has been a judicial reluctance to impinge upon areas which are seen as essentially matters of medical competence. In *Sidaway* v *Board of Governors of the Bethlem Royal Hospital and the Maudsley Hospital* (1984) (*page 314*) the Master of the Rolls accepted that the *Bolam* test was applicable in cases such as Mrs Sidaway's when the court was concerned to examine a failure of a surgeon to mention a one to two per cent risk that an operation could result in spinal cord damage. Evidence was adduced that not alerting a patient to this risk and therefore not warning the patient was in fact in accord with accepted medical practice. The Master of the Rolls expressed a caveat to the *Bolam* test after noting that *Bolam* had, in effect, been codified with s 1 Congenital Disabilities (Civil Liability) Act 1976. This section stipulates the need to have "due regard" to received professional opinion:

> " 'Due regard' involves an exercise in judgement, *inter alia*, whether 'received professional opinion' is engaged in the same exercise as the law. This qualification is analogous to that which has been asserted in the context of treating a trade practice as evidencing the proper standard of care in *Cavanagh* v *Ulster Weaving Company Limited* (1959) and in *Morris*

37

v *West Hartlepool Steam Navigation Company Limited* (1956) and would be equally infrequently relevant. In my judgement Skinner J was right to reject the approach of Professor Logue, which was not to refer to small risks if he thought that, in his hands, they were trivial. While it is true that he did so on the basis that none of the other medical witnesses adopted the same approach, I think that, in an appropriate case a judge would be entitled to reject a unanimous medical view if he were satisfied that it was manifestly wrong and the doctors must have been misdirecting themselves as to their duty in law. Another way of expressing my view of the test is to add just one qualifying word (which I have emphasised) to the law as Skinner J summarised it, so that it would read:

> 'The duty is fulfilled if the doctor acts in accordance with a practice *rightly* accepted as proper by a body of skilled and experienced medical men'" ([1984] 1 All ER at 1028 b-c).

It is interesting to note that the Master of the Rolls thought that this approach would be "infrequently relevant". Lord Bridge in the House of Lords came close to affirming this view when he attempted to meet the criticism expressed in the Canadian case of *Reibl* v *Hughes* (1980) (*page 297*) that to allow the medical profession itself to determine what risks it should disclose to a patient handed over the court's jurisdiction to practitioners:

> "It would follow from this that the issue whether non-disclosure in a particular case should be condemned as a breach of the doctor's duty of care is an issue to be decided primarily on the basis of expert medical evidence, applying the *Bolam* test. But I do not see that this approach involves the necessity 'to hand over to the medical profession the entire question of the scope of the duty of disclosure, including the question whether there has been a breach of that duty'. Of course, if there is a conflict of evidence, whether a responsible body of medical opinion approve of non-disclosure in a particular case, the judge will have to resolve that conflict. But, even in a case where, as here, no expert witness in the relevant medical field condemns the non-disclosure as being in conflict with accepted and responsible practice, I am of the opinion that the judge might in certain circumstances come to the conclusion that disclosure of a particular risk was so obviously necessary to an informed choice on the part of a patient that no reasonably prudent medical man would fail to make it" ([1985] 1 All ER at 663 a-c).

Accordingly the standard of care is one which the law determines, and the court reserves the right to itself to condemn an accepted practice as negligent. Examples of this judicial condemnation are limited (cf Singleton LJ's quotation from the trial judge in *Jones* v *Manchester Corporation* [1952] 2 All ER at 129 bc (*page 247*), *Clarke* v *Adams* (1950) (*page 181*). See Sachs LJ in *Hucks* v *Cole* (1968) (*page 241*)).

A similar judicial reticence is apparent when two or more modes of accepted practice are put before the court with each side's protagonist saying that the position of the other party is wrong. The courts have taken a view that medical knowledge and medical science is characterised by controversy and it is not for the courts to determine the current status of the development of medical debate. To this extent the court will decline to enter the affray between various proponents within detailed specialisms, each putting forward various theories and positions (*Moore* v *Lewisham Group Hospital Manage-*

ment Committee (1959) (*page 274*)). No negligence can be established if all that a plaintiff can demonstrate is that there is a competent body of medical opinion which takes the view that the mode of treatment in issue was wrong but is unable to refute the defendant's evidence that there is a body of competent practitioners who maintained that it was right (cf *Maynard* v *West Midlands Regional Health Authority* (1985) (*page 271*) applying the dicta of the Lord President Clyde in *Hunter* v *Hanley* (1955) (*page 243*)).

3. New forms of treatment and deviating from the norm

The Lord President Clyde in *Hunter* v *Hanley* (above) expressed the view that deviation from normal practice was not itself evidence of negligence:

"To establish liability by a doctor where deviation from normal practice is alleged, first of all it must be proved that there is a usual and normal practice; secondly it must be proved that the defender has not adopted that practice; and thirdly (and this is of crucial importance) it must be established that the course the doctor adopted is one which no professional man of ordinary skill would have taken if he had been acting with ordinary care" ([1955] SC at 206).

The Lord President thought that to take any different view would be disastrous as it would destroy inducements to progress. In 1957 Nathan and Barrowclough (*Medical Negligence*, Butterworth) expressed the following view still applicable today concerning deviation from accepted modes of practice and the ethics of new treatment research and experimentation:

"The practitioner who treads the well worn path, however, will usually be safer, as far as concerns legal liability, than the one who adopts a newly discovered method of treatment (*Crawford* v *Board of Governors of Charing Cross Hospital* (1953) (*page 188*)). Further medical men cannot be permitted to experiment on his patient: he ought not in general to resort to a new practice or remedy until its efficacy and safety had been sufficiently tested by experience (*Slater* v *Baker and Stapleton* (1767) (*page 317*)). On the other hand the courts will not press this proposition to a point where it stifles initiative and discourages advances in techniques . . . a line must be drawn between the reckless experimentation with a new and comparatively untried remedy or technique, and the utilisation of a new advance which carries with it wholly unforeseen dangers and difficulties" (at page 28).

Generally speaking, deviation from accepted practice is likely to result in a finding of negligence if the practitioner cannot establish a cogent reason for adopting the practice he did (*Holland* v *The Devitt and Moore Nautical College Limited* (1960) (*page 237*), *Landau* v *Werner* (1961) (*page 254*), *Stokes* v *Guest, Keen and Nettlefold (Bolts and Nuts)* (1968) (*page 322*), *Robinson* v *Post Office* (1974) (*page 301*), *Hotson* v *East Berkshire Health Authority* (1987) (*page 240*)).

In *Clark* v *MacLennan* (1983) (*page 180*), the significance of departing from an approved mode of practice was treated by the trial judge, Pain J, as having the effect of reversing the burden of proof so that once the plaintiff established a deviation the defendant had to disprove an inference of negligence. The case concerned the failure of an operation intended to relieve the stress incontinence of a mother following the birth of her daughter.

Evidence was adduced that it was normal practice to delay the operation in question until three months after birth, whereas the plaintiff in this case had been operated on approximately one month after the birth of her child. Pain J, interpreting the principles espoused in the case of *McGhee* v *National Coal Board* (1973), came to the view that:

> "Where there is a situation in which a general duty of care arises and there is a failure to take a precaution, and that very damage occurs against which the precaution is designed to be a protection, then the burden lies on the defendant to show that he was not in breach of duty as well as to show the damage did not result from his breach of duty. I shall therefore apply this approach to the evidence in this case." ([1983] 1 All ER at 427 g-h.)

The judge went on to find that the defendant had failed to establish that it was justified to perform the operation after only four weeks.

This approach with respect to the burden of proof was explicitly disapproved by the House of Lords in *Wilsher* v *Essex Area Health Authority* (1988) (*page 344*). In *Wilsher*, a case also tried by Pain J, the trial judge had applied the reasoning in *Clark* v *MacLennan* and had determined that the defendants in *Wilsher* were faced with the onus of proof in rebutting negligence. Lord Bridge, with whom the other four law lords agreed, said:

> "*McGhee* v *National Coal Board* (1973) laid down no new principle of law whatever. On the contrary it affirmed the principle that the onus of proving causation lies on the pursuer or plaintiff" ([1988] 2 WLR at 569 e).

Lord Bridge went on to express the view that the reasoning of Lord Wilberforce in *McGhee*, which gave clear support to Pain J's views both in *Clark* v *MacLennan* and in *Wilsher* v *Essex Area Health Authority*, was no more than a minority opinion which had no support from the other speeches in *McGhee*. It must therefore be accepted that *Clark* v *MacLennan* is not an authority for the proposition that in medical negligence cases, where a deviation from the accepted norm is proved, the defendant has the burden of proof in demonstrating that the treatment was not negligent. The plaintiff will always be required to prove negligence on the balance of probabilities in such cases. Deviation from accepted modes of practice, once proved, is, however, likely to impose a severe tactical evidential burden on a defendant even if, as a matter of law, the onus has not shifted on to the defendant.

Chapter 6

Causation

1. Introduction

If damages are to be recovered in tort or to be substantial in contract the plaintiff must, after having proved breach of duty, go on to prove that the harm and loss complained of were caused by the breach of duty. Just as the plaintiff is required to prove on the balance of probabilities that the acts or omissions complained of were a breach of the legal standard of care owed to him, he must also establish on the balance of probabilities that the resulting damage was occasioned by the breach. In law, linking the damage to the breach is considered as a question of causation. Even if a plaintiff establishes causation in this sense, to have a complete cause of action the damage alleged must be of a type of damage which the law recognizes as recoverable. Generally speaking, damage is recoverable if it is considered as being of a type which is reasonably foreseeable as likely to flow from the injury and which is not considered too remote to be recoverable. This chapter concentrates on the first question of causation since in cases of medical malpractice it is more frequently an issue. Questions of remoteness and foreseeability are not considered in any depth because they do not typically arise as difficulties in such cases.

2. The burden of proof, cause and material contribution

Most cases in personal injury litigation pose no factual or conceptual difficulty in relating the injury to a direct consequence of a negligent event. In such cases a simple lineal concept of cause is common-sensically obvious. If a previously healthy plaintiff damages a finger in an unguarded machine he need only prove negligence or breach of statutory duty on the part of the defendant, and the question of causation, the negligence leading to the loss, is self-evident. If the same injured plaintiff attends a casualty department or visits his general practitioner and receives negligent treatment, to found a cause of action against the doctors the plaintiff must be able to demonstrate that because of their negligence he suffered further injury. It is therefore more likely to be a problem for a plaintiff in a medical malpractice action to establish causation because he will usually be suffering from some symptoms or disease before he receives or fails to receive advice and treatment. The litigant will therefore have to rebut the argument that his post-negligent condition was not in fact aggravated by the tortious act but was an inevitable development of his presenting problems. In *Barnett* v *Chelsea and Kensington Hospital Management Committee* (1969) (*page 158*), Mrs Barnett received nothing in respect of the negligent treatment afforded to her husband because he would have died in any event irrespective of whether proper treatment had been afforded to him or not. The casualty officer should have examined Mr Barnett but his failure to do so given the volume of arsenic the patient had inadvertently drunk meant that no known antidote could have had a beneficial effect even if administered some five hours earlier. In *Robinson* v *Post Office* (1974) (*page 301*), Mr Robinson failed to establish negligence against Dr McEwan because even if the doctor had not been negligent in the manner in which he administered the anti-tetanus injection, proper adminis- tration of the drug would not have resulted in Mr Robinson's adverse reaction becoming known in any event. Similarly in actions where a plaintiff alleges there has been a negligent failure to inform the patient of risks inherent in treatment, the plaintiff must go on to persuade the trial judge that had he been appraised of the risks inherent in, say, an operation, he would then have declined to have had the operation. Accordingly in *Chatterton* v *Gerson* (1980) (*page 178*), Bristow J found that the plaintiff was a woman desperate for pain relief and even if she had been informed of all the risks in the nerve block operation she would still have had the operation. In *Gregory and Gregory* v *Pembrokeshire Health Authority* (1989) (*page 222*), Mrs Gregory gave birth to a mongoloid child following an amniocentesis test which had failed to take. The hospital negligently failed to tell Mrs Gregory of the failure of this test until she was very well advanced into her pregnancy. Rougier J found that had the plaintiff been informed earlier she would have accepted the advice that would have been given to her, namely not to proceed with a repeat test because any abortion that may have been subsequently required could only have been carried out more than twenty-four weeks into her pregnancy.

In *Smith* v *Barking, Havering and Brentwood Health Authority* (1989) (*page 318*), Miss Smith's damages were severely curtailed because of a failure to prove causation in this respect. The plaintiff suffered from a condition which was likely to cause her to become tetraplegic within one year if a certain operation was not carried out. However, the operation itself carried an inherent risk of up to twenty-five per cent of causing immediate tetraplegia. The surgeon negligently failed to disclose to the plaintiff the inherent risks in the operation. However, the trial judge, Hutchison J held that there was a strong probability that even if the plaintiff had been properly informed she would have agreed to the operation in any event. Accordingly the plaintiff was limited to damages to represent her shock and depression upon discovering, without prior warning of the prospect, that following the operation she had been rendered tetraplegic.

For further examples see *Burridge* v *Bournemouth and East Dorset Hospital Management Committee* (1965) (*page 173*), *Gauntlett* v *Northampton Health Authority* (1985) (*page 216*), *Hayward* v *Curwen* (1964) (*page 230*), *Hegarty* v *Tottenham Hospital Management Committee* (1976) (*page 231*), *Hulse* v *Wilson* (1953) (*page 243*), *Vernon* v *Bloomsbury Health Authority* (1986) (*page 333*).

These cases for the most part do not necessitate any significant departure from the simple lineal concept of cause. However, other types of actions may involve a more complex interrelationship of a number of causes, each operating simultaneously, and the court has to determine whether the tortious act is part of the combination of causes contributing to the plaintiff's condition. Often the existing state of medical knowledge is unable to be precise as to whether a cause is operating or not. In attempting to deal with the more complex class of case, the courts in medical malpractice actions have endeavoured to utilise those concepts of cause which have been developed in non-medical personal injury litigation concerned with the contraction of disease. If a plaintiff, for example, suffers a disease, say cancer or dermatitis or pneumoconiosis, it is often difficult to establish whether the disease is constitutional in origin or whether it results from exposure to substances which may cause the disease such as asbestos, brick dust or silica dust. Sometimes a substance which may cause a disease only becomes known as harmful at a later date, and the courts have to decide whether exposure to the substance before or after the date of knowledge when it was realised it was dangerous was the cause of the plaintiff's disease. If the exposure that caused the disease was before this date of knowledge, it may well not be negligent, if it was due to exposure after the date of knowledge then it possibly would be negligent. Similarly, some exposure to certain substances is lawful providing it is within certain threshold limits, and an issue may arise as to whether a disease could be contracted even below such limits of exposure. A victim of lung cancer may have to prove that it was the negligent exposure to asbestos that caused his disease and not merely his smoking habits, or that his breathlessness is due to asbestos-caused pleural disease rather than constitutional bronchitis. In dealing with these types of problems the courts have developed a concept of cause which does not rely simply on the "but for" lineal notion that had it not been for the accident the injury would not have occurred, or even if there had been no tort the injury would have occurred in any event. The courts have determined that in certain factual circumstances it will be enough to establish causation if the plaintiff can establish on the balance of probabilities that the negligent act materially contributed to or materially increased the risk of his injury or disease.

In *Bonnington Castings Ltd* v *Wardlaw* (1956) a steel dresser who was exposed to silica dust during the course of his employment contracted pneumoconiosis. The dust he inhaled came from two sources in the factory where he worked, one of which was due to a breach of statutory duty but the other source was from a non-negligent consequence of the production process. Some dust was therefore "tortious" and some was not. The question arose whether the "guilty" dust or the "innocent" dust caused his disease. The medical evidence was unable to determine this issue and could go no further than saying that both sources of dust contributed to the disease. This was so even though the greater amount of dust came from the innocent source. Lord Reid held that the "guilty" dust did cause the disease because it materially contributed to the disease process:

> "What is a material contribution must be a question of degree. A contribution which comes within the exception *de minimis non curat lex* is not material, but I think that any contribution which does not fall within that exception must be material" ([1956] AC at 621).

The case affirmed that it was for the plaintiff to prove on the balance of probabilities that there had been a material contribution to the disease from the tort.

In *McGhee* v *National Coal Board* (1973), the plaintiff contracted dermatitis allegedly due to the failure of his employers to provide him with washing facilities after the completion of his work which exposed him to brick dust. The defendants, on appeal, did not deny that the failure to provide washing facilities was a breach of duty but they denied causation. Again the medical evidence was inconclusive. This evidence could not establish that had the plaintiff been able to wash he could not have contracted the disease, but neither could the defendants prove that the effect of the brick dust and the absence of washing facilities did not materially increase the risk of the plaintiff contracting dermatitis. The House of Lords held that there was no difference between material contribution as in *Bonnington* (above) and materially increasing the risk of injury. The plaintiff accordingly succeeded. Lord Reid said:

> "It has always been the law that a pursuer succeeds if he can show that the fault of the defender caused or materially contributed to his injury. There may have been two separate causes but it is enough if one of the causes arose from the fault of the defender" ([1973] 1 WLR at 4 c-d).

Lord Wilberforce went further and suggested that in cases where neither the plaintiff nor the defendant could prove the precise causes of a disease and where the plaintiff had established that breach of duty involved an increase or risk of disease then it was for the defendant to prove that the damage was in fact caused by some other mechanism:

> "My Lords, I agree with the judge below to the extent that merely to show that a breach of duty increases the risk of harm is not, *in abstracto*, enough to enable the pursuer to succeed. He might, on this basis, still be met by successful defences. Thus, it was open to the respondents, while admitting or being unable to contest that, their failure had increased the risk, to prove, if they could, as they tried to do, that the appellant's dermatitis was 'non-occupational'. But the question remains whether a pursuer must necessarily fail if, after he has shown a breach of duty, involving an increase of risk of disease, he cannot positively prove that this increase of risk caused or materially contributed to the disease while his employers cannot positively prove the contrary. In this immediate case there is an appearance of logic in the view that the pursuer on whom the onus lies should fail — a logic which dictated that judgment below. The question is whether we should be satisfied in factual situations like the present, with this logical approach. In my opinion, there are further considerations of importance. First, it is a sound principle that where a person has, by breach of a duty of care, created a risk, and injury occurs within the area of that risk, the loss should be borne by him unless he shows that it had some other cause. Secondly, from the evidential point of view, one may ask, why should a man who is able to show that his employer should have taken certain precautions, because without them there is a risk, or an added risk, of injury or disease, and who in fact sustains exactly that injury or disease, have to assume the burden of proving more: namely, it was the addition to the risk caused by the breach of duty, which caused or materially contributed to the injury? In many cases, of which the present is typical, this is impossible to prove, just because honest medical opinion cannot segregate the causes of an illness between compound causes. And if one asks which of the parties, the workman or the employers, should suffer from this inherent evidential difficulty, the answer as a matter of policy or justice should be that it is the creator of the risk who, *ex hypothesi* must be taken to have foreseen the possibility of damage, who should bear its consequences." ([1973] 1 WLR at 6 c-g.)

In *Wilsher* v *Essex Area Health Authority* (1988) (*page 344*), the House of Lords affirmed the principle of causation that a plaintiff could in certain circumstances establish causality by demonstrating a material contribution and to this extent has confirmed the law as demonstrated in *McGhee* and *Bonnington*. The House of Lords however distinguished Lord Wilberforce as expressing a minority opinion on the question of the onus of proof and reversed the trial judge's ruling in law that it was for the defendants in this particular case to rebut causation. The plaintiff in *Wilsher* was born prematurely and was placed in a baby care unit and had oxygen administered to him. The oxygen required monitoring by a catheter which should have been located within an artery. A hospital doctor put the catheter into a vein and accordingly received from the monitor low gas readings. The mistake was repeated and on account of these errors the child was saturated with excess oxygen. The plaintiff developed an eye condition which resulted in near-blindness. This condition, retrolental fibroplasia (RLF) could be caused by a number of conditions which affect premature babies; and the infant plaintiff in fact suffered from all of these conditions (apnoea, hypercarbia, intra-ventricular haemorrhage, patent ductus arteriosus). The condition could also be caused by raised PO_2 levels in the blood which in turn could be caused by certain volumes of excess oxygen. The House of Lords, in analysing the judgment, held that there had been no clear finding of fact by the trial judge that the volume of excess oxygen administred to the plaintiff in this particular case was of such a volume that it caused or materially contributed to the plaintiff's virtual blindness. Accordingly the matter was sent for re-trial. It was not open as a matter of law to shift the onus to the defendants to show that the excess volume of oxygen did not cause or materially contribute to the blindness. The expert evidence on this issue at the trial was contradictory and there was no finding of fact as to whether the amount of oxygen administered through the negligence of the doctors was *capable* of having caused or materially contributed to the injury. Lord Bridge quoted extensively from Lord Wilberforce's reasoning in *McGhee* (above) and concluded:

"My Lords, it seems to me that both these paragraphs, particularly the words I have emphasised, amount to saying that in the circumstances the burden of proof of causation is reversed and thereby to run counter to the unanimous and emphatic opinions expressed in *Bonnington Castings Ltd* v *Wardlaw* (1956) to the contrary effect. I find no support in any of the other speeches for the view that the burden of proof is reversed and in this respect I think Lord Wilberforce's reasoning must be regarded as expressing a minority opinion." ([1988] 2 WLR at 567 bc.)

Lord Bridge refused to see any esoteric principle which altered the nature of the burden of proof of causation in cases where a relevant breach of duty had been established. He went on to quote the minority opinion of Sir Nicholas Browne-Wilkinson in the Court of Appeal in *Wilsher* ([1987] QB at 779):

"To apply the principle in *McGhee* v *National Coal Board* (1973) to the present case would constitute an extension of that principle. . . . In the present case the question is different. There are a number of different agents which could have caused the RLF. Excess oxygen was one of them. The defendants failed to take reasonable precautions to prevent one of the possible causative agents (eg excess oxygen) from causing RLF. But no one can tell in this case whether excess oxygen did or did not cause or contribute to the RLF suffered by the plaintiff".

It therefore remains necessary for a plaintiff to prove on the balance of probabilities that his injury was either directly caused by or was materially contributed to because of the act of negligence or breach of duty alleged. (See *Murray* v *Kensington and Chelsea and Westminster Area Health Authority* (1981) (*page 277*), *Kay* v *Ayrshire and Arran Health Board* (1987) (*page 251*).) Causation can be proved even when there are several so-called concurrent causes as long as the tortious act is proved to be one of the causes contributing to the injury and provided that the degree of its contribution is not so small that it ought to be dismissed as being so minimal that the law should take no account of it.

The application of this legal concept of causation appears to rule out an approach which would merely estimate the chances of a patient recovering from a disease or mishap had he been given the correct treatment. In *Kenyon* v *Bell* (1953) (*page 251*) the father of a sixteen month old girl who suffered an eye accident sued a casualty officer for allegedly negligent treatment and diagnosis he gave to the child. The doctor instructed a nurse to put drops into the eye and to powder the eye and advised that it was not necessary to return to the hospital or to consult a general practitioner. Approximately three months later the eye began to water and it was found that there was a severe internal haemorrhage, a detached retina and a bulged iris. The child lost the eye and the action included a claim for damages on the basis that the doctor's negligence either led to the loss of the eye or alternatively materially increased the chance of the eye being lost. At an interlocutory judgment, Lord Guthrie refused to incorporate the principles in the case of *Chaplin* v *Hicks* (1911), in which a model who was deprived of an opportunity to compete in a contest was awarded damages commensurate with her prospects of the chance of her winning the competition. Lord Guthrie held that the loss of a chance of saving the eye was not of itself a matter which could sound in damages. To found a cause of action the pursuer must prove facts from which the reasonable inference was that the eye would have been saved:

> ". . . now the pursuer has repeatedly used the word 'material' to qualify the chance of saving the eye by proper treatment. The significance of that word can only be assessed upon a consideration of expert evidence after proof. It may be that the chance of saving the eye by proper treatment was so material that the natural and reasonable inference is that its loss was due to the absence of such treatment" ([1953] SC at 129).

The views of Lord Guthrie in resisting any cause of action based upon less than such an inference were given specific approval in the House of Lords in the case of *Hotson* v *East Berkshire Health Authority* (1987) (*page 240*). When thirteen years old the plaintiff fell twelve feet from a rope he had been swinging on at school and suffered a serious hip injury which was not diagnosed until five days later. This failure, the defendants admitted, amounted to negligence. The plaintiff suffered from a condition known as avascular necrosis which the trial judge, Simon Brown J, found was seventy-five per cent likely to have occurred even if the defendants had diagnosed and treated the injury promptly. The trial judge found for the plaintiff on the basis that he had been deprived of a twenty-five per cent chance of recovering without the serious complications that had developed. He awarded him a quarter of the total damages, allowing therefore for the seventy-five per cent likelihood that the complications would have occurred in any event. The trial judge took the view that where a loss of a chance or risk was proved on the balance of probabilities, and provided that that loss was substantial, the plaintiff could recover even if the loss of that chance was below fifty per cent. The judge expressed the opinion that this finding was open to him because in effect he was concerned not with the question of causation and therefore liability, but only with the question of damages and was therefore in a position which courts routinely find themselves in, in cases of personal injury, where they have to quantify in monetary terms the chances of a plaintiff developing, for example, epilepsy or contracting osteo-arthritis in later life.

A very strong Court of Appeal (Sir John Donaldson MR and Dillon LJ and Croom-Johnson LJ) affirmed the persuasive reasoning of Simon Brown J in his careful analysis of the leading cases, including *McGhee* (above), and came to a view that where a plaintiff proved on the balance of probabilities that as a result of a failure to treat a patient timeously the patient lost a benefit of a substantial chance of avoiding long-term disability, the plaintiff was entitled to be compensated for the loss of that chance evaluated in terms of the percentage loss. The Master of the Rolls, Sir John Donaldson, said:

> "As a matter of common sense, it is unjust that there should be no liability for failure to treat a patient, simply because the chances of a successful cure by that treatment were less than fifty per cent, nor by the same token can it be just that if the chances of a successful cure only marginally exceed fifty per cent, the doctor or his employer should be liable to the same extent as if the treatment could be guaranteed to cure. If this is the law, it is high time it was changed, assuming that this court has the power to do so. Equally I am quite unable to detect any rational basis for a state of the law, if such it be, whereby in identical circumstances doctor A who treats a patient under the National Health Service, and whose liability therefore falls to be determined in accordance with the law of tort, should be in a different position from doctor B who treats a patient outside the Service and whose liability therefore falls to be determined in accordance with the law of contract, assuming of course, that the contract is in terms which imposes upon him neither more nor less than the tortious duty". ([1987] 2 WLR at 294.)

The Master of the Rolls went on to analyse the plaintiff's loss in this case as the loss of the benefit of timely treatment which he proved was of value. Dillon LJ thought nothing offensive in principle in allowing a loss of chance to sound in damages in tort as it already did in damages in contract as in *Chaplin v Hicks* (1911) and other leading cases. It was, however, offensive to common sense to limit a patient's cause of action to those cases where it could be proved that there was a fifty per cent chance or more, that is on the balance of probabilities, that the non-negligent treatment would have prevented the damage. Croom-Johnson LJ, thought, *inter alia*, that the case could be encompassed within the ordinary forms of the assessment of damages which were routinely subject to quantifying matters of chance.

The House of Lords allowed the defendant's appeal, reversing the trial judge and the unanimous opinions of the Court of Appeal. Moreover the House of Lords did so both on the question of causation and on the principle of the assessment of damages being proportionate to the percentage loss of chance. The House of Lords held that the proper application of the principles in *Bonnington* (above) and *McGhee* (above) required the plaintiff to establish on the balance of probabilities that the delay in treating him at least materially contributed to the development of his avascular necrosis. Therefore, because the trial judge had found as a fact that it was more likely than not (that is, seventy-five per cent likely) that the avascular necrosis would have occurred in any event, there had been a manifest failure to prove causation on the question of liability. Further, where a plaintiff did establish a material contribution and thereby established causality, he was entitled to the whole of the damages and not a proportion. Lord Bridge indicated that the trial judge:

"reached the conclusion that the question was one of quantification and thus arrived at his award to the plaintiff at one-quarter of the damages appropriate to compensate him for the consequences of avascular necrosis. It is here, with respect, that I part company with the judge. The plaintiff's claim was for damages for physical injury and consequential loss alleged to have been caused by the authority's breach of their duty of care. In some cases, perhaps particularly medical negligence cases, causation may be so shrouded in mystery that the court can only measure statistical chances. But that was not so here. On the evidence there was a clear conflict of what caused the avascular necrosis. The authority's evidence was that the sole cause was the original traumatic injury to the hip. The plaintiff's evidence, at its highest, was that the delay in treatment was a material contributory cause. This was a conflict like any other about some relevant past event, which the judge could not avoid resolving on the balance of probabilities. Unless the plaintiff proved on a balance of probabilities that the delayed treatment was at least a material contributory cause of the avascular necrosis he failed on the issue of causation and no question of quantification could arise. But the judge's finding of facts . . . are unmistakably to the effect that on the balance of probabilities the injury caused by the plaintiff's fall left insufficient blood vessels intact to keep the epiphysis alive. This amounts to a finding of fact that the fall was the sole cause of the avascular necrosis" ([1987] 3 WLR at 237 c-g).

The appeal was allowed on this narrow basis and is not authority for the wider proposition that in a claim for personal injury it is never appropriate for the plaintiff to show that he has a statistical chance less than even that but for the breach of duty he would not have had the injury.

Lord McKay's speech in *Hotson* averred to the outcome in *Kenyon* v *Bell* (1953) (*page 251*). In an unreported decision on the case that went on to proof, Lord Strachan held that the child's eye had been irreparably damaged at the initial injury. In Lord McKay's opinion it was proper to apply the same approach to the case of *Hotson*: it was more probable than not that the initial trauma caused the avascular necrosis. The Lord Chancellor's speech involved an interesting analysis of the differing approaches taken on the loss of a chance cases in the United States of America (cf *Herskovits* v *Group Health Cooperative of Puget Sound* (1983) (*page 233*), *Hamil* v *Bashline* (1978) and *Hicks* v *United States* (1966)). He expressed the view that:

". . . unless and until the House departs from the decision in *McGhee* your Lordships cannot affirm the proposition that in no circumstances can evidence of a loss of chance resulting from a breach of a duty of care found a successful claim of damage."

Lord Ackner further emphasised ([1987] 3 WLR at 248a) that where liability is established, the loss which the plaintiff sustained is payable in full and is not discounted by reducing the claim by the extent to which the plaintiff has failed to prove his case with one hundred per cent certainty. Accordingly:

> "The decision of Simon Brown J in the subsequent case of *Bagley* v *North Herts Health Authority* (*page 155*), reported only in (1986) 136 NLJ 1014 in which he discounted an award for a stillbirth, because there was a five per cent risk that the plaintiff would have had a still born child even if the hospital had not been negligent was clearly wrong". .

It must therefore follow that the manner in which Pain J reduced damages in *Clark* v *MacLennan* (1983) (*page 180*) was also wrong. In that case the trial judge heard evidence that if the operation to prevent the plaintiff's stress incontinence had been undertaken at the right time the general chance of it succeeding was approximately sixty-six per cent. Therefore, wrongly, he gave judgment for sixty-six per cent of the full value of the claim.

In establishing causation in terms of material contribution, therefore, a plaintiff must show on the balance of probabilities that the breach of duty materially contributed to the injury. In other words it must be established that it was more than fifty per cent likely to have operated as a cause. This is an entirely different issue to the question of proving the percentage degree of the causative effect of the tort *vis-à-vis* other concurrent non-tortious causes. If the saturation of oxygen, negligently administered to a child, materially contributed to a state of blindness it will be held to be a cause. This is assuming that the state of medical knowledge is unable to say precisely what did cause the blindness. As long as the medical evidence establishes that the tortious act amounted to *a* cause, it is not necessary for a plaintiff to be able to have to establish that it was *the* cause. Nor is it necessary for a plaintiff to establish in cases where there are a number of causes creating the condition precisely what causative power, that is ten per cent or twenty per cent or thirty per cent or more, was caused by the tortious act *vis-à-vis* the other non-tortious causes. All the plaintiff has to show is that the causative power was material, that is not *de minimis*. Conversely, and perhaps perversely, when analysing a plaintiff's prospects of the loss of a chance, the question appears to be not whether on the balance of probabilities the plaintiff lost a chance of recovery but whether on the balance of probabilities there was at least a fifty per cent prospect of him suffering as he did, even if the correct treatment had been afforded to him. For example, in *Mitchell* v *Hounslow and Spelthorne Health Authority* (1984) (*page 272*) an infant plaintiff sued in respect of spastic cerebral palsy caused by birth anoxia due to compression of the umbilical cord. The umbilical cord had prolapsed and the midwife had failed to apply pressure to the foetus in accord with normal standard practice. Kenneth Jones J accepted the expert evidence that if pressure had been applied to the foetus there was a sixty per cent chance that brain damage would have been avoided and therefore held the hospital authority liable for the midwife's negligence which was the *probable* cause of the plaintiff's condition. (See also *R* v *Vaccine Damage Tribunal, ex parte Loveday* (1985) (*page 295*) and *Loveday* v *Renton* (1988) (*page 262*).)

In summary, causation is established if the tort materially contributed to the injury. This will be so even if there are other non-tortious causes of greater causative power simultaneously contributing to the same injury. Moreover, as long as a plaintiff proves causation through material contribution, he will be entitled to one hundred per cent of his damages. Where, however, a plaintiff sues in respect of a chance that but for the tort the injury might not have occurred, he has to demonstrate that there was a prospect of more than fifty per cent of the injury not occurring but for the tort. If a plaintiff establishes the chance was over fifty per cent, he will be entitled to the whole of his damages.

3. Foreseeability, remoteness and breaking the chain of causation

For a plaintiff to recover damages, the court must be satisfied not only that there has been negligence or breach of duty and that negligence or breach of duty caused the loss, but also the damage occasioned must be of a type which is recognized in law as recoverable. Whether a type of damage is recoverable or not turns predominantly on the question whether the damage was a reasonably foreseeable consequence of the negligent act or whether it is held to be too remote. These concepts of reasonable foreseeability and remoteness have given rise to relatively complex legal debates. Part of the complexity no doubt arises because the concepts are used in very different contexts. Both remoteness and foreseeability are concepts which are applied to the question of whether there is a duty of care owed by one person to another. Similarly the question of remoteness is used in analysing the question of causation of an accident or incident as well as looking at the question whether the damage caused is too remote. When remoteness is applied to the question of causation, it is often found in conjunction with another concept which affords defendants a defence concerning the matter of causation, namely where a supervening event occasioned by the plaintiff or a third party is said to have broken the chain of causation and thereby relieved the defendant of the consequences of his breach of duty. A supervening force which is held to break the chain of causation is often known by the phrase *novus actus interveniens*. These concepts have on occasions been of significance in certain medical malpractice actions. Often the logic of these essentially legal concepts clearly interrelates with questions of public policy. As long ago as 1954, Lord Denning in *Roe* v *Minister of Health* (1954) (*page 301*) recognized the manner in which the concepts interrelated:

> "The first question in every case is whether there was a duty of care owed to the plaintiff and the test of duty depends, without doubt, on what you should foresee. There is no duty of care owed to a person when you could not reasonably foresee that he might be injured by your conduct: see *Hay (or Bourhill)* v *Young* (1943), *Woods* v *Duncan* (1946) per Lord Russell and per Lord Porter. The second question is whether the neglect of duty was a 'cause' of the injury in the proper sense of that term; and causation, as well as duty, often depends on what you should foresee. The chain of causation is broken when there is an intervening act which you could not reasonably be expected to foresee, see *Woods* v *Duncan* per Lord Simon, Lord McMillan and Lord Simmonds. It is even broken when there is an intervening omission which you could not reasonably expect. For instance in cases based on *Donoghue* v *Stevenson* (1932) a manufacturer is not liable if he might reasonably contemplate that an intermediate examination would probably be made. It is only when those two preliminary questions — duty and causation — are answered in favour of the plaintiff that the third question, remoteness of damage, comes into play. Even then your ability to foresee the consequences may be vital. It is decisive when there is intervening conduct by other persons: see *Stansbie* v *Troman* (1948), *Lewis*

v *Carmarthenshire County Council* (1953). It is only disregarded when the negligence is the immediate or precipitating cause of the damage, as in *Re Polemis* (1921) and *Thurogood* v *Van den Berghs and Jurgens Limited* (1951). In all these cases you will find that the three questions, duty, causation and remoteness run continually into one another. It seems to me that they are simply three different ways of looking at one and the same problem. Starting with the proposition that a negligent person should be liable, within reason, for the consequences of its conduct, the extent of his liabilities to be found by asking the one question: Is the consequence fairly to be regarded as within the risk created by the negligence? If so, the negligent person is liable for it, but not otherwise". ([1954] 2 QB 84–85.)

In medical malpractice actions, the question of remoteness is normally concerned with the question of negligence or breach of duty rather than with the foreseeable nature of the type of damage. In *Hothi* v *Greenwich Health Authority* (1982) (*page 239*) a plaintiff, who presented with a serious head injury, was given phenobarbitone and as a result developed a severe rash and symptoms known as Stevens-Johnson syndrome. The plaintiff sued on the basis that the phenobarbitone should not have been prescribed and that sensitivity tests should have been carried out beforehand. Croom-Johnson J held that it was a proper procedure to prescribe an anti-convulsant drug such as phenobarbitone and the chance of Stevens-Johnson syndrome occurring was so remote that no doctor could be negligent because of the very slight risk that some hypersensitive person might have an adverse reaction. In *Hyde* v *Tameside Area Health Authority* (1981) (*page 244*) a hospital patient suffered severe paralysis following a suicide attempt brought on by depression based upon an erroneous belief that he had cancer and was going to die. The plaintiff sued on the basis that proper care and attention would have led nurses and doctors to have noticed his depression and a psychiatrist should have been brought in. The trial judge found the defendants liable and awarded £200,000 damages. The Court of Appeal reversed the trial judge's decision and found that the nurses and doctors had used proper care. The appeal judges went on to say that, even if they were wrong, any error which might have been made did not amount to negligence. Further, Lord Denning suggested that the plaintiff's suicide attempt was in any event too remote a consequence of any error to be made the subject of damages. In *Prendergast* v *Sam and Dee Limited* (1989) (*page 290*), the plaintiff sued in respect of brain damage resulting from the dispensing of an erroneous prescription. The plaintiff's general practitioner had written out a prescription for three drugs including Amoxil tablets. This word was written in a manner that was difficult to read. The dispensing chemist, who was also sued, misread the prescription and dispensed Daonil. The Court of Appeal upheld the finding that the poor handwriting did constitute negligence. It also confirmed the reasoning that although other aspects on the prescription should have put the pharmacist on enquiry as being inconsistent with Daonil, the chain of causation was not broken and it was reasonably foreseeable that Daonil would be prescribed. In *De Freville* v *Dill* (1927) (*page 197*), the plaintiff sued a medical practitioner for negligently certifying her under the provisions of the Lunacy Act 1890. Dr Dill signed a statement saying the plaintiff was a person of unsound mind and a proper person to be taken charge of and detained for care and treatment. She was taken to a Justice of the Peace who, without examining her or calling in any other doctor, made a reception order. The jury found that Dr Dill had not acted with reasonable care and notwithstanding the fact that the Justice of the Peace had ordered the detention it was Dr Dill's certificate which was the cause of the plaintiff's detention. (See also *Edler* v *Greenwich and Deptford Hospital Management Committee and Another* (1953) (*page 203*).)

In *Emeh* v *Kensington and Chelsea and Westminster Area Health Authority* (1985) (*page 205*), the interrelationship of these concepts was particularly well illustrated. Mrs Emeh gave birth to a child with congenital abnormalities despite the fact that she had purportedly been sterilised approximately a year before. Park J held that the operation for sterilisation had been performed negligently but that the plaintiff was limited to damages which had accrued before she discovered her subsequent pregnancy. He took the view that the plaintiff's failure to have an abortion when she knew she was pregnant constituted a *novus actus interveniens* so as to eclipse the negligence of the surgeons. The Court of Appeal held that the plaintiff's refusal to have an abortion neither broke the chain of causation nor constituted a failure to mitigate her damages. The trial judge held that the plaintiff had acted in such an unreasonable way that the defendant's negligence could no longer be said to have been the cause of her damage. To this extent he dissented from the view expressed by Watkins J in *Sciuraga* v *Powell* (1979) (*page 312*). Slade LJ held that the judge had applied the correct test, namely whether the plaintiff had acted so unreasonably as to eclipse the defendant's wrongdoing, but he found himself in profound disagreement with the judge's view of the plaintiff's conduct. He went on to say:

"The judge, in saying that her failure to obtain an abortion was so unreasonable as to eclipse the defendants wrong doing was I think really saying that the defendants had the right to expect that, if they had not performed the operation properly, she would procure an abortion, even if she did not become aware of its existence until nearly 20 weeks of her pregnancy had elapsed. I do not, for my part, think that the defendants had the right to expect any such thing. By their own negligence, they faced her with the very dilemma which she had sought to avoid by having herself sterilised. For the reasons which I have attempted to give, I think they could and should have reasonably foreseen that if, as a consequence of the negligent performance of the operation she should find herself pregnant again, particularly after some months pregnancy, she might well decide to keep the child. Indeed for my part I would go even a little further. Save in the most exceptional circumstances, I cannot think it right that the court should ever declare it unreasonable for a woman to decline to have an abortion in a case where there is no evidence that there were any medical or psychiatric grounds for terminating the particular pregnancy." ([1985] 1 QB at 1024 f-h).

The defendants also argued that it was not reasonably foreseeable that the child would have been born with congenital abnormalities. Waller LJ dealt with this argument shortly:

"The next question which arises for consideration is the remoteness of the various things which then happened. In my view it is trite to say that if a woman becomes pregnant, it is certainly foreseeable that she will have a baby, but in my judgement, having regard to the fact that in a proportion of all births — between 1 in 200 and 1 in 400 were the figures given at the trial — congenital abnormalities might arise, makes this risk clearly one that is foreseeable, as the law of negligence understands it. There are many cases where even more remote risks have been taken to be foreseeable" ([1985] 1 QB at 1019 f-g).

Finally, the defendants argued that as a matter of public policy a part of the damages which the plaintiff sought should not be recoverable. The argument suggested that once the child is born, on assumption in the first instance that it is a healthy child, damages should not take into account the question of looking after such a child. The Lord Justices reviewed the cases of *Sciuraga* v *Powell* (1979) (*page 312*), *Udale* v *Bloomsbury Area Health Authority* (1983) (*page 329*) and *Thake* v *Maurice* (1986) (*page 327*) and concluded that there were no objections in law to damages in cases of so-called wrongful birth. Waller LJ quoted with approval the view of Lord Scarman in *McLoughlin* v *O'Brian* (1983) concerning the interrelationship of the judiciary and Parliament on questions of public policy:

"The distinguishing feature of the common law is this judicial development of formation of principle. Policy considerations will have to be weighed: but the objective of the judges is the formulation of principle. And, if principle inexorably requires a decision which entails a degree of policy risk, the court's function is to adjudicate according to principle, leaving policy curtailment to the judgement of Parliament. Here lies the true role of the two law making institutions in our constitution. By concentrating on principle the judges can keep the common law alive, flexible and consistent, and can keep the legal system clear of policy problems which neither they, nor the forensic process which is their duty to operate, are quick to resolve. If principle leads to results which are thought to be socially unacceptable, Parliament can legislate to draw a line or map out a new path" ([1985] 1 QB at 1021 in *Emeh*, and [1983] AC at 430 in *McLoughlin*).

Once a plaintiff establishes that the type of damage that occurs is reasonably foreseeable and is not considered too remote or against public policy, it does not matter that the extent of the injury was not reasonably foreseeable or that the injury occurred in an unforeseen manner. Accordingly in *Robinson* v *Post Office* (1974) (*page 301*) Mr Robinson was entitled to the whole of his damages from his employers, the Post Office, because of their original negligence causing the laceration to his shin. This negligent act gave rise to a reasonably foreseeable need for a tetanus injection. Although Dr McEwan had been negligent in the way in which he administered the injection, his negligent act was not causative because if he had waited the proper time before giving the injection in question, the plaintiff's particular susceptibility to the serum would not in any event have been made known. Therefore the doctor's negligence could not be considered a *novus actus interveniens* because it had no causative effect. Although the employers could not have foreseen that Mr Robinson had a particular susceptibility or allergy, the necessity for the injection was occasioned by their negligence and the plaintiff was entitled to recover (cf *Smith* v *Leech Brain & Co* (1962), a non-medical negligence case illustrating this principle). Had Dr McEwan's negligence been causative, the outcome may well have been different (see *Hogan* v *Bentinck West Hartley Collieries (Owners) Ltd* (1949)).

4. Contributory negligence

A partial defence to an action for damages arising out of medical malpractice is in principle afforded by the doctrine of contributory negligence. The Law Reform (Contributory Negligence) Act 1945 provides that where a person suffers damage, partly as a result of his own fault and partly as a result of another's fault, then the compensation received may be reduced in a proportion which the court thinks just and equitable having regard to his share in the responsibility for the damage. Fault is defined by s 4 of the Act as: "negligence, breach of statutory duty or other act or omission which gives rise to a liability in tort or would, apart from this Act give rise to the defence of contributory negligence". It is likely in the context of medical care that a partial defence of contributory negligence is available, no matter whether a plaintiff sues in tort or for breach of contract.

There is no reported UK medical malpractice case where an allegation of contributory negligence has succeeded. This absence may reflect the fact that in many cases the victim of a medical mishap is innocent. It may also reflect recognition that patients often have little knowledge or control over their treatment programme. Nevertheless, there are many situations in the context of medical care where allegations of contributory negligence may be made. The basis of the doctrine of contributory negligence arises not from any duty that a patient may owe to a doctor but from a generalised duty of self-care. The patient may be partly to blame for a mishap or for the degree of damage that follows from a mishap if he fails to take reasonable care for his own health and safety. Breach of duty of self-care must give rise to a foreseeable risk of damage, and the plaintiff's fault must be causative of some of the damage. In other words, the negligence on the part of the plaintiff must materially contribute to the injury. It is for the defendant to establish on the balance of probabilities that there has been contributory negligence. Once this is established, the percentage of fault held against the plaintiff will in practice be determined by looking not only at the causative effect of the behaviour but also at the relative degrees of blameworthy conduct. The standard of self-care will be what is reasonable in all the circumstances. Accordingly, a lower standard of care will be appropriate for those who are of tender or advanced years and for those who are sick or disabled.

In cases of medical malpractice, allegations of contributory fault could be made against a patient who, for example, failed to co-operate with a practitioner in fully answering questions designed to obtain a proper history. Equally, failures to keep appointments or leaving hospital against medical advice, or ignoring warnings, or failing to take heed of instructions concerning prescriptions or diet may in principle amount to contributory negligence. Failing to seek further help after a mishap has occurred or unreasonably refusing the treatment designed to mitigate the effects of a mishap may also result in a plaintiff's damages being reduced.

The Canadian case of *Crossman* v *Stewart* (1977) (*page 191*) is a good illustration. The partial defence of contributory negligence succeeded against a plaintiff who suffered irreversible eye damage from prolonged usage of a drug, known as chloroquine, originally prescribed by the defendant for a facial skin disorder. The plaintiff continued to use the drug without prescription by obtaining it from a salesman who visited her employer's medical practice. On the facts of the case, the defendant was held liable for failing to appreciate from material available to him that the plaintiff had been using the drug without prescription. However, the plaintiff was found to have been two-thirds to blame. Anderson J found the plaintiff negligent because she had obtained the drugs without obtaining prescription renewals and had not consulted a physician about them for almost two years. He went on to say:

"In my view, this is not a case where the apportionment of blame is so difficult that liability should be apportioned on a fifty-fifty basis. I hold that if the plaintiff had acted with any reasonable degree of prudence the permanent damage to her eyes would not have resulted. The defendant's failure to take the high standard of care was one of the causative factors but not the major cause. In those circumstances I hold the plaintiff was two-thirds to blame and the defendant one-third to blame".

Conversely, allegations of contributory fault failed in the Alberta case of *Bernier* v *Sisters of Service (St John's Hospital, Edson)* (1948) (*page 161*) where a patient suffered burns to her heels from hot-water bottles put into her bed during a recovery period from an appendicectomy. The defendants alleged that the plaintiff was partly to blame because she did not call for help in time, failed to disclose a possible vulnerability in her feet through having previously suffered from frost-bite, and left the hospital against medical advice. The judge dismissed all these allegations, indicating that the reason why she did not call for help was because her feet were de-sensitised due to the anaesthetic. Moreover, the failure to disclose the history of frost-bite was not unreasonable given the purpose of her visit to hospital, and the premature discharge was not causative of any damage.

Chapter 7

Res ipsa loquitur

In certain classes of injury or mishap the fact that the accident happened in the way it did is held to be so redolent of negligence as in effect to require the defendants to rebut a presumption that they were in breach of their duty. Obviously this presumption can be of great assistance to plaintiffs, even though the ultimate onus of proving negligence remains with them.

If the maxim applies, defendants can be in substantial difficulty in rebutting the evidential presumption that they were not in fact negligent. In this very limited class of cases, the mishap is said to speak for itself. The classical exposition of the principle was laid down by Erle CJ in *Scott* v *London and St Katherine Docks Co* (1865):

"There must be reasonable evidence of negligence. But where a thing is shown to be under the management of the defendant or his servants, and the accident is such as in the ordinary course of things does not happen if those who have the management use proper care, it affords reasonable evidence, in the absence of explanation by the defendants, that the accident arose from want of care" ([1865] 3 H & C at 601).

In medical cases, particularly where the treatment or operation is complex and the plaintiff may be unconscious at the time, this doctrine can be of particular significance. However, for the presumption to arise the accident must be more consistent with an act of negligence than any other explanation. In effect, this means that *res ipsa loquitur* is pertinent only in those cases where the plaintiff cannot prove what did cause the accident. Once there is evidence of what caused the accident, it becomes a question of legal judgment rather than presumption as to whether the act or omission amounted to negligence. The maxim is probably not strictly a doctrine of law creating a presumption but:

". . . a rule of evidence affecting onus, based on common sense, and its purpose is to enable justice to be done when the facts bearing on causation and on the care exercised by the defendants are at the outset unknown to the plaintiff and are or ought to be within the knowledge of the defendant" (per Lord Normand in *Barkway* v *South Wales Transport Company Limited* (1950)).

The maxim therefore applies when the circumstances of the occurrence are without further explanation more consistent with negligence than with any other cause. A plaintiff needs to demonstrate that the injury happened in an unexplained way, that the injury would not have happened in the ordinary way without negligence and the circumstances point to the liability of the defendant rather than any other person, that is, the incident causing the damage was in the management and control of the particular defendant sued. (See Charlesworth and Percy *On Negligence* (Sweet & Maxwell, 7th edition, 1983) pages 5–59.) Where the maxim is held to apply, the defendants have the onus of proving that they in fact were not negligent, and they may do this even though they cannot explain how the act occurred. The prime way in which defendants typically rebut this presumption is to adduce evidence that the act could have reasonably occurred without negligence. It is accordingly more accurate to state that the defendants need not disprove negligence; what they need to do is rebut the inference by indicating that other non-tortious reasonable causes exist and are just as, or more likely, to have caused the plaintiff's injury (*Moore* v *R Fox and Sons* (1956)).

In *Barkway* v *South Wales Transport Company Limited* (above) Asquith LJ expressed the issue of rebutting the inference of negligence in the following way:

"(i) If the defendants' omnibus leaves the road and falls down an embankment, and this without more is proved, then *res ipsa loquitur* there is a presumption that the event is caused by negligence on the part of the defendants, and the plaintiff succeeds unless the defendants can rebut this presumption.

(ii) It is no rebuttal for the defendants to show, again without more, that the immediate cause of the omnibus leaving the road is a tyre-burst, since the tyre-burst *per se* is a neutral event consistent, and equally consistent with negligence or due diligence on the part of the defendants. When a balance has been tilted one way, you cannot redress it adding an equal weight to each scale. The depressed scale will remain down . . .

(iii) To displace the presumption, the defendants must go further and prove, or it must emerge from the evidence as a whole either (a) that the burst itself was due to a specific cause which does not connote negligence on their part but points to its absence as more probable, or (b) if they can point to no such specific cause, that they used all reasonable care in and about the management of their tyres . . ." ([1948] 2 All ER at 471). (See also *Ng Chun Pui* v *Lee Chuen Tat* (1988).)

Before the development of the doctrine of vicarious liability, the maxim had less force within hospital settings because the act, for example, of leaving a swab in a body, could point to more than one person being negligent, such as occurred in *Morris* v *Winsbury-White* (1937) (*page 275*). In this case a portion of tube was left in the plaintiff's bladder. This tube may have been left in either by the contractual visiting surgeon or by a resident surgeon or resident nurses of the hospital. The tube may have been left in after the operation on 27 November 1933 or at any time up until the plaintiff's discharge on 10 February 1934. The plaintiff sued the contractual surgeon (as a matter of law at that time, the resident surgeons and the nurses were not deemed agents of the contractual visiting surgeon). Tucker J held that the maxim did not apply because the plaintiff was not in the control or charge or power of the defendant throughout the whole of the period in question.

Inroads were made on this restriction in *Mahon* v *Osborne* (1939) (*page 266*) where the Court of Appeal held by a majority that the maxim did apply in a case where a packing swab had been left in the patient's body. Scott LJ, in a dissenting judgment, did not think the maxim applied because the ordinary experience of mankind had no knowledge about the complications that can arise in emergency operations and therefore it would be unsafe to infer that such an event does not happen without negligence. He went on to say:

"How can the ordinary judge have sufficient knowledge of surgical operations to draw such an inference, or to apply the phrase in the judgment of *Scott* v *London and St Katherine Docks Co* (1865). What does he know of the 'ordinary cause of things' in a complicated abdominal operation" ([1938] 2 KB at 23).

McKinnon LJ disagreed and thought that the act of leaving the swab raised an inference both against the surgeon and the chief nurse:

"Five persons were concerned in the operation on March 4th: Mr Osborne (the surgeon), the anaesthetist, Nurse Ashburner (as chief or theatre nurse), Nurse Edmunds and Nurse Callaghan. The plaintiff, having no means of knowing what happened in the theatre, was in the position of being able to rely on the maxim *res ipsa loquitur* so as to say that some one or more of these five must have been negligent, since the swab was left in the abdomen in the deceased" ([1938] 2 KB at 38).

Goddard LJ concurred that the maxim applied, but did so on the narrow grounds that it was applicable to the surgeon because he was in command of the operation and therefore had overall control (at page 50).

In *Roe* v *Minister of Health* (1954) (*page 301*), McNair J at first instance held the maxim was not applicable because the treatment and operation in question were under the joint control of the anaesthetist and the theatre staff who were not responsible for each other's acts and the defendants were not responsible for the anaesthetist. The Court of Appeal held that the maxim did, in effect, apply. The judge's objections were undermined by the Court of Appeal finding that the hospital authorities were in fact vicariously liable for the acts of the anaesthetist. Lord Denning went further and suggested that even in cases where the negligence points to two persons possibly being at fault, the plaintiff could require each to rebut the inference:

"I do not think that the hospital authorities and Dr Graham (anaesthetist) can both avoid giving an explanation by the simple expedient of each throwing the responsibility onto the other. If an injured person shows that one or other or both of two persons injured him, but canot say which one of them it was, then he is not defeated altogether. He can call on each of them for an explanation: see *Baker* v *Market Harborough Industrial Co-operative Society* [1953] 1 WLR 1472" ([1954] 2 QB at 82). (But cf *Hawkins* v *Dhawan and Mishiku* (1987).)

Roe was a case where the defendants gave evidence that the plaintiff's paralysis arose out of phenol solution seeping through invisible cracks in glass ampoules used for anaesthetics, and that this did not arise through their negligence. The defendants therefore established the likely cause of the tragedy and rebutted the inference of negligence. It was held that they could not reasonably have been expected to have been aware of this sequence of events, given the state of knowledge obtaining at the time.

In *Cassidy* v *Ministry of Health* (1951) (*page 176*), Streatfield J had dismissed the case brought by the plaintiff on the basis that he had not proved negligence as the cause of his hand being rendered useless after an operation to relieve Dupuytrens contracture. The Court of Appeal held that the maxim did apply and Denning LJ put the matter in this way:

"If the plaintiff had to prove that some particular doctor or nurse was negligent, he would not be able to do it. But he was not put to that impossible task. He says, 'I went into the hospital to be cured of two stiff fingers. I have come out with four stiff fingers, and my hand is useless. That should not have happened if due care had been used. Explain it, if you can'. I am quite clearly of the opinion that that raises a prima-facie case against the hospital authorities: see per Goddard LJ in *Mahon* v *Osborne* [1939] 2 KB 14, 50. They have in no way explained how it could happen without negligence. They have busied themselves in saying that this or that member of staff was not negligent. But they have called not a single person to say that the injuries were consistent with due care on the part of all the members of their staff . . . they have not therefore displaced the prima-facie case against them and are liable to damages to the plaintiff" ([1951] 2 KB at 365–6).

In *Clarke* v *Worboys* (1952) (*page 181*), a patient suffered a burn on her buttock following electric coagulation treatment which involved passing a current through her body via a pad. The plaintiff could not say precisely how the burn was caused. McNair J held that it might have been caused by a number of factors including the possible susceptibility of the plaintiff. The Court of Appeal reversed this decision, holding that the burning would not have occurred if reasonable care had been used and that the case was one of *res ipsa loquitur*. In *Brazier* v *Ministry of Defence* (1965) (*page 169*) McNair J did, however, hold that the doctrine applied in circumstances where a needle broke and lodged in the plaintiff's right buttock. The defendants rebutted the inference of negligence by adducing evidence, which was accepted, to the effect that the needle probably broke due to a latent defect in the shaft of the needle, and therefore they avoided liability. (See also *Levenkind* v *Churchill-Davidson* (1983) (*page 259*).)

The application of the maxim will present few difficulties in relatively extreme and plain cases where, for example, the operation has been performed on the wrong limb, or on the wrong side of the body or where a prescription has been administered in the wrong dosage or the wrong drugs have been used or where test results are ascribed to the wrong patient. However, these are precisely the cases where liability is normally admitted or there is little difficulty in establishing negligence in any event. In *Garner* v *Morrell* (1953) (*page 215*) the swallowing or inhalation of a throat pack during the course of dental surgery was held to call for an explanation from the defendants. In *G* v *North Tees Health Authority* (1989) (*page 214*) a child's swab became contaminated with another swab because the same slide had been used for both swabs and this led to an investigation seeking to explain how the six year old girl's vaginal swab had active male sperm on it. Not surprisingly this case led to an admission of liability.

It is not, however, possible to be categorical about what may appear to be plain cases to the general public. The leaving of foreign objects in a patient's body is most likely to be found to be an act of negligence, but it cannot be stated in advance that the doctrine of *res ipsa loquitur* will always apply. In *Cooper* v *Nevill* (1961) (*page 186*), the Privy Council found that the trial judge was justified in finding that the leaving of an abdominal swab in a patient's body following a difficult emergency operation amounted to negligence. However, the court was of the view that it did not always follow that because such a mistake had been made that negligence had occurred. A mistake which would amount to negligence in a routine, so-called "cold operation" might not amount to negligence in an emergency, so-called "hot operation", where it may be no more than misadventure. The trial judge was also entitled to make a distinction between a restraining pack and a mopping pack, as these may indicate liability on different persons. Given the doctrine of vicarious liability as it now stands, such a distinction would be unlikely to alter the prospects of success of a plaintiff in such an action.

It appears reasonably well settled that in dentistry a fracturing of a jaw during certain operations does not give rise to an inference of negligence. In *Fish* v *Kapur* (1948) (*page 210*), a dentist left part of the root of a tooth in the jaw and also, by some unexplained means, fractured the jaw during extraction. The plaintiff relied on the doctrine of *res ipsa loquitur*, but Lynskey J held that the fact the fracture was caused in a process of extraction of the tooth was not of itself evidence of negligence. No doubt Mrs Fish's case was not helped by her own expert giving evidence that it was possible to fracture a jaw during an extraction without negligence. Similarly, in *Fletcher* v *Bench* (1973) (*page 210*) a dentist seeking to extract a molar broke a bone-burr leaving part of the burr inside the jaw. Ten days later the plaintiff's jaw fractured due to an infection that had arisen, and the burr was found at the very point of the fracture. The Court of Appeal held that the breaking of the drill and the fact that it was left there after the end of a difficult operation were not indicative of lack of care. In *Lock* v *Scantlebury* (1963) (*page 262*), the plaintiff suffered a dislocation to her jaw following the extraction of six teeth. This dislocation was not discovered by the defendant. Paull J held that the fact that the plaintiff's jaw had become dislocated during the extraction was not of itself proof of negligence. There was, however, held to be negligence in not subsequently discovering the dislocation.

Once the maxim is applicable, the rebuttal of the prima-facie case involves the defendant adducing an acceptable explanation. In *Saunders* v *Leeds Western Health Authority* (1985) (*page 310*), an infant plaintiff brought an action against the health authority and an anaesthetist, alleging negligent administration of anaesthetic during the course of a hip operation. After two hours the plaintiff's heart stopped for approximately thirty to forty minutes. The plaintiff relied on the doctrine of *res ipsa loquitur* and the defendants appeared to have conceded that the heart of a fit and healthy child did not stop under anaesthetics unless there was a want of care. The defendants, however, sought to explain the cardiac arrest as being due to a paradoxical air embolism travelling from the operation site and blocking a coronary artery. This was not accepted as a plausible explanation and the defendants were held to have failed to discharge the onus upon them.

Section C: Common types of action

Chapter 8

Failures in diagnosis

Whether a practitioner has fallen below the standard of skill and care required by law will always depend upon the particular facts of each case and the precise circumstances which give rise to the allegations. Although it is possible to delineate the legal principles which operate to appraise the facts in question (eg the duty and standard of care, issues of causation and damage), it is not possible to formulate in the abstract what will or what will not constitute negligence. The complex variety of circumstances which entail the need for medical care or advice obviously gives rise to the possibility that the administering of that advice and care could be undertaken in a proper or an improper manner. There are, however, certain categories of malpractice actions which arise reasonably routinely from the literature and case law and which do raise particular issues. This and the following two chapters examine, by way of illustrations, the approach of the courts in dealing with typical categories of cases. The categories which are examined are neither intended to be exhaustive nor do they claim to be truly representative of the volume of actions brought. They do, however, indicate something of the flavour of the ad hoc and situational approach which characterises the law of medical malpractice.

Diagnosis is the basis of clinical judgement as it determines, firstly, whether there is a need to treat and, secondly, the mode of treatment required. To make a proper diagnosis, the practitioner must, if possible, take a full history, conduct a proper examination and, where appropriate, organise tests. If the practitioner does this, he is unlikely to be liable for misdiagnosis as the courts recognize that diseases and injuries can present in atypical ways, that practitioners are not infallible and that in some cases the state of medical science and art may make diagnosis certain only with the benefit of hindsight.

A want of reasonable care has long been established as necessary to find against a doctor for misdiagnosis. In *Furstenau* v *Tomlinson* (1902) (*page 213*) a doctor diagnosed a skin infection as eczema and prescribed certain treatment which failed to alleviate the symptoms. The patient sought a second opinion and a correct diagnosis of scabies was made. The plaintiff sued the doctor for negligence. Walton J directed the jury that a mistake alone on Dr Tomlinson's part was not sufficient to enable the plaintiff to recover damages;

he needed to show a want of ordinary amount of skill. Dr Tomlinson's defence was that the original mischief was eczema and that if there was any concurrent scabies it was so masked by the eczema that it was impossible to diagnose it at that time. The jury found for Dr Tomlinson.

Nevertheless some misdiagnoses are such that no average doctor using a proper degree of skill and care and taking a proper history and making a proper examination ought to make. Accordingly, missing obvious fractures or common diseases or injuries is likely to result in a finding of negligence particularly against the general practitioner or the casualty officer who tend to be in the "front line" in these cases. According to Chapter 4 of *The Doctor and Negligence* (Pitman Medical, 1971) by Leahy-Taylor, the most common fracture missed in the five hundred cases looked at by the author in the Medical Protection Society files was the scaphoid and the most common dislocation missed was the hip, particularly when it presented with other major leg injuries. In *Hotson* v *East Berkshire Health Authority* (1987) (*page 240*), the defendants admitted liability in failing to diagnose a fracture of the left femoral epiphysis but the claim failed on the question of causation. Missing a diagnosis of a posterior dislocation of the right shoulder led to an admission of negligence in *Hughes* v *Hay* (1989) (*page 242*). In *Newton* v *Newton's Model Laundry Limited* (1959) (*page 280*) the court found the defendants negligent for failing to conduct properly an examination which overlooked a fractured patella which was broken in eleven places. Similarly, in *Patterson* v *Rotherham Health Authority* (1987) (*page 286*), a failure to diagnose a fracture within a knee resulted in an admission of liability. Missing a hole in a skull of between one-quarter and a half of an inch led to a finding of negligence against the casualty officer who failed to take an X-ray or to discover the fractured site in *McCormack* v *Redpath Brown and Co. Limited* (1961) (*page 263*). In that case a worker had been hit on the head by a spanner dropped by a colleague, but the casualty officer was apparently overworked and assumed that he was dealing with just another cut head. Similarly, overlooking eighteen fractured ribs and a broken collar bone led to liability in *Wood* v *Thurston* (1951) (*page 347*). In *Wood* the plaintiff presented in an intoxicated state saying that he had been pinned underneath a rear wheel of a lorry but assured the casualty officer he was all right and he wanted to go home.

Failing to appreciate the significance of a poisoned finger and therefore to prescribe antibiotics led to a finding of negligence against a general practitioner in *Hucks* v *Cole* (1968) (*page 241*); and missing a chip fracture in *Saumarez* v *Medway and Gravesend Hospital Management Committee* (1953) (*page 310*) was deemed negligent in circumstances where the plaintiff, who was a violinist, was complaining of pain in the finger.

In *Edler* v *Greenwich and Deptford Hospital Management Committee* (1953) (*page 203*), a casualty officer was found to have been negligent in failing to diagnose appendicitis in a young girl who died two days later. In *Burridge* v *Bournemouth and East Dorset Hospital Management Committee* (1965) (*page 173*), Cumming-Bruce J held there had not been negligence in failing to diagnose appendicitis on 9 October 1961 as the condition then had probably subsided. The subsequent day there was a flare-up which was properly diagnosed although the registrar failed to act on the diagnosis quickly enough.

Diagnoses of ailments in babies and children give rise to particular difficulties. In *Riddett* v *D'Arcy* (1960) (*page 299*), a month old baby who was icy cold and who had swelling round his eyes and exhibited a mauve type colour was diagnosed as having a cold rather than showing signs of heart failure due to staphylococcal pneumonia. The doctor was held negligent. In *Sa'd v Robinson and Dunlop; Sa'd v Ransley and Mid Surrey Health Authority* (1989) (*page 307*) Leggatt J found two general practitioners liable to an infant plaintiff for failing to diagnose significant damage to the oesophagus after the child had put her mouth to a spout of a hot teapot. Negligence was compounded in this case by failures in respect of a proper examination, timeous referral to hospital and failing to communicate adequate and full details to the hospital.

Cursory examination also resulted in liability against a general practitioner in *Patel v Adyha* (1985) (*page 284*), where a plaintiff suffered a collapse of her spine. The general practitioner failed to diagnose this condition and had never examined the plaintiff whilst undressed. Evidence was given that local stiffness or deformity would have been detectable with proper palpation or observation of the patient while she was bending.

In *Payne v St Helier Group Hospital Management Committee* (1952) (*page 287*), the patient was kicked in the abdomen by a horse. The casualty officer saw a bruise but concluded there was no internal injury. Mr Payne was allowed to go home and subsequently he developed a fatal degree of peritonitis. The court found that the doctor should have re-checked his own diagnosis after further observation or should have obtained a second opinion (cf *Chapman v Rix* (1960) (*page 177*)). Accordingly it may not be negligent to misdiagnose initially but negligence may follow if a re-diagnosis should properly have been made following changes and developments in the patient's signs and symptoms.

Alternatively there are many cases which indicate the limits imposed on a practitioner by the manner in which a patient relates his symptoms or indeed by the manner in which the symptoms are presented through the patient. In *Crivon v Barnet Group Hospital Management Committee* (1958) (*page 189*), a pathologist who diagnosed cancer was not held negligent when it transpired that the growth was in fact non-malignant. Evidence was adduced and accepted that such an error could have been made even by the greatest expert in the field, and a wrong diagnosis did not mean a negligent diagnosis. In *Whiteford v Hunter* (1950) (*page 340*), a surgeon diagnosed, during the course of an operation on a prostate, an inoperable degree of cancerous growth. The plaintiff was informed of this terminal condition which in fact turned out to be benign. The doctor was criticised for not taking a biopsy or not using an instrument called a cystoscope. Medical witnesses gave evidence that to use the type of cystoscope typically available in the United Kingdom at that time and in the particular circumstances of the operation would not have been acting in accord with the general and approved practice. Similarly no negligence was established in *Hulse v Wilson* (1953) (*page 243*) where a thirty year old man was diagnosed as suffering from a venereal disease when in fact he had cancer which necessitated the amputation of his penis. Finnemore J found the misdiagnosis had been made at a time when there was no reason to suspect the early stages of cancer, particularly in the light of this type of cancer being rare in a man of the plaintiff's age.

In *Warren v Greig; Warren v White* (1935) (*page 337*), the failure to diagnose leukaemia was not negligent. In *Sutton v Population Services Family Planning Programme Limited* (1981) (*page 324*), negligence was established in a nurse's failure to take steps to diagnose a highly malignant form of cancer. In

Vaughan v *Paddington and North Kensington Area Health Authority* (1987) (*page 332*), a false diagnosis of cancer which led to an unnecessary double mastectomy led to an admission of liability.

In *Maynard* v *West Midlands Regional Health Authority* (1984) (*page 271*), the House of Lords had affirmed the *Bolam* medical standard of care in cases of misdiagnosis. Lord Scarman quoted with approval the Lord President in *Hunter* v *Hanley* [1955] SLT at 217 (*page 243*) to the effect that to establish medical negligence in misdiagnosis a plaintiff had to prove a failure such that no doctor acting with ordinary skill and care would commit. The decision in *Maynard* to use a particular diagnostic procedure could not amount to negligence when a competent body of professional opinion would have used the same technique known as mediastinoscopy.

In *Barker* v *Nugent* (1987) (*page 157*), a general practitioner was held not to have been negligent in a case where he failed to diagnose meningitis in a three week old baby. The court, which heard the action eleven years later, found that the child had not been sufficiently ill to warrant hospitalization when the doctor examined it. The doctor was also held to have been entitled to bear in mind that the mother resided in a council home which had a nurse on its staff. In *Sadler* v *Henry* (1954) (*page 308*), a twenty-six year old woman died after suffering from localised meningitis which the G.P. had diagnosed as hysteria. Cassels J said that this was an error which others might well have made, and declined to find negligence.

The courts have also refused to find liability in cases where a school doctor misjudged the severity of a child's hepatitis (*Holland* v *The Devitt and Moore Nautical College Limited* (1960) (*page 237*)); where a finger infection was overlooked because the patient presented with a sprain (*Hogg* v *Ealing, Hammersmith and Hounslow Area Health Authority* (1982) (*page 236*)); where a ruptured Achilles' tendon was diagnosed as a partially ruptured Achilles' tendon (*Rouse* v *Kensington and Chelsea and Westminster Area Health Authority* (1982) (*page 303*)); where a ship's doctor diagnosed a mild rheumatic complaint instead of acute rheumatoid arthritis (*Pudney* v *Union-Castle Mail Steamship Company Limited* (1953) (*page 291*)). Neither did the striking temporal proof of error avail a widow in *Parkinson* v *West Cumberland Hospital Management Committee* (1955) (*page 283*). In this case a newly qualified doctor in his fourth day at a hospital had spent nearly one hour investigating a patient's complaint of chest pain. The patient left the hospital with two tablets of codeine and was told to return later for X-rays. The patient died a quarter of an hour later from massive coronary thrombosis. Ashworth J found the examination had been careful, and there were signs and symptoms pointing away from the serious condition.

Finally, the courts have required proper and reasonable grounds for the certification of a person as insane or mentally ill so as to warrant forced committal to a mental institution. A number of cases illustrate the duty that a doctor owed to someone who was not his patient but who was brought to his notice, often by relatives with the intention of having the person committed under the various Lunacy Acts. In *Hall* v *Semple* (1862) (*page 224*) a local physician and surgeon signed a certificate under the current Lunacy Act after one of them had seen the patient in an excited and rude state. The defendant had been told a number of adverse things about the plaintiff by the plaintiff's wife. The jury found the doctor had signed the certificate without reasonable grounds and without proper examination and enquiry. In *De*

Freville v *Dill* (1927) (*page 197*), a matrimonial dispute resulted in a husband alleging that his wife, the plaintiff, was of unsound mind. The defendant signed the relevant certificate under the Lunacy Act 1890, and as a result a Justice of the Peace committed her to a mental hospital. The hospital released her the following day, finding no grounds for her detention, and the jury indicated negligence on the part of the doctor in failing to act with reasonable care notwithstanding the fact that it was the plaintiff's husband and father-in-law who had employed the doctor. A similar duty was found to have existed but not to have been breached in *Everett* v *Griffiths* (1920) (*page 206*), where a twenty-three year old represented himself in person in court with remarkable forensic ability to demonstrate that he was not insane contrary to the defendant's diagnosis. However, the certifying medical practitioner was found in the case to have acted with reasonable care and in good faith. In *Harnett* v *Fisher* (1927) (*page 227*), a plaintiff was found to have been wrongfully confined in a lunatic asylum for nearly nine years because the certifying practitioner had acted negligently. A logical, but extremely harsh, application of the Limitation Act 1623 held he was time-barred in bringing his action. That Act allowed six years to bring an action, and because the plaintiff was not in fact insane he did not suffer from a disability so as to stop time running. Accordingly the six years had elapsed before he finally made his escape from the institution.

Leave to bring an action for wrongful certification under s 16(2) Mental Treatment Act 1930 was given in *Re Frost* (1936) (*page 212*), where the Court of Appeal upheld the view that to despatch a patient into an institution without medical examination and on the basis of behaviour contained in a short statement from the patient's doctor gave substantial grounds for indicating the doctor had acted without reasonable care. (For current cases see *Furber* v *Kratter* (1988) (*page 212*) and *Winch* v *Jones* (1985) (*page 346*).)

Chapter 9

Consenting, informing and advising

This chapter examines the case law that has arisen out of three areas concerning a medical practitioner's failure to communicate adequately with the patient. The first area concerns cases where there has been no proper consultation or discussion before treatment, with the result that the patient does not consent to the treatment or part of it. Secondly, many cases involve allegations of failure by the medical practitioner to disclose to the patient the inherent risks in the proposed mode of treatment, so that the patient consents without full knowledge of significant facts. The third area concerns alleged failure to give the patient adequate advice and warnings, whether in a therapeutic or a non-therapeutic context.

These failures of communication stem from the imbalance of knowledge, arguably accompanied by an imbalance of power, which is found at the base of the doctor/patient relationship. The courts, to some extent, have sought to redress this balance in two ways: firstly, by holding that any interference with a patient's body without his consent can amount to a battery; secondly, by deeming a practitioner to be negligent if he falls below the standard of due care in informing or advising his patient. In general, except in cases involving a total absence of consent, the medical standard of care based on generally approved medical practice tends to prevail over any doctrine rooted in a patient's right to know.

Despite the absence of hostile intent, it is good law that if a practitioner performs an operation or other treatment on a patient without the patient's consent, an action will lie for battery or trespass to the person. The intentional interference with a patient without legal justification amounts to an actionable assault. Cardozo J put the matter succinctly in an American case when he said:

"Every human being of adult years and sound mind has a right to determine what shall be done with his own body: and a surgeon who performs an operation without his patient's consent commits an assault for which he is liable in damages. This is true except in cases of emergency where the patient is unconscious and where it is necessary to operate before consent can be obtained" (*Schloendorff* v *Society of the New York Hospital* 105 NE 92 (NY 1914)).

As has been indicated in Chapter 1, the legal justification for determining that medical treatment on a person who is unconscious or who is mentally incompetent to give consent was determined by the House of Lords in *F* v *West Berkshire Health Authority* (1989) (*page 207*) as being based upon a doctrine of necessity whereby the practitioner acts in the best interests of the patient.

If a doctor therefore performs an operation which is of a non-emergency nature, and not one arising out of "necessity", without the consent of the patient, the doctor is likely to be liable in trespass. This is true even if the doctor has acted in what he thinks was the best interest of the patient. In *Hamilton* v *Birmingham Regional Hospital Board* (1969) (*page 226*), a forty year old Catholic woman was sterilised without her consent after the birth of her third child which, like the others, was born by caesarean section. Mrs Hamilton had not been consulted about the operation at all, and the defendants admitted liability. Liability was also conceded in *Devi* v *West Midlands Regional Health Authority* (1981) (*page 198*), where, following an operation to repair the tear in Mrs Devi's uterus, the surgeon took the undiscussed and unagreed decision to sterilise her. Similarly, in *Cull* v *Butler* (1932) (*page 192*), Mrs Cull succeeded in an action for breach of contract and trespass to the person after a surgeon performed a hysterectomy on her, despite her specific refusal to consent to that operation, having consented to a curettage only. It appears that the patient's specific instructions had become detached from her notes (see also *Leigh* v *Gladstone* (1910) (*page 258*), *Latter* v *Braddell* (1881) (*page 256*), *Freeman* v *Home Office* (1984) (*page 211*)).

In modern surgical operations, the consent from a patient which renders the medical bodily interference lawful is invariably written. In the National Health Service, a patient signs a consent form which contains a statement to the effect that the nature and purpose of the operation has been explained to him and consent is extended to alternative or further operations and anaesthetics that may be found necessary during the course of the operation. In such cases of written express consent, the extent of the consent will be subject to the construction of the actual words used and the actual operations undertaken. The consent cannot be construed as a *carte blanche* for the surgeon, as any additional and unintended surgical intervention must be deemed to have been necessary. Consent may also be oral, or in certain circumstances, implied. In *Beatty* v *Cullingworth* (1896) (*page 159*), the plaintiff, a nurse, was diagnosed as having a diseased right ovary which required removal. She consented to this operation but did not agree to the removal of both ovaries should the need arise. The defendant surgeon said he could not promise in advance not to remove the left ovary because it would depend on what he found upon examination. The plaintiff told the surgeon as she came into the operating theatre that he should not remove either of the ovaries if he found both were diseased. The defendant replied that that should be left to him and he understood the plaintiff's wishes and would not do anything that he did not have to do. The plaintiff failed to reply to the surgeon's last statement. The surgeon removed the left ovary, as he determined it was necessary to save her life. The jury were instructed that the central issue was whether there had been tacit consent, and in finding for the doctor it appears they did construe such a position.

In *Breen* v *Baker* (1956) (*page 170*), a plaintiff signed a consent form containing the words: "I agree to leave the nature and extent of the operation to be performed to the discretion of the surgeon". Barry J construed these words as wide enough to extend consent from the intended dilatation and curettage to cover a total hysterectomy which was performed after fibrosis was found during the operation.

These cases indicate that where there is no consent and where consent cannot be reasonably implied or where the bounds of consent have been exceeded in a non-emergency situation, an action will lie in trespass to the person against the practitioner. Where, however, the basis of the plaintiff's allegation is that inadequate information was given about the inherent risks of the treatment consented to, the courts have been quick to reject a cause of action in English law based on trespass. Consent is not vitiated by a failure to inform the patient fully of the details of the possible adverse consequences of the proposed operation so as to render the treatment an assault (*Chatterton* v *Gerson* (1980) (*page 178*), *Hills* v *Potter* (1984) (*page 233*), and *Sidaway* v *Board of Governors of the Bethlem Royal Hospital and the Maudsley Hospital* (1985) (*page 314*)). In such cases of alleged failure to disclose inherent risks, any cause of action that might exist has been held to lie in negligence.

It is clear law that part of a practitioner's duty of care is to give advice and information to a patient so that the patient understands the nature of the treatment proposed. The case law, however, illustrates the difficulty in determining just how much information a patient should receive; whether, for example, the curious should be told more than the uninquisitive, whether the doctor has a residual discretion to withhold or even distort information, and whether the standard of care in disclosure cases should be different in therapeutic and non-therapeutic circumstances.

In *Hatcher* v *Black* (1954) (*page 229*), the patient was not told that the partial thyroidectomy that she consented to carried a slight risk of permanent impairment to her voice. On the contrary, she was told there was no risk. The operation left her with a paralysed vocal cord. Denning LJ summed up to the jury in the following way:

> "What should a doctor tell a patient? The surgeon has admitted that on the evening before the operation he told the plaintiff that there was no risk to her voice when he knew that there was some slight risk; but that he did it for her own good because it was of vital importance that she should not worry . . . he told a lie; but he did it because in the circumstances it was justifiable . . . But the law does not condemn the doctor when he only does what a wise doctor so placed would do. And none of the doctors called as witnesses have suggested that the surgeon was wrong. All agreed that it was a matter for his own judgement. If they do not condemn him, why should you".

The jury returned a verdict for the defendant.

The standard of care implicit in Lord Denning's words to the jury was the one adopted in *Bolam* v *Friern Hospital Management Committee* (1957) (*page 166*), where, *inter alia*, a failure to warn a plaintiff of a slight risk of a fracture occurring during the administration of an ECT was held not to have been negligent because it accorded with a practice adopted by a competent body of medical opinion. This has come to be called the medical standard of care, and in disclosure cases the test is whether the quantity and quality of information disclosed to a patient is in accord with the practice adopted by either the profession as a whole or any responsible body of opinion within it. Accordingly, where information is generalised or where the risks are minimised or distorted, a defence will exist to an action for negligent disclosure if the practice accords with that of a respectable body of opinion within the profession. In *Waters* v *Park* (1961) (*page 337*), a plaintiff was sterilised in a particular manner which was known to carry a slight risk of failure but which was adopted because of a heart condition from which she suffered. The surgeon's practice was to inform a patient in these circumstances of the failure risk, but he did not tell the plaintiff after the operation because he had no opportunity to do so in privacy within a crowded ward. The defendant gave the plaintiff an appointment to come back in six weeks when he intended to tell her of the risk. The plaintiff never kept the appointment and she later conceived and required a further sterilisation. Her action failed on the basis that, notwithstanding it was this particular practitioner's practice and intent to disclose the risks to the plaintiff, there were two schools of thought about informing a patient, and in these circumstances the failure to tell the patient did not constitute negligence because there was a responsible body of opinion which would not have informed her in any event.

In *Wells* v *Surrey Area Health Authority* (1978) (*page 338*), a thirty-five year old Catholic mother, while exhausted during labour with her third child, was offered sterilisation and signed a consent form. She later sued in assault on the grounds that her consent was not valid because she signed it when she did not realise the implications because of her particular condition. This cause of action failed on the basis that she did know what the implications of signing a consent form were. The hospital, however, were found negligent for failing to give her proper advice and counselling which was an important preliminary to sterilisation.

Bristow J considered in *Chatterton* v *Gerson* (1980) (*page 178*) the duty of care owed to a patient in respect of disclosing risks in a proposed treatment, and concurred with the reasoning in *Bolam* (above) and *Hatcher* (above) that the doctor was required to explain what he intended to do in the way a careful and responsible doctor in similar circumstances would have done. Miss Chatterton suffered from severe pain emanating from an operation scar and sought the defendant's help in alleviating it. She underwent a nerve block operation which failed to stop the pain, and contended she was not warned that this operation could result in numbness and muscle weakness. The first operation was unsuccessful, and a second operation was undertaken with the defendant merely informing the patient that she knew what to expect. This operation not only failed to alleviate the severe pain but produced a loss of feeling in the right leg. Bristow J held that her claim in trespass failed because the doctor had explained in broad terms the nature of the operation, and her consent was therefore real. He also found that as a matter of fact the plaintiff had been given sufficient information in the circumstances and that the failure to warn about the loss of function in the leg was not unreasonable:

> "In my judgement there is no obligation on the doctor to canvass with the patient anything other than the inherent implications of the particular operation he intends to carry out. He is certainly under no obligation to say that if he operates incompetently he will do damage. The fundamental assumption is that he knows his job and will do it properly. But he ought to warn of what may happen by misfortune however well the operation is done, if there is a real risk of misfortune inherent in the procedure, as there was in the surgery of the carotid artery in the Canadian case of *Reibl* v *Hughes* (1980) (*page 297*). In what he says, any good doctor has to take into account the personality of the patient, the likelihood of a misfortune, and what in the way of warning is for the particular patient's welfare. I am not satisfied that Dr Gerson fell short of his duty to tell the plaintiff of the implications of this operation, properly carried out . . . there was no risk of significant damage to the motor nerves. There was not foreseeable risk

that her leg and foot would be deprived of sensation or control, nor am I satisfied that anything done in the course of the second injection caused that result." ([1980] 3 WLR at 1014 c-h.)

Similar principles were espoused in *Hills v Potter* (1984) (*page 233*). Mrs Hills sued for assault and battery and in negligence in respect of paralysis resulting from an operation designed to relieve a neck deformity. She claimed that she had not been properly informed of the risks inherent in the operation and that such failure vitiated her consent or alternatively amounted to negligence. Specifically the plaintiff contended that she had not been told of any risk of the possibility of anaesthetic complications, death or paralysis. The defendant doctor, as in *Chatterton* (above), could not remember precisely the warning he gave but thought that it would have been his normal advice which varied according to the ability of the patient to understand it but would have included the risks of death, anaesthetic mishap or paralysis which was likely to be temporary or transient. The judge, Hirst J, found that the defendant had given a detailed explanation of the operation, its risks and complications and this was in full accord with accepted practice. The judge went on to affirm the view that the standard of care applicable to questions of treatment and diagnoses was also that applicable to questions of advice. He rejected the plaintiff's arguments that there should be a higher standard of care in disclosure cases so that the practitioner had a duty to disclose sufficient information to found the basis of an informed consent as formulated in certain transatlantic cases. Hirst J said that the medical standard must always be one that is upheld by a substantial body of medical opinion which is both respectable, responsible and experienced in the particular field of medicine in issue. On the facts he went on to indicate the defendant's conduct would have in any event stood up to the much more rigorous so-called prudent patient test inherent in the doctrine of informed consent.

The House of Lords, in the leading case of *Sidaway v Board of Governors of the Bethlem Royal Hospital and the Maudsley Hospital* (1985) (*page 314*), further endorsed the approach in *Chatterton* and *Hills*, rejecting the applicability of the doctrine of informed consent. The doctrine, as established in the American case of *Canterbury v Spence* (1972) (*page 175*) and as discussed in the Canadian cases of *Reibl v Hughes* (1980) (*page 297*) and *Hopp v Lepp* (1980) postulates that the disclosure of risks should be made to any patient if the risk is material.

"A risk is thus material when a reasonable person, in what the physician knows or should know to be the patient's position would be likely to attach significance to the risk or cluster or risks in deciding whether or not to forgo the proposed therapy". (*Canterbury v Spence* (1972) 464 F 2d at 791.)

In *Sidaway*, the plaintiff suffered from persistent pain in her arms, and during the course of spinal surgery to relieve nerve root pressure the spinal cord was damaged causing severe disablement. The trial judge, Skinner J, found the surgeon, who had died before the trial, had not told the plaintiff of the risk of spinal cord damage although he had mentioned the possibility of disturbing a nerve root but not damage to the cord itself. Applying the *Bolam* test to the question of disclosure, the judge found that in failing to inform the plaintiff of the possibility of nerve cord damage the surgeon was acting in accord with a responsible body of competent neuro-surgeons who likewise never mentioned such risks so as to avoid frightening a patient. The risk of spinal cord damage was assessed at less than one per cent. The plaintiff's claim failed and the Court of Appeal affirmed the trial judge's view that the law in relation to failures in diagnosis and treatment also applied to failures in the realm of advice. Lord Donaldson, the Master of the Rolls, reviewed the leading transatlantic cases giving rise to the prudent patient test in the doctrine of informed consent, but declined to incorporate those principles into English law:

> "Once it is conceded, as of course it is, that a patient who is of sound mind sufficient age and capable of exercising a choice is entitled to grant or to withhold consent to treatment as he sees fit, the relationship of doctor and patient must carry with it some duty to give information to the patient which will enable him, if he is minded, to reach a rational decision. The problem is how to define the duty and having defined it, how to determine whether the duty has been discharged. . . . what information should be disclosed and how and when it should be disclosed is very much a matter for professional judgement, to be exercised in the context of the doctor's relationship with a particular patient in particular circumstances. It is for this reason that I would reject the American formulation of the duty by reference to a 'prudent patient' test". ([1984] 2 WLR at 790–791.)

The Master of the Rolls went on to indicate that the general duty of care included disclosing as well as withholding such information as was reasonable in all the circumstances to place the patient in a position to make a rational choice. The adoption of this so-called medical standard implicit in the *Bolam* test was not seen by the Master of the Rolls as abdicating responsibility to the medical profession. The practice held by the body of responsible practitioners had to be one that was rightly and properly held, and the court would not:

> "stand idly by if the profession by an excess of paternalism denies their patients real choice. In a word the law will not allow the medical profession to play God". ([1984] 2 WLR at 791 g-h.)

Lord Justice Browne-Wilkinson thought the American doctrine was rooted in a particular fiduciary relationship between doctor and patient in American law so that breach of the relationship vitiated consent. He found no such justification for the doctrine in English law. He went on to formulate a proposition that a doctor was under a duty to disclose to the patient information relevant to the decision the patient would have to take, and this would include the benefits and risks but would be subject to the emotional state of the patient as well as, of course, the degree of risk concerned. There was also an explicit recognition of policy:

> "It is inevitable that in considering this case one is acutely aware of the policy problem which it raises. In particular I have been very conscious of the need to ensure that the duty of care imposed by the law is not such as to inhibit the proper function of the medical profession in caring for the sick by exposing doctors to the threat of legal proceedings in which their actions will be judged by hindsight, not by reference to the standards of those skilled in the art, but by judge and jury. It is for this reason that I am not prepared to adopt the much stricter rules as to disclosure laid down in the transatlantic cases which involve an objective judgement both as to the materiality of the risk and the adequacy of the disclosure. It is common

knowledge that such rules have led to a large number of claims against doctors based on failure to warn; in consequence, a number of States in the USA have introduced legislation to modify the doctrine of informed consent" ([1984] 2 WLR at 801 a-d).

The House of Lords in *Sidaway* (*page 314*) affirmed the Court of Appeal's reasoning that the *Bolam* test was applicable in deciding whether a practitioner was negligent in failing to disclose inherent risks in treatment. The House of Lords, by a majority of four to one, indicated that to prove negligence in such cases a plaintiff must show that a practitioner, in failing to warn, fell below the standards of practice regarded as proper by a competent body of professional opinion and accordingly the doctor was not under a duty to warn a patient of any material risk. Only Lord Scarman dissented and embraced a modified version of the doctrine of informed consent:

". . . I think that English law must recognize a duty of the doctor to warn his patient of risk inherent in the treatment which he is proposing; and especially so, if the treatment be surgery. The critical limitation is that this duty is confined to material risk. The test of materiality is whether in the circumstances of the particular case the court is satisfied that a reasonable person in the patient's position will be likely to attach significance to the risk. Even if the risk be material the doctor will not be liable if upon a reasonable assessment of his patient's condition, he takes the view that a warning would be detrimental to his patient's health" ([1985] AC at 889g–890a).

Even applying this test, Lord Scarman would not have allowed the plaintiff's appeal.

Lords Keith, Bridge and Templeman did indicate two glosses, however, on the *Bolam* test. First, their Lordships were of the view that there might be circumstances where treatment involved such a substantial risk of grave consequences that notwithstanding the view of the responsible body of medical opinion, a patient should be told of the risk, as no prudent medical man should refrain from telling the patient of that type of risk:

". . . I am of (the) opinion that the judge might in certain circumstances come to the conclusion that disclosure of a particular risk was so obviously necessary to an informed choice on the part of the patient that no reasonably prudent medical man would fail to make it. The kind of case I have in mind would be an operation involving a substantial risk of grave adverse consequences, as for example, the ten per cent risk of a stroke from the operation which was the subject of the Canadian case of *Reibl* v *Hughes*. In such a case, in the absence of some cogent clinical reason why the patient should not be informed, a doctor, recognizing and respecting his patient's right of decision, could hardly fail to appreciate the necessity for an appropriate warning" (per Lord Bridge [1985] AC at 900 e-g).

Secondly, their Lordships indicated the position may be different if the patient specifically asked about risks:

"No doubt if the patient in fact manifested this attitude (of wishing to be informed of any risk) by means of questioning, the doctor would tell him whatever it was the patient wanted to know; but we are concerned here with voluntary unsought information about risks of the proposed treatment . . ." (per Lord Diplock [1985] AC at 895c).

Lord Bridge also indicated a similar view:

"I should perhaps add at this point, although the issue does not strictly arise in this appeal, that, when questioned specifically by a patient of apparently sound mind about risks involved in a particular treatment proposed, the doctor's duty must, in my opinion, be to answer both truthfully and as fully as the question requires" ([1985] AC at 898 b-c).

Thus in affirming the medical standard of care in disclosure cases, the House of Lords did manage to impose an outer limit on the practitioner's discretion and appear to have smoothed off some of the rougher edges of *Hatcher* v *Black* (1954) (*page 229*). It appears that it can no longer be part of the standard of care to lie to a patient in response to direct questioning.

An attempt to establish a different standard of care in cases concerning disclosure and advice in a non-therapeutic setting, as opposed to a therapeutic setting, was made in *Gold* v *Haringey Health Authority* (1987) (*page 219*). Mrs Gold was advised to undergo sterilisation after the birth of her third child. The operation was unsuccessful and she became pregnant again. She brought an action alleging, *inter alia*, a failure to warn her of the rate of unsuccessful sterilisations. She maintained that had she been informed of this failure rate her husband would have opted for a vasectomy instead. Schiemann J heard evidence that a substantial body of medical opinion at the time in question, 1979, would not have warned about the failure rate. If the *Bolam* test was applicable, therefore, the case would fail. The judge however drew a distinction between therapeutic and non-therapeutic settings and found the defendants liable. The Court of Appeal reversed the decision of the trial judge and applied the doctrine of law in *Sidaway* (above) to cover all aspects of the medical relationship, be this advice, diagnosis or treatment. Accordingly, advice in a contraceptive rather than a therapeutic context still fell to be considered within the *Bolam* medical standard of care. The plaintiff also failed on appeal in *Gold* with respect to an argument accepted by the trial judge that the representation that the operation was irreversible amounted to a misrepresentation because the sterilisation failed. The Court of Appeal held that, as in *Eyre* v *Measday* (1986) (*page 207*), the word irreversible was referable to the fact that the operation was incapable of being reversed and not a representation that sterility would be guaranteed (cf *Worster* v *City and Hackney Health Authority* (1987) (*page 348*)). The Court of Appeal in *Gold* also distinguished *Thake* v *Maurice* (1986) (*page 327*) where a surgeon had been held negligent in not warning the patient about the risk of the failure rate in vasectomy. That case was unusual because expert evidence was not adduced by either side. Accordingly, to succeed in an action in negligence for a failure to warn or advise in respect of risks inherent in a proposed mode of treatment, a plaintiff must show either that no respectable body of competent practitioners in the specialism in issue would fail to disclose the risk or that the risk was so obviously necessary to an informed choice that no prudent practitioner ought to fail to disclose it. It would appear that in rejecting the prudent patient test the House of Lords has given some authority to the prudent practitioner test.

Given this medical standard of care, it is perhaps not surprising that plaintiffs seldom succeed in such actions. In *Blyth* v *Bloomsbury Health Authority* (1987) (*page 166*), the plaintiff received an injection of the contraceptive Depo-Provera and was told of the side effects of menstrual irregularity and

73

irregular bleeding. The doctor however did not inform the plaintiff of other risks that the doctor knew about and that had been collated in the plaintiff's file. The medical witnesses gave evidence that in 1978 when the injection was given there was no need to pass on or to disclose such information, and the plaintiff's action therefore failed.

In *Buckle* v *DeLaunay* (1970) (*page 172*), a doctor told a patient to whom he had prescribed parnate not to eat cheese or marmite. The plaintiff ate cheese and died. In an action brought by the deceased's husband, an allegation was made that the warning was not adequate because it failed to mention the danger of not complying with the doctor's instructions which could be fatal. The warning however was held to be adequate.

In *O'Malley-Williams* v *Governors of National Hospital for Nervous Diseases* (1975) (*page 280*), the plaintiff underwent an aortagram to assist in the diagnosis of loss of vision to the right eye. He was not told of any risk inherent in the procedure. During the course of administering the aortagram, damage was caused which resulted in partial paralysis of the right hand. Bridge J held, *inter alia*, that the failure to warn of a remote risk where the patient had not raised the question was not negligent.

However, in *Smith* v *Barking, Havering and Brentwood Health Authority* (1989) (*page 318*), the plaintiff did establish a negligent failure to warn where a surgeon did not disclose that an operation to drain a cyst in the upper cervical canal carried with it an approximately twenty-five per cent risk of immediate tetraplegia. Without the operation the plaintiff might have been rendered tetraplegic in about one year, in any event. The operation did result in immediate and irreversible tetraplegia. Hutchison J held that a careful explanation was owed to the plaintiff before the operation, and the doctor had negligently failed to tell her, on the one hand, about the prospect of the twenty-five per cent risk and, on the other hand, the prospect of the risk if surgery was not undertaken. The plaintiff, however, failed to achieve substantial damages, for the judge further found that had proper disclosure been made the plaintiff would have been likely to have agreed to the operation in any event. She was awarded £3,000 for the shock and depression upon discovering without prior warning that she had been rendered tetraplegic. This case vividly illustrates the significance of the prudent practitioner test which the House of Lords in *Sidaway* (above) has imposed on the *Bolam* standard of care in disclosure cases. It also graphically illustrates the Pyrrhic nature of such a victory because, having cleared the hurdle of negligence, plaintiffs in this category of cases frequently fall at the hurdle of causation.

If a medical mishap does occur, the practitioner is most likely under a legal duty to explain to the patient what has occurred. Accordingly in *Gerber* v *Pines* (1935) (*page 216*), a doctor was found liable to a patient not because a needle broke during the course of an injection but because he failed timeously to inform the plaintiff that part of the needle had been left in her body. Du Parcq J found there had been a breach of duty for not informing the plaintiff at once of what had happened. Similarly, in *Cooper* v *Miron* (1927) (*page 185*) a dentist was found negligent for failing to inform a patient that part of one of her molars had broken off and disappeared down her throat. The Master of the Rolls, Sir John Donaldson, has also stipulated that it is part of a practitioner's duty to inform patients of what treatment they actually did receive, and in principle there appears to be nothing offensive to a patient seeking this information by an action for specific performance of such a duty to inform (*Lee* v *South West Thames Regional Health Authority* (1985) (*page 257*), *Naylor* v *Preston Area Health Authority* (1987) (*page 278*)). In *Naylor* the Master of the Rolls expressed the following view:

"I personally think that in professional negligence cases, and in particular in medical negligence cases, there is a duty of candour resting upon the professional man. This is recognized by the legal professions in their ethical rules requiring their members to refer the client to other advisors, if it appears that the client has a valid claim for negligence. This also appears to be recognized by the Medical Defence Union, whose view is that 'the patient is entitled to a prompt, sympathetic and above all truthful account of what has occurred': Journal of the Medical Defence Union, Spring 1987, p.23" ([1987] 1 WLR at 967 e-g).

Chapter 10

Substandard treatment

Many medical malpractice actions derive from accidents occasioned during the course of treatment or during after-care. In a review of five hundred cases contained within the Medical Protection Society files, Leahy-Taylor, in Chapter 4 of *The Doctor and Negligence* (Pitman Medical, 1971), formed the view that the most common incidents concerning allegations of substandard treatment arose in cases involving retained swabs and other instruments after operations, burns, anaesthetic mishaps and cases where the wrong operation was performed. The vast bulk of such cases never get to trial. The following illustrative categories of substandard care are not intended to be exhaustive but they do reflect the type of case that has tended to be litigated in the past and accordingly demonstrate the approach of the courts in certain factual situations.

1. Surgical and allied mishaps

The House of Lords confirmed in *Whitehouse* v *Jordan* (1981) (*page 341*) that the *Bolam* test was applicable to errors in the course of treatment procedures including childbirth and surgery. It is axiomatic that not every mistake or error during the course of an operation or treatment programme will amount to negligence. If the practitioner can establish that he was acting within a mode of practice that was accepted as proper by a responsible body of practitioners and that he was using the requisite degree of skill and care during the administering of the treatment, he would not be liable for a mistake that occurred. In *Whitehouse* the Court of Appeal reversed the decision of Bush J who found that Mr Jordan had delayed for too long before delivering a child by caesarean section and had pulled too hard and for too long with forceps. The House of Lords confirmed the Court of Appeal's ruling and in effect found that no error had been made by Mr Jordan, in the same way that no error had been made in the case of *Bolam*.

Where, however, errors have been found as facts, they quite frequently fall into a category of mistake which occurred notwithstanding the exercise of ordinary care and skill. In *Mose* v *North West Hertfordshire Health Authority* (1987) (*page 276*), a consultant orthopaedic surgeon operated to remove what was thought to be a cyst behind a child's right knee. The operation in fact revealed a tumour, and in removing the tumour three inches of the popliteal nerve was also removed, leading to a complete foot drop. The trial judge found that the surgeon had been negligent because he was not a person who was experienced in this type of work. Evidence was adduced that if an inexperienced surgeon discovered these circumstances the proper course

76

would have been to have closed the wound and called a specialist surgeon to investigate. The Court of Appeal reversed this finding on the basis that the surgeon was in fact experienced in this type of work and was entitled to conduct the operation.

In *White* v *Board of Governors of Westminster Hospital* (1961) (*page 340*), a surgeon who was operating on a child's squint inadvertently cut the retina while severing muscle and tendon attached by scar tissue. The eye shrunk and had to be removed. The plaintiff was held to be a victim of a mischance rather than of negligence. The scale of the operation was so fine that an error like this could occur notwithstanding that due skill, care and judgement had been exercised. In *O'Malley-Williams* v *Governors of National Hospital for Nervous Diseases* (1975) (*page 280*), an aortagram under a local anaesthetic proved difficult to administer. An attempt to pass the guide-wire through the femoral artery was abandoned and several attempts were required to pass it through the right axillary artery during which great pain was occasioned to the plaintiff. Bridge J held it was not negligent to continue to try to pass the wire because pain was not uncommon during this procedure under local anaesthetic. The plaintiff accordingly failed in his claim for damages arising out of partial paralysis of the right hand caused by nerve damage during the passing of the wire. In *Crawford* v *Board of Governors of Charing Cross Hospital* (1953) (*page 188*), no negligence was established against a doctor who had kept an arm extended at an angle of eighty degrees from the body during a transfusion. The result was a brachial palsy in the only good arm the plaintiff had. Knowledge that this was a dangerous method had only appeared in *The Lancet* six months previously.

Conversely, in *Patten* v *Birmingham Regional Hospital Board* (1955) (*page 286*) a house surgeon who not only removed part of the wrong finger but also failed in time to stitch fingers requiring treatment was found liable for the damage sustained to the hand. In *Cassidy* v *Ministry of Health* (1951) (*page 176*) a plaintiff, left with a virtually useless hand after an operation to relieve Dupuytrens contracture, established liability after the maxim *res ipsa loquitur* was held to apply. In *Saunders* v *Leeds Western Health Authority* (1985) (*page 310*) a four year old suffered a cardiac arrest while being operated upon. The doctrine *res ipsa loquitur* was held to apply, and the defendants failed to rebut the presumption of negligence. In *Croke* v *Wiseman* (1982) (*page 189*), the defendants admitted liability where an infant plaintiff suffered a cardio-respiratory failure while doctors were examining him. In *Wilsher* v *Essex Area Health Authority* (1988) (*page 344*) and in *Murray* v *Kensington and Chelsea and Westminster Area Health Authority* (1981) (*page 277*), negligence was established where premature babies were administered with excessive volumes of oxygen. In *Murray* no causation was established, and in *Wilsher* the House of Lords ordered a retrial on the question of causation. Negligence was also established in *Blackburn* v *Newcastle-upon-Tyne Health Authority* (1988) (*page 165*) when a plaintiff suffered severe brain damage after a tracheostomy tube became blocked with secretions. Either the medical or the nursing staff were negligent in failing to keep the tube clear.

The borderline between a negligent and a non-negligent mistake or error of judgement can be difficult to draw. (See *Whitehouse* v *Jordan* (1981) (*page 341*) for the classic exposition of this distinction.) Kilner-Brown J was faced with clear anguish in *Ashcroft* v *Mersey Regional Health Authority* (1983) (*page 153*) when he observed:

"This claim reveals a disgraceful state of affairs. Where an injury is caused which never should have been caused common sense and natural justice indicate that some degree of compensation ought to be paid by someone. As the law stands, in order to obtain compensation an injured person is compelled to allege negligence against a surgeon who may, as in this case, be a careful, dedicated person of the highest skill and reputation. If ever there was a case in which some reasonable compromise was called for, which would provide some amount of solace for the injured person, and avoid the pillorying of a distinguished surgeon, this was such a case" ([1983] 2 All ER 246 a-b).

The trial judge went on to find for the surgeon after applying the *Bolam* test in respect of an operation to remove granulated tissue from an eardrum. This was a routine operation for the surgeon which he had undertaken hundreds of times and had never caused the damage which was occasioned to the plaintiff, namely a severe paralysis of the facial nerve. The judge concluded:

". . . I am faced with the agonising question of deciding whether the probabilities are such that I am driven to say of Mr Siegler (the surgeon) that he has convinced himself that he did not use too much force when in fact he must have done so. It is not an easy problem and is a question of whether the proper inferences drawn from the primary facts are such that on this occasion Mr Siegler's belief in his carefulness is misplaced and that he did fall below the standard of care expected of him. In the end I have come to the conclusion that I cannot go so far".

Leahy-Taylor (ibid) provides examples of much clearer cases which have led to settlement. These cases are derived from files and not from reported hearings. They include examples of a patient's healthy testicle being removed in a mistaken belief that it was part of a hernial mass, an amputation being necessary following the ligation of a femoral artery during an operation for a varicose vein, the snipping of a new born baby's finger whilst cutting the umbilical cord, fatal accidents resulting from a patient being given the wrong type of blood, and a death caused by the application of Nupercaine jelly into a patient's anus in the mistaken belief it was Lignocaine. (See also *Waghorn* v *Lewisham and North Southwark Area Health Authority* (1987) (*page 334*).)

2. Needles and injections

Given the frequency of suturing and the routine use of injections in medical treatment, it is not surprising that mishaps occur which frequently give rise to allegations of negligence. The mere breaking of the needle of a hypodermic syringe is probably not indicative of negligence. In *Brazier* v *Ministry of Defence* (1965) (*page 169*), McNair J did, however, find that the breaking of a needle which remained lodged in the right buttock of the plaintiff required explanation. Mr Brazier alleged the one and a half inch fine needle broke because the ship's doctor treated it in a dagger-like fashion and stabbed him with it. This was rejected, and the defendant's explanation that a latent defect in the shaft of the needle caused the breaking was accepted. In *Gerber* v *Pines* (1935) (*page 216*), a needle broke during an injection into the gluteus maximus muscle, and the defendant, a general practitioner, failed to inform the plaintiff. The broken part was removed five days later. The trial judge found no negligence in the administration of the injection but did find there had been a failure in disclosing to the plaintiff that part of a needle remained in her. In *Corner* v *Murray* (1954) (*page 187*), a patient was left with most of the needle *in situ* after it broke while the doctor was extracting it. The trial judge accepted evidence that the breaking of a hypodermic needle was not an uncommon occurrence and could occur, as on this occasion, without any semblance of negligence. Similarly, a schoolgirl failed in her action against a nurse following the breaking of a number sixteen needle while injecting her thigh which left approximately an inch of the needle in the patient. The trial judge dismissed the allegation that a longer and thicker needle should have been used as this would have caused more pain, and attributed the accident to an unexpected movement on the plaintiff's part as opposed to any act of pushing the needle in too far (*Marchant* v *East Ham Borough Council* (1955) (*page 268*)). In *Hunter* v *Hanley* (1955) (*page 243*), an allegation that a needle used was too thin and fragile and that it had been withdrawn at a different angle from that at which it had been put in was rejected by the jury. (This matter was sent on appeal for retrial after a misdirection by the trial judge as to the standard of care.)

Although it may not be negligent if the needle breaks whilst in use, failure to cope adequately with the consequences can of course give rise to liability. In *Henderson* v *Henderson* (1955) (*page 232*), a surgeon broke the needle whilst stitching a girl's throat after a tonsillectomy, leaving approximately one half of an inch in the throat. The surgeon made efforts with his finger and with a scalpel to find the fragment and made an incision when he thought he had located it. This search went on unsuccessfully for approximately one hour. The result was that the child suffered scarring of the throat. The needle was eventually extracted by an electro-magnet at another hospital. The trial judge found the surgeon negligent for persisting with the search.

Prospects of succeeding in such actions appear slightly better when it is proved that the injection was entered in the wrong place or was extravenous when intended to be intravenous. Liability was proved in *Caldeira* v *Gray* (1936) (*page 174*) where a quinine injection resulted in damage to the sciatic nerve causing immediate lameness. Liability was conceded in *Daly* v *Wolverhampton Health Authority* (1986) (*page 193*), where an injection caused a permanent neuroma after damaging a nerve or blood vessel. McNair J in *Hayward* v *Curwen* (1964) (*page 230*) found neither negligence nor causation proved in a case where, following the injection of colchicine into the plaintiff's left arm, which caused no pain, the plaintiff developed median nerve palsy. The judge found that the correct vein had been chosen, that the manner of the injection was appropriate and it was not proved that any of the drug had been injected outside the vein. In *Prout* v *Crowley* (1956) (*page 291*), an extravenous injection did occur after the needle came out of a vein, allowing a small quantity of ferrivenin to penetrate surrounding tissue and to cause an abscess. The trial judge held that this happened without negligence and that when it did happen the doctor followed the correct procedure of applying a poultice as soon as he realised the mishap. The Court of Appeal upheld an appeal in a similar set of circumstances in *Williams* v *North Liverpool Hospital Management Committee* (1959) (*page 342*). Here pentothal was inadvertently extravenously injected into what was described as an exceedingly fat arm in which the vein was difficult to find. The plaintiff sued in respect of the abscesses that resulted, and the trial judge found for her. The Court of Appeal reversed the decision indicating that the doctor had taken all reasonable steps to ensure the needle was intravenous. The patient had not complained of pain and there was nothing to put him on notice that he had in fact missed the vein. The Court of Appeal declined, however, to interfere with the trial judge's finding in *Walker* v *South West Surrey District Health Authority* (1982) (*page 336*), where a nurse injected pethidine into the inside of a plaintiff's leg causing damage to a superficial nerve. They determined that no careful nurse or doctor would have chosen such a site without compelling reasons.

Injecting a patient at the wrong time may also give rise to liability if there are contra-indications which would cause the normally skilful doctor to wait. In *King* v *King* (1987) (*page 252*), the plaintiff was administered the second of a combined vaccination against cholera and typhoid by his general practitioner at a time when he appeared excited and had a small boil in front of his ear. Six hours later he suffered a stroke rendering him hemiplegic. The trial judge's finding that the doctor had been negligent in injecting his patient at a time when he had a temperature was rejected by the Court of Appeal. There was no proof that the excited state indicated a raised temperature, nor did the boil constitute a contra-indication. In *Hothi* v *Greenwich Health Authority* (1982) (*page 239*), no negligence was found where a patient was administered with an anti-convulsant drug after exhibiting signs of epilepsy. Unknown to the defendants, the plaintiff was suffering from a rare form of allergy to the drug which was deemed unforeseeable. In *Robinson* v *Post Office* (1974) (*page 301*), a doctor was negligent in the timing of his anti-tetanus serum injections but no damage flowed from his negligence.

Leahy-Taylor (ibid Chapter 4) describes, *inter alia*, cases that reached negotiated settlements where an iron preparation was injected into the deltoid area of the arm against the manufacturer's recommendation that it should have been administered into the buttocks, and where a child who was vaccinated during a quiescent phase of eczema developed generalised vaccinia producing keloid scarring.

3. Drugs and anaesthetic accidents

The administration of an incorrect drug or an incorrect volume of the drug, including anaesthetics, will normally give rise to liability. Frequently the mishap arises from a breakdown in communication between the practitioner who prescribed the drug and the practitioner who administered it. In *Collins* v *Hertfordshire County Council* (1947) (*page 182*), a junior house surgeon misheard a consultant's prescription and ordered from the pharmacist cocaine instead of procaine. As a result the patient was administered with a lethal dose. Hilbery J found the house surgeon, consultant and hospital liable. Similarly, where nurses misread a prescription and administered a lethal six ounces of paraldehyde instead of six drachms, they acted negligently (*Strangways-Lesmere* v *Clayton* (1936) (*page 323*)). A ward sister was also found negligent for allowing four extra injections of streptomycin over and above the thirty prescribed to a patient who as a consequence suffered permanent loss of balance (*Smith* v *Brighton and Lewes Hospital Management Committee* (1958) (*page 318*)).

In *Dwyer* v *Rodrick* (1983) (*page 202*), a general practitioner and a pharmacist were held negligent for diagnosing and dispensing a wholly inappropriate prescription of sixty Migril tablets, two to be taken every four hours as necessary, in respect of a patient suffering from migraine. The prescription was an obvious error and the pharmacist who dispensed the prescription failed to notice the error. The patient suffered gangrenous necrosis after taking thirty-six tablets in six days. Liability was apportioned 45 per cent to the doctor and 55 per cent to the chemist. In *Prendergast v Sam and Dee Limited* (1989) (*page 290*), the Court of Appeal upheld the trial judge's finding against a doctor and a chemist when a prescription of Amoxil was dispensed as Daonil. The pharmacist had made the error because the general practitioner's handwriting was poor enough to invite misreading. The trial judge held that the doctor's writing did amount to negligence because it reasonably permitted the misreading but also the pharmacist was negligent in failing to comprehend the incompatibility of Daonil given the other items that were on the prescription. Liability was apportioned 25 per cent to the doctor and 75 per cent to the chemist.

In *Junor v McNicol* (1959) (*page 248*), a failure to ensure an infant patient was given a suitable amount of penicillin was described as a mistake. The doctor who dispensed the penicillin, however, was held not to be acting outside the instructions of the consultant surgeon and was not negligent. In *Vernon v Bloomsbury Health Authority* (1986) (*page 333*), Tucker J rejected the plaintiff's allegation that she had been given an excessive quantity of gentamicin for an overly long period and found that the doctor had acted in conformance with a proper mode of treatment. (See also *Ackers v Wigan Area Health Authority* (1986) (*page 150*), *Jacobs v Great Yarmouth and Waveney Health Authority* (1984) (*page 245*).) A massive overdose in the order of a factor of thirty of penicillin in *Kay v Ayrshire and Arran Health Board* (1987) (*page 251*) led to an admission of negligence but the infant plaintiff failed to prove that his profound deafness was due to the consequence of the toxic effect of the penicillin.

An over-hasty withdrawal from prescribed drugs gave rise to liability in *Hatwell v South-West Metropolitan Regional Hospital Board* (1976) (*page 230*), where a plaintiff had Seconal and Valium immediately withdrawn by a psychiatrist upon admission to hospital. As a consequence the plaintiff suffered from violent tremors and had an epileptic fit during which she sustained a fractured jaw.

Anaesthetic mishaps can give rise to severe permanent brain damage and frequently raise the application of the maxim *res ipsa loquitur* (see *Thomas v Wignall* (1987) (*page 327*) and *Saunders v Leeds Western Health Authority* (1986) (*page 310*)). In *Gray v Mid Herts Group Hospital Management Committee* (1974) (*page 221*), a young boy suffered extensive brain damage and eventual death following a cardiac arrest during the course of a routine operation. Waller J found the anaesthetist negligent in failing to monitor adequately the boy's pulse and breathing pattern. In *Voller v Portsmouth Corporation* (1947) (*page 334*), a plaintiff who contracted meningitis following a spinal injection established liability on the basis that there must have been some defect in the hospital's aseptic technique and that such an infection could not have arisen without negligence on the hospital's part. (See also *Connolly v Camden and Islington Area Health Authority* (1981) (*page 183*), *Moser v Enfield and Haringey Area Health Authority* (1983) (*page 276*) and *Cunningham v Camberwell Health Authority* (1988) (*page 192*).)

Not all mishaps, however, will amount to negligence. In *Roe v Minister of Health* (1954) (*page 301*), the contamination of the anaesthetic was due to an unknown and unforeseen consequence of fractures in the glass ampoules which did not give rise to a foreseeable risk. In *Moore* v *Lewisham Group Hospital Management Committee* (1959) (*page 274*), a spinal anaesthetic was administered in circumstances where a body of medical opinion thought it should not be undertaken. However, evidence was received that an alternative body of medical opinion considered that it was a proper procedure. Barry J expressed sentiments which had been heard before and since:

"The courts could do not greater disservice to the community or the advancement of medical science than to place the hallmark of legality upon one form of treatment as opposed to another when there was a difference of informed medical opinion as to their merits".

4. Retained surgical products

The Medical Defence Union in a chapter headed "Perennial Pitfalls" in their 1983 annual report indicated that some 203 cases were reported to it from all over the world in respect of a variety of retained foreign bodies left in patients which included 70 instruments, 54 swabs and 23 sutures (see Giesen: 1988, page 139 footnote 79). Giesen provides interesting examples of tissues, swabs, sponges, packs, clamps, wires, tubes and forceps which illustrate the familiarity of this type of claim. It will be appreciated that once a plaintiff has proved that the retained body was left in as a result of the operation or treatment undertaken by the defendants, a good prospect of establishing liability arises. Accordingly most of these types of cases are settled. (cf Leahy-Taylor (ibid) for such examples involving a swab left in after a caesarean operation, a drain tube left in after a mastectomy, and a Spencer Wells clip left in after an operation.)

Reported cases frequently concerned the separate liabilities of the surgeon and the nursing staff. This distinction took on great significance before the development of the doctrine of vicarious liability on the part of the hospital. In 1931 the Court of Appeal refused to interfere with the jury's finding of negligence against a surgeon following the leaving of a surgical pack measuring eight inches by ten inches in a patient's body after a gall-stone operation (*James* v *Dunlop* (1931) (*page 245*)). Five years later a doctor who inadvertently left a surgical gauze in a patient was found negligent in *Dryden* v *Surrey County Council* (1936) (*page 201*). In *Mahon* v *Osborne* (1939) (*page 266*), the Court of Appeal ordered a retrial where a judge directed the jury that a surgeon in all abdominal operations had the duty of searching to ensure that all swabs had been removed. The test was deemed to be whether the surgeon had exercised reasonable skill and care, and this was to be determined in the light of all the circumstances of the particular case. By a majority the court held that the maxim *res ipsa loquitur* applied. In *Urry* v *Bierer* (1955) (*page 330*), a ten-inch surgical pack was left in a woman after a caesarean operation. The Court of Appeal rejected the surgeon's appeal which contended that he was entitled to rely on the nurse's count. In 1961 the Privy Council in *Cooper* v *Nevill* (*page 186*) determined that the leaving of a swab inside a patient obviously amounted to a mistake but it did not necessarily amount to negligence. The medical and nursing staff might be, in certain circumstances, engaged in an emergency race against time. It might accordingly be negligence in certain circumstances to search for a swab that is known to be missing if the patient's life is in grave danger. However, in *Cooper* there was no evidence to indicate precisely what type of mistake had in fact occurred. The Privy Council found the trial judge was justified in finding that whether it was a mopping or restraining pack the surgical team had been negligent. Similar considerations apply to other retained products. It is most likely the maxim *res ipsa loquitur* will apply but it cannot be said in advance of the facts whether the defendants will be able to rebut the presumption of negligence. In *Morris* v *Winsbury-White* (1937) (*page 275*), the maxim was held not to apply as the hospital was deemed not to be vicariously liable for the surgeon, and on the particular facts of that case the tube that was left in the patient's body could have been left in by the operating surgeon or alternatively by nurses or other resident surgeons. In *Hocking* v *Bell* (1948) (*page 234*), a doctor was found negligent for allowing a two-inch part of a tube to break off and to remain in a patient's body. The defendants conceded negligence in *Pask* v *Bexley Health Authority* (1988) (*page 284*) following the discovery, one year after the patient's stomach had been pumped, of two and a half feet of plastic tubing in her body.

5. Childbirth, sterilisation and contraception

Given the volume of prospective mothers receiving medical care throughout their pregnancy and at childbirth, it is not surprising that allegations of negligence frequently arise. This is not only because of the inherent hazards of childbirth itself, but also because of the variety of risks that can arise throughout pregnancy and at labour connected with drugs affecting the mother and foetus, anaesthetic mishaps during labour, accidents in the use of forceps and accidents during caesarean sections. The House of Lords in the leading cases of *Whitehouse* v *Jordan* (1981) (*page 341*) and *Sidaway* v *Board of Governors of the Bethlem Royal Hospital and the Maudsley Hospital* (1985) (*page 314*) has affirmed that the medical standard of care espoused in *Bolam* (1957) (*page 166*) applies to all aspects of diagnosis, treatment and advice in matters of pregnancy, childbirth, sterilisation and contraception.

In *Kralj* v *McGrath* (1986) (*page 253*), liability was admitted in respect of treatment described as horrific and totally unacceptable during the course of the birth of twins. In *Mitchell* v *Hounslow and Spelthorne Health Authority* (1984) (*page 272*), spasticity caused by a failure to deal adequately with a prolapsed umbilical cord in a baby girl was found to amount to negligence. In *Bull and Wakeham* v *Devon Health Authority* (1989) (*page 172*) a difficult twin birth was not properly supervised with registrar or consultant back-up. As a result the second twin was born seriously disabled. The hospital was found negligent in failing to provide an adequate system of obstetric cover which had given rise to a real risk that proper care could not be given after the birth of the first twin (see also *Ritter* v *Godfrey* (1919) (*page 299*), *Wilsher* v *Essex Area Health Authority* (1988) (*page 344*), *Murray* v *Kensington and Chelsea and Westminster Area Health Authority* (1981) (*page 277*) and *McKay* v *Essex Area Health Authority* (1982) (*page 265*)).

In *Leckie* v *Brent and Harrow Area Health Authority* (1982) (*page 257*), Mars-Jones J accepted that the maxim *res ipsa loquitur* applied to circumstances where a baby sustained a laceration to its face during the course of a caesarean section. The judge decided that such a cut could not have happened without negligence on the registrar's part.

In *Ackers* v *Wigan Area Health Authority* (1986) (*page 150*), a plaintiff received damages following a negligent failure to anaesthetise her during a caesarean section. Mrs Ackers was paralysed by a pre-operative relaxant but was conscious and receptive to sensation during the one and a quarter hour operation during which she was not able to communicate her plight to the medical or nursing staff. In *Jacobs* v *Great Yarmouth and Waveney Health Authority* (1984) (*page 245*) a similar type of claim was not proved. Mrs Jacobs alleged a negligent administering of anaesthetic for an operation for a hysterectomy resulting in her being conscious but paralysed right up until the first incision. The Court of Appeal held that the trial judge was justified in concluding that the plaintiff had been mistaken and had transposed her pre-operative and post-operative states of consciousness.

Failed sterilisations and vasectomies have given rise to litigation which has raised significant issues concerning the standard of care, particularly over the degree of disclosure required, and also difficult questions on causation and on damages. According to Capstick (*Patient Complaints and Litigation*, National Association of Public Health Authorities, 1985, page 68), by 1983 twenty per cent of married couples used sterilisation or vasectomy as a form of contraception. It is thought that the risks of re-canalisation of the fallopian tubes occur naturally in approximately one in 750 cases. Further risks may arise if the sterilisation technique was by way of clipping the fallopian tube, because occasionally the clip may be wrongly placed or may detach itself. The risk of re-canalisation is thought to be higher when the sterilisation is performed soon after delivery or abortion. Natural reversal following a vasectomy is thought to be in the region of about one in 5,000.

In *Emeh* v *Kensington and Chelsea and Westminster Area Health Authority* (1985) (*page 205*), a failed sterilisation was held to be due to negligence and breach of contract. The resultant birth of a congenitally deformed child was held to give rise to the right for damages for its so-called wrongful birth. The mother in this case refused to have an abortion, which was held by the trial judge to be a *novus actus interveniens* and a failure to mitigate her damages. The Court of Appeal reversed the trial judge's finding and said that it was not unreasonable for the plaintiff to decline to have an abortion. The Court of Appeal confirmed that it was not contrary to public policy to recover damages for the birth of a child whether healthy or abnormal. This decision of the Court of Appeal in effect approved *Thake* v *Maurice* (1985) (*page 327*), where at first instance Pain J had found both breach of contract and negligence in respect of a failed vasectomy which resulted in the birth of a healthy child, and awarded damages for the upkeep of the child. The Court of Appeal heard the defendant's appeal in *Thake* v *Maurice* after *Emeh*. The finding of negligence in *Thake* was upheld although the Court of Appeal reversed Pain J on the question of breach of contract. *Emeh* accordingly disapproved *Udale* v *Bloomsbury Area Health Authority* (1983) (*page 329*) where Jupp J had held it contrary to public policy to award damages for the birth of a healthy child. In *Udale* the defendants admitted liability for failing to clip each fallopian tube in a laparoscopic sterilisation. Similarly, liability for failed sterilisations was admitted in the cases of *Benarr* v *Kettering Health Authority* (1988) (*page 161*), *Chaunt* v *Hertfordshire Area Health Authority* (1982) (*page 179*) and *Williams* v *Imrie* (1988) (*page 342*).

Conversely in *Palmer* v *Eadie* (1987) (*page 282*), a plaintiff did not prove negligence or breach of contract where a vasectomy failed. The urologist had given adequate warning of the failure risk and no breach of duty arose in the practitioner's failure to discuss with the patient the actual mode of operation undertaken. In *Gold* v *Haringey Health Authority* (1987) (*page 219*), the Court of Appeal reversed the decision of Schiemann J who had found negligence in failing to disclose the failure rate in sterilisation. The trial judge had been persuaded to make a distinction between therapeutic and non-therapeutic settings, and thought the *Bolam* test did not apply to non-therapeutic settings which would include the arena of contraceptive advice. The Court of Appeal, in applying *Sidaway* v *Board of Governors of Bethlem Royal Hospital and the Maudsley Hospital* (1985) (*page 314*), said that no distinction could be made and the medical standard applied in both settings.

In *Venner* v *North East Essex Area Health Authority* (1987) (*page 332*), a doctor who had not carried out a dilataion and curettage during a sterilisation, and therefore allowed an undiagnosed pregnancy to continue, was not found negligent. The trial judge found it was neither necessary nor desirable to have a dilatation and curettage as a matter of course, and the doctor was acting in accord with an accepted mode of practice. In *Cronin* v *Islington Area Health Authority* (1987) (*page 190*), the plaintiff was sterilised following a caesarean delivery of her third child. The operation failed and she became pregnant again, and brought a case alleging negligence on the part of the consultant obstetrician who had not told her of the failure risks. Caulfield J dismissed the action, firstly on the basis that she had been warned. However, he also found that at this time in 1981 there was no duty to warn a patient that sterilisation might fail, since there was a substantial respectable body of medical opinion who would not have warned the patient in these circumstances. The judge went on to add that he did not accept the plaintiff's evidence that had she known about the failure risk she would have used contraception. She accordingly failed on the question of causation as well.

Unnecessary sterilisation led to liability in *Biles* v *Barking Health Authority* (1988) (*page 162*), as did sterilisation without consent in *Devi* v *West Midlands Regional Health Authority* (1981) (*page 198*).

6. Burns

A number of reported cases concern burns inadvertently occasioned to patients during the course of a variety of treatment requiring either the application of heat or of chemicals. Most are self-evidently negligent and raise the maxim *res ipsa loquitur*. In *Clarke* v *Worboys* (1952) (*page 181*), a patient undergoing electro-coagulation treatment suffered a severe burn on her buttock. The process involved passing a high frequency current via a pad. The Court of Appeal held that it was a case of *res ipsa loquitur*, and the presumption of negligence was not rebutted. In *Gold* v *Essex County Council* (1942) (*page 218*), a radiographer was found negligent in failing to protect a girl's face, causing disfiguring burns during treatment by Grenz rays for facial warts. Older cases are illustrated in *Ball* v *Caldwell* (1940) (*page 155*) (discolouration caused following irradiation on a breast lump); *Hall* v *Lees* (1904) (*page 223*) (burns by hot-water bottle); *Perionowsky* v *Freeman* (1866) (*page 288*) (scalded in a hip bath, no liability proved); *Smith* v *Pare* (1904) (*page 320*) (burns to the whole body following high frequency currents and X-rays); *Snell* v *Carter* (1941) (*page 320*) (burns which became gangrenous following oil and ray lamp treatment); and *Jones* v *Manchester Corporation* (1952) (*page 247*) (where before being administered a negligent lethal dose of pentothal, a patient suffered facial burns through contact with anaesthetics). Leahy-Taylor (Chapter 4) describes further cases which have led to settlement, involving, *inter alia*, tricholoracetic acid instead of adrenalin being used to prevent nasal bleeding and causing burns; a heat cradle being wrongly applied; diathermy electro-burns during a circumcision; and burns from suspension rods during a tonsillectomy.

7. Dentists

The normal medical standard of care applies to dental practitioners, and there is no legal significance in treating them in a separate category to, say, doctors, pharmacists or nurses. Even before the espousal and refinement of the *Bolam* standard of care, it had long been recognized that a dentist owed a patient the proper degree of skill and care of the averagely competent practitioner. In *Gordon* v *Goldberg* (1920) (*page 221*), the plaintiff sued a dentist on the grounds that two sets of artificial teeth which he had made for her did not fit and could not be adapted. Rowlatt J held that when people went to dentists they expected and contracted for skill and not for infallibility. In judging skill, account might be taken of the charges made, and the defendant in this case had charged very handsomely but the teeth he supplied were utterly unsatisfactory.

Where a dentist works in conjunction with a doctor, the dentist is to some extent entitled to rely upon the doctor's diagnosis of the patient's general health. In *Warren* v *Greig*; *Warren* v *White* (1935) (*page 337*), a dentist was asked by a general practitioner to examine a patient who appeared to be suffering from pyorrhoea. Both dentist and doctor advised extraction of all the patient's twenty-eight teeth. The patient died within twenty-four hours following persistent bleeding. Post-mortem examination revealed that the patient in fact had had leukaemia. McKinnon J held that where a dentist worked jointly with a general practitioner, it was not part of a dentist's duty to discover the general health of the patient, and the dentist had not been negligent. In *Tanswell* v *Nelson* (1959) (*page 325*), a patient had ten teeth removed resulting in locking of the jaw. The dentist sent her to her general practitioner who diagnosed an abscess and treated her with antibiotics. In fact the plaintiff had suffered osteomyelitis which was not discovered until X-ray at a hospital. McNair J held that the dentist was entitled to rely on the doctor's opinion of the patient's response to the antibiotic treatment and the taking of X-rays.

Accidents during extraction which are in the nature of dislocations or the fracturing of the jaw appear rarely to give rise to the doctrine of *res ipsa loquitur*. In *Fish* v *Kapur* (1948) (*page 210*), the plaintiff relied on the maxim on the basis that part of the root of a tooth had been left in her jaw, and the jaw was fractured during extraction. Evidence was adduced that this could happen without negligence and the claim failed. In *Lock* v *Scantlebury* (1963) (*page 262*), no negligence was held to arise where a jaw was dislocated during extraction. However, failure to diagnose the fact on subsequent visits was held to be in breach of the duty of care. In *O'Neill* v *Kelly* (1961) (*page 281*), a jaw bone was fractured during the use of a tool known as an elevator. However the trial judge rejected an inference that there must have been something wrong with the manner of the dentist's operation of the elevator and found as a fact that the fracture was due to a sudden jerk by the plaintiff. Similarly, in *Fletcher* v *Bench* (1973) (*page 210*), the Court of Appeal found no negligence arising out of a difficult extraction of an impacted tooth which resulted in part of a bone burr remaining in the patient's jaw after it had broken during drilling. The jaw later fractured after an infection set in, and did so at the point where the broken burr was eventually found.

A more clear-cut case where the maxim *res ipsa loquitur* arose is to be found in *Garner* v *Morrell and Another* (1953) (*page 215*), where the Court of Appeal held that the death of a patient arising out of the swallowing or inhalation of a throat pack during the course of an extraction called for explanation by the defendants. If a mishap does occur during dental treatment the dentist, like other practitioners, is under a duty to inform the patient of the problem. In *Cooper* v *Miron* (1927) (*page 185*), the crown of a molar tooth broke off and disappeared during the course of extraction. After the effects of the anaesthetic had worn off, the plaintiff complained of breathing difficulties but was allowed to go home without being told about the loss of part of her tooth. She subsequently contracted septic pneumonia due to the lodging of the piece of tooth in the bronchus, and died approximately three months later. The dentist was found liable by a jury after it had been directed that it was part of the duty of a dentist when an accident of this kind occurred to inform the plaintiff about it.

In *Connor* v *Fison-Clarke* (1987) (*page 185*), a dentist was found negligent in respect of extensive root therapy treatment and bridge work in the upper arch of the plaintiff's jaw which caused malocclusion within the lower teeth.

8. Hospital administration and organisation

Actions frequently arise based upon failures to organise or to implement a proper system of institutional treatment and after-care. It is likely that a hospital owes a non-delegable duty of care directly to a patient irrespective of any vicarious liability (*Cassidy* v *Ministry of Health* (1951) (*page 176*)). In *Wilsher* v *Essex Area Health Authority* (1987) (*page 344*), the Court of Appeal expressed a view that a health authority which conducted a hospital so that it failed to provide doctors of sufficient skill and experience to give proper treatment could be directly liable in negligence to the patient (see Chapter 1). Part of this duty was held to be to provide a proper obstetric back-up cover to cope with difficult births (*Bull and Wakeham* v *Devon Health Authority* (1989) (*page 172*)). Hospitals must also take steps to ensure their aseptic techniques are adequate so that equipment is properly sterile (*Voller* v *Portsmouth Corporation* (1947) (*page 334*)). Patients with or exposed to contagious diseases should be properly cared for and treated so that they do not spread infections to others (see *Heafield* v *Crane* (1937) (*page 231*) and *Marshall* v *County Council of the Parts of Lindsey, Lincolnshire* (1937) (*page 269*)). In *Vancouver General Hospital* v *McDaniel* (1935) (*page 331*), a patient sued after she contracted smallpox because she had to share the same floor as smallpox victims in a hospital and because she also came into contact with nurses who were nursing the smallpox patients. The plaintiff herself had been admitted because she was suffering from diphtheria. The hospital avoided liability predominantly on the *Bolam* test, albeit twenty years earlier, by adducing evidence that their system of sterilisation rather than isolation was in accord with general and approved practice. (See also *Salisbury* v *Gould* (1904) (*page 309*).)

While in the care of a hospital, patients must be adequately supervised so that they do not come to foreseeable harm. Leaving a disabled child momentarily with a hot inhalant did not amount to negligence in *Cox* v *Carshalton Group Hospital Management Committee* (1955) (*page 188*), as on those particular facts the child had managed the inhaler previously. In *Gravestock* v *Lewisham Group Hospital Management Committee* (1955) (*page 221*), judged by the standards of a prudent parent or schoolmaster, a hospital was found not to be negligent for leaving a nine year old child momentarily alone with the result that the child took the opportunity of running down the ward and injured herself. However, leaving a seven year old in a ward by an open window through which he fell was found negligent in *Newnham* v *Rochester and Chatham Joint Hospital Board* (1936) (*page 279*). Liability was also established in *Smith* v *Lewisham Group Hospital Management Committee* (1955) (*page 319*), where an eighty-six year old lady who was placed on a four-wheel trolley without any protective railings fell off after the nurse attending to her had left the cubicle to answer the telephone. (See also *Wilson* v *Tomlinson* (1956) (*page 345*).)

Particular problems arise concerning the degree of supervision required for patients who may harm themselves or injure others. The hospital wing of Winchester Prison was found not negligent in allowing a mentally defective inmate to attack a fellow patient in the hospital wing. The assailant had no previous record of such attacks and in the circumstances a failure to segregate was not deemed negligent (*Ellis* v *Home Office* (1953) (*page 205*)). In *Holgate* v *Lancashire Mental Hospitals Board* (1937) (*page 236*), negligence was established in respect of a decision to allow an inmate detained at His Majesty's pleasure to have extended leave during which he attacked a member of the public. In *Drummond* v *Wonford House Hospital (Incorporated)* (1928) (*page 200*), a mental nursing home was found negligent for failing to watch adequately a patient with acute melancholia. The patient forced herself through a ten-foot square window and in doing so fractured her arm and jaw.

In *Thorne* v *Northern Group Hospital Management Committee* (1964) (*page 328*), the court recognized that the degree of care and supervision with respect to a suicidal patient was greater than that normally required. However a claim brought by the widow of a patient who committed suicide after both the sister and the nurse had left the convalescent ward where the patient was being monitored was dismissed. The judge thought it likely that the patient was waiting for such an opportunity to avoid her supervisors and take her own life. Conversely in *Selfe* v *Ilford and District Hospital Management Committee* (1970) (*page 313*), a seventeen year old suicide risk recovered damages in respect of serious injuries resulting to him after a failed suicide bid. He was left momentarily in a ward which had an open window by his bed and he jumped out of it. Hinchcliffe J held that in the particular circumstances there was a need for a continuous observation. In *Size* v *Shenley Hospital Group Management Committee* (1970) (*page 316*), the Court of Appeal rejected a plaintiff's claim arising out of an attack perpetrated on him by an inmate of a mental hospital. The attacker, who shared a ward with the plaintiff but whose bed was near the nurse's desk, was, shortly before the attack, due to be taken to a secure ward following a hypomanic episode. He attacked just before the nurse could stop him, and it was held that in the circumstances the supervision had been adequate. In *Hyde* v *Tameside Area Health Authority* (1981) (*page 244*), the Court of Appeal reversed a finding of negligent supervision in respect of the care afforded to a patient in a general hospital who attempted suicide after wrongly thinking he had terminal cancer. The Court of Appeal held that any failure to assess the true significance of the patient's mental distress was at best an error in clinical judgement that did not amount to negligence.

Failure to supervise staff, including medical staff, may also, in principle, give rise to negligence (*Wilsher* v *Essex Area Health Authority* (1987) (*page 344*)).

Failure to take X-rays or to administer tests, particularly simple tests such as blood and urine samples, constituted a significant background in the five hundred cases looked at by Leahy-Taylor (ibid). In *Braisher* v *Harefield and Northwood Hospital Group Management Committee* (1966) (*page 169*), the then Master of the Rolls, Lord Denning, indicated that it was not in every case where there had been a failure to take an X-ray that negligence would arise. The plaintiff in that case presented at casualty with a complaint that he had knocked his arm on some metal. A wound was stitched but no X-ray was taken. The arm continued to be painful until a piece of metal close to the surface was removed. The Master of the Rolls indicated that there was no liability arising in this case, because the plaintiff had not told the nurse or casualty officer what in fact happened, namely that a piece of metal had flown off a machine, but had told them that he had knocked his arm on some metal. In *Tanswell* v *Nelson* (1959) (*page 325*), both a doctor and a dentist were found not to be negligent in failing to have an X-ray taken on a jaw which would have revealed developing osteomyelitis. With regard to the doctor, McNair J said that he had been presented with symptoms inconsistent with the osteomyelitis. Conversely, in *Kilburn* v *Swindon and District Hospital Management Committee* (1955) (*page 252*) a failure to X-ray a leg which had two fractures, and an arm which was also fractured, was held negligent (see also *McCormack* v *Redpath Brown and Co. Limited* (1961) (*page 263*) and *Elkan* v *Montgomery Smith* (1922) (*page 204*)).

Failure to carry out a blood test and amniocentesis in *Bagley* v *North Herts Health Authority* (1986) (*page 155*) and failure to establish a blood group in *Morgan* v *Gwent Health Authority* (1987) (*page 274*), led to admissions of liability on the part of the defendants. A system that resulted in a contamination of a child's vaginal swab with an adult's specimen carrying spermatozoa and which thereby resulted in an investigation concerning possible sexual abuse of the child was also undefended in *G* v *North Tees Health Authority* (1989) (*page 214*). Conversely, in *Whichello* v *Medway and Gravesend Hospital Management Committee* (1954) (*page 339*), a failure to take a culture from a wound which was to be treated by surgery rather than through antibiotics was held not to have been negligent in the light of the then current medical opinion.

Neglecting to take a history or a proper history from a patient will normally result in a breach of duty (see *Chin Keow* v *Government of Malaysia* (1967) (*page 180*)). Equally, failure to allow a patient to explain her particular problems and predicaments led to a consultant physician being held liable in *Horner* v *Scarborough, Bridlington, Malton and Whitby Group Hospital Management Committee* (1966) (*page 238*) for an over-hasty diagnosis and for failing to take an X-ray.

Failing to communicate a case history or to ensure that proper notes and test results are available to other practitioners may also result in findings of negligence. In *Coles* v *Reading and District Hospital Management Committee* (1963) (*page 182*), a cottage hospital was found to have been negligent in failing to ensure that a patient attended a general hospital in circumstances where although he was told to go to such a hospital, he was suffering from shock at the time and simply thereafter attended his general practitioner. Conversely, in *Chapman* v *Rix* (1960) (*page 177*), a doctor working at a cottage hospital was not held negligent for failing to communicate his findings and diagnosis to his patient's general practitioner. (See also *Bell* v *Secretary of State for Defence* (1986) (*page 160*).)

A casualty officer is under a general duty to attend to a bona fide patient presenting in a hospital, and failure to examine such a patient can lead to liability (*Barnett* v *Chelsea and Kensington Hospital Management Committee* (1969) (*page 158*)). A casualty officer has some small discretion so that he may properly delegate trivial injuries to a nurse or may decline to see someone who has already contacted his general practitioner and is merely seeking a second opinion (*Barnett* v *Chelsea and Kensington Hospital Management Committee* [1969] 1 QB at 436g-437).

9. General practitioners

A general practitioner has a duty to attend to a patient, which will include a person on his list as well as temporary residents. The doctor's terms and conditions, pursuant to his contract with the Family Practitioner Committee, also require the doctor, when requested, to attend to a person involved in an accident or an emergency in any place in his practice area. It is, however, debatable whether this last duty is owed directly to the injured person. In *Barnes* v *Crabtree* (1955) (*page 157*), Barry J directed a jury that in the case of a real emergency a doctor under the National Health Service scheme had an obligation to treat any patient who was acutely ill. Whether this duty to attend includes a home visit will depend on all the circumstances of the case. In *Barnes*, the plaintiff, who had a history of arguments with her general practitioner, called at her doctor's surgery on Christmas Day saying she was ill. The general practitioner told her there was nothing wrong with her, did not examine her, and told her to get another doctor if she was not satisfied. The plaintiff refused to leave the premises, and eventually she was removed by the police. She sued the doctor for failing to attend to her, and the jury found that there was no case to answer. Barry J had directed the jury that the doctor's obligation was to render all proper and necessary treatment to the patient, and this did not mean he was required to make full clinical examination on each occasion. A general practitioner must make proper provision for adequate locum cover and ensure that the stand-in doctors are properly informed about his patients (see *Farquhar* v *Murray* (1901) (*page 209*) and *Ball* v *Howard* (1924) (*page 156*)).

The general practitioner should also have an adequate system of dealing with possible emergency cases if they come into the surgery, and this will extend to being vicariously liable for the acts of his receptionist for any negligent failure to communicate an emergency to him (*Lobley* v *Going* (1985) (*page 261*)). A general practitioner is also probably under a duty to take reasonable steps to ascertain a patient's new address in circumstances when he makes a call at the old address, having been summoned by telephone and upon arrival at the address it is obvious that the patient has moved. In *Kavanagh* v *Abrahamson* (1964) (*page 250*), the doctor in these circumstances rang the door bell of the adjoining flats to see if he could ascertain the current address of his patient but met with no reply. The trial judge indicated that there was a measure of force in the criticism that the doctor might have done more but that of itself did not constitute negligence. In the same case the judge went on to find that the prescribing of compound codeine tablets without seeing the patient also did not, in the circumstances, amount to negligence.

Negligent prescription in *Dwyer* v *Rodrick* (1983) (*page 202*) led to liability against a general practitioner. The prescribing doctor was found liable for an obvious mistake but one of his colleagues was found not liable for failing to notice the mistake during a home visit. The second doctor did not have the medical notes with him and had failed to see the prescription and had also failed to see the bottle of tablets on the table in the plaintiff's bedroom. In *Prendergast* v *Sam and Dee Limited* (1989) (*page 290*), a general practitioner was found to be negligent with respect to his poor hand-writing which invited a misreading by the dispensing pharmacist, causing the plaintiff to suffer severe injuries because of the effects of the wrongly dispensed medicine.

In *Connolly* v *Rubra* (1937) (*page 184*), a general practitioner was held negligent for failing to take specimens of sputum and for failing to arrange for X-ray examination in respect of a patient who contracted undiagnosed tuberculosis from which he died.

Where a patient is under the care of a hospital, a general practitioner may, to a certain extent, rely on the diagnoses and advice given by the hospital doctors. Accordingly, in *Edler* v *Greenwich and Deptford Hospital Management Committee* (1953) (*page 203*), an eleven year old girl who had suffered nausea and stomach pain was examined by a casualty officer. The hospital doctor said there was nothing wrong with the girl but if she got worse her father should bring her back to the hospital. In fact the girl's mother took the child to her general practitioner who was told what the hospital doctor had said and formed the view that the child probably had gastric trouble. The following day the child deteriorated and was rushed to hospital, but she died of a ruptured appendix. The trial judge held that the hospital doctor had been negligent but the general practitioner had not been negligent in relying upon the hospital's diagnosis.

However, there can be no abdication of the general practitioner's responsibility, and a failure to ascertain precisely what treatment a patient did receive in hospital may lead to negligence. In *Coles* v *Reading and District Hospital Management Committee* (1963) (*page 182*), a man sustained a severe crushing injury to his finger, and attended a cottage hospital where the wound was cleaned and he was told to go to the general hospital. Mr Coles did not go to the hospital but the following day saw his own general practitioner who failed to ascertain what had happened at the hospital but simply redressed the wound. Accordingly no anti-tetanus injection was given. Sachs J found the hospital negligent for failing to give the injection and for failing to make sure the plaintiff attended the general hospital, but also found the general practitioner negligent for failing to make proper enquiry. (Further cases involving general practitioners are discussed in Chapter 8 in those actions based on failures in diagnosis.)

10. Nurses

Like other health care professionals, nurses are under a duty to exercise reasonable care and skill in all of the disparate tasks they undertake. Historically, like other skilled personnel, nurses were considered to be independent contractors, and an employing hospital was not automatically vicariously liable for their torts. Today the employing hospital authorities are both vicariously liable for, and also provide an indemnity to, nurses in respect of actions based on a breach of their duty of care. Accordingly in a case like *Fussell* v *Beddard* (1942) (*page 213*) where a patient died after a nurse wrongly prepared a 1% anaesthetic solution instead of a 0.1% solution, the employing hospital would be vicariously liable for this act assuming negligence was established. Where, however, a nursing agency supplies a nurse to an individual or to a hospital, the situation is less clear. The supplying agency is unlikely to be liable for the torts of the nurse during the course of her work. Much would depend upon the contractual terms, the representation made by the agency, and the steps taken by the agency to provide a competent nurse (see *Hall* v *Lees* (1904) (*page 223*)). If the nurse was working within a hospital, whether within the National Health Service or a private hospital, it is likely that the hospital would be liable for the nurse's tortious acts. Such liability could be founded on the fact that, given the degree of control of the nurse's activities, she was in law a servant of the hospital or in any event was the hospital's agent. Alternatively, the hospital may be found to be under a non-delegable duty to provide nursing services to the patient. (See the discussion on vicarious liability in Chapter 1.)

Typical actions involving nurses concern allegations that a patient has not been properly supervised. In *Selfe* v *Ilford and District Hospital Management Committee* (1970) (*page 313*), liability was established in a case where three nurses, who had been allocated to a ward containing a seventeen year old suicide-risk patient, had failed to provide continuous observation. One nurse went to the kitchen, another to the lavatory and a third nurse was attending to a patient when the plaintiff climbed up on to the roof of the hospital and jumped off. The court held that in these particular circumstances there was a requirement for constant observation. Conversely, in *Thorne* v *Northern Group Hospital Management Committee* (1964) (*page 328*), no negligence was established in circumstances where there had been a temporary gap in supervising a patient who committed suicide during a momentary absence of the nursing staff. In *Gravestock* v *Lewisham Group Hospital Management Committee* (1955) (*page 221*), a nursing orderly who had left a ward for a few moments to get the pudding course of a meal was found not to have been negligent in circumstances where a nine year old patient took the opportunity to run down the ward and to injure herself. In *Gauntlett* v *Northampton Health Authority* (1985) (*page 216*), allegations of inadequate supervision and inadequate note keeping were made against nursing staff in respect of a schizophrenic patient who set alight to herself four days after telling her husband that she might do so. The husband passed on this information to a nurse who failed to record the fact in the nursing notes. Evidence was given at the trial that a note ought to have been made and the trial judge, Kilner Brown J, held that the omission amounted to a negligent oversight. The Court of Appeal, however, reversed his decision and found that there had been no negligence. The notes already contained references to the patient's preoccupation with thoughts of fire, and the omitted information was better judged as an indication of her abnormal mind rather than a warning of her impending suicide attempt. The Court of Appeal held that, judged by the standards of the reasonably competent and experienced nurse, the omission was not negligent. In *Cox* v *Carshalton Group Hospital Management Committee* (1955) (*page 188*), McNair J found no negligence where a nurse had left a severely disabled thirteen year old girl alone for a few seconds with an inhaler which slipped and scalded her.

As with medical practitioners, many reported cases involving nurses feature allegations of substandard treatment and after-care. In *Powell* v *Streatham Manor Nursing Home* (1935) (*page 290*), the House of Lords restored the decision of the first instance judge, Horridge J, who found as a fact that a nurse had passed a rigid catheter vaginally and had caused a bladder perforation. In *Walker* v *South West Surrey District Health Authority* (1982) (*page 336*), the Court of Appeal declined to reverse the finding of H.H. Judge Vick that a midwife sister had injected, contrary to all good practice, pethidine into the inside of the plaintiff's right thigh. Negligence was also established in *Bayliss* v *Blagg* (1954) (*page 158*), where a matron had failed to notice a developing infection under a plaster cast which she had put on and which led to a child becoming severely disabled. In *Lowen* v *Hopper* (1950) (*page 263*), a failure to conduct a proper examination and to change a dressing led to a finding of negligence against a sister. (See also *Sutton* v *Population Services Family Planning Programme Limited* (1981) (*page 324*).)

No negligence was established against nursing staff in *Pickering* v *Governors of the United Leeds Hospital* (1954) (*page 288*) where an elderly patient developed severe bed sores following an operation on a fractured femur. The nursing staff were held to have been acting in accordance with the surgeon's instructions, as he had forbidden the turning of the plaintiff during the early stages after her operation. (Similar accusations of bed sores were made in *Biss* v *Lambeth, Southwark and Lewisham Area Health Authority* (1978) (*page 163*) in a case which was struck out for want of prosecution.) No liability was established in *Sullivan* v *Manchester Regional Hospital Board* (1957) (*page 324*) where a sister had failed to comprehend the significance of a patient's eye swelling following a nasal operation. The sister had attempted to reassure the patient and after four days asked a doctor to examine her.

Negligence in the dispensing of prescribed drugs was established in *Smith* v *Brighton and Lewes Hospital Management Committee* (1958) (*page 318*) where a sister had caused drugs to be administered beyond their prescribed course. The sister was criticised for failing to mark the intended termination of the treatment on the relevant notes. Nurses were also found negligent in the administration of a fatal dose of six ounces of paraldehyde instead of six drachms in *Strangways-Lesmere* v *Clayton* (1936) (*page 323*).

Where retained products are left in a patient following an operation, the nursing staff responsible for counting any of the products is likely to be liable for the oversight (see *Mahon* v *Osborne* (1939) (*page 266*), *James* v *Dunlop* (1931) (*page 245*), and *Urry* v *Bierer* (1955) (*page 330*)). The cases on retained surgical products indicate that a surgeon cannot simply rely on the nursing staff, but the corollary is that there is a high duty on the nurses in this context. Lord Justice Scott in *Mahon* v *Osborne* (above) said:

"The only matter on which I desire to say anything is on the relevance of the surgeon's duty with regard to the removal of packing swabs on any count by the nurses. His duty is undoubtedly to exercise care in the removal of the swabs, giving proper weight to the rare, but not impossible, risk of a swab having lost its Spencer-Wells clip. This risk, it is worth remembering, is one which depends not on the surgeon but on the nurses. It is their duty to see that each Spencer-Wells clip is in good order and that its safety catch is made well fast and the swab to which it is fastened is placed in the surgeon's hand. So, too, the check afforded by the count depends on the nurses. Those two risks are wholly external, both to the surgeon and to the patient. If an error has been committed, the surgeon cannot either control it or know it. Nonetheless, I do not doubt that over and above all the many signs of danger to the patient which are forcing themselves on his attention, the surgeon has to keep in his mind those two risks of error by the nurses. On the other hand, I do not think the surgeon should be deprived of all support from the count. In a difficult case, where he is anxious for the patient's sake to close the operation at the earliest possible moment, the fact that he is about to receive a check from the head sister, whom he knows to be careful, is one of the imponderable factors which he may properly have in mind, and indeed to have regard to it may sometimes save a patient's life." ([1939] 2 KB at 37.)

Nurses can, of course, also be negligent in the routine quasi-domestic aspects of their job. In *Trew* v *Middlesex Hospital* (1953) (*page 328*), a nurse was found to be negligent in the manner in which she placed a tray of tea on a patient's lap. In *Pargeter* v *Kensington and Chelsea and Westminster Health Authority* (1979) (*page 283*) the simple act of giving a patient a cup of tea was held in principle to be negligent if it was not done without trial sips in circumstances where a patient was recovering from an operation. The trial judge, however, found that it was highly unlikely that the nurse did not in fact give the patient trial sips of tea. Unfortunately the patient vomited the tea because of the particular type of pre-operative drug he had been given which resulted in his operative eye wound bursting.

11. Unregistered practitioners

Registered medical practitioners are qualified personnel pursuant to the provisions of the Medical Act 1983 in the case of doctors, and the Dentists Act 1984 in the case of dentists. A qualified practitioner has his name appearing on the register of either the General Medical Council or the General Dental Council, the regulatory bodies of the respective professions. Perhaps surprisingly, unqualified persons are not legally prevented from practising medicine, surgery or dentistry. Such practitioners, however, will commit an offence if they hold themselves out as being registered doctors (s 49 Medical Act 1983) or if they describe themselves as dentists, dental surgeons or dental practitioners (s 39 Dentists Act 1984).

The courts' attitude to non-qualified non-registered practitioners has been not only to protect the public from the dangers of quacks but also to recognize the contribution of unorthodox and alternative modes of healing, particularly when controlled by organised and respected institutions. Generally speaking, if a person becomes a patient of an unqualified practitioner, the practitioner will owe a duty of care to the patient to exercise the degree of skill which he claims to have. (See the striking facts of the Irish case of *Brogan* v *Bennett*

(1955) (*page 170*).) In *R* v *Crick* (1859) (*page 294*), a herb doctor was found guilty of manslaughter following the death of the child to whom he had prescribed lobelia from which she died. Pollock CB indicated to the jury that whereas it was not a crime to administer medicine, it was criminal to administer it in a risky and careless manner and in this respect there was no difference between the most regular practitioner and the greatest of quacks. Six years later, in *Jones* v *Fay* (1865) (*page 246*), a plaintiff succeeded in an action for damages arising out of a prescription of pills given to him by the defendant chemist which resulted in mercury poisoning. The defendant had dissuaded the plaintiff from seeking medical advice, and Baron Pigott directed the jury that if a person acted as if he was a medical practitioner then he would be judged by those standards and not by the standards of the chemist and druggist which in fact he was (see also *Markham* v *Abrahams* (1911) (*page 269*)).

In *Snell* v *Carter* (1941) (*page 320*), a masseur and medical electrician was found negligent in respect of treatment he gave to a patient which caused burns that eventually became gangrenous and apparently resulted in the patient's death from toxaemia. Evidence was given that the treatment was inadvisable and useless and that anyone with any medical knowledge would have realised the danger. The county court judge, H.H. Judge Scobell Armstrong, found the defendant negligent but added his sympathies on the basis that he was a person competent to perform work under a doctor's recommendations in all normal cases but this particular case had been unusual. This remark brought caustic comments from *The Lancet*:

"If comment can be added without disrespect to a careful and courteous tribunal, the decision and its rider exhibit the national compromise between two views of unqualified practice. One view resents any control of such practice, because unsupervised masseurs like the defendant may possess, or may at any moment discover, some therapeutic secret overlooked by orthodox medicine and because there is much more scientific truth in the world about us than is dreamt of in the registered medical practitioners philosophy. The other view is that it is unfair to the public to leave electrical or radiological treatment so utterly uncontrolled that an unqualified man can cause fatal burns to a patient suffering from disseminated sclerosis. On this view the sympathy is even more needed by the public than by the unqualified man." ([1941] 2 The Lancet at 321).

(See also *Smith* v *Lowry* (1935) (*page 319*), where a blind osteopath and masseur was found negligent for fracturing a five year old child's leg during manipulation.) Similar judicial views were expressed by Atkinson J in *Sones* v *Foster* (1937) (*page 321*). Mr Sones was awarded damages arising out of the negligent treatment afforded to him by a naturopath, medical herbalist and health practitioner which resulted in an above-knee amputation. Evidence was adduced that had the plaintiff been given proper treatment he would have required a below-knee amputation. The defendant never held himself out to be a registered practitioner, and the trial judge stressed to the jury that alternative practitioners did render a great public service and the more reputable of them had formed themselves into associations. Atkinson J also emphasised that orthodox practice did not have the monopoly on healing power. No one was compelled to consult an unorthodox practitioner, but anyone who did could expect to receive the average skill, knowledge and efficiency of the particular area of expertise claimed. The jury held that Mr Foster had fallen below these standards.

Conversely, where an unqualified practitioner makes unwarranted representations about his ability to cure, the courts are likely to find him in strict breach of contract. In *Walton* v *Lief* (1933) (*page 336*) an osteopath and naturopath represented that he could cure the plaintiff of a severe skin disease. The jury found a breach of contract and awarded damages equal to the fees paid. In *Shallard* v *Arline* (1939) (*page 313*), the defendant was held liable for a breach of contract and for fraudulent misrepresentation in respect of claims made that a facial rejuvenation programme was not only bound to work but was also harmless. The plaintiff in fact suffered severe burns which induced a mental breakdown. In *Hodson* v *Mellor* (1911) (*page 235*), the rather overblown representations made by an oculist were found to be in excess of the skill actually possessed. Mr Mellor claimed his system was based on irrefutable scientific principles which had long been justified by their outstanding success. His treatment of the plaintiff led to the worsening of her eye condition. Mr Mellor denied in evidence that his scientific experience had been gleaned from being a door-keeper at an eye hospital in Australia.

Section D: Damages

Chapter 11

General principles

The normal outcome of a successful action for a plaintiff in a medical malpractice case is compensatory financial redress known in law as damages. The assessment of the amount of damages is based upon the principles and methods of calculation evolved in the laws of contract and tort with particular reference to personal injury litigation. This chapter seeks to summarise these principles and to illustrate their application in certain cases concerning medical negligence and breach of contract. Most medical malpractice cases concern personal injury and resultant consequential losses and expenses. The following chapter looks at those cases which arise from the so-called wrongful birth of a child and which principally accrue from failed sterilisations and are not primarily based upon personal injury.

Once a litigant has proved a breach of duty and has shown that damage has resulted from that breach, the court will examine what monetary compensation should be awarded. Not every type of loss and expense will be recoverable. Just as a claim may fail on liability because the risk of the damage occurring was considered too remote, and was not therefore reasonably foreseeable, some types of damage are not recoverable because they are judicially determined as being too remotely connected to the negligent act. In the first concept of remoteness, concerned with questions of liability, there is no negligence or breach of contract because a practitioner should not reasonably be regarded as having to expect the unforeseeable. In the second usage, with respect to the quantum of damges, the courts have attempted to limit the consequences of a breach of duty to damage that is reasonably foreseeable as likely to flow from the negligence or breach of contract.

Whether a loss is considered as too remote is often inextricably connected with judicial reasoning that to recover certain types of losses would be offensive to public policy. For example, a married plaintiff who sustains a serious head injury as a result of negligence may develop personality changes or sexual disfunctions which cause an irretrievable breakdown of his marital relations resulting in a divorce. In *Pritchard* v *J.H. Cobden Limited* (1987), the court declined to allow a claim for the financial losses that followed divorce proceedings in a case where a thirty year old husband suffered brain damage in a road accident. Again, in *Meah* v *McCreamer* (1985 and 1986), a man who suffered a head injury in a road traffic accident which caused a propensity to attack women, and who consequently raped several women and was imprisoned for life, recovered compensation for the loss of his liberty. His further claim, however, for compensation to reflect the amount of damages which he personally had to pay to the victims of his rapes, in separate actions brought against him, were held not to be recoverable as being contrary to public policy and being too remote from the initial tortious act of the car collision. Woolf J held that the claim for indemnity in respect of the damages the plaintiff had to pay to his victims was essentially an indirect financial loss, and had the effect of imposing on the original tortfeasor liability in respect of injuries to persons owed no duty of care by the negligent car driver. To allow such a claim would be to impose a liability which was both indefinite in terms of the classes of person involved and, indeed, of an indefinite duration. It was also thought wholly inappropriate that criminal acts should be indemnified in such a manner.

A comparison of the two judgments of Woolf J in these separate actions is an instructive illustration of where a line has to be judicially drawn between what is recoverable, what is deemed too remote and what is deemed contrary to public policy. (See *Meah* v *McCreamer (No 2)* [1986] 1 All E R at 943.) In medical negligence cases, the courts drew this particular line when they struck out that part of a claim by an infant plaintiff who brought an action against doctors on the basis that, *inter alia*, she had been allowed to be born (see Chapter 4 and *McKay* v *Essex Area Health Authority* (1982) *(page 265)*). It is to be noted however that the courts recognize a claim in respect of raising a healthy or a non-healthy child who has been born due to breaches of duty concerning sterilisation, vasectomy, and abortion.

Once a type of damage is held not be too remote or not contrary to public policy, the plaintiff is entitled to compensation notwithstanding that the type of damage occurred in an unforeseeable way. A burn injury which was a reasonably foreseeable consequence of the defendant's negligence in *Smith* v *Leech Brain & Co.* (1962) led to the defendant being held liable for a cancer that developed as a result of the burn trauma. (See also *Hughes* v *Lord Advocate* (1963).) To this extent a tortfeasor is required in law to take the victim as he is found. In *Hatwell* v *South-West Metropolitan Regional Hospital Board* (1976) *(page 230)*, a plaintiff with clinical depression suffered a fractured jaw as a result of her medication being over-hastily withdrawn. The Court of Appeal confirmed that she was entitled to general damages for pain, suffering and loss of amenity which included her emotional distress and which should reflect the particular effect on the plaintiff's personality and constitutional predisposition. Similarly, in *Woodhouse* v *Yorkshire Regional Health Authority* (1984) *(page 347)*, a plaintiff with a hysterical personality sustained contracture deformities to her fingers. She was awarded damages that compensated her for her hysterical reaction which, albeit unexpected, was recoverable in law.

Once a plaintiff has established causation on the balance of probabilities, he does not have to show that one hundred per cent of his damages were caused by the negligent act. As indicated in Chapter 6, the approach of Pain J in *Clark* v *MacLennan* (1983) *(page 180)*, and Simon Brown J in *Bagley* v *North Herts Health Authority* (1986) *(page 155)*, was overruled by the House of Lords in *Hotson* v *East Berkshire Health Authority* (1987) *(page 240)*. Pain

J had awarded sixty per cent of the full value of Mrs Clark's claim on the basis that, had she had the operation at the proper time, there was still a risk of approximately one-third that it would have failed. Similarly, Simon Brown J had reduced a plaintiff's damages by five per cent in a case where a child was stillborn through the defendant's negligence. He accepted evidence that five per cent of births resulted in stillbirths and accordingly reduced the damages by this amount. In *Hotson* Lord Ackner specifically disapproved this approach:

> "Once liability is established, on the balance of probabilities, the loss which the plaintiff has sustained is payable in full. It is not discounted by reducing his claim by the extent to which he has failed to prove his case with one hundred per cent certainty. . . . To do so would be to propound a wholly new doctrine which has no support in principle or authority and would give rise to many complications in the search for mathematical or statistical exactitude" ([1987] 3 WLR at 248 a-c).

1. Heads of damage: general, special, provisional

The typical heads of damage in a medical malpractice case will accord with those in personal injury litigation which traditionally has separated so-called general from special damages. This distinction is analytically insignificant but is relevant for the purposes of pleading, procedure and the assessment of interest. Special damages are those losses and expenses that have actually been incurred and which can be calculated with reasonable precision at the date of the trial. They normally comprise specific losses of income, such as wages or profit, which arise as a result of the plaintiff being unable to work because of the injury, and also specific expenses that have been incurred because of the tort such as medical expenses, travel expenses, the costs of nursing care and attention, and damage to property or clothing. General damages are those which fall to be assessed and estimated, and accordingly involve a greater degree of judicial skill and discretion. General damages comprise the award made for the pain, suffering and loss of amenity occasioned by the breach of duty and also in respect of the future losses of income or profits and future expenses such as care and accommodation. The court, in assessing damages, must determine both past and present losses, some of which are entirely pecuniary and some of which are personal or non-pecuniary such as compensation for disfigurement and pain which has to be quantified in monetary terms.

The overriding principle is that a plaintiff should so far as is possible be put into a position he would have been in but for the injury done to him and thereby to compensate him for the harm done. This is normally done by the award of a once-and-for-all lump sum. In very limited circumstances, where new evidence comes to light, a party on appeal may be allowed to adduce new evidence if it is apparent that the plaintiff has been under-compensated or over-compensated. For example, in *Hughes* v *Hay* (1989) (*page 242*), the trial judge awarded a sum of £3,000 to cover the prospect of the plaintiff having difficulty in finding employment should he ever lose his job as a serving police officer. This award for disadvantage on the labour market was based on the assumption that he would in fact be fit enough to carry on for a further ten years in the police force. The plaintiff appealed and sought leave to have the court consider new evidence that he was in fact subsequently retired after the trial from the police force on medical grounds. The Court of Appeal allowed a retrial on the question of this discharge (see also *Reed* v *Oswal and Cleveland Area Health Authority* (1979) (*page 296*), *Mulholland* v *Mitchell* (1971)). The courts in fact will be slow to admit fresh evidence because they are governed by an overwhelming principle that there is an interest in litigation coming to an end. Accordingly a case will only be reopened in exceptional circumstances on the basis of fresh evidence (see Order 59 rule 10(2) of the Supreme Court Rules 1965 and *Murphy* v *Stone-Wallwork (Charlton) Limited* (1969), and *Jenkins* v *Richard Thomas & Baldwins Limited* (1966)).

An important inroad into the principle that damages will be awarded on a once and for all basis has been made through the provisions of s 6 Administration of Justice Act 1982 which has inserted s 32A into the Supreme Court Act 1981, thereby empowering the court to look again at a plaintiff's claim if a serious deterioration has occurred in a plaintiff's condition as a result of an injury for which he has already received some compensation. The powers to award so-called provisional damages took effect from 1 July 1985 and are governed by specific rules of court (see Order 37 Rules 7–10 of the Supreme Court Rules 1965 and the Practice Direction [1985] 1 WLR 961). Before these provisions, a plaintiff who had a risk of, for example, contracting lung cancer or mesothelioma because of a previous exposure to asbestos and who at the date of trial was suffering from only a minor form of breathlessness would receive compensation for the breathlessness together with some, normally small, award for the risk of contracting cancer in the future. This situation created potential injustice both for the plaintiff and for the defendant. If the plaintiff did contract cancer, the award was too little to cope with the disaster and, similarly, if the serious condition did not occur insurers felt they had compensated for an eventuality which had not materialised. The power of the courts to award provisional damages removes this uncertainty by allowing a plaintiff: (i) to receive damages on the basis of the pain and suffering and loss of amenity that he has already incurred and that he will suffer because of the ordinary consequences of the injury; and (ii) to recover further damages at a later date if specific risks of further injury materialise.

The Act accordingly allows, upon the matter being pleaded and proved, for a further award to be made when a plaintiff suffers a serious disease or deterioration as a result of the original tort which gave rise to the cause of action. Before it makes an order that a right exists for a subsequent further award, the court must be satisfied at the first trial that the plaintiff might, at some indefinite time, suffer a serious disease or deterioration. The court is required to specify in the order what the deterioration or disease is, and to indicate within what period of time the second application for damages must be made (see *Patterson* v *Ministry of Defence* (1987)). In *Hurditch* v *Sheffield Health Authority* (1989), the Court of Appeal held that a disagreement over medical evidence in respect of a worker's risk of contracting mesothelioma and lung cancer did not prevent a court entering judgment and making an award for provisional damages. In a case such as this the court held that the subsequent trial, should the plaintiff contract one of these diseases, could still hear evidence on causation and determine in the light of medical evidence whether the subsequent disease was attributable to the original asbestos exposure (see Purchas LJ [1989] 2 WLR at 839 d-h). These provisions, flexible and helpful as they are, will not assist in those cases where the disability flowing from an injury which has been compensated by an award turns out in fact to be worse than originally thought. The right to recover further damages arises only where nominated diseases or deteriorations have been stipulated in the order following a trial for provisional damages.

The principle of the lump sum award, as opposed to periodic payments, has also been called into question by commentators, particularly with regard to cases where very large awards have been made to severely injured plaintiffs who require constant care, attention and rehabilitation. In *Lim Poh Choo* v *Camden and Islington Area Health Authority* (1980) (*page 260*), Lord Scarman aired some of these concerns when he said:

"The course of this litigation illustrates with devastating clarity insuperable problems implicit in a system of compensation for personal injuries which . . . can yield only a lump sum . . . The award which covers past, present and future injury and loss must under our law be of a lump sum assessed at the conclusion of the legal process. The award is final, it is not susceptible to review as the future unfolds, substituting fact for estimation. Knowledge of the future being denied to mankind so much of the award as is attributed to future loss and suffering — in many cases the major part of the award — will almost surely be wrong. There is really only one certainty: the future will prove the award to be either too high or too low". ([1980] AC at 182h-183d.)

Lord Scarman went on to indicate that attempting to deal with this problem in the way that Lord Denning, the then Master of the Rolls, indicated in the Court of Appeal in *Lim's* case, via interim payments, was inappropriate. Such a proposal raised issues of social, economic and financial policy which were not amenable to judicial reform as they would almost certainly be controversial and could be resolved by legislation only. Problems of speculating what the precise degree of disability will be, what particular level of care a plaintiff may require, the degree of rehabilitation which will be necessary, and any particular special resources and accommodation that a plaintiff may need, have led some insurance companies to investigate the concept of structured compensation (see, for example, M. Wright Q.C. on structured compensation in Butterworth's Personal Injury Litigation Service Division s 1501). This concept seeks to award damages on the basis of an annuity or periodic payments which the courts would have the power to revise in cases where the plaintiff's condition had altered so as to warrant reappraisal. (See the Pearson Commission 1978 CMND 7054 paragraphs 555–576.) At present there is no power for a court to do this except by consent (see *Burke* v *Tower Hamlets Health Authority* (1989) (*page 173*), *Fournier* v *Canadian National Railway Company* (1927) and *Metcalfe* v *London Passenger Transport Board* (1938)). In cases where a plaintiff is unable to manage his own affairs and receives an award designed to compensate him for the rest of his working life and beyond, the danger of such a large award being dissipated is prevented if an order is made that the Court of Protection or a trust should administer the capital sum.

2. Pain, suffering and loss of amenity

The award made in respect of the physical pain and suffering and the effect on the lifestyle of the injured person necessarily focuses upon their particular consequences on that plaintiff. Accordingly, an award for the loss of a finger in an elderly retired person will be substantially lower than that for a young pianist whose promising career is blighted. However, given that there is no obvious equation between physical injury and financial compensation, these awards tend to have a strong aspect of conventionality about them. In effect, awards under this head of damage are within a flexible judicial range which is influenced but not constrained by previous reported comparable cases. These cases do not have the authority of precedents but are persuasive. They are reported principally in *The Quantum of Damages, Volume 2* (Sweet & Maxwell) by Kemp and Kemp, Personal Injury Reports, Current Law Year Books and Monthly Parts, and Halsbury's Monthly Reviews. In considering the level of damages in this respect, the judge is entitled to take a broad perspective of the effects of the injury including all aspects of past and future pain, discomfort, sickness, anxiety, loss of function, mental anguish, embarrassment, humiliation and, where appropriate, disfigurement. Loss of amenity may include the interference or cessation of leisure activities, sporting abilities, recreation and hobbies. If a particular career can no longer be followed then loss of enjoyment of work, if appropriate, may also sound in damages. Similarly, other losses such as the loss of enjoyment of family life, the loss of prospects of marriage, and losses through sexual malfunction will also be evaluated in money's worth.

If an injury or a disease is likely to shorten one's life, it is a matter statutorily singled out by s 1 Administration of Justice Act 1982 for a judge to consider. Damages specifically for the acceleration of one's own death as a separate head of damage, known as loss of expectation of life, were abolished by s 1 Administration of Justice Act 1982, but the same section went on to enjoin the court in the following way:

"If the injured person's expectation of life has been reduced by the injuries, the court, in assessing damages in respect of pain and suffering caused by the injuries, *shall* take account of any suffering caused or likely to be caused to him by awareness that his expectation of life has been so reduced" (s 1(1)(b) Administration of Justice Act 1982) (emphasis added).

Awards for pain, suffering and loss of amenity necessarily involve a value judgement about the worth of the loss of an eye, a leg or the loss of one's reason, but they are in theory meant to be substantial compensation rather than a token solace and as such are to be based on objective assessments of loss. This principle was espoused in *H. West & Son Limited* v *Shephard* (1964) and confirmed by the House of Lords in *Lim Poh Choo* v *Camden and Islington Area Health Authority* (1980) (*page 260*). In *Lim*, a plaintiff sustained brain damage of such a degree that she was not aware of the catastrophe that had befallen her, but was nevertheless held to be entitled to receive full damages in respect of the deprivation of the ordinary amenities of life. The fact of her being unaware of the loss did not eliminate the actuality of the deprivation. Dr Lim suffered a cardiac arrest when aged thirty-six after a minor operation as a result of admitted negligence which left her a "barely sentient human wreck". She was awarded, *inter alia*, £20,000 for pain, suffering and loss of amenity at her trial in December 1977 on the basis that she had suffered a total loss, objectively appraised, of the amenities of life. The fact that Dr Lim was unaware of her predicament was not a relevant matter; nor was the court concerned with the question of how the plaintiff would use the award.

Awards for pain, suffering and loss of amenity in a so-called "ordinary" case of tetraplegia or quadriplegia were given a guideline figure of £75,000 in *Housecroft* v *Burnett* (1986) (current value approximately £90,000) for a plaintiff who was not in pain, was fully aware of the disability, had a life expectancy of twenty-five years or more and had retained facilities of speech, sight and hearing but obviously needed help with bodily functions. Miss Housecroft was aged sixteen when she was rendered tetraplegic in a road traffic accident, and she was awarded £80,000 for pain, suffering and loss of amenity (current value approximately £96,600).

In *Aboul-Hosn* v *Trustees of the Italian Hospital* (1987) (*page 149*), a nineteen year old suffered irreversible brain damage reducing his mental age to two as a result of negligent treatment following an operation to remove a cyst. The plaintiff was awarded £85,000 (current value approximately £95,000) for pain, suffering and loss of amenity in circumstances where he could not walk except in a zombie-like fashion, his eyesight was severely impaired, he could not speak, he would never work or marry and he had some limited insight into his predicament. In *Thomas* v *Wignall* (1987) (*page 327*), a sixteen year old who suffered permanent brain damage after a negligently administered anaesthetic was awarded an agreed £60,000 (current value approximately £71,800) damages in respect of pain, suffering and loss of amenity. The plaintiff was left in a position of severe intellectual impairment with mood swings that made her occasionally aggressive; she was barely able to communicate, required a wheelchair and was frequently incontinent. In *Roberts* v *Johnstone* (1988) (*page 300*), an agreed figure of £75,000 (current value approximately £88,400) was awarded to a plaintiff who was born with a severe haemolytic disease and suffered grievous disabilities including brain damage due to the defendant's failure to give appropriate treatment to her mother during pregnancy. The infant plaintiff was hyperactive, incontinent, incapable of speech, was deaf, retarded and autistic. Earlier cases include *Croke* v *Wiseman* (1982) (*page 189*) where an infant plaintiff who suffered brain damage following a cardiac arrest during treatment was awarded £35,000 in 1979 (current value approximately £66,000) for severe quadriplegia. In *Connolly* v *Camden and Islington Area Health Authority* (1981) (*page 183*), an overdose of anaesthetic to a new-born baby rendered him epileptic, severely mentally disabled and unlikely to be able to walk properly. He was awarded £50,000 (current value approximately £88,500) for pain, suffering and loss of amenity. In *Moser* v *Enfield and Haringey Area Health Authority* (1983) (*page 276*), a four year old suffered irreversible brain damage following a negligent anaesthetic. The child had no insight into his condition of quadriplegia, was almost blind, was doubly incontinent and was unable to move. He had a life expectancy of approximately another twenty years. He was awarded £35,000 (current value £50,750).

In cases of less serious injuries, the judge will also be guided by comparable cases that may occur reasonably routinely in areas of non-medical personal injury. Many of these cases will present little difficulty in assessing. For example in *Mitchell* v *Liverpool Area Health Authority* (1985) (*page 273*), a one month old child who sustained circulation damage due to the defendant's negligence which resulted in an amputation of his arm below the elbow, was awarded £30,000 (current value approximately £36,000) general damages for pain, suffering and loss of amenity. The Court of Appeal thought that this award was at the top of the range but declined to interfere with it. In *Hoffman* v *Sofaer* (1982) (*page 235*), a forty-seven year old man was awarded £19,000 (current value approximately £28,000) for a severely impaired wrist and hand and a fused elbow resulting from the negligent treatment of his general practitioner. (See also *Connor* v *Fison-Clarke* (1987) (*page 185*), *McLoughlin* v *Greenwich and Bexley Area Health Authority* (1984) (*page 265*).)

Other cases encountered in the area of medical malpractice tend to be a little more removed from conventional personal injury. In *Ackers* v *Wigan Area Health Authority* (1986) (*page 150*), a plaintiff developed severe depression following a caesarean section for the delivery of her first child during which she was awake but unanaesthetised. She was unable to speak or inform the medical staff of her plight because she had been paralysed by a pre-operative relaxant drug. She was receptive to pain during the operation. She was awarded £12,000 general damages in June 1985 (current value approximately £14,400). In *Biles* v *Barking Health Authority* (1988) (*page 162*), Mrs Biles suffered clinical depression following a sterilisation which in fact proved to be unnecessary. She had thereafter undertaken many steps in attempting to conceive and had undergone many operations and tests which had caused pain and operation scarring. She had also developed severe sexual disfunction. She was awarded £45,000 (current value approximately £47,000). In *G* v *North Tees Health Authority* (1989) (*page 214*), a mother and daughter were each awarded £5,000 general damages for pain, suffering and loss of amenity (current value approximately £5,500), in circumstances where the infant plaintiff had been investigated for possible sexual abuse following the contamination of her vaginal swab with an adult's which had contained sperm. The child was examined and interviewed and as a result suffered nightmares and bedwetting. The mother had felt suicidal until the mistake was disclosed to her, and the affair had exacerbated her phobic anxiety state.

In *Morgan* v *Gwent Health Authority* (1987) (*page 274*), a plaintiff whose blood group was rhesus negative was negligently given a transfusion of rhesus positive blood which gave rise to potentially serious complications for any child that she might conceive. Only seventeen per cent of potential fathers would be compatible. The plaintiff received at first instance £8,000 which was increased to £20,000 (current value approximately £22,000) by the Court of Appeal whose judges were persuaded that the breakdown of her engagement was due to the fact of the complications which would occur if her fiancé fathered her children. In *Vaughan* v *Paddington and North Kensington Area Health Authority* (1987) (*page 332*), a middle-aged woman with two adult children was told that she had contracted breast cancer and she agreed to a double mastectomy. She required a number of operations to fit and remove prostheses. In fact Mrs Vaughan never did have cancer and she was awarded £25,000 (current value approximately £29,000) for pain, suffering and loss of amenity which included pain and restriction in the back and arms caused by the operations, and for the fear that she was going to die, which she had had for approximately two and a half years. (See also *Needham* v *Biograft Transplant Centre Ltd* (1983) (*page 279*).)

3. Loss of earnings and loss of earning capacity

A plaintiff who as a result of injuries has been unable to work is entitled to recover as special damages the value of lost wages or profits up to the date of trial. These losses will be net of tax and National Insurance contributions and the costs of earning the wages, such as travelling expenses. The loss of earnings may, however, include the monetary value of any benefits the plaintiff might have received, such as company cars and lost wage increases or lost prospects of promotion.

The loss of future earnings is considered as general damages, and the starting-point in its calculation is to consider the degree of disability. If a plaintiff will never be able to work again he is entitled to his full losses until retirement age together with any pension loss. The annual amount of a loss is determined at the date of the trial and is based on the annual income the plaintiff would have received net of tax and National Insurance. This sum, called the multiplicand, is then multiplied by a figure based upon the period of years during which the inability to work will persist; this figure is called the multiplier. If for example, a plaintiff loses earnings over a period of forty years, that number will determine a multiplier of approximately eighteen, which is considered appropriate by the court to account for the fact of accelerated receipt of the income. The theory behind the use of the multiplier and multiplicand is to provide the plaintiff with a lump sum which when invested will produce an annual income commensurate with the loss incurred. The courts work on a notional rate of return on the capital sum invested of approximately 4.5 per cent (see *Cookson* v *Knowles* (1978)). The multiplier may also be reduced to allow for other contingencies such as, for example, the unstable nature of the job or career the plaintiff was previously engaged in. The sum awarded is therefore meant to represent a capital amount which when invested will give an annual income equivalent to the plaintiff's lost income so that the interest and capital combined are exhausted at the end of the period when the plaintiff would no longer have worked. The courts have eschewed a fine actuarial-based calculation and have used the mode of calculation based upon the multiplier and multiplicand even where evidence indicates that in times of inflation it may undercompensate. The courts have rejected the taking into account of the fact of inflation both in the calculation of loss of future earnings and loss of future pension rights (see *Lim Poh Choo* v *Camden and Islington Area Health Authority* (1980) *(page 260)*, and *Auty* v *National Coal Board* (1985)).

A plaintiff with a reduced capacity to work will be awarded the difference between his pre-accident and post-accident working capacity, and will be under a duty to mitigate his loss by attempting to find suitable employment. In *Billingham* v *Hughes* (1949), the defendants were credited with an allowance representing the plaintiff's residual earning capacity as a radiologist in circumstances where his injury had meant that he could not pursue his career as a general practitioner.

A child injured at birth or at a very young age to a degree that the capacity to work is reduced or destroyed may claim for loss of earnings (see *Connolly* v *Camden and Islington Area Health Authority* (1981) *(page 183)*). In *Croke* v *Wiseman* (1982) *(page 189)*, the multiplier/multiplicand approach was used by basing the annual prospective loss on the national average wage; this was held to be justified by the Court of Appeal given the quality of the infant plaintiff's background. In *Moser* v *Enfield and Haringey Area Health Authority* (1983) *(page 276)*, a similar basis was used. Awards to infants for loss of future earnings are heavily discounted because of accelerated receipt, recognizing that they are receiving at trial sums which they would not in any event have earned until ten or more years later.

Some serious injuries reduce the life expectancy of plaintiffs. The loss of earnings in those years when the plaintiff will in fact be deceased but would have been alive and working had it not been for his injury is recoverable. Since *Harris* v *Empress Motors Limited* (1983), a plaintiff will normally be required to give credit for his living expenses in calculating what is called the "lost years" claim for future loss of earnings. The reasoning is that the costs of maintaining himself will not be required in those notional lost years when the plaintiff will not be alive. For a couple with no dependent children, the credit given in this respect is normally approximately fifty per cent of the net income. The percentage is lower if there are dependent children, approximately thirty per cent, and higher if the plaintiff is unmarried. In the case of a very young child, the lost years claim is likely to be small, if awarded at all (cf *Croke* v *Wiseman* (1982) (*page 189*)). The claim in respect of the lost years does not survive for the benefit of the estate of a plaintiff, having been specifically abolished by the provisions of s 4(2) Administration of Justice Act 1982 for death occurring after 1 January 1983. Any dependants of a deceased may, however, claim in respect of the loss of their dependency pursuant to the provisions of the Fatal Accidents Act 1976. Certain categories of dependants are also entitled to a statutory award of £3,500 in respect of bereavement where a wrongful act caused death. (See s 1A Fatal Accidents Act 1976 as amended by s 3(1) Administration of Justice Act 1982.)

In cases where the lost earnings of a young woman are being assessed, it is probably not necessary to take into account the prospects of her marriage in determining a multiplier, particularly where no account for the plaintiff's loss of the prospect of marriage has been taken in the award for general damages for loss of amenity (see *Hughes* v *McKeown* (1985), *Housecroft* v *Burnett* (1986) and *Thomas* v *Wignall* (1987) (*page 327*)).

Examples of the court's approach in determining loss of future earnings can be found in *Aboul-Hosn* v *Trustees of the Italian Hospital* (1987) (*page 149*) where the court accepted that a young man with four "A" levels and a place at university had a reasonable prospect of earning £18,000 per annum and applied a multiplier of 17 giving £306,000 loss of earnings. The plaintiff was also found to have lost reasonable prospects of having a company car, and £25,000 was added to the award in this respect. In *Moser* v *Enfield and Haringey Area Health Authority* (1983) (*page 276*), an infant plaintiff who was four and half years old at the date of an anaesthetic mishap, and was aged ten at the trial with a thirty years' life expectancy, was awarded £21,480 based on a multiplier of four years and a multiplicand of £5,370, being the net national average earnings at that date. No award was made for the lost years.

Often an injury results in a plaintiff being put at a disadvantage in relation to others in competing for jobs in the labour market. An injury may allow a plaintiff to continue working but may make him unsuitable for certain types of work and may, because of any continuing disability, make him less likely to get a job when competing with the fully able. The courts have recognized this as a basis for compensation, and an award is made in the circumstances for so-called disadvantage in the labour market and may be made whether a plaintiff is working or is unemployed at the date of the trial or indeed has not yet reached working age (see *Moeliker* v *A Reyrolle & Co. Limited* (1977), *Cooke* v *Consolidated Fisheries Limited* (1977)). The award takes into account the fact that the disadvantage, that is being unemployed or underemployed for longer periods because of the disability, may not happen at all, and if it does happen may occur at an indeterminate date. The award is often based on the annual value of the plaintiff's wage and accordingly can be substantial if the risk of the plaintiff losing his job is very great (see *Foster* v *Tyne & Wear County Council* (1986)). In *Mitchell* v *Liverpool Area Health Authority* (1985) (*page 273*), a one month old baby who suffered a below-elbow arm amputation was not awarded at first instance anything in respect of his claim for disadvantage on the labour market. The Court of Appeal held, however, that there there was a realistic prospect that he would not earn as much as he would have if he had had no disability, and awarded £5,000 which reflected the heavy discounting required for accelerated receipt.

4. Expenses

Expenses incurred up to the date of trial are recoverable as special damages, thereafter as general damages. A plaintiff is entitled to recover all expenses reasonably incurred or which will be reasonably incurred and which foreseeably arise out of injury suffered. Such expenses can range from the travelling costs of relatives visiting a plaintiff while in hospital, medical expenses, the cost of nursing care, the cost of domestic help, modifications to buildings, the extra costs of maintaining and running specially accommodated premises, appliances to aid the disabled, extra holiday costs incurred because of disablement, increased travelling and car costs, recompense for an inability to undertake household repairs, decorations or gardening, costs of physio-therapy and rehabilitation, to extra costs in respect of special clothing and bedding. In the case of a patient who is unable to manage his own affairs, the costs of a trust fund or the Court of Protection fees are also recoverable (cf *Moser* v *Enfield and Haringey Area Health Authority* (1983) (*page 276*), where £9,300 was awarded in this respect, and *Aboul-Hosn* v *Trustees of the Italian Hospital* (1987) (*page 149*) where £34,500 was awarded for Court of Protection fees in a claim totalling £1,032,000). If the Court of Protection is to administer the fund, the precise amount of the award cannot be determined in advance as the fees are charged on a sliding scale according to the amount administered. (See Rule 77 and the Appendix to the Court of Protection Rules 1984 SI 1984 No. 2035, *The Supreme Court Practice 1988, Volume 2*, at page 898.)

Future expenses are normally calculated on a multiplicand and multiplier basis wherever possible, and the normal starting point is the expected longevity of the plaintiff. In cases where nursing and domestic care is required, the multiplier may be larger than that for a loss of earnings claim because in some cases the life expectancy of a plaintiff may not be reduced below the normal retirement age.

Medical expenses can be recovered, even if a plaintiff could have used the National Health Service, because of the specific provisions of s 2(4) Law Reform (Personal Injuries) Act 1948. If, in fact, the National Health Service is used or is likely to be used in the future, the cost of private care is not recoverable. If a plaintiff has been in a National Health Service hospital, nursing home or other similar institution, he has to give credit for the savings in respect of his living expenses during that period of institutional care in respect of his award for loss of earnings (see s 5 Administration of Justice Act 1982 which came into force on 1 January 1983 in this respect).

If nursing and domestic care is rendered freely by a relative, the cost of giving that care is still recoverable notwithstanding that no money has changed hands (*Donnelly* v *Joyce* (1974)). The measure of nursing and other care gratuitously rendered may be the lost wages incurred by the carer if he/she had to give up a job to look after the disabled person (*Croke* v *Wiseman* (1982) (*page 189*)). In such a case where a job has been given up, the ceiling on the award is most likely to be the commercial rate which would be required to get a professional carer to do a similar job (see *Housecroft* v *Burnett* (1986)). Where the carer does not give up work, a claim still exists which will obviously depend on the level of care given; and again the ceiling on such an award is probably the going commercial rate (see *Cunningham* v *Harrison* (1973), *Aboul-Hosn* v *Trustees of the Italian Hospital* (1987) (*page 149*)). Future care and attention can amount to a considerable award of damages in those cases where a plaintiff needs constant or near-constant attention. In *Rialas* v *Mitchell* (1984), £143,552 was awarded for future nursing care and attention in respect of a seriously disabled child who was injured when he was six years old. The court held that it was not unreasonable for the child to be cared for at home, even though he could be cared for more cheaply in an institution. In *Aboul-Hosn* v *Trustees of Italian Hospital* (above), £76,650 was awarded for care up until the date of the trial, equivalent to four and three-quarter years at an annual value of £16,137. The cost of future care was divided into two periods. In the first period, where it was anticipated that the parents could cope with the help of a night auxiliary nurse, £234,102 was awarded. In the second period, where the plaintiff would be required to live in a home, a further £112,994 was awarded, plus £53,704 for costs of a rehabilitation programme and for assistance from physiotherapists, speech therapists and dietitians, making £400,800 for total costs of future care.

In cases where a large award is made for care, particularly with reference to institutional care, and also for loss of earnings, the courts have been careful to avoid duplication of awards in that an overlap may occur between the two heads of damage. If a plaintiff is in care in an institution, then notionally he does not require that part of his lost income which would be used for living expenses, because the plaintiff is catered for under the costs of institutional care (see *Lim Poh Choo* v *Camden and Islington Area Health Authority* (1980) (*page 260*)).

Just as inflation is ignored in the calculation of an award, so also is the possible effect of a higher rate of taxation being levied on the amount of interest generated by a large capital sum awarded. In *Hodgson* v *Trapp* (1988), the House of Lords overruled *Thomas* v *Wignall* (1987) (*page 327*) where the multiplier in respect of the loss of income and cost of future care was increased by one to reflect the higher risk of taxation that might accrue on the interest from the overall award. The House of Lords took the view that it would only be in rare circumstances where an increase in the multiplier would in fact be justified (per Lord Oliver [1988] 3 WLR at 1299–1300).

Where a plaintiff is required to purchase special accommodation to enable him to manage his domestic life in a reasonable fashion, he is not entitled to the purchase costs of the property but only to the additional annual cost during his lifetime of providing that accommodation, which is currently valued at two per cent of the net capital cost per annum. In addition, any costs in converting the property, which do not amount to betterment, are recoverable (*Roberts* v *Johnstone* (1988) (*page 300*)).

5. Deductions

The courts are required by statute to deduct certain statutory benefits paid to a victim who suffers a personal injury. The policy intention behind s 2 Law Reform (Personal Injuries) Act 1948 was to prevent a plaintiff from so-called double recovery. The Act in fact represents a political compromise and requires that one half of certain named benefits are to be deducted from the award for loss of earnings or disadvantage in the labour market for a period of five years from the date when the cause of action accrued. The named deductible benefits are sickness benefit, invalidity benefit, non-contributory invalidity pension and industrial disablement benefit which covers disablement gratuity and pension and hospital treatment allowance. The section also mentions injury benefit, which was abolished in April 1983. The argument that after the five year period has elapsed, the plaintiff should give credit for all of the benefits he continues to receive was roundly rejected in *Denman* v *Essex Area Health Authority* (1984) and *Jackman* v *Corbett* (1988) in favour of an alternative interpretation that the plaintiff should give no credit. A cause of action may be deemed to have accrued when damage which is more than negligible has occurred (*Cartledge* v *Jopling* (1963)). In some cases, therefore, it may be possible to argue where an injury or disease has been unattributed to the defendant's negligence or where there existed some small symptoms which were predominantly latent, that the five year period in question has run out before the benefits were paid. The benefits in question do fall to be deducted from an award for disadvantage in the labour market (see *Foster* v *Tyne and Wear County Council* (1986)). The relevant provision of the Law Reform (Personal Injuries) Act 1948 will be repealed by s 22 Social Security Act 1989 when it comes into force on a date to be appointed in 1990, and will have retrospective effect for accidents and injuries occurring on or after 1 January 1990.

The prevailing judicial attitude is currently towards deduction of other State benefits which are not stipulated within the 1948 Act. In *Hodgson* v *Trapp* (1988), the House of Lords unanimously held that both attendance and mobility allowances payable pursuant to s 35 and s 37A Social Security Act 1975 fell to be deducted in full for the whole period they were likely to be awarded (per Lord Bridge [1988] 3 WLR at 1285h–1286c). This reversed the Court of Appeal decision in *Bowker* v *Rose* (1978).

In the light of this mode of reasoning, full credit has to be given for certain benefits and receipts. These include statutory sick pay (*Palfrey* v *Greater London Council* (1985)); unemployment benefit (*Nabi* v *British Leyland (UK) Limited* (1980), *Westwood* v *Secretary of State for Employment* (1985)); supplementary benefit and family income supplement (which on 4 April 1988 were renamed income support and family credit respectively) (*Lincoln* v *Hayman* (1982), *Gaskill* v *Preston* (1981)).

Further, in *Hussain* v *New Taplow Paper Mill Limited* (1988), a plaintiff, who was injured through the negligence of his employers, was required to give credit for the income he received while off sick which was paid to him under a scheme of permanent health insurance, the premium for which was paid by his employers and to which he did not contribute. The situation was held to be different in *Berriello* v *Felixstowe Dock and Railway Company* (1989) where an Italian seaman, who remained accountable for sums he had received to a fund administered by the Italian State, did not have to give credit for those sums because there was in fact no double recovery. In *Colledge* v *Bass*

Mitchells & Butlers Limited (1988), the Court of Appeal held that redundancy payments made to an injured workman which arose because his injury made him more likely to be selected for redundancy did fall to be deducted from a loss of earnings claim. If, however, on different facts a plaintiff would in any event have been likely to have been made redundant, the redundancy payments would not fall to be deducted as they would properly reflect the monies paid for the previous service and loss of job.

There are two classes of receipts that may accrue to a plaintiff as a result of his injury and which are not required in law to be deducted from an award for damages. The first concerns insurance payments and pensions for which the plaintiff has contributed (*Bradburn* v *Great Western Railway Company* (1874), *Parry* v *Cleaver* (1970) and *Cunningham* v *Harrison* (1973)). The courts have considered as a matter of "justice, reasonableness and public policy" (per Lord Reid in *Parry* v *Cleaver* [1970] AC at 13), that premiums previously paid by an injured person to protect him against a contingency such as an injury should not fall to the credit of the tortfeasor, arising as they do out of the prudence and income of the victims. A State retirement pension falls into this category, as does a contributory disability pension (see *Hewson* v *Downs* (1970)). Where, however, a plaintiff is claiming for loss of pension as a head of damage, he is required to give credit for any disability pension he receives during the period for which he is claiming loss of the retirement pension (*Parry* v *Cleaver* (1970)).

The second class of exception is with respect to monies received through the benevolence of third parties motivated by sympathy for the misfortune of the plaintiff (see *Redpath* v *Belfast & Co Down Railway* (1947)).

In a Fatal Accidents Act 1976 claim, a widow was not required to give credit for her widow's pension which was paid to her on the death of her husband who was, at the time of death, in receipt of a retirement pension (*Pidduck* v *Eastern Scottish Omnibuses Ltd* (1989)). Section 4 Fatal Accidents Act 1976, as amended by s 3 Administration of Justice Act 1982, provides that:

> "In assessing damages in respect of a person's death or an action under this Act, benefits which have accrued or will or may accrue to any person from his estate or otherwise as a result of his death shall be disregarded".

Mrs Pidduck was not, on the wording of this Act, required to give any credit for the widow's pension she received because this arose on account of her husband's death. This was so notwithstanding the fact that she was entitled to, and did receive, a loss of dependency on her husband's own pension and was accordingly financially better off because of the death.

6. Interest

Interest is payable on the principle that a plaintiff is entitled to damages from the date when they accrued, and has therefore been kept out of money which is rightfully his, and which the defendants have continued to possess as an interest earning resource. A plaintiff is statutorily entitled to simple interest pursuant to s 35A Supreme Court Act 1981 in cases where damages for personal injuries exceed £200 (see also s 69 County Courts Act 1984). No interest, however, can arise on future losses of expenses, as no loss has been incurred at the date of trial. Interest for loss of earnings as special damages to the date of trial will run at one-half of the special account rate (formerly the short-term investment account rate) on the reasoning in *Jefford* v *Gee* (1970) that some of the loss had accrued immediately after the injury but some has accrued only immediately before the date of the trial, and one-half is a reasonable compromise. In those cases where the losses have accrued immediately after the accident, it would not be offensive in principle to allow the full rate from the date at which the loss fully accrued. There is, however, some dispute on this issue because of conflicting opinion of the Court of Appeal expressed in *Dexter* v *Courtaulds* (1984) and in *Prokop* v *The Department of Health and Social Security* (1985). It is, however, necessary to plead the special circumstances if the full rate is being argued for which in most cases would simply amount to the fact that the loss had accrued shortly after the tort.

In *Roberts* v *Johnstone* (1988) (*page 300*), the Court of Appeal held that nursing care expended before the trial was to be treated as special damage even where no one had been employed but the adoptive mother had undertaken the caring role, and interest would therefore run at the higher rate. Interest runs at a lower rate in respect of general damages for pain, suffering and loss of amenity, currently at two per cent from the service of the writ (*Birkett* v *Hayes* (1982), *Wright* v *British Railways Board* (1983)). There would appear to be no good reason why the low rate of two per cent should apply to the conventional award for bereavement in a Fatal Accidents Act 1976 claim. General damages for pain, suffering and loss of amenity are to some extent inflation proofed because they rise more or less in line with the rate of inflation. However, conventional awards do not increase in the same manner and the amount for bereavement is statutorily fixed at £3,500. (Before it was abolished, the conventional award for the loss of expectation of life did attract the full rate of interest.) Full interest was awarded on bereavement damages in *Prior* v *Bernard Hastie & Co* (1987).

7. Aggravated and exemplary damages

As has been indicated, damages in tort are primarily compensatory and not punitive. There are, however, very limited exceptions in cases where the defendant has acted in such a high-handed manner that the court thinks it proper to make a punitive award. Such awards, known as exemplary damages, are normally constrained to situations where a government body or department has acted oppressively or where the defendant has sought to make a profit from the tort perpetrated on the plaintiff (see *Rookes* v *Barnard* (1964) and *Cassell & Co. Limited* v *Broome* (1972)). Similarly, a punitive aspect to the award for damages may arise where the conduct of the defendant is so outrageous and perhaps motivated by spite and malice that the plaintiff's proper feelings of dignity and pride have been injured. These damages, known as aggravated damages, are more frequently awarded in defamation cases (see *Damages* (Sweet & Maxwell, 15th edition, 1988) by McGregor, at page 1029, paragraph 1623).

In medical mishap cases, the courts have indicated a reluctance to include an element of punitive damages in awards to plaintiffs. In *Kralj* v *McGrath* (1986) (*page 253*), Woolf J rejected the plaintiff's claim for aggravated damages arising out of an obstetric practice described as horrific and totally unacceptable:

"It is my view that it would be wholly inappropriate to introduce into claims of this sort, for breach of contract and negligence, the concept of aggravated damage . . . it would be difficult to see why it could not even extend to cases where damages are brought for personal injuries in respect of driving. If the principle is right, a higher award of damages would be appropriate in a case of reckless driving which caused injury than would be appropriate in cases where careless driving caused identical injuries. Such a result seems to me to be wholly inconsistent with the general approach to damages in this area, which is to compensate the plaintiff for the loss that she has actually suffered, so far as it is possible to do so, by the award of monetary compensation and not to treat those damages as being a matter which reflects the degree of negligence or breach of duty of the defendant. I do, however, accept that the effect on a mother who during the course of her labour undergoes unnecessary suffering may be greater if this results not in the birth of a normal child but a child who is in the unfortunate condition that Daniel was here. It would be easier for a mother to forget or adjust to the consequences of that distressing experience if she has the comfort of a normal child. If instead of having the satisfaction in the birth of a normal child she has the distress of the knowledge that the child is disabled, subject to the disabilities that Daniel was, it would be more difficult for her to overcome the consequences and the unnecessary suffering may have a greater impact on her". ([1986] 1 All ER at 61 e-h.)

Similarly, in *G* v *North Tees Health Authority* (1989) (*page 214*), no aggravated damages were awarded in the distressing circumstances where negligence led to the processing of a child as a possible victim of sexual abuse causing an aggravation of phobic anxiety in the child's mother and nightmares and enuresis in the child. In *Barbara* v *Home Office* (1984) (*page 156*), Leggatt J did make an award of £500 aggravated damages for the injury to the plaintiff's feelings in respect of a forcible injection by hospital officers on a prison inmate. However, the plaintiff's claim for exemplary damages was rejected on the basis that it did not follow that an act of mere negligence gave rise to such an award even if the victim regarded it as oppressive.

Chapter 12

Claims for wrongful birth

Where a woman conceives and gives birth to a child due to negligent advice or treatment concerning contraception, abortion, or sterilisation, the question arises whether damages can be recovered in respect of the costs of raising a child who would not otherwise have been born. In *Sciuraga* v *Powell* (1980) (*page 312*), the plaintiff contracted with a doctor to conduct a lawful termination of her pregnancy. The termination was negligently carried out and a child was born. The trial judge awarded damages in respect of the plaintiff's loss of earnings and for the impairment of her marriage prospects, accepting the view that the recovery of such damages was not contrary to public policy. The trial judge also rejected a defence that any damage which the plaintiff had suffered was caused not by the breach of contract but by the plaintiff declining to undergo a second attempt to terminate her pregnancy. The Court of Appeal varied certain aspects of the award but concurred in the view that the loss of future wages was recoverable. No claim was made in that case for the upkeep of the child.

Such a claim however was made and rejected by Jupp J in *Udale* v *Bloomsbury Area Health Authority* (1983) (*page 329*). The judge awarded £8,000 damages in total on the basis of the shock and anxiety that arose out of the unwanted pregnancy which had resulted from a negligent sterilisation. This sum included a claim in respect of the suffering caused by the pregnancy and birth itself, which was aggravated by the fear of having done the child inadvertent harm by taking drugs at a time when the mother was unaware she was pregnant. The judge rejected claims in respect of needing to extend the family accommodation to cater for the unplanned new arrival, for the baby's layette and for the cost of looking after the child up to the age of sixteen. Jupp J rejected these claims on the basis of public policy. The judge indicated that it would be highly undesirable that any child should learn that a court had publicly declared its life or birth to be a mistake and had awarded damages which could be conceived as proof of the child not being wanted. The judge also thought that if such claims were allowed it would create a subconscious pressure to encourage abortions by medical practitioners in order to avoid claims based on the cost of raising a child. The judge also inclined to the view that the birth of a child should be an occasion for rejoicing.

In *Thake* v *Maurice* (1985) (*page 327*), Pain J took a different view and made such an award in respect of the birth of a healthy child which had been born following a negligent vasectomy. The claim in this respect included the baby's layette (£717), and the upkeep of the child till aged seventeen (£5,960) together with the mother's loss of earnings in that period. On a cross-appeal,

113

the plaintiff further achieved general damages in the sum of £1,500 for the antenatal pain and suffering which Pain J had declined to award on the basis that the postnatal joy cancelled it out.

In *Emeh v Kensington and Chelsea and Westminster Area Health Authority* (1985) (*page 205*), the Court of Appeal preferred the view taken by Pain J to that taken by Jupp J and decided that it was not contrary to public policy to award damages for the wrongful birth of a child resulting in that case from a negligent sterilisation. Mrs Emeh, on appeal, received damages in respect of her own loss of earnings and the future costs of maintaining the child (£4,056, based on £507 per annum). She also received general damages for pain, suffering and loss of amenity in her own right for the normal birth and subsequent second sterilisation in the sum of £3,000. She further recovered the sum of £10,000 for her loss of amenity to cover the degree of future care that this child would need because it had been born with congenital deformities. The Court of Appeal in *Emeh* rejected the first instance reasoning of Park J who had determined that the plaintiff's failure to have an abortion when she found out that she was pregnant amounted to a *novus actus interveniens* or, alternatively, she had failed to mitigate her damages in not having the abortion. Purchas LJ, concurring with Lord Justices Slade and Waller, went on to analyse the public policy argument and saw it as misfounded:

"I see no reason for the court to introduce into the perfectly ordinary straightforward rules of recovery of damages, whether they are damages claimed for breach of contract or from tort, some qualification to reflect special social positions. If something has to be done in that respect, as Waller LJ cited from the speech of Lord Scarman in *McLoughlin v O'Brian* (1983), then that is a matter which falls more properly within the purview of Parliament." ([1985] 2 QB at 1028 e-g.)

The Court of Appeal in *Emeh* accordingly agreed with the reasoning of Pain J in *Thake v Maurice* (above) when he said:

"There remains some doubt whether the categories of public policy are now closed: see Cheshire and Fifoot's *Law of Contract*, 10th ed. (1981), page 318. However that may be, I take the view that a judge of first instance should hesitate long before attempting to ride this unruly horse in a new direction. In approaching this problem I firmly put sentiment on one side. A healthy baby is so lovely a creature that I can well understand the reaction of one who asks: how could its birth possibly give rise to an action for damages? But every baby has a belly to be filled and a body to be clothed. The law relating to damages is concerned with reparation in . money terms and this is what is needed for the maintenance of a baby". ([1985] 2 WLR at 230 e-g.)

In *Benarr v Kettering Health Authority* (1988) (*page 161*), Hodgson J awarded damages in respect of the educational costs (£19,534.32) of a child who was born as a result of a failed vasectomy. The judge said that the plaintiff was entitled to recover necessary expenses, of which private educational fees were an example, in circumstances where the plaintiff educated his children privately. Similarly in *Williams v Imrie* (1988) (*page 342*), Hutchison J awarded a plaintiff the costs of maintaining a child who was born following a negligent sterilisation. These costs amounted to £6,065 from the end of the fourth year of the child's life to the age of seventeen. The costs before that amounted to £485 in the first year of the child's life and £676 up until the end of the fourth year. A plaintiff has to give credit for child benefit in this respect. The mother was awarded £4,000 for pain, suffering and loss of amenity which included the discomfort of the pregnancy, the worry that the child she was bearing might have been injured, and a further sterilisation which led to a four to five inch scar. The award also included the loss of the mother's earnings. In *Kralj* v *McGrath* (1986) (*page 253*), damages were awarded in converse circumstances. In this case the plaintiff successfully argued that the loss of one of her twins through the negligence of the defendants meant that she would have to conceive again to produce a third child to create the family size she had always intended. Woolf J awarded her £18,000 in respect of her loss of earnings which would arise on account of that further pregnancy, rejecting the argument that such a contingency was too remote.

Section E: The practice of litigation

Chapter 13

Limitation and striking out for want of prosecution

The conduct of civil litigation is primarily determined by specific statutes such as the Supreme Court Act 1981 and the Limitation Act 1980 together with rules of court contained in the Rules of the Supreme Court 1965, and the County Court Rules 1981. Medical malpractice actions, like other civil prosecutions, are governed by these provisions and are rarely singled out for specific procedural determination (see for example RSC O 25 r 8). Nevertheless, actions involving an alleged breach of a medical duty of care do routinely raise certain procedural difficulties which merit particular attention. This section looks at the courts' approach to civil litigation in four selected areas: those concerning limitation, the striking out of claims for want of prosecution, the mechanisms of pre-action discovery and the exchange of expert reports with specific reference to medical negligence litigation.

1. Limitation

(a) The primary limitation period and the date of knowledge

Since the Limitation Act 1623, the legislature has determined that it is in the interests of the public good that litigation should be brought within specified periods of time. The principle behind the implementation of a statutory defence that an action after a certain time will be barred has been that stale claims frequently cause injustice because the probative value of the evidence that is adduced is fundamentally flawed due to the passage of time. Particularly in those cases where oral evidence is required, the recollection of events fades after appreciable distances of time, witnesses may have died or disappeared, and accordingly the factual basis of the claim may be extremely difficult to evaluate and indeed to defend. To prevent potential defendants being exposed to indeterminate liability, specific periods for specific causes of action have been statutorily imposed; they are currently contained in the consolidating statute of the Limitation Act 1980.

By the provisions of s 11 Limitation Act 1980, a three year primary limitation period arises in those actions for damages for negligence, nuisance or breach of a duty of care, whether contractual or otherwise, and which include or consist of a claim in respect of personal injuries. The three year period prescribed in this section runs from either the date when the cause of action accrued or from what is called the "date of knowledge" of the injured person. Accordingly, for the overwhelming majority of cases which are brought alleging a breach of the medical duty of care (and which do involve personal injury), the primary period is three years. In actions based upon negligence, the accrual of a cause of action is when damage (which is more than negligible) has occurred (per Lord Reid in *Cartledge* v *Jopling* [1963] AC at 771–2). In most cases, damage will flow immediately from the negligent act, as for example in anaesthetic and surgical mishaps. In other cases, however, such as those involving a negligent prescription of a drug which causes a delayed form of harm, damage may occur years after its prescription and ingestion. There can accordingly be a significant time gap between the negligent act and the creation of damage that is more than negligible. In contract, however, a cause of action is deemed to accrue when a breach has occurred which, in the case of a doctor, would be when the doctor prescribed the drug in question to his private patient (see *Gibbs* v *Guild* (1881)). This distinction fortifies the benefit of suing in negligence or collaterally in both contract and negligence.

Not all medical malpractice actions consist of or include damages for personal injury. For example, in a case like *Whiteford* v *Hunter* (1950) (*page 340*), where a plaintiff had been wrongly informed that he had inoperable terminal cancer and as a result closed down his engineering practice, sold his house and went abroad, the claim would be for financial and consequential losses. This particular action, which in fact was brought in time and which failed to establish any breach of duty, illustrates a potential category of treatment-based cases which do not result in personal injury. Similarly, a negligent report on the health of a person which injuriously affects a plaintiff's prospects of getting or keeping a job or becoming insured would not involve any claim for personal injury (see for example *Dawson* v *Scott-Brown* (1988) (*page 196*)).

By the provisions of s 2 and s 5 Limitation Act 1980, six years is allowed to bring an action based on tort or simple contract not involving personal injury. In cases concerned with the wrongful birth of a child, a mother normally has a claim for general damages arising out of the discomfort and suffering from the unplanned pregnancy itself, and, frequently, from a subsequent sterilisation which should not have been necessary had a prior sterilisation been undertaken properly. For the most part, however, the larger claim lies in respect of the consequential expenses and losses that arise from the requirement to maintain the unplanned child. It might be arguable in such a case that the costs of the upkeep of the child warrant a six year, rather than a three year, period of limitation. The matter is not free from doubt because of the alternative argument that both claims are closely connected to the "personal injury" of the wrongful birth (cf *Paterson* v *Chadwick* (1974) (*page 285*), *Ackbar* v *Green & Co* (1975)).

Personal injury is defined within s 38 Limitation Act 1980 as including any disease and any impairment of a person's physical or mental condition. Therefore any claim based on a psychological reaction to a medical breach of duty would be caught by the three year period. The wording of s 11 has been held to include any claim based on battery or trespass to the person, as this has been deemed to be a breach of duty. There is accordingly no benefit, in limitation terms, available to those small number of claims (eg *Cull* v *Butler* (1932) (*page 192*), *Devi* v *West Midlands Regional Health Authority* (1981) (*page 198*)) which may be properly brought as being founded in trespass to the person (see *Letang* v *Cooper* (1965) which concerned unintentional trespass to the person, and *Long* v *Hepworth* (1968) which concerned intentional assault).

(b) Date of knowledge

Previously strict periods of limitation found in earlier statutes worked patent injustice in those cases where the effect of the breach of duty was to cause a form of latent damage which only manifested itself in symptoms many years after the breach of duty. In extreme cases, a cause of action had expired before the injured person had any prospects of discovering the potential harm done to him. For example, s 2(1) Limitation Act 1939 allowed six years (for the most part) to bring an action in tort, whether it comprised a personal injury or not. In *Cartledge* v *Jopling* (1963), the plaintiff had in the course of his employment inhaled harmful dust which caused a form of injury which was undetectable by means of medical science until more than six years after the damage arose. Mr Cartledge was prevented from bringing an action, notwithstanding that his condition had substantially deteriorated, because of the strict interpretation of the limitation period:

"... a cause of action accrues as soon as the wrongful act has caused specific injury beyond what can be regarded as neglible, even when that injury is unknown to and cannot be discerned by the sufferer; and that further injury arising from the same act at a later date does not give rise to a further cause of action ... it seems to be unreasonable and unjustifiable in principle that a cause of action should be held to accrue before it is possible to raise any action ... a cause of action ought not to be held to accrue until either the injured person has discovered the injury or it would be possible for him to discover it if he took such steps as was reasonable in the circumstances" (per Lord Reid [1963] AC at 771–2).

This situation was partially remedied by the enactment of the Limitation Act 1963 which permitted a plaintiff, with leave of the court, to bring a claim beyond the limitation period if material facts concerning the cause of action were outside the actual or constructive knowledge of the plaintiff. The Limitation Act 1975 made a further modification to this principle of discovery by stipulating that it was not a material fact that a plaintiff, knowing the fact of his injury and its causation, did not know as a matter of law that he had a good cause of action.

These principles have now become consolidated within s 11(4) Limitation Act 1980, which allows time to run from the date of knowledge, and within s 14 Limitation Act 1980 which defines the date of knowledge. Time does not begin to run against a plaintiff until he has knowledge of four types of fact. The first fact concerns whether the plaintiff knew that the injury he sustained was significant, which is statutorily defined as whether the plaintiff felt it sufficiently serious to sue for damages in circumstances where a defendant who was good for the money would not contest liability. Put in this way, even the most trivial of injuries might appear to be "significant". Although the courts have indicated that to some extent they are prepared to look at the question of whether an injury is significant, partly from the perspective of the plaintiff (cf Lane LJ in *McCafferty* v *Metropolitan Police District Receiver* [1977] 2 All ER at 775, and *Young* v *GLC and Massey* (1987)), the fact that an injury later turns out to be more severe than was foreseen will not be enough to stop the clock running. Accordingly, in *Miller* v *London Electrical Manufacturing Company Limited* (1976), dermatitis contracted by a worker was held to be significant, notwithstanding that he later developed a much more serious form of eczema-based skin disease.

Secondly, time does not run against a plaintiff until he knows that his injury was attributable to the act of the defendant. Attribution here means factual not legal causation, because s 14 specifically provides that knowledge that an act or omission "did not as a matter of law involve negligence, nuisance or breach of duty is irrelevant". In *Wilkinson* v *Ancliff BLT Limited* (1986), attribution was interpreted as meaning not definitely caused by but being capable of being attributed to. This accorded with an earlier interpretation found in *Davis* v *Ministry of Defence* (1985). In medical malpractice actions, therefore, a plaintiff may be held to know within the meaning of the section if he appreciates in general terms that the particular treatment, advice, or omission was capable of being attributed to his disability, even where the particular facts of what specifically went wrong or how and where the precise error was made are not known to the plaintiff.

The third and fourth factual requirements stipulated in the section require that the plaintiff knows the identity of the defendant and any other person who might be vicariously liable for the acts or omission which caused the personal injury. In medical negligence and breach of contract cases, this is most unlikely to cause any difficulties, given the vicarious liability of hospital authorities for their nursing and medical staff. Even in cases of private treatment where the vicarious liability may be less clear, it is normally possible to determine the identity of potential defendants.

Section 14 also imposes a duty on the plaintiff to take reasonable steps to acquire knowledge. In effect the plaintiff will be fixed with a constructive knowledge that might reasonably have been inferred from facts that were observable or ascertainable by the plaintiff directly or from facts that he could have ascertained with the help of medical or other expert advice which it is reasonable for him to consult. The court will therefore enquire into what, if any, steps the plaintiff did take which he reasonably ought to have taken by himself, or with the help of others to determine whether the injury was significant, attributable to the act or omission in question and caused by the particular defendants sued. What is reasonable will vary according to the subjective capabilities of the particular plaintiff in question. The test, however, is to a certain extent objective. In *Davis* v *City and Hackney Health Authority* (1989) (*page 195*), a plaintiff who was born suffering from spasticity in June 1963 issued a writ on 1 April 1987. At the age of seventeen he had asked his mother what had caused his disabilities, and she thought that his birth may have been mishandled but did not encourage him to claim damages. In September 1985, the plaintiff consulted solicitors and on or about 26 November 1986 an expert reported that the plaintiff's mother had been given an injection of ovametrin which caused the plaintiff's spasticity. The plaintiff was allowed to bring the action because the date of knowledge was determined by the court to be when he learned of the contents of the expert's report. The trial judge, Jowitt J, indicated that in view of the plaintiff's disabilities, which included a serious speech defect, the delay in failing to take legal advice was not unreasonable. The judge said:

"The test is an objective one. The question is, looked at objectively, when might he, the plaintiff, reasonably have been expected to acquire those facts referred to in paragraph b of subsection 3. In other words one applies an objective test, but it is an objective test applied to the kind of plaintiff I am here dealing with, with his disability, and looking at his age and his circumstances and the difficulties he has faced".

In *Waghorn* v *Lewisham and North Southwark Area Health Authority* (1987) (*page 334*) the plaintiff served a writ in 1985 in respect of an operation that occurred on 31 March 1977 which was intended to lengthen the plaintiff's perineum and tighten the introitus. In fact the operation did the opposite, and shortened the perineum and further opened the introitus. The plaintiff had ascertained as early as 4 April 1977 that the mishap had occurred. The trial judge found that the plaintiff knew, therefore, that her injury was significant in April 1977 and time ran against her from then. It was not material that she did not have expert medical advice, because she had observed the mishap and obviously knew it was significant.

However, by the specific words of s 14, the plaintiff will not be prejudiced if he has been given wrong advice by his experts (*Marston* v *British Railways Board* (1976)). Such bad advice, however, will only stop the clock running if it concerns the factual basis of the claim. If a plaintiff receives bad legal advice to the effect that he has no cause of action in law, this would not prevent time running against him, because whether the plaintiff has a correct or an incorrect belief that he has a good cause of action or no cause of action at all is not a relevant consideration under the section. It might well, however, be the case that if the legal advice which is wrong concerns a failure to take certain steps to uncover material facts, the plaintiff will not be prejudiced by such bad advice because it is not essentially legal (*Central Asbestos Company Limited* v *Dodd* (per Lord Salmon [1973] AC at 556–6), *Fowell* v *National Coal Board* (1986), and *Farmer* v *National Coal Board* (1985)).

In fatal cases, the Limitation Act provides by s 12 a period of three years from the date of the deceased's death for the dependants to bring an action pursuant to the provisions of the Fatal Accidents Act 1976. Alternatively, the deceased's dependants have three years from the date of knowledge as defined in s 14 of the Act if this is later. Similarly, by s 11(5), the deceased's estate can bring an action three years after the death or three years from the date of the personal representative's date of knowledge. Claims brought by the estate in this respect would be limited to general damages for pain, suffering and loss of amenity before death and special damages that arose up to the date of death together with any funeral expenses. Claims under the Fatal Accidents Act 1976 would include loss of dependency. Section 13 provides the possibility of different periods applying to different dependants. In those cases where the cause of action is time barred, both the estate and the dependants may bring an application pursuant to s 33 Limitation Act 1980 for an order that the time limits be applied. This matter is considered below.

In those small number of cases where the cause of action does not consist of or include any damages in respect of personal injuries, plaintiffs in medical malpractice actions may be able to rely on the provisions of the Latent

Damage Act 1986. This Act has added s 14B to the Limitation Act 1980. Section 14B contains similar provisions to s 14 concerning the date of knowledge in non-personal injury actions based on tort. Such actions may now be brought six years from the date when the cause of action accrued or three years from the date of knowledge subject to a stop gap period of fifteen years.

If a plaintiff is under a disability when a cause of action accrues, time does not run pursuant to the provisions of s 28 Limitation Act 1980 until the disability ceases. By s 28(6) any such action would be time barred three years after the disability ceased in cases concerning personal injury. A minor is considered to be under a disability until reaching the age of eighteen, pursuant to s 1(1) Family Law Reform Act 1969. Accordingly, an infant plaintiff has until the age of twenty-one to issue a writ (an action is begun when the writ is issued, not when it is served, which can be up to a year later) in respect of any action consisting of or including a claim for personal injuries (*Tolley* v *Morris* (1979)). An infant plaintiff is almost immune, therefore, from having his action struck out for want of prosecution but there can be evidential difficulties both for plaintiffs as well as for defendants in leaving actions for many years until they are prosecuted. In *Bull and Wakeham* v *Devon Health Authority* (1989) (*page 172*), an action was commenced in 1979 by a mother for herself and for the benefit of her child in respect of the child's birth in 1970 which resulted in the child being rendered quadriplegic. The trial was heard eight years later by which time the consultant had died, and the mother's own claim for damages was dismissed as statute barred. The child, however, did in this case recover damages in respect of a negligent system of obstetric cover.

A person is also under a disability if he is of unsound mind and, by reason of mental disorder within the meaning of s 1(2) Mental Health Act 1983, is incapable of managing his own affairs. In *Blackburn* v *Newcastle Area Health Authority (No. 2)* (1988) (*page 165*), a plaintiff required four firms of solicitors before he finally got his case on liability to trial in October 1987 following a cause of action accruing in October 1976 arising out of severe brain damage. Again, such plaintiffs are protected from time running against them and therefore having an action dismissed for want of prosecution. However, the court did take account of the delay by restricting interest to six years rather than eleven. Mr Blackburn was entitled to both the Court of Protection charges and receiver's fees which arose because he was unable to conduct his own affairs. If a mental disability intervenes after the accrual of a cause of action, time continues to run (*Purnell* v *Roche* (1927)). However, in those cases where a plaintiff suffers from an intervening mental disability, there is specific power within the provisions of s 33 Limitation Act 1980 to consider this as a factor in determining whether the time limit should be overridden.

Although the definition of mental disorder within s 1(2) Mental Health Act 1983 is broad (it includes mental illness, arrested or incomplete development of mind, psychopathic disorder and any other disorder or disability of mind), it did not avail the plaintiff in *Dawson* v *Scott-Brown* (1988) (*page 196*). In this action the plaintiff, an ex-Royal Navy seaman, alleged negligence against his surgeon-commander in respect of a report some thirteen years before he issued proceedings, which led to the plaintiff being discharged from the Navy in October 1974 on grounds of mental ill-health. The Master struck out the writ on the basis that the limitation defence was bound to succeed. The Court of Appeal concurred with this decision, indicating that being invalided out of the Navy did not make him unable to manage his own affairs pursuant to the provisions of s 28 Limitation Act 1980, and he was therefore not under a disability as from the date of discharge. The plaintiff also argued that there had been concealment and, therefore, according to the provisions of s 32(1(b) Limitation Act 1980, time ran only when the concealment could with reasonable diligence have been discovered. The Court of Appeal said that, although the defendant had not disclosed his report to the plaintiff and had made it direct to the Navy, there was no question of the matter being deliberately concealed.

From 1 January 1989, an individual has the right to see any report prepared by a medical practitioner, which has been or is to be supplied for employment purposes or for insurance purposes, pursuant to the Access to Medical Reports Act 1988. Section 2 of the Act defines employment purposes as including a report by an existing or a potential employer. The Act requires the employer or insurer to seek the consent of the subject of the report before seeking such a report from a medical practitioner. The subject of the report, by s 4, has a right of access to the report before it is supplied and has a right to correct errors. Access to the report may be withheld if, in the opinion of the medical practitioner, allowing the subject to read the report would be "likely to cause serious harm to the physical or mental health of the individual or others or would indicate the intentions of a practitioner in respect of the individual" (s 7(1)). A similar right on the part of the medical practitioner to withhold the report arises where the report would be likely to reveal information about another person or to reveal the identity of another person who has supplied information to the practitioner about the individual concerned. The county court is conferred with the jurisdiction to hear applications where the subject of the report claims a breach of the requirements of the Act.

(c) The discretion to allow a time-barred action to proceed

Judicial experience has produced an awareness that strict periods of limitation, even when they are accompanied by provisions concerning knowledge and discoverability of a cause of action, can still work injustice. A stark example is contained in the case of *Harnett* v *Fisher* (1927) (*page 227*) where a plaintiff who was negligently certified as of unsound mind and detained, pursuant to the powers of the Lunacy Act 1890, for nearly nine years in an institution was rendered remediless by the provisions of the Limitation Act 1623. Mr Harnett, a Kentish farmer, had taken a "toxin given him by a quack" which caused transient insanity (see *Harnett* v *Bond* (1925) for the background facts). As a result of this he was originally properly detained, but thereafter wrongly redetained on the basis of the defendant simply watching him from the window when he was in the street. Mr Harnett brought his cause of action against the doctor in 1922 after making his escape from the institution some seven months earlier. A jury held that he had been wrongly detained for nine years, and awarded him substantial damages of £500. The House of Lords, however, confirmed the Court of Appeal's views that the action was time barred because, under the Limitation Act 1623, he had six years to bring the action and that time ran from 10 November 1912 when the negligent act and the damage, the loss of liberty, occurred. Because Mr Harnett never was insane, he could not rely on the disability provisions of s 7 of that Act. The plaintiff argued his own case with great skill and learning in the House of Lords, but their Lordships felt unable to accept his arguments that if he was treated in law as though he were mad then at least he should have the benefits of that detriment and the defendant should be estopped from saying his action was time barred when he never had an opportunity to consult his solicitors because of his incarceration. His case was dismissed with costs against him.

Because of many cases, like *Harnett*, albeit less extreme on their facts, s 33 Limitation Act 1980 contains provisions for the court to set aside the time limit of three years from the date of the cause of action or from the date of knowledge in those cases which consist of or include damages for personal injury if it is satisfied that it is equitable to do so. Even today, *Harnett's* case might not be decided differently, as his damages did not consist of or include a claim for personal injury, and accordingly s 33 would have no applicability.

Section 33(1) requires the judge to consider the respective prejudices that the plaintiff and defendant will suffer if he allows an action to proceed or if he refuses to disapply ss 11 and 12 of the Act. In one sense prejudice is obvious. The plaintiff is prejudiced if he loses the right to sue, and the defendant is prejudiced if he loses the limitation defence. Equally, however, the strength of the merits on liability of the plaintiff's case will be important in weighing this prejudice. If a plaintiff has a hopeless case as far as can be judged, then barring the action does not cause much prejudice. Prejudice to the defendant possibly arises in those cases where there is little possibility, because of the delay, of properly resisting the claim because of the unavailability of documents, evidence or witnesses. Prejudice in this respect may be assumed after a period of five years or more (*Buck* v *English Electric Co. Limited* (1977)). The court's discretion is entirely unfettered and is not restricted to the particular matters set out in s 33(3); nor is it limited to the occasional "hard" case (*Conry* v *Simpson* (1983), *Firman* v *Ellis* (1978), *Simpson* v *Norwest Holst Southern Limited* (1980), *Taylor* v *Taylor* (1984)).

The discretion within s 33 does not, however, empower the court to disapply the time limits pursuant to that section in cases where a writ has been issued but has not been served within the one year allowed, or where an action has been struck out for want of prosecution and the time limit has expired (*Chappell* v *Cooper* (1980), *Walkley* v *Precision Forgings Limited* (1979)). The House of Lords has determined in such cases that the prejudice that arises is deemed not to flow from the provisions of the Limitation Act but from the actions or inactions of the plaintiff's legal advisers in failing to pursue an action rather than failing to start the action. Accordingly, if a solicitor fails to initiate an action, the judge is entitled to look at the matter within the provisions of s 33; whereas if a writ, albeit issued, is not served, then s 33 does not apply. Lord Diplock in *Walkley* v *Precision Forgings Limited* (above) did indicate there might be exceptional circumstances in which a court would allow a time-barred action to proceed where a writ had been issued but not served, but these were effectively limited to cases of estoppel by his own reasoning in *Deerness* v *Keeble & Son (Brantham) Limited* (1983).

Section 33(3) provides six matters which the court ought to take into account in applying its discretion, and the case law that has arisen pursuant to this section is illustrative of how the matter is approached.

Section 33(3)(a) looks at the length of and the reasons for the delay on the part of the plaintiff. In *Buck* v *English Electric Co. Ltd* (1978), a pneumoconiosis case, the plaintiff was allowed to proceed sixteen years after the onset of her late husband's disease and ten years since he knew that it was significant. The court was impressed by his attitude which was to continue working and to avoid what he thought was "sponging" on his employers by bringing an action against them. Similarly, in *McCafferty* v *Metropolitan Police District Receiver* (1977), the plaintiff, who enjoyed his job, attempted to cope with his hearing difficulties by regarding them as a nuisance, and did not wish to sour relations with his employer. He was allowed to proceed with his action despite the fact that it was started in 1974 in respect of deafness and tinnitus that probably resulted from working conditions as far back as 1948 which had caused symptoms certainly since 1969. No doubt the type of injury sustained is significant, so that a plaintiff who waited six years before issuing in respect of a back injury at work was not given leave to proceed (*Davies* v *British Insulated Callender's Cables* (1977)).

Section 33(3)(b) specifically enjoins the court to look at what effect the delay has had on the evidence that is likely to be adduced. The mere fact of a very long delay will not necessarily be fatal to an application. If the case is one of a number which the defendants have previously defended or fully investigated and have taken proofs concerning the conditions of work or the system of work, then these matters would push the balance of advantage and disadvantage in the favour of the plaintiff (*Simpson* v *Norwest Holst Southern Limited* (1980)). Where the incident was isolated, was not reported, or did not result in the proofing of witnesses or the retention of evidence, then the defendants would be severely prejudiced (see, for example, *Mahon* v *Concrete (Southern) Limited* (1979), where relevant X-rays had been destroyed). Accordingly in *Waghorn* v *Lewisham and North Southwark Area Health Authority* (1987) (*page 334*), the court exercised its discretion and disapplied the provisions of s 11 Limitation Act 1980 in a case where a plaintiff knew a medical mishap had occurred in 1977 but did not serve a writ until 1985. The trial judge determined that the defendants had known about the plaintiff's complaints from 1978 and all the hospital records except for the nursing notes had been preserved. Although it was true that two further surgical procedures in 1980 and in 1983 had obscured what in fact had happened in 1977, the judge found that the evidence was only marginally less cogent and exercised his discretion in favour of the plaintiff.

Section 33(3)(c) requires the court to consider the conduct of the defendant after the cause of action arose, particularly in respect of how he responded to any request that the plaintiff made. Obstructive behaviour on the part of the defendant personally, or the defendant's solicitors or insurers, may tip the balance in the plaintiff's favour (*Thompson* v *Brown Construction (Ebbw Vale) Limited* (1981)). In *Mills* v *Dyer-Fare* (1987) Steyn J regarded a five-month delay in producing medical notes as a relevant factor in considering the exercise of his discretion under s 33.

Section 33(3)(d) specifically allows the court to consider the duration of any disability of the plaintiff arising after the date of the accrual of the cause of action. Mr Harnett in *Harnett* v *Fisher* (above) would not have fared better had this provision been in force in 1927 as his action did not concern personal injury. The disability can refer only to mental disability, as disability on account of minority cannot arise after the date of the accrual of the cause of action. (cf *Dawson* v *Scott-Brown* (1988) (*page 196*)).

Section 33(3)(e) requires investigation into how the plaintiff acted once he knew that his injury was attributable to the acts of the defendants and gave rise to a cause of action. This date could well be later than the s 14 date of knowledge, because consideration can be given at this stage to the actual date when the plaintiff realised that the facts in question amounted to a cause of action in law.

Finally, s 33(3)(f) investigates the steps, if any, taken by the plaintiff to obtain expert advice, and the nature of that advice he received. Accordingly, a plaintiff will be disadvantaged if he failed to take an opportunity of seeking advice which was readily available, as in the case of *Casey* v *J. Murphy & Sons* (1979) where a worker who had contracted dermatitis could have obtained trade union backed legal services. The court is allowed at this stage to enquire into legal advice given, and legal professional privilege can be waived for this purpose so that, for example, negative advice given by counsel can be looked at (*Jones* v *G.D. Searle & Co. Limited* (1978)). Whether a plaintiff has a prospective cause of action against his legal advisers for alleged negligence in pursuing a claim will be a pertinent matter for the court to look into.

Given the wide-ranging investigation which a s 33 application generates, it is difficult to say in advance whether an order to disapply the time limits will be made. In most medical malpractice actions, a degree of record keeping should preserve some cogent evidence. There may also be a recognition of the factual complexities that can arise in both formulating and appraising a claim. Again the court may allow some indulgence in respect of the natural reluctance of many patients to take issue with their doctors. Moreover, the often grave difficulty in obtaining proper expert evidence may help a plaintiff who finds himself statute barred. In *Birnie* v *Oxfordshire Health Authority* (1982) (*page 163*), a plaintiff who had become permanently paraplegic following treatment for pain relief in December 1972 issued a writ alleging negligence in August 1979. During this period of seven years, the plaintiff had become depressed and suicidal and had also contracted gangrene which resulted in an amputation. It was conceded that his claim was statute barred by approximately December 1976, but he relied on s 33 Limitation Act 1980. Glidewell J held that the delay before the plaintiff contacted his solicitors in 1977 was understandable because of the extreme difficulties the plaintiff had experienced, but that one year of the subsequent delay was inexcusable. The defendant was prejudiced because he was not insured and he had this action hanging over him. Alternatively, there were reasonably good notes available, and in balancing all the factors the judge allowed the action to proceed.

Conversely, in *Goodman* v *Fletcher* (1982) (*page 220*), the plaintiff's claim was struck out as statute barred in circumstances where a writ was issued in March 1978 in respect of allegedly negligent treatment in July 1973. The plaintiff had learnt in approximately September 1974, and certainly by February 1975 that the diet prescribed for her by the defendant in respect of her allergies was inappropriate. Her claim was therefore *prima facie* statute barred. The Court of Appeal held that there had been great delay and it would be impossible for the relevant doctor at a trial in 1983 to have an accurate recollection of consultations which took place ten years earlier. The Court of Appeal considered this delay fatal to the exercise of discretion under s 33.

2. Dismissal for want of prosecution

Once an action is started by the issue of a writ, the court prescribes time limits for subsequent stages in the litigation, such as the service of the writ and statement of claim, the time for the defence and other pleadings to be completed, the period during which discovery and inspection of documents must take place, the date for a hearing for directions of the conduct of the action and, finally, for the setting down of the action for trial. The court has specific powers contained in RSC O 25 r1(4) to dismiss an action for failure to take out a summons for directions within one month of when the pleadings are deemed to have closed. (In medical negligence actions, the automatic directions which apply to other personal injury actions pursuant to RSC O 25 r5 do not apply.) The court has similar powers for failure to serve a statement of claim (RSC O 19 r1), for default of discovery (RSC O 24 r16(1)) and for default of setting down (RSC O 34 r2). In addition, the court retains an inherent power to dismiss an action for default in complying with the rules or in failing to prosecute the action. Disobeying a so-called peremptory order of the court, so that a party is held to have been guilty of intentional and contumelious conduct, may result in the action being struck out. More frequently, it is dilatory conduct which results in applications to strike out for inordinate and inexcusable delay on the part of the plaintiff. Actions may be struck out if such improper delay gives rise to a substantial risk that it is not possible to have a fair trial of the issues, or is such that the defendants have suffered serious prejudice (*Birkett* v *James* (1978), *Allen* v *Sir Alfred McAlpine & Sons Limited* (1968) and *Department of Transport* v *Chris Smaller (Transport) Ltd* (1989)).

Delay which is deemed to be culpable in this context is that which has occurred after the limitation period has expired, and an action will not be dismissed for delay if there is still time to commence another action within the limitation period. The power to dismiss an action arises even in those cases where liability has been admitted and indeed a payment into court has been made, if the delay is such that it makes it difficult or impossible to have a fair trial on the quantum of damages (*Gloria* v *Sokoloff & Others* (1969), *Paxton* v *Alsopp* (1971)). Delay is considered to be inordinate if it is materially longer than that which is normally regarded by the courts and legal practitioners as acceptable. Delay is usually inexcusable when it is caused by the plaintiff or the plaintiff's advisers, and the defendant has not caused or contributed to the delay (*Austin Securities* v *Northgate and English Stores Limited* (1969)). Delay can occur when things are being done in a desultory fashion, and although the defendants must not contribute to the delay they are entitled to let "sleeping dogs" lie (*Lev* v *Fagan* (1988)).

Prejudice primarily connotes evidential difficulties occurring because of the delay, involving the loss of witnesses, the failing of recollections particularly in accident cases, and the loss of the pertinent detail to rebut allegations of negligence or breach of duty. Prejudice of a financial nature may arise, however, in those cases where it can be demonstrated and proved that the delay has caused an increase in the level of damages the plaintiff is likely to receive. In certain circumstances, because annual wage increases may be above the rate of inflation and because the multiplier has not diminished at the same rate as the years of delay in getting the case to trial, a plaintiff might be financially better off because he delayed (*Hayes* v *Bowman* (1988)). In assessing whether the delay has caused serious prejudice, the court is entitled to look at the whole period of the delay from the cause of action. Whereas it is recognized that the delay in issuing within the limitation period is legitimate, the courts have stressed that if a plaintiff starts an action late in the day he must thereafter proceed with reasonable diligence. Moreover, the additional prejudice compared to that degree of prejudice which has already occurred before the issuing of the writ need not be great but only more than minimal (*Birkett* v *James* (1978), *Department of Transport* v *Chris Smaller (Transport) Limited* (1989)). Further, in *Leniston* v *Phipps* (1988), Stuart-Smith LJ indicated that:

> "Where prolonged culpable delay follows prolonged delay in the issue of or service of proceedings, the court may readily infer that memories and reliability of witnesses has further deteriorated in the period of culpable delay". (See also *James Investments (Isle of Man) Limited and Spartina Properties Limited* v *Phillips Cutler Phillips Troy (A Firm)* (1987).)

In medical negligence cases, prejudice may also arise because the practitioners, or the hospitals where they practise, have the nuisance of an action hanging over them for many years. In *Biss* v *Lambeth, Southwark and Lewisham Area Health Authority (Teaching)* (1978) (*page 163*) Lord Denning indicated that businesses may be prejudiced by not being able to conduct their affairs with confidence because they have an action hanging over them, and similarly hospitals were after a time entitled to some peace of mind and entitled to close their files and to tell their staff that they will no longer be needed to fight a very stale claim. In *Biss* the plaintiff suffered from bed sores in 1965, allegedly from negligent nursing care, and was granted leave to start proceedings out of time in February 1975 under the provisions of the then Limitation Act 1963. Pleadings closed in July 1975; in March 1977 the defendants sought to strike out the claim for want of prosecution. The Court of Appeal concurred with the Master who struck out the claim, finding there had been inordinate and inexcusable delay and serious prejudice. The prejudice in question was predominantly the Sword of Damocles hanging over the authority's head. In *Department of Transport* v *Chris Smaller (Transport) Limited* (1989), the House of Lords expressed caution in allowing the mere fact of anxiety which accompanies all litigation to constitute serious prejudice. The eleven and a half years' delay in *Biss* was considered exceptional (per Lord Griffith [1989] 2 WLR at 587h and *Eagil Trust Company Limited* v *Pigott-Brown* [1985] 3 All ER at 124).

In *Joseph* v *Korn* (1984) (*page 248*), an action was brought by the mother of the deceased, alleging that the negligence of a general practitioner's receptionist led to the death of her son on 30 December 1971. The writ was issued on 23 December 1974, and the action was dismissed in March 1984 for want of prosecution. In dismissing the action, the Court of Appeal held that, notwithstanding the fact that there had been a full documented hearing shortly after the death instigated by the health authority, the claim thirteen years later still involved disputed questions of fact.

In *Mansouri* v *Bloomsbury Health Authority* (1987) (*page 268*), the Court of Appeal upheld a dismissal of an action which was founded on a cause of action in June 1979 with a writ issued in June 1982. Counsel was asked to advise in March 1984 but was unable to do so, and a subsequent counsel, after requesting a further medical report, gave an opinion in May 1985. The matter was struck out in July 1985, a little over six years after the cause of action, on the grounds of inordinate delay. In *Rosen* v *Marston* (1984) (*page 303*), the plaintiff alleged negligent treatment in an operation for varicose veins in March 1977, and issued a writ in 1980. Approximately three years later, during which time nothing was done, an application was made to the defendants for the hospital notes, and they replied with an application to strike out. The Court of Appeal upheld the striking out on the basis of approximately two and a half years of unwarranted delay which caused prejudice to the defendant because his recollection would be impaired and because he had suffered an unnecessary two years of anxiety and distress.

However, in *Westaway* v *South Glamorgan Health Authority* (1986) (*page 338*), although a delay was held to be inordinate and inexcusable, no prejudice was thought to have arisen in a case brought on the basis of a failure to diagnose a fracture which occurred in May 1976. The writ was issued in April 1979, the statement of claim served in June 1979, and a defence eventually filed in 1983 after the defendants had indicated an intention to settle. The plaintiff's solicitors failed to respond to a request for quantification of the claim, and the defendants issued in June 1985 a summons to dismiss the action. The Court of Appeal held that no prejudice had arisen because the substance of the claim was a failure to diagnose a fracture which must substantially be a matter of record. Draconian as the power to strike out is, practitioners have experienced an increasing judicial willingness to exercise this power in recent years.

Chapter 14

Pre-action discovery and expert evidence

1. Pre-action discovery

One procedural process by which a plaintiff can speed up the evaluation and formulation of a prospective cause of action is by obtaining before the issue of a writ the relevant medical and other records which are crucial to appraising whether the mishap in question gives rise to a reasonable cause of action. The power of the court to make an order for pre-action discovery is contained within the provisions of s 33 Supreme Court Act 1981 and RSC O 24 r 7A. These provisions were, in the words of the Master of the Rolls, Sir John Donaldson, "designed to facilitate settlements and to avoid fruitless actions" (*Lee* v *South West Thames Regional Health Authority* [1985] 1 WLR at 847c). The right exists for a person who is "likely" to be a party in an action in which a claim for personal injuries is "likely" to be made to obtain an order, before the action is commenced, against a person who is "likely" to be another party and who is "likely" to have documents in his possession, to peruse the documents if they are related to the issues arising out of the claim. In *Dunning* v *United Liverpool Hospitals' Board of Governors* (1973) (*page 201*), the likelihood of a plaintiff suing was construed as being in terms of a reasonable prospect; a mere speculative prospect would not be sufficient. In *Paterson* v *Chadwick* (1974) (*page 285*) a claim in respect of personal injuries was deemed in this context to include a claim against the plaintiff's solicitors for failing to sue in respect of an anaesthetic accident, and pre-action discovery was allowed against the hospital where the accident occurred. Similar powers are contained in s 33 Supreme Court Act 1981 and RSC O 29 r 7A *vis-à-vis* any case (ie, not restricted to personal injury cases) for property to be inspected, photographed, preserved, or placed in the court's custody, and to have samples taken from, or experiments conducted on those pieces of property which may be the subject matter of proceedings. However, by s 35(4) Supreme Court Act 1981, these facilities only bind the Crown in actions of personal injuries or death.

These provisions are most important in medical malpractice actions because they allow a plaintiff to have access to medical and nursing notes and to all the relevant material such as X-rays, test results, reports, letters and so on that have been compiled during the course of treatment and are contained in the relevant records. They would also, in certain cases, afford an opportunity to inspect or test a particular machine. Such information may be vital to a potential litigant as it forms the basis of the instructions to his legal and medical experts. In many cases, assessing the prospects of success is difficult indeed without sight of such records. The recent tendency has been for hospital authorities, in particular, to release such information without the issuing of a summons, provided that the intended claim contains a proper level of detail (see the Department of Health and Social Security Circular CH 8216 for the official attitude regarding the disclosure of such information). Sometimes, however, it will not be possible to give any more that a brief outline of the circumstances of the mishap. Although the courts' approach is to avoid what they deem to be fishing exercises, it has been recognized that at this early stage a plaintiff may not be able to condescend to details until after the information in question has been received, and that, of course, the prime object of this power is to assess a case before litigation (*Shaw* v *Vauxhall Motors Limited* (1974)).

Section 33(2) Supreme Court Act 1981 enables the documents to be received by the applicant's legal advisers and any medical or other professional adviser, and may restrict disclosure to the prospective plaintiff on the basis that such disclosure might cause detriment to the patient's health and well-being. This wording reverses the decision in *McIvor* v *Southern Health and Social Services Board* (1978) and restores the decision in *Dunning* v *United Liverpool Hospitals' Board of Governors* (1973) (*page 201*). (Both these cases were concerned with earlier similar provisions contained in s 32(1) Administration of Justice Act 1970.) There is, therefore, no power to restrict disclosure to a medical expert, and the previous attitude of health authorities seeking to impose such a condition in cases of voluntary disclosure has no foundation in law.

In *Harris* v *Newcastle Health Authority* (1989) (*page 228*), the Court of Appeal determined that pre-trial disclosure of hospital records under s 33(2) Supreme Court Act 1981 should normally be given when the conditions are satisfied, notwithstanding that there may be a strong defence of limitation. This case concerned a plaintiff who was born in October 1959 and was operated on in 1961 for a squint. The operation was unsuccessful, and four years later a further operation was performed but this did not wholly rectify the defect of the eyelid being closed and caused further pain. In February 1987 the plaintiff was encouraged to start an action, and she sought disclosure of the records. Both the district registrar and the judge refused the application on the grounds that the limitation defence was bound to succeed. The Court of Appeal, however, indicated that the application should in fact be granted because although there was a strong limitation defence the plaintiff's case was not clearly doomed to fail. Lord Justice Kerr said:

"If it is plain beyond doubt that a defence of limitation will be raised and will succeed then it seems to me that the court must be entitled to take that matter into account . . . but I would accept that in the normal run of cases even where a defence of limitation has a strong prospect of success, like here, it is very difficult for a court, on limited material, before pleadings and discovery, to conclude at that stage that the situation is such that the proposed action is bound to fail . . . so in general I would accept the submission of counsel that issues relevant to limitation should not enter into consideration on applications for pre-trial discovery".

In suitable cases, the professional adviser may include a so-called specialist scientific co-ordinator even if that person might be controversial. This was the situation in *Davies* v *Eli Lilly & Co.* (1987) (*page 193*) where a journalist known to be critical of the drug industry was deemed a fit person to attempt to co-ordinate the massive documentation involved in a case where over a thousand plaintiffs were suing in respect of Benoxaprofen ("Opren"). This case concerned discovery after the issue of proceedings, but the principle is applicable to pre-commencement actions.

Because a pre-commencement order against a potential defendant causes expense which may not be recoverable if an action is not initiated, RSC O 62 r 3(12) provides that defendants should normally have their costs unless the court thinks it inappropriate. In those cases where reasonable requests have been made by letter to health authorities who have refused or failed in a reasonable time to respond, the courts have denied the defendants their costs and on occasions given the plaintiff costs. Accordingly, in *Hall* v *Wandsworth Health Authority* (1985) (*page 224*), where there had been bad dilatory conduct, the applicant recovered her costs having written to the defendants and given them a six week period for the documents to be produced. Similarly, in *Jacob* v *Wessex Regional Health Authority* (1984) (*page 244*), the defendants had to pay the costs of an application where the plaintiff had pointed out that it would be a waste of public legal aid money if an application had to be made for the relevant documents. The application did become necessary: although the defendants conceded the notes, they wanted their costs which, in the event, the plaintiff was awarded.

If a prospective plaintiff wishes to have notes from someone who is not going to be a party, there is no power for a pre-commencement order to be made against a non-prospective third party. Once an action is started, s 34 Supreme Court Act 1981 empowers the court to order discovery of documents or inspection of property against a non-party in a personal injury action. In *Walker* v *Eli Lilly & Co.* (1986) (*page 335*), Hirst J held that in circumstances where a plaintiff was suing a drug manufacturer, the plaintiff was entitled to his hospital notes and records kept by the health authority; and the judge indicated that health authorities and medical practitioners should readily respond to such requests from advisers of a plaintiff in cases where there is no particular consideration of confidentiality. (See also *O'Sullivan* v *Herdsmans* (1987).)

Rules of the Supreme Court O 24 r7A(6) preserves the right of a prospective defendant to claim privilege in respect of certain classes of documents held which the plaintiff may require. An example of such a document may be a report which was commissioned and compiled following a medical mishap. If the dominant purpose of this report was the anticipated legal action that would be brought by the victim, then such a document is privileged (*Waugh* v *British Railways Board* (1980)). The court will scrutinise such a claim for privilege and will not necessarily be content with what appears on the face of a document. Accordingly, in *Lask* v *Gloucester Health Authority* (1985) (*page 256*), a report which was made following an accident and in accord with the demands of a National Health circular with the purpose of preventing further accidents but also to assist the defendants in anticipated litigation was found not to be privileged. This was so despite affidavit evidence emphasising the significance of the documents in defending possible claims.

Privilege was, however, sustained in *Lee* v *South West Thames Regional Health Authority* (1985) (*page 257*). This case involved a child who sustained brain damage due to a lack of oxygen following treatment he received after an accidental scalding injury at home. During the variety of treatments at different hospitals, the plaintiff was taken from a hospital within the jurisdiction of the Hillingdon Area Health Authority by an ambulance crew for which the defendants were responsible. There was a possibility that something happened during the course of the ambulance journey, and the ambulance crew submitted a report to Hillingdon Area Health Authority. The defendants disclosed the existence of the report but claimed privilege. Technically this privilege was not their own but that of Hillingdon Area Health Authority. The court, however, with "undisguised reluctance" held that the two possible causes of action against the ambulance crew and against the hospital were not independent of each other and that Hillingdon Area Health Authority had not waived its own right of privilege, and the defendants could rightfully refuse to disclose the document. The Master of the Rolls, Sir John Donaldson, indicated in no uncertain terms that he thought there was something wrong if the plaintiff's mother could not get the document and begin to understand what had gone wrong and what had exactly caused the brain damage to her son. In this case, the Master of the Rolls thought that there might be an alternative route to obtaining the document. He indicated that *Sidaway* v *Board of Governors of Bethlem Royal Hospital and the Maudsley Hospital* (1985) (*page 314*) was authority for the proposition that medical practitioners owed patients a duty of care to inform them what treatment was going to be given them when they specifically asked. The Master of the Rolls, *obiter*, indicated that such a duty may exist when a patient asks what treatment he did in fact receive. It might, therefore, be possible to seek specific performance of a breach of an implied contractual term to inform. In *Naylor* v *Preston Area Health Authority* (1987) (*page 278*) the Master of the Rolls "entirely repudiated" a view that such a cause of action would only arise in contractual cases but thought also it was a legal or equitable right arising in tort and therefore available to National Health Service patients.

2. The disclosure of evidence: expert and lay witnesses

Given the central importance in medical malpractice actions of the medical expert's views whether a particular act or omission constituted a breach of duty, it is of crucial importance, particularly for plaintiffs, to know in advance of the trial what the defendants' experts are contending. Until the important case of *Naylor* v *Preston Area Health Authority* (1987) and the modification of RSC O 38 r 37 which took effect from October 1987, medical expert evidence on the question of liability was not normally disclosed between the parties. The Court of Appeal in *Naylor* unanimously determined that it was in the interests of refining the issues in dispute, saving costs and increasing the prospects of settlement to order simultaneous disclosure before trial of experts' reports (and the academic literature on which they relied) on the question of liability. Before this case, medical negligence actions were exempt from the norm favouring mutual disclosure of expert evidence. Before *Naylor*, the position depended upon the Court of Appeal's construction of the then rules in *Rahman* v *Kirklees Area Health Authority* (1980). In that case Cumming-Bruce LJ rejected the principle of usual exchange between experts on the basis explicitly contained in the rules that applied at that time that it would involve the defendants giving away the factual basis of their defence. The Master of the Rolls, Sir John Donaldson, expressed the view in *Naylor* that:

> "In practical terms *Rahman's* case is now best forgotten" ([1987] 1 WLR at 965h).

Many of the Court of Appeal's views in *Naylor* arose out of the difficulties that were experienced in *Wilsher* v *Essex Area Health Authority* (1987) (*page 344*). In *Wilsher* the normal course of events took place and there was no exchange of experts' reports on liability before trial. The Master of the Rolls in *Naylor* described the outcome of *Wilsher* as a "total disaster". Lord Justice Mustill in *Wilsher* eloquently expressed discontent:

"In the result that parties realised soon after the case began that they had misunderstood what the case was about. As was stated before us, it was fought 'in the dark'. It lasted four weeks instead of the allotted five days, which not only imposed great pressure of time on all concerned, but meant that the scheduling of the expert witnesses was put quite out of joint. The judge had nothing to read beforehand except some pleadings which told him nothing. The evidence of the plaintiff and the defendants' witnesses came forward in no sort of order, sometimes by instalments. Nearly 150 pages of medical literature was put in, without prior exchange, or any opportunity for proper scrutiny. All this could have been avoided if there had been adequate clarification of the issue before the trial . . . I believe that practitioners do their clients and the interest of justice no service by continuing to pursue the policy of concealment . . . to me it seems wrong that in this area of law, more than in any other, this kind of forensic blind man's bluff should continue to be the norm" ([1987] 2 WLR at 461).

The current RSC O 38 r 37 makes the disclosure of expert evidence reports the norm, in that unless the court considers there are special reasons for not doing so it will direct mutual disclosure which will normally be simultaneous. Some guidance was given by the Court of Appeal in *Naylor* as to what would constitute special reasons for not making the normal order for mutual disclosure. Sir Frederick Lawton expressed the following opinion:

"I have no hesitation at all in saying that in most actions for medical negligence there should be a direction for the substance of expert medical reports to be exchanged. In some cases, however, there may be good reasons why they should not be exchanged. The particulars of negligence may be so vague that it would be unfair to the defendants to expect their experts to deal with them until such time as the plaintiff had disclosed, either by further particulars or by his own experts' reports, exactly what his case was. In such a case a sequential direction for disclosure would be appropriate . . . (in some cases) disclosure might enable the plaintiff, or his medical experts, to trim their evidence; but this is only likely to happen if there is a substantial dispute about primary facts or there is reason to think that the plaintiff's medical experts have mistakenly based their opinions on clinical findings which the defendants can prove, or think they can prove, were wrong. Another type of case is that in which the defendants are in possession of evidence, referred to in the expert medical reports, which goes to prove that the plaintiff is alleging that he is suffering from a non-existent disability or is exaggerating his symptoms or that his disability is due to an earlier trauma which he has not disclosed. The value of such evidence would be lost if the plaintiff became aware of it before trial. Since actions for medical negligence tend to raise difficult issues and vary greatly in complexity, I doubt whether directions for disclosure should ever be made automatically" ([1987] 1 WLR at 975h–976d).

Since these observations, a radical alteration in the Rules of the Supreme

Court has been made, allowing the court to order exchange of non-expert witnesses in all types of action in all the divisions of the High Court. By amendment (Rules of Supreme Court Amendment 1988 SI No. 1340) RSC O 38 r 2A now applies not only to the Chancery, Commercial, Admiralty or Official Referees Courts but to all the divisions of the High Court. Order 38 Rule 2A(2) allows the court at any stage, if it thinks fit for the purpose of disposing fairly and expeditiously of the case and to save costs, to direct that any party must serve on any other party, on such terms as the court thinks just, written statements of the oral evidence which the party intends to lead on any issues of fact to be decided at the trial. This is a remarkable incursion into the arena of open justice which may well result in the precise nature of each side's case being precisely known in medical malpractice actions before the trial begins. The rule is specifically designed to create a fair and expeditious hearing, to eliminate the element of surprise and to procure proper settlements. This provision may also reduce interlocutory hearings and, for example, the need for extensive interrogatories. It is also hoped that the provision will tend to isolate the real issues in dispute and may cause parties to admit certain facts. Similar considerations as those which Lawton LJ in *Naylor* (above) indicated may apply in determining whether an order should be made or not. It is expected that the normal order would be for simultaneous disclosure in those cases where it was deemed fit to make any order at all in respect of the exchange of witness proofs. In addition, it is expected that these twin developments of the norm of mutual expert disclosure on liability and potential disclosure of the lay witnesses' proofs will substantially alter the conduct of future medical malpractice actions.

PART II

Medical negligence cases

List of case subjects

Abortion
Re B (page 154); C (page 174); Chaunt (page 179); Cunningham (page 192); Re P (page 281); Paton (page 285); Sciuraga (page 312).

Adjournment of trial
Slater v Maidstone H.A. (page 317); Taylor (page 326).

Advice
Colston (page 183); Connolly v Rubra (page 184); Department of Health (page 198); Edler (page 203); Goodman (page 220); Jones v Fay (page 246); Wells (page 338); Willson (page 343).

After-care
Aboul-Hosn (page 149); Ali (page 151); Corder (page 186); Harrington (page 228); Hocking (page 234); Lock (page 262); Pargeter (page 283); Pickering (page 288); Powell (page 290); Sayer (page 311); Sullivan (page 324).

Aggravated damages
Barbara (page 156); G (page 214); Kralj (page 253).

Alternative practitioner
Brogan (page 170); Gladwell (page 218); Gordon (page 221); Hodson (page 235); R v Crick (page 294); R v Jones (page 294); Ruddock (page 305); Shallard (page 313); Smith v Lowry (page 319); Snell (page 320); Sones (page 321); Walton (page 336).

Anaesthetics
Ackers (page 150); Allan (page 152); Brown (page 171); Chatterton (page 178); Collins (page 182); Connolly v Camden (page 183); Crawford (page 188); Davis v LCC (page 196); Fussell (page 213); Gray (page 221); Hall v Wandsworth (page 224); Halushka (page 225); Hopley (page 238); Jacobs (page 245); Jones v Manchester Corporation (page 247); Lock (page 262); Moore (page 274); Paterson (page 285); Roe (page 301); Saunders (page 310); Thomas (page 327); Williams v North Liverpool (page 342).

Appendicitis
Ball v Howard (page 156); Burridge (page 173); Edler (page 203).

Apportionment of liability
Dwyer (page 202); Jones v Manchester Corporation (page 247); Prendergast (page 290).

Assault (qv **Battery** and **Trespass**)
Beatty (page 159); Breen (page 170); Davies v Horton Road (page 194); Halushka (page 225); Latter (page 256); Leigh (page 258); Marshall v Curry (page 270); Smith v Pare (page 320).

Battery (qv **Assault** and **Trespass**)
Allan (page 152); Barbara (page 156); Chatterton (page 178); Devi (page 198); Hills (page 233); Reibl (page 297).

Bedsores
Birnie (page 163); Biss (page 163); Pickering (page 288).

Blood donor
Lowen (page 263).

Blood transfusion
Malette (page 267); Morgan (page 274); Roberts (page 300).

Brain damage
Aboul-Hosn (page 149); Bell v Gateshead (page 160); Connolly v Camden (page 183); Croke (page 189); Cunningham (page 192); Gray (page 221); Lim Poh Choo (page 260); Moser (page 276); Thomas (page 327).

Breach of contract
Drummond (page 200); Edwards (page 204); Everard (page 206); Eyre (page 207); Gordon (page 221); McGrath (page 264); Michael (page 272); Morris (page 275); Sciuraga (page 312); Shallard (page 313); Thake (page 327); Walton (page 336).

Burden of proof
Harrington (page 228); McCormick (page 264); Pargeter (page 283); Wilsher (page 344).

Burns
Ball v Caldwell (page 155); Bernier (page 161); Clarke v Adams (page 181); Clarke v Worboys (page 181); Cox (page 188); Davis v LCC (page 196); Gold v Essex (page 218); Goode (page 220); Hall v Lees (page 223); Jones v Manchester (page 247); Shallard (page 313); Smith v Pare (page 320); Snell (page 320).

Caesarian
Ackers (page 150); Burke (page 173); Leckie (page 257); Sayer (page 311); Urry (page 330).

Cancer
Clarke v Worboys (page 181); Crivon (page 189); Herskovits (page 233); Hulse (page 243); Smith v Pare (page 320); Sutton (page 324); Vaughan (page 332); Whiteford (page 340).

Cardiac arrest
Ali (page 151); Blackburn (No.1) (page 165); Gray (page 221); Halushka (page 225); Lim Poh Choo (page 260); Saunders (page 310).

Cardio-respiratory arrest
Croke (page 189); Cunningham (page 192).

Casualty officer (qv **Hospital doctor**)
Barnett (page 158); Braisher (page 169); Edler (page 203); Jones v Manchester (page 247); Kilburn (page 252); McCormack (page 263); Payne (page 287); Wood (page 347).

Causation
Barnett (page 158); Bernier (page 161); Bonthrone (page 168); Burridge (page 173); Canterbury (page 175); Chatterton (page 178); Cooper v Miron (page 185); Cronin (page 190); De Freville (page 197); Edler (page 203); Elkan (page 204); Gauntlett (page 216); Gregory (page 222); Hayward (page 230); Hegarty (page 231); Herskovits (page 233); Hocking (page 234); Hotson (page 240); Hulse (page 243); Jacobs (page 245); Karp (page 249); Kavanagh (page 250); Kay (page 251); Kenyon (page 251); Levenkind (page 259); Loveday (page 262); Lowen (page 263); Marchant (page 268); Mitchell v Hounslow (page 272); Murray (page 277); O'Neill (page 281); R v (ex parte Loveday) (page 295); Reibl (page 297); Rich (page 298); Robinson (page 301); Smith v Barking (page 318); Smith v Brighton (page 318); Sones (page 321); Stokes (page 322); Thorne (page 328); Vernon (page 333); Walton (page 336); Wilsher (page 344).

Childbirth
Bagley (page 155); Bell v Gateshead (page 160); Brown (page 171); Bull (page 172); Burke (page 173); Davis v City (page 195); Hall v Wandsworth (page 224); Kralj (page 253); Leckie (page 257); Mitchell v Hounslow (page 272); Murray (page 277); R v Bateman (page 292); Rich (page 298); Ritter (page 299); Sayer (page 311); Slater v Maidstone (page 317); Urry (page 330); Walker v S.W. Surrey (page 336); Whitehouse (page 341).

Child death
Gray (page 221); Riddett (page 299).

Child patient
Cox (page 188); Gravestock (page 221); Newnham (page 279).

Chiropodist
Colston (page 183).

Circumcision
Abrahams (page 149).

Communication
Bell v Secretary of State (page 160); Chapman (page 177); Coles (page 182); Corder (page 186); Farquhar (page 209); Gregory (page 222); Hucks (page 241); Ritter (page 299); Sa'd (page 307).

Confidentiality
Davies v Eli Lilly (page 193); Tarasoff (page 325).

Congenital Disabilities (Civil Liability) Act 1976
McKay (page 265).

Consent
Allan (page 152); Re B (page 154); Beatty (page 159); Breen (page 170); Chatterton (page 178); Cull (page 192); Davies v Horton Road (page 194); Devi (page 198); F (page 207); Freeman (page 211); Gillick (page 217); Halushka (page 225); Hamilton (page 226); Hills (page 233); Latter (page 256); Malette (page 267); Marshall v Curry (page 270); Re P (page 281); Sankey (page 309); Smith v Pare (page 320); Wells (page 338); Worster (page 348).

Consultant
Collins (page 182); Horner (page 238); Hothi (page 239); Hughes (page 242); Hulse (page 243); Junor (page 248); Moore (page 274); Mose (page 276); Perionowsky (page 288); Pickering (page 288); Reed (page 296); Rosen v Edgar (page 302).

Contraceptive advice
Blyth (page 166); Gillick (page 217); Gold v Haringey (page 219).

Contra-indications
Bonthrone (page 168); King (page 252); Loveday (page 262).

Contributory negligence
Bernier (page 161); Crossman (page 191).

Costs
Davies (Joseph Owen) (page 195); Hall v Wandsworth (page 224); Jacob (page 244); Ritter (page 299); Sa'd (page 307).

Cottage hospital
Chapman (page 177); Coles (page 182); Hogg (page 236).

Court of Protection
Blackburn (No.2) (page 165); Cunningham (page 192).

Criminal liability
R v Bateman (page 292); R v Crick (page 294); R v Jones (page 294).

Crown Proceedings Act 1947
Bell v Secretary of State (page 160).

Damages
Aboul-Hosn (page 149); Ackers (page 150); Allan (page 152); Bagley (page 155); Barbara (page 156); Bell v Gateshead (page 160); Benarr (page 161); Biles (page 162); Blackburn (No.2) (page 165); Burke (page 173); Chaunt (page 179); Connolly v Camden (page 183); Connor (page 185); Croke (page 189); Cunningham (page 192); Daly (page 193); Devi (page 198); Emeh (page 205); G (page 214); Gray (page 221); Hamilton (page 226); Hatwell (page 230); Herskovits

Routley (page 304); S v Distillers (page 305); Stevens (page 322); Stokes (page 322); Vancouver General Hospital (page 331).

Duty of care to third party
Sankey (page 309); Tarasoff (page 325); Urbanski (page 330).

Duty to inform of mishap
Cooper v Miron (page 185); Gerber (page 216).

Duty to treat
Barnes (page 157); Barnett (page 158).

ECT
Bolam (page 166); Davies v Horton Road (page 194).

Emergency
Malette (page 267); Marshall v Curry (page 270).

Epilepsy
Hatwell (page 230); Hothi (page 239); Lepine (page 259); McCormick (page 264).

Error of judgement
Ashton (page 154); Furstenau (page 213); Parkinson (page 283); Whitehouse (page 341).

Examination
Barnes (page 157); Barnett (page 158); Kavanagh (page 250); Kilburn (page 252); Latter (page 256); Newton (page 280); Patel (page 284); Riddett (page 299); Wood (page 347).

Experimentation
Halushka (page 225); Karp (page 249); Slater v Baker (page 317).

False imprisonment
Frost (page 212); Furber (page 212); Routley (page 304).

Father's status
C (page 174); Paton (page 285).

Foetus' rights
C (page 174); Paton (page 285).

Force feeding
Leigh (page 258).

Foreign
Allan (page 152); Bernier (page 161); Canterbury (page 175); Crossman (page 191); Goode (page 220); Haines (page 223); Halushka (page 225); Herskovits (page 233); Karp (page 249); Lepine (page 259); Malette (page 267); Reibl (page 297); Tarasoff (page 325); Urbanski (page 330).

Foreseeability
Allan (page 152); Hothi (page 239); Hyde (page 244); Prendergast (page 290); Robinson (page 301); Sidaway (page 314); Size (page 316); Urbanski (page 330).

Fractures
Bolam (page 166); Davies v Horton Road (page 194); Dransfield (page 199); Elkan (page 204); Fish (page 210); Fletcher (page 210); Fowler (page 211); Hartley (page 229); Hotson (page 240); Junor (page 248); Kilburn (page 252); Lanphier (page 255); McCormack (page 263); McGrath (page 264); McLoughlin (page 265); Newton (page 280); O'Neill (page 281); Patterson (page 286); Sabapathi (page 306); Saumarez (page 310); Seare (page 312); Slater v Baker (page 317); Smith v Lowry (page 319); Tyndall (page 329); Westaway (page 338); Wilson (page 345); Wood (page 347).

Fraud
Karp (page 249); Shallard (page 313).

Fresh evidence
Hughes (page 242); Reed (page 296).

Gangrene
> Birnie (page 163); Dwyer (page 202); Fowler (page 211); Junor (page 248); Sones (page 321).

General practitioner
> Ball v Caldwell (page 155); Ball v Howard (page 156); Barker (page 157); Barnes (page 157); Buckle (page 172); Chapman (page 177); Coles (page 182); Connolly v Rubra (page 184); Corner (page 187); Dwyer (page 202); Edler (page 203); Farquhar (page 209); Gerber (page 216); Goode (page 220); Hoffman (page 235); Hucks (page 241); Joseph (page 248); Kavanagh (page 250); King (page 252); Langley (page 255); Lobley (page 261); Patel (page 284); Prendergast (page 290); R v Bateman (page 292); Riddett (page 299); Robinson (page 301); Sa'd (page 307); Sadler (page 308); Tanswell (page 325); Warren (page 337).

Gratuitous service
> Goode (page 220).

Heart transplant
> Karp (page 249).

Hospital administration
> Bagley (page 155); Bull (page 172); Collins (page 182); Cull (page 192); G (page 214); Heafield (page 231); Hopley (page 238); Jones v Manchester Corporation (page 247); McCormack (page 263); McLoughlin (page 265); Marshall v Lindsey C.C. (page 269); Smith v Lewisham (page 319); Vancouver General Hospital (page 331); Voller (page 334); Wilsher (page 344).

Hospital doctor (qv **Casualty officer; House surgeon; Registrar**)
> Kenyon (page 251); Newton (page 280); Parkinson (page 283); Patterson (page 286); Rouse (page 303); Sankey (page 309); Saumarez (page 310); Stevens (page 322); Tyndall (page 329).

Hospital resources
> R v (ex parte Collier) (page 293); R v (ex parte Hincks) (page 295); R v (ex parte Walker) (page 293).

House surgeon (qv **Hospital doctor**)
> Collins (page 182); Junor (page 248); Patten (page 286).

Hysterectomy
> Breen (page 170); Chaunt (page 179); Cull (page 192).

Infection
> Bayliss (page 158); Fletcher (page 210); Heafield (page 231); Marshall v Lindsey C.C. (page 269); Vancouver General Hospital (page 331); Voller (page 334).

Informed consent
> Canterbury (page 175); Karp (page 249); Reibl (page 297).

Injections
> Akerele (page 151); Allan (page 152); Brazier (page 169); Caldeira (page 174); Chin Keow (page 180); Corner (page 187); Daly (page 193); Freeman (page 211); Gale (page 215); Gerber (page 216); Hayward (page 230); Hunter (page 243); Jacobs (page 245); Kay (page 251); King (page 252); Marchant (page 268); Pargeter (page 283); Paterson (page 285); Prout (page 291); Robinson (page 301); Smith v Brighton (page 318); Voller (page 334); Walker v S.W. Surrey (page 336); Williams v North Liverpool (page 342).

Interests of patient
> F (page 207); Marshall v Curry (page 270).

Interrogatories
> Ali (page 151).

Judicial review
> R v (ex parte Collier) (page 293); R v (ex parte Hincks) (page 295); R v (ex parte Walker) (page 293).

Operation

Optician

Osteopath

Overdose

Pain relief

Parental objections

Patient's history

Pathologist

Penicillin

Pharmacist

Physiotherapist

Plastic surgeon

Pleadings

Post-traumatic stress disorder

Pregnancy

Prescription

Hothi (page 239); Jones v Fay (page 246); Kavanagh (page 250); Prendergast (page 290); R v Crick (page 294); Rhodes (page 298); Smith v Brighton (page 318); Strangways-Lesmere (page 323); Vernon (page 333).

Prison inmate
Barbara (page 156); Ellis (page 205); Freeman (page 211); Holgate (page 236); Leigh (page 258).

Privilege
Lask (page 256); Lee (page 257).

Prudent patient test
Canterbury (page 175); Reibl (page 297).

Psychiatric patient
De Freville (page 197); Drummond (page 200); Ellis (page 205); Everett (page 206); F (page 207); Re Frost (page 212); Furber (page 212); Gauntlett (page 216); Haines (page 223); Hall v Semple (page 224); Harnett (page 227); Hatwell (page 230); Routley (page 304); Size (page 316); Tarasoff (page 325); Winch (page 346).

Psychiatrist
Bolam (page 166); Gale (page 215); Hatwell (page 230); Landau (page 254).

Psychologist
Haines (page 223).

Public Health Officer
Salisbury (page 309).

Public policy
Emeh (page 205); Hyde (page 244); Sciuraga (page 312); Thake (page 327); Udale (page 329).

Quadriplegia
Brown (page 171); Moser (page 276).

Radiographer
Gold v Essex (page 218).

Receptionist
Joseph (page 248); Lobley (page 261).

Registrar (qv **Hospital doctor**)
Burridge (page 173); Chaunt (page 179); Jones v Berkshire (page 246); Leckie (page 257); Murray (page 277); O'Malley-Williams (page 280); Rosen v Edgar (page 302); Whitehouse (page 341); Wilsher (page 344).

Representation
Brogan (page 170); Edwards (page 204); Hodson (page 235); Markham (page 269); Ruddock (page 305); Shallard (page 313); Walton (page 336); Worster (page 348).

Representative action
Davies v Eli Lilly (page 193); Davies (Joseph Owen) (page 195).

Res ipsa loquitur
Brazier (page 169); Brown (page 171); Cassidy (page 176); Clarke v Worboys (page 181); Cooper v Nevill (page 186); Corner (page 187); Fish (page 210); Fletcher (page 210); Garner (page 215); James (page 245); Leckie (page 257); Levenkind (page 259); Lock (page 262); Lowen (page 263); Mahon (page 266); Morris (page 275); O'Malley-Williams (page 280); Roe (page 301); Saunders (page 310); Voller (page 334); Woodhouse (page 347).

Retained surgical product
Cooper v Nevill (page 186); Dryden (page 201); Garner (page 215); Hocking (page 234); James (page 245); Mahon (page 266); Morris (page 275); Needham (page 279); Pask (page 284); Urry (page 330).

Right to know treatment received
Lee (page 257); Naylor (page 278).

Risk disclosure
Blyth (page 166); Bolam (page 166); Canterbury (page 175); Chatterton (page 178); Cronin (page 190); Davies v Horton Road (page 194); Eyre (page 207); Gold v Haringey (page 219); Halushka (page 225); Hatcher (page 229); O'Malley-Williams (page 280); Palmer (page 282); Reibl (page 297); Sankey (page 309); Sidaway (page 314); Smith v Barking (page 318); Thake (page 327); Waters (page 337); Worster (page 348).

Scarring
Daly (page 193); Pask (page 284); Vaughan (page 332); Williams v Imrie (page 342).

School doctor
Holland (page 237).

School fees
Benarr (page 161); Williams v Imrie (page 342).

Second opinion
Connolly v Rubra (page 184); Crivon (page 189); Payne (page 287); R v Bateman (page 292).

Segregation
Ellis (page 205); Heafield (page 231).

Settlement of claim
Pimm (page 289); Stevens (page 322).

Sexual abuse
G (page 214).

Ship's doctor
Pudney (page 291).

Smallpox
Salisbury (page 309); Vancouver General Hospital (page 331).

Solicitor's negligence
Paterson (page 285).

Standard of care
Akerele (page 151); Ashcroft (page 153); Ashton (page 154); Blyth (page 166); Bolam (page 166); Brogan (page 170); Buckle (page 172); Chin Keow (page 180); Clark (page 180); Crivon (page 189); Crossman (page 191); Dransfield (page 199); Everett (page 206); F (page 207); Gale (page 215); Gauntlett (page 216); Gold v Haringey (page 219); Gordon (page 221); Gravestock (page 221); Haines (page 223); Hancke (page 226); Hartley (page 229); Hatcher (page 229); Hodson (page 235); Holgate (page 236); Holland (page 237); Hucks (page 241); Hunter (page 243); Hyde (page 244); Jones v Fay (page 246); Landau (page 254); Lanphier (page 255); Lepine (page 259); Lobley (page 261); Loveday (page 262); Mahon (page 266); Markham (page 269); Maynard (page 271); Moore (page 274); Mose (page 276); Munro (page 277); Nickolls (page 280); O'Malley-Williams (page 280); Palmer (page 282); Pargeter (page 283); Parkinson (page 283); Prout (page 291); Pudney (page 291); R v Crick (page 294); R v Jones (page 294); Rhodes (page 298); Rich (page 298); Sadler (page 308); Seare (page 312); Selfe (page 313); Sidaway (page 314); Size (page 316); Snell (page 320); Stokes (page 322); Tanswell (page 325); Tarasoff (page 325); Vancouver General Hospital (page 331); Venner (page 332); Warren (page 337); Waters (page 337); Whichello (page 339); White (page 340); Whiteford (page 340); Whitehouse (page 341); Williams v Ward (page 343).

State of knowledge
Gale (page 215); Hopley (page 238); Palmer (page 282); Roe (page 301); Stokes (page 322).

Sterilisation
Biles (page 162); Devi (page 198); F (page 207); Hamilton (page 226); Wells (page 338); Worster (page 348).

146

Sterilisation (failed)
Chaunt (page 179); Cronin (page 190); Emeh (page 205); Eyre (page 207); Gold v Haringey (page 219); Jones v Berkshire (page 246); Udale (page 329); Venner (page 332); Waters (page 337); Williams v Imrie (page 342).

Striking out
Dawson (page 196); Department of Health (page 198); Goodman (page 220); McKay (page 265); Rosen v Marston (page 303).

Substandard treatment
Aboul-Hosn (page 149); Abrahams (page 149); Ackers (page 150); Ali (page 151); Ashcroft (page 153); Ball (page 155); Bell v Gateshead (page 160); Bernier (page 161); Blackburn (No 1) (page 165); Blackburn (No 2) (page 165); Bolam (page 166); Breen (page 170); Burridge (page 173); Caldeira (page 174); Colston (page 183); Connor (page 185); Drummond (page 200); Edgar (page 203); Everard (page 206); Fowler (page 211); Furber (page 212); Gladwell (page 218); Gold v Essex (page 218); Goode (page 220); Goodman (page 220); Gray (page 221); Hartley (page 229); Hatwell (page 230); Hegarty (page 231); Hodson (page 235); Hoffman (page 235); Horner (page 238); Hotson (page 240); Junor (page 248); Kralj (page 253); Leckie (page 257); Lowen (page 263); Mitchell v Hounslow (page 272); Mitchell v Liverpool (page 273); Munro (page 277); Murray (page 277); Patten (page 286); Pippin (page 289); Powell (page 290); R v Bateman (page 292); R v Jones (page 294); Roberts (page 300); Robinson (page 301); Ruddock (page 305); Smith v Lewisham (page 319); Smith v Lowry (page 319); Sones (page 321); Sutton (page 324); Trew (page 328); Tyndall (page 329); Urbanski (page 330); Waghorn (page 334); Walker v S.W. Surrey (page 336); Willson (page 343); Wilsher (page 344); Wilson (page 345); Wood (page 347).

Suicide risk
Haines (page 223); Hyde (page 244); Selfe (page 313); Thorne (page 328).

Supervision
Cox (page 188); Drummond (page 200); Ellis (page 205); Gauntlett (page 216); Gravestock (page 221); Holgate (page 236); Hyde (page 244); Jones v Manchester (page 247); Lepine (page 259); Selfe (page 313); Size (page 316); Smith v Lewisham (page 319); Thorne (page 328).

Surgeon
Ashcroft (page 153); Beatty (page 159); Cassidy (page 176); Clark (page 180); Cooper v Nevill (page 186); Devi (page 198); Hancke (page 226); Henderson (page 232); Hills (page 233); James (page 245); Karp (page 249); Levenkind (page 259); Mahon (page 266); Michael (page 272); Morris (page 275); Mose (page 276); Munro (page 277); Needham (page 279); Nickolls (page 280); Pippin (page 289); Rosen v Marston (page 303); Seare (page 312); Sidaway (page 314); Slater v Baker (page 317); Smith v Barking (page 318); Sullivan (page 324); Urbanski (page 330); Urry (page 330); Waghorn (page 334); Whichello (page 339); White (page 340); Whiteford (page 340); Willson (page 343); Woodhouse (page 347).

Test subject
Halushka (page 225).

Tests
Connolly v Rubra (page 184); G (page 214); Gregory (page 222); Hothi (page 239); Marshall v Lindsey C.C. (page 269); Vernon (page 333); Whichello (page 339); Whiteford (page 340).

Thalidomide
Distillers v Thompson (page 199); S v Distillers (page 305).

Trespass to person (qv **Assault** and **Battery**)
Cull (page 192); F (page 207); Freeman (page 211); Michael (page 272); Slater v Baker (page 317).

Tuberculosis
Brogan (page 170); Connolly v Rubra (page 184); Maynard (page 271).

Aboul-Hosn v Trustees of the Italian Hospital and Others

Damages: substandard treatment: after-care: brain damage

Hirst J. (1987) PMILL Vol 3 No 7

On 30 September 1982, on the eve of his nineteenth birthday, the plaintiff (Samer Aboul-Hosn) underwent an operation at the National Hospital for Nervous Diseases for the removal of a colloid cyst from his brain. He had been transferred for the operation from the Italian Hospital to which he returned the next day. During the ensuing fortnight it was observed by computerised scanner that his ventricles were still abnormally enlarged due to a recurrence of hydrocephalus, ie raised intracranial fluid pressure. Between 15 and 17 October he suffered a progressive deterioration of this condition. It was correctly diagnosed but incorrectly treated.

The plaintiff sued the Italian Hospital and three doctors responsible for his treatment. He agreed not to pursue his claim against the Italian Hospital. The three doctors admitted liability.

Before the operation and its aftermath, the plaintiff was a bright and personable young man with four "A" levels, a place at university and the prospect of a successful career. He suffered catastrophic and irreversible brain damage. His mental age had shrunk to that of a two year old. He could not speak, his eyesight was drastically impaired, and he walked in a zombie like fashion. He would never be able to work or marry. There was evidence that deep within him he had some insight into his appalling predicament.

Held: the plaintiff was awarded damages for:

Pain, suffering and loss of amenities	£ 85,000
Parents' past care and expenditure	£ 100,700
Future care in all its aspects	£ 400,800
Housing needs	£ 48,100
Future loss of earnings (including car)	£ 331,000
Court of Protection fees	£ 34,500
Agreed interest	£ 31,550
Total (rounded)	£1,032,000

See pages 103, 106, 107, 108.

Abrahams v Snowman

Substandard treatment: operation: circumcision

Ridley J (with special jury). [1910] 2 BMJ 1565

The plaintiff (Mr Abrahams) was the father of a young Jewish boy. Dr Snowman was a member of the Initiation Society, established for the purpose of carrying out the rite of circumcision among Jewish people. Mr Snadon performed the operation of circumcision on the plaintiff's son under Dr Snowman's supervision. The child was then taken to his mother. Later in the day the Society's nurse found that there was a great deal of haemorrhage. Dr Snowman was called for, but was not at home, so another doctor was called in to stop the bleeding.

The child gradually wasted and suffered from marasmus. The plaintiff sued Dr Snowman, alleging negligent performance of the operation. Evidence was given that the operation had been properly performed and that the marasmus was due to malnutrition.

Held: Ridley J described the case as grossly exaggerated, to say the least. He directed the members of the jury that if in their opinion the child's condition was brought about by reason of the negligent manner in which Dr Snowman performed or assisted at the operation, then their verdict should be for the plaintiff.

The jury returned a verdict for the defendant.

Ackers v Wigan Area Health Authority

Substandard treatment: childbirth: caesarian: anaesthetics: damages: post-traumatic stress disorder

Russell J. [1986] CLY 1048

The plaintiff (Mrs Ackers) was aged twenty-six when her first child was delivered. A caesarian section operation was needed. Owing to the hospital's negligence, she was not anaesthetised but was paralysed by pre-operation muscle relaxant drugs. The surgeon and theatre staff were unaware of her plight. During the one and a quarter hour operation she was fully conscious, felt every sensation and was terrified and distressed by artificial ventilation of her lungs.

She developed a severe reactive depression. For the first three months after birth she had negative feelings towards her child. When she became pregnant again a further caesarian was necessary; for ten weeks she suffered terror and misery in fear of what lay ahead. Thereafter she suffered continuing depression, mood changes, irritability, phobia of general anaesthetics and hospitals, and severe insomnia. She was also afraid of further pregnancy, which seriously impaired her sexual relationship with her husband. She was unable to face the required surgery for painful and embarrassing varicose veins and bladder cyst.

A course of abreactive therapy was planned. This would have involved her reliving her experiences and would have been very unpleasant. The prognosis was guardedly optimistic.

Held (June 1985): the plaintiff was awarded £12,000 general damages for pain, suffering and loss of amenities. Other elements of her damages were £1,700 for the cost of future psychiatric treatment and agreed special damages of £75. Her total award was £13,775 plus interest.

See pages 81, 84, 104.

Akerele v R

Manslaughter: standard of care: injections: drugs

Privy Council. [1943] AC 255, [1943] 1 All ER 367

Dr Akerele was a qualified medical practitioner in Nigeria. On 6 and 7 May 1941 he treated fifty-seven children in Asaga. With a few exceptions, they were suffering from yaws. He injected nearly all of them with sobita which consisted of sodium bismuth tartrate. Ten of the children died.

Dr Akerele was charged with the manslaughter of one of them, Kalu Ibe. The trial judge found that he negligently prepared too strong a mixture of sobita. The boy had died from stomatis induced by bismuth poisoning. Dr Akerele was convicted and sentenced to imprisonment with hard labour.

Held: the single act of mixing too strong a solution in making up the preparation of sobita did not amount to criminal negligence. The negligence to be imputed depends on the probable, not the actual, result. The fatal consequences to the ten children did not convert carelessness into criminal negligence.

See page 34.

Ali v St Mary's Private Hospital and Another

Substandard treatment: cardiac arrest: after-care: interrogatories

Court of Appeal. 21 October 1981

Mohammed Abdel Rahman Ali, an asthmatic, came to the U.K. from Khartoum to have a complicated tonsillectomy. On 13 September 1975 this was successfully carried out at St Mary's Private Hospital. However, a few hours after returning to his bed, Mr Ali suffered a cardiac arrest and died.

The plaintiff (his widow) sued St Mary's Hospital and the anaesthetist, Dr Lahiri. Interrogatories were administered to Dr Lahiri. Sheldon J gave her leave to administer seven interrogatories to the hospital for answer by their matron.

Held: interrogatories will not be allowed unless they are necessary for fairly disposing of the action, and will not generally be allowed where the information can or will be proved by a witness at the trial so that the interrogatories will not save costs. On an undertaking from the defendants to call the nurses who attended the deceased during the last few hours of his life, the first interrogatory was deleted and the others were varied.

Per Stephenson LJ: "In a case of this kind brought by the widow of a man who has died in hospital, there may be a good many things which the plaintiff cannot possibly know but which must be within the knowledge of the defendant hospital, and that is the kind of case, rather like an unwitnessed fatal accident or an accident in which the plaintiff is knocked unconscious, in which interrogatories as to the facts are ordered to enable the plaintiff to prove her case."

Allan v Mount Sinai Hospital et al.

Anaesthetics: consent: battery: injections: damages: foreseeability: foreign

Ontario High Court of Justice (Linden J). (1980) 109 DLR (3d) 634

In November 1972, the plaintiff (Venita Allan) entered the Mount Sinai Hospital in Toronto for a dilatation and curettage operation. When she first met Dr Hellman, the anaesthetist, in the hall outside the operating room, she said to him: "Please don't touch my left arm. You'll have nothing but trouble there". Dr Hellman's response was: "We know what we are doing".

The plaintiff was then wheeled into the operating room where Dr Hellman injected sodium pentothal and the other required anaesthetic chemicals into her left arm. He had no trouble in finding a vein. However a short time later he noticed that the needle had slipped out. This caused part of the solution to leak into the tissue of the arm interstitially, instead of entering the vein.

The normal consequence of injecting some sodium pentothal into the tissue of the arm, as a result of a needle slipping out of the vein, is that the patient has a sore arm for a day or two. Instead the plaintiff suffered a very severe reaction. She sued Dr Hellman for damages in battery and negligence. Her action against the hospital and other defendants did not proceed.

Held: (i) Dr Hellman exercised reasonable skill throughout. Needles can slip out without fault. He had not been negligent;

(ii) the administration of an anaesthetic is a surgical operation which constitutes a battery, unless the patient consents to it. The plaintiff did not consent: she expressly instructed Dr Hellman not to start the anaesthetic in her left arm. He had committed a battery;

(iii) because his responsibility was founded in battery, Dr Hellman was liable for all of the consequences flowing therefrom, be they foreseeable or unforeseeable. Even if nothing at all had gone wrong, he would have been required to pay nominal damages.

See page 6.

Appleby v Sleep

Pharmacist: prescription

Court of Appeal. [1968] 2 All ER 265, [1968] 1 WLR 948

In April 1967 Mrs Magee took a National Health Service prescription to the Ferry Pharmacy in Hythe. This was owned by the defendant, Mr Ernest Sleep. She was handed a bottle of penidural syrup as prescribed for her child. A few days later she saw a lump in the medicine as it came out of the bottle and found this to be a piece of glass.

Mr Sleep was a registered pharmaceutical chemist who was engaged under a contract with the National Health Service Executive Council for Hampshire. They subsequently paid him for supplying the medicine. He was prosecuted under s 2 Food and Drugs Act 1955.

Held: Mr Sleep was not liable. There was no sale by him to the patient. His contract with the National Health Service Executive Council was a contract for services, not a contract of sale.

Per Lord Parker CJ: "The first thing that is clear is that there will have been no sale by the chemist to the patient, the person presenting the prescription. Not only has that been so held, but it is clearly the case, because the patient is not paying for the medicine or drugs, and that is so even if there is a prescription charge."

See page 14.

Ashcroft v Mersey Regional Health Authority

Standard of care: surgeon: operation: substandard treatment

Kilner Brown J. [1983] 2 All ER 245

In January 1978 the plaintiff (Mrs Ashcroft) submitted herself to an operation on her left ear. It was performed by Mr Joseph Siegler, a surgeon of long experience and high reputation. The operation was for the removal of granulated tissue adhering to part of the ear drum, and is regarded as routine and perfectly safe. In this case, there was no bony covering to the facial nerve, the ear drum was close to the nerve and the granulations extended to the nerve. Mr Siegler got the forceps to bite on the facial nerve because he was searching for granulations which extended that far. The nerve was damaged and the plaintiff was left with a partial paralysis of the left side of the face.

The plaintiff's expert testified that the accident could only have happened due to negligence by Mr Siegler, and maintained that damage to the nerve was done by excessive force in the use of forceps. This was denied by Mr Siegler who was satisfied that he was using the forceps as he always did. He was supported by an eminent ear surgeon who also considered that he had not been negligent.

Held: it had not been proved that Mr Siegler fell below the standard of care expected of him. The plaintiff's case failed.

Per Kilner Brown J: "The question for consideration is whether on a balance of probabilities it has been established that a professional man has failed to exercise the care required of a man possessing and professing special skill in circumstances which require the exercise of that special skill. If there is an added burden, such burden does not rest on the person alleging negligence; on the contrary, it could be said that the more skilled a person is, the more the care that is expected of him. It is preferable in my judgement to concentrate on and to apply the test which has long been established in the law and to avoid all commentary or gloss".

See pages 25, 37, 77–78.

Ashton v Alexander and Trent Regional Health Authority

Standard of care: error of judgement: dentist: operation

Court of Appeal. 29 January 1988

In 1982 the plaintiff (Geoffrey Ashton) underwent an operation under general anaesthetic for removal of an unerupted molar tooth in his left lower jaw. This was carried out at Lincoln County Hospital by Mr Alexander who employed a hammer and chisel. The tooth was successfully elevated, but the plaintiff sustained a displaced fracture of the lower left jaw.

The plaintiff sued Mr Alexander and the hospital authority in the Lincoln County Court. Mr Alexander accepted in evidence that the likely cause was either excessive force on the chisel or insufficient removal of bone from the jaw causing fracture on elevation and that, if so, "I would have fallen below my usual standard". The Recorder found: "the first defendant accepted fault on his part. I hold that he was negligent".

Held: an error of judgement may, or may not, be negligent. The admission of a mistake does not equal an admission of negligence. The Recorder failed to apply the appropriate test of whether the error was one that would not have been made by a reasonably competent professional person professing to have the standard and type of skill that the defendant held himself out as having, and acting with ordinary care. Thus the defendants' appeal was allowed and a new trial ordered.

In Re B (a minor) (Wardship: Sterilisation)

Consent: abortion: minor: wardship

House of Lords. [1988] 1 AC 199, [1987] 2 All ER 206, [1987] 2 WLR 1213

B, a seventeen year old girl, was mentally retarded and epileptic. Her ability to understand speech was that of a six year old, and her ability to express herself that of a two year old. She lived under a care order at a residential institution for the mentally handicapped. She began to show signs of sexual awareness and drive, exemplified by provocative approaches to male staff and members and other residents and by touching herself in the genital area. She would be terrified, distressed and violent during normal labour, and if she underwent a caesarian section would be likely to pick at the operational wound and tear it open. She had an antipathy to small children. Any child born to her would have to be taken for fostering or adoption. She was unaware of sexual intercourse and its relationship to pregnancy. It was not feasible to discuss contraception with her. The only appropriate course offering complete protection was for her to undergo sterilisation by occluding the fallopian tubes. She did not have the mental capacity to consent to this.

Consequently the Sutherland Borough Council, in whose care she was, applied to make her a ward of court and for leave to be given for her to undergo a sterilisation operation. The Court of Appeal upheld the decision of Bush J to give leave for the operation to be carried out.

Held: in the exercise of wardship jurisdiction, the court's first and paramount consideration is the well being, welfare or interests of the ward herself. The necessity was to decide the right course in the best interests of the ward. The decision to grant leave for the sterilisation operation was correct.

See page 6.

Bagley v North Herts Health Authority

Childbirth: hospital administration: damages

Simon Brown J. (1986) 136 NLJ 1014

The plaintiff (Mrs Bagley) was a married woman who became pregnant. She suffered from a condition of blood incompatibility. This was known to the defendant's maternity hospital to which she was admitted to have the child. The hospital intended to perform a blood analysis followed by an amnio-centesis which would probably have led to the induction of birth. The hospital failed to carry out that procedure, and after over ten hours' labour the plaintiff gave birth to a still-born child. The defendant (North Herts Health Authority) admitted liability.

The plaintiff suffered from severe depression, and her marriage was adversely affected. If the hospital had not been negligent, she would have had a ninety-five per cent chance of giving birth to a normal child. The risk of mortality in any subsequent pregnancy was about fifty per cent.

Held: the plaintiff was awarded general damages of £17,100 (£18,000 discounted by five per cent for the five per cent risk that she would have had a still-born child even if the hospital had not been negligent) to compensate her for:

(i) her loss of the satisfaction of bringing her pregnancy, confinement and labour to a successful, indeed joyous, conclusion;

(ii) the loss associated with the physical loss of the child; the hospital's negligence frustrated her plans to enlarge her family, and her decision not to attempt a further pregnancy was reasonable;

(iii) the illness brought on the plaintiff by her great misfortune; she had suffered a great deal over the four years to trial, and this suffering was likely to continue, although with psychiatric treatment it would diminish and possibly resolve.

N.B. In *Hotson v East Berkshire Area Health Authority*, Lord Ackner stated that the discount of five per cent in this case was clearly wrong. The plaintiff had established causation on the balance of probabilities and should have been awarded the full £18,000.

See pages 49, 89, 98, 99.

Ball v Caldwell

General practitioner: X-ray: burn: substandard treatment

Singleton J. [1940] 1 BMJ 750

In early 1933 the plaintiff (Miss Mabel Ball) injured her left breast. She consulted Dr Caldwell, a general practitioner, who gave her X-ray treatment.

The condition cleared up until October 1934 when she consulted Dr Caldwell again. He found a hard lump and decided to irradiate it. He used an induction-coil apparatus with a coolidge tube working at 150 KV, giving one-third of a skin erythema dose. On 13 November he saw her again and gave her double the previous dose. He was in and out of the room during treatment, but never further away than the adjoining room.

The plaintiff suffered skin discolouration which made it impossible for her to wear low-cut dresses or a bathing costume. She sued Dr Caldwell. Expert evidence was given that her discolouration was due to a healed X-ray burn.

Held: the plaintiff's condition resulted from Dr Caldwell's negligence.

Ball v Howard

General practitioner: appendicitis

Bailache J. [1924] 1 The Lancet 253

The plaintiff (Mr Ball) was operated on by Mr Howard for appendicitis. He requested that a specialist be called in, but Mr Howard said that this was not necessary. Initially the plaintiff made good progress after the operation, but then complications arose. A consulting surgeon was called in and performed another operation. The plaintiff made a good recovery from this.

He sued Mr Howard.

Held: Mr Howard was liable because he had committed two errors of judgement:

(i) in not attending at once to the plaintiff's call;

(ii) by going away without leaving proper instructions what to do.

See page 90.

Barbara v Home Office

Battery: injection: prison inmate: aggravated damages

Leggatt J. (1984) 134 NLJ 888

The plaintiff (Mr Barbara) was arrested for an offence of possessing an offensive weapon. He was remanded in custody for a week at Brixton Prison so that a report on his mental condition could be prepared. Hospital officers there forcibly injected him in the buttock with a tranquillising drug called Largactil. He claimed damages for trespass to the person. The Home Office admitted liability.

Held: (i) he was awarded £100 general damages for his physical injury and £500 by way of aggravated damages for injury to his feelings and dignity;

(ii) his claim for exemplary damages was rejected. Mere negligence should not be visited by an award of exemplary damages just because it resulted in a trespass which could, from the point of view of the person affected by it, be regarded as oppressive.

See pages 5, 112.

Barker v Nugent

Diagnosis: general practitioner: meningitis: duty of care

Rougier J. [1987] 3 MLJ 182

On 2 December 1975 the plaintiff child was delivered with the aid of forceps. On 10 December, when he weighed 2750g, he was discharged with his seventeen year old mother to a home run for unsupported mothers by the London Borough of Ealing. On 18 December she took the baby to Dr Nugent, a general practitioner, because of a bulging fontanelle, but when Dr Nugent saw him this had gone. On 23 December the baby weighed only 2450g. At about 6.00pm Dr Nugent conducted an apparently thorough examination and prescribed dicyclomine hydrochloride to stop vomiting after feeding. However the baby vomited up his evening and night feeds. Around 6.00am on 24 December the baby was awake with staring eyes. He uttered high-pitched cries and had convulsions.

The baby was taken to hospital where meningitis was diagnosed. This resulted in irreversible brain damage. Years later he sued Dr Nugent.

Held: the key issue was the baby's condition when Dr Nugent examined him on 23 December. The delay of over eleven years to trial gravely impaired the quality of evidence. It had not been established that Dr Nugent negligently failed to realise that the baby was sufficiently ill to merit immediate hospital admission. He was entitled to take account of the fact that the baby was in a council home with a nurse on its staff. The home had his telephone number and he lived nearby.

Judgment for the defendants.

See page 64.

Barnes v Crabtree

General practitioner: duty to treat: examination

Barry J (with jury). [1955] The Times 1–2 November

Around 2.20pm on Christmas Day 1952, the plaintiff (Miss Irene Barnes) called at the surgery of her general practitioner, Dr Crabtree. She had a history of quarrels with previous doctors and during visits to Dr Crabtree. When he opened his door, she said "I am ill". He told her that there was nothing wrong with her, and that if she was not satisfied she could get another doctor, and closed the door. Thereafter she peered through the window of his sitting-room and rang the bell again. He warned her that he would call the police. She responded by lying down in his porch. Dr Crabtree summoned the police who removed her. She sued him for failing to treat her.

Held: Barry J directed the jury that in a case of real emergency a doctor under the National Health Service scheme was under an obligation to treat any patient who was acutely ill. The doctor's obligation was to render all proper and necessary treatment to the patient. In a case of chronic illness, when he had been seeing the patient frequently, this did not mean that he was required to make a full clinical examination each time the plaintiff asked for it.

The jury found that Dr Crabtree had no case to answer.

See page 90.

Barnett v Chelsea and Kensington Hospital Management Committee

Casualty officer: duty to treat: causation

Nield J. [1969] 1 QB 428, [1968] 1 All ER 1068, [1968] 2 WLR 422

Around 8.00am on 1 January 1966, three night watchmen presented themselves at the casualty department of St Stephen's Hospital. They met the nurse on duty. One of them told her that they had been vomiting continuously since drinking tea at 5.00am. Another, Mr Barnett, did not speak but lay down, on armless chairs placed together, with his head resting on his hand. It was obvious that all three men were feeling ill. After several minutes the nurse agreed to telephone the casualty officer and told him, "There are three men complaining of vomiting after drinking tea". The doctor replied "Well, I am vomiting myself and I have not been drinking. Tell them to go home and go to bed and call in their own doctors". They drove away. Mr Barnett died a few hours later around 1.30pm.

It was found that the death was due to arsenical poisoning. There was no reasonable prospect of a suitable antidote being delivered before the death. The plaintiff's widow (Mrs Barnett) sued for damages.

Held: (i) since the defendants provided and ran the casualty department to which the deceased presented himself with a complaint of illness or injury, they owed him a duty to exercise the skill and care to be expected of a nurse and casualty officer;

(ii) the defendants through their casualty officer were negligent and in breach of their duty, in that he did not see and examine the deceased and did not admit him to the wards and treat him;

(iii) but since the deceased would have died of the poisoning even if he had been treated with all care, the plaintiff had failed to establish, on the balance of probabilities, that the defendants' negligence caused his death.

Per Nield J: "It is not, in my judgement, the case that a casualty officer must always see the caller at his department. Casualty departments are misused from time to time. If the receptionist, for example, discovers that the visitor is already attending his own doctor and merely wants a second opinion, or if the caller has a small cut which the nurse can perfectly well dress herself, then the casualty officer need not be called. However, apart from such things as this. . . the duty of a casualty officer is in general to see and examine all patients who come to the casualty department of the hospital."

See pages 9, 25, 41–42, 90.

Bayliss v Blagg and Another

Diagnosis: nurse: infection

Stable J. [1954] 1 BMJ 709

In November 1949 the plaintiff (Christine Bayliss), a very young girl, became ill. In June 1950 she was taken to Gringley-on-the-Hill Children's Hospital and was put on to a frame to keep her left hip still. At the beginning of

January 1952 the matron, Mrs Bertha Blagg, put her left leg into a plaster cast. Her father testified that she "changed into an adult overnight". When he suggested to Mrs Blagg that the plaster was too tight, she snubbed him by saying, "This is not the first plaster I have put on". On 15 January the plaintiff's toes turned blue.

When the plaster cast was removed on 16 January, there was swelling in the plaintiff's left calf and foot. The skin had an unhealthy look, and there was a grey pallor in the calf. The leg began to improve after the plaster was off, but at the end of January it became discoloured and the tissues of the calf started breaking down. The plaintiff became a cripple for life.

She sued Mrs Blagg and the hospital authority. Evidence was given at the trial that the leg became infected under the plaster.

Held: although the plaster had been put on with care and skill, there had subsequently been a high degree of negligence over a protracted period of time. The matron, Mrs Blagg, did not observe for herself or heed the warnings she received of the marked degree of deterioration practically from the moment the plaster was put on.

See page 93.

Beatty v Cullingworth

Consent: surgeon: operation: assault

Hawkins J (with jury). [1896] 2 BMJ 1525

In August 1892 the plaintiff (Alice Beatty), a hospital nurse, consulted Dr Cullingworth, senior obstetric physician at St Thomas' Hospital. He advised her that she had an inflamed cyst of the right ovary and that it was necessary to remove it. She consented to removal of the right ovary but told him that she could not agree to removal of the left ovary as well, since this would prevent her from having children. Dr Cullingworth doubted that removal of the left ovary would be necessary but added that it was impossible to be sure until the operation was proceeding and that he could not bind himself by any promise not to remove it. When the plaintiff entered the operating theatre she said "Dr Cullingworth, if you find both ovaries diseased you must remove neither". He replied "You really must leave that to me, nurse. I know your wishes; you may be sure I shall not remove anything that I can help". She made no reply but got on to the operating table and submitted to the anaesthetic. During the operation he found that the left ovary was thick, opaque and diseased and deemed it necessary to remove it in order to save her life.

The plaintiff sued Dr Cullingworth for removing the left ovary wrongfully and without her consent, and for assault.

Held: Hawkins J directed the jury that if a medical man undertook an operation, it was a humane thing for him to do everything in his power to remove the mischief, provided that he had no definite instructions not to operate. The main question was whether the plaintiff had given a tacit consent.

The jury returned a verdict for the defendant.

See page 67.

Bell and Others v Gateshead Area Health Authority

Childbirth: damages: substandard treatment: brain damage

Alliott J. (1986) Kemp & Kemp Vol 2: 1–518/1B

Kathryn Bell was born in 1978. Her skull was fractured during an induced birth. She suffered catastrophic brain damage. She was aged eight at the date of trial and had an expectation of life of thirty-two years. Her mental state was that of an infant of less than six months, and her physical skills those of one of less than twelve months. Her vision was minimal. She had moderate spasticity of her lower limbs. She could stand with help and walk a few steps with support. She could not care for herself and wore nappies. She could perceive sensations such as pain, heat or cold and could be comforted by being lifted or cuddled. Her disabilities were permanent. Her mother cared for her for almost the entire period before trial.

Held: the plaintiff was awarded (October 1986):

(i) general damages of £60,000 for pain, suffering and loss of amenities;

(ii) £50,000 for past care and attention, reached by adding to her mother's lost earnings a sum of £80 per week and rounding down the resultant figure of £50,780;

(iii) £20,000 for her own future loss of earnings (£4,000 x 5);

(iv) £220,000 for future care and attention (multiplier 14).

Other heads of damages brought the total award up to £426,500.

Bell v Secretary of State for Defence

Communication: Crown Proceedings Act 1947: military hospital

Court of Appeal. [1986] 1 Q B 322, [1985] 3 All ER 661, [1986] 2 WLR 248

Trooper Wayne Bell, aged twenty, was serving with the 15/19 King's Royal Hussars stationed in Germany. Between 6.10pm amd 6.40pm on 11 November 1978 he fell while engaged in some horseplay in barracks and received a blow to the head. At 7.30pm he was seen by an army doctor, Major Herbert, who recorded that he was suffering from the effects of drink and that he had a head injury. By 10.00pm, his condition was causing such concern that he was returned to the medical reception centre. When Major Herbert saw him again before midnight, he sent him to a German civilian hospital accompanied by a nursing sister who knew little, if anything, about his case. Trooper Bell died of his injuries.

The plaintiff (his father) sued on the grounds that his death was due to the negligence of army medical staff. He alleged, *inter alia*, that Major Herbert caused his son to be admitted to the German civilian hospital with an inaccurate and misleading case history and without any reference to the head injury. There was a trial on the preliminary issue on whether s 10 Crown Proceedings Act 1947 gave the defendant immunity.

Held: the plaintiff was entitled to allege that the death of Trooper Bell was due to a failure or omission to provide complete records to the civilian hospital. This failure or omission was suffered by him at the civilian hospital when he was no longer on Crown land. Therefore the defendant could not claim immunity under s 10 of the 1947 Act.

N.B. The Crown Proceedings (Armed Forces) Act 1987 abolished the immunity under s 10 of the 1947 Act with effect from 15 May 1987, but does not operate retrospectively.

See page 90.

Benarr and Another v Kettering Health Authority

Vasectomy (failed): wrongful birth: damages: school fees

Hodgson J. (1988) 138 NLJ 179

The plaintiffs (Mr and Mrs Benarr) decided that they did not want any more children. Consequently in June 1981 Mr Benarr had a vasectomy operation at one of the defendant's hospitals. The operation proved unsuccessful, for in October 1983 Mrs Benarr gave birth to a child, Catherine.

The plaintiffs sued the health authority. During the trial, the parties came to terms as to liability and most of the heads of damages. The issue of damages for Catherine's education remained outstanding.

Held: (i) if the victim of a negligent vasectomy is a father who in any event would have privately educated his children, he is entitled to be compensated for what in the circumstances of that family could properly be called necessary. Therefore Mr Benarr was entitled to be compensated for the future expense of Catherine's education;

(ii) on the basis of accountancy evidence that the average cost of this education in the fourteen years between the ages of four and seventeen inclusive was £2,441.79 per annum, with the lower fees falling in the earlier years, a multiplier of 8 was appropriate, so that the sum awarded for Catherine's future education was £19,534.32.

See pages 84, 114.

Bernier v Sisters of Service (St John's Hospital, Edson)

Burns: nurses: substandard treatment: contributory negligence: causation: foreign

Alberta Supreme Court. [1948] 1 WWR 113

On 5 September 1946, the plaintiff (Mrs Evelyn Bernier) was admitted for an appendicectomy to St John's Hospital, Edson, in Canada. She did not mention that she had ever had frostbite in her feet or heels. At 10.18am on 6 September she was given a spinal anaesthetic. Her appendix was duly removed. At 11.05am she was returned to the surgical ward.

One nurse filled two hot-water bottles, one covered and one uncovered, testing the temperature by moving her hand in the running water from the tap. Another nurse placed the bottles inside the foot of the bed. At 11.30am both nurses left the ward without letting the sister know that there were hot-water bottles in the bed. Over the next twenty minutes the plaintiff started to moan and cry. Soon after midday, the bottles were removed.

By then the plaintiff had suffered third degree burns to both her heels. On 23 September she left St John's Hospital against her hospital doctor's advice. She sued the hospital authority which denied liability and alleged contributory negligence.

Held: (i) the hospital staff had been negligent in failing to test the hot-water bottles with a thermometer, in placing at least one of them in direct contact with the feet of an anaesthetised patient and in not having a nurse in almost constant attendance on a patient coming out of spinal anaesthesia;

(ii) the plaintiff was not guilty of contributory negligence. She had no reason to think that even if her feet had been frost bitten such a fact was a subject matter for disclosure on entering the hospital, or that her feet might be burned with a hot-water bottle. The allegation of failure on her part to communicate her pain was of little importance, since the damage was fully done by the time sensibility returned. Although she left the hospital on 23 September against medical advice and with the possibility of infection setting in, no such infection resulted from this.

See page 55.

Biles v Barking Health Authority

Sterilisation: damages: post-traumatic stress disorder

Webster J. [1988] CLY 1103

In 1973 the plaintiff, then aged nineteen, was sterilised. In 1979 she was told that this sterilisation had been unnecessary. Since then she had taken all steps to conceive, including four *in vitro* fertilisation attempts, and had to be assumed to be permanently sterile. Her treatment had included four full laparotomies, six laparoscopies, two painful hysterosalpingograms, many blood tests and injections. She had suffered a very painful ectopic pregnancy. There was a tender scar across her lower abdomen above the bikini line. Her sexual function was impaired, with dyspareunia and loss of libido, although a course of psycho-sexual therapy had led to a good prognosis on sexual function. Since 1980 she had suffered post-traumatic disorder causing clinical depression and anxiety.

Held: general damages (October 1987) for pain, suffering and loss of amenities were £45,000 in a total award of £52, 269.73.

N.B. This case is sometimes entitled *Biles v North East Thames Health Authority*.

See pages 85, 104.

Birnie v Oxfordshire Health Authority and Another

Limitation: bedsores: gangrene: pain relief

Glidewell J. [1982] 2 The Lancet 281

In December 1972 the plaintiff (Mr Birnie), who had severe pain in his side and legs, was admitted to a pain clinic under the care of Mr Lloyd, a specialist in pain relief. Mr Lloyd carried out barbotage on two occasions. After the second barbotage, on 19 December 1972, the plaintiff was permanently paralysed in his two lower limbs.

He became severely depressed and on 6 October 1973 he attempted suicide. He was in hospital between 6 October and 23 December 1973 during which period severe bedsores and gangrene developed.

The plaintiff needed further surgery, including a chordotomy in November 1974 and, due to gangrenous sores, the amputation of his right leg in July 1975. In 1977 he spent a week in a Scottish hospital where the doctor and nurses were critical of those who had allowed the bedsores to develop. In August 1977 he consulted solicitors. His depressive state continued until 1978.

The writ was issued in August 1979. It was accepted that the three year limitation periods covered by it expired not later than 19 December 1975 and 23 December 1976 respectively. The plaintiff relied on s 33 Limitation Act 1980.

Held: (i) in considering the delay, the plaintiff's state of health and state of mind had to be taken into account. For much of the time he was sunk in depression which produced inertia of will. The delay before he consulted solicitors was understandable. After he had consulted solicitors there had been a two year delay before the writ was issued, and ten to twelve months of this delay were without valid excuse;

(ii) so far as prejudice to the defendants was concerned, there was substantial documentation, although recollection was needed with regard to the barbotage and this was affected by the passage of time. Mr Lloyd was prejudiced in that he had the claim hanging over his head and was not insured. The nursing notes on the plaintiff's bedsores were available;

(iii) the prejudice to the plaintiff outweighed the prejudice to the defendants or the effect of delay on the cogency of evidence. The scale tipped in the plaintiff's favour even when the inexcusable delay by the solicitors was added. He was granted leave to proceed under s 33 Limitation Act 1980.

See page 125.

Biss v Lambeth, Southwark and Lewisham Area Health Authority (Teaching)

Dismissal for want of prosecution: bedsores: nurses

Court of Appeal. [1978] 2 All ER 125, [1978] 1 WLR 382

In March 1965 the plaintiff (Mrs Biss) contracted multiple sclerosis. She awoke at home to find that she could not move her legs. She was taken to

Lewisham Hospital where she lay paralysed and helpless on her back. Bedsores developed and were very painful. She accused the nursing staff of negligence.

In 1966 she made an abortive attempt to claim damages, but her legal aid certificate was discharged after negative advice from Counsel. In 1973 she was encouraged through the Multiple Sclerosis Society to renew her claim. She obtained legal aid again.

In February 1975 she was granted leave to proceed under the Limitation Act 1963 and issued a writ alleging negligence by Lewisham Hospital. Pleadings were closed in July 1975. In November 1975 the hospital gave particulars of its defence and served on the plaintiff a request for further and better particulars. These were never supplied. Nine months later, in September 1976, she changed her solicitors. Subsequently she declined to travel to see her medical expert at Stoke Mandeville Hospital. The case was not set down for trial.

In March 1977 the defendants issued a summons to dismiss for want of prosecution. The Master granted it, but on appeal the judge (Sir Norman Richards) allowed the action to proceed.

Held: the defendants' appeal was allowed.

Per Lord Denning MR: "Prejudice to a defendant by delay is not to be found solely in the death or disappearance of witnesses or their fading memories or in the loss or destruction of records. There is much prejudice to a defendant in having an action hanging over his head indefinitely, not knowing when it is going to be brought to trial. Like the prejudice to Damocles when the sword was suspended over his head at the banquet . . .

"Likewise the hospital here. There comes a time when it is entitled to have some peace of mind and to regard the incident as closed. It should not have to keep in touch with the nurses: saying 'We may need you to give evidence'; or to say to the finance department: 'We ought to keep some funds in reserve in case this claim is persisted in'; or to say to the keepers of records: 'Keep these files in a safe place and don't destroy them as we may need them'. It seems to me that in these cases this kind of prejudice is a very real prejudice to a defendant when the plaintiff is guilty of inordinate and inexcusable delay since the issue of the writ: and that it can properly be regarded as more than minimal. And when this prejudice is added to the great and prejudicial delay before writ (as the House of Lords says it may be: see *Birkett* v *James*) then there is sufficient ground on which to dismiss the action for want of prosecution.

"Applying this principle, I am clearly of opinion that this action should be dismissed for want of prosecution. It would be an intolerable injustice to the hospital—and to the nurses and staff—to have to fight it out twelve years after the incident—when they quite reasonably regarded it as closed eleven years ago. . .

"One word more. It is, I believe, accepted on all hands, that if the plaintiff is guilty of inordinate and inexcusable delay before issuing the writ, then it is his duty to proceed with it with expedition after the issue of the writ. He must comply with the Rules of Court and do everything that is reasonable to bring the case quickly for trial. Even a short delay after the writ may in many circumstances be regarded as inordinate and inexcusable: and give a basis for an application to dismiss for want of prosecution. So in the present case the delay of nine months was properly admitted to be inordinate and inexcusable. "It is a serious prejudice to the hospital to have the action hanging over its head even for that time. On this simple ground I think this action should be dismissed for want of prosecution. I would allow the appeal, accordingly".

See pages 93, 127.

Blackburn v Newcastle-upon-Tyne Health Authority (No.1)

Substandard treatment: nurses: cardiac arrest

Lawton J. (1988) PMILL Vol 4 No 7

On 30 September 1976 the plaintiff (Keith Blackburn), then aged thirty-four, entered the Newcastle General Hospital. He was suffering from pneumonia and pleurisy and was admitted to the Intensive Care Unit. From the start he had difficulty with his breathing. On 4 October a tracheostomy tube was inserted by means of a hole in his windpipe. On 5 and 6 October it was noted that large amounts of thick blood-stained sputum were being sucked out. The 6 October note read "tracheostomy tube appears to be crusted, requiring a lot of humidification". On 7 October the plaintiff's lips became blue, meaning that not enough oxygen was getting through. On 8 October he suffered a cardiac arrest. The registrar who was called to attend ordered the removal of the tracheal tube and noted "Old tube blocked with blood-stained se-cretions".

The plaintiff had suffered severe brain damage. He was left grossly disabled in thought, movement and speech, and with a childlike personality. He sued the hospital authority.

Held: the hospital staff had been negligent. By the evening of 7 October it should have been clear that not enough oxygen was getting to the plaintiff's brain. The tube had started to get crusted up on 7 October, but the crusting was not removed before 3.25pm on 8 October. The nursing and medical staff should have been alive to the danger of the tracheal tube becoming blocked. Someone had not sucked it out as regularly or frequently as (s)he should have done.

See page 77.

Blackburn v Newcastle Area Health Authority (No. 2)

Substandard treatment: cardiac arrest: damages: Court of Protection

Owen J. [1988] QBD 1 August

The plaintiff (Keith Blackburn) suffered severe brain damage in October 1976. He successively instructed three firms of solicitors who issued his writ in 1979 but failed to make substantial progress with his case. A fourth firm took over in 1986 and pursued the case to a trial on liability in October 1987. Lawton J found that the defendant health authority had been negligent.

At the subsequent hearing on quantum some heads of damages were agreed but there were areas of dispute over, *inter alia*, the Receiver's fees and interest.

Held: (i) as the defendants had caused the plaintiff's mental incapacity, they must compensate him for both the Court of Protection charges and the Receiver's fees. The family was entitled to appoint a solicitor as Receiver;

(ii) there had been gross delay. The case, if properly handled, should have come to trial in 1982. The period for interest on special damages should be abridged to six years from October 1976. General damages would attract interest from the date of service of the writ in 1981 to October 1984.

See page 121.

Blyth v Bloomsbury Health Authority

Contraceptive advice: risk disclosure: standard of care

Court of Appeal. (1987) PMILL Vol 3 No 2

In May 1978 the plaintiff (Mrs Blyth) was referred to University College Hospital for antenatal care. When she was admitted there in December 1978 for the birth of her baby, she received a vaccination against rubella and an injection of the contraceptive Depo-Provera. She suffered bleeding and menstrual irregularity due to the Depo-Provera.

Soon after the plaintiff received the rubella vaccine, Dr Burt, a member of the hospital staff, discussed Depo-Provera with her and told her of the side effect of irregular bleeding. Dr Burt did not tell her all the information available to the hospital which Dr Law had collated in her files. Medical experts testified that there was no need to do so.

The plaintiff sued the hospital authority and her general practitioner. The trial judge (Leonard J) found in her favour against the hospital authority.

Held: Dr Burt and the hospital were not negligent in failing to pass on more information. Irregular bleeding was the side effect that was known and recognized in 1978. The plaintiff was told about it. None of the expert witnesses suggested that the defendants were under any duty to provide her with the full picture of the information in Dr Law's files.

See pages 73–74.

Bolam v Friern Hospital Management Committee

Standard of care: psychiatrist: risk disclosure: fractures: substandard treatment: ECT

McNair J (with jury). [1957] 2 All ER 118, [1957] 1 WLR 582

In August 1954 the plaintiff (John Bolam) was readmitted to Friern Hospital, a mental hospital. He was suffering from depression and on August 19 and 23 was treated for this condition by electro-convulsive therapy (ECT). ECT was carried out by placing electrodes on each side of the head and passing an electric current through the brain. If no relaxant drug is administered, one of the effects of ECT is to precipitate violent convulsive movements in the form of a fit in the patient, with muscular contractions and spasms attended by a very slight risk of bone fracture.

The defendants' doctors did not warn the plaintiff of the risks of the treatment. On August 23 the treatment was given to the plaintiff by Dr Allfrey who, in accordance with the hospital's normal practice, did not administer a relaxant drug or apply any form of manual restraint. The treatment was given to the plaintiff while he was lying on the couch. Dr Allfrey's precautions were to support his chin, to hold his shoulders and to place a gag in his mouth, while the nurses were present on either side of the couch to prevent him from falling off. He suffered bilateral fractures of the acetabula.

The plaintiff alleged that the defendants were negligent in:

(a) failing to administer to him, before the current was passed through his brain, a suitable relaxant and/or drugs;

(b) failing to provide sufficient manual control of his convulsive movements while undergoing the fit; and

(c) failing to warn him of the risks he was running when he consented to the treatment.

Expert witnesses agreed that there was a large body of competent medical opinion that was opposed to the use of relaxant drugs and that it was also the view of some competent and respected doctors that the more restraint there was the more likelihood there was of fracture. The plaintiff's expert thought that a patient should be warned of the risk of fracture, but the defendants' doctors took the view that it was not desirable to warn a patient of the risk unless he asked about it.

Held: In directing the jury, McNair J stated:

". . where you get a situation which involves the use of some special skill or competence, then the test as to whether there has been negligence or not is not the test of the man on the top of a Clapham omnibus, because he has not got this special skill. The test is the standard of the ordinary skilled man exercising and professing to have that special skill. A man need not possess the highest expert skill; it is a well established law that it is sufficient if he exercises the ordinary skill of an ordinary competent man exercising that particular art.

"A doctor is not guilty of negligence if he has acted in accordance with a practice accepted as proper by a responsible body of medical men skilled in that particular art. . . Putting it the other way round, a doctor is not negligent, if he is acting in accordance with such a practice, merely because there is a body of opinion that takes a contrary view". . .

When dealing with warning about risks, McNair J added:

"Having considered the evidence on this point, you have to make up your minds whether it has been proved to your satisfaction that when the defendants adopted the practice they did (namely, the practice of saying very little and waiting for questions from the patient), they were falling below a proper standard of competent professional opinion on this question of whether or not it is right to warn. . .

"If you do come to the conclusion that proper practice requires some warning to be given, the second question which you have to decide is: if a warning had been given, would it have made any difference? The only man who can really tell you the answer to that question is the plaintiff, and he was never asked the question."

The jury returned a verdict for the defendants.

See pages 7, 8, 25, 29–30, 33, 34–35, 36, 37, 68, 69, 70, 71, 72, 73, 74, 76, 83, 85.

Bonthrone v Millan and Others

Vaccine damage: causation: contra-indications

Scotland, Court of Session. [1985] 2 The Lancet 1137

A boy was born on 4 October 1975. When he was examined six weeks later, he was found to be very large but normal. On 25 February 1976 he had his first DTP vaccine. A six month report by a health visitor showed him to be normal but overweight. On 4 May a second dose of DTP was given. On 10 May he had a spasm and, after further fits, was admitted to hospital. When discharged on 22 June, he had greatly deteriorated and his brain damage was severe.

The vaccine damage tribunal accepted that probably his brain damage was caused by pertussis vaccine, so £10,000 compensation was paid to his parents under the Vaccine Damage Payments Act 1979. The parents also sued for negligence, alleging that after the first vaccine the baby began to vomit regularly about half an hour or more after a feed and that he began to move his left arm in an unusual way. They blamed the general practitioner for administering the second vaccination without asking about symptoms which had emerged since the first, and the health visitor for not reporting the symptoms to the GP's group practice.

Held: (i) the defendants had not been negligent. The health visitor had neither seen nor been told by the mother of the regular vomiting or the arm movements. Nor was it established that the GP had failed to ask reasonable questions before the second vaccination;

(ii) it was not proved that the second vaccination was the cause of the spasms and brain damage.

Per Lord Jauncey: "When about fifty per cent of infantile spasms and other encephalopathic symptoms occurring at this age are cryptogenic, it seems to me difficult to say that these symptoms are more likely to be attributable to vaccine than any one of the unknown causes".

See page 23.

Braisher v Harefield and Northwood Hospital Group Management Committee and Another

Diagnosis: casualty officer: X-ray: patient's history

Court of Appeal. [1966] 2 The Lancet 235

A piece of metal flew off a machine and entered the plaintiff's arm where it became embedded in fatty tissue. The plaintiff went to hospital where he told a nurse and the casualty officer that he had knocked his arm on some metal. The casualty officer examined the wound and inserted seventeen stitches, but he did not see the foreign body. Nor was its presence detected when the stitches were taken out. No X-ray was taken.

The plaintiff's arm continued to cause him pain. Eventually the foreign body rose to the surface and was removed. He sued the hospital authority and the casualty officer. The trial judge found that they had not been negligent.

Held: as the plaintiff said that he had knocked his arm, there was no negligence in not taking X-rays. The appeal was dismissed.

Lord Denning MR observed that in some of the earlier cases doctors had been criticised for not having X-rays taken, with the result that they were sometimes taken unnecessarily. This case showed that the court did not always find that there had been negligence because a patient had not had an X-ray; it depended on the circumstances of each case.

See page 89.

Brazier v Ministry of Defence

Injection: res ipsa loquitur: needle breaking

McNair J. [1965] 1 Lloyds Rep 26

In December 1956 the plaintiff (Reginald Brazier), a deep-sea diver, contracted an infected right hand while clearing up wrecks in the Suez Canal. He was treated in the sick bay of HMS Forth. When the sick bay attendant, Mr Bradbere, gave him by syringe an injection of procaine penicillin, the fine one and a half inch needle broke and lodged in the plaintiff's right buttock. In October 1960 it shifted to such a position in his groin that it caused him very severe pain and compelled him to give up his diving work.

The plaintiff sued the Ministry of Defence, alleging that Mr Bradbere held the syringe as if it were a dagger and plunged the needle into his buttock from a distance of twelve to eighteen inches, and that he failed to take proper care.

Held: (i) there was no stabbing by Mr Bradbere with the syringe held in a closed fist; the insertion of the needle was done in the proper recognized manner;

(ii) the evidence of the needle lodging in the plaintiff's right buttock required an explanation from the defendants as to how it could happen without negligence;

(iii) they established that it probably happened due to a latent defect in the shaft of the needle, not by some misalignment of the cylinder and the needle at the moment of insertion or during the process of injection.

Judgment for the defendants.

See pages 59, 78.

Breen v Baker

Consent: hysterectomy: assault: substandard treatment

Barry J. [1956] The Times 27 January

In November 1947 the plaintiff (Mrs Breen), who had had a fibroid in her uterus for years, suffered a heavy period and other symptoms. She consulted Miss Baker, a surgeon at Elizabeth Garrett Anderson Hospital. She signed a form consenting to an operation and which stated, "I agree to leave the nature and extent of the operation to be performed to the discretion of the surgeon". On 11 December 1947, after a dilatation and curettage, Miss Baker performed on the plaintiff a total hysterectomy.

The plaintiff sued Miss Baker for assault, alleging that the hysterectomy was performed without her consent, and for negligence in deciding to carry it out.

Held: (i) the plaintiff's consent was not limited to curettage, so there was no assault;

(ii) as the defendant was justified in diagnosing fibrosis from the curettings, she was not negligent in deciding to remove the uterus.

See page 67.

Brogan v Bennett

Alternative practitioner: standard of care: representation: tuberculosis

Irish Supreme Court. [1955] IR 119

From January to June 1950 Christopher Brogan was treated in County Longford Tuberculosis Hospital for tuberculosis of both lungs and made good progress towards an eventual recovery. Then there came into his hands a pamphlet entitled "T.B. CONQUERED by Mr J.H. Bennett. . .of Kelly & Bennett, Divining Specialists, Longford". His uncle and aunt visited Mr Bennett who produced a bullet on the end of a string, said he was going to "X-ray" the patient, caused the pendulum to oscillate and pronounced the case to be a fairly bad one. He said that he could guarantee to cure Christopher Brogan and make him fit for work in three months' time. He told them his fees were £100 for a rich person and £20 for a poor person. After negotiations, he agreed to take £20 by instalments for the cure of Christopher Brogan.

Mr Bennett insisted that he leave hospital forthwith and return home. He prescribed medicine combined with what was in effect a starvation diet and said that the patient was to have no other food. He never made any detailed enquiry as to Mr Brogan's symptoms; nor did he ever visit him to ascertain his condition. Christopher Brogan left the hospital against his doctor's advice, underwent the rigorous diet and took the medicine which Mr Bennett supplied. His colour became darker, and his face became larger. In September Mr Bennett pronounced him cured. In fact Christopher Brogan was emaciated, and the condition of his lungs showed gross deterioration. On 15 October he died.

His father sued Mr Bennett. The trial judge found as facts that: at no time did the defendant hold himself out as having any professional or academic qualifications in medicine; he represented himself as having special skill and knowledge in the diagnosis, treatment and cure of tuberculosis; in fact the defendant possessed no special skill or knowledge in the diagnosis or treatment of tuberculosis; the death of Christopher Brogan was directly due to his acceptance of the ignorant advice given him by the defendant and to his adoption of the deleterious treatment prescribed by the defendant.

Held: if a person is induced to become a patient of an unqualified person on the recommendation that that person is skilled, the latter owes a duty to use care in exercising the skill and administering the treatment which he has offered. He is not expected to employ the degree of skill which would be expected from a qualified man. He is only liable for failure to employ such skill as he said he had. The defendant was liable because he failed to manifest the skill that he professed in the treatment of tuberculosis.

See pages 28, 94.

Brown v Merton, Sutton and Wandsworth Area Health Authority (Teaching)

Childbirth: anaesthetics: quadriplegia: res ipsa loquitur: pleadings

Court of Appeal. [1982] 1 The Lancet 159

In January 1979 the plaintiff (Mrs Carol Brown) went into St George's Hospital, Tooting, to be delivered of a child. In the course of preparation for giving birth, she underwent an epidural anaesthesia. She felt severe pain when receiving the second dose of epidural and developed quadriplegia.

The plaintiff sued the health authority and relied on the maxim *res ipsa loquitur*. In the defendants' Further and Better Particulars of the Defence, "They admit that the maxim quoted is applicable. Enquiries are still being made in an endeavour to find out whether the onus of proof imposed by that maxim can be discharged by the Defendants".

Held: as the pleadings stood, there was no issue on liability; the only issue was as to damage. Therefore the correct order in respect of expert medical evidence was that the plaintiff and the defendants do mutually disclose their medical reports relating to the condition and prognosis of the plaintiff within a limited period, that such reports be agreed if possible, and that if those reports are not agreed the parties be at liberty to call medical witnesses limited to those whose reports have been so disclosed—limited to one witness by agreement.

Buckle v DeLaunay

General practitioner: prescription: warning: standard of care

Geoffrey Lane J. [1970] 2 The Lancet 145

In 1963 and April 1966 Mrs Buckle attended her general practitioner, Dr DeLaunay, for nervous troubles and depression. On 20 June 1966 she was more distressed and felt that she was going to die, so he prescribed parnate, to be taken three times a day in doses of ten milligrammes. He gave her his usual verbal warning about cheese and parnate, saying: "You must not eat cheese or marmite. That would be serious". Mrs Buckle understood the warning. However she proceeded to eat some cheese.

On 24 June 1966 she died in hospital as a result of a massive cerebral haemorrhage which was caused by the ingestion of cheese on top of parnate. The plaintiff (her husband) sued Dr DeLaunay.

Held: the danger of parnate reacting unfavourably with cheese was well known, so it was Dr DeLaunay's duty to warn Mrs Buckle of the dangers of eating cheese and to see that she understood the warning. He was under no duty to mention any danger to her, let alone the danger of death. The warning was adequate. Dr DeLaunay had not been negligent.

See page 74.

Bull and Wakeham v Devon Health Authority

Childbirth: hospital administration: limitation

Court of Appeal. [1989] 1 The Lancet 738

In 1969 a woman of twenty became pregnant. A twin pregnancy was diagnosed when she was admitted to hospital at 4.30pm on 21 March 1970. She was thirty-three weeks pregnant but her waters had broken thirteen hours earlier. One twin was "vertex in brim" and the other was a breach presentation. She was seen by a senior house officer who was new to the job and by a registrar with five years' experience.

At about 7.30pm the first twin was born. The S.H.O. asked for the registrar on call to be urgently summoned. Brisk vaginal bleeding indicated an emergency. The hospital's gynaecology department was over a mile away. When the registrar had not arrived after twenty-five minutes, the consultant was summoned. He came as quickly as he could, but an hour had by then elapsed since the birth of the first twin. The second twin (the plaintiff) was then delivered. He seemed hypoxic and pale. At eighteen months, profound mental disability and spastic quadriplegia were diagnosed.

His mother commenced court action nine years later. It took another eight years for the case to come to trial. Memories had long faded, and the consultant had died. The mother's claim for her own damages was dismissed as statute-barred. The trial judge (Tucker J) found in favour of the plaintiff. The hospital authority appealed.

Held: the hospital's negligence had caused the plaintiff's brain damage. The system of obstetric cover had given rise to a real inherent risk that an obstetrician might not have attended reasonably promptly after the birth of the first twin. There had been no proved explanation for the inordinate delay.

See pages 83, 87, 121.

Burke v Tower Hamlets Health Authority

Childbirth: caesarian: damages

Drake J. [1989] The Times 10 August

The plaintiff (Elaine Burke) sustained brain damage during a caesarian operation at the London Hospital. She applied for an order that her damages should take the form of periodical payments. The defendant health authority objected.

Held: the court has no power to order periodical payments instead of a lump sum, except where both parties consent. The order could not be made in the face of the defendant's opposition.

See page 101.

Burridge v Bournemouth and East Dorset Hospital Management Committee

Diagnosis: appendicitis: registrar: substandard treatment: causation

Cumming-Bruce J. [1965] 1 The Lancet 1065

At about 6.00am on 9 October 1961 the general practitioner to the plaintiff (Mr Burridge) sent for an ambulance and telephoned the hospital stating that it was an acute case of appendicitis. The plaintiff was put to bed in a ward. Soon afterwards his pain subsided. At 8.10am he was seen by the house surgeon who considered his symptoms and history insufficient to arouse suspicions of an inflamed appendix. He was examined during the day by the house surgeon again and twice by the surgical registrar.

At 10.00am on 10 October the plaintiff was examined by the surgical registrar. At 11.00am he was examined by the senior surgical registrar who at once diagnosed appendicitis and operated at 12.15pm, removing the gangrenous appendix.

The plaintiff sued the hospital authority, alleging that the delay in performing the appendicectomy permitted the appendix to rupture causing severe peritonitis.

Held: (i) it seemed probable that an acute obstruction of the appendix in the early hours of 9 October subsided but that the condition flared during the night of 9–10 October. There was no factor compelling a diagnosis of appendicitis while the plaintiff was in hospital on 9 October, and the hospital staff had not been negligent then;

(ii) the surgical registrar negligently failed to take any steps after 10.00am on 10 October. However the resultant delay of one hour did not cause any part of the damage.

Judgment for the defendants.

See pages 42, 62.

C and Another v S and Others

Abortion: foetus' rights: father's status: parental objections

Court of Appeal. [1988] 1 QB 135, [1987] 1 All ER 1230, [1987] 2 WLR 1108

In 1985 Mr C, a postgraduate student, met Miss S, a university student. In October 1986 their child was conceived. Miss S was X-rayed twice, on one occasion unshielded, before a scan showed in January 1987 that she was pregnant. In February her college doctor and a hospital consultant duly signed the certificate required under the Abortion Act 1967.

Mr C (the first plaintiff) applied on his own behalf and on behalf of the foetus named as "a child *en ventre sa mère*" (the second plaintiff) for orders restraining Miss S from having the abortion or harming the foetus and the area health authority from carrying out the abortion or harming the foetus. Miss S was at least eighteen weeks' pregnant.

His case was that termination of the pregnancy at that stage would involve a criminal offence under s 1(1) Infant Life (Preservation) Act 1929, the provisions of which are unaffected by the Abortion Act 1967. The medical evidence was that a foetus of a gestational age between eighteen and twenty-one weeks could be said to demonstrate real and discernible signs of life but, if delivered then, would never be able to breathe.

Heilbron J dismissed the applications and held that a foetus cannot until birth be a party to court action. The first plaintiff appealed.

Held: the foetus was not "a child capable of being born alive" within the meaning of s 1(1) of the 1929 Act. Accordingly the termination of the pregnancy would not constitute a criminal offence. The appeal was dismissed.

See page 31.

Caldeira v Gray

Injection: substandard treatment

Privy Council. [1936] 1 All ER 540, [1936] The Times 15 February

In March 1930 the respondent (Frederick Gray) was being treated in Trinidad for malaria by the appellant (Dr Caldeira). Dr Caldeira gave him a quinine injection by inserting the needle of a hypodermic syringe into his right buttock. Immediately Mr Gray got off the operation bed, he walked with a dropped right foot and had to cling to Dr Caldeira for support. Mr Gray was permanently lamed. He sued Dr Caldeira on the ground that he had travelled beyond the safe area for injection and injured his sciatic nerve.

Held: the trial judge's finding of negligence was upheld.

See page 79.

Canterbury v Spence and Washington Hospital Center

Risk disclosure: informed consent: prudent patient test: causation: foreign

U.S. Court of Appeals, District of Columbia Circuit (1972) 464 F 2d 772

In December 1958 the plaintiff (Jerry Canterbury), aged nineteen, began to experience severe pain between his shoulder blades. He was referred to Dr Spence, a neurosurgeon. In early February 1959 a myleogram was performed. Following this, Dr Spence told the plaintiff that he would have to undergo a laminectomy to correct what he suspected was a ruptured disc. The plaintiff neither objected to the proposed operation nor probed into its exact nature. When his widowed mother asked if the operation was serious, Dr Spence replied "not any more than any other operation". She signed a consent form. He did not tell either of them that there was a one per cent risk of paralysis inherent in the laminectomy operation.

Dr Spence performed the laminectomy on 11 February 1959 at the Washington Hospital Center. On 12 February the plaintiff fell from his hospital bed. A few hours after the fall, the lower half of his body was paralysed. He became permanently disabled.

The plaintiff sued Dr Spence and the hospital on the ground, *inter alia*, that Dr Spence negligently failed to disclose a risk of serious disability inherent in the operation. At the end of the plaintiff's case in chief, the trial judge directed that verdicts for the defendants be entered. The plaintiff appealed.

Held: (i) every human being of adult years and sound mind has a right to determine what shall be done with his own body. True consent is the informed exercise of a choice. This requires a reasonable divulgence by physician to patient to make such a decision possible. The physician must warn of dangers lurking in the proposed treatment and impart information which the patient has every right to expect;

(ii) any definition of the scope of the duty to disclose in terms purely of medical professional standards is at odds with the patient's prerogative to decide on projected therapy himself. The law itself must set the standard for adequate disclosure;

(iii) the test for determining whether a particular peril must be divulged is its materiality to the patient's decision. A risk is material when a reasonable person, in what the physician knows or should know to be the patient's position, would be likely to attach significance to the risk or cluster of risks in deciding whether or not to forgo the proposed therapy. The main factors are the incidence of injury and the degree of harm threatened. A very small chance of death or serious disablement may well be significant;

(iv) the issue of causation should be resolved on an objective basis: in terms of what a prudent person in the patient's position would have decided, if adequately informed of all significant perils. The patient's testimony on this is relevant but should not dominate the findings;

(v) the jury should be the final arbiter of whether Dr Spence's non-disclosure was reasonable under the circumstances. A retrial was ordered.

See page 70.

Cassidy v Ministry of Health

Operation: surgeon: vicarious liability: res ipsa loquitur

Court of Appeal. [1951] 2 KB 343, [1951] 1 All ER 574

The plaintiff (Michael Cassidy) was a fifty-six year old labourer when in 1948 he found that the little finger and the ring finger of his left hand were becoming stiff and bent inwards. His panel doctor, Dr Flanagan, diagnosed Dupuytrens contracture and sent him to Walton Hospital. On 8 April 1948 he was operated on there by Dr Fahrni, a full-time assistant medical officer of the hospital. After the operation a nurse bandaged his hand and arm to a splint. The plaintiff complained of exceptional pain and was seen by Dr Ronaldson, a house surgeon, who instructed that morphia be administered. On 12 April Dr Fahrni examined the hand and decided to leave the splint and bandage as they were. Thereafter the plaintiff continued to complain of excessive pain, but Dr Fahrni told him he must put up with it. When the splint was finally removed a fortnight after the operation, it was found that the plaintiff had lost the use of all four fingers which had become stiff and bent into the hand.

The plaintiff sued the hospital authority. The trial judge (Streatfield J) dismissed his claim.

Held: the evidence showed a prima-facie case of negligence which had not been rebutted. The defendants were liable whichever of their employees had been negligent.

Per Denning LJ: "When hospital authorities undertake to treat a patient and themselves select and appoint and employ the professional men and women who are to give the treatment, they are responsible for the negligence of those persons in failing to give proper treatment, no matter whether they are doctors, surgeons, nurses or anyone else.

". . . . . I think it depends on this: Who employs the doctor or surgeon? Is it the patient or the hospital authorities? If the patient himself selects and employs the doctor and surgeon, as in *Hillyer's* case, the hospital authorities are, of course, not liable for his negligence, because he is not employed by them. Where, however the doctor or surgeon, be he a consultant or not, is employed and paid, not by the patient, but by the hospital authorities, I am of opinion that the hospital authorities are liable for his negligence in treating the patient. . .

"If the patient had to prove that some particular doctor or nurse was negligent, he would not be able to do it, but he was not put to that impossible task. He says: 'I went into the hospital to be cured of two stiff fingers. I have come out with four stiff fingers, and my hand is useless. That should not have happened if due care had been used. Explain it, if you can'. I am quite clearly of the opinion that that raises a *prima-facie* case against the hospital authorities".

See pages 8, 10–12, 25, 58–59, 77, 87.

Chapman v Rix

Diagnosis: cottage hospital: general practitioner: communication

House of Lords. [1960] The Times 22 December

In October 1955 Edward Chapman, a butcher employed by Sainsbury's, was boning a piece of beef with a boning knife when the knife slipped and caused a wound in his abdomen. A telephone call for a doctor was made to Brentwood District Hospital, a general practitioners' (or "cottage") hospital. Dr Rix received the call and promptly went to Sainsbury's shop. He felt around the wound and decided that it was glancing, forming the view that the knife had not penetrated the abdominal wall. At the hospital he conducted a further examination with a probe, told Mr Chapman that the wound was superficial and sent him home with emphatic instructions to see his own doctor, Dr Moore, that evening and to tell him what had happened and what had been done.

When Dr Moore called, Mr Chapman complained of stomach pains and nausea. Dr Moore did not know that Brentwood Hospital was a general practitioners' hospital and was under the impression that the diagnosis of a superficial wound had emanated from the casualty department of a fully staffed hospital. Consequently he thought Mr Chapman was suffering from a digestive disorder and prescribed liquid paraffin.

The next day Mr Chapman was worse. Dr Moore ordered him to be taken to Oldchurch Hospital where fulminating peritonitis was diagnosed. An operation was performed which revealed a half-inch wound of the small bowel. Unfortunately the diagnosis had come too late and Mr Chapman died on 23 October.

The plaintiff (his widow) claimed damages against Dr Rix. The trial judge (Barry J) found that Dr Rix's diagnosis was wrong but not negligent, as it was extremely difficult to ascertain the depth of an abdominal wound. Nor was Dr Rix negligent in not sending Mr Chapman to hospital, since close observation could be carried out at home by a nurse or a relation apprised of symptoms for which he or she must watch. However he considered that Dr Rix was negligent in not contacting Dr Moore to inform him of the exact nature of his findings.

Held: Dr Rix had given the patient emphatic instructions (which were carried out), an object of which must have been to guard, by observation, against the outside chance that penetration of the peritoneal cavity had occurred. If he had contacted Dr Moore direct, it was doubtful that he would have told him more than that after observation and probing he had concluded that there was no penetration. Dr Rix was not liable.

See pages 25, 63, 90.

Chatterton v Gerson and Another

Risk disclosure: consent: battery: causation: pain relief: anaesthetics

Bristow J. [1981] 1 QB 432, [1981] 1 All ER 257, [1980] 3 WLR 1003

In February 1974 the plaintiff (Miss Elizabeth Chatterton) underwent, at the age of fifty-five, a nylon darn repair operation for an inguinal hernia. Subsequently she suffered severe and chronic intractable pain around the post-operative scar in her right groin.

She was then referred to Dr Gerson, a consultant anaesthetist who ran a pain clinic at the Royal Sussex County Hospital. He advised an intrathecal phenol solution injection to block the pain. He told her that this would involve numbness over an area larger than the pain source itself, and might involve temporary loss of muscle power. The plaintiff consented, and Dr Gerson performed the operation in August 1974. After temporary relief the pain returned and she became numb down her right leg.

In February 1975 Dr Gerson put her name down for a repeat intrathecal block. He did not repeat his warning, simply telling her that the second operation would be a repeat of the first and she knew what to expect. In June 1975 the plaintiff had the second intrathecal phenol solution nerve block operation. Afterwards she continued to suffer acute pain in the scar area and could not tolerate clothing in contact with it. She also lost feeling in her right leg and could only move around with a stick.

She sued Dr Gerson and the East Sussex Health Authority for (i) battery, alleging that her consent to the operation was vitiated by lack of consent, and (ii) negligence, not in treatment, but in an alleged failure to give a reasonable explanation of the nature and implications of the operation.

Held: (i) (Battery) "It is clear law that in any context in which consent of the injured party is a defence to what would otherwise be a crime or a civil wrong the consent must be real . . . In my judgement what the court has to do in each case is to look at all the circumstances and say 'Was there a real consent?' I think that justice requires that in order to vitiate the reality of consent there must be a greater failure of communication between doctor and patient than that involved in a breach of duty if the claim is based on negligence. When the claim is based on negligence the plaintiff must prove not only the breach of duty to inform, but that had the duty not been broken she would not have chosen to have the operation. Where the claim is based on trespass to the person, once it is shown that the consent is unreal, then what the plaintiff would have decided if she had been given the information which would have prevented vitiation of the reality of her consent is irrelevant.

"In my judgement, once the plaintiff is informed in broad terms of the nature of the procedure which is intended, and gives her consent, that consent is real, and the cause of the action on which to base a claim for failure to go into risks and implications is negligence, not trespass. . . it would be very much against the interests of justice if actions which are really based on a failure by the doctor to perform his duty adequately to inform were pleaded in trespass.

"In this case in my judgement, even taking the plaintiff's evidence at its face value, she was under no illusion as to the general nature of what an intrathecal injection of phenol solution nerve block would be, and in the case of each injection her consent was not unreal";

(ii) (Negligence) the duty of the doctor is to explain what he intends to do, and its implications, in the way a careful and responsible doctor in similar circumstances would have done. Dr Gerson did not fall short of his duties in this respect. Moreover the plaintiff had not proved that, even if she had been further informed, she would have chosen not to have the operation since the whole picture was of a lady desperate for pain relief.

Her action failed both in battery and in negligence.

See pages 3, 4, 5, 42, 68, 69–70.

Chaunt v Hertfordshire Area Health Authority

Sterilisation (failed): registrar: abortion: hysterectomy: damages

Park J. (1982) 132 NLJ 1054

In February 1973 the plaintiff, who had a complicated gynaecological history, was admitted to hospital for a laparoscopic sterilisation. This operation was performed by a registrar on the misunderstanding that it was not a difficult case. In or about June 1974 she became pregnant. In August 1974 the pregnancy was terminated and a laparoscopic sterilisation was performed by a consultant in private practice. She experienced some pain for two to three days following the sterilisation. Later her periods became painful and their frequency increased. On finding also that fibroids were present in her uterus, her doctor and specialist advised vaginal hysterectomy.

The hysterectomy was performed in July 1975. Afterwards the plaintiff suffered intraperitoneal bleeding which the defendants failed to detect for five days. On 6 July a laparotomy was performed and two and a half litres of blood were sucked from her abdominal cavity. On 8 July she was transferred to Hammersmith Hospital where the diagnosis was "post-operative bacteriods infection with septacaemia, general peritonitis, bronchopneumonia and pleurisy".* She was on artificial respiration in intensive care and was finally discharged on 11 September 1975. In January 1977 she was readmitted to Hammersmith Hospital because of pelvic infection. She was treated with antibiotics but continued to have periodical bouts of pelvic infection thereafter.

Held (February 1982): (i) general damages of £2,000 were awarded for the negligent sterilisation, for the unwanted pregnancy and the two further operations in August 1974. However no damages were awarded for the hastened hysterectomy, since the plaintiff would have needed this anyway at some stage;

(ii) general damages of £5,000 were awarded in respect of the negligent after-care following the hysterectomy for the septicaemia etc and bouts of pelvic infection.

*N.B. This quotation is reproduced intact from the law report, although the authors are advised that the normal formulation would be "post-operative bacterial infection with septicaemia".

See page 84.

Chin Keow v Government of Malaysia and Another

Injection: penicillin: patient's history: standard of care

Privy Council. [1967] 1 WLR 813

In April 1960 Madam Chu Wai Lian, an amah employed at a social hygiene clinic in Kuala Lumpur, spoke to the staff nurse there about an ulcer on her right ankle and swollen glands in her thigh. The nurse took her to Dr Devadason, the medical officer in charge of the clinic. After he had examined her, she was given an injection of procaine penicillin from which she died within an hour. Her mother, the appellant, claimed damages.

In 1958 the deceased had been given a penicillin injection from which she suffered adverse reactions. This led to her outpatient card being endorsed with the warning "allergic to penicillin". Dr Devadason did not enquire into her medical history and ascertain this. He admitted that he knew of the possibility of a person developing hypersensitivity to penicillin after a previous injection and that he had been told by the nurse that the deceased had had a penicillin injection some years ago. He testified that he carried on because he had had no mishaps before.

Held: the test of negligence, as propounded in *Bolam* v *Friern Hospital Management Committee*, was based on the standard of the ordinary competent practitioner exercising ordinary professional skill. Consequently, evidence from witnesses of the highest professional standing or references to writings of distinguished medical authorities were not necessary. The evidence of medical witnesses at the trial made it clear that Dr Devadason was negligent in failing to make appropriate enquiry before causing the penicillin injection to be given.

See pages 36, 89.

Clark v MacLennan and Another

Operation: surgeon: departing from orthodox practice: standard of care

Peter Pain J. [1983] 1 All ER 416

On 11 June 1975 the plaintiff (Jacqueline Clark) gave birth to her first child at the John Radcliffe Hospital in Oxford. Within two days she was found to be suffering from stress incontinence. On 1 July Professor Turnbull and his senior registrar, Mr MacLennan, decided that an anterior colporrhaphy operation was desirable. Mr MacLennan performed this operation on 10 July, four weeks after the birth. A substantial haemorrhage occurred, and the repair initially effected by the operation later broke down. Despite two subsequent operations, the plaintiff's stress incontinence became permanent.

She sued Mr MacLennan and the Oxfordshire Area Health Authority. The complaint pursued at trial was that the operation was performed too soon. There was a general practice among gynaecologists that an anterior colporrhaphy should not be ordinarily performed until at least three months after birth, partly because time might heal and partly to reduce the risk of haemorrhage and breakdown of the operation.

Held: the departure from standard gynaecological practice was unjustified, and the defendants were in breach of their duty of care. Judgment for the plaintiff.

See pages 25, 39–40, 49, 98–99.

Clarke v Adams

Physiotherapist: burns: warning

Slade J. (1950) 94 SJ 599

The plaintiff (Mr Clarke) was treated by Mr Adams, a physiotherapist, for a fibrositic condition of his left heel. Before applying the treatment, Mr Adams warned him: "When I turn on the machine I want you to experience a comfortable warmth and nothing more; if you do, I want you to tell me." As a result of the treatment, the plaintiff suffered injury by burning which led to his left leg being amputated below the knee.

Held: the apparatus was not defective but it was dangerous because burns caused by it could lead to serious consequences. There should have been a warning of danger, to the effect that the plaintiff's safety depended on his informing Mr Adams the moment he felt more than a comfortable warmth. Judgment for the plaintiff.

See pages 13, 25, 38.

Clarke and Another v Worboys and Others

Burns: cancer: mastectomy: res ipsa loquitur

Court of Appeal. [1952] The Times 18 March

In January 1947 the plaintiff (Mrs Helena Clarke) was found to be suffering from carcinoma of the breast. Consequently in February 1947 she underwent an operation at the Luton and Dunstable Hospital for removal of her right breast. The operation was successful, but as extensive bleeding was expected electro-coagulation was applied. This involved the passing of a high-frequency alternating current through the patient's body via a pad placed on her right buttock. A severe burn was caused on this buttock, which caused permanent injury to the muscles.

The plaintiff sued the hospital authorities. Her case was that the hospital staff had not prepared the rod properly by moistening it in a saline solution before application. The trial judge (McNair J) dismissed the claim.

Held: this was a case of *res ipsa loquitur*. The accident was one of a kind which did not normally happen if reasonable care was used, and the evidence was that, if the apparatus was applied properly, burning was unknown. The hospital staff were negligent.

See pages 59, 85.

Coles v Reading and District Hospital Management Committee and Another

Cottage hospital: communication: warning: general practitioner

Sachs J. (1963) 107 SJ 115, [1963] The Times 31 January

Mr Coles, aged twenty-one, went to a cottage hospital after a lump of coal fell on his finger at work and severely crushed it. A nurse cleaned and covered his wound and told him to go to Battle Hospital for further treatment. He did not go, either because it was not clearly explained to him or because he was suffering from shock. Instead, the next day he saw his own doctor who did not ask what had happened at the hospital but simply redressed the wound. No anti-tetanus injection was given to him. He died of toxaemia due to tetanus infection. His father claimed damages.

Held: (i) it was well known that, in cases such as this, failure to take anti-tetanus injection precautions could cause death. It was for the cottage hospital to give the anti-tetanus injection or to ensure that the patient got proper treatment. Mr Coles should have been given a document to take to Battle Hospital, stating what had been done and what should be done, with particular reference to anti-tetanus injections. Even if Mr Coles had realised that he had to go to Battle Hospital, but was not told of the importance of going or the danger in failing to do so, the hospital authorities would still have been negligent;

(ii) Mr Coles' doctor probably assumed that the hospital had done everything necessary, but he should have made some enquiries. Even if the doctor had considered giving an anti-tetanus injection and decided that it was not necessary, he would have been neglecting elementary precautions. He too was negligent.

See pages 25, 90, 91.

Collins v Hertfordshire County Council and Another

House surgeon: negligent prescription: anaesthetics: hospital administration: pharmacist: consultant: vicarious liability

Hilbery J. [1947] 1 KB 598, [1947] 1 All ER 633

In April 1945 James Collins had an extensive growth on his jaw which required a serious operation. This was performed at the Wellhouse Hospital in Barnet by Mr Hunt, a visiting surgeon employed part-time by the hospital. The hospital also employed as a full-time resident junior house surgeon Miss Knight, a final year student who had passed her examination in pharmacology but who was not then a qualified doctor.

The evening before the operation Miss Knight telephoned Mr Hunt to ascertain his orders. He ordered for Mr Collins 1 per cent procaine with 1–200,000th adrenalin. Miss Knight misheard procaine as cocaine. She went to the hospital pharmacist without any written order and told him to make up 1 per cent cocaine with the usual quantity of adrenalin. He dispensed to her 1 per cent cocaine with 1–20,000th adrenalin. Mr Hunt omitted to check that the solution was correct and so injected into Mr Collins a lethal dose which killed him. His widow claimed damages.

Held: (i) the hospital authority was responsible for the hospital's dangerous and negligent system in the provision of drugs, whereby an unqualified person was able to obtain a dispensation for an extraordinary quantity of a dangerous drug without any prescription or order signed by a qualified person, and for the pharmacist's negligence in participating in this and failing to verify the order;

(ii) the hospital authority was also vicariously liable for Miss Knight's negligence as an employed resident junior house surgeon, but not for the negligence of Mr Hunt as visiting surgeon;

(iii) liability for the damages was apportioned equally between the hospital authority and Mr Hunt.

N.B. It is submitted that, following the cases of *Cassidy* v *Ministry of Health* and *Roe* v *Minister of Health*, the hospital authority would now be held vicariously liable for Mr Hunt's negligence.

See pages 25, 80.

Colston v Frape

Chiropodist: diagnosis: substandard treatment: advice

Barnstaple County Court. [1941] 1 The Lancet 490

The plaintiff (Mrs Colston) visited Mr Frape, a chiropodist, for treatment for corns. She knew he was a chiropodist and not a surgeon. He advised her that her toes needed treatment. When she returned to him for this purpose, he took her foot in both hands and twisted and jerked it. She suffered pain and was unable to walk as well as before. The plaintiff sued Mr Frape for damages for negligence.

Held: Mr Frape had been negligently wrong, either in his diagnosis or in the action taken to remedy the trouble diagnosed; "if he did not know, he ought to have advised Mrs Colston to see a doctor".

Connolly v Camden and Islington Area Health Authority

Anaesthetics: overdose: damages: brain damage

Comyn J. [1981] 3 All ER 250

In August 1976, when he was seventeen days old, the plaintiff (Liam Connolly) was to undergo an operation at University College Hospital. He was given a serious overdose of anaesthetic.

He was reduced to being very severely mentally abnormal. He became subject to epilepsy. He was doubly incontinent. He could walk up to a maximum of one hundred yards, falling over frequently. He had a squint attributable to his brain damage. He was only capable of speaking a few words. He would never be able to work or marry and required constant care and supervision. He had feelings of affection and would become aware of his plight.

The plaintiff sued the hospital authority who admitted liability. When his case came to trial, he was aged four and three-quarters, and was expected to live to twenty-seven and a half.

Held: (i) general damages (April 1981) for pain, suffering and loss of amenities were assessed at £50,000;

(ii) the appropriate multiplier for cost of future care was 13¼;

(iii) on an agreed loss of earnings figure of £3,000 per annum, £7,500 was awarded for loss of the plaintiff's earnings during his shortened life span;

(iv) he was entitled to claim damages for loss of earnings during the lost years of his life, but on the material before the court this claim was assessed at nil.

The total award was £220,007.

See pages 81, 103, 105.

Connolly v Rubra

General practitioner: diagnosis: advice: tuberculosis: tests: second opinion

Court of Appeal. [1937] 1 The Lancet 1005

In December 1930 Matthew Connolly suffered from an attack of coughing and called in Dr Rubra. He told him that his coughing was severe and accompanied by spasmodic attacks, that he had a raised temperature at night and spat blood which formed streaks in the sputum, that he had lost weight, and that in July 1929 he had had an attack of haemoptysis while bathing. He suffered from considerable bronchitis and when Dr Rubra was called in, was spitting so much blood that he kept a bowl by his bed. Dr Rubra treated him for bronchitis, but did not advise any special diet or treatment and did not have the sputum examined. Mr Connolly's condition got gradually worse in 1931 and by February 1932 he was seriously ill. Dr Rubra continued conservative treatment and dissuaded him from seeing a specialist. When Mr Connolly was finally examined by a specialist in March 1933, it was found that he had tuberculosis from which he died.

The plaintiff (his widow) sued Dr Rubra who died before trial. Expert witnesses agreed that when there was blood in the sputum, tuberculosis could not be eliminated without further investigation. The trial judge (Greaves-Lord J) found that Dr Rubra had been negligent.

Held: if a general practitioner has any doubt whether or not there are signs of tuberculosis, it is his obvious duty to make further examination. If he is not confident of his own judgement, he should call in an expert. To enable the expert's opinion to be of value, the doctor must take many specimens of the sputum, arrange an X-ray examination and continually watch the patient. Dr Rubra had done none of these things, so the trial judge's decision was justified.

See page 91.

Connor v Fison-Clarke

Dentist: substandard treatment: damages

Rose J. [1987] QBD 9 October

The plaintiff went to Mr Fison-Clarke as her dentist between 1974 and 1980. In 1975 he carried out extensive root therapy treatment and bridgework in her upper arch.

From about mid-1981 the plaintiff began to suffer symptoms due to malocclusion: the poor fit of the bridge in relation to the trimmed crowns and the teeth of the lower jaw. The temporo-mandibular joints had become deranged. She suffered pain and tenderness over those joints, aching at the sides of the head, headaches and pain and tenderness in the neck. This pain and suffering lasted until mid-1984. From mid-1983 she also suffered some cosmetic impairment due to receding gums. She had to undergo remedial dentistry until the summer of 1985. The remedial treatment was more prolonged than should have been necessary due to the effects of years of malocclusion on the temporo-mandibular joints. She had continuing pain and discomfort in her right temporo-mandibular joint; it was possible that some of this might become permanent. She was aged forty-five at trial.

Held: (i) Mr Fison-Clarke was negligent in respect of the fit of the bridge in relation to the trimmed crowns on which it rested and in relation to occlusion within the lower teeth;

(ii) general damages (October 1987) were assessed at £4,000 for pain, suffering and loss of amenities. The plaintiff was also awarded £5,337 agreed special damages in respect of the cost of remedial treatment and other expenses.

See pages 87, 104.

Cooper v Miron and Another

Dentist: duty to inform of mishap: X-ray: causation

McCardie J (with special jury). [1927] 2 BMJ 40, [1927] 2 The Lancet 35

In May 1925 Edith Cooper, aged thirty, went to the National Dental Hospital to have three teeth extracted. The operation was undertaken under nitrous gas by Mr Davy, a third-year student, in the presence of Mr Miron, a registered dentist. During the operation, the crown of one molar broke off and disappeared down her throat. When she recovered from the anaesthetic, she complained to her sister of difficulty in breathing. However she was allowed to go home. No one at the hospital told her about the missing bit of tooth, and no arrangements were made for her further examination or treatment at the hospital. She contracted septic pneumonia, due to impaction of the piece of tooth in a bronchus, and died on 27 August.

The plaintiff (her mother) sued Mr Miron and the hospital superintendent.

Held: McCardie J directed the jury that one of the issues was whether Miss Cooper's life would have been saved if proper steps had been taken in time. Another was whether Mr Miron was guilty of negligence in not informing

Miss Cooper or her friends what had taken place and in not taking steps to ascertain where the broken piece of tooth actually was. There seemed to be no doubt what was the duty of a dentist when an accident of this kind happened. He must tell the patient what had happened, and must take steps, by X-rays, to locate the foreign body and to have it removed if it was in a place of danger to the patient. Yet Miss Cooper left the hospital with no idea what had happened, and nothing was said about it to her sister who was with her.

The jury found that negligence had been proved against Mr Miron and that Miss Cooper's death resulted from this.

See pages 26, 74, 87.

Cooper v Nevill and Another

Operation: surgeon: retained surgical product: res ipsa loquitur

Privy Council. [1961] The Times 10 March

Mr Nevill operated on the appellant (Mrs Rosetta Cooper) at a hospital managed by the Kenya European Hospital Association. He successfully performed a difficult emergency operation. However an abdominal swab was left in her body. Consequently she suffered for months much physical pain and acute mental distress and had to undergo another major operation.

Held: once it was undisputed that a swab had been left in the body, there must have been some mistake made by both Mr Nevill and the hospital authorities. Although there must have been some mistake, it did not necessarily follow that there was negligence. The whole team was engaged in a race against time. A mistake which would amount to negligence in a "cold" operation might be no more than misadventure in a "hot" one. But there was no evidence to suggest what kind of mistake this would be.

The trial judge was justified in finding: "If the pack was a mopping pack, it was negligence on the part of the person who used it, whether it was Mr Nevill or his assistant, to lose control of it and leave it in the body. If it was a restraining pack, having regard to the small number used and their obvious position, the absence of movement and the lack of any particular need for haste at the conclusion of the operation, it was negligence on the part of Mr Nevill not to remove it, the responsibility being, as he admits, upon him to do so, and there being no justification for the departure from the normal routine".

See pages 59–60, 82–83.

Corder v Banks

Plastic surgeon: after-care: operation: communication

McNair J. [1960] The Times 9 April

In 1952 the plaintiff (then Miss Stella Corder) was a twenty-nine year old typist. She was distressed at what she regarded as a disfiguring condition below her eyes. Mr Banks, a plastic surgeon with rooms in Harley Street, agreed to operate on her under a local anaesthetic on the basis that she would be an out-patient. The operation was correctly performed.

It was clear that the first forty-eight hours after the operation were of crucial importance as during that period bleeding might occur and, if it was not attended to properly, irreversible damage might result. Consequently proper directions had to be given to an out-patient by the surgeon, as were given by Mr Banks, and the surgeon or a properly qualified substitute had to be available to deal with any untoward developments.

On the first day after the operation Miss Corder suffered substantial bleeding from the stitches. This continued intermittently for a day or so. She telephoned Mr Banks' consulting rooms but he never learned of her condition. Prudent surgical practice required that the bleeding be dealt with properly by a skilled surgeon. The plaintiff suffered definite and marked facial disfigurement.

Held: if a surgeon who adopted a course of letting a patient go home and was relying on a telephone message from the patient to deal with an unexpected emergency that might arise, it was essential that the telephone should be adequately covered in the sense that messages would be received and transmitted to the surgeon. There was a failure by Mr Banks to keep his telephone adequately covered or a failure by those for whom he was responsible to inform him of the message. That failure amounted to professional negligence.

Corner v Murray

General practitioner: injection: needle breaking: res ipsa loquitur

H. H. Judge Tudor Rees. [1954] 2 BMJ 1555

In September 1951 the plaintiff (Arthur Corner) sustained a back injury at work. His general practitioner, Dr Murray, injected a local anaesthetic into the site of the injury. At the conclusion of the injection Dr Murray was about to withdraw the hypodermic needle from his body, when it broke off close to the mount. He was unable to extract the broken portion of needle and sent the plaintiff to the Central Middlesex Hospital. The piece of needle was removed there by operation the next day.

The plaintiff sued Dr Murray in the High Court, alleging that he had been negligent in administration of the injection. The case was transferred to the Brentford County Court. Expert evidence was given that the breaking of hypodermic needles was a not uncommon occurrence, the risk of which had to be accepted, and that this could occur without any negligence on the part of the doctor.

Held: there had been no negligence, or any semblance of negligence, on the part of Dr Murray. The plaintiff's case was dismissed.

See page 79.

Cox v Carshalton Group Hospital Management Committee

Child patient: nurse: supervision: burns

Court of Appeal. [1955] The Times 29 March

The plaintiff (Valerie Cox), aged thirteen, was a child patient at Queen Mary's Hospital for Children, Carshalton. She suffered severely from poliomyelitis. She could not move her legs at all or sit up without being propped up, and could just move her arms a little. The method that the nurses devised for giving her an inhalant was to prop her up in bed with pillows, put a pillow on her lap, and a tray on the pillow, on which stood the bottle, which did not move at all easily. That method was tried successfully under supervision for two months, the child putting her hands on either side of the bottle.

In December 1952 the night nurse woke the child at 6.30am and gave her the inhaler. The nurse then had to go to the sluice about ten paces along the corridor. While she was out of the room, the inhalation bottle, filled with scalding liquid, fell on to the plaintiff's legs.

The plaintiff sued the hospital authority. The trial judge (McNair J) dismissed her claim.

Held: the positioning of the inhaler was carefully and properly done. The more difficult question was whether the little girl ought to have been left alone at all while taking the inhalant with the boiling water in it, helpless as she was. It might have been negligence in the early stages before it had been seen that she could manage the inhaler. But the trial judge was right in holding that when she had managed it quite well herself for a couple of months it could not be negligence on the part of the nurse, who had all the children under her care, to leave the room for a few seconds.

See pages 25, 88, 93.

Crawford v Board of Governors of Charing Cross Hospital

Anaesthetics: blood transfusion: standard of care: medical literature

Court of Appeal. [1953] The Times 8 December

In 1950 the plaintiff (Robert Crawford) was admitted to Charing Cross Hospital for an operation to remove his bladder due to widespread growth of a tumour. He had only one effective arm (the left); the right had been useless to him since an attack of infantile paralysis long before.

The operation was performed in July 1950 and involved a transfusion of blood. The anaesthetist, Dr Clausen, kept the plaintiff's left arm extended at an angle of eighty degrees from the body so that the transfusion could be performed. Afterwards the plaintiff found that his left arm suffered a loss of power due to brachial palsy.

An article had appeared in *The Lancet* in January 1950 on the subject of the operation. Dr Clausen had not read this article. The trial judge (Gerrard J) in effect held that failure to keep himself familiar with the technical journals was negligence on his part. The testimony of the medical expert had shown no negligence by Dr Clausen.

Held: there was no evidence of negligence. It would be putting much too high a burden on a medical man to say that he must read every article in the medical press.

See pages 37, 39, 77.

Crivon v Barnet Group Hospital Management Committee and Others

Cancer: diagnosis: pathologist: standard of care: second opinion: X-rays

Court of Appeal. [1958] The Times 19 November

In May 1950 the plaintiff (Mrs Myra Crivon) was operated on at the Wellhouse Hospital for the removal of a small lump in her breast. A specimen taken was submitted to the hospital's assistant pathologist, Dr Cogman, who reported that it looked as if she had cancer. The report was put in a paper clip above her bed in hospital. She saw it, looked up the meaning of "carcinoma" and was very troubled.

On the basis of the report, Mrs Crivon eventually went to the Mount Vernon Hospital where she underwent deep X-ray therapy very intensively for a few weeks. It was then discovered that the original diagnosis of cancer was not agreed with by senior pathologists at the Wellhouse Hospital. Also the Mount Vernon pathologist reported that he did not think it was malignant cancer. The deep X-ray treatment was stopped. One of the sequels was that the condition of the skin had become marked and the surface destroyed. There were other potential hazards attendant on the therapy.

The trial judge (Hilbery J) dismissed the plaintiff's case.

The effective issue on her appeal was her allegation of negligent diagnosis. Professor Scarff, an eminent expert, had testified at trial that he would not even say that the diagnosis was wrong and that he might on that slide have come to the same conclusion himself.

Held: it was not negligent for a pathologist to appear to have come to a wrong decision which a great expert might himself have reached. A wrong diagnosis did not necessarily mean an unskilful or negligent diagnosis.

Once cancer was diagnosed, speed of treatment was essential. The mere fact that a second opinion was not taken and that there was no further check at Mount Vernon did not make out a case of negligence.

See pages 25, 63.

Croke v Wiseman

Cardio-respiratory arrest: brain damage: damages

Court of Appeal. [1981] 3 All ER 852, [1982] 1 WLR 71

The plaintiff (James Croke) was born in March 1972. In December 1973 he became feverish with symptoms of croup and was taken to Northwick Park Hospital. While the doctors were examining him there, he suffered cardio-respiratory arrest. This resulted in brain damage giving rise to blindness, paralysis in all four limbs, double incontinence and inability to stand or speak. His mother gave up work as a teacher for several years in order to look after him. He was aged seven and a half at trial in November 1979, and was expected to live to forty. The hospital authority admitted negligence.

Held: (i) the award by the trial judge (Michael Davies J) of £35,000 for general damages for pain, suffering and loss of amenities was correct;

(ii) the judge was entitled to take into account the fact that Mrs Croke would lose pension rights as a teacher and to award the plaintiff £7,000 for that as part of the costs of future parental care;

(iii) as the child's life expectancy was 32–33 years, the multiplier for the cost of future parental and nursing care should be reduced to 14 and the total award under this head to £119,000;

(iv) the plaintiff should be awarded damages for his loss of earnings during the period that he will live but not during the lost years of his life. The judge was justified in assessing this at £5,000 per annum, the national average male adult wage;

(v) The plaintiff's maximum working life from the ages of 18–40 would be 22 years, and, taking into account at least 11 years' accelerated receipt from the age of 7, the multiplier for future loss of earnings should be reduced to 5.

See pages 77, 103, 105, 106, 108.

Cronin v Islington Area Health Authority

Sterilisation (failed): risk disclosure: warning: causation

Caulfield J. [1987] 1 The Lancet 638

In May 1981 the plaintiff (Mrs Cronin) discussed with her consultant obstetrician the possibility of sterilisation. She was pregnant with her third baby who was due for delivery by caesarean section. The consultant suggested sterilisation to be carried out at the same time as the caesarean delivery. She consented, and this was done. The plaintiff and her husband subsequently took no precautions against pregnancy. In 1983 she gave birth to another baby.

The plaintiff sued the hospital authority. She alleged that she was not warned of the possibility of sterilisation failure and that, had she been warned, while she would have undergone the operation she and her husband would have used birth control afterwards.

Held: her claim was dismissed because:

(i) she had in fact been warned before the sterilisation operation of the risk of failure, both by the consultant and by the house officer who took her consent;

(ii) there was in 1981 no duty to warn a patient that sterilisation might fail, since at that time there was a substantial respectable body of medical opinion which would not have warned a patient in those circumstances;

(iii) the judge did not accept that the plaintiff, once sterilised, would have resorted to contraception.

See page 85.

Crossman v Stewart

Drugs: standard of care: contributory negligence: foreign

British Columbia Supreme Court. (1977) 5 CCLT 45

In January 1962, the plaintiff (Mrs Margaret Crossman) was referred to Dr Stewart, a dermatologist, in respect of a facial skin disorder. He diagnosed it as being discoid lupus erythematosus and prescribed a drug known as chloroquine or Aralen. The plaintiff continued to consult him until June 1962, and he gave her further prescriptions of the drug.

When her supply of the drug ran out, the plaintiff obtained a continued supply in an unorthodox manner. She was employed as a medical receptionist by another doctor and obtained the drug without a prescription from the salesman who supplied this doctor with his drug requirements. Dr Stewart did not know about this.

In December 1962, when attending a medical convention, Dr Stewart was alerted to the fact that in some case patients who had consumed the drug over long periods had suffered irreversible damage to the retina of the eye, causing blindness or near-blindness. Consequently in January 1963, he called in the plaintiff and referred her to Dr Johnston, an eye specialist.

Dr Johnston's report in February 1963 contained the following passages: "She gives a history of having had this medication for the past thirteen to fourteen months. . . slit lamp examination of the cornea revealed moderate central bilateral superficial keratopathy. . . Impression. Bilateral superficial keratopathy. . . which suggests a sequela of chloroquine therapy."

The plaintiff was informed that the results of Dr Johnston's examination were negative. From March 1963 to March 1965 she continued to take the drug without Dr Stewart's knowledge. In March 1965 she consulted him again and continued on chloroquine therapy under prescription from him until September 1965.

In April 1966 signs of retinal damage were found. In 1968 it was determined that this was irreversible. By 1971 the plaintiff was nearly blind. She sued Dr Stewart.

Held: (i) the standard of care, having regard to the inherent dangers involved in the use of the drug, must be very high. Dr Stewart had breached the high standard of care required through:

(a) failure to peruse carefully the report of Dr Johnston, which stated that the plaintiff had been taking the drug for over a year;

(b) failure to discern from the presence of corneal changes that the probability of recent consumption of the drug existed;

(ii) the plaintiff was guilty of contributory negligence in:

(a) obtaining prescription drugs from an unorthodox source;

(b) continuing to use drugs on a prolonged basis without obtaining "prescription" renewals;

(c) continuing to use the drugs on a prolonged basis without consulting the prescribing physician;

(iii) the plaintiff was two-thirds to blame and the defendant one-third to blame, so she was only entitled to recover one-third of the value of her claim.

See pages 54–55.

Cull v Butler and Another

Hysterectomy: consent: breach of contract: trespass to person: hospital administration

Lord Chief Justice (with jury). [1932] 1 BMJ 1195

In 1929 the plaintiff (Mrs Ellen Cull), who was prone to epileptic fits, became pregnant. Two of her previous three pregnancies had failed. Not being well, she saw Mr Butler at the Royal Surrey County Hospital in Guildford. He advised removal of her uterus. After discussion with her doctor, Dr Cranstoun, it was decided that she should undergo instead the operation of curetting. Dr Cranstoun wrote to the hospital, stating that curetting was desired and that she refused the major operation. His letter reached the hospital office but became detached from other papers relating to the case. It remained unseen by Mr Butler who proceeded to perform a hysterectomy. The plaintiff sued Mr Butler and the hospital authority.

Held: the jury found that:

(i) there was a negligent breach of contract on the part of the hospital authorities;

(ii) there was a trespass on the part of Mr Butler, through the hospital authority's negligence.

See pages 5, 67,118.

Cunningham v Camberwell Health Authority

Abortion: cardiac arrest: damages: Court of Protection: brain damage

Otton J. [1988] QBD 21 July

In January 1983 the plaintiff (Mrs Cunningham), then aged forty, was admitted to Dulwich Hospital for the termination of a pregnancy and sterilisation. An operation was carried out the next day to complete a spontaneous abortion. Immediately afterwards she had a cardiac arrest and a temporary failure of blood flow and oxygen supply to the brain.

The plaintiff suffered extensive brain damage. She had total loss of movement in her limbs. There was gross impairment of speech and communicative thought. She was unable to care for herself and required full-time care and supervision. She had a total loss of amenity, but was aware to some extent of her surroundings and still derived some pleasure from the company of her husband and three children. Her future life expectancy was fifteen years from trial.

She sued the hospital authority who admitted liability. Many heads of damages were agreed between counsel.

Held: (i) general damages (July 1988) for pain, suffering and loss of amenities were assessed at £75,000;

(ii) the appropriate multiplier for loss of future earnings and various future expenses was 8;

(iii) as the damages fund would be administered by the Court of Protection, whose charges formed part of the damages, the defendants were not liable to pay additional damages to cover the fees of independent financial advisers.

The total award was £655,126.

See page 81.

Daly v Wolverhampton Health Authority

Injection: scarring: damages

Deputy Judge Patrick Bennett QC. [1986] CLY 1050

The plaintiff (Miss Daly) was aged twenty-three when she developed a permanent neuroma on her thigh due to damage to a nerve and/or blood vessel caused by an injection at one of the defendant's hospitals. Initially she suffered bruising and blistering and required daily dressings for over six weeks due to discharge from the wound. By the time of the hearing four years later, she still suffered an aching or burning sensation in her thigh after walking for more than half an hour or standing for any length of time; this was likely to resolve eventually. She was left with a permanent round scar on her thigh, which was "visible, unsightly and nasty"; it embarrassed her and inhibited her from swimming or sunbathing.

Held (June 1986): general damages for pain, suffering and loss of amenities were assessed at £6,000.

See page 79.

Davies v Eli Lilly & Co and Others

Discovery: representative action: confidentiality: drugs

Court of Appeal. [1987] 1 All ER 801, [1987] 1 WLR 428

The plaintiff (Joy Davies) was one of over one thousand plaintiffs claiming damages for personal injuries due to Opren, the drug benoxaprofen. The first five defendants were the U.S. manufacturers of the drug and their U.K. subsidiaries (the "Lilly defendants"). The sixth and seventh defendants were the Committee on Safety of Medicines and the Department of Health and Social Security as the licensing authority under the Medicines Act 1968.

As the number and complexity of the documents to be produced on discovery

193

necessitated special assistance, the plaintiffs' solicitors engaged Mr Charles Medawar, a medical writer and journalist with a wide knowledge of medical and scientific specialities, to act as a specialist coordinator of the medical and scientific documents. The defendants objected to his being allowed to inspect their documents, on the grounds that he had published matter highly critical of the pharmaceutical industry in general and the Lilly defendants in particular.

Held: (i) in relation to the requirement of RSC O 24 r 9 that a party allow "the other party" to inspect the documents in his list, in the special circumstances of this extensive complex and important litigation, the previously recognized categories of agent should be extended to include someone doing the work described as being done by Mr Medawar;

(ii) on the additional evidence now available, Mr Medawar would not breach the duty of confidentiality and should be allowed to inspect the disclosable documents on giving to the court the following express undertakings:

(a) to preserve the confidentiality of the defendants' disclosed documents in terms which reflect what would otherwise be his implied obligation;

(b) not without the leave of the court or the consent of the defendants to publish or communicate anything (other than to the plaintiffs and their advisers) about the drug benoxaprofen as manufactured or marketed by the defendants under whatever name or about the role of the defendants in marketing or licensing it, subject, however, to a right to publish such matter in written form not less than twenty-eight days after giving the defendants a sight of the terms of the intended publication unless restrained by further order of the court. This undertaking should expire on 31 December 1992 unless earlier varied by the court.

See pages 130–131.

Davies v Horton Road and Coney Hills Hospital Management Committee and Another

Disclosure of risks: consent: assault: warning: fracture: ECT

Hallett J. [1954] 1 BMJ 883

In June 1951 the plaintiff (Charles Davies) suffered from insomnia and throat trouble. His general practitioner referred him to Dr Logan at the Gloucester Royal Hospital. Dr Logan advised five treatments of electro-convulsive therapy (ECT). He told the plaintiff that there was a possible risk of fractures or of dislocation of the jaw. He said that there was a risk, but it was a risk worth taking. During ECT the plaintiff received a crush fracture of his eighth dorsal vertebra.

He sued Dr Logan and the hospital authority for damages for assault and negligence, alleging that he had not been warned that the treatment might result in injury. Dr Logan testified as to his warning and said that relaxants had not then been introduced.

Held: (i) Dr Logan warned the plaintiff appropriately about the risks of the treatment. There had been no assault;

(ii) the treatment was administered carefully and efficiently in the usual and proper way. There had been no negligence.

Davies (Joseph Owen) v Eli Lilly & Co and Others

Representative action: costs: drugs

Court of Appeal. [1987] 3 All ER 94, [1987] 1 WLR 1136

The plaintiff (Joseph Davies) was one of about 1,500 plaintiffs claiming damages for personal injuries due to taking Opren. About a thousand of the plaintiffs were legally aided. The plaintiff's action was selected for the purpose of giving directions applicable to all the actions. Hirst J ordered that any costs incurred by the plaintiff in a lead action should be borne proportionately by each of the plaintiffs in the other actions.

Held: RSC O 62 r 3(3), which stated the normal rule that costs should "follow the event", did not preclude the order made. It meant that the costs discretion be exercised "according to who wins" and did not prohibit an exercise of the discretion before the end of the case.

Per Sir John Donaldson MR: "Put simply, but for present purposes wholly accurately, legal aid helps out those who lose cases, not those who win them. Legal aid makes 'out and out' grants to those who lose cases. It only makes loans to those who win them".

Davis v City and Hackney Health Authority

Childbirth: limitation

Jowitt J. (1989) PMILL Vol 5 No 6

The plaintiff (Mr Davis) was born a spastic in June 1963. He could only move with considerable difficulty, and his speech was seriously affected. When he was about seventeen, he asked his mother what caused this. She replied that she thought his delivery might have been mishandled but discouraged him from claiming damages. In February 1983 he left his home to live with other disabled people. In August 1985 he met in a pub a law student who advised him that something could possibly be done in his case. In September 1985 he consulted solicitors. On 26 November 1986 they received a report from Professor Taylor.

The plaintiff's writ was issued on 1 April 1987. His case was that his mother was given an injection of Ovametrin which caused his spasticity. The defendant health authority pleaded limitation.

Held: (i) the date of the plaintiff's knowledge for the purpose of s 11(4)(b) Limitation Act 1980 was 26 November 1986 or a few days after that when the contents of Professor Taylor's report were communicated to him;

(ii) in view of his disability, the plaintiff had not been delaying unreasonably in failing to take legal advice earlier than he did. Consequently he should not be fixed with any earlier date of knowledge under s 14(3). His claim was not statute-barred.

Per Jowitt J: "I turn now to section 14(3). The test is an objective one. The question is, looked at objectively, when might he, the plaintiff, reasonably have been expected to acquire those facts referred to in paragraph (b) of subsection (3). In other words one applies an objective test, but it is an objective test applied to the kind of plaintiff I am here dealing with, with his disability, and looking at his age and his circumstances and the difficulties he has faced".

See pages 119–120.

Davis v London County Council

Nurses: anaesthetics: burns: vicarious liability

Lush J (with jury). (1914) 30 TLR 275

In October 1912 the plaintiff (Miss Davis) became a pupil in the "babies class" at Barnsbury Park elementary school. In November the doctor told her mother that an operation was necessary for the removal of her adenoids and tonsils. On the teacher's advice the child was sent to the Islington Medical Treatment Centre, and a fee of one shilling was paid to London County Council. The operation took place on 13 December. When the child was brought back to her mother, her face was swathed in bandages and her lips blistered. The nurse who brought her back told Mrs Davis that some of the anaesthetic had been spilled and had burned the child's cheek. The operation had been performed by one doctor at the centre, with a second doctor acting as anaesthetist.

The Islington Medical Treatment Centre was conducted by a number of Islington doctors under an agreement as to the treatment of schoolchildren with the London County Council, who paid contributions varying with the amount of work done to the children. The doctors provided the premises and had the power to refuse cases. The plaintiff sued the London County Council. It was admitted that anaesthetic had been spilled, but negligence was denied.

Held: (i) the jury found that the anaesthetist had not been guilty of negligence;

(ii) Lush J stated that a contrary verdict would have imposed no liability on the London County Council, as it had discharged its duty to the plaintiff when it engaged competent professional men to perform the operation.

See page 10.

Dawson v Scott-Brown

Medical report: limitation: striking out

Court of Appeal. 18 October 1988

The plaintiff (Richard Dawson) was an able-seaman in the Royal Navy. Surgeon-Commander Scott-Brown reported on his medical condition. His reports led to the plaintiff being discharged from the Royal Navy on the grounds of mental ill-health in October 1974.

In July 1987 the plaintiff issued a writ, alleging negligence in relation to Surgeon-Commander Scott-Brown's reports and treatment. The Master struck out his Statement of Claim and dismissed the action.

Held: (i) the fact that the plaintiff was invalided out of the Navy on the ground of mental ill-health did not mean that he was incapable of managing his affairs, so the extension of time in s 28(1) Limitation Act 1980 did not apply;

(ii) the Surgeon-Commander took no steps to conceal what he was reporting. While he did not disclose the reports to the plaintiff, this was because it was to the Navy that the reports were made. Thus the plaintiff could not rely on s 32(1)(b) Limitation Act 1980.;

(iii) the Master was entitled to conclude that, since the limitation defence was almost inevitably bound to succeed, the action was an abuse of the process of the court and should be dismissed.

See pages 117, 121–122, 124.

De Freville v Dill

Negligent certification: psychiatric patient: duty of care: causation

McCardie J. (1927) 96 LJKB 1056

In 1917 the plaintiff (Muriel de Freville) married the son of a Gloucestershire vicar. The marriage became unhappy. In June 1926 she visited the vicarage where her husband and small son were staying. Her husband put her out of the house, so she re-entered by the servants' entrance. She was detained in the servants' hall while someone telephoned to summon Dr Dill, a Stroud doctor who was medical attendant to the vicar and his wife. When Dr Dill arrived, he spent a few hours with the plaintiff and telephoned the relieving officer who brought a certificate appropriate to the Lunacy Act 1890. Dr Dill completed and signed it, stating that the plaintiff "was a person of unsound mind and a proper person to be taken charge of and detained under care and treatment".

Consequently the plaintiff was taken to a Justice of the Peace who, without examining her or calling in another doctor, made a reception order. She was driven to Gloucester Mental Hospital where she spent the night. The next day the hospital decided no ground existed for her detention. She was discharged and sued Dr Dill for negligent certification.

Held: (i) the jury found that Dr Dill had not acted with reasonable care;

(ii) McCardie J held that Dr Dill owed the plaintiff the duty of reasonable care, even though he was never employed by her and had acted on behalf of her husband or father-in-law;

(iii) McCardie J further held that, notwithstanding the Justice's omissions, Dr Dill's certificate was the cause of the plaintiff's detention.

See pages 51–52, 64–65.

Department of Health and Social Security v Kinnear and Others

Vaccine damage: striking out: advice

Stuart-Smith J. [1984] The Times 7 July, (1984) 134 NLJ 886

Section 26 of the National Health Service Act 1946 had given the DHSS and local health authorities a discretion whether arrangements should be made to immunise people against diseases other than smallpox and diphtheria. Pursuant to this, acting in good faith, the DHSS had adopted a policy of promoting immunisation against whooping cough.

Victims of the whooping cough vaccine, who had suffered injury as a result of a reaction to inoculation, sued the DHSS, the manufacturers of the vaccine and the relevant regional health authorities. Their Statements of Claim were partly based on the department's formulation and promotion of its policy. They also alleged that the DHSS had given negligent or misleading advice to local health authorities concerning the circumstances in which such inoculations should be performed and the criteria to be applied in deciding whether an individual should be inoculated.

The DHSS applied under RSC O 18 r 19 to have the Statements of Claim in six actions struck out on the basis that they disclosed no reasonable cause of action.

Held: the policy could not give rise to a cause of action. It was within the limits of the DHSS discretion and the result of its bona fide exercise. Even allegations of negligence against DHSS employees—eg in failing to submit relevant reports to those taking the policy decisions—could not found a cause of action against the department.

However, steps of an "operational" rather than a "policy" nature were actionable if taken negligently. It was arguable that allegations about negligent and misleading advice by the DHSS as to the manner and circumstances in which immunisations were to be performed were in the "operational" category. Therefore these allegations would not be struck out.

See page 22.

Devi v West Midlands Regional Health Authority

Operation: surgeon: sterilisation: battery: consent: damages

Court of Appeal. 9 December 1981

In June 1975 the plaintiff (Sheela Devi), a twenty-nine year old Sikh, underwent at the defendant's hospital in Walsall an abdominal operation to repair perforation in her uterus. The surgeon performing the operation decided then and there to perform a sterilisation operation as the abdomen was opened, since he thought this to be in the plaintiff's interest. In fact, there had been no discussion with her as to whether a sterilisation should be contemplated. The defendants admitted liability for sterilising her without her consent.

The sterilisation caused her considerable shock and upset. It also prevented her from having two more children to add to the four she already had. In May

1980 the trial judge (Kilner Brown J) awarded her £4,000 general damages to cover these aspects.

The plaintiff had been emotionally upset since the operation. She suffered from total loss of libido, and had ceased to have sexual intercourse with her husband except on rare occasions. He had since died. She showed marked signs of hysteria, and a diagnosis of hysterical hypochondriasis was made. There was also an element of exaggeration. Improvement was expected. The trial judge awarded £2,750 under this head.

Held: there were no grounds for interfering with either the judge's assessments or with his total award of £6,750 general damages for pain, suffering and loss of amenities.

See pages 5, 67, 85, 118.

Distillers Co (Biochemicals) Ltd v Laura Anne Thompson

Drugs: warning: jurisdiction: thalidomide

Privy Council. [1971] AC 458, [1971] 1 All ER 694, [1971] 2 WLR 441

In August 1961, when Laura Thompson's mother was pregnant, her doctor in New South Wales prescribed for her Distaval, the principal ingredient of which was thalidomide. She obtained it from a chemist in New South Wales and took it. There were no warnings of danger on the printed matter supplied with the drug. In April 1962 Laura Thompson (the plaintiff) was born without arms and with defective eyesight.

Distillers, an English company incorporated in Great Britain, obtained the substance thalidomide in bulk from its German manufacturers and used it to manufacture the drug Distaval. They sold it to an Australian company which marketed it in New South Wales. The plaintiff sued both Distillers and the Australian company in the Supreme Court of New South Wales.

Held: (on appeal by Distillers): the alleged negligence of failure to give a warning that Distaval could be dangerous if taken in the first three months of pregnancy occurred in New South Wales and injured the plaintiff there. Consequently her cause of action arose in the New South Wales jurisdiction and she could sue Distillers there.

See page 28.

Dransfield v Rotherham and Mexborough Hospital Management Committee and Another

Fracture: operation: standard of care

Court of Appeal. 19 February 1976

The plaintiff (Colin Dransfield) suffered a fracture of his left humerus in 1922 or 1923. Metal plates were inserted to hold it in position and metal bands were put round the broken bone. Around 1960, suppurations from the arm developed. The plaintiff's general practitioner referred him to Rotherham

Hospital. He was seen there by Dr Murray who recommended an operation to remove the metal objects. Dr Murray performed this in April 1968. During the course of the operation, damage was caused to the radial nerve in the plaintiff's left arm and he suffered from a dropped left wrist.

The plaintiff sued Dr Murray and the hospital authority. His expert asserted that the radial nerve should have been exposed at the start of the operation. The defence expert and Dr Murray testified that the radial nerve was embedded in thick fibrous growth that had built up over the bone and that the proposed course would have been more dangerous than the one adopted.

Held: the trial judge (Pain J) was entitled to prefer the evidence of the defendants and to hold that Dr Murray did not fall in any way below the duty of a competent doctor in the circumstances. The fact that surgical operations involve risks and that in the course of an operation one of the risks materialises does not mean that those conducting the operation have been at fault. There was no possible ground for suggesting that the judge was wrong in holding that the defendants were not negligent.

Drummond and Another v Wonford House Hospital (Incorporated)

Psychiatric patient: supervision: breach of contract: substandard treatment

Avory J (with jury). [1928] 1 BMJ 287, [1928] 1 The Lancet 411

After the birth of her third child, the plaintiff (Mrs Drummond) had become obsessed with the idea that she had committed an unspeakable crime and had expressed intense dislike for her husband and children. On the advice of Dr Grant Wilson, she was removed to a mental nursing home in Exeter. Dr Grant Wilson told Dr Morton, medical superintendent of the home, of the suicidal tendencies exhibited by her. He said that she was extremely restless and agitated, and that she had delusions of persecutions and all the symptoms of acute puerperal melancholia. He suggested that she should enter the hospital as a voluntary patient but that if Dr Morton thought that was not safe he would certify her as a lunatic.

The plaintiff was watched unceasingly until her second night. Dr Morton then withdrew the night nurse and substituted visits every half hour. In the absence of a nurse, the plaintiff broke the glass of a window and forced herself through an aperture measuring less than ten inches square and through the bars guarding the window. She struck an iron balustrade and fractured her arm and jaw.

When the plaintiff recovered her mental balance, she and her husband sued the proprietors of the nursing home for negligence and breach of contract.

Held: Avory J directed the members of the jury that the defendants owed a duty to take reasonable care and to exhibit reasonable skill in the treatment of all patients admitted to their institution. They had to ascertain whether the defendants had been guilty of negligence and whether Dr Morton, knowing what he did, was right in withdrawing the night nurse on the second night.

The jury returned a verdict for the plaintiffs.

See page 88.

Dryden v Surrey County Council and Another

Operation: retained surgical product: nurses

Finlay J. [1936] 2 All ER 535

Dr Stewart performed a minor operation on the plaintiff (Mrs Dryden) at the defendant's hospital at Epsom. She remained in hospital for a week. Two days later she was examined by Dr Keble, her general practitioner, who extracted from her body a black evil-smelling sausage of surgical gauze. This was plugging that Dr Stewart left in her after the operation. She contracted pyelitis and cystitis.

The plaintiff alleged negligence against Dr Stewart and the hospital nurses. She claimed, *inter alia*, that she had a swelling which could be detected by anyone swabbing, that she had a profuse and foul-smelling discharge and that she was sent home without her temperature being taken. Both the hospital anaesthetist and Dr Stewart saw her several times after the operation. They saw nothing wrong, and she made no complaint to them. Dr Keble did not detect the discharge until he extracted the gauze.

Held: (i) Dr Stewart had negligently left the gauze in the plaintiff's body;

(ii) the nurses were not negligent. They had no reason to know that the gauze had been left in, so they were under no duty to remove it. As the plaintiff's temperature had pursued a normal course, it was unnecessary for them to take it again on the morning on which she left the hospital.

See page 82.

Dunning v United Liverpool Hospitals' Board of Governors

Discovery

Court of Appeal. [1973] 2 All ER 454, [1973] 1 WLR 586

In April 1963 the applicant (Mrs Florence Dunning) developed a cough and was admitted to the Royal Infirmary at Liverpool for further investigations. She became gravely ill in hospital and her personality changed. The doctors were at first uncertain of the diagnosis and treated her with different drugs. When she left hospital after seventeen weeks, her walking and memory were impaired and she was a different woman altogether.

In 1969 she was granted legal aid limited to getting a medical opinion. The hospital refused to disclose her clinical notes to her medical expert unless it was assured that no action would be brought against it. The assurance was not given, so the clinical notes were not produced. Her expert reported that his assessment had been considerably hampered by their absence.

The applicant issued an originating summons under s 31 Administration of Justice Act 1970. By it she asked for an order that the hospital should disclose the medical records and case notes that it had about her treatment.

Held: they should be produced to the plaintiff's medical adviser or such medical consultant as he should advise.

Per Lord Denning MR: "I think that we should construe 'likely to be made' as meaning 'may' or 'may well be made' dependent on the outcome of the discovery. One of the objects of the section is to enable a plaintiff to find out—before he starts proceedings— whether he has a good cause of action or not. The object would be defeated if he had to show—in advance—that he had already got a good cause of action before he saw the documents."

Per James LJ: "In order to take advantage of the section, the applicant for relief must disclose the nature of the claim he intends to make and show not only the intention of making it but also that there is a reasonable basis for making it. Ill-founded, irresponsible and speculative allegations or allegations based merely on hope would not provide a reasonable basis for an intended claim in subsequent proceedings."

See pages 129, 130.

Dwyer v Rodrick and Others

General practitioner: prescription: pharmacist: gangrene: apportionment of liability

Court of Appeal. [1983] The Times 12 November

The plaintiff (Mrs Joan Dwyer) suffered persistent pain in her neck. On 20 November 1973 Dr Rodrick diagnosed migraine and prescribed sixty Migril tablets, two to be taken every four hours as necessary. This prescription was a patent mistake. It was taken on the same day to the shop of Cross Chemists (Banbury) Ltd where a qualified pharmacist dispensed the tablets without noticing the error. On 23 November Dr Jackson, Dr Rodrick's partner, visited the plaintiff at her home. He did not have her clinical notes with him, so he did not know she had been prescribed Migril. He did not discover this on his visit and prescribed Stemetil for her complaint of vomiting. When Dr Jackson visited her again on 26 November he discovered that she had taken thirty-six Migril tablets in six days. She suffered gangrenous necrosis and loss of part of each toe, peripheral nerve damage and other serious injuries.

The trial judge (Stuart-Smith J) held all three defendants liable in negligence and apportioned liability at 45 per cent to Dr Rodrick, 15 per cent to Dr Jackson and 40 per cent to Cross Chemists. Dr Jackson appealed.

Held: Dr Jackson did not see the Migril bottle. He was not negligent in not finding out on 23 November that the plaintiff was taking Migril.

N.B. It had been agreed between counsel that, if Dr Jackson's appeal should succeed, Cross Chemists would accept the extra 15 per cent liability. Thus the final apportionment was 45 per cent to Dr Rodrick and 55 per cent to Cross Chemists.

See pages 80–81, 91.

Edgar v Lamont

Duty of care: breach of contract: substandard treatment

Scotland, Court of Session. [1914] SC 277

In June 1913 Mrs Jessie Edgar cut her finger. Dr Lamont was sent for. She was under his care for the next fortnight. She suffered great pain and finally had to have the finger amputated.

She sued Dr Lamont, alleging that this was due to his improper treatment. He argued that it was a claim for breach of contract and that his contract was with her husband who had agreed to pay for his services.

Held: Mrs Edgar was entitled to sue. A doctor owes a duty to the patient, whoever has called him in and whoever is liable for his bill, and it is for breach of that duty that he is liable.

See pages 7, 25.

Edler v Greenwich and Deptford Hospital Management Committee and Another

Diagnosis: appendicitis: casualty officer: general practitioner: causation: advice

Finnemore J. [1953] The Times 7 March

Iris Edler, aged eleven, became ill with abdominal pains and vomiting on Saturday 7 July 1951. She was ill throughout the night. On Sunday 8 July the plaintiff (her father) took her to the Miller Hospital in Greenwich where she was examined by Dr Hewlett-Clarke, the casualty officer, who was told about the pains and vomiting. When asked where the pain was, she put her hand over the middle of her stomach and moved it to and fro. She winced every time that her abdomen was touched on examination. The doctor then carried out a rectal examination and said afterwards that there was nothing wrong with the girl but if she got worse that day her father should bring her back to the hospital.

She remained ill. On 9 July her mother went to see the family's panel doctor, Dr Mehta, who, on being told what the hospital doctor had said, thought it was probably gastric trouble. On 10 July she got worse and Dr Mehta arranged her immediate admission to hospital where under operation there was found an advanced state of peritonitis and a ruptured and gangrenous appendix. The child died. Her father sued the hospital management committee and Dr Mehta.

Held: (i) Dr Hewlett-Clarke was negligent in failing to diagnose appendicitis. It was no defence to say that he told the father to bring the child back if she got worse, because the father was sent away with the idea that nothing was wrong. Everything that ensued was due to the faulty diagnosis;

(ii) as Dr Mehta was told that the hospital had said that there was nothing wrong, it was impossible to say that he was negligent. There was nothing that provided an excuse for Dr Hewlett-Clarke's negligence or a break in the chain of causation.

See pages 52, 62, 91.

Edwards v Mallan

Dentist: representation: breach of contract

Court of Appeal. [1908] 1 KB 1002

The plaintiff sued in the High Court, alleging as follows in her Statement of Claim:
"1. The plaintiff has suffered damage from the negligence and unskilfulness of the defendant as a surgeon dentist employed for reward by the plaintiff to extract one of her teeth.

2. The plaintiff in February 1907 was suffering from toothache, and went to the defendant to have a tooth extracted by the defendant's 'painless process', and on February 18 the defendant or his operator or other representative agent did extract the said tooth, but so unskilfully that broken portions of the said tooth were left in the jaw, whereby illness, pain and suffering were caused to the plaintiff."

Held: there was no allegation of a breach of contract to use a painless process. The action was simply an action based on unskilful dentistry. Thus it was an action in tort, not contract (and so could be remitted to the county court under s 66 County Courts Act 1888 (since repealed) if the plaintiff had no visible means of paying the defendant's costs).

See page 25.

Elkan v Montgomery Smith

Diagnosis: fracture: X-ray: causation

McCardie J. [1922] 1 The Lancet 548

The plaintiff (Mrs Elkan) injured her ankle in a fall. She consulted Dr Montgomery Smith. No X-ray was taken for a considerable time. She continued to place weight on her ankle. When an X-ray was finally taken, it showed that there had been a fracture of the lower end of the fibula, and of the lower end of the shaft of the tibia with partial dislocation backwards of the foot near the ankle-joint.

The plaintiff became lame and sued Dr Montgomery Smith, alleging that he had opposed X-ray examination and that his treatment had made her worse.

Held: (i) Dr Montgomery Smith had in fact recommended the employment of X-rays, and had diagnosed and treated the case with proper care;

(ii) the plaintiff's lameness was due not to the treatment but to her own conduct in over-working the ankle.

Judgment for the defendant.

See page 89.

Ellis v Home Office

Duty of care: prison inmate: supervision: segregation: psychiatric patient

Court of Appeal. [1953] 2 All ER 149, [1953] 3 WLR 105

In July 1949 the plaintiff (Mr Ellis) was in Winchester prison awaiting trial. Under suspicion of illness, he was in the hospital wing. One morning the only prison officer in attendance left the wing for a period. While he was away, a prisoner named Hamill went into the plaintiff's cell and hit him violently on the head at least twice with some implement. Hamill was convicted of unlawfully wounding the plaintiff.

In April 1949 Dr Fenton, the prison medical officer, had learned that Hamill might well be mentally defective. He kept him in the hospital wing for observation. However, when Dr Fenton examined Hamill he did not think that he was likely to commit an act of violence. Hamill did not have a previous record of such acts.

The plaintiff sued the Home Office for failing to segregate Hamill and failing to safeguard the plaintiff against him. The trial judge (Devlin J) dismissed the claim.

Held: the mere fact that Hamill was mentally defective did not make him likely to commit an act of violence. Dr Fenton had no reason to anticipate this. The plaintiff's case failed.

See pages 26, 88.

Emeh v Kensington and Chelsea and Westminster Area Health Authority and Others

Sterilisation (failed): wrongful birth: novus actus interveniens: damages: public policy

Court of Appeal. [1985] 1 QB 1012, [1985] 2 WLR 233

In May 1976 the plaintiff (Kathleen Emeh), a married woman who already had three healthy children, underwent an abortion and sterilisation operation at St. Stephen's Hospital. In January 1977 she learned that she was 18–20 weeks pregnant. She decided against another abortion. When her baby Elizabeth was born, it was found to be congenitally abnormal. The trial judge (Park J) held that the sterilisation operation had been performed negligently and in breach of contract.

Held: (i) the plaintiff's refusal to undergo an abortion was not so unreasonable as to eclipse the surgeon's negligence. Save in the most exceptional circumstances, the court should not declare it unreasonable for a woman to decline to have an abortion in a case when there is no evidence that there were any medical or psychiatric grounds for terminating the particular pregnancy. Consequently the defendants' plea of *novus actus interveniens*

205

failed, as did their argument that the plaintiff had failed to take reasonable steps to minimise the damage;

(ii) it is not contrary to public policy to recover damages for the birth of a child, whether healthy or abnormal;

(iii) the plaintiff was awarded:

(a) £3,000 for pain and suffering up to trial in December 1982;

(b) £10,000 for future pain, suffering and loss of amenity, including the extra care to be given to the child over the years;

(c) £7,000 for the plaintiff's loss of future earnings;

(d) £1,736 for the cost of maintaining the child up to trial;

(e) £507 per annum with a multiplier of 8 for the future cost of maintaining her;

(f) the cost of a second sterilisation operation;

(g) the cost of a layette (£248).

See pages 31, 52–53, 84, 114.

Everard v Hopkins

Substandard treatment: breach of contract: duty of care

Coke CJ (with Croke J). (1615) 2 Bulst 332

In December 1611 the servant of the plaintiff (Mr Everard) was hurt by a cartwheel. The plaintiff agreed with Mr Hopkins, a common surgeon, that Mr Hopkins would undertake the cure for a fee of five marks. The treatment caused the servant more pain and left him lame and unable to work.

The plaintiff sued Mr Hopkins, alleging that he had been negligent and had applied unwholesome medicines to the servant's wounds.

Held: the pleading was neither good nor formal. In view of the nature of the contract, the plaintiff ought to have pleaded that he had paid the money. The servant could not base an action upon the plaintiff's contract with Mr Hopkins, but he could bring a case for the negligent application of unwholesome medicines.

The court was inclined to be of opinion for the plaintiff, but as the pleading was defective no judgment was given. The case was adjourned and then settled.

Everett v Griffiths and Another

Psychiatric patient: negligent certification: standard of care

Court of Appeal. [1920] 3 KB 163

In early 1919 the plaintiff (Mr Everett), then aged twenty-three, was residing with his parents in Islington. On 21 March, following a complaint by his mother, he was removed to Islington workhouse and detained in the observation ward. On 24 March Dr Anklesaria, the medical officer of the workhouse, who had examined and visited the plaintiff several times and had watched him through the peep-hole, certified him to be insane and a proper person to be detained. Pursuant to the Lunacy Act 1890, the plaintiff was sent on 27 March to Colney Hatch mental asylum where he remained until his escape on 9 April.

He was subsequently accepted to be sane and represented himself in court with remarkable forensic ability. However the Lord Chief Justice entered judgment for the defendants.

Held: Dr Anklesaria was under a duty to the plaintiff to act with good faith and reasonable care. His good faith was accepted, and there was no evidence that he was negligent.

See page 65.

Eyre v Measday

Sterilisation (failed): breach of contract: risk disclosure

Court of Appeal. [1986] 1 All ER 488

In 1978 the plaintiff (Mrs Mary Eyre), then aged thirty-five, consulted Mr Measday, a gynaecological surgeon. It was agreed that he should carry out a sterilisation by laparoscopy. She was to undergo this on a budget scheme as a private patient who made a modest payment. Mr Measday performed the operation competently. However in April 1979 the plaintiff discovered that . she was pregnant, and in October 1979 she gave birth to a fine healthy boy.

Mr Measday did not mention that there was a chance of 2–6 in 1,000 that pregnancy might occur following the operation. He emphasised the irreversibility of the procedure. The plaintiff sued him for breach of contract or warranty to render her irreversibly sterile. The trial judge (French J) found in favour of Mr Measday.

Held: (i) the contract was a contract to perform a laparoscopic sterilisation rather than to render her absolutely sterile. The reference to irreversibility simply meant that the operative procedure was incapable of being reversed; it was not a guarantee that the operation was bound to sterilise the appellant;

(ii) in the absence of any express warranty, the court should be slow to imply against a medical man an unqualified warranty as to the results of an intended operation. It is most unlikely that a responsible medical man would intend to give a warranty of this nature, as distinct from an undertaking that he would perform the operation with reasonable care and skill.

See pages 15, 73.

F v West Berkshire Health Authority and Another

Psychiatric patient: consent: sterilisation: trespass to person: interests of patient: standard of care

House of Lords. [1989] 2 All ER 545

F, aged thirty-six, suffered from serious mental disability. She had the verbal capacity of a child of two and the general mental capacity of a child of four.

Since 1967 she had been a voluntary in-patient at a mental hospital. She formed a sexual relationship with a male patient there. From a psychiatric point of view, it would have been disastrous for her to conceive a child. There was a serious objection to each of the ordinary methods of contraception.

F's mother, acting as her next friend, sought against the health authority a declaration that the absence of consent would not make sterilisation of F an unlawful act. The trial judge (Scott Baker J) granted the declaration. The Court of Appeal dismissed the Official Solicitor's appeal.

Held: (i) no court has jurisdiction to give or withhold consent to such an operation in the case of an adult;

(ii) however the court has jurisdiction to declare the lawfulness of such a proposed operation. Although such a declaration is not necessary, in practice the court's jurisdiction should be invoked;

(iii) the application should be by way of originating summons issuing out of the Family Division of the High Court. The applicants should normally be those responsible for the care of the patient or those intending to carry out the proposed operation. The patient must always be a party and must normally be a respondent. Subject to the judge's discretion, the hearing will be in chambers but the decision and reasons will be given in open court;

(iv) to be lawful, in the absence of consent, the operation or other treatment concerned must be in the best interests of the patient, either to save the patient's life or to ensure improvement or prevent deterioration in her physical or mental health. In making such decisions, the doctor must act in accordance with a responsible and competent body of professional opinion;

(v) the judge had been right to grant the declaration sought.

Per Lord Brandon: "At common law a doctor cannot lawfully operate on adult patients of sound mind, or give them any other treatment involving the application of physical force however small (which I shall refer to as 'other treatment'), without their consent. If a doctor were to operate on such patients, or give them other treatment, without their consent, he would commit the actionable tort of trespass to the person. There are, however, cases where adult patients cannot give or refuse their consent to an operation or other treatment. One case is where, as a result of an accident or otherwise, an adult patient is unconscious and an operation or other treatment cannot be safely delayed until he or she recovers consciousness. Another case is where a patient, though adult, cannot by reason of mental disability understand the nature or purpose of an operation or other treatment. The common law would be seriously defective if it failed to provide a solution to the problem created by such inability to consent. In my opinion, however, the common law does not fail. In my opinion, the solution to the problem which the common law provides is that a doctor can lawfully operate on, or give other treatment to, adult patients who are incapable, for one reason or another, of consenting to his doing so, provided that the operation or other treatment concerned is in the best interests of such patients. The operation or other treatment will be in their best interests if, but only if, it is carried out in order to either save their lives or to ensure improvement or prevent deterioration in their physical or mental health. . .

"With respect to the Court of Appeal, I do not agree that the *Bolam* test is inapplicable to cases of performing operations on, or giving other treatments to, adults incompetent to give consent. In order that the performance of such operations on, and the giving of such other treatment to, such adults should be lawful, they must be in their best interests. If doctors were to be required, in deciding whether an operation or other treatment was in the best interests of adults incompetent to give consent, to apply some test more stringent than the *Bolam* tests, the result would be that such adults would, in some circumstances at least, be deprived of the benefit of medical treatment which adults competent to give consent would enjoy. In my opinion it would be wrong for the law, in its concern to protect such adults, to produce such a result."

Per Lord Goff: "I feel bound to express my opinion that, in principle, the lawfulness of the doctor's action is, at least in its origin, to be found in the principle of necessity. This can perhaps be seen most clearly in cases where there is no continuing relationship between doctor and patient. The doctor in the house who volunteers to assist a lady in the audience who, overcome by the drama or by the heat in the theatre, has fainted away is impelled to act by no greater duty than that imposed by his own Hippocratic oath. Furthermore, intervention can be justified in the case of a non-professional, as well as a professional, man or woman who has no pre-existing relationship with the assisted person, as in the case of a stranger who rushes to assist an injured man after an accident. In my opinion, it is the necessity itself which provides the justification for the intervention.

"I have said that the doctor has to act in the best interests of the assisted person. In the case of routine treatment of mentally disordered persons, there should be little difficulty in applying this principle. In the case of more serious treatment, I recognize that its application may create problems for the medical profession; however, in making decisions about treatment, the doctor must act in accordance with a responsible and competent body of relevant professional opinion, in the principles set down in *Bolam* v *Friern Hospital Management Committee*."

See pages 5, 6–7, 33, 66.

Farquhar v Murray

Diagnosis: general practitioner: communication: locum

Scotland, Second Division. [1901] SLT 45, (1901) 3 F 859, 38 ScLR 642

Mr Farquhar, an Edinburgh grocer, alleged that on 9 April 1900 a finger of his right hand was scratched by a rusty nail. The finger having swollen, he consulted Dr Murray, his regular medical attendant. Dr Murray pronounced the finger to be affected with erysipelas. He prescribed a medicine to be taken and an ointment to be applied; he also told Mr Farquhar to poultice the finger with linseed and oatmeal. He called again on 10 April and directed Mr Farquhar to continue the poulticing and to use the medicines until he called again the next day.

Dr Murray never came. On 25 April Mrs Farquhar wrote to him. This led to a visit on 26 April from Dr Mackenzie who stated that Dr Murray was away on holiday, that he was looking after his practice in his absence and that Dr Murray had not left any message about the case. When Dr Mackenzie examined the finger, he said that it had been too long poulticed and wrote out a prescription. Eventually the finger had to be amputated.

Mr Farquhar sued Dr Murray, averring that "the defender carelessly and grossly neglected his duty to the pursuer as his patient by failing to visit him as he had promised to do after giving directions for the treatment of his finger. The defender further absented himself suddenly from home without any communication to the pursuer of his intention to do so, and without making any arrangement for medical attendance on the pursuer during his absence. There was thus, on the part of the defender, a culpable want of attention and care, and a gross neglect of his professional duty". The Lord Ordinary dismissed the action as irrelevant.

Held: the case was relevant and fit to be tried.

See page 90.

Fish v Kapur and Another

Dentist: fracture: res ipsa loquitur

Lynskey J. [1948] 2 All ER 176

In May 1946 a wisdom tooth was troubling the plaintiff (Mrs Fish). She went to the premises occupied by Mr S.K. Kapur and asked him to remove the tooth. She saw a nurse who took her into the surgery and placed her in the dentist's chair. The defendant dentist, Mr I.K. Kapur, came in and she was given an anaesthetic. In the extraction, he left part of the root of the tooth in the jaw. Also, by some means unexplained, the jaw was fractured.

The plaintiff called at trial Dr Devas, a doctor of medicine, who said in evidence that it is possible to fracture a jaw during extraction without any negligence. Her other expert, Mr Siggers a dental surgeon, testified that when one is extracting teeth, fractures may occur without fault on the part of the dentist and equally one may leave in the root of the tooth without any blame attaching to him. The defendant did not give evidence. The plaintiff relied on the doctrine of *res ipsa loquitur*.

Held: the fact that the fracture was caused in the process of extraction of the tooth was not in itself any evidence of negligence. There was nothing left on which a finding of negligence could be based. The plaintiff's case must fail.

See pages 25, 60, 86.

Fletcher v Bench

Dentist: fracture: infection: X-ray: res ipsa loquitur

Court of Appeal. [1973] 4 BMJ 118

On 12 September 1968 the plaintiff visited his dentist at his Twickenham surgery. The dentist set to work to remove the plaintiff's lower third right molar under local anaesthetic. The tooth was impacted and did not respond to forceps. The dentist used a bone-burr. While he was drilling the bone, the bone-burr broke leaving a bit of it inside the jaw. Ultimately with another burr the dentist removed the bone around the tooth and got it out with forceps. He was unable to find the bit of broken burr.

On 13 September the plaintiff visited the dentist in much pain; he was suffering from swelling and stiffness of the jaw. Away on holiday the plaintiff twice saw another dentist who found that the socket was infected, dressed it and alleviated the pain. On 22 September the plaintiff's jaw fractured due to the infection. When he visited his dentist again on 23 September, the socket was badly infected. An X-ray showed that the broken bit of burr was stuck at the very point of fracture. On 26 September the tip of the bone-burr was finally removed.

The plaintiff sued his dentist. The trial judge dismissed the claim.

Held: the breaking of the drill and the fact that it was left there at the end of a difficult operation were not indicative of a lack of care. After 13 September, the plaintiff did not see his dentist again until 23 September by which date the fracture had already occurred. The defendant was not liable.

See pages 60, 87.

Fowler and Another v South-West Metropolitan Regional Hospital Board and Another

Fracture: substandard treatment: penicillin: gangrene

Pilcher J. [1955] 2 BMJ 387

In February 1952 the plaintiff (Mrs Irene Fowler) fell in her garden. She sustained a fracture of both bones in the right forearm, and there was a small punctured wound caused by the bones. She was taken to the Yeatman Hospital, Sherborne, where she was treated by Dr McIntosh. The fracture was reduced. An unpadded plaster cast was applied to the plaintiff's arm, but she was not given any penicillin injections. Her arm became infected with gas gangrene and had to be amputated.

The plaintiff and her husband sued Dr McIntosh and the health authority.

Held: the defendants were liable in negligence. It was impossible to absolve Dr McIntosh from some responsibility for his failure to treat the plaintiff with a course of penicillin injections. Good practice demanded that a fracture of that kind should not be enclosed at once in an unpadded cast. The fitting of a close and unpadded plaster immediately after the reduction of the fracture interfered with the circulation, creating a condition in which the preventive and curative effects of free circulation provided by nature were removed.

Freeman v Home Office

Prison inmate: consent: injection: trespass to person

Court of Appeal. [1984] QB 524, [1984] 1 All ER 1036, [1984] 2 WLR 130

The plaintiff (David Freeman) was serving a life sentence at Wakefield Prison. He behaved in a disruptive way, suffered from bouts of depression and attempted suicide on a number of occasions. In August 1972 Dr Xavier, a prison medical officer, prescribed Stelazine to be taken orally. The plaintiff refused to take it. Between September and December 1972 he received injections of Serenace and Modecate prescribed by Dr Xavier. He alleged that these injections were administered against his will and by force and sued for trespass to the person.

Held: where in a prison setting a doctor has the power to influence a prisoner's situation and prospects, a court must be alive to the risk that what may appear to be a real consent may not in fact be so. Essentially the matter is one of fact. The trial judge (McCowan J) rejected the plaintiff's evidence and justifiably found that he had consented.
See page 67.

Re Frost

Psychiatric patient: negligent certification: duty of care: leave to sue: false imprisonment

Court of Appeal. [1936] 2 All ER 182

Robert Frost was a pauper aged seventy-five. On Saturday 24 August 1935 he buried his wife. Afterwards he was in a very excitable condition and drank heavily. On the request of Mr Frost's daughter, Dr Dean wrote: "Please receive into hospital Robert John Frost of 11 Warriker Street, aged about 75 years. He requires hospital treatment. Requires to be kept under observation."

On 25 August after receiving this letter by hand, an official at the Anlaby Road Institution, Kingston-upon-Hull, dispatched an ambulance with a driver and an attendant to Mr Frost's home. Without his consent they took him away to the institution. Dr Todd, the senior medical officer, issued a certificate for his detention, although he had not personally examined him. He was kept in a mental ward for four days.

Mr Frost was subsequently examined by two independent doctors who found no sign of mental incapacity. He applied unders s 16(2) Mental Treatment Act 1930 for leave to bring court action against the Kingston-upon-Hull Corporation for false imprisonment and wrongful detention. Goddard J granted this application.

Held: there was sufficient evidence to justify the judge in concluding that through their acting only upon Dr Dean's letter and failing to get any medical man or expert to examine Mr Frost before they took him to the mental ward, there were substantial grounds for the contention that the appellants acted without reasonable care.
See page 65.

Furber v Kratter and Others

Psychiatric patient: leave to sue: substandard treatment: false imprisonment

Henry J. [1988] The Times 21 July

The plaintiff was a mental patient detained under a hospital order at Moss Side Special Hospital. After a violent and unprovoked attack on a ward sister, she was placed under a "seclusion" regime for sixteen days. That meant that she was locked alone in a side room off the ward. The room was furnished simply with a mattress. She was naked during the sixteen days.

She applied under s 139 Mental Health Act 1983 for leave to sue the three hospital staff responsible for negligence and false imprisonment. She alleged that during the sixteen days she had been denied nursing care, clothing, reading and writing materials. She further alleged that the regime of seclusion was imposed not as a treatment but as a punishment in order to humiliate her.

Held: (i) she was entitled to sue in negligence, because if her allegations of wrongful imposition of the regime were substantiated it was eminently arguable that general damages for discomfort, suffering and loss of amenities could be recoverable;

(ii) she was entitled to sue for false imprisonment, even though she was already detained under a hospital order by sentence of the court, because it was possible for a regime to be so intolerable and prejudicial that it would render unlawful an imprisonment which had been lawful.
See page 65.

Furstenau v Tomlinson

Diagnosis: error of judgement: mistake

Walton J (with special jury). [1902] 2 BMJ 496

The plaintiff (Mr Furstenau) was suffering from a skin infection. Dr Tomlinson diagnosed this as eczema. In spite of the remedies supplied and prescribed, the plaintiff's condition got worse and he finally sought a second opinion. The doctor whom he then consulted diagnosed scabies. The plaintiff's wife was also found to be suffering from this.

The plaintiff sued Dr Tomlinson, alleging negligence and ignorance. The defence was that the original mischief was eczema, and that if there were any concurrent scabies the latter was so masked by the former that it was impossible for anyone to diagnose it at that time.

Held: Walton J directed the jury that a mistake alone on Dr Tomlinson's part was not sufficient to enable the plaintiff to recover damages; negligence and the want of an ordinary amount of skill had to be proved before the jury could find for the plaintiff.

The jury returned a verdict for the defendant.
See pages 61–62.

Fussell v Beddard

Anaesthetic: nurses: overdose: duty of care: vicarious liability

Lewis J. [1942] 2 BMJ 411

Mrs Fussell had to undergo an operation for removal of gall-stones. The surgeon and the anaesthetist, Mr Beddard, decided that anaesthesia should be induced by an epidural nerve block with decicaine. Mr Beddard told a sister that decicaine would be used and instructed her to prepare a solution of 0.1 per cent. She was highly qualified and had been in charge of the theatre for six years. Believing that she was carrying out his instructions, she prepared a solution of 1 per cent. Mrs Fussell died of the overdose.

The plaintiff (her widower) sued Mr Beddard.

Held: the anaesthetist did not owe a duty to do more than state clearly to a responsible and efficient sister the anaesthetic he required. Mr Beddard had not been negligent.

N.B. It is submitted that, following the cases of *Cassidy* v *Ministry of Health* and *Roe* v *Minister of Health*, on the same facts today a patient suing a health authority which is vicariously liable for any negligence on the part of the anaesthetist or the sister might reasonably expect to succeed.
See page 92.

G v North Tees Health Authority

Hospital administration: tests: post-traumatic stress disorder: sexual abuse: damages: aggravated damages

Eastham J. [1989] FCR 53

A six year old girl was being treated by a hospital for a skin complaint. When she attended on 6 February 1986, her mother reported to the doctor that the child was suffering from a vaginal discharge. A vaginal swab was taken. It was reported to have active male sperm on it, indicating sexual intercourse. The child was admitted to hospital and subjected to a very painful internal examination, since it was thought that she might have been sexually abused for about two years. She also underwent a series of interviews by police officers and social workers.

On 10 February it was discovered that a mistake had been made. The practice at the hospital was to use one slide for two swabs. The slide upon which the child's swab was put was also used for a swab for an older person who had obviously had sexual intercourse. The mother was promptly informed of the error. She and her daughter sued the health authority who admitted liability.

The mother, a single parent, was extremely upset and depressed. Her family reacted badly, and she felt suicidal until the mistake was discovered. She suffered an exacerbation of a phobic anxiety state. She improved after counselling. The prognosis was promising.

The child suffered nightmares and enuresis. She became preoccupied with sexual assaults and her genital organs, and developed a fear of doctors and dread of the police. She responded well to counselling. However future gynaecological examinations might make her anxious.

Held: the case could adequately be dealt with by compensatory damages without awarding aggravated damages. The mother and child were awarded general damages of £5,000 each (December 1987).
See pages 26–27, 59, 89, 104, 112.

Gale v Cowie

Psychiatrist: injection: drugs: medical literature: standard of care: state of knowledge

Lawton J. [1965] 2 The Lancet 1341

In December 1960 the plaintiff (Mr Gale) consulted Dr Cowie, a psychiatrist. The plaintiff complained of anxiety and depression for which another doctor had prescribed him Amytal and Nardil. Dr Cowie agreed to treat him, telling him not to take the pills before he came for treatment. On 27 January 1961, in the course of treatment, Dr Cowie injected him with Methedrine. The plaintiff felt greatly distressed, thought that he was about to die and lost consciousness. His depression was aggravated.

The plaintiff sued Dr Cowie. Evidence was given that, at the time of the injection, no medical writer had drawn attention to the risks of injecting Methedrine into a patient who had taken Nardil. The danger was first described in 1962.

Held: in view of the absence of published warning, at the time of the injection, about the dangers of the combination of Methedrine and Nardil, Dr Cowie should not be blamed for not appreciating that the combination would bring about the unfortunate consequences that followed. He had not been negligent.
See page 37.

Garner v Morrell and Another

Dentist: operation: retained surgical product: res ipsa loquitur

Court of Appeal. [1953] The Times 31 October

In April 1948 Charles Garner attended the surgery of the defendants, Arnold Morrell and William Morrell, for the purpose of having teeth extracted. One defendant performed the operation of extraction, and the other administered the anaesthetic. During the course of the operation, a throat pack which had been inserted in Mr Garner's mouth was swallowed or inhaled by him. In consequence he died of asphyxia. His widow claimed damages.

Held: there was ample evidence to support the finding of the trial judge (Sellers J) that the throat pack was too short. The occurrence of the accident called for an explanation from the defendants, and the explanation offered by them had largely broken down. The accident could and should have been avoided; and the fact that a similar accident had never happened before was against the defendants.
See pages 59, 87.

Gauntlett v Northampton Health Authority

Psychiatric patient: supervision: nurses: standard of care: causation

Court of Appeal. 12 December 1985

In September 1979 the plaintiff (Mrs Pamela Gauntlett), then aged twenty-four, suffered the latest in a series of mental breakdowns. On 14 September she took an overdose of tranquillising tablets and was admitted to Northampton General Hospital. She expressed bizarre and florid delusions about Jesus Christ having a stake driven through his heart, vampires, snakes etc and said that she would have to die.

On 15 September she was transferred to St Crispin's Hospital, a mental hospital, where a diagnosis of schizophrenia was made. When her husband left her after a visit on 16 September, she handed him a box of matches, saying "You had better take these because I may set fire to myself". He told a nurse who did not record it.

On 20 September the plaintiff went to the washroom and toilet by herself. She there set fire with a box of matches to the tee-shirt which she was wearing, burning herself badly and leaving severe and unsightly scarring.

She sued the health authority for inadequate supervision. The trial judge (Kilner Brown J) found in her favour.

Held: (i) the trial judge did not ask himself the key question: "should a reasonably competent and experienced nurse have foreseen that if she omitted to make a note of this incident, there was a risk that the patient might not be closely supervised and might, if she got the opportunity, set her clothes on fire?" or " is this an omission which no reasonably competent and skilled nurse would make in the circumstances of this case?" His finding of negligence could not be justified;

(ii) causation had not been established. It had not been shown that a note of the matches incident would probably have resulted in the plaintiff being accompanied by a nurse to the washroom on every occasion, and so prevented her from setting light to her clothes.
See pages 25, 42, 92–93.

Gerber v Pines

Injection: general practitioner: needle breaking: duty to inform of mishap

Du Parcq J. [1935] SJ 13

The plaintiff (Mrs Rebecca Gerber) was undergoing a course of injections for her rheumatism by Dr Pine at his surgery. Six had been given successfully when on 11 August, while he was injecting into the muscle known as the gluteus maximus, the needle broke. He was unable to get it out of the plaintiff's body and did not initially tell her that it was there. On 16 August it was removed by operation. The plaintiff sued Dr Pines who testified that the breaking of the needle was due to a sudden muscular spasm.

Held: no negligence in the performance of the injection was proved against Dr Pines, and there was apparently nothing wrong with the needle. However, as a general rule, a patient in whose body a doctor found that he had left some foreign substance was entitled to be told at once. There was a breach of duty and negligence on the doctor's part in not at once informing either the patient or her husband on the day of the accident.

See pages 26, 74, 78–79.

Gillick v West Norfolk and Wisbech Area Health Authority and Another

Consent: minors: contraceptive advice: parental objections

House of Lords. [1986] AC 112, [1985] 3 All ER 402, [1985] 3 WLR 830

The Department of Health and Social Security issued a circular to area health authorities. This contained advice that a doctor consulted at a family planning clinic by a girl under sixteen would not be acting unlawfully if he prescribed contraceptives for the girl, so long as in doing so he was acting in good faith to protect her against the harmful effects of sexual intercourse. It further advised that in exceptional cases the doctor could prescribe contraceptives without consulting the girl's parents or obtaining their consent, if in the doctor's clinical judgement it was desirable to prescribe contraceptives.

The plaintiff (Mrs Victoria Gillick), who had five daughters under the age of sixteen, brought an action seeking (i) against the DHSS and the area health authority a declaration that the advice contained in their circular was unlawful, and (ii) against the area health authority a declaration that a doctor employed by it could not give contraceptive advice or treatment to any of her children aged under sixteen without the plaintiff's consent. The Court of Appeal granted the declaration sought.

Held: the declarations had been wrongly granted. A girl under sixteen did not, merely by reason of her age, lack legal capacity to consent to contraceptive advice and treatment by a doctor. A doctor had a discretion to give such advice or treatment without her parent's consent, provided that the girl was old enough to have sufficient understanding and intelligence to enable her to understand fully what was being proposed.

Per Lord Fraser of Tullybelton: "It seems to me verging on the absurd to suggest that a girl or boy aged fifteen could not effectively consent, for example, to have a medical examination of some trivial injury to his body or even to have a broken arm set. Of course the consent of the parents should normally be asked, but they may not be immediately available. Provided the patient, whether a boy or a girl, is capable of understanding what is proposed, and of expressing his or her own wishes, I see no good reason for holding that he or she lacks the capacity to express them validly and effectively and to authorise the medical man to make the examination or give the treatment which he advises."

Per Lord Scarman: "Parental right yields to the child's right to make his own decisions when he reaches a sufficient understanding and intelligence to be capable of making up his own mind on the matter requiring decision. . . . In the light of the foregoing I would hold that as a matter of law the parental right to determine whether or not their minor child below the age of sixteen

217

will have medical treatment terminates if and when the child achieves a sufficient understanding and intelligence to enable him or her to understand fully what is proposed. It will be a question of fact whether a child seeking advice has sufficient understanding of what is involved to give a valid consent in law. Until the child achieves the capacity to consent, the parental right to make the decision continues save only in exceptional circumstances. Emergency, parental neglect, abandonment of the child or inability to find the parent are examples of exceptional situations justifying the doctor proceeding to treat the child without parental knowledge and consent; but there will arise, no doubt, other exceptional situations in which it will be reasonable for the doctor to proceed without the parent's consent."

Per Lord Templeman: "I accept also that a doctor may lawfully carry out some forms of treatment with the consent of an infant patient and against the opposition of a parent based on religious or any other grounds. The effect of the consent of the infant depends on the nature of the treatment and the age and understanding of the infant. For example, a doctor with the consent of an intelligent boy or girl of fifteen could in my opinion safely remove tonsils or a troublesome appendix."

See pages 6, 27.

Gladwell v Steggall

Alternative practitioner: duty of care: substandard treatment

Vaughan J. (1839) 5 Bing N Cas 733

The plaintiff was a ten year old girl. While working in the fields with her father in the 1830s, she complained of a pain in the knee and went home. Her mother sent for the defendant who, though a clergyman, practised also as a medical man. He attended the plaintiff, with disastrous consequences for her.

Held: having accepted employment by the plaintiff as a surgeon, the defendant negligently carried out his duties as such. Judgment for the plaintiff.
See pages 7, 25.

Gold and others v Essex County Council

Radiographer: burns: substandard treatment: vicarious liability

Court of Appeal. [1942] 2 KB 293, [1942] 2 All ER 237

In June and July 1940 the plaintiff (Ruth Gold), then aged five, was taken by her mother to Oldchurch Hospital for treatment for warts on her face. The visiting dermatologist, Dr Burrows, ordered treatment by Grenz rays. This was given by Mr Mead, a qualified radiographer who was employed by the hospital as a technical assistant. While the plaintiff was undergoing treatment, her face was covered with a lead-lined rubber cloth which protected all but the affected part of her face. This happened on some five occasions.

As the warts did not yield to this treatment, Dr Burrows prescribed applications of double the strength. On 11 July 1940 the plaintiff's mother took her again for treatment. Mr Mead was in a hurry. Instead of getting the lead-lined cloth, he covered the child's face with only a piece of ordinary lint. Her face was severely burnt, and she suffered permanent disfigurement. The trial judge (Tucker J) found that Mr Mead was negligent.

Held: as the radiographer, Mr Mead, was employed by the defendant hospital authority under a contract of service, the authority was liable for his negligence. This was so even though his work was of a skilful or technical nature. In this legal context, he was in exactly the same position as a nurse.
See pages 10–11, 25, 85.

Gold v Haringey Health Authority

Sterilisation (failed): standard of care: risk disclosure: warning: contraceptive advice

Court of Appeal. [1987] 2 All ER 888, [1987] 3 WLR 649, [1987] 1 FLR 125

In 1979 the plaintiff (Mrs Phyllis Gold) was pregnant with her third child. She and her husband were discussing his having a vasectomy. Miss Witt, a consultant at the North Middlesex Hospital, suggested that she be sterilised. None of the hospital doctors mentioned the failure rate of the operation which was about six per thousand if carried out immediately after childbirth. On 19 August 1979 the plaintiff gave birth to a daughter, Nicola. On 20 August Dr Arzanghi performed the sterilisation operation at North Middlesex Hospital. The operation did not succeed, for in October 1982 the plaintiff gave birth to her fourth child, Darren.

Her claim that the operation was carried out negligently was rejected by the trial judge (Schiemann J). She also alleged negligence in failing to disclose that the operation had a failure rate, saying that if she had known this she would not have had the operation and her husband would have been vasectomised instead. The unanimous medical evidence was that a substantial body of doctors would not have given any warning about the failure rate in 1979. However the judge found that the *Bolam* test applied only to advice given in a therapeutic context and not to advice given in a contraceptive context. He found that the defendants had been negligent in not warning the plaintiff that the operation might not succeed.

Held: there was no reason to distinguish between advice given in a therapeutic context and advice given in a non-therapeutic context. The *Bolam* test applied to contraceptive advice as well as to therapeutic advice. As there was a body of responsible medical opinion which would not have given any warning as to the failure of female sterilisation, the defendants were not liable.
See pages 73, 85.

Goode v Nash

General practitioner: duty of care: gratuitous services: substandard treatment: burns: foreign

Supreme Court (South Australia). (1979) 21 SASR 419

On 25 May 1974 the Lions Clubs of Southern Districts were conducting glaucoma screenings at the Willunga District Hall. Mr W.P. Nash, aged twenty-four, presented himself for testing. The tests were free and Mr Goode, an experienced general practitioner, was giving his services free of charge. Dr Goode placed a hot tonometer upon Mr Nash's left eye.

Mr Nash suffered a burn which left him with scarring of the cornea and reduced vision. He sued Dr Goode.

Held: Dr Goode must have been negligent. It may be that he left the tonometer in the sterilising flame for longer than usual, or that he allowed less time than usual for it to cool, or perhaps there was a combination of both. Although he was engaged in a valuable community service, entirely on a voluntary basis, he was liable to pay damages.
See pages 8, 27–28.

Goodman v Fletcher and Others

Limitation: advice: substandard treatment: striking out

Court of Appeal. 4 October 1982

The plaintiff (Miss Goodman) suffered from a number of allergies. In June and July 1973 she consulted Dr Buisseret who advised her to go on a gluten-free diet. In September 1974 she learned that he had recommended this on an empirical basis, that is, he wanted to see what was going to happen. In February 1975 she was discharged from the Peace Memorial Hospital with a dietary recommendation that included gluten.

In March 1978 she issued a writ against Dr Buisseret (among others). In April 1981 she served an inadequate Statement of Claim. A substitute Statement of Claim was served in November 1981, alleging that Dr Buisseret's advice was negligent and wrong. In April 1982 her case was struck out as statute-barred.

Held: (i) the plaintiff probably knew in September 1974 that Dr Buisseret's diagnosis and advice were in error, and she certainly knew it by February 1975. Thus her case was prima facie statute barred by s 11 Limitation Act 1980;

(ii) the delays had been great, and it would be impossible for Dr Buisseret at a trial in 1983 to have an accurate recollection of the consultations ten years earlier in 1973. The delay was fatal to any exercise of discretion under s 33 of the 1980 Act.
See page 125.

Gordon v Goldberg

Dentist: alternative practitioner: breach of contract: standard of care

Rowlatt J. [1920] 2 The Lancet 964

In the absence of her usual dentist, who was serving in the army, the plaintiff (Mrs Gordon), aged nearly eighty, consulted Mr Goldberg who practised dentistry but was not upon the Dental Register. She had been attracted by his advertisement describing himself as "D.D.S. American Dentistry". He made her two sets of artificial teeth for which she paid him sums of £31 15s and £40. Neither fitted her, and she suffered great pain.

The plaintiff sued Mr Goldberg. Expert evidence was given that the teeth did not fit, that they were wanting in articulation between the upper and lower jaws, and that it was impossible to adapt them.

Held: Mr Goldberg was liable. When people went to dentists they expected and contracted for skill, not for infallibility. In judging skill, account might be taken of the charges made. Mr Goldberg had charged very handsomely, but the teeth that he supplied were utterly unsatisfactory.
See pages 17, 86.

Gravestock and Another v Lewisham Group Hospital Management Committee

Supervision: child patient: standard of care: nurses

Streatfield J. [1955] The Times 27 May

Pauline Gravestock (the plaintiff) was a nine year old patient in Lewisham Hospital. On 13 August 1952 the orderly left the ward for a few minutes in order to get the pudding course of a meal. Contrary to the rules, the plaintiff ran down the the ward and, swinging on the swing doors, tripped on the stud and was seriously injured.

Held: on the purely disciplinary side, the duty of a hospital was no higher than that of a school. The duty of the defendant should not be measured by any more severe standard than that of a schoolmaster, which was that of an ordinary prudent parent. Measured by the scales of the prudent parent, the defendants had provided adequate supervision.
See pages 25, 88, 92.

Gray v Mid Herts Group Hospital Management Committee

Anaesthetics: cardiac arrest: substandard treatment: damages: child death: brain damage

Waller J. [1974] The Times 30 March

Edward Gray was born in September 1968. In October 1969 he entered St Alban's City Hospital for an inguinal hernia operation. He was given 5 mg of Omnopon as a premedication. Difficulty in breathing was the first untoward sign to be observed. He had a cardiac arrest due to anoxia.

Edward had suffered widespread brain damage in the operation. He became blind and deaf, showing a typical picture of spastic paraplegia. From time to time he had fits, and he was doubly incontinent. He sometimes had periods of crying which could not be stopped. While he was not aware of his surroundings, he had a slight reaction to familiar and friendly touch. He died due to his brain damage in July 1972. His father sued the hospital authority.

Held: (i) careful monitoring would have given warning in time to avoid the consequences that followed. The anaesthetist was not keeping a good look-out on the chest and re-breathing bag, and he was not continually monitoring the pulse. The hospital authority was liable for the anaesthetist's negligence;

(ii) taking into account the child's very young age, his comparatively long two and three-quarter year period of survival, and his slight reaction to touch, general damages were assessed (March 1974) at £5,000 for his loss of amenities. A further £500 was awarded for loss of expectation of life.
See page 81.

Gregory and Gregory v Pembrokeshire Health Authority

Pregnancy: tests: communication: causation

Court of Appeal. 31 January 1989

In autumn 1979 the plaintiff (Mrs Jacqueline Gregory), then aged twenty-eight, was pregnant with her second child. Her own first child was normal, but when in her forties her mother had produced a mongol. On 19 November Dr Davies performed an amniocentesis test at Withybush Hospital and sent the sample to a laboratory at Cardiff. On 7 December the laboratory informed the hospital that the sample had not produced sufficient cultures to make testing possible. By then the plaintiff was twenty-one weeks and two days into her pregnancy. The hospital staff omitted to tell her that the test had failed until she saw Dr Davies in February 1980. When her baby was born in April, he turned out to be a mongol (a Downs Syndrome baby).

Mr & Mrs Gregory sued the hospital authority. The trial judge (Rougier J) found that (i) the failure of the hospital staff to inform the plaintiff at the earliest practicable moment that the amniocentesis test had failed to produce a result was a breach of their duty of care to her, but (ii) if timeously informed she would have accepted the advice that Dr Davies would have given not to proceed with a repeat test, since any abortion resulting from this would have had to be carried out more than twenty-four weeks into her pregnancy. Accordingly, he dismissed her claim.

Held: this was *par excellence* a case in which the judge's impression of the plaintiff and Dr Davies was of the utmost importance, since he had to evaluate the likely impact of Dr Davies' advice on her. There were no grounds for interfering with the judge's findings.
See page 42.

Haines v Bellissimo et al

Psychiatric patient: suicide risk: diagnosis: standard of care: foreign: psychologist

Ontario High Court of Justice (Griffiths J). (1978) 82 DLR(3d) 215

Robert Haines was born in 1931. He first suffered from schizophrenia in 1954. In November 1971 he commenced treatment at the McMaster University Medical Centre where a diagnosis of chronic residual schizophrenia was made. Dr Bellissimo, a psychologist with a doctorate in clinical pyschology, was designated as his therapist. In 1974 Mr Haines' mental health deteriorated: he suffered from hypomania and depression and became socially disruptive.

On 28 June 1974 Mrs Haines, his wife, discovered in the garage of their house a shotgun which he had purchased on 24 June. She told Dr Bellissimo who saw Mr Haines. Mr Haines assured him that he had no immediate plan for suicide. After Dr Bellissimo had threatened to call the police, Mr Haines finally handed over the gun to him. Weighing all factors, such as that there had been no recent stressful situations and no immediate suicide plans, Dr Bellissimo decided not to hospitalize him.

On 29 June Mr Haines secretly bought another shotgun. On 1 July he entered the garage and shot himself to death. The plaintiff (Mrs Haines) sued Dr Bellissimo and the medical centre for failing to prevent his suicide.

Held: the duty and standard of care imposed on a psychiatrist, or a clinical psychologist applying therapy in a specialised capacity in a hospital environment, is the same required of physicians in all fields of medicine and surgery. If the patient's mental condition and actions were such that a reasonably prudent psychiatrist or psychologist would under the circumstances have anticipated a suicide attempt, then the concept of reasonable care in treatment requires the therapist to take all reasonable steps, including hospitalization of the patient if necessary, to prevent or reduce the risk of self-destruction. Dr Bellissimo's opinion on 28 June that there was no immediate risk of suicide was reasonable. He had not been negligent in deciding not to hospitalize Mr Haines.
Judgment for the defendants.

Hall and Wife v Lees and Others

Nurses: burns: vicarious liability

Court of Appeal. [1904] 2 KB 602

The plaintiff (Mrs Hall) needed a serious operation. Her surgeon asked the Oldham Nursing Association for two nurses to attend on her during the operation. After the operation, while the plaintiff was still under anaesthetic, a very highly heated hot-water bottle came into immediate contact with her body, instead of being shielded by a blanket as it should have been. She was severely burnt. One or both of the nurses had been negligent.

The object of Oldham Nursing Association was "to supply aid and instruction in skilled nursing by nurses located in Oldham". The Association's rules provided, *inter alia*, that "when at a case the nurse shall not absent herself from duty without permission from the patient's friends" and that "only such cases shall be undertaken as are attended by a medical man, whose instructions the nurses must implicitly follow". A printed form was sent with each nurse, including a report on her "to be filled in by employer".

Held: the Association never undertook to nurse the female plaintiff, but only to supply duly qualified nurses for that purpose. The nurses were not the servants of the Association for the purpose of nursing the patient, and the Association was not liable for their negligence.
See pages 85, 92.

Hall v Semple

Psychiatric patient: negligent certification: duty of care

Crompton J (with jury). (1862) 3 F&F 337

The plaintiff (Richard Hall) was a respectable tradesman aged fifty-six. His marriage had proved very unhappy, and there were bitter dissensions and disturbances between him and his wife. Since 1856 she had been making efforts to get him certified as a lunatic. On 28 July 1862 she consulted Dr Semple, a local physician. She told him that the plaintiff slept with a drawn sword by his bedside and had threatened to stab her and, further, that he laboured under the delusions that she was ruining him and improperly associating with other men. Dr Semple saw the plaintiff at his shop the same day, found him excited and rude, and left after ten minutes. On 29 July Dr Semple discussed the plaintiff with Mr Guy, a surgeon whom Mrs Hall had been consulting, and without further examination or enquiry, they signed certificates under the Lunacy Acts that the plaintiff was of unsound mind. The next night he was seized and forcibly carried to an asylum.

Soon after his release in mid-August, the plaintiff sued Dr Semple. Evidence was given at the hearing that the sword was only an old theatrical sword which hung up in his bedroom where Mrs Hall did not sleep anyway, and that she had in fact been pawning items and running into debt. The plaintiff denied accusing her of adultery.

Held: Crompton J directed the jury that a man may hate and detest his wife very much and yet not be a madman. The question was whether Dr Semple acted negligently in signing the certificate without reasonable grounds and without proper examination and enquiries.
The jury returned a verdict for the plaintiff.
See page 64.

Hall and Others v Wandsworth Health Authority

Childbirth: anaesthetics: discovery: costs

Tudor Price J. [1985] The Times 16 February, (1985) PMILL Vol 1 No 7, (1985) 129 SJ 188

In December 1982 Mrs Patricia Hall gave birth to twin daughters in St

George's Hospital. During labour she was given an epidural injection on two occasions. Since then she had recurring episodes of paralysis and other disabilities. She contemplated court proceedings.

On 1 June 1984 her solicitors wrote a full letter before action to the hospital administrator, requesting production to them of the hospital notes and other records. They gave proper undertakings of confidentiality. They stated that if they had not, within six weeks of the date of the letter, been notified of consent to disclose the documents, and within a further fourteen days received the documents, they would commence proceedings.

They received no disclosure, so on 4 October 1984 they issued an originating summons pursuant to s 33(2) Supreme Court Act 1981. On 5 November, Master Creightmore ordered disclosure within twenty-eight days. Only in February 1985 were copies of case notes finally disclosed.

Held: it was clear from the wording of RSC O 62 r 3(12) that normally the defendant to such an application will have his costs paid by the plaintiff. In a small number of cases, the conduct of the defendant will justify the court in ordering him to pay his own costs. Mrs Hall's case was a worse example of dilatory conduct by the defendants. The six weeks suggested by her solicitors were a reasonable period. There was no reasonable excuse for failure to disclose the record to them before the hearing by the Master. The defendants should pay her costs of this hearing.

N.B. In two associated cases, in which the defendant's delays were less pronounced, the Master's decision not to make any order as to costs was upheld.

See page 131.

Halushka v University of Saskatchewan et al

Consent: test subject: anaesthetics: assault: cardiac arrest: risk disclosure: foreign: experimentation

Saskatchewan Court of Appeal. (1965) 53 DLR (2d) 436

In August 1961 the plaintiff (Walter Halushka), a student at the University of Saskatchewan, was told that he could earn fifty dollars by being the subject of a test at the University Hospital. He reported to the anaesthesia department where Professor Wyant told him that a new drug was to be tried out, that electrodes would be attached to his arms, legs and head, and that it was a perfectly safe test. Professor Wyant also told him that an incision would be made in his left arm and that a catheter would be inserted into his vein. The plaintiff agreed to undergo the test and signed a form of consent.

On 23 August he underwent the test which involved a new anaesthetic agent known commercially as Fluoromar. The described procedure was followed except that the catheter, after being inserted into his left arm, was advanced towards his heart. At 11.32am the anaesthetic agent started to be administered to him. At 12.25pm he suffered a complete cardiac arrest and was unconscious for four days. As a result of the experiment, Professor Wyant concluded that as an anaesthetic agent Fluoromar had too narrow a margin of safety and it was withdrawn from clinical use in the University Hospital.

The plaintiff sued Professor Wyant and the university for assault and negligence. Professor Wyant had not informed him that the new drug was in fact an anaesthetic of which he had no previous knowledge, nor that there was a risk involved with the use of an anaesthetic, nor that as far as he knew no test using Fluoromar had been conducted before.

Held: the duty imposed upon those engaged in medical research to those who offer themselves as subjects for experimentation is at least as great, if not greater than, the duty owed by the ordinary physician or surgeon to his patient. There can be no exceptions to the ordinary requirements of disclosure in the case of research as there may well be in ordinary medical practice. The researcher does not have to balance the probable effect of lack of treatment itself. The example of risks being properly hidden from a patient when it is important that he should not worry can have no application in the field of research. The subject of medical experimentation is entitled to a full and frank disclosure of all the facts, probabilities and opinions which a reasonable man might be expected to consider before giving his consent. There was ample evidence on which the jury was entitled to find that the plaintiff had given no effectual consent. The defendants were liable in trespass.
See page 26.

Hamilton v Birmingham Regional Hospital Board and Another

Sterilisation: consent: damages

Cusack J. [1969] 2 BMJ 456

The plaintiff (Mrs Katie Hamilton) was forty years old and the mother of three sons aged eleven, eight and two. All her children had been delivered by caesarian section. On the occasion of the delivery of her third child in June 1966, she was sterilised without her consent. She had never been asked whether she wanted to be sterilised. Liability was admitted by the hospital authority and by Dr Keates who performed the operation.

The plaintiff, a Roman Catholic, said that if she had been advised that having further children might be dangerous to her health or life she still would have declined sterilisation, preferring to put her own life at risk. The sterilisation had deprived her of the chance of having more children and of deciding whether to do so.

Held: (April 1969): general damages of £750 were awarded.
See pages 5, 67.

Hancke v Hooper

Surgeon: vicarious liability: standard of care

Tindal CJ (with jury). (1835) 7 C&P 81

In June 1834 the plaintiff (Mr Hancke), who was a whitesmith, went into the shop of Mr Hooper, who was a surgeon in the London Road, and asked to be bled. Two of Mr Hooper's apprentices were in the shop, and he himself was engaged in an adjoining back parlour. The plaintiff told the young men that he had a disease in his head, for which he had been bled before, and found relief from it. Upon this, he was bled by the senior apprentice in the presence of the other. The bleeding took place in the basilic vein, where it appeared from an old cicatrix that the plaintiff had been bled before. During the operation the apprentices observed the blood to flow more freely than usual, so they called for Mr Hooper who came in and told them when to stop and himself tied up the plaintiff's arm.

The plaintiff suffered considerable swelling and discolouration of the arm and was confined to bed for a month. Surgeons testified that all the appearances were consistent with proper performance of the operation.

Held: Tindal CJ directed the jury: "The defendant is responsible for the act of his apprentice; therefore the question is whether you think the injury which the plaintiff has sustained is attributable to a want of proper skill on the part of the young man, or to some accident. A surgeon does not become an actual insurer; he is only bound to display sufficient skill and knowledge of his profession."
The jury returned a verdict for the defendant.

See page 34.

Harnett v Fisher

Psychiatric patient: negligent certification: limitation

House of Lords. [1927] AC 573

The appellant (Mr Harnett) was a Kentish farmer. On 10 November 1912 Dr Fisher, a country doctor, was asked by another doctor to examine him. From a window he watched the appellant for a short time in the street and took note of his demeanour. Subsequently he made an attempt to get into conversation with him. As a result he signed a certificate in the form required by the Lunacy Act 1890, in which he pronounced the appellant to be of unsound mind. On the petition of the appellant's brother, a Justice of the Peace made a reception order on the same day. The appellant was confined in a lunatic asylum and licensed houses for lunatics until he escaped on 15 October 1921. On 31 May 1922 he started court action against Dr Fisher.

Held: the appellant was not of unsound mind, and Dr Fisher had acted negligently. However, the appellant was debarred from recovering damages by the Limitation Act 1623, since the six years limitation period ran from the date of his detention on 10 November 1912. As he was never insane, time was not prevented from running by reason of disability.
See pages 65, 122–123, 124.

Harrington v Essex Area Health Authority

Operation: after-care: burden of proof

Beldam J. [1984] The Times 14 November

Complications occurred after an operation to the plaintiff. He alleged that the defendants were negligent in their treatment of him.

Held: as it was impossible to select between two possible explanations for these complications, the plaintiff had failed to discharge the burden of proof. The defendants were not liable.

Harris v Newcastle Health Authority

Operation: discovery: limitation

Court of Appeal. [1989] 2 All ER 273, [1989] 1 WLR 96

The plaintiff (Veronica Harris) was born in October 1959. She suffered from a squint in her left eye. Around April 1961 her parents consulted Mr Lake who conducted an operation either at the Fleming Memorial Hospital or at the Royal Victoria Infirmary. The result was that her eyelid became nearly closed.

In 1965 Mr Howard was consulted. He performed a further operation. This resulted in some cosmetic improvement, with the eyelid opening more. However she since suffered pain which became progressively worse.

In February 1987 a nurse suggested to the plaintiff that the problem was not of natural origin. Indeed, the plaintiff had always connected it with the operation which she had had as a small child. She consulted solicitors who applied for pre-trial disclosure of the hospital records under s 33(2) Supreme Court Act 1981. The district registrar and the judge (Staughton J) refused on the ground that there was no point in ordering pre-trial discovery when a limitation defence was virtually bound to succeed.

Held: the plaintiff's counsel had stated that proceedings were likely to be instituted, so the jurisdictional requirements of s 33(2) were satisfied. Although there was a strong limitation defence, the plaintiff's case was not clearly doomed to failure. The application for pre-trial discovery should be granted.

Per Kerr LJ: "If it is plain beyond doubt that a defence of limitation will be raised and will succeed, then it seems to me that the court must be entitled to take that matter into account. . . But I would accept that in the normal run of cases, even where a defence of limitation has a strong prospect of success, like here, it is very difficult for a court, on limited material, before pleadings and discovery, to conclude at that stage that the situation is such that the proposed action is bound to fail and therefore frivolous, vexatious or otherwise ill-founded. So in general I would accept the submission of counsel that issues relevant to limitation should not enter into consideration on applications for pre-trial discovery".

See page 130.

Hartley and Another v Jackson and Lewin

Fracture: X-ray: standard of care: substandard treatment

Horridge J (with special jury). [1933] 1 The Lancet 1148, [1933] 1 BMJ 942

On 30 July 1931 the plaintiff, aged seventeen, sustained a compound fracture of the femur in a traffic accident. On 3 August he was admitted to the defendants' nursing home. The fracture was reduced there. On 7 August the plaintiff's injured leg slipped off the foot of the bed, due to its not having been properly fixed, and was twisted. On 20 August his father removed him from the home. On 21 August his family doctor advised him that the result of the reduction operation was very bad and that, unless something was done, the plaintiff would become a cripple for life.

The plaintiff and his father sued the nursing home's owners who were a Kings Lynn surgeon and his partner. Expert evidence was given that the fracture had never been properly set, that an X-ray should have been taken to see the effect of the correction and that traction should have been applied to keep the bones in position.

Held: Horridge J directed the jury that the law applicable to the case was simple. A man who professed to be a consulting surgeon must use due care and skill. It would not follow that he did not use due care and skill merely because some other surgeon would have given different treatment. The surgeon gave no guarantee that his treatment would succeed; he was not negligent merely because it did not succeed. Nor was he negligent because he adopted a method which others would not have adopted, provided that his method was not in itself negligent and improper.

The jury found that the defendants had been negligent, both in relation to the incident on 7 August and otherwise.

Hatcher v Black and Others

Operation: risk disclosure: standard of care

Denning LJ (with jury). [1954] The Times 2 July

In November 1951 the plaintiff (Mrs Celia Hatcher) had been suffering from goitre. She was referred to St. Bartholomew's Hospital where she saw Dr Black. He diagnosed a toxic goitre and discussed with her the possible alternatives, an operation in hospital or medical treatment with drugs. He pointed out that it would take a long time by drugs and did not tell her that there was a slight risk to her voice involved in the operation. Mr Tuckwell performed on her a partial thyroidectomy at the hospital. Her left vocal cord was paralysed, and she alleged that the operation had permanently damaged her voice.

Held: Lord Justice Denning directed the jury:

(i) that it was for them to say whether Dr Black had told her that there was no risk whatsoever, or he may have prevaricated to put her off, as many a good doctor would rather than worry her. Even if he told her, that was not necessarily a matter for censure; the law did not condemn a doctor when he only did what a wise doctor so placed would do;

(ii) all the doctors testifying had said that damage to the laryngeal nerve was a well-known hazard in such an operation, notwithstanding all care, and there was no suggestion that Mr Tuckwell had done anything that he ought not to have done.

The jury returned a verdict for the defendants.

See pages 35, 68, 73.

Hatwell v South-West Metropolitan Regional Hospital Board

Epilepsy: psychiatrist: drugs: psychiatric patient: substandard treatment: damages

Court of Appeal. 5 November 1976

In 1969 the plaintiff (Miss Ruth Hatwell) was suffering from severe endogenous depression. She had been taking drugs known as Seconal and Valium, prescribed by her general practitioner. On 23 December 1969 she was admitted to Belmont Hospital and seen by a psychiatrist, Dr Markus. He ordered the withdrawal of all drugs from her forthwith.

On 24 December the plaintiff suffered from violent tremors. In the afternoon she had an isolated attack of grand mal epilepsy, with the result that she fell and fractured her jaw. She suffered substantial pain and emotional distress. She was left with deviation of her jaw two units to the left on opening. There was also an area of anaesthesia below the malar prominence of her left cheek.

The trial judge (Norman Richards J) held that Dr Markus' medical treatment had been negligent in that, having regard to the nature and extent of the drugs prescribed by the general practitioner, if there was to be a withdrawal of drugs it should not have been so immediate and so complete. He awarded her general damages (December 1975) of £600 for pain, suffering and loss of amenities.

Held: the general damages should be increased to £1,000. The damages payable should be referable to the plaintiff's actual personality, even if, as a result of that personality, the damages were greater than they would have been for someone in a less vulnerable condition. The defendants had to take the plaintiff as they found her.

See pages 81, 98.

Hayward v Curwen

Injection: drugs: causation

McNair J. [1964] The Times 29 January

The plaintiff (Tom Hayward) had for some years been a sufferer from disabling attacks of gout. He had been under the care of Dr Wilson, a consultant specialist in physical medicine, who had prescribed colchicine at first orally and later by intravenous injection. On 19 August 1959, Dr Wilson being ill, Dr Curwen visited the plaintiff at his home and injected the drug intravenously into his left arm. The plaintiff told Dr Curwen at the time that this caused him no pain or discomfort. However he later developed median nerve palsy.

Held: (i) Dr Curwen had not been shown to be negligent in the choice of vein in which to inject; nor was he negligent in asking the plaintiff to grip his own left arm in order to distend the vein. Dr Curwen's belief that if any of the drug injected intravenously had been accidently injected into the tissues outside the vein the patient would have experienced pain was reasonable;

(ii) with regard to causation, it had not been shown that the median nerve palsy was due to colchicine injected accidently outside the vein, rather than to the growth of a haematoma.
See pages 42, 79.

Heafield v Crane and Another

Hospital administration: duty of care: infection: warning: segregation

Singleton J. [1937] The Times 31 July

The plaintiff (Mrs Marjorie Heafield) entered the Ashby-de-la-Zouche Cottage Hospital to have a baby. One of the hospital rules was that no infectious case should be kept at the hospital. After the birth of her child, she was removed from the maternity ward to a general ward. A woman there was found later to be suffering from puerperal fever. The plaintiff caught if from her. She became crippled in the hips, and one of her shoulders and a wrist were also affected. She sued Mr Crane, the hospital chairman, in his representative capacity and also Dr Hart who had attended her in the hospital.

Held: (i) the hospital authorities ought to have known that the hospital was dangerous, but no warning was given to the plaintiff. They failed in their duty to her when they placed her in a ward where there was a deeply suspicious case;

(ii) Dr Hart had in the hospital a patient who was a gravely suspicious case. He ought to have isolated that patient to prevent the infection spreading. When he found that the plaintiff had been put in the same ward as that patient, it was his duty to have her removed and do everything to prevent her becoming infected. He also had neglected his duty towards her.
See pages 12, 26, 87.

Hegarty v Tottenham Hospital Management Committee and Others

Substandard treatment: nurses: causation

Court of Appeal. 20 February 1976

On 1 April 1969 Patrick Hegarty, a thirty year old labourer, contracted measles. On 5 April he was admitted to St Ann's Hospital, Tottenham. On 9 April polyneuritis was diagnosed. It was feared that he might develop pneumonia. By 13 April he was having difficulty with his breathing and was placed in a Kelleher rotating alligator tank respirator (or iron-lung). Thick white secretions were removed from his throat. Apart from short periods of removal for X-ray, he remained in the iron lung until he died on 17 April. Broncho-pneumonia was found on autopsy.

His widow sued the hospital authority and three of the doctors. The trial judge (Swanwick J) found that the doctors were negligent in failing to operate the iron lung in such a manner as to prevent the inhalation and pooling of secretions; and that the pooling of these secretions caused the broncho-pneumonia which killed the patient.

Held: (i) as the supposed failure was never part of the plaintiff's substantive case, as it was never put to the main doctor concerned, and as it cast more than a suspicion of negligence upon the nursing staff against whom the plaintiff made no allegations at all, the conclusion of negligence could not be allowed to stand;

(ii) the plaintiff had not established that the pooling of the secretions was the cause of the broncho-pneumonia. The most that could be said was that such pooling might perhaps have occurred and might perhaps have precipitated the broncho-pneumonia.
See page 42.

Henderson v Henderson

Surgeon: operation: needle breaking: departing from orthodox practice

Lord Guthrie (Scottish Court of Session). [1955] 1 BMJ 672

In March 1951 Marion Henderson underwent an operation for the removal of her tonsils and adenoids. This was performed by Mr Henderson, a surgeon, at Maryfield Hospital, Dundee. Severe bleeding occurred at the end of the operation, and Mr Henderson took measures to control this by stitching. While he was doing so, the needle broke, and two-thirds of it, about half an inch in length, remained in the child's throat. A stitch was inserted with a fresh needle, and the bleeding was brought under control.

At that point the bulb in the headlamp used by Mr Henderson failed, plunging the theatre into almost total darkness. Replacement of the bulb took only a few seconds, and continuous anaesthesia by gas was administered while the broken needle was sought. Mr Henderson probed the child's soft palate with his finger and the blunt end of forceps. After about fifteen minutes he thought he felt the needle and made an incision with a scalpel. The needle was not found and a stitch was inserted in the incision. The search lasted unsuccessfully for an hour.

Next day the missing part of the needle was removed at another hospital by an electro-magnet. The child had received severe scarring of her throat during the earlier efforts to find it. She sued Mr Henderson.

Held: although normally meticulous, Mr Henderson had negligently departed from proper surgical procedure in the circumstances. It should have occurred to him that prolonged probing and stretching of the fibres would have serious and possibly permanent consequences. Had he exercised the care and skill

reasonably to be expected of a surgeon, after a few minutes he would have desisted from his blind search.
See page 79.

Herskovits v Group Health Cooperative of Puget Sound

Cancer: diagnosis: causation: damages: foreign: loss of chance

Supreme Court of Washington. 664 P 2d 474 (Wash. 1983)

In early 1974 Leslie Herskovits attended the Group Health Cooperative with complaints of pain and coughing. Chest X-rays revealed infiltrate in the left lung. Rales were present. The chest pain and coughing became persistent and chronic by December 1974. He was treated with cough medicine.

In June 1975 Mr Herskovits visited Dr Ostrow for a second medical opinion. Within three weeks, Dr Ostrow's evaluation and direction to Group Health led to the diagnosis of cancer. In July 1975 his diseased lung was removed, but no radiation or chemotherapy was instituted. In March 1977 Mr Herskovits died at the age of sixty.

The plaintiff (his widow) sued the hospital authority, alleging failure to make an early diagnosis of the lung cancer. The trial court granted the defendant's motion for summary judgment for dismissal, on the basis that Mr Herskovits probably would have died from lung cancer even if the diagnosis had been made earlier.

Counsel agreed that for the purpose of the appeal the court was to assume that the failure to diagnose cancer in December 1974 and the consequent six months delay reduced Mr Herskovits' chances of survival from 30 per cent to 25 per cent. It was undisputed that he had less than a 50 per cent chance of survival at all relevant times.

Held: (i) a 14 per cent reduction, from 39 per cent to 25 per cent, in the deceased's chances of survival, was sufficient evidence of causation to allow the jury to consider the possibility that the delay in diagnosing the cancer was the proximate cause of death;

(ii) this reduced chance of survival did not necessitate total recovery for all damages caused by the death; rather, damages should be awarded based only on damages caused directly by premature death, such as lost earnings and additional medical expenses etc.

Per Dole J: "To decide otherwise would be a blanket release from liability for doctors and hospitals any time there was less than a 50 per cent chance of survival, regardless of how flagrant the negligence".

See page 48.

Hills v Potter and Another

Surgeon: risk disclosure: battery: consent

Hirst J. [1983] 3 All ER 716, [1984] 1 WLR 641

In January 1974 the plaintiff (Mrs Sylvia Hills) underwent at the Radcliffe

Infirmary an operation performed by Mr Potter for spasmodic torticollis, a deformity of the neck. As a result of the operation she was paralysed from the neck downwards. No negligence in performance of the operation was alleged.

Mr Potter had seen the plaintiff in September 1973 and explained what the operation involved. He said that any major operation, such as this one, carried certain risks but they should not be exaggerated. There was always a small risk of the patient dying or something going wrong with the anaesthetics and a risk of paralysis or at least weakness to the arms and legs, which might only be temporary or transient.

The plaintiff sued Mr Potter and the hospital authority for:

(a) negligently failing to provide her with all appropriate information as to the risk; and

(b) assault and battery on the basis that her consent was not real. None of the three surgical experts said that they would have given more detail than Mr Potter.

Held: as Mr Potter's practice accorded with that upheld by a substantial body of respectable and responsible medical opinion, he was not negligent. The plaintiff's undoubted consent to the operation that was in fact performed negatived any possibility of liability for assault and battery.
See pages 4, 5, 68, 70.

Hocking v Bell

Operation: after-care: retained surgical product: causation

Privy Council. [1948] WN 21

In March 1938 Dr Bell performed a thyroidectomy on the plaintiff (Mrs Stella Hocking). Her case was that a few days later, when Dr Bell undertook the removal of a rubber drainage tube from her wound, he negligently left *in situ* a portion of its inner end, which broke off, and never got it out. She alleged that the foreign body, enclosed in a suppurating cavity, brought about violent and painful attacks of tetany and that in October 1939, during a particularly severe tetanic spasm, a portion of tube was carried into her mouth due to the bursting out from her left tonsil of the abscess surrounding the foreign body. Dr Bell denied that this was possible.

Held: it could not be said that no reasonable jury could have reached the jury's verdict, namely that Dr Bell had negligently injured the plaintiff by leaving in the site of the operation a portion of rubber tube somewhat less than two inches long. There was no adequate ground for ordering a new trial, and the verdict should be restored.
See page 83.

Hodson v Mellor

Alternative practitioner: substandard treatment: representations: standard of care

Manchester County Court. [1911] 1 BMJ 1489

In 1908 the plaintiff (William Hodson) had a cataract in his right eye. It had not developed to the stage when an operation could be performed. He obtained through a newspaper advertisement a booklet which stated: "Mr William Mellor, the famous eye specialist, rightly claims to have been the recipient of more unsolicited praise from people he has cured than any man in the country . . . The 'William Mellor' system of eye treatment is based on irrefutable scientific principles which have long been justified by their outstanding success".

The plaintiff saw Mr Mellor who examined his eye, and said he could cure it without an operation and guaranteed that he would do so. Over two years Mr Mellor gave him drops for the eye and some medicines and pills. The drops inflamed the eye which became worse.

The plaintiff sued Mr Mellor for negligence and breach of contract. Mr Mellor testified that he had practised as an oculist in Manchester for sixteen or seventeen years. He admitted that he had been in Perth, Australia, but denied that he had ever been a door-keeper at the eye hospital there or that his sole scientific experience had been gained in that capacity.

Held: this was a case in which a person held himself out to possess skill which he did not possess and, by means of very optimistic advertisements, he persuaded people to come and consult him. The judge found for the plaintiff. See pages 17, 96.

Hoffman v Sofaer

General practitioner: substandard treatment: damages

Talbot J. [1982] 1 WLR 1350

In August 1976 the plaintiff (Mr Hoffman), an American then aged forty-seven, was visiting London. He was right handed and had pain in the right arm which he attributed to lifting heavy luggage. He consulted Dr Sofaer, a general practitioner, who diagnosed tennis elbow. Dr Sofaer administered lignocaine, hydrocortisone and hyaluronidase by injection. He later admitted liability for negligent treatment.

The plaintiff experienced further pain in his elbow and became feverish. An abscess formed in the region of his right elbow, which necessitated multiple incisions under general anaesthesia. In September 1976 he returned to the United States. His right upper arm was wasted, and an operation was performed to save it. X-rays taken in October 1977 showed absence of the radial head and solid fusion of the right elbow at an angle of 75° of flexion. Owing to the condition of his arm, in January 1978 he suffered a fall which resulted in a transverse undisplaced supracondylar fracture of the right humerus. He was left with an arthrodesed elbow and severe impairment of wrist and hand function. He was greatly limited in do-it-yourself tasks and his work. He had difficulty in writing and could no longer pursue his hobby of photography.

Held: (i) general damages for pain, suffering and loss of amenities were assessed at £19,000 (May 1981);

(ii) judgment for all the plaintiff's other damages—eg loss of earnings, medical expenses, loss of holiday, cost of employing others to perform his former work in the home—was given in U.S. dollars, as that was the currency in which his losses were suffered.
See pages 103–104.

Hogg v Ealing, Hammersmith and Hounslow Area Health Authority and Another

Cottage hospital: diagnosis: nurses: patient's history

Forbes J. [1982] 4 MLJ 174

On 3 October 1975 the plaintiff, then aged eleven, cut his left hand on some glass, and a splinter entered his palm below the ring finger. His mother removed the splinter and disinfected the hand. On 9 October he fell on his left hand, bending back the ring and middle fingers. By 10 October the ring finger was swollen. He was seen by a nurse at the casualty department of a cottage hospital. An X-ray revealed no bony injury; lead lotion was applied, and he was told to return next day if necessary. As the swelling was worse, his mother took him back to the cottage hospital in the afternoon where an orthopaedic surgeon, who was holding a clinic there, saw him for three to four minutes and diagnosed a soft tissue injury to the proximal interphalangeal joint.

Two days later the plaintiff's hand was very swollen and he was admitted to another hospital as an in-patient. He was left with a permanently flexed ring finger which did not respond to physiotherapy. He sued alleging a negligent failure to diagnose and treat the infection at the cottage hospital.

Held: neither the nurse nor the surgeon was told of the earlier injury on 3 October. Consequently there were no grounds for suspecting an infection in the hand when they saw the plaintiff. They had not been negligent.
See page 64.

Holgate and Another v Lancashire Mental Hospitals Board, Gill and Robertson

Prison inmate: duty of care: supervision: standard of care

Lewis J (with jury). [1937] 4 All ER 19

John Lawson had very early in life shown criminal tendencies. After convictions for wilful damage, indecent assault, housebreaking and theft, he was sent to a reformatory school. He was then tried and acquitted for attempted rape. Within two months he was charged with robbery with violence and two cases of indecent assault. In February 1927 he was ordered to be detained during His Majesty's pleasure and was sent to the Calderstone Institution.

An application was made for him to go out on licence to the house of his brother who would have taken a holiday and been at home to look after him. This application was refused. When it was later repeated and granted, no enquiries were made of the brother nor undertakings sought from him. In June 1936, during his leave, Lawson visited the house of the plaintiffs (Mr and Mrs Holgate) where Mrs Holgate was alone. She gave him food and began to mend a garment at his request, when he struck her on the head and hand with a piece of wood, causing severe injury.

The plaintiffs sued Lancashire Mental Hospitals Board, Dr Gill (the superintendent) who had agreed to Lawson's initial leave, and Dr Robertson (the acting superintendent) who had granted an extension of it.

Held: Lewis J directed the jury that they should not find negligence if the defendants were only guilty of an error of judgement. The question was whether, bearing in mind the care and control of mental defectives which they must exercise, the defendants failed to take reasonable care.

The jury found that all three defendants were negligent.

See pages 26, 88.

Holland v The Devitt and Moore Nautical College Limited and Another

School doctor: diagnosis: vicarious liability: medical literature: standard of care

Streatfield J. [1960] The Times 4 March

Peter Holland had suffered from mild attacks of epilepsy since the age of three. In May 1954, when he was a fifteen year old pupil at the Devitt and Moore Nautical College, he was stricken with infective hepatitis. Dr Thomas, the school medical officer, concluded that it was a mild case. He put the boy on a full fat-free diet and glucose and kept him in bed. Peter told him that he felt perfectly well: there was no nausea, no vomiting and his appetite was normal. He showed continued improvement, even after being allowed to get up in his room, although without completely recovering. Dr Thomas allowed him to go home for the school half-term holiday on 5 June, partly because he feared that the emotional disturbance of refusing this might adversely affect the epilepsy. The day after his return to school, Peter had a relapse. His disease progressed, and in 1957 he died of cirrhosis of the liver. His father sued the college and Dr Thomas.

According to its prospectus, the college held itself out as providing medical attention including treatment in the sick-bay. Dr Thomas had to visit the college on Tuesdays and Fridays and attend the boys in the sick-bay when sent for.

Held: (i) the college had undertaken to provide treatment in the sick-bay, and that could not be read as limited to treatment by the sister. Therefore if Dr Thomas was negligent, the college would be vicariously liable;

(ii) all the doctors had agreed that the general practitioner in charge of the case was in the best position to judge, and that statements in textbooks were no substitute for his judgement. Not only was there no negligence, but also no mistake was made in the first stage. It was the cruellest misfortune that, in spite of all indications to the contrary, the disease had turned out to be more severe than thought.

See pages 39, 64.

Hopley v British Transport Commission and Others

Anaesthetics: operation: state of knowledge: medical literature: hospital administration

Pilcher J. [1960] 2 The Lancet 1452

In January 1954 Mr Hopley was knocked down by a lorry and seriously injured. He was admitted to hospital and needed an operation. He was anaesthetised with an explosive mixture of oxygen, nitrous oxide and cyclopropane. While he was on the operating table, it became necessary to deepen anaesthesia, and the anaesthetist decided to change from an open to a closed circuit. For this purpose he had to remove the terminal metal cylinder of the breathing tube from a metal orifice on the anaesthetics trolley. As he did so a spark, caused by a static electrical charge on the apparatus, ignited the anaesthetic and an explosion took place. As a result Mr Hopley, whose lungs had been full of the gas, died about one and a half hours later.

The plaintiff (his widow) sued the lorry driver's employers, the anaesthetist and the hospital authority. Evidence was given that in 1947 an authoritative textbook on anaesthesia, dealing with the risk of sparks, recommended that the relative humidity of an operating theatre should not be less than sixty per cent when explosive anaesthetics were being used. When the explosion occurred, however, the humidity in the theatre was twenty-five per cent or less. This was due to a minor failure of the air conditioning plant two days before the operation, which could easily have been put right.

Held: (i) the anaesthetist was entitled to assume that the humidity was correct; his first duty was to a patient who was in a bad state. It would be wrong to convict him of negligence;

(ii) the hospital authority was liable for failing to maintain the correct humidity.

See page 37.

Horner v Scarborough, Bridlington, Malton and Whitby Group Hospital Management Committee

Consultant: substandard treatment: patient's history: diagnosis: physiotherapist

Edmund Davies J. [1966] 2 The Lancet 47

On 6 March 1961 the plaintiff, then aged seventy-six, found that she could not move her left leg and had pain from the hip downwards. She had had osteoarthritis of the knee joints for many years but had led a fairly active life.

After visits on 7 and 14 March, her general practitioner referred her on a non-urgent basis to the temporary consultant physician at the local hospital's rheumatism clinic. He mentioned that she had asked for a wheelchair.

When the consultant saw her on 24 March, he gave her a gruff reception, would not let her explain about her leg and said "You must get up and walk. You cannot have a chair" (a wheelchair on the NHS). Although she demonstrated her inability to walk, he did not examine her knee. He wrote to her general practitioner, referring to her "unwillingness" to move, and stating that the provision of a wheelchair would "complete her downfall". He sent her to the physiotherapy department for walking exercises and short-wave diathermy.

She attended five times between 7 and 17 April. She was supported in walking by two physiotherapists. They stated that it was difficult to say whether she was limping and that she complained of pain. The walking exercises were not continued after the second visit, but the diathermy was persisted in until the physiotherapists referred her back to the clinic.

The plaintiff was then seen by a different consultant who, after an X-ray, diagnosed a displaced fracture of the neck of the femur. After an unsuccessful attempt at pinning, an arthroplasty was performed on 2 May. She sued the hospital authority, the temporary consultant and the physiotherapists.

Held: (i) the temporary consultant had jumped too hastily to the conclusion that the plaintiff was unwilling, rather than unable, to do what was asked of her on 24 March. She was complaining of such pain and presented such signs as should have led to a thorough examination by the temporary consultant and an X-ray forthwith. The hospital authority was liable for his negligence;

(ii) the physiotherapists were governed and influenced by the view of the plaintiff's condition implicit in the consultant's instructions. They should not have detected that something was radically wrong. They had not been negligent.
See page 89.

Hothi v Greenwich Health Authority and Another

Consultant: prescription: tests: foreseeability: epilepsy

Croom-Johnson J. [1982] 2 The Lancet 1474

At 10.00pm on 28 June 1976 the plaintiff (Mr Hothi), then aged twenty-four, was admitted to hospital with a severe head injury. He was deeply unconscious. A brain scan was ordered. On 29 June Mr Neil-Dwyer, consultant neurosurgeon, took control of the case. At 12.30pm slight twitching and chewing of the jaw on the right side were observed. Mr Neil-Dwyer believed that there were signs of focal epilepsy and that there was a need to reduce oedema in the brain. Phenobarbitone was given three times a day, and later a decompression operation was performed. The plaintiff continued to take phenobarbitone until his discharge on 26 July when he was provided with a supply for two further weeks.

After he went home, the plaintiff developed a severe rash on the trunk. He suffered persistent symptoms of Stevens-Johnson syndrome. He sued the health authority and Mr Neil-Dwyer, contending that phenobarbitone should not have been prescribed and/or that sensitivity tests should have been carried out beforehand.

Held: the defendants were not liable. Where there was epilepsy, it was correct to prescribe an anticonvulsant. Phenobarbitone was a proper drug for the purpose and had been prescribed in the correct quantity. The plaintiff's adverse reaction to it was not foreseeable. The chance of Stevens-Johnson syndrome was so remote that no doctor could be negligent because there was a very slight risk that some hypersensitive person might have an adverse reaction.
See pages 51, 80.

Hotson v East Berkshire Health Authority

Diagnosis: substandard treatment: loss of chance: fracture: causation: damages

House of Lords. [1987] AC 750, [1987] 2 All ER 909, [1987] 3 WLR 232

On 26 April 1977 the plaintiff (Stephen Hotson), then aged thirteen, was playing in the school lunch hour. He climbed a tree to which a rope was attached, lost his hold on the rope and fell some twelve feet to the ground. Within hours he was taken to St Luke's Hospital, Maidenhead. The hospital staff examined him but failed to diagnose he had sustained an acute traumatic fracture of the left femoral epiphysis. He was sent home and for five days was in severe pain. On 1 May 1977, when he returned to the hospital, X-rays of his hip disclosed the correct diagnosis. He suffered an avascular necrosis of the epiphysis, causing disability of the hip joint with a virtual certainty of future osteoarthritis. He sued the health authority who admitted negligence in failing to diagnose the injury on 26 April 1977.

The trial judge (Simon Brown J) made the following findings of fact:

"(1) Even had the health authority correctly diagnosed and treated the plaintiff on 26 April there is a high probability, which I assess as a seventy-five per cent risk, that the plaintiff's injury would have followed the same course as it in fact has, that is, he would have developed avascular necrosis of the whole femoral head with all the same adverse consequences as have already ensued and with all the same adverse future prospects.

"(2) That seventy-five per cent risk was translated by the health authority's admitted breach of duty into an inevitability. Putting it the other way, their delay in diagnosis denied the plaintiff the twenty-five per cent chance that, given immediate treatment, avascular necrosis would not have developed.

"(3) Had avascular necrosis not developed, the plaintiff would have made a very nearly full recovery.

"(4) The reason why the delay sealed the plaintiff's fate was because it allowed the pressure caused by haemarthrosis—the bleeding of ruptured blood vessels into the joint— to compress and thus block the intact but distorted remaining vessels with the result that even had the fall left intact sufficient vessels to keep the epiphysis alive (which, as finding (1) makes plain, I think possible but improbable) such vessels would have become occluded and ineffective for this purpose".

On the basis of these findings, he awarded the plaintiff £150 for his pain and suffering from 26 April to 1 May plus twenty-five per cent of the £46,000 damages attributable to the avascular necrosis as compensation for loss of the twenty-five per cent chance of a recovery. The Court of Appeal dismissed the defendant's appeal against this latter element.

Held: in determining what happened in the past, the court decides on the balance of probabilities. Anything that is more probable than not is treated as a certainty. Unless the plaintiff proved on a balance of probabilities that the delayed treatment was at least a material contributory cause of the avascular necrosis, he failed on the issue of causation and no question of quantification could arise. The judge's findings of fact were that on a balance of probabilities the injury caused by the plaintiff's fall left insufficient blood vessels intact to keep the epiphysis alive. This amounted to a finding of fact that the fall was the sole cause of the avascular necrosis. The appeal was allowed on the ground that the plaintiff failed to establish that the health authority's negligence caused his avascular necrosis and its consequences.

Per Lord Ackner: "Once liability is established, on the balance of probabilities, the loss which the plaintiff has sustained is payable in full. It is not discounted by reducing his claim by the extent to which he has failed to prove his case with one hundred per cent certainty. The decision of Simon Brown J in the subsequent case of *Bagley* v *North Herts Health Authority*, reported only in (1986) 136 NLJ 1014, in which he discounted an award for a stillbirth, because there was a five per cent risk that the plaintiff would have had a stillborn child even if the hospital had not been negligent, was clearly wrong. In that case, the plaintiff had established on a balance of probabilities, indeed with near certainty, that the hospital's negligence had caused the stillbirth. Causation was thus fully established. Such a finding does not permit any discounting. To do so would be to propound a wholly new doctrine which has no support in principle or authority and would give rise to many complications in the search for mathematical or statistical exactitude.

"Of course, where the cause of action has been established, the assessment of that part of the plaintiff's loss where the future is uncertain involves the evaluation of that uncertainty. In *Bagley*, if the child had, by reason of the hospital's breach of duty, been born with brain injury, which could lead in later life to epilepsy, then it would have been a classic case for the evaluation, inter alia, of the chance of epilepsy occurring and discounting, to the extent that the chance of that happening fell below 100 per cent, what would have been the sum of damages appropriate if epilepsy was a certain consequence."

See pages 14, 16, 39, 46–49, 62, 98, 99

Hucks v Cole and Another

General practitioner: diagnosis: communication: penicillin: standard of care

Court of Appeal. (1968) 118 NLJ 469, (1968) 12 SJ 483, [1968] The Times 9 May

The plaintiff (Mrs Hucks) was under the care of Dr Cole, a general practitioner with a diploma in obstetrics, during and after her confinement. On 4 October 1963 her ring finger became swollen and a sore developed on it with several yellow spots. Dr Cole told her it was nothing to worry about and did not inform the maternity hospital where, on 10 October, she gave birth. On 11 October the hospital, alarmed by the condition of her finger and the fact that one of her toes was similarly affected, isolated her from other patients. On 12 October a bacteriological test was taken and an antiobiotic, tetracycline, administered to her. The bacteriological report indicated that she was suffering from fulminating septicaemia. On 16 October the five day course of tetracycline ended. However, although her lesions had not fully healed, Dr Cole did not then begin a course of penicillin treatment or prescribe antibiotics for her. The plaintiff's voice was permanently impaired.

Held: Dr Cole was to be judged as a general practitioner with a diploma in obstetrics. He had allowed the plaintiff to enter hospital with a septic finger and had not notified the hospital of her condition. He failed at the appropriate time to put her on to penicillin or more antibiotics. He had been negligent.

Per Lord Denning MR: "A doctor is not to be held negligent simply because something has gone wrong. He is not liable for mischance or misadventure; or for an error in judgement. He is not liable for taking one choice out of two or favouring one school rather than another. He is only liable when he falls below the standard of a reasonably competent practitioner in his field. . . . ."

Sachs LJ, concurring, said that when the evidence showed that a lacuna in professional practice existed by which risks of grave danger were knowingly taken, then however small the risks, the courts must anxiously examine that lacuna, particularly if the risks could be easily and inexpensively avoided.

See pages 35, 38, 62.

Hughes v Hay and Another

Consultant: diagnosis: damages: fresh evidence

Court of Appeal. 13 April 1989

In April 1982 the plaintiff (Barry Hughes), then a serving police officer, was involved in a road traffic collision in which he fell from his motor cycle and injured his right shoulder. About three weeks later his general practitioner referred him to Mr Hay, a consultant orthopaedic surgeon. Mr Hay did not diagnose the true nature of the injury which was a posterior dislocation of the right shoulder joint. In consequence the plaintiff was left with a substantial disability instead of a minor one.

The plaintiff sued the other motor cycle rider and Mr Hay. Liability was admitted. In May 1988 the trial judge (Hugh Carlisle QC) awarded damages which included £3,000 in respect of the future disadvantages of the plaintiff on the open labour market, on the assumption that he would be able to serve out his remaining ten years in the police force. In June the plaintiff appealed. In September 1988, following a medical examination, he was discharged from the police on medical grounds.

Held: this was a classic case for the exercise of the Court of Appeal's discretion in favour of the plaintiff. Justice would not be done unless the additional development of his discharge from the police force became the subject matter of a retrial.
See pages 62, 99–100.

Hulse v Wilson and Others

Cancer: diagnosis: consultant: causation

Finnemore J. [1953] 2 BMJ 890

In 1948 the plaintiff (Daniel Hulse), then aged about thirty, underwent tests for venereal disease in Birmingham Hospital. He was also seen by Dr Wilson at West Bromwich Hospital. The pain increased, and in January 1949 the plaintiff was admitted to West Bromwich Hospital where they still thought that he was suffering from venereal disease. Mr Kirkham performed a minor operation, which disclosed an ulcer, and sent the plaintiff home three days later. In March he saw another surgeon who diagnosed cancer. In July his penis was amputated.

The plaintiff sued the hospital doctors and the hospital authority for negligently diagnosing venereal disease instead of cancer.

Held: (i) there was no reason for Dr Wilson to suspect cancer in the early stages, and at that time there was no reason for the case to be treated as urgent;

(ii) Mr Kirkham did not delay too long in satisfying himself that venereal disease was not the cause, since such a cancer was extremely rare, especially in a young man;

(iii) even if Mr Kirkham had immediately diagnosed cancer, it was not proved that the amputation could have been avoided.
Judgment for the defendants.
See pages 42, 63.

Hunter v Hanley

Injections: needle breaking: diagnosis: standard of care

Scotland, First Division. [1955] SLT 213, [1955] SC 200

Mrs Hunter suffered from chronic bronchitis for which Dr Hanley was treating her by a course of twelve injections of procaine penicillin into her buttocks with a size sixteen needle. In November 1951, during the twelfth injection, the needle broke as Dr Hanley was withdrawing it and the end remained embedded in Mrs Hunter's body.

She sued Dr Hanley for his alleged failure to use a suitable hypodermic needle. The trial judge directed the jury that "gross negligence" must be proved. The jury returned a verdict for Dr Hanley.

Held: the direction was inaccurate, so the jury's verdict could not stand. A new trial was ordered.
Per the Lord President (Clyde): "In the realm of diagnosis and treatment there is ample scope for genuine difference of opinion and one man clearly is not negligent merely because his conclusion differs from that of other professional men, nor because he has displayed less skill and knowledge than others would have shown. The true test in establishing negligence in diagnosis or treatment on the part of a doctor is whether he has been proved to be guilty

of such failure as no doctor of ordinary skill would be guilty of if acting with ordinary care. The standard seems to be the same in England".

See pages 34, 39, 64, 79.

Hyde v Tameside Area Health Authority

Standard of care: diagnosis: foreseeability: public policy: supervision: suicide risk

Court of Appeal. [1981] The Times 16 April

On 7 February 1972 the plaintiff (Mr Hyde) tried to kill himself. He was in a ward on the third floor of the general hospital at Ashton-under-Lyne. In the middle of the night he got out of bed, smashed the window and jumped out on to the roadway. He survived but had total paralysis of the arms, body and legs, and loss of bladder and bowel control.

When admitted on 26 January, the plaintiff was suffering from a very painful right shoulder. On 31 January he was treated with cervical traction, but the pain was so severe it had to be discontinued. During a blizzard on 1 February he got out of bed, put on a pullover and slippers and attempted to discharge himself. Hospital notes for 2 February showed that he was then more composed. Another patient testified that from 1 to 4 February the plaintiff got terribly depressed and was crying. Thereafter he was seriously ill in body. It subsequently emerged that he thought (wrongly) that he had cancer and was going to die.

It was alleged that if the plaintiff had been treated carefully, the nurses and doctors would have noticed his depression and called in a psychiatrist who through treatment might have prevented the suicide attempt. The trial judge (Lincoln J) found liability against the health authority and awarded the plaintiff £200,000 damages.

Held: the nurses and doctors had treated the plaintiff with the utmost care and competence. Even if this finding was wrong, in failing to assess the true significance of his mental distress, they had only made an error of clinical judgement which was not such an error as to amount to negligence. Moreover the plaintiff's suicide attempt was too remote a consequence of an error to be the subject of damages.

Lord Denning MR expressed the view that the policy of the law should be to discourage actions in respect of suicides and attempted suicides. Lord Justice Watkins and Lord Justice O'Connor concurred in allowing the appeal on the ground that the evidence did not establish any breach of duty by the hospital.

See pages 25, 51, 89.

Jacob v Wessex Regional Health Authority

Discovery: legally aided plaintiff: costs

Master Turner. [1984] CLY 2618

The plaintiff asked for disclosure of various hospital documents. There ensued comprehensive correspondence from the plaintiff's solicitors as to the relevant authorities and the reasonableness of the request. They pointed out that, as the plaintiff was legally aided, an application would result in unnecessary public expense. The health authority refused the disclosure.

Consequently the plaintiff applied for specific discovery pursuant to s 33 Supreme Court Act 1981 and RSC O 24 r 7A. Before the hearing of the application, the health authority agreed to disclose the hospital documents but claimed its costs pursuant to RSC O 62 r 3 (12).

Held: the circumstances were appropriate for the court to "otherwise direct". The health authority should pay the plaintiff's costs of the application in any event.
See page 131.

Jacobs v Great Yarmouth and Waveney Health Authority

Anaesthetics: injection: causation

Court of Appeal. 29 March 1984. [1984] 1 The Lancet 1249

In July 1976 the plaintiff (Mrs Shelagh Jacobs) underwent an operation for hysterectomy at Lowestoft Hospital. Dr King-Davies, the anaesthetist, administered 3.5ml of althesin to her, a small woman weighing 7 stone 5 lb. She alleged that he negligently missed the vein so that, although she was paralysed by a subsequent injection of pavulon, she remained conscious and aware of the operative procedures right up to the minute of the first surgical incision for the operation itself.

Held: the trial judge (Forbes J) was justified in concluding that the plaintiff's allegation was mistaken, and that the more probable explanation of her experience was that as she regained consciousness of the operation, not realising that it had already taken place, she became aware of a number of incidents and had transposed them in her mind to the period before the operation.
See pages 81, 84.

James v Dunlop

Surgeon: retained surgical product: nurses: res ipsa loquitur

Court of Appeal. [1931] 1 BMJ 730

On 11 December 1928 Dr Dunlop operated on Mr James and removed some gall-stones. Mr James remained ill, and on 20 March 1929 a second operation was performed by Dr Burrell. He discovered a surgical pack in Mr James' body. Having been left there in the first operation, it set up a fistula from which he died on 27 March.

The plaintiff (his widow) sued Mr Dunlop. The evidence at trial was that between three and five packs had been inserted and that the pack which had been left was eight inches by ten inches. Dr Dunlop said that he asked "Are all the swabs out?" and heard a female voice answer "Yes", but he was not sure to whom the voice belonged. The jury found negligence proved.

Held: the fact that counting might be exercised by some other people did not

245

absolve the doctor from the necessity of making some reasonable search before he put any question to the nurse with regard to the count. Any jury who had felt the towelling pack and seen the size of it would conclude that it was careless not to have taken it out. Moreover they had not been satisfied on the evidence that a suitable assurance had been given.

Dr Dunlop's appeal was dismissed.

See pages 82, 93.

Jones v Berkshire Area Health Authority

Registrar: sterilisation (failed): wrongful birth: damages

Ognall J. [1986] QBD 2 July

In 1977, the plaintiff (Mrs Jones), then aged twenty-six, agreed to surgical sterilisation. Mr Woofson, a surgical registrar, performed the operation. In summer 1978, the plaintiff started to feel generally unwell, tired, dizzy and occasionally afflicted by "blackouts". Her girth increased and she missed her periods. She feared that she was suffering from cancer, perhaps of the womb. When she consulted her general practitioner in August 1978, he told her that she was twenty-eight weeks pregnant. In January 1979, she gave birth by caesarian section to a healthy baby girl.

The plaintiff sued the hospital authority on the basis that at no time was she advised that, despite the sterilisation operation, there was a small risk that she might conceive and that, had she known this, when she became unwell she would have suspected pregnancy, consulted her general practitioner and had an abortion. The trial judge accepted her evidence and found that the health authority was liable.

Held: general damages (July 1986) for pain, suffering and loss of amenities were assessed at £2,750 to cover the plaintiff's fear that she had cancer and the need for a caesarian operation. The total award was £32,963.

Jones v Fay

Pharmacist: negligent prescription: advice: standard of care

Pigott B (with jury). (1865) 4 F&F 525

The plaintiff (Mr Jones) was a painter. In May 1864 he went to the shop of Mr Fay, a chemist and druggist, and complained of pain in the stomach, called painter's colic. Mr Fay prescribed and dispensed a preparation of bluepill. The plaintiff collected these pills on several further occasions. Whenever he asked if he should have medical advice, Mr Fay dissuaded him from it and said that he would set him right. The plaintiff suffered severe salivation and subsequently contracted bronchitis and dropsy, aggravated by the weakness caused by the salivation.

He sued Mr Fay. Evidence was given that the bluepill contained a large proportion of mercury. Mr Fay claimed that he had administered rhubarb pills, not bluepill.

Held: Pigott B directed the jury that if a person acts as medical practitioner, he is liable although he is only a chemist. The question was whether the pills that Mr Fay gave the plaintiff were bluepill, for it was admitted that such treatment would have been improper in a case of colic.

The jury returned a verdict for the plaintiff.

See page 95.

Jones v Manchester Corporation and Others

Anaesthetics: burns: overdose: hospital administration: casualty officer: supervision: apportionment of liability

Court of Appeal. [1952] 2 KB 852, [1952] 2 All ER 125

In January 1950, William Jones was burnt about the face at work. He was taken to Ancoats Hospital where he was seen by two young doctors. Dr Sejrup, a house surgeon who had qualified in 1947, was acting as casualty officer. Dr Wilkes, who had obtained her degrees in 1949, was acting as anaesthetist that day, but she had no special qualifications as such and not much experience. The two young doctors decided to clean up Mr Jones' face under an anaesthetic. Dr Wilkes first applied nitrous oxide gas with oxygen by means of a mask over his face, thereby rendering him unconscious. When it was realised that the mask would be in the way, it was decided to switch to pentothal. Dr Wilkes injected the ordinary dose given to a person who has not had any anaesthetic (ten cubic centimetres). She allowed only ten seconds between the first five cubic centimetres and the second five, whereas she knew she ought to have allowed thirty seconds. By the time she had finished, Mr Jones was dead.

The trial judge (Oliver J) awarded the plaintiff widow damages against Mr Jones' employers, Manchester Corporation, in respect of the burns to his face. He held that Dr Wilkes and the hospital authority were liable in respect of his death.

Held: (i) the death was caused through negligence in the administration of the anaesthetic;

(ii) the employer cannot have an indemnity, if he himself has contributed to the damage or bears some part of the responsibility. It would be extremely unjust if hospital authorities, by getting inexperienced doctors to perform their duties for them, without adequate supervision, should be able to throw all responsibility on to those doctors as if they were fully experienced practitioners. The hospital board was not entitled to an indemnity against Dr Wilkes;

(iii) Dr Wilkes was not entitled to a complete indemnity from the hospital board, since it was admitted that she was negligent to a degree that was inexcusable even in an inexperienced person;

(iv) the proportion of responsibility for the damage should be twenty per cent to Dr Wilkes and eighty per cent to the hospital board.

See pages 25, 36, 38, 86.

Joseph v Korn and Another

General practitioner: vicarious liability: receptionist: dismissal for want of prosecution

Court of Appeal. 31 July 1984

The son of the plaintiff (Mrs Joseph) died of gastro-enteritis on 30 December 1971. She alleged that this was due to negligence by the child's general practitioner and his receptionist. Following a complaint, there was a full hearing by the appropriate health authority committee in 1972. The plaintiff's writ was issued on 23 December 1974. In March 1984 her action was dismissed for want of prosecution.

Held: there had been inordinate delay which was at least partly the plaintiff's fault. The delay had prejudiced a fair trial of the action, which would have to take place at least thirteen years after the event. Although there was a full transcript of the enquiry evidence, there were still disputed questions of fact. The plaintiff was refused leave to appeal.
See page 127.

Junor v McNicol and Others

Diagnosis: consultant: house surgeon: penicillin: fracture: substandard treatment: gangrene

House of Lords. [1959] The Times 26 March

On 2 July 1953 James Junor, then aged six, fell fom a gate and fractured his left forearm, sustaining also a small wound on his inner forearm. After treatment locally, his mother took him to the Raigmore Hospital where he was seen by Dr McNicol, a house surgeon, and Mr Murray, a consultant in orthopaedic surgery. Mr Murray's diagnosis was a greenstick fracture of both bones of the forearm "potentially compound" by which he meant that it was possible that the small wound communicated with the fracture. He instructed reduction of the fracture and a dry dressing on the wound, but said nothing to Dr McNicol about penicillin. She interpreted his instructions as meaning that the fracture was to be treated as a simple fracture. When the boy was in the theatre, she administered half a million units of penicillin and gave him anti-tetanus serum. She authorised his discharge on 3 July.

James' condition deteriorated on 5 July. He was hurried back to hospital and his arm was amputated in the shoulder joint, as gangrene had set in with such severity as to threaten his life. His father sued Dr McNicol and the hospital authority.

Held: there was no doubt that a mistake had been made in letting the boy out of hospital and he had not been given adequate treatment with penicillin. Dr McNicol's primary duty was to carry out the consultant's instructions unless they were manifestly wrong. In view of the opinion which the consultant had conveyed with regard to the wound, this was not a case in which she should have disregarded what she believed her instructions to be. Dr McNicol had not been negligent.
See pages 37, 81.

Karp v Cooley and Liotta

Heart transplant: surgeon: operation: informed consent: fraud: experimentation: causation: foreign

U.S. Court of Appeals, Fifth Circuit. (1974) 493 F 2d 408

In March 1969, Haskell Karp was admitted to St Luke's Episcopal Hospital in Houston, after a long and difficult ten-year history of cardiac problems. Tests showed that he had triple vessel disease where all three coronary arteries were occluded. Electrocardiograms showed evidence of extensive scarring and damage, and chest X-rays showed enormous cardiac enlargement. His pacemaker was about to fail.

Soon after Mr Karp's admission, Dr Denton Cooley recommended a heart transplant. Mr Karp rejected this, preferring "some alternative procedure". A wedge excision was considered but not performed. In late March Dr Cooley began to discuss with Mr Karp another alternative, involving the temporary implant of the first totally mechanical heart, to which after at least two discussions Mr Karp signed the following consent on 3 April:

". . . In the event cardiac function cannot be restored by excision of destroyed heart muscle and plastic reconstruction of the ventricle and death seems imminent, I authorise Dr Cooley and his staff to remove my diseased heart and insert a mechanical cardiac substitute. I understand that this mechanical device will not be permanent and ultimately will require replacement by a heart transplant. I realise that this device has been tested in the laboratory but has not been used to sustain a human being and that no assurance of success can be made. . . ".

Dr Cooley told Mr Karp that the chances of the wedge excision procedure failing were thirty per cent and that the mechanical heart had kept a calf alive for more than forty hours. He did not discuss with Mr Karp the number of animals in which the device had been tested.

When Mr Karp entered the operating room on 4 April he was near death, "mottled and blue". The operation began with Dr Cooley as chief surgeon and Dr Liotta as first assistant. Dr Cooley performed a wedge excision but, due to extensive scarring of the heart, there was not enough healthy muscle remaining to form an efficient pump to support Mr Karp's life. Consequently, his heart was removed and the mechanical device was inserted. He responded well and remained alive.

Subsequently a donor was found. The heart transplant operation was performed on 7 April, about sixty-four hours after the mechanical device had been implanted in Mr Karp. He died on 8 April, some thirty-two hours after the transplant surgery.

The plaintiff (his widow) sued Dr Cooley and Dr Liotta on the grounds of fraud, lack of informed consent, negligent surgery and negligent experimentation. The district court directed verdict and entered judgment for the defendants. The plaintiff appealed.

Held: (i) the plaintiff's reliance on what she was and was not told was misplaced. Consent of the wife for the husband's operation has no significance under Texan law unless she is legally authorised to give such consent. The relationship of husband and wife does not itself create such a legal authorisation;

(ii) what was significant was what Mr Karp was told. The consent form was consistent with Dr Cooley's testimony. Each step of the three-step operation was specifically set out in the consent form signed by Mr Karp. Moreover, as death was imminent after the wedge excision procedure, there was no causal relationship between the harm and the alleged lack of informed consent to the mechanical heart;

(iii) there was no evidence of fraud; the district court had been right to direct a verdict for the defendants on the fraud counts;

(iv) a specialist like Dr Cooley is bound to exercise the degree of skill and knowledge that is ordinarily possessed by similar specialists. Since the expert testimony provided no evidence of negligent surgical acts or omissions by the defendants, a directed verdict for both defendants was proper;

(v) an action for experimentation must be measured by traditional malpractice evidentiary standards based on how a reasonably careful and prudent physician would have acted under the same or similar circumstances. The record contained no evidence that Mr Karp's treatment was other than therapeutic. A directed verdict for the defendant was warranted.

Kavanagh v Abrahamson

General practitioner: duty of care: prescription: examination: causation

Fenton Atkinson J. (1964) 108 SJ 320

Mr and Mrs Kavanagh (the plaintiff) had been National Health patients of Dr Abrahamson for some years. They moved without notifying him. A few months later the plaintiff called at his surgery and told him that her husband did not feel well and might have caught influenza. He gave her a prescription for compound codeine tablets with instructions.

The next day the plaintiff called again at the surgery and asked him to visit Mr Kavanagh who had got worse. Later that day Dr Abrahamson visited the address on his records but obtained no reply to repeated ringing of the doorbell. He realised that the Kavanaghs must have moved and rang the doorbell of an adjoining flat. As there was no answer, he left to pay other urgent visits.

Two days later the plaintiff called at the surgery. Dr Abrahamson visited Mr Kavanagh who turned out to have bronchitis and died in hospital two days later.

Held: (i) there was a measure of force in the criticism that Dr Abrahamson might have done more than he did after calling and finding that the Kavanaghs had moved. However that was not, in itself, a negligent failure;

(ii) no doubt it was unusual to prescribe without seeing the patient, but so prescribing compound codeine tablets was not negligence in the absence of evidence that they made any difference.

See page 91.

Kay v Ayrshire and Arran Health Board

Injection: overdose: causation: penicillin: meningitis

House of Lords. [1987] 2 All ER 417

On 28 November 1975 Andrew Kay, then aged two and a half, was admitted to Seafield Children's Hospital in Ayr. Tests led to a diagnosis on 29 November of pneumococcal meningitis. The consultant paediatrician in charge of the case, Dr McCure, instructed that 10,000 units of penicillin be injected intrathecally. The injection was carried out shortly after noon by Dr Adam-Strump, a senior house officer. By mistake he injected 300,000 units of penicillin. The massive overdose rapidly produced toxic effects. The child went into convulsions and later developed a degree of hemiparesis. Dr Adam-Strump realised his mistake immediately and remedial measures were urgently instituted. These were successful in saving Andrew's life, and by 1 December the immediate ill effects of the overdose appeared to have been surmounted. He was discharged from hospital on 24 December. His parents before then had begun to suspect that he had been suffering from deafness. This proved to be the case. He suffered profound bilateral deafness.

His father sued on his behalf the hospital authority who admitted liability for Dr Adam-Strump's negligence. The authority contended that the consequences of his negligence were limited to the convulsions and hemiparesis and denied that the overdose had caused the deafness. Expert evidence was given at the hearing that, whereas deafness was a common sequel of meningitis, in no recorded case had an overdose of penicillin caused deafness.

Held: this was not a case of two competing causes of damage. The medical evidence simply failed to prove any causal link between the penicillin overdose and the deafness. The weight of the evidence was that the deafness was caused by meningitis. The father's appeal was dismissed.
See pages 19, 46, 81.

Kenyon v Bell

Diagnosis: hospital doctor: causation: loss of chance

Scotland, Court of Session. [1953] SC 125

On 15 March 1951 Mr Kenyon found his sixteen month old daughter Emily lying on the kitchen floor of his house in Dundee. Her head was resting upon a broken cup, and the lower lid of her left eye was cut and bleeding profusely. She was taken by two neighbours to the Dundee Royal Infirmary where she was seen by Dr Bell, the resident medical officer there. One of the neighbours informed him of the circumstances, and Dr Bell instructed a nurse to put drops into the child's eye and to apply a powder. No other treatment was ordered. He informed the neighbour that it was not necessary to consult the family doctor or to return to the infirmary.

The child's eye began to water around the end of June 1951. She was taken to her family doctor who at once ordered her removal to Dundee Royal Infirmary. It was found that there was severe internal haemorrhage in the left eye, which had a detached retina and a bulged iris. The eye was removed on 10 July 1951.

Mr Kenyon sued Dr Bell on the basis that as a result of his alleged negligence the child lost her eye or alternatively lost a material chance that her eye would be saved.

Held: (i) the loss of a chance of saving the eye was not of itself a matter which would warrant a recovery of damages;

(ii) if however the chance of saving the eye by proper treatment was so material that the natural and reasonable inference was that its loss was due to the absence of such treatment, this would entitle the case to succeed.

N.B. This reasoning was followed by the House of Lords in *Hotson v East Berkshire Health Authority*.

See pages 46, 48.

Kilburn v Swindon and District Hospital Management Committee

Diagnosis: casualty officer: X-ray: examination: fractures: damages

Pilcher J. [1955] 2 BMJ 145

The plaintiff (Frederick Kilburn) fell from his scooter. He was a "mountain of a man" weighing twenty-two stone. He arrived at Savernake Hospital, near Marlborough, in a very dirty state, wearing half a dozen coats and jumpers and not having shaved for a week. Mr Wheeler, the acting casualty officer, concluded that he had been shaken up. Sticking plaster was put on his knees, and he was given a cup of tea and sent on his way.

Two and a half hours later, the plaintiff was admitted to the Royal Berkshire Hospital, Reading, where he was X-rayed, and it was discovered that he had sustained two fractures in his left knee and a fracture of the right wrist. He sued the Savernake Hospital Authority.

Held: (i) Mr Wheeler's examination was not a proper one, and could not be expected to discover what was wrong. The hospital authority was liable for his negligence;

(ii) the damages would necessarily be small (£20), because the treatment which the plaintiff ought to have received at Savernake Hospital he did in fact receive about three hours later at the Reading Hospital.

See page 89.

King v King

General practitioner: injection: contra-indications

Court of Appeal. 9 April 1987. [1987] 1 The Lancet 991

In 1980 the plaintiff (Jeffrey King), a generally fit man aged twenty-two, was planning a holiday in Morocco. The travel agents recommended that he should be inoculated against typhoid and cholera. On 8 May Dr King, his general practitioner, gave him an injection of a combined vaccination against cholera and typhoid. When the plaintiff attended for the second injection on 29 May, he was excited and had a small boil in front of his right ear. Six hours after the second injection, he suffered a stroke which left him with marked right-sided hemiplegia.

He sued Dr King. The trial judge (Rose J) found that it was negligent of Dr King to have given him the second injection because there were indications that should have caused him to postpone it, namely a temperature and the boil. Dr King appealed.

Held: the fact that the plaintiff was excited (shortly before his holiday) did not justify the judge's inference that he was probably suffering from a raised temperature. There was no evidence that the presence of a boil alone led to an increased risk of a stroke. Dr King had not been negligent.
See page 80.

Kralj and Another v McGrath and Another

Childbirth: substandard treatment: damages: aggravated damages: post-traumatic stress disorder

Woolf J. [1986] 1 All ER 54

The plaintiffs (Sally and Peter Kralj) had their first daughter in 1977. They had planned a family of three. In 1979 Mrs Kralj became pregnant again. It was arranged that her confinement would take place on a private basis at St Theresa's Hospital in Wimbledon under Mr McGrath, a consultant obstetrician. Tests showed that Mrs Kralj was expecting twins, one of which was in the transverse position. She was admitted to St Theresa's on 19 March 1980. After 8.00pm Mr McGrath set up a drip of Syntocinon to accelerate labour, and at 10.05pm the first twin, Thomas, was born. No anaesthetist was present.

After a slight lull, the contractions started again. Mr McGrath told Mrs Kralj to push, and the next thing she experienced was dreadful pain. She realised that Mr McGrath had put his arm inside her, entering by the vagina. She tried to stop him but hospital staff were holding her down. This lasted for forty minutes. She was then taken down to the operating theatre, and the second twin Daniel was delivered by caesarian section. He was born in an extremely debilitated state and died eight weeks later due to brain damage.

Mrs Kralj suffered vaginal bleeding for three months. She also had the caesarian scar. She suffered pain, as a result of which it was about two years before she could enjoy sexual intercourse. She suffered nervous shock as a result of seeing and being told what had happened to Daniel and grief due to his death.

Mr Kralj sued Mr McGrath and St Theresa's Hospital on behalf of Daniel's estate. Mrs Kralj sued for her injuries and financial loss. The claims were brought in tort and in contract. Liability was admitted by both defendants. The treatment was described at the hearing as horrific and totally unacceptable.

Held: (i) it would be wholly inappropriate to introduce into claims of this sort the concept of aggravated damages. This would be inconsistent with the general compensatory approach to damages in this area;

(ii) Mrs Kralj was entitled to be compensated for the shock she suffered as a result of being told of what had happened to Daniel and of seeing him during her visits, but damages for her grief and suffering at his death were not payable;

(iii) so far as her distress at Daniel's disabilities and grief over his death worsened the consequences of her own injuries, the court could take this into account;

(iv) she was awarded (June 1985) £10,000 general damages for her pain, suffering and loss of amenities;

(v) the expected additional pregnancy to have the third child and the attendant financial losses were reasonably foreseeable and not too remote. She was awarded £18,000 for future loss of earnings on an agreed multiplicand of £5,360 per annum.

See pages 83, 111–112, 115.

Landau v Werner

Psychiatrist: departing from orthodox practice: standard of care

Court of Appeal. (1961) 105 SJ 1008

In March 1949 Dr Landau, a psychiatrist, undertook the treatment of the plaintiff (Miss Werner), a middle-aged spinster in an anxiety state. Psychotherapeutic consultations took place twice a week in his consulting rooms. By the end of July the plaintiff felt much better. However, she had fallen deeply in love with Dr Landau and told him that for that reason she had decided not to continue with the treatment. He thought she was not yet well. Between August 1949 and March 1950 he took her out to tea and dinner in restaurants and visited her once in her bedsitting room; they also discussed spending a holiday together. By March 1950 the plaintiff's condition had deteriorated. Dr Landau resumed formal treatment but finally abandoned it as of no avail.

The plaintiff sued Dr Landau. The trial judge (Barry J) found that he had been negligent.

Held: the real question was whether the social meetings, and discussion about a holiday together, were bad and negligent practice in the sphere in which the doctor worked. The medical evidence was all one way in condemning social contacts, and the doctor had failed to convince the trial judge that his departure from standard practice was justified. The judge had reasonably decided that his unwise treatment had led to the grave deterioration in the plaintiff's health. It was negligent and in breach of the doctor's duty to his patient.

Per Sellers LJ: "A doctor's duty is to exercise ordinary skill and care according to the ordinary and reasonable standards of those who practise in the same field of medicine. The standard for the specialist is the standard of the specialists."

See pages 25, 39.

Langley v Campbell

General practitioner: diagnosis: loss of chance

Cusack J. [1975] The Times 6 November

Mr Langley had been sent by his employers to Uganda and returned on 1 July 1970. On the evening of 9 July he felt unwell with fever headache and alternate sweating and shivering. Dr Campbell, his general practitioner, called the next day. He was told that Mr Langley had just returned from Uganda and that he had suffered malaria during the war. Dr Campbell diagnosed influenza and prescribed accordingly. He called again on 11, 13 and 15 July. Mr Langley continued to deteriorate, so his family called in another doctor who had him transferred immediately to hospital where two Asian doctors immediately diagnosed malaria. He died on 18 July.

The plaintiff (his widow) sued for damages. The medical evidence was that if malaria had been diagnosed by 13 July, or even 15 July, and treatment put in hand, there would have been a good chance of recovery.

Held: if a general practitioner knew that a patient he thought had influenza had just come back from the tropics and was not getting better, he should have considered that it might be a tropical disease of some kind. Dr Campbell had fallen short of the standard of care to be observed by a general practitioner in his position and was negligent.

See page 37.

Lanphier and Wife v Phipos

Fracture: diagnosis: standard of care

Tindal CJ (with jury). (1838) 8 C&P 475

In September 1835 the plaintiff (Mrs Lanphier) was walking in a field when she came across a cow and, in her alarm, tripped and fell on her right wrist. She called in Mr Phipos, a surgeon and apothecary, who said that he thought the small bone of the arm was broken. He put splints on and bound her arm from the elbow to the wrist, leaving the hand hanging down. The swelling and inflammation of the arm spread over the next seven weeks, but Mr Phipos continued to say that it was going very well.

Another surgeon, Mr Vandenburgh, was called in. He found that there was a fracture of the small bone of her arm and a partial dislocation of the third bone of the palm of her hand. He put on longer splints which supported the hand and sent some lotion which reduced the swelling and inflammation. However the plaintiff had so lost the use of it that she could not use a knife or fork, or dress or undress herself with it. She sued Mr Phipos.

Held: Tindal CJ directed the jury: "Every person who enters into a learned profession undertakes to bring to the exercise of it a reasonable degree of care and skill. He does not undertake, if he is an attorney, that at all events you shall gain your case, nor does a surgeon undertake that he will perform a cure; nor does he undertake to use the highest possible degree of skill. There may be persons who have higher education and greater advantages than he has, but he undertakes to bring a fair, reasonable, and competent degree of skill, and you will say whether, in this case, the injury was occasioned by the want of such skill in the defendant. The question is, whether this injury must be referred to the want of a proper degree of skill and care in the defendant or not."

The jury returned a verdict for the plaintiff.

See page 34.

Lask v Gloucester Health Authority

Discovery: privilege

Court of Appeal. [1985] The Times 13 December

The plaintiff (Mrs Margaret Lask) sued for disclosure of a confidential accident report. National Health Service circulars required this to be completed by health authorities, both for the use of solicitors if litigation arose in respect of the accident, and also to enable action to be taken to avoid a repetition of the accident. The form itself referred only to the former purpose.

Held: the dominant purpose of its preparation had not been for submission to solicitors in anticipation of litigation. Therefore the report was not subject to legal professional privilege and should be disclosed to the plaintiff.

See page 131.

Latter v Braddell and Others

Consent: examination: assault

Court of Appeal. (1881) 50 LJQB 448

The plaintiff was a domestic servant of Captain and Mrs Braddell. Mrs Braddell requested Dr Sutcliffe to examine the plaintiff, in order to ascertain whether she was pregnant. The plaintiff objected, but undressed on Dr Sutcliffe's orders and submitted to an examination. Dr Sutcliffe used no violence or threats. He merely examined her and ascertained that she was not pregnant. Captain and Mrs Braddell were not present.

The plaintiff sued all three of them for assault. At the trial the judge directed a verdict for Captain and Mrs Braddell, and the jury found for Dr Sutcliffe.

Held: (i) to make out an assault by Dr Sutcliffe, the plaintiff had to show that he used violence or the threat of it. There was no evidence of this, and the jury were entitled to find that she submitted;

(ii) there was no evidence that Captain and Mrs Braddell authorised Dr Sutcliffe to examine the plaintiff without her submission.

The plaintiff's appeal was dismissed.

See page 67.

Leckie v Brent and Harrow Area Health Authority

Childbirth: registrar: substandard treatment: caesarian: res ipsa loquitur

Mars-Jones J. [1982] 1 The Lancet 634

When the infant plaintiff's mother was admitted to hospital, difficulty with the birth was expected due to a posterior lie and an undescended head. After an unsuccessful trial of labour, signs of foetal distress were observed and a caesarean section was required for urgent delivery. The operation was performed by a registrar. When he made the incision, the baby sustained on her left cheek a cut of 1.5 cm which penetrated full-thickness skin. The wound was sutured after she was handed to the paediatrician.

She sued the hospital authority, alleging that the registrar had been negligent and relying on the maxim *res ipsa loquitur*. Expert evidence was given that such a cut was extremely rare. Also the defendants' expert admitted that a cut of 2 mm should not occur.

Held: the hospital authority was liable. The cut could not have happened without negligence on the registrar's part.

See page 83.

Lee v South West Thames Regional Health Authority

Discovery: disclosure of report: privilege: duty of care: right to know treatment received

Court of Appeal. [1985] 2 All ER 385, [1985] 1 WLR 845

In April 1983 the plaintiff (Marlon Lee), then aged one, was severely scalded by boiling water in a domestic accident. He was taken to University College Hospital (North East Thames R.H.A.). On the same day the hospital sent him to the burns unit at Mount Vernon Hospital (Hillingdon A.H.A.). Next day he developed respiratory problems. He was put on a respirator and sent back to University College Hospital still on a respirator in an ambulance of the London Ambulance Service (South West Thames R.H.A.). When he was weaned from the respirator about three days later, he was found to have very severe brain damage, probably due to lack of oxygen.

Marlon's mother, acting as his next friend, applied for pre-action discovery under RSC O 24 r 7A against all three health authorities. South West Thames claimed legal privilege in respect of a memorandum prepared by the ambulance crew. The hospital records had suggested that there was a problem in the ambulance transfer. Mount Vernon Hospital had asked the London Ambulance Service for the report with a view to obtaining legal advice on the hospital's liability to Marlon. Thus South West Thames primarily were advancing Hillingdon's claim to privilege.

Held: the cause of action asserted against South West Thames was not a wholly independent cause of action, but arose out of the same incident as that which rendered Hillingdon a likely defendant. The principle is that a defendant or potential defendant shall be free to seek evidence without being obliged to disclose the result of his researches to his opponent. Hillingdon had not waived its rights to privilege. Disclosure could not be ordered.

Per Sir John Donaldson MR: "We reach this conclusion with undisguised reluctance, because we think that there is something seriously wrong with the law if Marlon's mother cannot find out what exactly caused this brain damage.

"A doctor is under a duty to answer his patient's questions as to the treatment proposed. We see no reason why this should not be a similar duty in relation to hospital staff. This duty is subject to the exercise of clinical judgement as to the terms in which the information is given and the extent to which, in the patient's interests, information should be withheld. Why, we ask ourselves, is the position any different if the patient asks what treatment he has in fact had? . . .

"If the duty is the same, then if the patient is refused information to which he is entitled, it must be for consideration whether he could not bring an action for breach of contract claiming specific performance of the duty to inform. In other words, whether the patient could not bring an action for discovery, albeit on a novel basis".

See pages 16–17, 26, 74–75, 129, 131–132.

Leigh v Gladstone and Others

Prison inmate: force feeding: assault

Lord Alverstone CJ (with jury). (1910) 26 TLR 139

On 22 September 1908 the plaintiff (Mrs Marie Leigh), a suffragette, was convicted on charges of resisting the police and disturbing a meeting held by Mr Asquith and was sentenced to four months' imprisonment with hard labour. She was sent to Winson-Green Prison where she declined food. Between 25 September and 30 October Dr Helby, the prison medical officer, subjected her to forcible feeding, sometimes through the mouth and sometimes through the nose.

The plaintiff claimed damages for assault and an injunction against Mr Gladstone (the Home Secretary), Dr Helby and the prison governor. Dr Helby testified that on 25 September she was looking ill, her pulse was high, her breath was unpleasant, and that he considered it dangerous to allow her to starve any further.

Held: Lord Alverstone CJ directed the jury that it was the duty of the prison officials to preserve the health of the prisoners, and *a fortiori* to preserve their lives. If they forcibly fed the plaintiff when it was not necessary, the defendants ought to pay damages. The medical evidence was that at the time she was first fed it had become dangerous to allow her to abstain from food any longer.

The jury returned a verdict for the defendants.

See page 67.

Lepine v University Hospital Board; Lepine v Monckton

Epilepsy: supervision: standard of care: foreign

Alberta Supreme Court. (1965) 54 DLR (2d) 340

The plaintiff (Mr Lepine) had suffered from epilepsy for ten years. This took two forms: grand mal seizures, and automatism. On 17 July 1961 he had a seizure at a hotel, headed for a fire escape and was stopped. He was strapped to a stretcher and taken to the University Hospital where he was put in the ward for Dr Monckton's patients on the fourth floor. During the next week he had approximately twenty-eight epileptic seizures of which seventeen were automatisms.

In the early morning of 24 July the plaintiff became difficult, noisy and psychotic. At 9.50 am he was found wandering outside the hospital and told the police: "The nuts in the hospital have a bomb." While he was being returned to the hospital he bolted, knocked over a little girl and hit a sergeant. He told the police to go ahead and shoot him, he had nothing left. When they got him back to the ward, the orderly left to get a nurse and doctor.

The plaintiff, who had been sitting beside a window, went to the bathroom. Just as he returned, Dr Monckton came in and spoke to him. The plaintiff, with his head down, walked to the chair which was near the window, stepped up on it and jumped through the glass and fell to the pavement four storeys below, where he suffered very serious injuries.

He sued Dr Monckton and the hospital authority. The trial judge found that the hospital was negligent but not Dr Monckton.

Held: (i) the hospital negligently failed to provide constant supervision which would have prevented the plaintiff's final jump and his escape which led to it;

(ii) Dr Monckton, who was the only one with the training and experience to assess the level of supervision necessary for the plaintiff's safety, shared in the hospital's negligence and was jointly liable.

Levenkind v Churchill-Davidson

Operation: surgeon: res ipsa loquitur: causation

Kenneth Jones J. [1983] 1 The Lancet 1452

The plaintiff (Malcolm Levenkind), aged nineteen, had recurrent dislocations of his right shoulder. On 16 July 1976 Mr Churchill-Davidson, an orthopaedic surgeon, performed a Putti-Platt repair. The musculocutaneous nerve was damaged during the operation. The plaintiff lost the use of the muscles in the right upper arm, and the biceps became wasted and functionless.

He sued Mr Churchill-Davidson for negligence and relied on the maxim *res ipsa loquitur*.

Held: the defendant, an experienced surgeon, did not expose the musculo-cutaneous nerve. On the balance of probabilities, the injury was caused by traction. Traction with no more than normal force could have caused the lesion, and that would not have involved negligence. Mr Churchill-Davidson was not liable.

See page 59.

Lim Poh Choo v Camden and Islington Area Health Authority

Operation: cardiac arrest: damages: brain damage

House of Lords. [1980] AC 174, [1979] 2 All ER 910, [1979] 3 WLR 44

In February 1973 the plaintiff (Dr Lim Poh Choo) was a thirty-six year old senior psychiatric registrar. She was admitted to the Elizabeth Garrett Anderson Hospital for a dilatation and curettage operation. When she was in the recovery room after the operation, she suffered a cardiac arrest. The health authority admitted liability.

The plaintiff, who was described as a remarkably intelligent doctor, had a future career in psychiatry ahead of her. Following the operation, she suffered from extensive and irremediable brain damage. This left her only intermittently, and then barely, sentient. She was totally dependent on others.

Held: (i) compensation should as nearly as possible put the party who has suffered in the same position as he would have been if he had not sustained the wrong. An attack on the total of damages awarded as being excessive, merely by reason of its size, must fail. It is necessary to show that one or more of the component items of the award are wrong;

(ii) the fact of unconsciousness does not eliminate the actuality of the deprivation of the ordinary experiences and amenities of life; and it is of no concern to the court to consider any question as to the use that will thereafter be made of the money awarded. As the plaintiff's loss of the amenities of her good and useful life was total, the trial judge's award in December 1977 of £20,000 general damages for pain, suffering and loss of amenities was suitably substantial and not excessive;

(iii) the plaintiff was entitled to an award for loss of earnings, since a genuine deprivation (be it pecuniary or non-pecuniary in character) is a proper subject of compensation. This is subject to a deduction in respect of the expenses of earning the income that has been lost;

(iv) the correct approach for taking account of the plaintiff's living expenses was to deduct the "domestic element" from the cost of care. Damages for the cost of future care must be assessed on the basis that capital as well as income is to be used in meeting the expenditure;

(v) only in exceptional cases will the risk of future inflation be brought into account in the assessment of damages for future loss. It is pure speculation whether inflation will continue at present, or higher, rates, or even disappear. Inflation is best left to be dealt with by investment policy;

(vi) after discounting for accelerated payment, the contingency that the plaintiff may not live out her full expectation of life, and the availability of capital as well as income to meet the cost of care, the multiplier of the trial judge (Bristow J) of 18 for the cost of future care was reduced to 12 from the date of the House of Lords judgment in June 1979;

(vii) as it was necessary to fix the multiplier for loss of future earnings by reference to pre-accident rather than post-accident expectation of life, the trial judge's multiplier of 14 should not be varied;

(viii) after taking into account fresh evidence of the cost of future care, the House of Lords reduced the trial judge's total award to £229,298.64 plus interest.

See pages 101, 102, 105, 108.

Lobley v Going and Others

General practitioner: vicarious liability: receptionist: standard of care

Court of Appeal. 9 December 1985

At about 9.00 am on 2 January 1979 the plaintiff (Simon Lobley), aged twenty-two months, started to suffer with a sore throat. Around 11.00 am his father rang the surgery of the family's general practitioners, Dr Going and Dr Nunn, and it was suggested that the child be brought to the early evening surgery. They arrived around 5.00 pm. The surgery was busy. Mr Lobley, who had left Simon sitting down with his wife, told the receptionist, Mrs Porter, his name and that he had rung earlier about his son. Mr Lobley said "He has got worse; he is having a bit of difficulty in breathing". Mrs Porter asked him to take a seat. Mr Lobley added "We would like to get in as soon as possible because of his breathing", to which Mrs Porter replied "OK, I'll see what I can do". They sat for a quarter of an hour whereupon Mr Lobley successfully insisted that Simon be seen immediately.

When Dr Going saw the child, he consulted Dr Nunn and telephoned for an ambulance. Simon suffered a hypoxic interlude on the way to hospital. His condition was promptly diagnosed there as epiglottitis. The consultant paediatrician and his registrar attempted to insert a tube into the child's lungs. While they were doing this, he had a cardiac arrest. He suffered irreparable brain damage with very serious disabilities.

The trial judge (Kenneth Jones J) dismissed his claim for negligence against Dr Going, Dr Nunn and the hospital authority. He appealed solely on the basis that Dr Going and Dr Nunn were vicariously liable for the negligence of their receptionist, Mrs Porter.

Held: if it is brought to a receptionist's attention that a small child has been brought to a surgery in an ill condition, with respiratory difficulties about which the parents are genuinely concerned, it is her duty to inform a doctor immediately, and if she fails to do so she is guilty of negligence. However it is not enough for the parent to indicate a measure of concern about the child and then expect the receptionist to embark on enquiries as to the exact basis of such concern. It had not been clearly communicated to Mrs Porter that she was being called upon to deal with an emergency. The trial judge was justified in concluding that she had not been negligent.

See page 90.

Lock v Scantlebury and Another

Dentist: anaesthetics: diagnosis: after-care: res ipsa loquitur

Paull J. [1963] The Times 25 July

On 14 November 1960 the plaintiff (Miss Betty Lock) was seen by Mr Dawson, a dentist admitted about two years previously who was employed by Mr Scantlebury as his assistant. Mr Dawson extracted six teeth from her upper jaw and two from the lower while Mr Scantlebury administered the anaesthetic.

After the extraction, the plaintiff visited a doctor who gave her pain-killing tablets. On 4 December she visited Mr Dawson and complained that she could not speak properly or eat, and said that she was sure there was something wrong with her face. He examined her and told her that she was getting along nicely and told her to visit him again later. When she did so, after more pain-killers from her doctor, Mr Dawson again did not discover any dislocation and was prepared to do a filling. She turned round and walked out.

Eventually it was discovered that her jaw was dislocated. In June 1961, at Mount Vernon Hospital the dislocation was got back into place manually. She sued Mr Scantlebury and Mr Dawson.

Held: the plaintiff's jaw had become dislocated during the extraction, which of itself was not proof of negligence. However there had been negligence in failing, either on that day or on two subsequent visits, to discover that the dislocation had taken place.

See pages 60, 86.

Loveday v Renton and Another

Vaccine damage: contra-indications: causation: standard of care

Stuart-Smith LJ. [1988] The Times 31 March

In 1970 and 1971, when she was a baby, the plaintiff (Susan Loveday) was treated with whooping-cough vaccine by Dr Renton. She suffered permanent brain damage.

She sued Dr Renton on the basis that the vaccine was administered in disregard of one or more of the contra-indications. She put forward four suggested biological mechanisms to explain the alleged link between the vaccine and her brain damage, one of which was febrile convulsions.

The most important epidemiological evidence was derived from the National Childhood Encephalopathy Study. This supported the theory that diphtheria tetanus pertussis (DTP) vaccine sometimes caused febrile convulsions.

Held: all four suggested biological mechanisms were improbable. The study did not provide evidence that febrile convulsions following the DTP vaccine caused permanent brain damage.

The plaintiff had failed to show on the balance of probabilities that pertussis vaccine could cause permanent brain damage in young children. It was possible that it did; the contrary could not be proved. But in the result the plaintiff's claim failed.

(*Obiter*): even if the preliminary issue of causation had been resolved in her favour, any plaintiff would face insuperable difficulties in proving negligence on the part of the doctor or nurse who administered the vaccine.

See pages 22, 23, 49.

Lowen v Hopper and Another

Nurses: substandard treatment: res ipsa loquitur: blood donor: causation

Hilbery J (with jury). [1950] 1 BMJ 792

The plaintiff (Mrs Ivy Lowen) gave blood eight times without ill effect at the Rochford Municipal Hospital. Dr Hopper, the hospital medical officer, took her blood on the ninth occasion. The plaintiff reported to the sister after the operation that she was losing an undue quantity of blood. However the sister did not examine her thoroughly or replace the sodden dressing. The plaintiff's right arm became septic and she was left with a long permanent scar.

She sued Dr Hopper and the hospital authority. Dr Hopper was dismissed from the case for lack of evidence of negligence.

Held: Hilbery J directed the jury that the mere fact that the plaintiff's arm became septic after the operation did not of itself establish negligence. If they believed that there had been a want of reasonable skill and care, they would have to decide whether that was the cause of the arm becoming septic. There was some evidence from which they might infer that germs had entered the plaintiff's system from blood-soaked dressing.

The jury found that the hospital had been negligent.

See page 93.

McCormack v Redpath Brown & Co Ltd and Another

Diagnosis: casualty officer: X-rays: fracture: hospital administration

Paull J. [1961] The Times 24 March

In April 1957 the plaintiff (Edward McCormack) was working as a steel erector at Vauxhall Motors in Luton for his then employers Redpath Brown & Co Ltd. He was hit on the head by a spanner accidentally dropped from above by a fellow workman. The spanner cut right through the plaintiff's cap and made a gash about one inch long well above the normal hair line but where he was was very nearly bald. He was taken to the Luton and Dunstable Hospital where he was attended to by the casualty officer, his wound cleaned and three or four stitches inserted. He was given a letter to his doctor and left.

He suffered from headaches and dizziness. In January 1958 he was examined by a neurologist attached to the West End Hospital for Nervous Diseases who diagnosed a depressed fracture of the skull. X-rays showed that there was a hole in his skull between a quarter and a half inch in diameter and that a piece of bone had been forced through into the brain itself. An operation took place in March 1958. He sued both his employers, who admitted liability, and the hospital authority who denied negligence.

Held: the casualty officer had been negligent in:

(1) failing to arrange for an X-ray to be taken; and

(2) failing to discover the hole in the plaintiff's skull.

It appeared that he was overworked and unjustifiably assumed that this was just another cut head. The hospital authority was responsible for the consequences of his failure.

See pages 62, 89.

McCormick v O'Connor

Epilepsy: diagnosis: burden of proof

Court of Appeal. 20 November 1978

The plaintiff (Alistair McCormick) had been a serving officer in the Royal Air Force. Air Vice-Marshal O'Connor diagnosed that he was suffering from epilepsy and paranoia. This put an end to his career in the R.A.F. He sued the Air Vice-Marshal for negligent diagnosis.

In 1966 the plaintiff had received a head injury in a road accident and had suffered at least two epileptic attacks in consequence. He had falsely alleged that his passenger Dr Drinkwater interfered with his driving. He had formed an obsessive desire to expose Dr Drinkwater and manifested other paranoid tendencies.

Held: all the medical evidence was one way, against the allegations of negligence. The trial judge (Mars-Jones J) had been correct to find that Air Vice-Marshal O'Connor was not liable.

McGrath v Kiely and Powell

Medical report: breach of contract: fracture: damages

Irish High Court. [1965] IR 497

In December 1959 the plaintiff (Margaret McGrath) was involved in a motor accident. She sustained injuries which included a fracture to her left clavicle. She instructed Mr Powell, a solicitor, to conduct her claim for damages against the drivers concerned and told him of the fracture. For the purposes of her claim, he commissioned and paid for a full medical report on her injuries from Professor Kiely, who had set the fractured clavicle in plaster. His report did not mention it.

She commenced High Court action against the two drivers. Her fractured clavicle was not pleaded. Counsel only learned of it on the morning of the hearing. A decision was taken to proceed without relying on it, since the alternative was an adjournment with substantial costs. The jury awarded £1,000 general damages.

The plaintiff then sued Professor Kiely and Mr Powell.

Held: (i) each defendant was in breach of his contract with the plaintiff;

(ii) if the fractured clavicle had been taken into account, the jury would have awarded the plaintiff a further £100 general damages, so she was entitled to judgment for £100 against both defendants.

See page 27.

McKay and Another v Essex Area Health Authority and Another

Wrongful birth: diagnosis: Congenital Disabilities (Civil Liability) Act 1976: striking out

Court of Appeal. [1982] 1 QB 1166

In February 1975 the plaintiff (Mary McKay) was conceived. Her case was that while in her mother's womb she was infected with rubella (German measles). Her mother consulted Dr Gower-Jones who took blood samples that were submitted to a hospital laboratory. It was alleged that, despite this, Dr Gower-Jones informed her mother that she and her unborn child had not been infected with rubella during the pregnancy and that she need not consider an abortion. The plaintiff was born in August 1975 with severe congenital disabilities.

She sued Dr Gower-Jones and the hospital authorities. It was not disputed that she was entitled to bring a claim against the doctor for negligently causing her injuries by failing to inject globulins into her mother. She also claimed against both defendants for "entry into a life in which her injuries are highly debilitating, and distress, loss and damage".

Held: this latter claim was for "wrongful life". There was no duty to the foetus to cause its death. Such a proposition was wholly contrary to the sanctity of human life. Moreover the claim was impossible to value, since it involved a comparison with a state of non-existence. The Master was right to strike it out under RSC O 18 r 19(1) as disclosing no reasonable cause of action.

Per curiam: The effect of the Congenital Disabilities (Civil Liability) Act 1976 was that no child born after its passing could have a right of action for "wrongful life".

See pages 29, 30–31, 83, 98.

McLoughlin v Greenwich and Bexley Area Health Authority

Hospital administration: damages: fracture

McNeill J. (1984) 134 NLJ 383

The plaintiff (Mrs McLoughlin), aged sixty-four, was a voluntary patient in a psychiatric hospital. She slipped on a wet patch of the ward floor.

She sustained a trochanteric fracture of the left femur, with bruising on the flank, and a Colles fracture of the right wrist. She underwent operative processes to repair her fractures, and the fracture of the left femur had to be dealt with by a pinning device. Her left leg was permanently shortened by 9 cm and, even wearing a surgical boot, she was left with a severe limp. She relied on a tripod walking stick and a wheelchair for more than very short distances but had led a fairly immobile life out of preference before the accident. The left wrist had been her dominant wrist but had thickened and a "dinner-fork" deformity had developed which slightly restricted movement so that, for example, she was unable to lift a teapot. No improvement was expected.

The plaintiff sued the health authority.

Held: general damages (July 1983) for pain, suffering and loss of amenities were assessed at £10,000.

See page 104.

Mahon v Osborne

Surgeon: operation: retained surgical product: nurse: standard of care: res ipsa loquitur

Court of Appeal. [1939] 2 KB 14

In March 1937 Thomas Mahon, a twenty-four year old labourer, was operated on for a duodenal ulcer by Mr Osborne, resident surgeon at Park Hospital in Manchester. During the operation, swabs were used to pack off the adjacent areas in the patient's abdomen. At the end of the operation, Mr Osborne removed all the swabs of which he was aware. He asked the theatre sister whether the swab count was correct, and she told him that it was. He then sewed up the opening in Mr Mahon's body.

In June 1937 Mr Mahon again became acutely ill. A further operation became necessary. In the course of this a packing swab, left in at the first operation, was discovered lying just under the part of the liver which is close to the stomach. It had caused an abscess which led to Mr Mahon's death the next day.

His mother sued Mr Osborne and the theatre sister. The jury found that Mr Osborne had been negligent, but not the theatre sister.

Held: the trial judge had been wrong to direct the jury that there was a positive rule of English law, to be enforced in all abdominal operations, imposing on the surgeon a duty to search and make sure he has removed all the swabs. The issue was whether in all the circumstances of the operation the surgeon failed to exercise reasonable care with regard to the removal of packing swabs. A new trial was ordered.

Per Goddard LJ: "I think it right to say that in my opinion the doctrine of *res ipsa loquitur* does apply in such a case as this, at least to the extent I mention below. The surgeon is in command of the operation, it is for him to decide what instruments, swabs and the like are to be used, and it is he who uses them. The patient, or, if he dies, his representatives, can know nothing about this matter. There can be no possible question but that neither swabs nor instruments are ordinarily left in the patient's body, and no one would venture to say that it is proper, although in particular circumstances it may be excusable, so to leave them. If, therefore, a swab is left in the patient's body, it seems to me clear that the surgeon is called on for an explanation, that is, he is called on to show not necessarily why he missed it but that he exercised due care to prevent it being left there."

See pages 57–58, 82, 93–94.

Malette v Shulman et al

Emergency: duty of care: consent: damages: blood transfusion: foreign

Ontario High Court of Justice. (1988) 47 DLR (4th) 18

On 30 June 1979 the plaintiff (Mrs Malette) was seriously injured in a road accident. She was taken to Kirkland District Hospital where she was treated by Dr Shulman. She showed signs of hypovolaemic shock, bled profusely and was becoming critically ill. As she was virtually unconscious and unable to speak, a nurse searched her purse and found a Jehovah's Witness card which (in an agreed English translation of the French) read as follows:

NO BLOOD TRANSFUSION!

> As one of Jehovah's witnesses with firm religious convictions, I request that no blood or blood products be administered to me under any circumstances. I fully realise the implications of this position, but I have resolutely decided to obey the Bible command: Keep abstaining . . . from blood" (Acts 15: 28, 29). However, I have no religious objection to use the non-blood alternatives, such as Dextran, Haemacel, PVP, Ringer's Lactate or saline solution.

The contents of this card were communicated to Dr Shulman. When the plaintiff's condition deteriorated, he decided to administer blood and did so personally. When the plaintiff's daughter arrived, she objected to the administration of blood and expressed her conviction that the plaintiff wanted no blood. The daughter signed "A Consent to Treatment and a Release of Liability Form" specifically prohibiting blood transfusions. Dr Shulman continued to administer them with a view to saving the plaintiff's life.

On July 1 the plaintiff was taken to Toronto General Hospital where the blood transfusions were discontinued. On 11 August she was discharged. She sued Dr Shulman, the hospital and four nurses for negligence and assault.

Held: (i) there was no negligence in the diagnosis, and the treatment was carried out in a competent, careful and conscientious manner;

(ii) the card constituted a valid restriction of Dr Shulman's right to treat the plaintiff. The administration of blood by him constituted battery;

(iii) this was not a case for punitive damages. General damages payable by Dr Shulman for the plaintiff's mental distress were assessed at $20,000.

Per Donnelly J: "A conscious, rational patient is entitled to refuse any medical treatment and the doctor must comply, no matter how ill advised he may believe that instruction to be."

See page 6.

Mansouri v Bloomsbury Health Authority

Dismissal for want of prosecution: legally aided plaintiff

Court of Appeal. [1987] The Times 20 July

The plaintiff (Mrs Mina Mansouri) claimed damages for negligent medical treatment by Bloomsbury Health Authority in June 1979. In June 1982 she instructed solicitors, Duke-Cohan & Co, and a writ was issued. The writ was served in June 1983 and the Statement of Claim in July 1983. In August 1983 she was granted a legal aid certificate "limited to preparation of papers for counsel and obtaining counsel's opinion upon merits and quantum after a conference which the assisted person should attend".

She attended a conference with counsel, J. Singh, in March 1984. He then left for India and in June 1984 the papers were transferred to his colleague Miss N Mathew. She wanted a further medical report which was received in February 1985 and sent to her. In March 1985 the defendant's solicitors decided to apply to strike out the action. Miss Mathew's opinion was received in May 1985 and sent to the Law Society in June 1985 when the limitation on the legal aid certificate was removed.

In July 1985 Master Waldman struck out the plaintiff's action for want of prosecution.

Held: it was well established that if there was a delay before the issue of the writ, it was all the more incumbent on the plaintiff's legal advisers to bring the action to trial speedily. It was not satisfactory for the solicitors simply to send chasers to counsel once a month. A situation in which counsel's opinion was received only in May 1985 constituted inordinate delay. The Master's order was correct.

See pages 127–128.

Marchant v East Ham Borough Council and Another

Injection: needle breaking: causation

Pearson J. [1955] 2 The Lancet 973

The plaintiff, a fifteen year old schoolgirl, developed a blister on her heel which became septic. She went to a hospital clinic where a doctor advised an injection of penicillin. She was told to sit. While the nurse was giving her an intramuscular injection, using a No 16 needle, the plaintiff made a sudden movement. The needle broke and remained embedded in her thigh. The needle was 30/32 of an inch long and broke 1/32 of an inch from the mount.

The plaintiff was left with a three and a half inch scar on the thigh. She sued the hospital authority and the nurse.

Held: if a longer and thicker needle had been used, it would have caused more pain and thereby have been more likely to cause a convulsive reaction. It was not proved that the needle had been pushed in too far; the accident was due to an unexpected movement on the plaintiff's part. It would not be right to use a thicker needle and inflict extra pain on all patients to meet the possible contingency that one of them might flinch as this girl had. The nurse had not been negligent.

Judgment for the defendants.

See page 79.

Markham v Abrahams

Optician: standard of care: representation: diagnosis

Lord Chief Justice (with special jury). [1911] 1 BMJ 703

In 1907 the plaintiff (Miss Markham) was having trouble with her eyes and suffering from pain, dizziness and difficulty in reading. She went to the shop of Mr Thomas who practised in Manchester under the style of Wood Abrahams, describing himself as an "eyesight and spectacle specialist" and a "qualified optician". One of his assistants prescribed spectacles. As these were unsatisfactory, the plaintiff returned more than once and in 1909 saw Mr Thomas. Later that year she consulted an ophthalmic surgeon who found that she was suffering from conical cornea of long standing.

She sued Mr Thomas, alleging that if he had exercised reasonable care and been possessed of sufficient skill he should have seen that it was a case of disease and not one of ordinary short sight. For Mr Thomas it was contended that he did not profess to be a person able to diagnose and cure diseases of the eye, but was simply a maker and seller of spectacles.

Held: the Lord Chief Justice told the jury that the plaintiff admitted she had not been influenced by Mr Thomas' description of himself as an eyesight specialist and that she knew an optician was not an oculist. Conical cornea was very rare. Could they say, in view of the fact that opticians carried on a well-known trade, that they were under any obligation to discover disease? He directed the jury that, to find in favour of the plaintiff, they must be satisfied that the defendant had been negligent as an optician, or had taken on himself and had not performed duties outside those of an optician.

The jury returned a verdict for the plaintiff.

See pages 28, 95.

Marshall v County Council of the Parts of Lindsey, Lincolnshire

Hospital administration: infection: tests: warning: vicarious liability

House of Lords. [1937] AC 97

On 4 July 1933 Mrs Franklin, a patient at Cleethorpes Maternity Home, developed a high temperature and was taken to Grimsby General Hospital. On her removal, the ward in which she had been lying and the nurses who had been in contact with her were disinfected. The hospital diagnosed puerperal fever. On 5 July this diagnosis was communicated to the matron of the home and to Dr Stott, its medical superintendent. The normal precaution of taking swabs from the throats of all persons who had been in contact with Mrs

Franklin, in order to ascertain whether any such person was a carrier, was not taken.

On 12 July the plaintiff (Mrs Mary Marshall) was admitted to the home. Neither she nor her husband was told about Mrs Franklin's case. On 13 July the plaintiff's child was born. On 17 July she herself suffered a very severe attack of puerperal fever. She sued the county council responsible for the nursing home.

Held: (i) there was ample evidence to support the jury in finding that the nursing home was in breach of duty in admitting the plaintiff without ascertaining whether or not there was a carrier in the staff by taking swabs from all the nurses who had been in contact with Mrs Franklin, and that as the plaintiff had been admitted before this was ascertained, she or her husband or her doctor ought to have been informed of the facts in order to decide whether to enter the home and under what precautions;

(ii) the defendants were responsible for Dr Stott's negligence; it was no excuse in law for them to say they were misled by his advice.

See pages 10, 87.

Marshall v Curry

Operation: consent: emergency: assault: interests of patient

Nova Scotia Supreme Court. [1933] 3 DLR 260

In 1929 the plaintiff (Mr Marshall), a master mariner, sent for Dr Curry. It was agreed that Dr Curry would perform an operation to remove a hernia in his left groin. When Dr Curry opened the inguinal canal, the plaintiff's left testicle appeared and was found grossly diseased. Dr Curry deemed it necessary to remove the testicle, not only to cure the hernia but also because if not removed the testicle might have become gangrenous and caused blood poisoning.

Dr Curry told the plaintiff of the removal of the testicle one or two days after the operation. The plaintiff sued him for negligence and assault.

Held: (i) Dr Curry had performed the operation skilfully. The condition of the testicle could not reasonably have been anticipated before the operation. He had not been negligent;

(ii) where a great emergency that could not be anticipated arises, it is better to put consent altogether out of the case and to rule that it is the surgeon's duty to act in order to save the life or preserve the health of the patient. Despite the absence of express and possibly of implied consent on the plaintiff's part, Dr Curry had acted in the interest of his patient for the protection of his health and possibly his life. The removal was in that sense necessary. Dr Curry was not guilty of assault.

See page 6.

Maynard v West Midlands Regional Health Authority

Tuberculosis: diagnosis: operation: standard of care

House of Lords. [1985] 1 All ER 635, [1984] 1 WLR 634

The plaintiff (Blondell Maynard), a West Indian lady, was treated at East Birmingham Hospital in 1970 by Dr Ross, a consultant physician, and Mr Stephenson, a consultant surgeon. They recognized that tuberculosis was the most likely diagnosis. But in their opinion there was an unusual factor, viz, swollen glands in the mediastinum unaccompanied by any evidence of lesion in the lungs, which meant that Hodgkin's disease was a possible danger. They therefore decided that she should undergo the diagnostic operation of mediastinoscopy. During the course of this the plaintiff's left laryngeal recurrent nerve was damaged, with resulting paralysis of the left vocal cord.

The plaintiff sued the hospital authority. No negligence in the performance of the operation was alleged. Her case was that the diagnosis of tuberculosis should have been so clear that the consultants were guilty of an error of judgement amounting to negligence in requiring the operation to be undertaken.

Held: the Court of Appeal had been right to reverse the trial judge's finding of negligence.

Per Lord Scarman: "A case which is based on an allegation that a fully considered decision of two consultants in the field of their special skill was negligent clearly presents certain difficulties of proof. It is not enough to show that there is a body of competent professional opinion which considers theirs as a wrong decision, if there also exists a body of professional opinion, equally competent, which supports the decision as reasonable in the circumstances. It is not enough to show that subsequent events show that the operation need never have been performed, if at the time the decision to operate was taken it was reasonable in the sense that a responsible body of medical opinion would have accepted it as proper. I do not think that the words of Lord President (Clyde) in *Hunter* v *Hanley* [1955] SLT 213 at page 217 can be bettered:

"'In the realm of diagnosis and treatment there is ample scope for genuine difference of opinion and one man is not negligent merely because his conclusion differs from that of other medical men . . . The true test for establishing negligence in diagnosis or treatment on the part of a doctor is whether he has been proved to be guilty of such failure as no doctor of ordinary skill would be guilty of if acting with ordinary care . . .'

"I would only add that a doctor who professes to exercise a special skill must exercise the ordinary skill of his speciality. Differences of opinion and practice exist, and will always exist, in the medical as in other professions. There is seldom any one answer exclusive of all others to problems of professional judgement. A court may prefer one body of opinion to the other, but that is no basis for a conclusion of negligence.

". . . I have to say that a judge's 'preference' for one body of distinguished professional opinion to another also professionally distinguished is not sufficient to establish negligence in a practitioner whose actions have received the seal of approval of those whose opinions, truthfully expressed, honestly held, were not preferred. If this was the real reason for the judge's finding, he erred in law even though elsewhere in his judgment he stated the law

271

correctly. For in the realm of diagnosis and treatment, negligence is not established by preferring one respectable body of professional opinion to another. Failure to exercise the ordinary skill of a doctor (in the appropriate speciality, if he be a specialist) is necessary."

See pages 33, 37, 39, 64.

Michael v Molesworth

Surgeon: breach of contract: trespass to person: damages

Singleton LJ. (1950] 2 BMJ 171

The plaintiff (Mr Michael) suffered from a hernia. He consulted Mr Molesworth, senior surgeon at the Royal Victoria Hospital, Folkestone. Mr Molesworth told the plaintiff that his minimum fee for a privately performed operation would be 25 guineas but that there were no private wards in Folkestone. He sought to make it clear to the plaintiff that he would be in a public ward in the Folkestone Hospital, and he did not undertake to carry out the operation personally.

On 23 March 1948, the operation was performed, with complete success, by the house surgeon, Mr Ribet. When the plaintiff discovered that Mr Ribet had operated, he sued Mr Molesworth for breach of an alleged oral agreement to operate and for procuring a trespass upon him by Mr Ribet. He testified that he had been shocked that an apprentice had practised his skill on him without his consent when he had engaged a craftsman.

Held: (i) there had been no breach of contract by Mr Molesworth. He had not agreed to carry out the operation himself, and he probably did not realise that the plaintiff expected him to do so;

(ii) Mr Ribet had operated without consent. The wording of the form that the plaintiff had signed did not debar him from bringing an action. There had been a technical trespass for which the plaintiff was awarded nominal damages of £1.

N.B. Most modern consent forms state that no assurance has been given to the patient that the operation will be performed by any particular practitioner.

Mitchell v Hounslow and Spelthorne Health Authority

Childbirth: nurses: substandard treatment: causation

Kenneth Jones J. [1984] 1 The Lancet 579

In March 1979 Mrs Mitchell, expecting her first baby, was admitted to hospital in labour. After the admission procedure, she was given an enema and shown to the toilet. No one showed her the emergency bell. While she was there, the membranes ruptured and the umbilical cord prolapsed and emerged beyond the introitus.

She called out for help, but there was no one in the adjoining admission room. It was some minutes before she was found by her husband and another nurse. No pressure was applied, no warm saline gauze was wrapped round the protruding cord, and no other first-aid treatment was carried out until she reached the operating theatre. A caesarian section was performed, and a girl was born.

The infant plaintiff suffered spastic cerebral palsy caused by birth anoxia due to compression of the umbilical cord. She sued the health authority for failing to provide proper care after prolapse of the cord. The expert evidence was that if pressure had been applied to the foetus there was a sixty per cent chance that brain damage would have been avoided. All the specialists agreed that once the prolapse was discovered, first-aid treatment should have been given.

Held: the failure to apply pressure for about ten minutes constituted a failure of what should have been normal standard practice in the circumstances by a competent midwife. The hospital authority was liable for that negligence which was the probable cause of the plaintiff's condition.

See pages 49, 83.

Mitchell v Liverpool Area Health Authority (Teaching)

Substandard treatment: damages

Court of Appeal. 13 June 1985

The plaintiff (Anthony Mitchell) was born in August 1981. When one month old, he sustained damage to the circulation of his right arm. The defendants admitted liability.

The plaintiff's right arm had to be amputated at elbow level. Consequently he would be barred from certain manual and industrial trades requiring bi-manual digital skills, such as plumbing, and some types of intricate bench or assembly work. Occupations requiring work on ladders or scaffolding would be unsuitable. However, it seemed he would have very good power in his left hand and many jobs would be open to him.

In November 1984 the trial judge (Russell J) awarded him £30,000 general damages for pain, suffering and loss of amenities, but refused to add anything in relation to future loss of earnings or diminished potential in the labour market.

Held: (i) the court would not interfere with the award of £30,000 general damages for pain, suffering and loss of amenities, although it was very much at the top end of the range;

(ii) the judge had been in error in declining to make any award in respect of future financial loss. There was a real risk that the plaintiff would not be able to earn as much as if he had no disability. It was impossible to compute this arithmetically. After substantially discounting for acceleration, an award of £5,000 was appropriate under this head.

See pages 103, 107.

Moore v Lewisham Group Hospital Management Committee

Anaesthetics: consultant: standard of care

Barry J. [1959] The Times 5 February

In January 1956 the plaintiff (Mrs Flora Moore) was a healthy and active woman aged sixty-eight, but for some fifteen months she had been suffering from bouts of pain in the upper abdomen. She was admitted to Lewisham Hospital for a cholecystectomy operation. Dr Piney, the consultant anaesthetist, decided upon spinal anaesthesia supplemented by a light general anaesthetic. The next morning it was discovered that her left leg was paralysed and there was, for a time, acute urinary trouble. She made some improvement, but no further progress was expected.

The plaintiff sued the hospital authority for negligence. No criticism was made of the manner in which the anaesthetic was administered. Her case was that, owing to the known risk of permanent neurological damage, a spinal anaesthetic should not have been used for her operation. Some highly informed medical practitioners held the view that the risks involved in the use of spinal anaesthesia could never be justified; others justified its use for certain operations but not for those such as removal of the gall bladder; and there were yet others who denied the possibility of neurological damage in the absence of some contamination of the drug used.

Held: it was impossible to find that Dr Piney's decision to use spinal anaesthesia was negligent. It was one which could have been made by a competent and properly informed anaesthetist exercising a proper degree of skill and care.

See pages 38–39, 82.

Morgan v Gwent Health Authority

Diagnosis: blood transfusion: damages

Court of Appeal. 8 December 1987. [1988] 2 The Lancet 519

The plaintiff (Caroline Morgan) was born in 1958. She did not know that her blood group was rhesus negative. In 1978 she underwent a small nasal operation at St Lawrence Hospital, Chepstow. She was given a transfusion of rhesus positive blood. The hospital authority admitted liability, since the hospital had negligently failed to ascertain what her blood group was.

The incompatibility produced a sensitivity to the rhesus antigen which could create very serious complications in pregnancy to the foetus, though not to the mother. The chances that any future husband would be compatible in the sense that no problem could arise was seventeen per cent; that any foetus would be rhesus positive (the foetus having rhesus positive blood causes the problem) was fifty-nine per cent; that the child would be severely affected was twenty per cent. Treatment of the child could avoid the consequences of stillbirth or serious disability in most cases, at the cost of her submitting to very tiring treatment during pregnancy.

The plaintiff discovered what had happened in 1980 when she had an abortion. In 1981 she became engaged, but in 1982 tests showed that there would be complications if any child was conceived by her fiancé, and in 1984 the engagement was broken off. Her choice of husband and thus her chances of marriage were restricted. She wanted a family and felt anxiety which would become acute during a pregnancy.

In November 1986 the trial judge (Boreham J) awarded her £8,000 general damages.

Held: the award should be increased to £20,000. The judge was mistaken in not holding that the negligent transfusion had been a major cause of the break-up of her engagement. A major factor was the reasonable anxiety which she would have to face about prospects of marriage, about prospects of telling the man concerned of her condition, and about problems of her reduced ability to bear a healthy child by a father not himself a rhesus negative.

See pages 89, 104.

Morris v Winsbury-White

Surgeon: retained surgical product: breach of contract: res ipsa loquitur

Tucker J. [1937] 4 All ER 494

In November 1933 the plaintiff (Arthur Morris) consulted Mr Winsbury-White, a surgeon specialising in genito-urinary diseases, who diagnosed prostate trouble. Mr Winsbury-White agreed to give the case his personal attention, and the plaintiff entered St Paul's Hospital. On 27 November there was performed the usual preliminary operation, which consisted of draining off the bladder, and on 18 December Mr Winsbury-White performed the main operation. The plaintiff remained in hospital until 10 February 1934.

He visited Mr Winsbury-White there on 28 March and 11 April when, as a result of an X-ray, Mr Winsbury-White performed an operation and found that a major part of a tube had been left in the bladder and a small portion in the perineum. The plaintiff continued to suffer great discomfort from periodical leaking. He sued Mr Winsbury-White for breach of contract and negligence.

Held: (i) the medical officers and nursing staff are not the agents of a specialist surgeon who comes in and performs an operation, in so far as they are performing their ordinary hospital duties;

(ii) the tube must have got in between 27 November and 10 February while the plaintiff was being dealt with and treated at the hospital by numerous nurses and sisters and two resident medical officers and being visited occasionally by Mr Winsbury-White. The doctrine of *res ipsa loquitur* was inapplicable to the facts of the case;

(iii) the agreement to give the case his personal attention did not place any additional material duty on Mr Winsbury-White who had carried out his obligations under the contract and was not guilty of negligence.

See pages 16, 57, 83.

Mose v North West Hertfordshire Health Authority

Consultant: surgeon: operation: standard of care

Court of Appeal. 26 November 1987

The plaintiff (Garrie Mose) was born in March 1976. In 1978 his parents noticed a lump behind his right knee. It increased in size. He was examined by Mr Hirschowitz, a consultant orthopaedic surgeon, at West Hertfordshire Hospital, who reasonably concluded that it was probably a cyst.

On 8 September 1980 Mr Hirschowitz performed an operation to excise the lump. In the process, he found that it was not a cyst but was either a schwannoma or a neurofibroma. He proceeded to remove it but in doing so also removed three inches of the lateral popliteal nerve. The plaintiff suffered a "complete foot drop".

He sued the hospital authority. The expert evidence at trial was that when a surgeon inexperienced in work on peripheral nerves comes inadvertently on a nerve expanded by a tumour, or apparently connected inextricably with a tumour, he or she should ideally restrict the procedure to a small biopsy or should close the wound without further action, and that the patient should then be sent to a surgeon experienced in work on peripheral nerves. Mr Hirschowitz testified that he operated on peripheral nerve lesions about once a week, although he had only occasionally treated a peripheral nerve tumour. The trial judge (Mr Anthony Hidden QC) held that he had been negligent in proceeding to remove the tumour which was found to be a plexiform neurofibroma.

Held: the central flaw in the judge's reasoning was that, contrary to what he thought, the description "a surgeon inexperienced in work on peripheral nerves" did not apply to Mr Hirschowitz. The finding of negligence could not be justified.

See pages 76–77.

Moser v Enfield and Haringey Area Health Authority

Operation: quadriplegia: damages: brain damage

Michael Davies J. (1983) 133 NLJ 105

In October 1976 the plaintiff (Robert Moser), then aged four, entered hospital for a minor operation. It went wrong and he was deprived of oxygen, thereby suffering irreversible brain damage. From being a bright child, he became severely mentally subnormal and was unlikely to have any insight into his condition. He also became quadriplegic and quite unable to look after himself. His life expectancy was a further twenty years to the age of thirty.

He sued the health authority who admitted liability.

Held (November 1982): the plaintiff was awarded:

(i) general damages of £35,000 for pain, suffering and loss of amenities;

   (ii) £132,000 for future nursing care, based on a multiplicand
        of £12,000 and a multiplier of 11, and on the basis of his
        being indefinitely cared for at home, not in an institution;
  (iii) £21,480 for loss of earnings, based on a multiplicand of
        £5,370 and a multiplier of 4;
   (iv) £10,098 for equipment, based on a multiplicand of £918
        and a multiplier of 11;
    (v) £13,750 for private physiotherapy: £1,250 x 11;
   (vi) £25,000 for the cost of having his house altered or of
        moving to a bungalow suitable for his long-term care;
  (vii) other items which resulted in a total award of £273,958
        plus Court of Protection charges.

See pages 81, 103, 105, 106, 107.

Munro v Oxford United Hospitals and Another

Operation: surgeon: substandard treatment: standard of care

Oxford County Court. [1958] 1 BMJ 167

When the plaintiff (Sheila Munro), then aged seven, was undergoing a tonsillectomy, the gag slipped. The surgeon was taken by surprise, and four of her front teeth were knocked out. Two of the teeth were second teeth, and as a result of their loss she had to wear a denture.

The plaintiff sued the surgeon and the hospital authority. Expert evidence was given that it was a matter of no difficulty to check and correct slipping of a gag.

Held: the defendants were liable. The operation was a normal one without complications, and it was a normal part of the surgeon's duty to prevent the gag from slipping. The only reasonable inference was that the surgeon had shown a lack of attention and alertness which fell short of the standard of care which it was reasonable to expect in the circumstances, and that the force required to dislodge the teeth had come from the surgeon's hands.

Murray v Kensington and Chelsea and Westminster Area Health Authority and Another

Childbirth: registrar: substandard treatment: causation

Court of Appeal. 11 May 1981

On Saturday 4 January 1975 the plaintiff (Robert Murray) was born in Westminster Hospital. He was a tiny baby, born prematurely after twenty-eight weeks, and weighed two and a half pounds. He was placed in an incubator. In the evening the house doctor, Dr Murfitt, increased the oxygen in the incubator from twenty-one per cent to thirty per cent. When a registrar took over on the morning of Monday 6 January, the extra oxygen was discontinued.

On 7 January the baby became very poorly, suffering breathlessness and other symptoms. For the next three to four weeks, the oxygen content in the incubator was maintained at between thirty and forty per cent, and sometimes one hundred per cent oxygen was administered for short periods. The baby was kept alive, but it was later discovered that all the extra oxygen had left him totally blind.

His next friend sued the hospital authority. The trial judge (May J) found negligence proved but not causation.

Held: (i) as the baby did not initially suffer from breathing difficulties, it was negligent to subject him to an oxygen-enriched atmosphere for the first thirty-six hours; and harm from this was reasonably foreseeable. There was no subsequent negligence;

(ii) the trial judge was justified in concluding that the plaintiff had not discharged the onus of proving that this initial excess oxygen had materially contributed to his blindness.

See pages 46, 77, 83.

Naylor v Preston Area Health Authority

Disclosure of experts' reports: duty of care: right to know treatment received: medical literature

Court of Appeal. [1987] 2 All ER 353, [1987] 1 WLR 958

Mrs Naylor was admitted to hospital in Preston for the birth of her child. She had a history of epilepsy. Four days after the birth she had an epileptic fit while taking a bath, and drowned. The administrator of her estate sued the health authority.

In this and three other cases, the plaintiffs appealed against the refusal of an order for the advance disclosure of the reports of all expert medical witnesses on liability issues which would be relied upon at the trial.

Held: in all four cases, the issues would be refined, costs would be saved and the chances of a consensual resolution of the dispute would be enhanced by an order for pre-trial disclosure of the substance of the expert evidence. This should be accompanied by an identification of any medical or scientific literature, published or unpublished, to which the experts intended to refer. In none of the four cases were there any grounds to depart from the norm of simultaneous disclosure.

Per Sir John Donaldson MR: "I personally think that in professional negligence cases, and in particular in medical negligence cases, there is a duty of candour resting upon the professional man . . . In my judgement, still admittedly and regretfully *obiter*, it is but one aspect of the general duty of care, arising out of the patient-medical practitioner or hospital authority relationship and gives rise to rights both in contract and tort".

N.B. The subject matter of the appeals would now be governed by the revised RSC O 38 r 37.

See pages 17, 26, 75, 132–134.

Needham v Biograft Transplant Centre Ltd and Another

Surgeon: operation: retained surgical product: damages

Hobhouse J. [1983] The Times 16 February

The plaintiff (Arthur Needham), aged fifty-seven, was a builder who was going bald. The Biograph Transplant Centre claimed that it could combat baldness with a new technique by which bald patches were removed and hair-bearing skin was drawn over them. In April 1981 Mr Clamp, a surgeon, carried out the operation at Biograft's clinic. A swab of gauze was inadvertently left under the plaintiff's skin.

The plaintiff went straight to bed and stayed there for five days. He was in considerable pain and could not sleep. His face was badly swollen and he had black eyes. When he was on holiday in Majorca the next week, there appeared on his neck a lump which frequently wept and twice burst. The wound continued to discharge for the rest of the holiday, causing discomfort and embarrassment. A further operation was performed to remove the swab. The plaintiff made a good recovery but was left with scars on his head where hair did not grow.

He sued the Biograft Transplant Centre and Mr Clamp. Both admitted liability.

Held: general damages (February 1983) for pain, suffering and loss of amenities were assessed at £1,500. The plaintiff's total award was £3,903.

See page 104.

Newnham and Another v Rochester and Chatham Joint Hospital Board

Child patient: hospital administration: supervision: nurses

Talbot J (with jury). [1936] The Times 28 February

In December 1934 the plaintiff (Charles Newnham), aged seven, was suffering from scarlet fever. He was admitted to St William's Hospital in Rochester and placed in a ward on the ground floor. During the late afternoon of his second day he was in bed a few feet from a window, the lower part of which was open. In the absence of a nurse, he fell out of the window and dropped about seventeen feet on to the ground below. As a result, his forehead was badly disfigured and both feet became flat, requiring special supports.

Held: the hospital staff were negligent in leaving the boy unattended near the open window.

See page 88.

Newton v Newton's Model Laundry Ltd and Others

Fracture: diagnosis: hospital doctor: examination

Salmon J. [1959] The Times 3 November

On 29 September 1954 the plaintiff (Vernon Newton) went up to inspect tanks in the roof of the laundry which he managed. He slipped and fell twelve feet on to the concrete floor below. He was taken to Acton Hospital where he was seen by Dr Potasnick who did not diagnose the broken patella in his left knee. The plaintiff suffered excruciating pain until the fracture was diagnosed on 16 October 1954. When an operation was performed, it was found that the bone was broken into eleven pieces.

Held: Dr Potasnick had been negligent. He had failed to examine the plaintiff's left knee properly.

See page 62.

Nickolls v Ministry of Health and Another

Surgeon: standard of care: operation

Gorman J. [1955] The Times 4 February

In December 1944 the plaintiff (Mrs Winifred Nickolls) underwent an operation by Mr Joll at the Royal Free Hospital. He was suffering from cancer at the time and knew that he had the disease. Her recurrent laryngeal nerves were damaged in the operation. Mr Joll died a few weeks later.

The plaintiff sued the Ministry of Health and the Royal Free Hospital alleging that Mr Joll was unfit for the task.

Held: Mr Joll was fit to perform the operation. The evidence did not make out a case of negligence against him.

See page 37.

O'Malley-Williams v Governors of National Hospital for Nervous Diseases

Registrar: operation: diagnosis: risk disclosure: standard of care: res ipsa loquitur

Bridge J. [1975] 1 BMJ 635

In 1968 the plaintiff (Mr O'Malley-Williams), an accomplished pianist, sought treatment at the National Hospital for Nervous Diseases. He had been afflicted by recurrent episodes of loss of vision in the right eye. Stenosis of the right carotid artery was diagnosed. To confirm the diagnosis, the hospital decided to perform an aortagram. The plaintiff was not informed of any risk.

The operation was performed under local anaesthetic by a registrar, Dr Bland. He successfully punctured the femoral artery in the patient's right groin with the Seldinger needle, but then met an obstruction before the guide wire had travelled more than five or six inches up the artery. Therefore he abandoned the femoral route and decided to insert the catheter by way of the right axillary artery. Before that artery was successfully punctured, Dr Bland had to make a number of passes and the plaintiff suffered great pain.

Thereafter, the trouble with the vision in the plaintiff's right eye was successfully treated with anti-coagulants. However he suffered neurological complications which led to partial paralysis of his right hand. He sued the hospital.

Held: (i) even severe pain was by no means uncommon with aortagrams under local anaesthesia, so it was not negligent of Dr Bland to continue trying to get into the artery;

(ii) *res ipsa loquitur* did not apply, since the injury sustained was recognized as an inherent risk of the treatment undergone;

(iii) a failure to warn of remote risks, where the patient had not raised the question, was not negligence.

Judgment for the defendants.

See pages 74, 77.

O'Neill v Kelly

Dentist: fracture: causation

Davies LJ. [1961] The Times 15 December

On 4 September 1957 the plaintiff (Mrs Patricia O'Neill) attended the surgery of Mr Kelly, a young dentist who had just qualified. In trying to remove a tooth in her lower jaw, he took the crown off. He told her that he must take out the root and gave her a local injection. After he failed to remove the root with forceps, the plaintiff wanted to go home but finally consented to remain. He proceeded to use an elevator three or four times. During its use the plaintiff was jumping, and the nurse had to hold her head down. Mr Kelly then felt a movement of the elevator and something gave. In consequence the plaintiff was taken to Guy's Hospital where it was discovered that she had fractured a jaw bone. She sued Mr Kelly for using the elevator negligently.

Held: the plaintiff had failed to make out a case of negligence. There had been nothing abnormal about Mr Kelly's use of the elevator. The plaintiff, being excitable and nervous, had jerked her head at the last moment and this had caused the fracture.

See pages 86–87.

Re P (a Minor)

Consent: abortion: minor: wardship: parental objections

Butler-Sloss J. (1981) 80 LGR 301

In August 1966, Shirley was born. In 1979 she was convicted of theft and committed to the care of Lewisham Borough Council. In 1980 she conceived and gave birth to a baby boy. She lived with him in a single room in a mother and child unit. In 1981, at the age of fifteen, she became pregnant again. She wanted an abortion and understood the implications. Her general practitioner and hospital consultant were in favour of an abortion. Her father, a Seventh Day Adventist, opposed it, partly on religious grounds.

The Lewisham Borough Council applied to make Shirley a ward of court and sought an order that the pregnancy, which had lasted eleven weeks, be terminated.

Held: (i) it was appropriate for the local authority to have placed the problem before the court under wardship proceedings;

(ii) the case came within the Abortion Act 1967. The continuance of the pregnancy would involve injury to the mental health of Shirley and her existing child, and that risk was undoubtedly much greater than the risk of the pregnancy being terminated;

(iii) the parents' feelings must be considered as a factor in the case, and their religious objections must be taken into account. However Shirley's welfare must be paramount. The parents' objections could not weigh against her needs so as to prevent the termination.

The applications were granted.

See page 6.

Palmer and Palmer v Eadie

Vasectomy (failed): warning: risk disclosure: standard of care: state of knowledge

Court of Appeal. 18 May 1987

By 1980 the plaintiffs (Mr and Mrs Palmer) had had four children and three aborted pregnancies. Mr Palmer consulted Mr Eadie, a consultant urologist, about a vasectomy. Mr Eadie warned him that the operation, though likely to be successful, carried with it the risk of failure. He performed the vasectomy. Mr Palmer had two successive zero sperm counts. However in 1983 the plaintiffs had another child.

They sued Mr Eadie. The evidence was that in 1980 the vasectomy operation could be carried out in two ways, either by 3–4 centimetre excisions, or by 1.5 centimetre excisions with other steps. If 3–4 centimetres were excised, it was more difficult to reverse the operation. However in 1980 it was thought that, if after either method was used, there were two successive zero sperm counts, then there was no chance that the operation had failed. The trial judge (Hollings J) dismissed the plaintiffs' claim.

Held: (i) as the trial judge accepted that Mr Eadie had warned Mr Palmer of the risk of failure, there was no breach of contract;

(ii) it was not negligent of Mr Eadie not to discuss with Mr Palmer the choice between the two methods of excision, at a time when nobody thought there was a risk provided that there were two consecutive zero counts.

See pages 84–85.

Pargeter v Kensington and Chelsea and Westminster Health Authority

Injection: drugs: after-care: nurses: standard of care: burden of proof

Forbes J. [1979] 2 The Lancet 1030

The plaintiff (Mr Pargeter) was admitted to hospital for the removal of a cataract in his left eye. At 2.00 pm on the day of the operation he received an injection of 15 mg of papaveretum, with an anti-emetic drug, as pre-operative medication. Further injections of 10 mg of papaveretum, without an anti-emetic drug, were administered by nursing staff after the operation at 4.35 pm, when the plaintiff was in some pain, and at 11.30 pm, to "settle" him. When he awoke the next morning at 7.15, he was offered a cup of tea, drank it and vomited immediately. His left eye burst open and he lost the sight in it.

The plaintiff sued the hospital authority. Evidence was given at trial that everything must be done to stop the patient from coughing or vomiting after an open eye operation. Evidence was also given that it was wholly wrong nursing practice to give tea to a patient recovering from an anaesthetic, unless it was first established that he could tolerate liquid by giving him controlled sips of water.

Held: (i) as there was a respectable body of medical opinion which took the view that papaveretum should be administered, even though there was an opposing school of thought, the hospital staff were not negligent in using it;

(ii) if a patient were given tea without trial sips, especially after having had papaveretum without an anti-emetic, that would be negligent nursing practice. However it was highly improbable that this precaution was not taken.

Judgment for the defendants.

See page 94.

Parkinson v West Cumberland Hospital Management Committee and Another

Diagnosis: hospital doctor: standard of care: error of judgement

Ashworth J. [1955] 1 BMJ 977

Soon after 4.00 am on 11 July 1973 Mr Parkinson, aged thirty-nine, went to the Workington Infirmary and complained of chest pains. Dr Graham, a newly qualified doctor in his fourth day there, examined him for nearly an hour. Then he discharged Mr Parkinson, giving him two tablets of codeine and telling him to return later for X-ray examination. A quarter of an hour later, Mr Parkinson was found dead in a street near the hospital. He had died of a massive coronary thrombosis.

The plaintiff (his widow) sued the hospital authority and Dr Graham.

Held: Dr Graham made a mistake, but he had not been negligent. His examination had been careful, and there were signs and symptoms pointing away from a serious condition.

See page 64.

Pask v Bexley Health Authority

Retained surgical product: scarring: damages

Court of Appeal. [1988] CLY 1098

In July 1981 the plaintiff, then aged twenty-three, having taken tablets and alcohol, was admitted to hospital to have her stomach pumped out. A year later it was discovered that two and a half feet of plastic tubing had been left in her body. The tubing had worked its way into the bottom of her left lung.

When the plaintiff was discharged in July 1981, she suffered severe breathlessness and dreadful pains in her body, coughed violently and brought up blood and phlegm. She endured appalling discomfort and pain for the next year. The operation to remove the tube left a very large scar running from underneath her left breast and up her back almost to the base of her neck. It was thirty-six centimetres long, ugly and permanent. It was also tender, causing pain and discomfort if she should knock it or wear tight clothing. The plaintiff's health improved after the operation but she still suffered from breathlessness and had repeated chest infections. The infections would recur, and she would suffer discomfort for the rest of her life. She needed help from her mother with housework.

She sued the health authority who admitted liability. In October 1987 the trial judge (Caulfield J) awarded her £25,000 for her pain and suffering, to include an element to enable her to pay those who help her in future, and £17,500 for the disfigurement and discomfort resulting from her scar.

Held: the court would not interfere with the total award of £42,500 general damages, although it might have been preferable not to split it up into two constituents.

See page 83.

Patel v Adyha

General practitioner: examination: diagnosis

Court of Appeal. 2 April 1985

In September and October 1975 the plaintiff (Mrs Patel) went three times to her general practitioner, Dr Adyha, and complained of pains in her back. He only examined her once when he inserted his hand underneath her dress and placed it on her back. He did not ask her to take her dress off. She was given analgesics on each visit. In March 1976 there was a collapse of her spine. She was found to be suffering from a tubercular condition and there was kyphus.

The plaintiff sued Dr Adyha. There was expert evidence that a suitable examination would have found either local spinal deformity or local stiffness detectable on palpation or bending. The trial judge found in her favour.

Held: (i) the trial judge was right to accept that Dr Adyha negligently failed to carry out a proper examination which would have revealed the need to obtain specialist advice and led to treatment;

(ii) the plaintiff could not be criticised for not seeking further medical advice before March 1976 since she did not know that she had a serious condition and the mere prescription of analgesics signalled that hers was a case for patience and fortitude rather than treatment.

See page 63.

Paterson v Chadwick

Anaesthetics: injection: discovery: solicitor's negligence

Boreham J. [1974] 1 WLR 890

In February 1969 the plaintiff (Mrs Sarah Paterson) attended Northampton Hospital for dental treatment. An anaesthetic injection was given to her. She sustained a serious and permanent disability of her left hand. She alleged that this was due to the injection having been negligently carried out.

She instructed solicitors to claim damages for her. They did not start court action, so her claim became statute barred in February 1972. Thereafter she consulted other solicitors and in February 1973 a writ was issued against her former solicitors for negligence and breach of contract.

The plaintiff applied by summons pursuant to s 32(1) Administration of Justice Act 1970 and RSC O 24 r 7A for an order for disclosure by the hospital authority of medical records and other documents relating to her treatment at Northampton Hospital.

Held: there was a clear and firm connection between her professional negligence claim and her personal injuries. Thus she was "a person who is a party to proceedings in which a claim in respect of personal injuries to a person is made" within the words of s 32(1) of the 1970 Act. As such, she was entitled to the order for disclosure.

N.B. Section 32((1) Administration of Justice Act 1970 has been replaced by s 34(2) Supreme Court Act 1981.

See pages 117, 129.

Paton v British Pregnancy Advisory Service Trustees and Another

Abortion: father's status: foetus' rights: parental objections

Sir George Baker P. [1979] 1 QB 276, [1978] 2 All ER 987, [1978] 3 WLR 687

On 8 May 1978 Mrs Joan Paton's general practitioner confirmed that she was pregnant. She applied for and obtained the necessary medical certificate entitling her to an abortion within the terms of the Abortion Act 1967. On 16 May she left the matrimonial home. On 17 May she filed a petition for divorce.

The plaintiff, her husband William Paton, applied for an injunction to restrain the British Pregnancy Advisory Service and Mrs Paton from causing or permitting an abortion to be carried out on her. It was accepted that there had been correct compliance with the provisions of the Abortion Act 1967.

Held: (i) the foetus cannot have a right of its own until it is born and has a separate existence from its mother;

(ii) personal family relationships in marriage cannot be enforced by the order of a court. The Abortion Act 1967 gives no right to a father to be consulted in respect of a termination of a pregnancy. The plaintiff, whether as husband or father, had no legal right to stop his wife having the abortion or to stop the doctors from carrying it out.

Per Sir George Baker P: "It would be quite impossible for the courts in any event to supervise the operation of the Abortion Act 1967. The great social responsibility is firmly placed by the law upon the shoulders of the medical profession."

N.B. Mr Paton's subsequent application to the European Commission of Human Rights was also dismissed: *Paton* v *United Kingdom* [1980] 3 EHRR 408.

See page 31.

Patten v Birmingham Regional Hospital Board and Others

House surgeon: operation: substandard treatment

Stable J. [1955] 2 The Lancet 1336

The plaintiff (Mrs Lily Patten), a factory operative, was injured at work when a power press suddenly descended and caught her right hand. An orthopaedic surgeon at the hospital advised that part of the middle finger should be amputated. The operation was carried out by a house surgeon who by mistake removed the tip of the little finger. Also, an operation for the suture of a severed tendon in the injured finger was performed too late, and all three middle fingers were bent in towards the palm. Nineteen months after the operation the whole of the middle finger was amputated.

The plaintiff sued her employers, the hospital authority and the house surgeon.

Held: the hospital authority was liable with the house surgeon who made the grave blunder for substantially the whole of the condition of the plaintiff's injured hand.

See page 77.

Patterson v Rotherham Health Authority

Diagnosis: hospital doctor: fracture: damages

Court of Appeal. 20 May 1987

On 29 August 1982 the plaintiff (Angela Patterson), then aged twenty-two, fell from her horse in a show-jumping competition. She suffered a fracture of the tibia within her left knee joint. She was immediately taken to Rotherham

District General Hospital where they failed to diagnose the fracture until she returned there on 13 September. An operation was carried out on 14 September.

The plaintiff suffered acute pain in the fortnight after the accident. The delay made it impracticable to attempt to repair the medial collateral ligament. There was continuing pain and discomfort in her knee, and worsening osteoarthritic changes which would eventually require an arthroplasty. If the operation had been immediately performed, her disability would have been twenty per cent; instead it was fifty per cent.

She sued the health authority who admitted negligently failing to diagnose the fracture. In July 1986 the trial judge (French J) awarded her £24,000 general damages including the cost of arthroplasty.

Held: (i) the judge was entitled to conclude that the future need for an arthroplasty had been caused by the delay in treatment; £2,500 was appropriate as a discounted sum of this future cost;

(ii) £1,000 was appropriate for the needless pain and suffering during the fortnight after the accident;

(iii) the award for the subsequent extra suffering and loss of amenities caused by the defendant's negligence could not properly exceed £15,000;

(iv) the total award for general damages should be £18,500.

See page 62.

Payne v St Helier Group Hospital Management Committee and Another

Diagnosis: casualty officer: second opinion

Donovan J. [1952] The Times 12 November

On 10 July 1950 Reginald Payne was kicked in the abdomen by a horse. His general practitioner sent him for examination to the Sutton and Cheam Hospital. He was examined there nine and a half hours after the accident by Dr Perkins, the hospital's casualty officer. Dr Perkins noted a bruise about the size of a man's hand on Mr Payne's abdomen but concluded that there was no internal injury. He sent Mr Payne home and told him to go to bed and to call his own panel doctor if he should experience pain.

By 28 July 1950 Mr Payne was very ill and was admitted to hospital where two operations were later performed on him; first a lumbar incision, and then a laparotomy which revealed a condition of general peritonitis. Mr Payne died from this condition nine days later on 30 August 1950. His widow sued Dr Perkins and the hospital authority.

Held: (i) the hospital was not negligent in respect of the system that it provided for the examination of abdominal injury;

(ii) Dr Perkins ought to have found that Mr Payne was suffering from pain, shock and rigidity of the abdomen. It was wholly unreasonable for him to send Mr Payne home and not to detain him for observation and examination by a consultant. Dr Perkins had failed to exercise reasonable care in his diagnosis and treatment. He was negligent and the hospital authority was vicariously liable;

(iii) the hospital authority was granted an indemnity against Dr Perkins in respect of the whole of the damages and two-thirds of the costs.

See pages 36, 63.

Perionowsky v Freeman and Another

Consultant: nurses

Cockburn CJ (with jury). [1866] 4 F & F 977

In May 1865 the plaintiff (Mr Perionowsky) suffered a disease and became a patient at St George's Hospital. Mr Freeman and Mr Holmes, two surgeons there, ordered that he should have a hot hip bath. They went on to attend other patients in the ward and were not present when nurses put the plaintiff into the bath. He was somewhat scalded.

The plaintiff sued the two surgeons. Evidence was given that it was usual hospital practice for doctors to leave it to nurses to see to the baths.

Held: such matters should be left to nurses. The surgeons would not be liable for the negligence of the nurses, unless near enough to be aware of it and to prevent it.

The jury returned a verdict for the defendants.

See page 85.

Pickering v Governors of the United Leeds Hospital

Operation: after-care: nurses: consultant: bedsores

Slade J. [1954] 1 The Lancet 1075

The plaintiff (Mrs Pickering), aged eighty-two, was admitted to hospital after falling and fracturing a femur. She was mentally alert and in no way senile, but weighed about fifteen stone and suffered from a mild form of Parkinson's disease. Her operation lasted one and a half hours, and she needed a subsequent blood transfusion lasting ten hours. The surgeon forbade the turning of the plaintiff on to her side in the early stages after the operation. Later he directed that she should be moved on to her right side. She developed severe bedsores while in hospital, and two operations had to be performed in a nursing home for removal of gangrenous tissue.

The plaintiff sued the hospital authority, alleging that the nursing staff failed to keep the bed dry and failed to change her position. The orthopaedic officer testified that he examined the bed at least once every day and always found it dry. The only direct evidence of the bed being wet was that of the plaintiff's daughter who said she did nothing about it.

Held: the plaintiff had failed to make out her allegations. The question of changing the plaintiff's position was one for the surgeon, not the nurses. There had been no negligence on the part of the nursing staff.

See page 93.

Pimm v Roper

Diagnosis: duty of care: settlement of claim

Bramwell B. [1862] 2 F&F 783

The plaintiff (Mr Pimm) was injured while a passenger in a train that collided. At the station the railway company's staff sent him to Mr Roper, the railway company's surgeon. The plaintiff, whose face was bleeding, told Mr Roper that he was injured in his face and arm. Mr Roper made the usual applications for these visible wounds. On the plaintiff's next visit, considering that he was more frightened than hurt, Mr Roper sent him to the railway company's authorities who gave him £5 which he accepted in settlement.

Next day the plaintiff came again and got Mr Roper to examine his abdomen. It was discovered that it was ruptured. The plaintiff's claim against the railway company for further damages failed due to the settlement. He then sued Mr Roper.

Held: there was no proof of any injury sustained by the plaintiff as a result of any neglect on the part of Mr Roper to examine him. Examination was the only duty that had been proved. There was no further ground of action.

See page 7.

Pippin and Wife v Sheppard

Surgeon: duty of care: substandard treatment

Court of Exchequer. (1822) 11 Price 400

The declaration stated that the Defendant, Mr Sheppard, followed and carried on the art, mystery and occupation of a surgeon – that Defendant, afterwards, and etc at Bristol aforesaid, was retained and employed as such surgeon for a certain reasonable reward to be to him therefore paid, to treat, attend to, and cure divers grievous hurts, cuts and etc just before then by the plaintiff Mrs Pippin had and received: and the said Defendant then and there entered upon the treatment and cure of her; yet Defendant afterwards so carelessly, negligently, improperly and unskilfully, conducted himself in that behalf, and then and there so carelessly and etc applied his care and treatment in and upon a certain wound and etc of the said wife, that by means thereof the said wound became and was grievously aggravated and made worse, and was thereby then and there made and rendered violently and dreadfully inflamed and etc to the danger of the wife, and that her life was greatly despaired of, and that by means thereof she suffered great pain and etc and was forced to submit to painful surgical operations in and about the treatment of the said wound by other and more skilful surgeons.

Held: the declaration was a sufficient pleading. It was not necessary to state by whom the defendant was retained and employed. Nor did the declaration need to allege that it was the duty of the defendant, or that he undertook or engaged, properly or skilfully to conduct himself in the treatment and cure of the said wounds.

See pages 7, 24–25.

Powell v Streatham Manor Nursing Home

After-care: nurses: substandard treatment

House of Lords. [1935] AC 243

In January 1930 the plaintiff (Helena Powell) entered the defendants' nursing home as a paying patient. Dr Kirkland performed the operation of hysterectomy on her. Soon afterwards it was found that her bladder had been punctured.

The plaintiff sued the defendants in the name of the nursing home. She testified at trial that one of the nurses there, in attempting to relieve her of urine after the operation, used a rigid catheter and passed it not into the urethra (as she ought to have done) but into the vagina, and continued forcing the catheter through the suture, which had been made to complete the operation, until it perforated the bladder.

The trial judge (Horridge J) believed her evidence and decided the case in her favour. The Court of Appeal reversed his judgment.

Held: it was impossible to say that the trial judge was wrong in believing the plaintiff and therefore finding that the defendants had negligently punctured her bladder. His judgment should be restored.

Per Viscount Sankey LC: "the judge of first instance is not the possessor of infallibility and, like other tribunals, there may be occasions when he goes wrong on a question of fact; but first and last and all the time, he has the great advantage, which is denied to the Court of Appeal, of seeing the witnesses and watching their demeanour."

See page 93.

Prendergast v Sam & Dee Limited and Others

General practitioner: pharmacist: prescription: foreseeability: apportionment of liability

Court of Appeal. [1989] The Times 14 March. 1 MLR 36

In December 1983 the plaintiff (James Prendergast), an asthmatic who was starting to get a cold, consulted his general practitioner, Dr Miller. Dr Miller wrote out a prescription for three drugs including twenty-one 250 mg Amoxil tablets to be taken three times a day. The word Amoxil was written, not very legibly, in lower case. The plaintiff took the prescription to the pharmacy of Sam & Dee Limited where Mr Kozary misread the prescription and dispensed twenty-one 5 mg tablets of Daonil, a drug to control diabetes by reducing the sugar content of the blood. After taking six Daonil tablets, the plaintiff suffered hypoglycaemia which led to unconsciousness and irreparable brain damage.

He sued Sam & Dee Limited, Mr Kozary and Dr Miller. The trial judge (Auld J) found all the defendants liable and apportioned liability of seventy-five per cent to Sam & Dee Limited and Mr Kozary, and twenty-five per cent to Dr Miller. Dr Miller appealed.

Held: (i) a prescription which is so written as to invite or reasonably permit misreading by a pharmacist under ordinary working conditions (which may be less than ideal) falls below the necessary standard. Dr Miller's poor writing came within this category;

(ii) although other aspects of the prescription, such as the dosage and number of tablets, should have put Mr Kozary on inquiry as being inconsistent with Daonil, the chain of causation was not broken and it was reasonably foreseeable that Daonil would be prescribed;

(iii) the trial judge did not err in his allocation of liability between the defendants.

See pages 51, 81, 91.

Prout v Crowley and Another

Injection: standard of care

G Glynn Blackledge QC. [1956] 1 BMJ 580

In June 1952 the plaintiff (Mrs Catherine Prout) was being treated for anaemia as an in-patient at Walton Hospital, Liverpool. On three previous occasions Dr Crowley had successfully injected ferrivenin into a vein of the antecubital fossa of her right arm. On the fourth occasion the plaintiff complained of pain after he had injected about 1 ml. He realised that the point of the needle had come out of the vein, so he immediately withdrew the needle and ordered poultices to be applied to her arm. A small quantity of the ferrivenin had entered the tissues surrounding the vein. This caused an abscess to develop.

The plaintiff sued Dr Crowley and the hospital authority.

Held: the extravenous injection of a small quanitity of solution could happen without any negligence on the part of the operator. Dr Crowley had followed the correct technique and had stopped the injection as soon as he realised that the point of the needle was outside the vein. He had not been negligent.

See page 79.

Pudney v Union-Castle Mail Steamship Company Ltd and Another

Ship's doctor: diagnosis: standard of care

Devlin J. [1953] 1 Lloyds Rep 73

In April 1948 the plaintiff (David Pudney), then aged twenty-five, was an assistant pantryman in the defendant's ship travelling from London to Cape Town. On 9 April he was taken ill with rheumatic pains and was treated by Dr Fairley, the ship's surgeon. He developed a high temperature and suffered a sore throat. There was no swelling of his joints, the fever subsided, but his pains remained. Dr Fairley advised the plaintiff to be discharged from the ship at Cape Town on 24 April and repatriated. His diagnosis was one of a mild rheumatic complaint.

The plaintiff deteriorated thereafter. In October 1949, after he had been examined by a number of doctors, it was discovered that he was suffering from acute rheumatoid arthritis. This left him a permanent cripple. He sued Dr Fairley and the shipping company, alleging that Dr Fairley should have guarded against potential dangers, of which rheumatoid arthritis was one, and advised immediate rest until the diagnosis was complete.

Held: Dr Fairley had not been negligent. It was impossible to diagnose a mild rheumatic atttack as rheumatoid arthritis until swellings in the joints appeared. Following an apparently mild attack of rheumatism with a high temperature, it was not practicable to insist on the patient remaining in bed or going to hospital.

See page 64.

R v Bateman

Childbirth: substandard treatment: general practitioner: criminal liability: manslaughter: second opinion

Court of Appeal. [1925] 94 LJKB 791

On 23 July Dr Bateman, a general practitioner, was called in by the midwife to attend Mary Ann Harding on her confinement. He administered chloroform and attempted, properly but unsuccessfully, to effect delivery by the use of instruments. He then proceeded with his hands to perform the operation known as "version", using of necessity considerable force. He worked at this operation for an hour and then delivered the child which was dead. In removing the placenta, he mistakenly removed with it a portion of the uterus. He visited the patient twice daily, but despite requests by the husband and the midwife, did not remove her to the infirmary until 28 July. She grew gradually weaker and died on 30 July.

On a post-mortem examination, The bladder was found to be ruptured, the colon was crushed against the sacral promontory, there was a small rupture of the rectum, and the uterus was almost entirely gone. Dr Bateman was prosecuted for manslaughter. The charges of negligence made against him were, in substance: (i) causing the internal ruptures in performing the operation of "version"; (ii) removing part of the uterus along with the placenta; (iii) delay in sending the patient to the infirmary. He was convicted and sentenced to six months' imprisonment.

Held: in order to establish criminal liability, the facts must be such that, in the opinion of the jury, the negligence of the accused went beyond a mere matter of compensation between subjects and showed such disregard for the life and safety of others as to amount to a crime against the State and conduct deserving punishment.

The conviction was quashed, as there was no evidence to support the first charge, and it was uncertain whether the jury would have convicted on the second and third charges alone.

See page 34.

R v Central Birmingham Health Authority, ex parte Collier

Judicial review: hospital resources: duty of care

Court of Appeal. 6 January 1988

Matthew Collier was born in June 1983 with a missing heart valve: "a hole in his heart". By-pass surgery did not achieve the desired progress. In September 1987 his surgeon at the Children's Hospital advised that Matthew "desperately needed" open heart surgery. He was placed at the top of the waiting list but, due to a shortage of intensive care beds and nurses, months passed without the operation being performed.

His father, Barry Collier, sought leave to apply for judicial review in respect of an alleged "decision of the Central Birmingham Health Authority . . . not to conduct an operation and/or provide proper medical care for his baby boy Matthew Collier".

Held: it was not for the court to allocate financial resources. There was no evidence that the health authority had acted unreasonably or in breach of any public duty. It would not be right for the court to intervene by means of judicial review.

See page 28.

R v Central Birmingham Health Authority, ex parte Walker

Judicial review: duty of care: hospital resources

Court of Appeal. [1987] The Independent 26 November

The applicant's baby required an operation. On 20 October 1987 the Central Birmingham Health Authority accepted this, but decided that it was unable to conduct the operation at that time.

Leave to apply for judicial review of this decision was refused by Macpherson J. The applicant appealed.

Held: the decisions of National Health Service authorities were amenable to judicial review, but the court's discretion to intervene must be used extremely sparingly. Leave was refused.

Per Sir John Donaldson MR: "It is not for this court, or indeed any court, to substitute its own judgement for the judgement of those who are responsible for the allocation of resources. This court could only intervene where it was satisfied that there was a prima-facie case, not only of failing to allocate resources in the way in which others think that resources should be allocated, but of a failure to allocate resources to an extent which was 'Wednesbury unreasonable' (see *Associated Provincial Picture Houses* v *Wednesbury Corporation* [1948] 1 KB 223, [1947] 2 All ER 680), to use the lawyers' jargon or, in simpler words, which involves a breach of a public law duty. Even then, of course, the court has to exercise a judicial discretion. It has to take account of all the circumstances of the particular case with which it is concerned."

See page 28.

R v Crick

Alternative practitioner: prescription: overdose: criminal liability: standard of care

Pollock CB (with jury). [1859] 1 F&F 519

Mrs Orpin took a child named William Hardwicke to Mr Crick, a herb doctor. He examined the child and gave Mrs Orpin a bottle of infusion of lobelia inflata. He advised her to give the child two teaspoonfuls of the infusion three times a day. She gave the child some doses of the infusion for several days. Then she ceased, as she thought that he had got better. The child died, three weeks after Mr Crick saw him, and more than a week after the last dose had been administered.

Mr Crick was prosecuted. Medical witnesses testified that the child had died of overdoses of lobelia.

Held: Pollock CB directed the jury: "it is no crime for anyone to administer medicine, but it is a crime to administer it so rashly and carelessly as to produce death; and in this respect there is no difference between the most regular practitioner and the greatest quack . . . on the evidence it appeared that the child got better while the medicine was being administered to it. If the prisoner had been a medical man I should have recommended you to take the most favourable view of his conduct, for it would be most fatal to the efficiency of the medical profession if no one could administer medicine without a halter around his neck; and although I cannot speak of a person in the prisoner's position in language as strong, still he ought not to be responsible unless it has been proved with reasonable certainty that he caused the death by the careless administration of the drug."

The jury returned a verdict of not guilty.

See page 95.

R v Jones

Alternative practitioner: substandard treatment: criminal liability: standard of care

Charles J. [1938] 1 BMJ 1401

A twenty-three year old school teacher, who had suffered from diabetes for four years, was on a strict diet and was taking insulin. On the advice of a friend she consulted an "osteopath and radiologist" named Herbert Jones. He told her that she had not got diabetes and had never had it, but that she was suffering from anaemia. He advised her to starve herself for four days and take nothing but orange juice. This she did, discontinuing her insulin, and within three days she had lost seven pounds. Her father telephoned Mr Jones who replied that she should continue with her treatment until he saw her in a few weeks' time. On that day she went into a coma and, despite hospital treatment, she died a week after the consultation.

Mr Jones was committed for trial at the Gloucestershire Assizes. He testified that he had taken up the science of healing twenty-three years ago, when he had cured by the laying of hands a man who was dying of consumption, but admitted that he had no experience in diabetes.

Held: Charles J remarked that Mr Jones' conduct was a danger to the State and the public. If it had not been for his good character he would have been bound to send him to prison for a long term, not only to correct him but also to deter others who might be likely to undertake the treatment of sick folk without proper knowledge. A sentence of six months' imprisonment was imposed.

R v Secretary of State for Social Services and Others, ex parte Hincks and Others

Judicial review: hospital resources: duty of care

Wien J. (1979) 123 SJ 436

The applicants were orthopaedic patients at a Birmingham Hospital. They had waited for treatment for periods longer than was medically advisable. This was due to a shortage of facilities arising, in part, from a decision on grounds of cost not to build a new block on the hospital.

The applicants sought against the Secretary of State and the hospital authorities declarations that they were in breach of their duties under the National Health Service Act 1977: under s 1 to continue to promote a comprehensive health service designed to secure improvement in health and the prevention of illness, and under s 3 to provide accommodation facilities and services for those purposes.

Held: (i) it was not the court's function to direct Parliament what funds to make available to the health service and how to allocate them. The Secretary of State's duty under s 3, to provide services "to such extent as he considers necessary" gave him a discretion as to the disposition of financial resources. The court could only interfere if the Secretary of State acted so as to frustrate the policy of the Act, or as no reasonable Minister could have acted. No such breach had been shown in the present case;

    (ii) the application was also dismissed in relation to the regional and area health authorities.

N.B. The applicant's appeal to the Court of Appeal was dismissed.

See page 28.

R v Vaccine Damage Tribunal, ex parte Loveday

Vaccine damage: causation

Court of Appeal. [1985] 2 The Lancet 1137

In 1970 a seven week old baby was seen at a clinic, where notes were made referring to "hypotonia" and "a miserable little baby". On 16 April, when she was medically examined for the purposes of adoption, a general practitioner found no abnormality. On 13 May he gave her a first DTP vaccination. On 22 June a squint was observed. On 1 July 1970 and 1 January 1971 she was given two more doses of DTP. Subsequently she was found to be seriously brain damaged.

She claimed compensation under the Vaccine Damage Payments Act 1979. Her claim was rejected by a vaccine damage tribunal whose members did not accept that vaccination had caused her disability. A High Court judge quashed the tribunal's decision and remitted the case for further review by another tribunal. He refused to direct the tribunal to find as a matter of law that the child was entitled to a payment. The mother appealed to the Court of Appeal.

Held: the appeal was dismissed. It was impossible for the court to conclude that the child's condition resulted inevitably from vaccination. The state of her health before vaccination was not established on the evidence. The court was not prepared to direct the tribunal to pronounce in favour of the claimant, although in principle it might be possible to do so in a different case in the future.

See pages 23, 49.

Reed v Oswal and Cleveland Area Health Authority

Operation: consultant: fresh evidence

Court of Appeal. 22 November 1979

In June 1970 the plaintiff (Mrs Mary Reed) underwent a stapedectomy operation by Mr Oswal at the North Riding Infirmary, Middlesbrough. Following the operation, which was intended to improve the hearing of her right ear, she suffered from almost complete paralysis of the facial muscles on the right side of her face. She sued Mr Oswal and the hospital authority. In November 1978 the trial judge (Jones J) gave judgment for the defendants.

As a result of local publicity about the trial, the plaintiff learned afterwards about Mrs Addison on whom Mr Oswal performed a mastoidectomy in July 1970. This left Mrs Addison with total paralysis of the right side of her face. The plaintiff appealed, applying for leave to adduce fresh evidence about Mrs Addison's operation.

Held: the fresh evidence was credible and could not have been obtained with reasonable diligence for use at the trial. However if given, it would probably not have had an important influence on the result. The drill used by Mr Oswal cut Mrs Addison's facial nerve, which was not how the plaintiff's injuries were caused. The facts of the two operations were not similar enough for evidence about Mrs Addison's operation to be of probative value in the plaintiff's case. The plaintiff's appeal and application were dismissed.

See page 100.

Reibl v Hughes

Operation: risk disclosure: informed consent: battery: prudent patient test:
causation: foreign

Supreme Court of Canada. (1980) 114 DLR (3d) 1

The plaintiff (John Reibl) suffered from headaches and high blood pressure. He was referred to Dr Hughes, a neurosurgeon, and an arteriogram was taken. This showed that his left carotid artery had narrowed so as to permit only fifteen per cent of the normal blood flow through the artery, which leads to the brain. Dr Hughes advised an operation and told the plaintiff that he would be better off to have the operation than not to have it. Dr Hughes did not tell him that the operation involved a four per cent risk of death and a further ten per cent risk of having a stroke.

The plaintiff consented to the operation which was intended to remove an occlusion in the left carotid artery. Dr Hughes performed it competently in March 1970, but the plaintiff suffered a massive stroke which left him paralysed on the right side of his body and also impotent. Alleging that his was not an "informed consent", he sued Dr Hughes for damages in battery and negligence.

Held: (i) the facts did not justify the imposition of liability for battery. An action for battery does not arise where there has been consent to the very surgical procedure carried out upon the patient, and the only failure is a breach of the duty of disclosure of attendant risks. Actions for battery in respect of surgical or other medical treatment should be confined to cases where there has been no consent at all or where, emergency situations aside, the surgery or treatment has gone beyond that to which there was consent;

(ii) the relationship between surgeon and patient gives rise to a duty of the surgeon to make disclosure to the patient of all material risks attending the recommended surgery. A surgeon, generally, should answer any specific questions posed by the patient as to the risk involved and should, without being questioned, disclose to him the nature of the proposed operation, its gravity, any material risks and any special or unusual risks attendant upon the performance of the operation. Even if a certain risk is a mere possibility which ordinarily need not be disclosed, yet if its occurrence carries serious consequences, for example, paralysis or even death, it should be regarded as a material risk requiring disclosure. The risks attending the surgery in question of a stroke, of paralysis, and indeed of death, were without question material risks. Dr Hughes had been negligent in not disclosing them;

(iii) the objective standard is the preferable one on the issue of causation. It must take into account any special considerations affecting the particular patient. The test is what the average prudent person, the reasonable person in the plaintiff's particular position, would agree to or would not agree to, if all material and special risks of going ahead with the surgery or forgoing it were made known to him. As the plaintiff was at no immediate risk without the operation and was within one and a half years of earning pension benefits if he continued at his job, a reasonable person in his position would probably have opted against surgery at that time. The plaintiff succeeded on causation.

See pages 38, 69, 70, 72.

Rhodes v Rowbotham

Prescription: standard of care

Hilbery J. [1935] 1 BMJ 622

The plaintiff (Kenneth Rhodes) was treated by Dr Rowbotham for asthma for six weeks from June 1933. Dr Rowbotham attempted to stop his asthma spasms by spraying the plaintiff's nose on six occasions with ten per cent solution of cocaine. On one occasion, when the plaintiff was going away, Dr Rowbotham filled his atomiser with cocaine to spray his nose, warning him that it was not to be used indiscriminately but only for the relief of asthma. Dr Rowbotham also once left a bottle of percaine at his house. The cocaine sprays relieved the asthma.

The plaintiff sued Dr Rowbotham alleging that as a result of the treatment he had become a cocaine addict.

Held: the plaintiff had not become a drug addict. Dr Rowbotham's treatment was perfectly sound and up to date. He had not been negligent.

Rich v Pierpont

Childbirth: duty of care: causation: standard of care

Earle CJ (with jury). [1862] 3 F&F 35

In December 1861 the plaintiff (Mrs Rich) was pregnant. Her husband hired Mr Pierpont to attend to her as accoucheur. Mr and Mrs Rich were teetotallers and expressly desired Mr Pierpont not to give spirits. On 11 and 12 December the plaintiff retained nothing in her stomach and suffered from nausea and exhaustion. Mr Pierpont did not then direct stimulants and support, due to Mr Rich's aversion to the use of spirits. When he saw the plaintiff again in the early hours of 13 December, he desired to give her a little gin in warm water. The nurse brought him a bottle containing some colourless fluid of which, supposing it to be gin, he gave the plaintiff half a drachma in warm water. When it was discovered that the fluid was not gin but tartaric acid, Mr Pierpont again suggested the use of a little gin and water. Mr Rich still objected and said that he would rather his wife should die than take it. Disagreement ensued, the result of which was that the plaintiff did not have the spirits. The delivery on 14 December proved abortive, the child being dead.

Held: Earle CJ directed the jury that it was not enough to make Mr Pierpont liable because some medical men, of far greater experience and ability, might have used a greater degree of skill, nor even that he might possibly have used some greater degree of care. The question was whether there had been a want of competent care and skill to such an extent as to lead to the bad result. The mistake about the tartaric acid turned out to have been of no consequence.

The jury delivered a verdict for the defendant.

See page 34.

Riddett v D'Arcy

General practitioner: diagnosis: examination: child death

Southampton County Court. [1960] 2 BMJ 1607

On Sunday 18 January 1960 the plaintiff (Mr Riddett) called Dr D'Arcy, a general practitioner, to see his month old baby. The baby was icy cold, displayed a mauve colour and swelling about the eyes, and was breathing irregularly. Dr D'Arcy discerned only a runny nose, diagnosed that the baby had a cold and recommended a dose of castor oil.

In the evening of the next day, Dr Nally, a partner of Dr D'Arcy, called and saw the baby. He immediately sent for an ambulance. The baby died in hospital of staphylococcal pneumonia.

Held: it should have been apparent to Dr D'Arcy that the baby was sick. Symptoms of heart failure had been present, but Dr D'Arcy's examination was insufficiently close to enable him to notice them. He had been negligent.

See pages 62–63.

Ritter v Godfrey

Childbirth: communication: costs

Court of Appeal. [1919] 2 The Lancet 1163

Mrs Ritter was pregnant with her first child. Dr Godfrey, an obstetrician, had to deal with a double breach presentation, requiring quick action on his part. The nurse in attendance did not inform him of a material fact on his arrival. Consequently he made a mistaken diagnosis. The baby died at birth.

The plaintiff (Mr Ritter), a barrister, complained. Dr Godfrey wrote in response a heated and argumentative fifteen page letter containing a detailed reply and an emphatic repudiation of liability.

The plaintiff sued Dr Godfrey. The trial judge (McCardie J) found that he had not been negligent. He dismissed the plaintiff's claim but, referring to the letter with disapproval, refused to order the plaintiff to pay Dr Godfrey his costs. Dr Godfrey appealed.

Held: the discretion to disallow costs was not absolute but must be exercised in accordance with certain principles. A judge should give costs to a successful defendant, unless he had either brought about the litigation, or had done something connected with the institution or conduct of the suit calculated to cause unnecessary litigation, or had done some wrongful act in the course of the transaction of which the plaintiff complained. Dr Godfrey's letter accurately explained what had occurred and did not give the plaintiff any reasonable grounds for believing that he had a good cause of action. It would be a negation of justice to hold that Dr Godfrey was disentitled to his costs merely because he had retaliated with some warmth. His appeal was allowed.

See page 83.

Roberts v Johnstone and Another

Blood transfusion: substandard treatment: damages

Court of Appeal. [1988] 3 WLR 1247

The plaintiff (Sandra Roberts) was born in November 1981. Her mother's blood group was rhesus negative. In 1975 she had erroneously received a blood transfusion of rhesus positive blood. The father's blood group was rhesus positive. The defendants knew about these matters. Nevertheless they failed to give appropriate treatment to the mother during pregancy. Consequently the plaintiff was born with a severe form of haemolytic disease.

From May 1984 the plaintiff's care was entrusted to Mr and Mrs Woodward who legally adopted her. Their cottage was unsuitable for her, so it was sold for £18,000 and a bungalow purchased for £86,500. The conversion cost of the bungalow was £38,284 of which £10,000 was due to "betterment" rather than the plaintiff's needs.

Mrs Woodward cared for the plaintiff full time and would continue to do so. Mr Woodward assisted and served as a relief for her.

The plaintiff sued the obstetrician and the health authority who admitted liability. In July 1986 the trial judge (Alliott J) awarded her £335,000 damages and interest, including £75,000 general damages for pain, suffering and loss of amenities.

Held: (i) the damages to be awarded in respect of the specially purchased accommodation should be the additional annual cost of providing it. A rate of 2 per cent should be applied to the full difference of £68,500, a figure of £1,370 which, applying the multiplier of 16, equals £21,920. To this should be added the net conversion costs of £28,284;

(ii) the judge was arithmetically correct in awarding £9,152 in respect of Mrs Woodward's care to trial: 2.2 years at £80 per week over 52 weeks. This head, relating to the notional cost of services performed by someone else, was recoverable as special and not general damages. Interest should have been awarded at the rate appropriate to special damages;

(iii) there was no need for two people to care for the plaintiff all the time, but Mr Woodward was entitled to some recompense for the services he had to provide if his wife was to be engaged or on call for 24 hours a day. These should be assessed at £20 per week for 46.5 weeks a year;

(iv) some relief one night a week should be allowed to enable both Mr & Mrs Woodward to be absent from home together if they so wished, so £20 per week should be allowed for night-sitting relief.

The total award was increased to around £400,000 damages and interest.

See pages 103, 108, 111.

Robinson v Post Office and Another

General practitioner: injection: substandard treatment: causation: foresee-ability: novus actus interveniens: departing from orthodox practice

Court of Appeal. [1974] 2 All ER 737, [1974] 1 WLR 1176

On 15 February 1968 the plaintiff (Keith Robinson), a joiner employed by the Post Office, was descending an oily ladder at work when he slipped and sustained a laceration some three inches long on his left shin. About eight hours later he saw his general practitioner, Dr McEwan, who enquired what anti-tetanus injections he had previously had. Dr McEwan sent the plaintiff to a chemist for anti-tetanus serum (ATS) and, on his return, gave him an injection of it. On 25 February the plaintiff became delirious and suffered brain damage. As a result of the injection, he had contracted encephalitis.

He sued the Post Office and Dr McEwan. Evidence was given at the trial that there was a reputable school of thought which considered that administration of ATS was appropriate in the case of a non-immunised patient with a contaminated wound over six hours old. However it was common ground that in the case of a patient who had already had an injection of ATS the correct procedure was to administer just below the skin a test dose and wait half an hour to see whether the patient showed any reaction. Dr McEwan knew that the plaintiff had had an ATS injection in 1955 but did not follow this procedure.

Held: (i) Dr McEwan had not been negligent in injecting ATS, since in doing so he had acted in accordance with a practice accepted as proper by a responsible body of medical men;

(ii) he had negligently diverged from proper practice in respect of administration of the test dose;

(iii) as an adverse reaction would not have manifested itself in the standard half hour, Dr McEwan's negligence had not caused or contributed to the encephalitis, so he was not liable to pay damages to the plaintiff;

(iv) since the accident and the need for an anti-tetanus prophylactic were reasonably foreseeable, the Post Office could not rely on the doctor's negligence as a *novus actus interveniens* and were liable to the plaintiff both for the skin wound and the encephalitis.

See pages 39, 42, 53, 80.

Roe v Minister of Health and Another; Woolley v Same

Anaesthetics: res ipsa loquitur: vicarious liability: medical literature: state of knowledge

Court of Appeal. [1954] 2 QB 66

On 13 October 1947 the plaintiffs (Cecil Roe and Albert Woolley) were operated on at Chesterfield and North Derbyshire Royal Hospital for minor complaints. The anaesthetist, Dr Graham, had been appointed as visiting anaesthetist to the hospital. He carried on a private anaesthetic practice, but with another anaesthetist he was under an obligation to provide a regular anaesthetic service for the hospital.

In each case phenol, in which the glass ampoules containing the anaesthetic had been immersed, percolated through invisible cracks in each ampoule. It contaminated the spinal anaesthetic that was given to the plaintiffs. The risk of this happening was first drawn to the attention of the medical profession by a book published in 1951.

Each plaintiff developed a condition of spastic paraplegia and was permanently paralysed from the waist down. Each sued Dr Graham and the hospital authority. The trial judge found for the defendants.

Held: (i) the hospital authority was liable for Dr Graham's acts;

(ii) the maxim *res ipsa loquitur* applied;

(iii) the hospital had explained how the accident occurred; applying the standard knowledge to be imputed to competent anaesthetists in 1947, Dr Graham was not negligent in failing to appreciate the risk.

Per Lord Denning: (i) "I think that the hospital authorities are responsible for the whole of their staff, not only for the nurses and doctors, but also for the anaesthetists and surgeons. It does not matter whether they are permanent or temporary, resident or visiting, whole-time or part-time. The hospital authorities are responsible for all of them. The reason is because even if they are not servants, they are the agents of the hospital to give the treatment. The only exception is the case of consultants or anaesthetists selected and employed by the patient himself."

(ii) "The judge has said that those facts do not speak for themselves, but I think that they do. They certainly call for an explanation. Each of these men is entitled to say to the hospital: 'While I was in your hands something has been done to me which has wrecked my life. Please explain how this has come to pass' . . . I approach this case, therefore, on the footing that the hospital authorities and Dr Graham were called on to give an explanation of what has happened."

(iii) "But I think that they have done so . . . I do not think that their failure to foresee this was negligence. It is so easy to be wise after the event and to condemn as negligence that which was only a misadventure . . . We must not look at the 1947 accident with 1954 spectacles. The judge acquitted Dr Graham of negligence and we should uphold his decision".

See pages 8, 11, 35, 37, 50–51, 58, 81–82.

Rosen v Edgar

Operation: consultant: registrar: vicarious liability

Tucker J. (1986) 293 BMJ 552

The plaintiff (Mrs Margaret Rosen) was referred by her general practitioner for treatment of a bunion as a National Health Service patient to the clinic of Mr Edgar, consultant, at the Middlesex Hospital. In February 1977 she saw a senior registrar in out-patients. In June 1978 the same senior registrar operated on her.

Acting without solicitors, she issued a writ against Mr Edgar. She claimed that the operation was negligently performed and indeed deliberately done to cripple her. She considered that Mr Edgar was liable because he was in charge of the senior registrar.

Held: Mr Edgar was not liable. He had no responsibility in law for what was done in the operation. An employee is not vicariously liable for the acts of another employee, even if that other employee is junior to him and in some senses answerable to him.

N.B. The appropriate defendants were the senior registrar and the local health authority.

See page 9.

Rosen v Marston

Surgeon: operation: limitation: striking out for want of prosecution

Court of Appeal. 15 March 1984

In March 1977 the plaintiff (Mrs Margaret Rosen) was operated on for varicose veins in both legs by Mr Marston at the Middlesex Hospital. She alleged that this left her with a scar from the middle of her right leg to the ankle.

In early 1980 she issued a writ endorsed with a Statement of Claim. A Defence was served. The pleadings were closed in October 1980. The plaintiff consulted solicitors at the Mary Ward Legal Centre. No further steps in the action were taken until February 1983 when Mr Marston's solicitors, on learning that a request had been made to the hospital for release of the operation case notes, applied for the case to be struck out for want of prosecution. Hirst J reversed the Master's decision to strike out.

Held: (i) the delay of two and a half years in a case in which the writ was issued shortly before the expiry of the limitation period was excessive. The judge was in error in so far as he took the view that the plaintiff had a good excuse because she entrusted her case to persons who claimed legal qualifications who failed her;

(ii) there was prejudice to Mr Marston, not only because his recollection was likely to be significantly impaired, but also because the action with its potential threat to reputation and the attendant anxiety and distress would be hanging over his head for more than two years longer than it should have been.

The case was struck out for want of prosecution.

See page 128.

Rouse v Kensington and Chelsea and Westminster Area Health Authority

Diagnosis: hospital doctor: warning

Court of Appeal. 26 January 1982

On 16 May 1976 the plaintiff (Mr Rouse) injured his left foot playing football.

The next day he was seen at the Casualty Department at Westminster Hospital by Dr Roskovek, who noted "Tender over upper part of Achilles tendon and pain there on flexion of ankle. Treatment. Elastoplast for 10 days." On 1 June he returned to the Casualty Department where Dr Mirza removed the elastoplast and noted "Pain in the tendon Achilles on walking. Treatment: Crepe bandage".

When the plaintiff was seen at the Orthopaedic Clinic on 1 October, Mr Andrews diagnosed a ruptured Achilles tendon. The plaintiff needed three operations. His left foot was seriously disfigured and partly deformed.

He sued the health authority, alleging negligence by the two casualty officers on 17 May and 1 June. The trial judge (Boreham J) dismissed his claim.

Held: (i) the trial judge was entitled to conclude that the initial injury was a partially ruptured Achilles tendon and that the casualty officers had not been negligent in their diagnosis;

(ii) there was no reason to interfere with his finding that their treatment was the proper treatment;

(iii) there was no evidence that they failed to give the plaintiff a warning, if such was needed, to be careful with his injured foot.

See page 64.

Routley v Worthing Health Authority and Others

Psychiatric patient: leave to sue: negligent certification: duty of care: false imprisonment

Court of Appeal. 14 July 1983

The plaintiff (David Routley), then aged twenty, was extremely distressed following the death of his mother in May 1979. The family general practitioner, Dr Lewis, referred him to Dr Vaudrey, a consultant psychiatrist at the Graylingwell Hospital, who saw the plaintiff in December 1979 and February 1980.

As a result of letters from the plaintiff's father, Dr Lewis requested Dr Vaudrey to make a domiciliary visit which he did late in the evening of 15 July 1981. The plaintiff returned from the opera at 10.30 pm. Dr Vaudrey was waiting for him. The plaintiff refused to see him and rushed past him up the stairs to his room. Dr Vaudrey stated that he was "making strange noises". The plaintiff's father told him that the plaintiff had fought with his younger brother, broken furniture and threatened to kill both the father and the brother. Dr Vaudrey decided that the plaintiff should be admitted to a psychiatric hospital for treatment under s 26 Mental Health Act 1959 and completed the s 26 recommendation papers.

On 16 July Dr Vaudrey telephoned Dr Lewis with his advice, and reported what had happened. Dr Vaudrey also telephoned a mental welfare officer to ask him and Dr Lewis to make arrangements for the plaintiff's admission. On 17 July Dr Lewis and the mental welfare officer went to the plaintiff's home, with police and ambulance in attendance. They talked to the plaintiff, mostly through locked doors. When he tried to run out of the back door, three police constables jumped on him and forcibly strapped and handcuffed him to the stretcher. Dr Lewis signed the s 26 recommendation.

The plaintiff was detained at Graylingwell Hospital for eighteen days. It subsequently transpired that he was not suffering from any mental illness. He sought leave to sue Dr Vaudrey, Dr Lewis and others for negligence and false imprisonment. Wood J refused his application.

Held: the plaintiff had substantial grounds for contending that the recommendations which led to his admission were made by both doctors without reasonable care. He should be granted leave to bring court action against them.

Ruddock v Lowe

Alternative practitioner: representations: substandard treatment

Crompton J (with jury). [1865] 4 F&F 519

In the early 1860s Mr Lowe was the proprietor of an "anatomical museum" in the Strand. He circulated among those who entered the museum a pamphlet in which he had held himself out as a master in the art of healing sexual disorders. He denounced the use of mercury or mineral medicines and stated "I never undertake a case unless I can guarantee a perfect cure". To which he added his address, "Dr" Lowe, at the "Strand Museum".

In December 1865 the plaintiff (Mr Ruddock) was induced by the pamphlet to consult "Dr" Lowe who said it was a "very bad case" and gave him medicine and charged him two guineas. After many further visits, medicines and fees, the plaintiff found that he was getting worse instead of better, his mouth becoming sore and his teeth loose in his head.

He sued Mr Lowe. The expert evidence was that the medicine contained a great deal of mercury and that the plaintiff was suffering under excessive salivation. Mr Lowe, who was not a duly qualified doctor, denied that he had ever seen or treated the plaintiff.

Held: Crompton J directed the jury that the substantial issue was whether Mr Lowe did undertake to and did treat the plaintiff, since there was no doubt that the supposed treatment was grossly improper.

The jury returned a verdict for the plaintiff.

See pages 17, 28.

S and Another v Distillers Company (Biochemicals) Ltd; J and Another v Same

Drugs: thalidomide: damages: duty of care

Hinchcliffe J. [1969] 3 All ER 1412, [1970] 1 WLR 114

The drug thalidomide was first marketed in the U.K. in 1958. It was withdrawn in December 1961, after it had been shown that if taken during the fifth and eighth weeks of pregnancy the drug could cause damage to the embryo. Writs were issued on behalf of about sixty deformed infants and their parents. The issue of liability was settled, with approval of the court, on the basis that the defendant would pay forty per cent of the appropriate figure for damages.

D.J., aged eight, was born without any viable limbs and was in the category of those children who had been most badly affected by the drug.

R.S., aged seven, was born without arms and was in the middle of the category of injuries.

Mrs S, his mother, had been depressed, anxious and worried.

Held: (1969) (i) the appropriate figure for D.J.'s general damages for pain, suffering and loss of amenities was £28,000. Total award £52,000 less 60 per cent;

(ii) the award for R.S.' pain, suffering and loss of amenities was £18,000. Total award £32,000 less 60 per cent;

(iii) Mrs S was awarded general damages of £5,000 for grievous shock, future travelling expenses, special clothes for the boy and loss of wages. Total award £7,250 less 60 per cent.

See page 28.

Sabapathi v Huntley

Fractures: diagnosis: X-ray: libel/slander

Privy Council. [1938] 1 WWR 817

On 27 January 1933 Mr Huntley, a planter, and his wife were involved in a serious road accident in Ceylon. They were taken to the Government Hospital at Karawanella where they were treated by Dr Sabapathi, the district Medical Officer. Dr Sabapathi examined them on admission and visited them twice on 28 January. They left hospital on 29 January, and Mr Huntley wrote a letter of gratitude to Dr Sabapathi on 1 February.

On 7 February Mr and Mrs Huntley visited a doctor in Colombo who did not make a diagnosis but arranged for them to be X-rayed. The X-rays showed that they had suffered fractures in the accident. Mr Huntley wrote a letter of complaint, alleging negligence and incompetence against Dr Sabapathi. This letter was publicly discussed at a meeting of the Planter's Association and was published in the Ceylon Daily News.

Dr Sabapathi sued Mr Huntley for damages for libel and slander. Mr Huntley pleaded justification. The Supreme Court reversed on appeal the trial judge's finding in favour of Dr Sabapathi.

Held: it is not necessarily the case that, after a road accident, the attending physician must advise resort to a radiologist and that, if he omits to do so, he displays both incompetence and negligence. The advisability of an X-ray examination must always depend on the circumstances, in particular the condition of the patient, the character of the injuries and the accessibility of the apparatus. Dr Sabapathi's treatment had been competent and careful. He was entitled to damages.

Sa'd v Robinson and Dunlop; Sa'd v Ransley and Mid Surrey Health Authority

General practitioner: diagnosis: communication: damages: costs

Leggatt J. (1989) PMILL Vol 5 No 4

Around 5.45 am on 18 July 1980 the plaintiff (Zeena Sa'd), then aged nineteen months, put her mouth to the spout of a teapot which had just been placed on a low table. Her mother was absent answering the telephone, but four other adults were present. The resulting pain and screams caused Mrs Sa'd to take Zeena to the doctor's surgery within ten minutes.

Dr Robinson examined the child who was trying to vomit and had mucus in her mouth. He noted a scalded lip, recorded "swallowed hot tea", prescribed a painkiller together with an antacid, and said that the child would be "O.K.".

By about 8.00 pm she had not significantly improved, so Mrs Sa'd telephoned the surgery where her call was redirected to Dr Dunlop, a partner of Dr Robinson. She related the facts. He told her that the previous medication would take about two hours to work and did not seem unduly concerned.

About two hours later, following a further telephone call from Mrs Sa'd, Dr Dunlop promptly attended and examined the child, checking her respiration and pulse. He advised that she should be in hospital where she could be observed. He telephoned the hospital to warn that she had drunk something hot some hours before, had a possibility of respiratory problems and should be kept in.

Around 10.45 pm the hospital S.H.O. in paediatrics recorded the child's condition as grave. Dr Ransley, the consultant paediatrician, was summoned by telephone. He managed to insert an intravenous line, but the obstruction was becoming more complete due to the mucus. The child then had an anoxic fit. As soon as the fit was over, Dr Ransley inserted an endotracheal tube, but by that time apnoea had persisted for an indefinite period. The plaintiff suffered gross and irreversible brain damage.

The plaintiff through her father sued Dr Robinson and Dr Dunlop. Dr Robinson issued Third Party proceedings against Mrs Sa'd on the grounds that she allowed the child to reach the teapot and failed to give him a full and proper history. Mrs Sa'd in turn served a Second and Third Party Notice on Dr Ransley and the hospital authority. The plaintiff added the three Third Parties as defendants. A fortnight before the trial Dr Robinson discontinued the Third Party proceedings against Mrs Sa'd but declined to grant an indemnity.

Held: (i) Dr Robinson had been negligent. He had failed to appreciate the significance of ingestion of tea and potential damage to the oesophagus leading to the obstruction. He should have referred the plaintiff to hospital immediately;

(ii) Dr Dunlop was also liable. The telephone call and subsequent visit should have prompted admission of the plaintiff to hospital. His subsequent examinations were also inadequate, as was his description to the hospital of the plaintiff's condition;

(iii) neither Mrs Sa'd, Dr Ransley nor the hospital authority had been negligent;

(iv) the plaintiff was awarded total damages of £535,000 which included general damages, future schooling and care and Court of Protection costs;

(v) Dr Robinson and Dr Dunlop were ordered to pay on the standard basis the plaintiff's costs of proceeding against them and also to indemnify the plaintiff, under a Sanderson Order, in respect of the costs of the other three defendants;

(vi) Dr Robinson was ordered to pay on an indemnity basis the whole of the costs of the Third Party proceedings, the costs of the proceedings against Dr Ransley and the hospital authority up to discontinuance of the Third Party proceedings, and the costs subsequently incurred by Mrs Sa'd continuing to and including trial.

See page 63.

Sadler v Henry

General practitioner: diagnosis: meningitis: standard of care

Cassels J. [1954] 1 BMJ 1331

On 25 April 1952 Kathleen Sadler, aged twenty-six, went to see Dr Henry at his surgery. She gave a history of having had a cold earlier and complained of earache. Dr Henry examined her right ear with an auriscope, took her temperature (99°F), looked and felt behind her ear, and saw partial inflammation of the right eardrum. He saw no discharge or sign of perforation, diagnosed "catarrhal drum" and prescribed drops to relieve the pain and a sedative.

He was called on 26 April, and was told that she had a headache and some vomiting, and that she heard "rushing noises like the sea" in her head. He examined her ear through the auriscope, thought it slightly improved and ordered glucose and codeine tablets.

At 6.30 pm on 27 April Dr Henry called and made a thorough examination. He could find nothing clinically wrong. Her temperature was again 99°F, and she was worried and emotional. He thought she had acute hysteria. At 8.45 pm she became irrational, and he arranged for her admission to hospital. At 11.50 pm she died from acute meningitis due to suppurative otitis media.

Her father sued Dr Henry.

Held: there were no signs or symptoms which could reasonably have led Dr Henry to suspect localised meningitis. His diagnosis of hysteria was a mistake, but one which others might well have made. He had failed in the difficult circumstances of the case to diagnose the real condition, which the necropsy disclosed. However he had not been negligent.

See page 64.

Salisbury v Gould

Diagnosis: public health officer: damages: smallpox: negligent certification

Grantham J (with jury). [1904] 1 BMJ 282

The plaintiff (Mrs Salisbury) was a dressmaker in Lambs Conduit Street, Holborn. In September 1901 her child was taken ill. Dr Gould was sent for and diagnosed smallpox. The next day he returned with Dr Bond, the Medical Officer of Health for Holborn and, following a further examination, notified the authorities that the child was suffering from smallpox. In consequence, a magistrate's order was obtained, pursuant to which the child was forcibly removed to the "sheds" at Rotherhithe. The child was detained there for three days and then returned as suffering from chickenpox only.

The plaintiff sued Dr Gould, claiming that she had lost customers due to it being known amongst them that an ambulance had taken away her child from the house in which she carried on her business. For the defence it was contended that Dr Gould acted bona fide and that he was compelled under the provisions of the Public Health Acts to notify the case as soon as he was of opinion that it was one of smallpox.

Held: the jury found that Dr Gould had acted properly in giving the notification certificate, and returned a verdict in his favour.

See page 88.

Sankey v Kensington and Chelsea and Westminster Area Health Authority

Hospital doctors: operation: consent: risk disclosure: duty of care to third party

Tudor Evans J. [1982] QBD 2 April

The plaintiff (Mr Sankey), who suffered from hypertension, had had left-sided headaches for several years. An X-ray of his skull showed that the pituitary fossa was grossly eroded. He was admitted to Westminster Hospital for further tests. On 3 July 1975 Dr Gibberd advised an arteriogram to identify the nature of the lesion in the pituitary fossa. He explained the procedure and told the plaintiff that the main risks were because of his high blood pressure which could be made worse; he told him that the procedure was risky because of the hypertension and the vascular disease associated with it. Dr Gibberd separately saw the plaintiff's wife and advised her that the arteriogram should be done but that it would be risky. He left a junior doctor, Dr Truter, to obtain the plaintiff's signed consent to the operation. Dr Truter told the plaintiff that, because of his raised blood pressure, the risks were a little greater than normal. After the arteriogram was performed, the plaintiff became highly disturbed and then lapsed into coma; he had a number of major epileptic fits.

The plaintiff sued the hospital authority. By the end of the hearing, his case was solely that his consent to the arteriogram had been negligently obtained without his having been given any or adequate warning of the risks involved. Evidence was given that the arteriogram involved a risk of a stroke which in a normal patient was well under two per cent and was not substantially increased in the plaintiff's case. The majority of experts testified that they would mention risks without using the word "stroke".

Held: (i) the question of warning had to be judged by competent responsible medical opinion. Dr Gibberd gave the plaintiff a very full and wholly acceptable description of what was involved in the procedure and a warning of the risks involved;

(ii) Dr Gibberd very properly left the signing of the consent form to be obtained by a junior doctor. Competent medical practice does not require a second warning, although in fact Dr Truter gave one;

(iii) there is no duty in law to give warning of risks to the relative of an adult patient, certainly if the patient himself has been warned. Even so, Dr Gibberd warned Mrs Sankey.

Judgment for the defendants.

Saumarez v Medway and Gravesend Hospital Management Committee

Fracture: diagnosis: hospital doctor: X-rays

Havers J. [1953] 2 BMJ 1109

In July 1949 the plaintiff (Julie Saumarez), a violinist, fell and sustained a fracture of the base of the proximal phalanx of the left thumb and a chip fracture of the base of the distal phalanx of the middle finger of the left hand. From 15 July to 1 October she was treated by Dr Theobalds at the Sheppey General Hospital. She complained several times about her finger and told him that an X-ray examination at the London Hospital had revealed a chip fracture. Nevertheless he only treated her for the thumb fracture and did not discover or diagnose the chip fracture to the finger.

As a result the bone set in a crooked position, making it impossible for her to play the violin properly. She sued the hospital authority.

Held: Dr Theobalds should have discovered the injury on his first examination. If he had discovered it, his duty would have been to make a further clinical and X-ray examination. It was even more incumbent upon him to make further enquiries, since the plaintiff had complained of injury to the finger. He had been negligent.

See page 62.

Saunders v Leeds Western Health Authority and Another

Operation: anaesthetics: cardiac arrest: res ipsa loquitur

Mann J. (1985) 129 SJ 225, (1986) PMILL Vol 1 No 10

The plaintiff, when four years old, underwent an operation to correct a congenitally dislocated hip. During the operation she suffered a cardiac arrest lasting thirty to forty minutes. In consequence her brain was permanently damaged by hypoxia, and she became permanently quadriplegic, mentally retarded and blind.

She sued the health authority and the anaesthetist. At trial she relied on *res ipsa loquitur*. Evidence was given that the heart of a fit child did not arrest under anaesthesia if proper care was taken in the anaesthetic and surgical processes. The defendants sought to explain the cardiac arrest by the effect of a paradoxical air embolism travelling from the site of the operation to block a coronary artery.

Held: *res ipsa loquitur* applied, so the plaintiff need not show the specific cause of the arrest. The defendants' explanation was rejected. The inevitable inference was that proper monitoring would have disclosed significant signs, including a forewarning of the arrest. The defendants had been negligent.

See pages 60, 77, 81.

Sayer v Kingston and Esher Health Authority

Childbirth: caesarian: pleadings: after-care

Court of Appeal. 9 March 1989

On 19 February 1980 the plaintiff (Pauline Sayer) gave birth to her second child by caesarian section in one of the defendants' hospitals. There were various complications, and two further operations were necessary.

In January 1983 she sued the health authority. Her writ and Statement of Claim were limited to complaints of what happened on 18–19 February, the period of the operation itself. In September 1988, on the eve of her trial, she applied to amend her Statement of Claim.

The amendment, which she obtained leave from the judge to make, deleted the complaints about the caesarian section operation altogether. It substituted three new complaints:

- (i) that she was allowed to spend too long in the second stage of labour before the operation;
- (ii) that her condition was not monitored closely enough after the operation; and
- (iii) that a follow-up operation on 26 February should have been performed by a specialist urologist.

The defendants appealed against the judge's order granting leave to amend.

Held: (i) the amendments arose out of substantially the same facts, although not the same facts, as those already pleaded, so the judge had discretion to allow the amendment under s 35(5) Limitation Act 1980 and RSC O 20 r 5(5);

(ii) the judge acted within his discretion in allowing the amendment, since the defendants' main witnesses were still available and full and detailed medical records were in existence.

Sciuraga v Powell

Abortion: wrongful birth: breach of contract: damages: public policy

Court of Appeal. 24 July 1980. (1979) 123 SJ 406

In April 1972 the plaintiff (Miss Florence Sciuraga), a polio sufferer then aged twenty-two, contracted with Dr Powell that he would terminate her pregnancy for a fee of £150. He failed to remove the foetus which she had been carrying for some seven weeks, and he did not tell her what had happened. When she found out, he repaid her the £150 and offered to try again. She refused and in December 1972 was delivered of a baby boy by caesarian section.

The plaintiff sued Dr Powell for breach of contract. In May 1979 the trial judge (Watkins J) found that he had performed the operation negligently and in breach of contract and rejected the defence that no damages were recoverable on the ground of public policy. He awarded the plaintiff £7,000 for loss of earnings to date of trial, £7,500 for future loss of earning capacity, £3,500 for impairment of her marriage prospects and £750 for her pain and distress. Dr Powell appealed on quantum.

Held: (i) her loss of future earnings should be assessed by deducting from her figure of £4,000 per annum for a full-time audio-typist the £2,000 per annum that she could earn in the part-time work to which her young son's presence limited her, reducing the gross loss of £2,000 to £1,400 net of tax and applying a multiplier of 3. To the resultant figure of £4,200 should be added payments of £550 for child minder, a total of £4,750;

(ii) as the presence of the child impaired her marriage prospects to some extent, but not greatly, in view of other factors, the judge's award under this head should be reduced to £1,500.

See pages 31, 52, 53, 113.

Seare v Prentice

Fracture: surgeon: diagnosis: standard of care

Ellenborough CJ. (1807) 8 East 348

In April 1805 the plaintiff (Mr Seare) fell from a horse. He dislocated his elbow and fractured his arm. He attended the village surgeon, Mr Prentice, and told him that his arm was broken. Mr Prentice said that he thought the arm which was swollen, was not broken. He applied vinegar to it and bound it with tape. About nine days later Mr Prentice set the elbow. The plaintiff continued in a crippled state until July 1805 when another surgeon instituted a cure.

The plaintiff sued Mr Prentice for negligent, ignorant and unskilful treatment. The trial judge directed the jury to consider the issue of negligence and that unskilfulness alone would not suffice. They returned a verdict for the defendant.

Held: an ordinary degree of skill is necessary for a surgeon. A surgeon could also be liable for crass ignorance. However as the plaintiff's expert specifically imputed the failure of the cure to negligence and the jury duly considered this, the court could not order a new trial.

N.B. The distinction between carelessness, unskilfulness and ignorance is no longer pertinent. They simply constitute different ways of failing to achieve a proper standard of care.

See page 34.

Selfe v Ilford and District Hospital Management Committee

Suicide risk: nurses: supervision: standard of care

Hinchcliffe J. [1970] The Times 26 November, (1970) 114 SJ 935

In June 1966 the plaintiff (Alan Selfe), then aged seventeen, left for work but could not face it and took an overdose of sleeping pills. He told his mother that he had done so, and the family doctor arranged for him to be admitted to King George's Hospital, Ilford. He was put in a ward on the ground floor with an unlocked window behind him. There were twenty-seven patients in the ward. He was grouped together with the three other suicide risks at one end.

There were three nurses allocated to the ward. Each knew that the plaintiff was a suicide risk and was to be kept under constant supervision. One nurse was in charge of the ward. Without a word to the nurse in charge, another nurse went to the lavatory and a nursing auxiliary went to the kitchen. Neither could see into the main ward. The charge nurse answered a call for assistance by a patient and went to him.

The plaintiff then climbed through the window, walked along a grass path and climbed up some steps on to a roof from which he threw himself to the ground. He became a paraplegic and sued the hospital authority.

Held: the hospital's duty of reasonable care demanded adequate supervision, which included continuous observation by duty nurses in the ward. To leave unobserved a seventeen year old youth with suicidal tendencies and an unlocked window behind his bed was asking for trouble. The hospital had been negligent.

See pages 12, 25, 88, 92.

Shallard v Arline and Another

Alternative practitioner: burns: representations: breach of contract: fraud

Cassels J. [1939] 2 The Lancet 215

The plaintiff (Mrs Shallard) was a middle-aged lady whose husband had died in December 1937. Miss Arline persuaded her to try the Gustavson treatment at her Knightsbridge clinic. She was given a pamphlet about his facial and other rejuvenation treatment which was described as absolutely harmless and certain in its effects. She was told that her condition was good except for toxins in her body, which toxins the Gustavson treatment would remove. His fee would be two hundred guineas.

On 14 March 1938 the plaintiff entered the clinic. Mr Gustavson administered the treatment. She was put to bed, and there was applied to her face some substance which burned her. She was given tablets which made her vomit. Next day there was similar treatment. Her eyes became painful. She was placed in a bath of Epsom salts. On 18 March bandages were taken off, which tore the skin from her forehead and neck, leaving them sore and bleeding. She was in pain until 28 March when she insisted on being driven home.

Her skin was thickened and had a mask-like appearance. She suffered a nervous breakdown. She sued Miss Arline and Mr Gustavson. Mr Gustavson, a Swede, left the country and did not return for the trial.

Held: the defendants were liable for negligence, breach of contract and fraud. They had divided the proceeds of a fraudulent scheme for extracting money from a middle-aged woman in indifferent health.

N.B. Miss Arline's appeal to the Court of Appeal was dismissed.

See pages 17, 96.

Sidaway v Board of Governors of Bethlem Royal Hospital and the Maudsley Hospital and Others

Surgeon: operation: risk disclosure: standard of care: foreseeability

House of Lords. [1985] AC 871, [1985] 1 All ER 643, [1985] 2 WLR 480

The plaintiff (Mrs Amy Sidaway) was complaining of very persistent pain in the right arm and shoulder and also pain in the left forearm. In October 1974 she was admitted to the Maudsley Hospital where a myleogram was performed. Mr Falconer decided that pressure on the fourth cervical nerve root was the cause of her pain and decided to operate. The operation consisted of a laminectomy of the fourth cervical vertebra and a facetectomy or foraminectomy of the disc space between the fourth and fifth cervical vertebrae. Mr Falconer freed the fourth cervical nerve root by removing the facets from the fourth vertebra and used a dental drill to free the nerve within the foramen. The plaintiff's spinal cord was damaged. She suffered severe disability.

She sued the hospital authority and the surgeon's estate. The operation had not been negligently performed. Her claim was based on failure to warn her of the risk of damage to the spinal cord. The two specific risks were damage to a nerve root and damage to the spinal cord. Evidence at trial was that the combined risk was between one and two per cent, and that the risk of damage to the spinal cord alone, the more serious risk, was less than one per cent. The trial judge found that Mr Falconer mentioned the possibility of disturbing a nerve root and the consequences of doing so but not the danger of spinal cord damage. The medical witnesses agreed that they would mention that there was a small risk of untoward consequences and of an increase of pain instead of relief. It was a practice accepted as proper by a responsible body of competent neuro-surgeons not to frighten a patient by talking about death or paralysis. The trial judge dismissed the plaintiff's claim.

Held: as there was a responsible body of medical opinion which would have warned the plaintiff in substantially the same terms as Mr Falconer had done, her claim failed.

Per Lord Diplock: "What we do know, however, and this is in my view determinative of this appeal, is that all the expert witnesses specialising in neurology . . . agreed that there was a responsible body of medical opinion which would have undertaken the operation at the time the neuro-surgeon did and would have warned the patient of the risk involved in the operation in substantially the same terms as the trial judge found on the balance of probabilities the neuro-surgeon had done, ie without specific reference to risk of injuring the spinal cord . . .

"No doubt if the patient in fact manifested this attitude by means of questioning, the doctor would tell him whatever it was the patient wanted to know; but we are concerned here with volunteering unsought information about risks of the proposed treatment failing to achieve the result sought or making the patient's physical or mental condition worse rather than better. The only effect that mention of risks can have on the patient's mind, if it has any at all, can be in the direction of deterring the patient from undergoing the treatment which in the expert opinion of the doctor it is in the patient's interest to undergo. To decide what risks the existence of which a patient should be voluntarily warned and the terms in which such warning, if any, should be given, having regard to the effect that the warning may have, is as much an exercise of professional skill and judgement as any other part of the doctor's comprehensive duty of care to the individual patient, and expert medical evidence on this matter should be treated in just the same way. The *Bolam* test should be applied."

Per Lord Bridge: "I should perhaps add at this point, although the issue does not strictly arise in this appeal, that, when questioned specifically by a patient of apparently sound mind about risks involved in a particular treatment proposed, the doctor's duty must, in my opinion, be to answer both truthfully and as fully as the questioner requires . . .

"The issue whether non-disclosure in a particular case should be condemned as a breach of the doctor's duty of care is an issue to be decided primarily on the basis of expert medical evidence, applying the *Bolam* test. But I do not see that this approach involves the necessity 'to hand over to the medical profession the entire question of the scope of the duty of disclosure, including the question whether there has been a breach of that duty'. Of course, if there is a conflict of evidence as to whether a responsible body of medical opinion approves of non-disclosure in a particular case, the judge will have to resolve that conflict. But even in a case where, as here, no expert witness in the relevant medical field condemns the non-disclosure as being in conflict with accepted and responsible medical practice, I am of opinion that the judge might in certain circumstances come to the conclusion that disclosure of a particular risk was so obviously necessary to an informed choice on the part of the patient that no reasonably prudent medical man would fail to make it. The kind of case I have in mind would be an operation involving a substantial risk of grave adverse consequences, as, for example, the ten per cent risk of a stroke from the operation which was a subject of the Canadian case of *Reibl v Hughes* 114 DLR (3d) 1. In such a case, in the absence of some cogent clinical reason why the patient should not be informed, a doctor, recognizing and respecting his patient's right of decision, could hardly fail to appreciate the necessity for an appropriate warning."

Per Lord Templeman: "In my opinion a simple and general explanation of the nature of the operation should have been sufficient to alert Mrs Sidaway to the fact that a major operation was to be performed and to the possibility that something might go wrong at or near the site of the spinal cord or the site of the nerve root causing serious injury. If, as the judge held, Dr Falconer probably referred expressly to the possibility of damage to a nerve root and to the consequences of such damage, this warning could only have reinforced the possibility of something going wrong in the course of a delicate operation performed in a vital area with resultant damage. In view of the fact that Mr Falconer recommended the operation, Mrs Sidaway must have been told or could have assumed that Mr Falconer considered that the possibilities of damage were sufficiently remote to be ignored. Mrs Sidaway could have asked questions. If she had done so, she could and should have been informed there was an aggregate risk of between one per cent or two per cent risk of some damage either to the spinal cord or to a nerve root resulting in injury which might vary from irritation to paralysis. But to my mind this further information would only have reinforced the obvious, with the assurance that the maximum risk of damage, slight or serious, did not exceed two per cent. Mr Falconer may reasonably have taken the view that Mrs Sidaway might have been confused, frightened or misled by more detailed information which she was unable to evaluate at a time when she was suffering from stress, pain and anxiety. A patient may prefer that the doctor should not thrust too much detail at the patient."

See pages 4–5, 15, 17, 33, 37–38, 68, 70–73, 74, 83, 85, 132.

Size v Shenley Hospital Group Management Committee

Psychiatric patient: supervision: nurses: standard of care: foreseeability

Court of Appeal. [1970] 1 The Lancet 313

In January 1962 the plaintiff (Mr Size) was a detained patient in Shenley Hospital where the treatment was permissive. M, who was suffering from manic depressive psychosis, was a patient in the same open ward, his bed being near the nurse's desk. M had relapsed into a hypomanic phase and was due to be transferred to a closed ward at 6.00 pm. Between 4.30 pm and 5.00 pm he assaulted and injured the plaintiff. The nurse was just too late to prevent this.

The plaintiff sued the hospital authority, alleging that M had made attacks on two previous occasions. The trial judge dismissed his case, finding that the hospital did not know of any previous attacks.

Held: (i) the judge was entitled to conclude that the foreseeable risk was minimal. Thus the hospital was not to be blamed for not transferring M sooner or for not giving him more sedation;

(ii) nor should M have been more closely supervised. He was a bed patient close to the nurse's desk, and the nurse was only just too late to stop the damage. The plaintiff had suffered a misfortune for which the hospital was not liable.

See pages 88–89.

Slater v Baker and Stapleton

Surgeon: departing from orthodox practice: fractures: experimentation:
trespass to person

Wilmot CJ. (1767) 95 ER 860, (1767) 2 Wils KB 359

The plaintiff (Mr Slater) broke one of his legs. It was set and started to heal. He then consulted Mr Stapleton, an apothecary, who called in Mr Baker, a surgeon from St Bartholomew's Hospital. Mr Baker put on the plaintiff's leg a heavy steel contraption with teeth intended to stretch and extend his leg. He took up the plaintiff's foot in both his hands and nodded to Mr Stapleton. Mr Stapleton took the plaintiff's leg on his knee and the leg cracked.

The plaintiff's leg had been fractured again and for the next three to four months he suffered gravely. He sued Mr Baker and Mr Stapleton. The trial jury found in his favour.

Held: (i) there was a joint undertaking by both the defendants;

(ii) the objection that the action ought to have been brought in trespass was rejected;

(iii) in performing on the plaintiff the first experiment with this new instrument, the defendants had acted ignorantly and unskilfully contrary to the known rule and usage of surgeons.

The judgment for the plaintiff was upheld.

See pages 5, 39.

Slater v Maidstone Health Authority

Childbirth: adjournment of trial

Michael Davies J. [1987] The Times 2 December

The infant plaintiff was born in 1980. Medical negligence was alleged to have occurred during the birth. The health authority was sued. In June 1986 the trial date was fixed for 7 December 1987. On 1 December 1987 the plaintiff's application for an adjournment was heard.

Held: (i) the application for an adjournment was granted in view of the health authority's consent. If the case were tried in December 1987, that would have been bad enough because of the delay. The case was now said not to be ready. If the health authority had opposed the application, it would have been refused. The doctors against whom the negligence was alleged had had the case hanging over them for seven years. It was an appalling situation;

(ii) where an application was made in the High Court by one party to an action to stand the case out of the date fixed for the trial, the lay parties to the particular case should attend court when the application was made so that the reason for the need to defer the case could be explained to them by the court and not, subsequently, by their legal representatives.

Smith v Barking, Havering and Brentwood Health Authority

Surgeon: risk disclosure: causation: damages

Hutchison J. (1989) PMILL Vol 5 No 4

In April 1970, when the plaintiff (Sharon Smith) was nine years old, Mr Fairburn performed on her at the Oldchurch Hospital an operation to drain a cyst in the upper cervical canal. In 1979 she began to experience a recurrence of her symptoms of weakness and loss of sensation in her limbs. Mr Fairburn reluctantly decided that a further operation was advisable, although he regarded it as difficult. On the one hand, if nothing was done, the plaintiff could well become tetraplegic within a year. On the other hand, the operation itself carried an inherent risk of up to twenty-five per cent of immediate tetraplegia. He did not inform the plaintiff of the risks or discuss the dilemma with her. When he carried out the second operation in January 1981, she suffered damage to the spinal cord resulting in immediate and permanent tetraplegia.

The plaintiff sued the hospital authority on the grounds of Mr Fairburn's failure to warn her of the risks inherent in the operation.

Held: (i) the situation obviously called for careful explanation to the plaintiff. Mr Fairburn negligently omitted to tell her either of the inherent risk of immediate tetraplegia or that she was destined to become tetraplegic if she did not have the operation;

(ii) the strong probability was that the plaintiff, if suitably informed, would have agreed to the operation, since it was her only chance of avoiding tetraplegia in the near future;

(iii) she was therefore only entitled to £3,000 general damages to compensate her for her shock and depression upon discovering—without prior warning—that she had been rendered tetraplegic.

See pages 42, 74.

Smith v Brighton and Lewes Hospital Management Committee

Prescription: nurse: injections: overdose: causation

Streatfield J. [1958] The Times 2 May

In May 1954 the plaintiff (Mrs Florence Smith) had a severe attack of boils and was admitted to hospital. On 13 May Dr Vickery, the house surgeon, ordered a course of thirty streptomycin injections to be administered at intervals of eight hours. The last injection should have been given at 10.00 pm on 23 May. In fact the plaintiff received four more injections than had been ordered. Her final injection was at 6.00 am on 25 May.

On 26 May she experienced a sense of giddiness and suffered a permanent loss of balance. She sued the hospital authorities.

Held: (i) the two nurses who administered the last four injections had no reason at the time to suppose that the doses were other than those prescribed by a doctor, so they had not been negligent;

(ii) the blame lay with the ward sister who alone had known that the injections had exceeded the prescribed dose. It would have been simple for her to draw a red line, a star or some other red danger signal in a diary or treatment sheet, indicating the time when the prescription was to end. The injury was foreseeable. She had been negligent;

(iii) it was the last injection which probably did the damage. The hospital authority was liable.

See pages 80, 93.

Smith v Lewisham Group Hospital Management Committee

Hospital administration: supervision: substandard treatment

Gorman J (with jury). [1955] The Times 21 June

In March 1953 the plaintiff (Mrs Emma Smith), then aged eighty-six, was admitted to Lewisham Hospital. She was suffering from acute cholecystitis, was in a frail condition and was in considerable pain. On admission she was placed on a four-wheeled trolley, about two feet wide and two and a half feet high, the top of which had no edge or rail or other protection. The nurse attending her in her cubicle left her in order to answer the telephone. The plaintiff fell off the trolley and broke a thigh. She sued the hospital authority.

Held: the jury found that the hospital staff had been negligent in leaving the plaintiff unattended on the trolley.

See page 88.

Smith v Lowry

Alternative practitioner: osteopath: X-ray: fractures: substandard treatment: masseur

Talbot J (with jury). [1935] 1 BMJ 743

The plaintiff (Sheila Smith) had rheumatic fever when she was five. Four years later she complained of pains in her leg, which were attributed to rheumatism. In August 1931, when she was aged eleven, her parents consulted Captain Lowry, a blind osteopath and masseur. When he was manipulating her under anaesthetic, a cracking noise was heard. She was sent to hospital where it was found that the neck of her left thigh had been fractured. She was left with permanent disability in her left hip.

The plaintiff sued Captain Lowry. An X-ray taken a year earlier in 1930 had revealed a displacement of the neck of the thigh-bone on both sides. Expert evidence was given that a manipulation which would cause no injury to a normal child might fracture the thigh of a child suffering from displacement, and that if an X-ray had been taken before the treatment it would have disclosed the dangers of manipulation to a man who knew his work.

Held: (i) the jury found that Captain Lowry had been negligent, so the plaintiff was awarded damages for her injuries;

319

(ii) they dismissed Captain Lowry's counterclaim for the balance of his fee.

See page 95.

Smith v Pare

Cancer: burns: X-rays: assault: consent

Lawrence J (with special jury). [1904] 1 BMJ 1227

In 1899 Mrs Pare underwent an operation for a non-cancerous growth on her left breast. In March 1903 she consulted Dr Smith who thought that she was suffering from cancer and advised a combined treatment by X-rays and high-frequency currents. Mr Pare told him that he would not agree to any treatment which caused his wife pain. Dr Smith was supposed to obtain the consents of her regular doctor and the surgeon who had operated earlier, but these were never forthcoming. Nevertheless the treatment was pursued. X-rays were applied over the whole of Mrs Pare's body and caused burns to her skin. In June 1903 her husband assaulted Dr Smith on the steps of his private hospital.

Dr Smith sued Mr Pare for damages for assault. Mr Pare counterclaimed damages for negligence. Expert evidence was given that Mrs Pare was in fact suffering from septic pneumonia and that the X-rays should have been stopped as soon as damage to the skin commenced. Mr Pare testified that he had decided to assault Dr Smith after he had seen the burns from which his wife was suffering.

Held: (i) the jury found that Mr Pare did not consent to the X-ray part of the treatment, which was improper, negligent and unskilful;

(ii) they awarded Dr Smith £2 damages for the assault (which had already been paid into court) and Mr Pare £100 damages on the counterclaim.

See page 85.

Snell v Carter

Alternative practitioner: burns: standard of care: masseur

H.H. Judge Scobell Armstrong. [1941] 2 The Lancet 321

Miss Winifred Snell, aged thirty-two, suffered from disseminated sclerosis. She consulted Mr Carter who described himself as a masseur and medical electrician. He agreed to carry out four treatments a week at 7s 6d per treatment. Two treatments were given on successive days; Miss Snell's back was massaged with oil, and ray lamps were used. Soon after the second treatment, the skin began to come off her back which was severely burned. The burns became gangrenous and, after suffering great pain, Miss Snell died of toxaemia.

The plaintiff (her mother) sued Mr Carter. Expert evidence was given that ray treatment was inadvisable and useless; the disease made the skin sensitive to heat. It was said that anyone with medical knowledge would realise the danger of ray treatment in such a case.

Held: Mr Carter had been negligent.

See pages 85–86, 95.

Sones v Foster

Alternative practitioner: naturopath: substandard treatment: causation:
gangrene

Atkinson J (with jury). [1937] 1 BMJ 250

The plaintiff (Mr Sones) had a corn on the little toe of his left foot. When this became septic, he consulted Mr Foster, a naturopath, and spent nine weeks in Mr Foster's house under treatment at eight guineas a week. On 17 August, when he arrived, an attendant sprayed the foot with antiseptic and administered a hot compress, applying a poultice at about midnight. During the first six days Mr Foster used a nail brush, which caused intense pain, about five times a day, and had then sprayed the foot and applied hot compresses. On one occasion Mr Foster inserted the foot in antiseptic and cut off a quantity of skin, afterwards pressing the foot by force into almost boiling water. Other operations were performed for cutting off mortified skin under the foot and toes, and a little toe which had become necrotic. On 22 October the plaintiff was taken to St Bartholomew's Hospital where his left leg was amputated above the knee.

He sued Mr Foster for negligence. Expert evidence was given that he was suffering from arteriosclerosis and had gangrene as far back as the ankle. If an operation had been performed when the plaintiff first went to Mr Foster, it would probably have been safe to amputate seven inches below the knee. The nail brush was not good treatment and was likely to do harm.

Held: Atkinson J directed the jury that, although the orthodox medical profession liked to think itself the sole repository of knowledge of the art of healing, there were undoubtedly unorthodox practitioners who rendered great public service. Professional osteopaths were an example, and the same might be said of naturopaths, who combined herbalism and nature treatment, and the more reputable of them had formed themselves into associations which did their best to create standards. No one need consult these practitioners unless he liked; a patient who consulted one had the right to expect the average skill, knowledge and efficiency of the body of naturopaths to which the practitioner belonged.

The jury found that Mr Foster had been negligent in his advice and treatment. The plaintiff was awarded general damages for his pain, suffering and loss of amenities, plus a return of most of the fees he had paid.

See pages 28, 95–96.

Stevens v Bermondsey and Southwark Group Hospital Management Committee and Another

Diagnosis: hospital doctor: X-ray: settlement: duty of care

Paull J. (1963) 107 SJ 478

In May 1957 the plaintiff (Mr Stevens) sustained injury when he was thrown off his bicycle after a borough council roadsweeper had pushed his broom into the plaintiff's bicycle wheel. He was examined at hospital by a casualty officer. The plaintiff told him that he was suffering severe pain in his back and asked for an X-ray. He was not X-rayed, however, because the doctor thought that there was nothing seriously wrong. On his fourth visit to the hospital he still complained of the pain in his back, and the doctor prescribed a course of physiotherapy.

On the strength of this medical advice, the plaintiff settled his claim for negligence against the borough council at £125. Later, when he was seen by another doctor at another hospital, he was diagnosed as suffering from spondylolisthesis, a congenital affliction hitherto free of symptoms, which had been activated by the fall from his bicycle.

The plaintiff sued the casualty officer and the health authority. One head of claim was that, but for their negligence, he would have claimed and recovered a much larger sum from the borough council.

Held: the plaintiff was not entitled to damages under this head. A doctor's duty was limited to the sphere of medicine, and he had nothing to do with the sphere of legal liability unless he examined with an eye to liability. Unless there were special circumstances, he was not required to contemplate or foresee any question connected with a third party's liability to his patient.

See page 27.

Stokes v Guest, Keen and Nettlefold (Bolts and Nuts) Limited

Works doctor: state of knowledge: warning: duty of care: standard of care: causation

Swanwick J. [1968] 1 WLR 1776

From 1950 to 1965 Sidney Stokes worked as a tool setter/operator at G.K.N.'s Darlaston factory. His job involved him in intermittently leaning over machines in such a way as to bring the lower part of his stomach and the top of his thighs into contact with a film of cooling or cutting oil (of the type accepted as containing carcinogenic elements) which escaped on to the part of the machine over which a tool-setter would lean. His boilersuits got soaked with oil down the front, his trousers underneath got oily, and his underpants often had discoloured oil patches down the front. He developed an epithelioma of the scrotum from which he died in 1966.

In July 1960 the Factory Inspectorate had issued a leaflet, Form 295, entitled "The Effects on the Skin of Mineral Oil", specifically describing warts on the scrotum, indicating that they might develop into skin cancer and should therefore be reported to a doctor without delay, warning against putting oily rags in trouser pockets, and contemplating that there might be periodical examinations by works doctors of which workers should avail themselves. In

January 1961 Dr Lloyd, the full-time factory medical officer, learned that Mr Ward, another tool setter operator at the same works, was suffering from scrotal cancer and traced the cause as heavy contamination of overalls at work by mineral oil.

Dr Lloyd rejected the suggestion of periodical medical examinations, even when made by the coroner at the inquest on Mr Ward's death in 1963. Nor did he circulate Form 295. His only measure was to address the Works Council later in 1963, stressing personal hygiene and mentioning cancer, but not mentioning the scrotum or warts or reporting.

Held: (i) a factory doctor is to be judged by the standards of a physician in the medical aspects of his work; the economic and administrative aspects are covered by the general principles of employers' liability;

(ii) the defendants were responsible for Dr Lloyd's negligence in:

(a) not instituting after the discovery of Mr Ward's condition and *a fortiori* after his death six-monthly periodic medical examinations of tool-setters at the Darlaston works; and

(b) not issuing at these same times direct to the workers either Form 295 or an equivalent notice calling attention to the existence of a risk of cancer of the scrotum, describing the symptoms and recommending immediate reference to the factory doctor or general practitioner;

(iii) these measures would probably have saved Mr Stokes' life.

See page 39.

Strangways-Lesmere v Clayton

Prescription: overdose: nurses: vicarious liability

Horridge J. [1936] 2 KB 11

In May 1935 Mrs Strangways-Lesmere was admitted to the Weymouth and District Hospital for an operation. The house surgeon wrote out on the bed card that six drachms of paraldehyde were to be administered. A piece of paper with the instructions that the paraldehyde was to be six drachms in nine ounces of water was handed to Nurse Miles. She poured out a dose of six ounces of paraldehyde and Nurse Chapman checked this. Neither of them looked at the bed card. Consequently six ounces, rather than six drachms, of paraldehyde were administered to Mrs Strangways-Lesmere. She died without recovering consciousness.

The plaintiff (her husband) sued the nurses Miles and Chapman and the hospital authority.

Held: the nurses were guilty of negligence. Nurse Miles misread the note that was handed to her. Both the nurses ought to have looked at the bed card when measuring out a dose.

N.B. Following the cases of *Cassidy v Ministry of Health* and *Roe v Minister of Health*, the judge's further finding that the hospital authority was not liable for the nurses' negligence would not be good law today.

See pages 10, 80, 93.

Sullivan v Manchester Regional Hospital Board and Another

Operation: after-care: nurses: diagnosis: surgeon

Lynskey J. [1957] 2 BMJ 1442

In September 1953 the plaintiff (Mrs Sullivan) underwent an operation by Mr Evans at Accrington Victoria Hospital for the removal of nasal polypi. When she recovered from the anaesthetic, her right eye was swollen and remained so for several days. She asked the ward sister several times if her eye "would be all right" and accepted reassurance that it would be. Two days after the operation, she noticed that her eyeball had the appearance of red jelly and that she could not see. Four days after the operation, the ward sister asked the resident surgical officer to examine her because the swelling still persisted. This led to her transfer to the care of an eye specialist.

The plaintiff had suffered damage to the optic nerve with loss of sight. She sued Mr Evans and the hospital authority, alleging that Mr Evans had been negligent in the performance of the operation and that the nursing staff had failed for four days to act on her complaints. Expert evidence was given that the occurrence of such bleeding behind the eye did not signify lack of skill on the part of the surgeon.

Held: (i) Mr Evans had not been guilty of any lack of reasonable skill and care;

(ii) the nursing staff had not been negligent in failing to recognize the significance of the plaintiff's appearance and her complaint that she could not see.

Judgment for the defendants.
See page 93.

Sutton v Population Services Family Planning Programme Ltd and Another

Cancer: diagnosis: nurses: damages: substandard treatment

McCowan J. [1981] The Times 7 November, [1981] 2 The Lancet 1430

The plaintiff suffered cancer. The negligence of a nurse employed by the first defendants caused the cancerous growth to be detected and removed too late. Since the cancer was highly malignant, an earlier removal would not have eradicated it. However its recurrence would have been delayed for four years during which the plaintiff would have led a normal life and worked full-time. In addition, her menopause was prematurely brought forward.

Held: (i) the plaintiff was awarded damages for four years' loss of future earnings plus the conventional figure for four years' expectation of life;

(ii) she was further awarded £1,000 for the suffering caused by the premature arrival of her menopause;

(iii) since she would have undergone the same operations and treatment four years later, there could be no extra award of damages for pain and suffering.
See pages 25, 63, 93.

Tanswell v Nelson and Others

Dentist: general practitioner: diagnosis: X-rays: standard of care

McNair J. [1959] The Times 11 February

On 26 October 1954 the plaintiff (Mrs Gwendoline Tanswell) had ten teeth removed by her dentist Mr Nelson. Consequently she suffered a locking of the jaws accompanied by intense pain and swelling of the cheek and face. Mr Nelson treated her with irrigation of the mouth and hot washes. Her condition did not improve.

On 5 November Mr Nelson sent the plaintiff to her doctor Dr Cree, who diagnosed dental abscess with infection spreading up into the parotid gland, and treated her with antibiotics. On 9 November Dr Cree told Mr Nelson that he was satisfied the abscess was coming to a head. Dr Cree continued to treat her until 29 November when he arranged for her to go into hospital.

It emerged that the plaintiff had suffered trismus, a locking of the jaws, and osteomyelitis of the jaw. She became a frail and sick person. She sued Mr Nelson and Dr Cree on the grounds that each in turn failed to have X-ray films taken of her jaw and to send her to hospital until it was too late.

Held: (i) the taking of X-rays by Mr Nelson probably would not have told him anything he did not know already. A dentist was entitled to rely upon a doctor's opinion of the patient's general response to antibiotic treatment, unless that opinion was clearly inconsistent with facts observed by the dentist;

(ii) many of the symptoms shown by the plaintiff were inconsistent with developing osteomyelitis. They were not such as should have led Dr Cree to suspect it.

See pages 86, 89.

Tarasoff et al v The Regents of the University of California et al

Psychiatric patient: duty of care to third party: warning: confidentiality: standard of care: foreign

Supreme Court of California. (1976) 551 P (2d) 334

In August 1969 Prosenjit Poddar was a voluntary outpatient receiving therapy at Cowell Memorial Hospital in the University of California at Berkeley. The plaintiffs' case was that Poddar informed Dr Moore, his therapist there, that he was going to kill an unnamed girl, readily identifiable as Tatiana Tarasoff, when she returned home from spending the summer in Brazil; that Dr Moore decided that Poddar should be committed for observation in a mental hospital and requested the assistance of the police department in securing Poddar's confinement; that police officers took Poddar into custody but, satisfied that he was rational, released him on his promise to stay away from Tatiana; that Dr Powelson, Dr Moore's superior, then directed that no further action be taken to detain Poddar; and that Dr Moore did not warn Tatiana or her parents.

On 27 October 1969, shortly after her return from Brazil, Poddar went to Tatiana Tarasoff's home and killed her there. The plaintiffs (her parents) sued, *inter alia*, Dr Moore, Dr Powelson and the university. These defendants had statutory immunity from liability for failing to confine Poddar. The plaintiffs alleged that they were negligent in failing to warn of the danger.

Held: (i) the defendant therapists could not escape liability merely because Tatiana herself was not their patient. When a therapist determines, or pursuant to the standards of his profession should determine, that his patient presents a serious danger of violence to another, he incurs an obligation to use reasonable care to protect the intended victim against such danger. The discharge of his duty may require the therapist to take one or more of various steps, depending upon the nature of the case. Thus it may call for him to warn the intended victim or others likely to apprise the victim of the danger, to notify the police, or to take whatever other steps are reasonably necessary under the circumstances. Thus the plaintiffs' causes of action could be amended to allege that Tatiana's death proximately resulted from the defendants' negligent failure to warn Tatiana or others likely to apprise her of the danger;

(ii) the broad rule of privilege protecting confidential communications between patient and psychotherapist does not apply if the psychotherapist has reasonable cause to believe that the patient is in such a mental or emotional condition as to be dangerous to himself or to the person or property of another, and that disclosure of the communication is necessary to prevent the threatened danger. The protective privilege ends where the public peril begins.
See page 27.

Taylor v Glass

Vaccine damage: meningitis: adjournment of trial

Court of Appeal. 24 April 1979

The plaintiff (David Taylor) was born in June 1970. When he was one year old, Dr Glass gave him a vaccination against diphtheria and other illnesses. A little later he was taken ill with meningitis. This illness left him permanently incapacitated.

The plaintiff sued Dr Glass who admitted liability. There was a major issue as to his expectation of life, which his own experts suggested was normal, but which Dr Glass' experts said was limited to fifteen years. Only one of his five experts had seen the plaintiff.

The case had been on the warned list at the Newcastle District Registry two or three times. It reached the top of the list, with the result that it was expected to be heard on 26 April 1979. A vacation judge granted the defendant's application for an adjournment on the ground that his expert witnesses could not attend court then.

Held: the vacation judge had been under a misapprehension as to the listing arrangements in Newcastle. By making suitable arrangements the defendant could either obtain the attendance of his original medical experts or, as only one of them had seen the plaintiff, could get substitute doctors who would be equally capable of helping the court in matters of theoretical opinion. The original date in the list should be restored.

Thake and Another v Maurice

Vasectomy (failed): breach of contract: wrongful birth: risk disclosure: damages: public policy

Court of Appeal. [1986] QB 644, [1986] 1 All ER 479, [1986] 2 WLR 337

In 1975 the plaintiffs (Mr and Mrs Thake) had four children with a fifth on the way. They arranged with Mr Maurice that he would carry out a vasectomy operation on Mr Thake for £20. Mr Maurice told them that the vasectomy operation was irreversible, subject to a possible operation to restore fertility, and did not warn them that there was a chance of the vasectomy failing to sterilise Mr Thake. He performed it in October 1975. Late recanalisation occurred, and in autumn 1978 Mrs Thake was informed to her surprise that she was five months' pregnant. She declined a late abortion, and a daughter Samantha was born to her in April 1979.

The plaintiffs sued Mr Maurice for breach of contract and negligence. The trial judge (Peter Pain J) found for them on liability and awarded £6,677 agreed damages for the cost of the layette and of Samantha's upkeep to the age of seventeen, plus an agreed sum of £2,000 to Mrs Thake for loss of earnings, but he refused to make any award of general damages for pain and suffering.

Held: (i) sterility was the expected result of the operation, but that did not mean that a reasonable person would have understood the defendant to be giving a binding promise that the operation would achieve its purpose. Accordingly there was no breach of contract;

(ii) in the absence of expert evidence of standard practice, the judge was entitled to conclude that Mr Maurice's failure to warn amounted to an inadvertent breach of his duty of care to the plaintiffs. The consequence that Mrs Thake would not appreciate that she had become pregnant at an early enough stage to enable her to have an abortion was reasonably foreseeable. Mr Maurice was liable in negligence;

(iii) the joy of having the child should be set off against the time, trouble and care inevitably involved in her upbringing. But the pre-natal distress, pain and suffering stood in a separate category and she should be compensated for this by the agreed sum of £1,500.
See pages 14–15, 31, 53, 73, 84, 113–114.

Thomas v Wignall and Another

Anaesthetics: damages: brain damage

Court of Appeal. [1987] 1 All ER 1185, [1987] 2 WLR 930

In March 1976 the plaintiff (Linda Thomas), then aged sixteen, underwent a routine operation for removal of her tonsils in the University Hospital of Wales in Cardiff. The anaesthetic went wrong. She sued the health authority and the anaesthetist who admitted liability for negligence.

The plaintiff suffered permanent brain damage. She became very seriously disabled. She was confined to a wheelchair and would need constant care and attention for the rest of her life. She was not aware of what had happened to her. She was incontinent and had serious behavioural problems. She was not expected to live beyond the age of fifty-five.

In December 1985 the trial judge (Hutchison J) awarded the then record sum of £679,264 damages. The principal items were agreed general damages of £60,000 for pain, suffering and loss of amenities, £49,000 for past and future loss of earnings, £25,000 for conversion of a house to her requirements and £502,500 for the past and future cost of the plaintiff's care.

Held: the award was affirmed and the defendant's appeal dismissed.
See pages 81, 103, 106, 108.

Thorne v Northern Group Hospital Management Committee

Suicide risk: supervision: nurses: causation

Edmund Davies J. (1964) 108 SJ 484

Mrs Thorne was a patient in a general hospital. The plaintiff (her husband) told the ward sister that she had threatened suicide. She was a suspected depressive. The hospital transferred her to one wing of two in a convalescent ward.

On 16 August 1960 she was due to be removed at 10.00am to an outside neurosis unit for further investigation. At 8.45am a nurse saw her sitting by her bed. At 9.00am the nurse and ward sister left the wing temporarily. Mrs Thorne walked out of the hospital, went to her home and committed suicide. The plaintiff sued the hospital authority.

Held: the degree of care and supervision required of hospital staff in relation to a patient with known or, perhaps, even suspected suicidal tendencies was greater than that called for in relation to patients generally. However, Mrs Thorne was set upon making her escape for the purposes of self-destruction and it was highly conceivable that she kept a wary eye on the nurses and seized her opportunity immediately their backs were turned and had absented themselves temporarily. That did not connote negligence on the part of the nurses.

Judgment for the defendants.
See pages 12, 88, 92.

Trew v Middlesex Hospital

Nurses: substandard treatment

Gerrard J. [1953] 1 The Lancet 343

The plaintiff (Mr Trew), a private patient, was sitting in bed in the Middlesex Hospital. He had one leg in a sling and the other on a pillow. Considering this, he was sitting as upright as he comfortably could. A nurse, who was a small brisk woman in a hurry, placed a tea tray on his lap. The tray tilted and hot water from the jug was spilt on to the plaintiff.

He sustained burns and sued the hospital.

Held: the nurse had been negligent. She "breezed into the room, put down the tray and went out, giving the patient no time to protest".
See page 94.

Tyndall v Alcock

Fracture: hospital doctor: substandard treatment

Court of Appeal. [1928] 1 BMJ 528

In July 1926 the plaintiff (Phyllis Tyndall), then aged eight, fell from a donkey and sustained a fracture of the lower end of the left humerus. She was taken to Gloucester where she was treated by Dr Alcock, first at a nursing home and later in the Gloucester Infirmary. He manipulated the bones into position and was satisfied that the fracture had been properly reduced. The arm was then suspended from the shoulder, and an X-ray was taken. The next day the hand was a little swollen, so the bandages were loosened. By the fifth day there was more discolouration. Dr Alcock realised that the circulation was obstructed, so the bandages were loosened further and the strapping removed. The plaintiff developed Volkmann's contracture. Her left arm became fixed at the elbow, resulting in permanent impairment of movement.

Her claim against Dr Alcock was heard before Shearman J and a special jury. The jury found that Dr Alcock had been negligent in failing to set the bone properly and in his subsequent treatment. He appealed to the Court of Appeal.

Held: the jury were the persons put there by the constitution to try actions involving questions of negligence. Since there was evidence before them on which they were entitled to find either way, it was impossible for a Court of Appeal to interfere with the result.

Udale v Bloomsbury Area Health Authority

Sterilisation (failed): wrongful birth: damages: public policy

Jupp J. [1983] 2 All ER 522, [1983] 1 WLR 1098

By 1977 the plaintiff (Mrs Muriel Udale) and her husband had four children, all daughters. In October 1977 she underwent an operation for laparoscopic sterilisation. The operation failed. In June 1978 she was told that she was pregnant. In November 1978 she gave birth to a healthy baby boy.

She sued the hospital authority. The surgeon, who should have placed a metal clip on each fallopian tube in order to close it, in fact placed the right-hand clip, not on the fallopian tube but on a nearby ligament. The defendants admitted liability.

Held: (i) the plaintiff was awarded (February 1983) £8,000 general damages to compensate her for:

(a) the shock and anxiety of an unwanted pregnancy;

(b) her anger at the thwarting of her decision not to have further children;

(c) the ordinary symptoms of pregnancy during the first three and a half months to June 1978, thought by her to be illness or disease, and the taking of unnecessary drugs to overcome them;

(d) the subsequent symptoms of pregnancy and the fear after its diagnosis that the drugs may have harmed or deformed the child;

(e) an operation for resterilisation two or three days after the birth;

(f) an operation in September 1982 to remove the sterilisation clip on the left side;

(ii) she was also awarded £1,025 agreed damages in respect of her loss of earnings for eleven months, made necessary by the pregnancy and birth.

N.B. In view of the Court of Appeal decisions in *Emeh* v *Kensington and Chelsea and Westminster Area Health Authority* and *Thake* v *Maurice*, the judge's decision to reject the cost of the child's upbringing on the ground of public policy is not good law.
See pages 31, 53, 84, 113.

Urbanski v Patel et al; Firman et al v Patel

Surgeon: substandard treatment: duty of care to third party: foreign: foreseeability

Manitoba Queen's Bench (Wilson J). (1978) 84 DLR (3d) 650

In April 1975 Mrs Shirley Firman entered the Gimli Hospital for a tubal ligation. As she had felt occasional abdominal discomfort, it was agreed that Mr Patel, the surgeon, should explore for and if necessary remove any ovarian cyst causing this. Instead, by mistake, he removed her only kidney.

Mrs Firman's father, Victor Urbanski, donated one of his own kidneys. This was implanted in May 1976. Unfortunately Mrs Firman's body rejected the kidney, and she had to go back on to dialysis.

Mr and Mrs Firman and Mr Urbanski sued Mr Patel who admitted negligence. He conceded liability to the Firmans but not to Mr Urbanski.

Held: in the light of today's medicine, kidney transplant is an accepted remedy in renal failure. The transplant must be viewed as an expected result, something to be expected as a consequence of loss of normal kidney function. It was entirely foreseeable that one of Mr Firman's family would be invited, and would agree, to donate a kidney for transplant: an act according with the principle developed in the many "rescue" cases. Mr Patel was liable to Mr Urbanski as well as the Firmans.
See page 27.

Urry v Bierer and Another

Childbirth: caesarian: retained surgical product: surgeon: nurses

Court of Appeal. [1955] The Times 15 July

The plaintiff (Mrs Ellen Urry) underwent an operation by Mr Bierer, a gynaecological surgeon, for delivery of a child by lower caesarian section. The

Harley Street Nursing Home Limited provided the surgical packs which were about ten inches square. The sister counted them before and after use. One was left in the plaintiff's body.

The plaintiff sued the nursing home and Mr Bierer. The nursing home admitted liability for the sister's count having been wrong. The trial judge (Pearson J) found Mr Bierer and the nursing home liable in equal shares. Mr Bierer appealed.

Held: the patient was entitled to expect that the surgeon would do what is reasonable to ensure that packs were removed from the body before he asked the sister if the count was correct. The one was independent of the other. The sister's count was an additional check for the protection both of the patient and of the surgeon. That it failed occasionally only emphasised the need for diligence on the part of the surgeon in that respect. Mr Bierer had insisted that he was entitled to rely on the sister's count, and his technique did not include any particular effort to remember or have himself reminded of the location of particular packs. He fell far short of the standard of care required of him and was equally liable with the sister.
See pages 82, 93.

Vancouver General Hospital v McDaniel and Another

Hospital administration: duty of care: infection: smallpox: standard of care

Privy Council. (1935) 152 LT 56, (1934) WN 171

On 17 January 1932 Annabelle McDaniel, aged nine, who was then suffering from diphtheria, was admitted to the Infectious Diseases Hospital in Vancouver. At that time there was smallpox in Vancouver. Between 18 and 29 January seven smallpox patients were admitted and placed in rooms on the same floor. The hospital's policy was to deal with this by a system of sterilisation rather than isolation. Nevertheless on 29 January Annabelle was removed to another floor on her doctor's request.

On 12 February she was diagnosed as suffering from smallpox. She suffered personal disfigurement and sued the hospital, alleging negligence in juxtaposing the smallpox patients on the same floor as her and in allowing nurses who also nursed the smallpox patients to attend on her. The trial judge found in her favour.

Held: the system adopted by the hospital was in accord with general if not universal practice in Canada and the United States. A defendant charged with negligence can clear himself if he shows that he has acted in accord with general and approved practice. The hospital had established this and was not liable.
See pages 87–88.

Vaughan v Paddington and North Kensington Area Health Authority

Cancer: diagnosis: scarring: mastectomy: damages

Boreham J. (1987) PMILL Vol 3 No 9

In July 1981 the plaintiff (Mrs Vaughan), a middle aged woman with two adult children, had a lump in her right breast. She was referred to St Mary's Hospital where after a biopsy she was told that she had cancer of the breast. In September both her breasts were removed in a mastectomy operation. There was persistent bleeding. In October the prosthesis in the right breast was removed, and in December 1981 the left prosthesis was removed. She underwent unsuccessful plastic surgery to reconstitute the nipples. A further operation was required in February 1984 to insert a larger prosthesis in her left breast.

It was then discovered that she had never had cancer at all. She sued the health authority who admitted that they had been negligent.

The plaintiff was left with scars which had once been very unsightly but had been substantially improved by cosmetic surgery. She suffered permanent pain and restriction of movement of her back and arms. She was very sensitive to the removal of her breasts. For two and a half years she had been led to believe that she had cancer, and there were times when she thought that she was going to die.

Held: (i) she was awarded (October 1986) £25,000 general damages for pain, suffering and loss of amenities;

(ii) she was also awarded £3,000 in respect of her inability to do her housework, £15,000 for the cost of future help, £13,870 for wages lost to date of trial, £36,000 for future loss of earnings as a chambermaid and miscellaneous expenses of £105.32.
See pages 64, 104.

Venner v North East Essex Area Health Authority and Another

Sterilisation (failed): pregnancy: standard of care

Tucker J. [1987] The Times 21 February, [1987] 1 The Lancet 638

The plaintiff (Mrs Venner) was a married woman born in August 1954. She had four children aged at trial between five and fourteen. She sued the first defendants (North East Essex A.H.A.) and the second defendant (Mr Donald Morrison, a gynaecologist) arising out of the birth of the youngest child.

The plaintiff used the contraceptive pill and conceived on withdrawal from it. In 1978 she became pregnant when she forgot to take the pill. The second defendant terminated that pregnancy. He declined to sterilise her at the time in view of her age (then twenty-four).

In 1980 the second defendant agreed to sterilise the plaintiff. Owing to the risk of thrombosis, he told her to come off the pill one month before the operation. He advised her that either she should abstain from sex or her husband should use a sheath. Neither precaution was taken.

On the morning of the operation the second defendant checked that the plaintiff still wanted the operation. He told her that the operation would not terminate any pregnancy and asked whether she might be pregnant; she replied that she was certain that she was not. The operation took place on the twenty-seventh day of her menstrual cycle. No dilatation and curettage (D and C) was performed.

In fact the plaintiff was pregnant. She later gave birth to a healthy child. An expert called on her behalf at the trial said that he always performed a D and C and that, if this had been done, the plaintiff would probably not have remained pregnant.

Held: the defendants were not negligent. The second defendant was justified in advising the plaintiff to come off the pill before the operation. It was neither necessary nor desirable for a D and C to be performed as a matter of course.
See page 85.

Vernon v Bloomsbury Health Authority

Prescription: tests: causation

Tucker J. [1986] 3 MLJ 190

In the summer of 1982 the plaintiff went on holiday to Taiwan and Australia where she contracted two infections. She continued to feel unwell and was admitted to hospital. On 16 and 17 November her condition was diagnosed as subacute bacterially negative endocarditis. All attempts to grow an organism from blood culture failed. She was given a nineteen day course of 1.2g of intravenous benzylpenicillin four-hourly plus a loading dose of gentamicin (160mg intravenously) followed by 120mg eight-hourly (360mg) per day. She weighed 64kg. The treatment lasted from 17 November to 6 December. The hospital monitored the trough levels of her blood up to 29 November but did not monitor the peak levels at all. Her temperature remained normal throughout.

Soon after the end of the treatment, the plaintiff suffered symptoms of irreversible bilateral vestibular damage. She sued the hospital authorities, alleging that she had been given excessive amounts of gentamicin for too long and that they had not monitored her blood levels adequately.

Held: the dose given was a proper one, and the hospital had acted in the plaintiff's best interests by continuing treatment for nineteen days. Extra monitoring would have had no effect on the outcome, since probably no danger would have been revealed. The hospital doctors had conformed with a proper standard of treatment. The defendants were not liable.
See pages 42, 81.

Voller v Portsmouth Corporation

Injection: infection: hospital administration: meningitis: res ipsa loquitur

Birkett J. (1947) 203 LTJ 264

In April 1944 the plaintiff (Edwin Voller) fractured a femur while playing football and was admitted to St Mary's Hospital, Portsmouth. Dr Hans, senior resident medical officer, gave him a spinal injection of Nupercaine in the ward with a needle and syringe. A few days later the plaintiff was diagnosed as suffering from meningitis. Owing to the injection, he became permanently disabled, both legs being paralysed.

The plaintiff sued the hospital authority and three of the hospital doctors.

Held: (i) the surface skin of the plaintiff was properly cleansed before the operation and Dr Hans prepared himself in the approved way by washing his hands and did all that was required. There was no evidence of negligence against the three doctors;

(ii) as the bacillus entered the plaintiff's body from without at the moment of the injection, there must have been some breach of the aseptic technique at the hospital. The only remaining source of infection was in the apparatus used for the operation. This was within the control of the hospital and its staff. The infection would not have arisen without negligence on their part and must have been due to a breach of the aseptic technique. The hospital authority was liable.
See pages 81, 87.

Waghorn v Lewisham and North Southwark Area Health Authority

Surgeon: operation: substandard treatment: limitation

S.N. McKinnon QC.[1987] QBD 23 June

The plaintiff (Mrs Waghorn) went to Guy's Hospital because she had a very short perineum which was causing marital problems. Her case was that she requested an operation which would lengthen the perineum and tighten the introitus, whereas instead on 31 March 1977 Mr Thomkinson performed an operation which shortened the perineum and opened the introitus further. On 4 April 1977, upon examining herself, she ascertained what had happened.

In May 1978 the plaintiff complained to Guy's Hospital through the Community Health Council. In September 1978 she notified the hospital health authority of her claim for damages. In May 1979 she instructed solicitors who commissioned a report from Mr Coden, a consultant obstetrician and gynaecologist. Following Mr Coden's report, counsel was instructed in December 1979 and advised that there had been no negligence in the 1977 operation.

In July 1980 Mr Coden performed a further operation on the plaintiff. In January 1982 he advised that if her narrative was correct the hospital might have been at fault. In February 1982 her solicitors advised her that she could have a claim. In April 1983 she changed her solicitors. Sometime in 1983 Mr

Coden operated again. In April 1984 the writ was issued. It was not served until nearly a year later. There was a preliminary trial of the limitation defence.

Held: (i) the plaintiff knew that her injury was significant in April 1977. Time began to run against her then. It was immaterial that she did not have supporting expert medical advice until 1982. Accordingly her action had been brought outside the primary period specified by s11 Limitation Act 1980;

(ii) part of the delay (from early 1982 onwards) was inexcusable. However, the defendants knew about the plaintiff's complaints in 1978, and all the hospital records except for the nursing notes had been preserved. Further surgery in 1980 and 1983 had obscured the surgical procedures that were undertaken in 1977. Even so, the evidence had been rendered only marginally less cogent by the delay since 1980. The potential prejudice to the plaintiff, who would be left effectively without a remedy, outweighed that to the defendant. The court's discretion under s33 Limitation Act 1980 was exercised in the plaintiff's favour to allow her action to proceed.
See pages 78, 120, 124.

Walker v Eli Lilly & Co

Discovery: drugs

Hirst J. (1986) 136 NLJ 608

The plaintiff was claiming damages against Eli Lilly & Co and others for personal injuries resulting from alleged side-effects of the drug Opren. She applied under s34(2) Supreme Court Act 1981 against a health authority, which was not a party to the action, seeking discovery of her hospital and medical notes and records of the relevant treatment carried out. During extensive correspondence, which had lasted nearly a year, the health authority had been reluctant to release these documents.

Held: the plaintiff's application for discovery was granted.
Per Hirst J: "Availability of such notes and records is, of course, essential both to the plaintiff and defendants and, indeed, to the court itself, for the proper conduct and disposal of the litigation. . . .

"Where, as in the present case, no special consideration of confidentiality is invoked, the court will almost certainly order disclosure if a summons should become necessary. It is, therefore, very much to be hoped that in future health authorities and medical practitioners will respond readily and promptly to any requests for disclosure in such cases, so that unnecessary expense and delay can be avoided.

"Needless to say, where in any case special considerations arise, such as a particular reason for confidentiality, the authority or medical practitioner would be fully justified in having the matter tested in court.

"One problem which arose in the present case, and which may arise elsewhere, was the anxiety on the part of the health authority that any documents disclosed might subsequently be used against them; it will, I hope, be some reassurance on this score for me to emphasise that, under well-established principles, there is an implied undertaking by a party seeking discovery in legal proceedings that documents so obtained will be used only for the purpose of those proceedings and for no other purpose".

See page 131.

Walker v South West Surrey District Health Authority

Childbirth: injection: nurse: substandard treatment: damages

Court of Appeal. 17 June 1982

On 22 March 1978 the plaintiff (Mrs Danielle Walker) went into St Luke's Hospital to have her third child. At about 11.00pm on 23 March she was given an injection of pethidine by the midwife, Sister Dyer. Dr Champion noted on 24 March: "also complaining of paraesthesia of the right leg. L1, L2. distribution distal to the injection site of pethidine", with a drawing showing an area of paraesthesia extending from about the middle of the thigh down to the ankle and an arrow pointing to an injection site on the inner side of the right thigh.

The injection damaged a superficial nerve, leaving the plaintiff with an area of numbness in her right leg. She sued the hospital authority. The trial judge (H.H. Judge Vick) found in her favour and awarded £1,000 damages.

Held: the judge had been right to accept the plaintiff's evidence that the injection was given to her on the inner side of the right thigh. No careful nurse or doctor would give an injection there in the absence of some compelling reason. It was clearly negligent.

See pages 80, 93.

Walton v Lief and Another

Alternative practitioner: representations: naturopath: osteopath: breach of contract: causation: damages

Lord Chief Justice (with special jury). [1933] 1 BMJ 132, [1933] 2 The Lancet 147

The plaintiff (Mrs Eleanor Walton) suffered from lupus erythematosus. In February 1932 Mr Stanley Lief MNCA, an osteopath and naturopath, warranted that he would cure her completely if she undertook his treatment. She spent five weeks at his sanatorium in Champneys where she was subjected to a starvation diet and repeated light treatment from a mercury vapour lamp. She then underwent further treatment from him at Park Lane. Her face and scalp became permanently disfigured.

The plaintiff sued Mr Lief and his company, Natural Healing Ltd, for breach of warranty and negligence. He explained in evidence that MNCA meant "Member Nature Cure Association" of which he was president. Expert testimony was that starvation treatment was a bad preface to any local treatment and that ultra-violet rays were irritating unless applied in very small doses. Lupus erythematosus had an inherent tendency to flare up, and it was doubted whether ultra-violet rays would cause it to do so.

Held: (i) the jury found that Mr Lief was in breach of his warranty to effect a complete cure of her disease, and assessed her damages under this head as the amount of the bill;

(ii) the jury also found that he had been negligent in his treatment and awarded one farthing damages (possibly because they decided that the negligence had little causative effect).
See pages 17, 96.

Warren v Greig; Warren v White

Dentist: general practitioner: diagnosis: standard of care

McKinnon J. [1935] 1 The Lancet 330

Mr Warren was under treatment for lumbago and sciatica. His doctor, observing the presence of pyorrhoea, advised a dental examination. A dentist was called in and, on the joint advice of doctor and dentist, Mr Warren consented to the extraction of his teeth. All twenty-eight teeth were extracted in one operation at 2.00pm with the doctor administering the anaesthetic. Bleeding persisted despite remedial measures.

At 5.55pm Mr Warren was removed to hospital where he died within twenty-four hours. Post-mortem examination revealed acute leukaemia. The plaintiff (his widow) sued the dentist and the doctor.

Held: (i) the mere performance of a mass extraction was not negligence. When a dentist was acting in conjunction with a doctor, it was no part of the dentist's duty to discover the general health of the patient or to search for abnormal signs. The dentist had not been negligent;

(ii) having regard to the rarity of acute leukaemia, it was not necessary to carry out a blood test as a safeguard against the possibility of the patient suffering from it. The doctor failed to find the disease without having been negligent.
Judgment for the defendants.
See pages 63, 86.

Waters and Another v Park

Sterilisation (failed): risk disclosure: standard of care

Havers J. [1961] The Times 15 July

The plaintiff (Mrs Waters) had a weak heart and was advised that she should have an operation for hysterectomy and sterilisation. An operation for sterilisation (but not for hysterectomy) was performed on 29 May 1956 by Mr Park at Selly Oak Hospital, Birmingham. In view of her cardiac trouble, he used a less efficient method of sterilisation that carried a slight risk of failure.

Mr Park's standard practice was to tell a patient of this risk. However, he did not tell the plaintiff in hospital because she was in an extremely congested ward with beds down the middle and no source of privacy. Instead he gave her an appointment to see him about six weeks after her discharge from hospital so that he could tell her then. She never kept the appointment.

On 3 July 1957 the plaintiff gave birth to a still-born child and had to undergo a further operation for sterilisation. She sued Mr Park.

Held: there was no generally approved practice at the time about telling patients of the risk; there were two schools of thought. In the light of current medical practice and opinion, a surgeon did not fall short of the proper standards of his profession if, in circumstances such as these, he did not tell the patient that there was a slight risk or did not advise her to use contraceptives. The risk of pregnancy within six weeks was very slight, and the chances were generally only about six in one thousand. There were reasons which made it impracticable for Mr Park to tell the plaintiff in the ward. He had not committed any breach of duty by not telling her afterwards of the slight risk of failure.
See pages 68–69.

Wells v Surrey Area Health Authority

Sterilisation: consent: advice: damages: loss of chance

Croom Johnson J. [1978] The Times 29 July

The plaintiff (Mrs Doreen Wells), a Roman Catholic, was thirty-five years of age and having trouble with her third pregnancy. It was the defendant hospital's practice, if a woman who already had two or three children needed a caesarian operation, to offer to sterilise her at the same time. Sterilisation had not been mentioned during the antenatal period and was first suggested to the plaintiff when she was in labour. There was no medical necessity. The hospital did not counsel her about the sterilisation, and she was in a state of some exhaustion when she consented.

The baby was born alive and well, but the plaintiff bitterly regretted the sterilisation. She sued the hospital authority.

Held: (i) the plaintiff understood the implication of the operation when she signed a consent form authorising the hospital to carry it out. Her claim for assault failed;

(ii) counselling is an important preliminary to sterilisation. The hospital had been negligent in failing to give her proper advice about it;

(iii) she was awarded (July 1978) £3,000 general damages, covering the loss of a "somewhat remote chance" of having another baby.
See page 69.

Westaway v South Glamorgan Health Authority

Dismissal for want of prosecution: diagnosis: fracture

Court of Appeal. 9 June 1986

On 29 May 1976 the plaintiff (Brian Westaway) fell in his garden and injured his left ankle. On the same day he attended Cardiff Royal Infirmary. In

March 1977 he wrote to the health authority to complain of his treatment. His writ was issued in April 1979 and served in June 1979. The Statement of Claim was served in April 1980. The defendants' solicitors persistently indicated a willingness to settle the case. They served the Defence in May 1983. In October 1983 the plaintiff amended his Statement of Claim to allege failure to diagnose a Pott's fracture and the consequent provision of inappropriate treatment. The amended Defence was served in January 1984. The defendants' solicitors still indicated that they regarded it as a case for full liability settlement. The plaintiff's solicitors failed to respond to a request for quantification. In June 1985 the defendants issued a summons to dismiss the action for want of prosecution.

Held: (i) the delay was inordinate and parts of it were inexcusable;

(ii) as the only negligence now relied upon was the failure to diagnose the Pott's fracture at the plaintiff's original attendance at Cardiff Royal Infirmary, which must be substantially if not entirely a question of the medical records and expert evidence, there was no particular prejudice to the defendants. The general principle that all delay is prejudicial was not enough to require the drastic step of dismissing the action.
See page 128.

Whichello v Medway and Gravesend Hospital Management Committee and Another

Surgeon: operation: tests: standard of care

Ashworth J. (1954) 108 SJ 55

In 1958 the plaintiff (Mr Whichello) underwent an operation for appendicitis and was discharged from hospital. Four days later he was readmitted for a second operation as the wound was infected. The surgeon in charge of the case did not order a culture to be taken. The wound did not heal properly and a third operation was performed. Still the wound did not heal. A fourth operation was undertaken and antibiotics were administered, after which the wound healed and the plaintiff was discharged from hospital.

He sued the health authority and the surgeon, alleging that they were negligent in failing to take a culture or administer antibiotics earlier than they did. Expert evidence was given at trial that a culture would have been an essential step, had a decision then been made to treat the infection by administering antibiotics, but was not a necessary prerequisite of the treatment followed, namely an operation to reopen and drain the wound. It was realised that antibiotics, in some circumstances, had disadvantages greater than those the antibiotics were intended to cure.

Held: it would have been wise to take a culture before the second operation. The surgeon had, however, decided to dispose of the case by surgery and, in view of the state of medical opinion then, he was not negligent in doing that. It was one thing to say that it was wiser to take a step, quite another to say that it was negligent not to do so. The defendants were not liable.
See page 89.

White v Board of Governors of Westminster Hospital and Another

Surgeon: operation: standard of care

Thompson J. [1961] The Times 26 October

The plaintiff (Robert White) suffered from an inveterate squint in his right eye. In June 1955, when he was nine years old, Mr McAuley performed a cosmetic operation on him at the Westminster Hospital. In the course of the operation, while cutting muscle and tendon attached by scar tissue, Mr McAuley unintentionally cut through to the retina. The eye became shrunken and useless and had to be removed.

The plaintiff sued Mr McAuley and the hospital authority.

Held: the plaintiff was the victim of mischance. The scale of the parts involved was very small, and Mr McAuley exercised due skill, care and judgement. He had not been negligent.
See page 77.

Whiteford v Hunter

Surgeon: operation: diagnosis: standard of care: cancer: tests

House of Lords. [1950] WN 553, (1950) 94 SJ 758

In March 1942 the plaintiff (Mr Whiteford), a consulting engineer, entered an English hospital and was seen by Mr Hunter, a consulting surgeon. The plaintiff's bladder was emptied and drained. In April Mr Hunter operated on him, with a view to removing his prostate. Near the base of the bladder he saw what he described as an indurated mass about the size of a palm of a man's hand. At no stage did he use a cystoscope or make a biopsy. He concluded that the plaintiff was suffering from inoperable cancer and so informed his wife, intimating that his life could only last a matter of months.

In this belief, the plaintiff closed down his practice, sold his home and went to the United States. A cystoscope examination there, followed by pathological analysis, showed the presence of chronic cystitis and a benign prostate hypertrophy. There was no trace of cancer.

The plaintiff sued Mr Hunter. His two main criticisms were:

(1) that no cystoscope was used before the opening of the bladder; and

(2) no specimen of the growth was taken in order to test microscopically whether it was cancerous or not.

All the English medical witnesses testified that it was against approved practice in England to use a cystoscope where there was acute urinary retention, and that when the bladder was drained and collapsed, it was difficult if not impossible to use one effectively unless it were of the flushing type, an instrument which was rare in England in 1942 and which Mr Hunter did not possess. Mr Hunter testified that a biopsy would have involved a serious risk of perforating the bladder wall and that, if the condition were cancerous, an unhealing ulcer would supervene.

Held: a defendant charged with negligence can clear himself if he shows that he acted in accord with general and approved practice. Mr Hunter was not negligent in not using a cystoscope. He explained why he did not make a biopsy. His actions conformed to the proper professional practice of the time. He was not liable.
See pages 63, 117.

Whitehouse v Jordan and Another

Childbirth: registrar: standard of care: error of judgement

House of Lords. [1981] 1 All ER 267, [1981] 1 WLR 246

Mrs Whitehouse had been seen during her pregnancy by a number of doctors at Queen Elizabeth Hospital, Edgbaston. She was a small woman aged thirty and had been identified as a difficult case. On 31 December 1969 Professor McLaren recorded that he thought the outlet was tight and that a trial labour would be needed. When she was admitted to hospital on 6 January 1970 it was noted that she was carrying a "fair-sized baby".

Mr Jordan, a senior registrar of near consultant status, embarked on a trial of forceps delivery at 11.45pm on 6 January. He was trying to see whether, with the use of forceps, a delivery *per vaginam* was possible. After pulling with five or six contractions, he decided that a vaginal delivery would be too traumatic. Consequently he proceeded to perform a caesarian section.

The baby (Stuart Whitehouse) was born apnoeic. He was made to breathe after thirty-five minutes, by which time irreversible brain damage had occurred. He sued Mr Jordan and the hospital authority. The trial judge (Bush J) concluded that Mr Jordan had negligently pulled too long and too hard with the forceps, thereby causing the brain damage. The Court of Appeal reversed the finding of negligence.

Held: the view of the judge who saw and heard the witnesses as to the weight to be given to their evidence is always entitled to great respect. However in this case the important facts were almost all inferences from the primary facts and, in determining what inferences should be drawn, an appellate court is just as well placed as a trial judge. There was not sufficient evidence to justify a finding that Mr Jordan had been negligent.

Per Lord Edmund-Davies: "to say that a surgeon committed an error of clinical judgement is wholly ambiguous, for, while some such errors may be completely consistent with the due exercise of professional skill, other acts or omissions in the course of exercising clinical judgement may be so glaringly below proper standards as to make a finding of negligence inevitable. . . Doctors and surgeons fall into no special category and, to avoid any future disputation of a similar kind, I would have it accepted that the true doctrine was enunciated and by no means for the first time, by McNair J in *Bolam* v *Friern Hospital Management Committee*. . . . . The test is the standard of the ordinary skilled man exercising and professing to have that special skill. If a surgeon fails to measure up to that standard in any respect ('clinical judgement' or otherwise), he has been negligent and should be so adjudged".

Per Lord Wilberforce: "While some degree of consultation between experts and legal advisers is entirely proper, it is necessary that expert evidence presented to the courts should be, and should be seen to be, the independent product of the expert, uninfluenced as to form or content by the exigencies of litigation. To the extent that it is not, the evidence is likely to be not only incorrect but self-defeating."
See pages 32–33, 35–36, 76, 77, 83.

Williams v Imrie

Sterilisation (failed): wrongful birth: damages: school fees: scarring

Hutchison J. (1988) PMILL Vol 4 No 3

In July 1979 the plaintiff, then aged thirty-two, underwent a sterilisation operation which was unsuccessful. She subsequently became pregnant. This caused her considerable distress, as she did not know the reason for the symptoms she was suffering. Her medical advisers believed that a clip had worked free from her fallopian tube. This in turn caused the plaintiff to worry for the well-being of the child she was carrying. Nevertheless she gave birth to a healthy daughter. Immediately after the birth she had to undergo a further sterilisation operation which led to a four to five inch-long scar across her abdomen. The pregnancy and birth caused financial worries and problems, particularly as the plaintiff, who already had two young children, felt unable to continue her part-time work.

Held: (i) (April 1987) general damages for pain, suffering and loss of amenities were assessed at £4,000;

(ii) the remaining damages consisted of £485 for the costs attributable to the birth to the end of the first year, £676 for the costs of maintaining the child to the end of its fourth year, £6,065 for the costs of maintaining the child from its fifth to seventeenth year, and £5,970 for loss of earnings to when the plaintiff was able to resume work.
The total award was £17,197.

See pages 84, 114–115.

Williams v North Liverpool Hospital Management Committee and Others

Anaesthetics: injection

Court of Appeal. [1959] The Times 17 January

In October 1955 the plaintiff (Mrs Alice Williams) was to undergo an operation for varicose veins at Bootle Hospital. Dr Pratt attempted to induce anaesthesia by means of intravenous injections of pentothal into one of her arms. She was exceedingly fat. This made the veins more difficult to find; a further handicap was that fat was not sensitive to pain. Dr Pratt found the vein on either the first or second prick and aspirated by withdrawing the plunger to check that there was blood in the cylinder. He then injected up to 5 c.c. of pentothal. A substantial part of the pentothal went into the tissues which were injured. When Dr Pratt appreciated that he had not succeeded in anaesthetising her with the pentothal, he injected a saline solution into the tissues to counteract the irritant effect of the pentothal.

The plaintiff suffered from an abscess which was caused by the first or second injection of pentothal. She sued the hospital authority and Dr Pratt. The trial judge (Elwes J) found in her favour.

Held: Dr Pratt could not have taken any further steps to ensure that the needle was in the lumen of the vein. The plaintiff did not manifest any pain to put him on enquiry. There was no basis for a finding of negligence against him.
See pages 79–80.

Williams v Ward

Works doctor: diagnosis: standard of care

Grantham J (with special jury). [1901] 2 BMJ 505

The plaintiff (Mr Williams) was an Aberdare collier. On 25 August 1900, while he was working in the pit, his left arm was fractured between the wrist and the elbow by the fall of a heavy stone. He was seen by Dr Ward, the works doctor, who put the injured limb in splints and bandages. On 17 September the plaintiff went to the works surgery with his father who was getting anxious due to the appearance of certain swellings on the arm. They saw Dr Ward who said it would be all right and promised to put the limb in plaster, which he did on 24 September. When the limb was subsequently freed, the swelling was still apparent. Dr Ward suggested that plaster of Paris should be used again. Instead the plaintiff was taken by his father to Liverpool where he was placed under the care of Dr Jones who operated.

The plaintiff sued Dr Ward, alleging negligence in that the bones of the arm had not been placed in position and could not, therefore, be properly set. The Works Committee approached Dr Ward and suggested that he should pay some compensation.

Dr Ward made a promise of some kind at the time, but later wrote to the Committee to say that anything he should give would be quite voluntary, as Dr Jones' report completely exonerated him from blame. Dr Jones testified that Dr Ward's treatment was perfectly proper and denied that he had ever mentioned the existence of negligence to the plaintiff or his father.

Held: the jury returned a verdict for the defendant.

Willson v McKechnie

Surgeon: operation: substandard treatment: advice

Thesiger J. [1973] 2 The Lancet 163

In May 1968 the plaintiff (Mr Willson) was suffering from back pain. It improved during bed rest from 4 May to 21 May, but worsened on mobilisation from 21 May to 2 June. Between 2 June and 13 June his symptoms improved. The myelogram showed a disc protrusion at L3–L4 level. A lumbar puncture revealed a high protein count in the cerebro-spinal fluid of 160 mg per 100 ml. Some functional overlay was suspected.

On 14 June Mr McKechnie operated on the plaintiff for what turned out to be a minor lumbar disc protrusion. Within three hours the plaintiff developed low paraplegia. He suffered permanent partial incapacity in the use of his legs and sued Mr McKechnie.

Held: Mr McKechnie had been too quick to advise an operation. Conservative treatment by bed rest had not been sufficiently tried. He had not given enough weight to the plaintiff's improvement in the one and a half weeks before the operation. The disastrous result was the kind of damage to be feared. Operating in these circumstances amounted to negligence.

Wilsher v Essex Area Health Authority

Hospital administration: substandard treatment: registrar: causation: burden of proof

House of Lords. [1988] 1 All ER 871, [1988] 2 WLR 557

At 11.25pm on 15 December 1978 the plaintiff (Martin Wilsher) was born at the Princess Alexandra Hospital, Harlow. He was a tiny baby, and his birth was nearly three months early. He could not breathe effectively and needed extra oxygen.

In order to monitor the partial pressure of oxygen (PO_2) in the arterial blood of a young baby, it is standard practice to pass a catheter through the umbilical artery into the aorta. Some time after 1.00am on 16 December Dr Wiles, a senior house officer, inserted the catheter into a vein instead of an artery. The monitor was then connected, and a blood sample was drawn through the catheter. This and subsequent samples were mixtures of arterial and venous blood instead of pure arterial blood, so they gave false readings of the level of PO_2 in the arterial blood.

Dr Wiles arranged for an X-ray and called Dr Kawa, a registrar, to inspect what he had done. Neither doctor realised that the configuration of the catheter disclosed by the X-ray meant that it must be following the line of a vein. At about 10.00am on 16 December Dr Kawa decided to change the catheter. Dr Wiles withdrew the old catheter, and Dr Kawa inserted the new one. Again it was inserted in a vein. A further X-ray was taken and inspected, but again the error in placing the catheter was not realised.

The misplaced catheters gave readings of PO_2 well below the true level of PO_2 in the arterial blood. This led to increased levels of oxygen being administered in an attempt to raise the PO_2 level. Consequently, by the time, around 8.00am on 17 December, that Dr Wiles realised that the catheter was in the wrong place and it was duly changed and inserted in an artery, the baby's PO_2 levels had been excessive for about eight to twelve hours.

He needed extra oxygen for another eleven weeks. He suffered unduly high levels of PO_2 in his arterial blood on five subsequent occasions between 20 December 1978 and 23 January 1979.

The plaintiff contracted retrolental fibroplasia (RLF) and was nearly blind.

He sued the health authority, alleging that this was due to an excess of oxygen in his bloodstream during the early weeks. The trial judge (Peter Pain J) found in his favour.

The Court of Appeal affirmed the judge's decision, in so far as it was based on negligence affecting the first period (16–17 December) though not any subsequent period. The majority held that a hospital doctor's duty of care is to be assessed in relation to the post which he occupies. It was not suggested that inserting the catheter into a vein instead of an artery amounted to negligence. The Court of Appeal held that the trial judge was right to find that Dr Kawa had been negligent in failing to appreciate that the catheter was not situated in an artery, but that Dr Wiles was entitled to rely on his work being checked by Dr Kawa and that Dr Wiles had not been negligent.

The defendant health authority appealed. There was no dispute on negligence before the House of Lords. The sole issue for their decision was causation.

Held: (i) the onus of proving causation was on the plaintiff who had to establish that the raised level of PO_2 in his arterial blood before 8.00am on 17 December 1978 probably caused or materially contributed to his RLF. The mere fact that excess oxygen was one of a number of different factors which could have caused the RLF raised no presumption that it caused or contributed to it in this case;

(ii) as the primary conflict of opinion between the experts as to whether excess oxygen during the relevant period probably caused or materially contributed to the plaintiff's RLF could not be resolved by reading the transcript of their evidence, there was no alternative but to order a retrial.
See pages 13, 25, 33, 36, 40, 45, 77, 83, 87, 89, 133.

Wilson v Tomlinson

Fracture: substandard treatment

Ashworth J. [1956] 2 The Lancet 1154

The plaintiff, a sixty-two year old woman, visited Dr Tomlinson for a course of treatment for her neck and right arm. On about the sixth visit, when she was still suffering from considerable pain, he asked her to lie on a couch in a cubicle for manipulative treatment to her neck. On the couch, which was covered in Rexine, there was a blanket which was not tied with tapes but was to some extent kept in position on the right side by a flange along the side of the cubicle against which it was pressed. The top of the couch was 2ft 9½in. from the floor, and it was impossible for the patient to reach the floor when in a sitting position.

When the treatment was finished, Dr Tomlinson indicated that she should get off the couch. The plaintiff had reached a sitting position and was swinging her legs around to the left, when the blanket came away and both she and the blanket fell to the floor. She sustained a fractured wrist and sued Dr Tomlinson.

Held: where there was a displaced or loose blanket on Rexine, a person on top of it who moved her legs around on it was likely to slip. Dr Tomlinson was dealing with a lady aged sixty-two who was not well and whose right arm was

giving her trouble. He should have known that a patient of that age and in that condition required assistance in getting off the couch. In the exercise of reasonable care, he should have placed himself at the side of the couch to help her. He had been negligent.
See page 88.

Winch v Jones and Others

Psychiatric patient: leave to sue: negligent certification

Court of Appeal. [1985] 3 All ER 97, [1985] 3 WLR 729.

In October 1978 the applicant (Mary Winch) was admitted to the North Wales Hospital for treatment pursuant to recommendations under s 26 Mental Health Act 1959. Such an admission authorised the detention of the patient for up to twelve months. The necessary recommendations were made by Dr Hayward, the medical officer of Risley Remand Centre, and Dr Bishop, a general practitioner. On admission to North Wales Hospital, the applicant came under the care of Dr Jones. She spent twelve months subject to the s 26 admission either at the hospital or on leave from it.

She applied to the High Court for leave to sue the doctors and their employers. She complained that Dr Hayward and Dr Bishop failed to exercise reasonable care in diagnosing that she suffered from paranoia and in recommending that she be admitted to a mental hospital. Her complaint against Dr Jones was that he failed to give any or adequate consideration to discharging her before the order came to an end twelve months after her admission. Otton J refused her application for leave under s 139 Mental Health Act 1983.

Held: her applications should be granted, as her complaints deserved fuller investigation.

Per Sir John Donaldson MR: "The section is intended to strike a balance between the legitimate interest of the applicant to be allowed, at his own risk as to costs, to seek the adjudication of the courts upon any claim which is not frivolous, vexatious, or an abuse of process, and the equally legitimate interests of the respondent to such an application not to be subjected to the undoubted exceptional risk of being harassed by baseless claims by those who have been treated under the Acts. In striking such a balance, the issue is not whether the applicant has established a prima-facie case or even whether there is a serious issue to be tried, although that comes close to it. The issue is whether, on the material immediately available to the court, which, of course, can include material furnished by the proposed defendants, the applicant's complaint appears to be such that it deserves the further investigation which will be possible if the intended applicant is allowed to proceed".
See page 65.

Wood v Thurston and Others

Fractures: diagnosis: casualty officer: examination: substandard treatment

Pritchard J. [1951] The Times 25 May

On 6 August 1948 John Wood had been drinking with friends after work. After leaving a public house, he crawled on all fours underneath a lorry. As he did so the lorry started to move and one of its rear wheels pinned Mr Wood to the ground, although he was released before it went completely over him.

He walked to the casualty department of Charing Cross Hospital where he was examined by Dr Thurston. He was intoxicated but not drunk. He told Mr Thurston what had happened and said that there was nothing wrong with him and that he wanted to go home. Dr Thurston treated him for a nose bleed. He felt Mr Wood's chest but in a cursory manner, and allowed him to travel in a taxi to his home.

In the early hours of 7 August, Mr Wood was admitted to West Middlesex Hospital where he died at about 7.00am. Post-mortem examination showed that he had a broken collar bone, eighteen fractured ribs and badly congested lungs. The plaintiff (his widow) sued Dr Thurston and the hospital authority.

Held: (i) Dr Thurston did not examine Mr Wood with the care that was demanded in the circumstances. If a stethoscope had been used, it was almost inevitable that Mr Wood's true condition would have been discovered;

     (ii) Mr Wood would not have died if he had been kept immobile. His death was caused by Dr Thurston's negligence.
See page 62.

Woodhouse v Yorkshire Regional Health Authority

Surgeon: operation: res ipsa loquitur: damages

Court of Appeal. 12 April 1984. [1984] 1 The Lancet 1306

On 28 January 1976 the plaintiff (Elizabeth Woodhouse), a keen pianist, was admitted to Scarborough General Hospital with a subphrenic abscess. On 31 January and 10 February she was operated on under general anaesthetics by Mr Fletcher, a consultant surgeon. Her left ulnar nerve was damaged during the first operation and her right ulnar nerve during the second. She was left with severe contracture deformities of her fingers. She also suffered from a hysterical condition.

The plaintiff sued the hospital authority. It was agreed that ulnar nerve damage is a well recognized hazard of operating under anaesthesia and great care must be taken to ensure that it does not occur. The trial judge (Russell J) found that the defendants had been negligent.

Held: (i) the plaintiff had suffered injuries which ought not to occur if standard precautions had been taken. The judge inferred that these precautions could not have been taken and, in the absence of any explanation for failing to take them, he was entitled to conclude that such a failure was negligent;

(ii) the defendants were liable for the plaintiff's hysteria as well as her organic injuries. The tortfeasor takes the victim as he finds her. The defendants had damaged a plaintiff with a hysterical personality. As a result they had caused greater damage than might have been expected, but in law they were responsible for it.

See page 98.

Worster v City and Hackney Health Authority

Sterilisation: consent: risk disclosure: representation

Garland J. [1987] The Times 22 June

The plaintiff signed a consent form for a sterilisation operation. It included the words: "This is to certify that we, the undersigned, agree to this operation of sterilisation being performed on. . . . . and we understand this means we can have no more children."

The defendant health authority's consultant gynaecologist, Mr John Woolf, did not warn the plaintiff that a sterilisation operation by the Pomeroy method was subject to a small possibility of failure.

Held: the wording on the consent form was not a negligent representation capable of being understood as an assurance of success. The plaintiff's claim was dismissed.

See pages 15, 73.

APPENDIX

List of statutory materials included in Appendix

1. Congenital Disabilities (Civil Liability) Act 1976

Civil liability to child born disabled

1.—(1) If a child is born disabled as the result of such an occurrence before its birth as is mentioned in subsection (2) below, and a person (other than the child's own mother) is under this section answerable to the child in respect of the occurrence, the child's disabilities are to be regarded as damage resulting from the wrongful act of that person and actionable accordingly at the suit of the child.

(2) An occurrence to which this section applies is one which—

   (a)   affected either parent of the child in his or her ability to have a normal, healthy child; or

   (b)   affected the mother during her pregnancy, or affected her or the child in the course of its birth, so that the child is born with disabilities which would not otherwise have been present.

(3) Subject to the following subsections, a person (here referred to as "the defendant") is answerable to the child if he was liable in tort to the parent or would, if sued in due time, have been so; and it is no answer that there could not have been such liability because the parent suffered no actionable injury, if there was a breach of legal duty which, accompanied by injury, would have given rise to the liability.

(4) In the case of an occurrence preceding the time of conception, the defendant is not answerable to the child if at that time either or both of the parents knew the risk of their child being born disabled (that is to say, the particular risk created by the occurrence); but should it be the child's father who is the defendant, this subsection does not apply if he knew of the risk and the mother did not.

(5) The defendant is not answerable to the child, for anything he did or omitted to do when responsible in a professional capacity for treating or advising the parent, if he took reasonable care having due regard to then received professional opinion applicable to the particular class of case; but this does not mean that he is answerable only because he departed from received opinion.

(6) Liability to the child under this section may be treated as having been excluded

or limited by contract made with the parent affected, to the same extent and subject to the same restrictions as liability in the parent's own case; and a contract term which could have been set up by the defendant in an action by the parent, so as to exclude or limit his liability to him or her, operates in the defendant's favour to the same, but no greater, extent in an action under this section by the child.

(7) If in the child's action under this section it is shown that the parent affected shared the responsibility for the child being born disabled, the damages are to be reduced to such extent as the court thinks just and equitable having regard to the extent of the parent's responsibility.

Liability of woman driving when pregnant

2. A woman driving a motor vehicle when she knows (or ought reasonably to know) herself to be pregnant is to be regarded as being under the same duty to take care for the safety of her unborn child as the law imposes on her with respect to the safety of other people; and if in consequence of her breach of that duty her child is born with disabilities which would not otherwise have been present, those disabilities are to be regarded as damage resulting from her wrongful act and actionable accordingly at the suit of the child.

Disabled birth due to radiation

3.—(1) Section 1 of this Act does not affect the operation of the Nuclear Installations Act 1965 as to liability for, and compensation in respect of, injury or damage caused by occurrences involving nuclear matter or the emission of ionising radiations.

(2) For the avoidance of doubt anything which—

   (a) affects a man in his ability to have a normal, healthy child; or

   (b) affects a woman in that ability, or so affects her when she is pregnant that her child is born with disabilities which would not otherwise have been present,

is an injury for the purposes of that Act.

(3) If a child is born disabled as the result of an injury to either of its parents caused in breach of a duty imposed by any of sections 7 to 11 of that (nuclear site licensees and others to secure that nuclear incidents do not cause injury to persons, etc.), the child's disabilities are to be regarded under the subsequent provisions of that Act (compensation and other matters) as injuries caused on the same occasion, and by the same breach of duty, as was the injury to the parent.

(4) As respects compensation to the child, section 13(6) of that Act (contributory fault of person injured by radiation) is to be applied as if the reference there to fault were to the fault of the parent.

(5) Compensation is not payable in the child's case if the injury to the parent preceded the time of he child's conception and at that time either or both of the parents knew the risk of their child being born disabled (that is to say, the particular risk created by the injury).

Interpretation and other supplementary provisions

4.—(1) References in this Act to a child being born disabled or with disabilities are to its being born with any deformity, disease or abnormality, including predisposition (whether or not susceptible of immediate prognosis) to physical or mental defect in the future.

(2) In this Act—

   (a) "born" means born alive (the moment of a child's birth being when it first

has a life separate from its mother), and "birth" has a corresponding meaning; and

    (b) "motor vehicle" means a mechanically propelled vehicle intended or adapted for use on roads.

(3) Liability to a child under section 1 or 2 of this Act is to be regarded—

    (a) as respects all its incidents and any matters arising or to arise out of it; and

    (b) subject to any contrary context or intention, for the purpose of construing references in enactments and documents to personal or bodily injuries and cognate matters,

as liability for personal injuries sustained by the child immediately after its birth.

(4) No damages shall be recoverable under either of those sections in respect of any loss of expectation of life, nor shall any such loss be taken into account in the compensation payable in respect of a child under the Nuclear Installations Act 1965 as extended by section 3, unless (in either case) the child lives for at least 48 hours.

(5) This Act applies in respect of births after (but not before) its passing, and in respect of any such birth it replaces any law in force before its passing, whereby a person could be liable to a child in respect of disabilities with which it might be born; but in section 1 (3) of this Act the expression "liable in tort" does not include any reference to liability by virtue of this Act, or to liability by virtue of any such law.

(6) References to the Nuclear Installations Act 1965 are to that Act as amended; and for the purposes of section 28 of that Act (power by Order in Council to extend the Act to territories outside the United Kingdom) section 3 of this Act is to be treated as if it were a provision of that Act.

Crown application

5. This Act binds the Crown.

Citation and extent

    6.—(1) This Act may be cited as the Congenital Disabilities (Civil Liability) Act 1976.

    (2) This Act extends to Northern Ireland but not to Scotland.

2. Limitation Act 1980

Sections 1, 2, 5, 10, 11, 12, 13, 14, 28, 32, 33, 35 and 38

(As amended by, *inter alia*, the Mental Health Act 1983, Administration of Justice Act 1985, Latent Damage Act 1986 and Consumer Protection Act 1987)

PART I
ORDINARY TIME LIMITS FOR DIFFERENT CLASSES OF ACTION

Time limits under Part I subject to extension or exclusion under Part II

1.—(1) This Part of this Act gives the ordinary time limits for bringing actions of the various classes mentioned in the following provisions of this Part.

(2) The ordinary time limits given in this Part of this Act are subject to extension or exclusion in accordance with the provisions of Part II of this Act.

Actions founded on tort

2. An action founded on tort shall not be brought after the expiration of six years from the date on which the cause of action accrued.

Actions founded on simple contract

5. An action founded on simple contract shall not be brought after the expiration of six years from the date on which the cause of action accrued.

Actions for sums recoverable by statute

10.—(1) Where under section 1 of the Civil Liability (Contribution) Act 1978 any person becomes entitled to a right to recover contribution in respect of any damage from any other person, no action to recover contribution by virtue of that right shall be brought after the expiration of two years from the date on which that right accrued.

(2) For the purposes of this section the date on which a right to recover contribution in respect of any damage accrues to any person (referred to below in this section as "the relevant date") shall be ascertained as provided in subsections (3) and (4) below.

(3) If the person in question is held liable in respect of that damage—

    (a) by a judgment given in any civil proceedings; or

    (b) by an award made on any arbitration;

the relevant date shall be the date on which the judgment is given, or the date of the award (as the case may be).

For the purposes of this subsection no account shall be taken of any judgment or award given or made on appeal in so far as it varies the amount of damages awarded against the person in question.

(4) If, in any case not within subsection (3) above, the person in question makes or agrees to make any payment to one or more persons in compensation for that damage (whether he admits any liability in respect of the damage or not), the relevant date shall be the earliest date on which the amount to be paid by him is agreed between him (or his representative) and the person (or each of the persons, as the case may be) to whom the payment is to be made.

(5) An action to recover contribution shall be one to which sections 28, 32, 35 of this Act apply, but otherwise Parts II and III of this Act (except sections 34, 37 and 38) shall not apply for the purposes of this section.

Actions in respect of wrongs causing personal injuries or death

11.—(1) This section applies to any action for damages for negligence, nuisance or breach of duty (whether the duty exists by virtue of a contract or of provision made by or under a statute or independently of any contract or any such provision) where the damages claimed by the plaintiff for the negligence, nuisance or breach of duty consist of or include damages in respect of personal injuries to the plaintiff or any other person.

(2) None of the time limits given in the preceding provisions of this Act shall apply to an action to which this section applies.

(3) An action to which this section applies shall not be brought after the expiration of the period applicable in accordance with subsection (4) or (5) below.

(4) Except where subsection (5) below applies, the period applicable is three years from—

    (a)   the date on which the cause of action accrued; or

    (b)   the date of knowledge (if later) of the person injured.

(5) If the person injured dies before the expiration of the period mentioned in subsection (4) above, the period applicable as respects the cause of action surviving for the benefit of his estate by virtue of section 1 of the Law Reform (Miscellaneous Provisions) Act 1934 shall be three years from—

    (a)   the date of death; or

    (b)   the date of the personal representative's knowledge; whichever is the later.

(6) For the purposes of this section "personal representative" includes any person who is or has been a personal representative of the deceased, including an executor who has not proved the will (whether or not he has renounced probate) but not anyone appointed only as a special personal representative in relation to settled land; and regard shall be had to any knowledge acquired by any such person while a personal representative or previously.

(7) If there is more than one personal representative, and their dates of knowledge are different, subsection (5)*(b)*above shall be read as referring to the earliest of those dates.

11A.—(1) This section shall apply to an action for damages by virtue of any provision of Part I of the Consumer Protection Act 1987.

(2) None of the time limits given in the preceding provisions of this Act shall apply. to an action to which this section applies.

(3) An action to which this section applies shall not be brought after the expiration of the period of ten years from the relevant time, within the meaning of section 4 of the said Act of 1987; and this subsection shall operate to extinguish a right of action and shall do so whether or not that right of action had accrued, or time under the following provisions of this Act had begun to run, at the end of the said period of ten years.

(4) Subject to subsection (5) below, an action to which this section applies in which the damages claimed by the plaintiff consist of or include damages in respect of personal injuries to the plaintiff or any other person or loss of or damage to any property, shall not be brought after the expiration of the period of three years from whichever is the later of—

    (a)   the date on which the cause of action accrued; and

    (b)   the date of knowledge of the injured person or, in the case of loss of or damage to property, the date of knowledge of the plaintiff or (if earlier) of any person in whom his cause of action was previously vested.

(5) If in a case where the damages claimed by the plaintiff consist of or include damages in respect of personal injuries to the plaintiff or any other person the injured person died before the expiration of the period mentioned in subsection (4) above, that subsection shall have effect as respects the cause of action surviving for the benefit of his estate by virtue of section 1 of the Law Reform (Miscellaneous Provisions) Act

1934 as if for the reference to that period there were substituted a reference to the period of three years from whichever is the later of—

    (a)   the date of death; and

    (b)   the date of the personal representative's knowledge.

(6) For the purposes of this section 'personal representative' includes any person who is or has been a personal representative of the deceased, including an executor who has not proved the will (whether or not he has renounced probate) but not anyone appointed only as a special personal representative in relation to settled land; and regard shall be had to any knowledge acquired by any such person while a personal representative or previously.

(7) If there is more than one personal representative and their dates of knowledge are different, subsection (5)*(b)* above shall be read as referring to the earliest of those dates.

(8) Expressions used in this section or section 14 of this Act and in Part I of the Consumer Protection Act 1987 have the same meanings in this section or that section as in that Part; and section 1(1) of that Act (Part I to be construed as enacted for the purpose of complying with the product liability Directive) shall apply for the purpose of construing this section and the following provisions of this Act so far as they relate to an action by virtue of any provision of that Part as it applies for the purpose of construing that Part."

Actions under the Fatal Accidents Act 1976

12 (1) An action under the Fatal Accidents Act 1976 shall not be brought if the death occurred when the person injured could no longer maintain an action and recover damages in respect of the injury (whether because of a time limit in this Act or in any other Act, or for any other reason).

Where any such action by the injured person would have been barred by the time limit in section 11 or 11A of this Act, no account shall be taken of the possibility of that time limit being overridden under section 33 of this Act.

(2) None of the time limits given in the preceding provisions of this Act shall apply to an action under the Fatal Accidents Act 1976, but no such action shall be brought after the expiration of three years from—

    (a)   the date of death; or

    (b)   the date of knowledge of the person for whose benefit the action is brought;

whichever is the later.

(3) An action under the Fatal Accidents Act 1976 shall be one to which sections 28, 33 and 35 of this Act apply, and the application to any such action of the time limit under subsection (2) above shall be subject to section 39; but otherwise Parts II and III of this Act shall not apply to any such action.

Actions under s 12 in relation to different dependants

13.—(1) Where there is more than one person for whose benefit an action under the Fatal Accidents Act 1976 is brought, section 12(2)*(b)* of this Act shall be applied separately to each of them.

(2) Subject to subsection (3) below, if by virtue of subsection (1) above the action would be outside the time limit given by section 12(2) as regards one or more, but not all, of the persons for whose benefit it is brought, the court shall direct that any person as regards whom the action would be outside that limit shall be excluded from those for whom the action is brought.

(3) The court shall not give such a direction if it is shown that if the action were brought exclusively for the benefit of the person in question it would not be defeated

by a defence of limitation (whether in consequence of section 28 of this Act or an agreement between the parties not to raise the defence, or otherwise).

Definition of date of knowledge for purposes of sections 11 and 12

14 (1) Subject to subsection 1A below, in sections 11 and 12 of this Act references to a person's date of knowledge are references to the date on which he first had knowledge of the following facts—

(a) that the injury in question was significant; and

(b) that the injury was attributable in whole or in part to the act or omission which is alleged to constitute negligence, nuisance or breach of duty; and

(c) the identity of the defendant; and

(d) if it is alleged that the act or omission was that of a person other than the defendant, the identity of that person and the additional facts supporting the bringing of an action against the defendant;

and knowledge that any acts or omissions did or did not, as a matter of law, involve negligence, nuisance or breach of duty is irrelevant.

(1A) In section 11A of this Act and in section 12 of this Act so far as that section applies to an action by virtue of section 6(1)(a) of the Consumer Protection Act 1987 (death caused by defective product) references to a person's date of knowledge are references to the date on which he first had knowledge of the following facts—

(a) such facts about the damage caused by the defect as would lead a reasonable person who had suffered such damage to consider it sufficiently serious to justify his instituting proceedings for damages against a defendant who did not dispute liability and was able to satisfy a judgment; and

(b) that the damage was wholly or partly attributable to the facts and circumstances alleged to constitute the defect; and

(c) the identity of the defendant;

but, in determining the date on which a person first had such knowledge there shall be disregarded both the extent (if any) of that person's knowledge on any date of whether particular facts or circumstances would or would not, as a matter of law, constitute a defect and, in a case relating to loss of or damage to property, any knowledge which that person had on a date on which he had no right of action by virtue of Part I of that Act in respect of the loss or damage.

(2) For the purposes of this section an injury is significant if the person whose date of knowledge is in question would reasonably have considered it sufficiently serious to justify his instituting proceedings for damages against a defendant who did not dispute liability and was able to satisfy a judgment.

(3) For the purposes of this section a person's knowledge includes knowledge which he might reasonably have been expected to acquire—

(a) from facts observable or ascertainable by him; or

(b) from facts ascertainable by him with the help of medical or other appropriate expert advice which it is reasonable for him to seek;

but a person shall not be fixed under this subsection with knowledge of a fact ascertainable only with the help of expert advice so long as he has taken all reasonable steps to obtain (and, where appropriate, to act on) that advice.

Special time limit for negligence actions where facts relevant to cause of action are not known at date of accrual

14A (1) This section applies to any action for damages for negligence, other than one to which section 11 of this Act applies, where the starting date for reckoning the period of limitation under subsection (4)*(b)* below falls after the date on which the cause of action accrued.

(2) Section 2 of this Act shall not apply to an action to which this section applies.

(3) An action to which this section applies shall not be brought after the expiration of the period applicable in accordance with subsection (4) below.

(4) That period is either—

    (a)   six years from the date on which the cause of action accrued; or

    (b)   three years from the starting date as defined by subsection (5) below, if that period expires later than the period mentioned in paragraph *(a)* above.

(5) For the purposes of this section, the starting date for reckoning the period of limitation under subsection (4) *(b)* above is the earliest date on which the plaintiff or any person in whom the cause of action was vested before him first had both the knowledge required for bringing an action for damages in respect of the relevant damage and a right to bring such an action.

(6) In subsection (5) above "the knowledge required for bringing an action for damages in respect of the relevant damage" means knowledge both—

    (a)   of the material facts about the damage in respect of which damages are claimed; and

    (b)   of the other facts relevant to the current action mentioned in subsection (8) below.

(7) For the purposes of subsection (6) *(a)* above, the material facts about the damage are such facts about the damage as would lead a reasonable person who had suffered such damage to consider it sufficiently serious to justify his instituting proceedings for damages against a defendant who did not dispute liability and was able to satisfy a judgment.

(8) The other facts referred to in subsection (6) *(b)* above are—

    (a)   that the damage was attributable in whole or in part to the act or omission which is alleged to constitute negligence; and

    (b)   the identity of the defendant; and

    (c)   if it is alleged that the act or omission was that of a person other than the defendant, the identity of that person and the additional facts supporting the bringing of an action against the defendant.

(9) Knowledge that any acts or omissions did or did not, as a matter of law, involve negligence is irrelevant for the purposes of subsection (5) above.

(10) For the purposes of this section a person's knowledge includes knowledge which he might reasonably have been expected to acquire—

    (a)   from facts observable or ascertainable by him; or

    (b)   from facts ascertainable by him with the help of appropriate expert advice which it is reasonable for him to seek;

but a person shall not be taken by virtue of this subsection to have knowledge of a fact ascertainable only with the help of expert advice so long as he has taken all reasonable steps to obtain (and, where appropriate, to act on) that advice.

Overriding time limit for negligence actions not involving personal injuries

14B (1) An action for damages for negligence, other than one to which section 11 of this Act applies, shall not be brought after the expiration of fifteen years from the date (or, if more than one, from the last of the dates) on which there occurred any act or omission—

    (a)   which is alleged to constitute negligence; and

(b) to which the damage in respect of which damages are claimed is alleged to be attributable (in whole or in part).

(2) This section bars the right of action in a case to which subsection (1) above applies notwithstanding that—

(a) the cause of action has not yet accrued; or

(b) where section 14A of this Act applies to the action, the date which is for the purposes of that section the starting date for reckoning the period mentioned in subsection (4) *(b)* of that section has not yet occurred;

before the end of the period of limitation prescribed by this section.

PART II
EXTENSION OR EXCLUSION OF ORDINARY TIME LIMITS

Extension of limitation period in case of disability

28 (1) Subject to the following provisions of this section, if on the date when any right of action accrued for which a period of limitation is prescribed by this Act, the person to whom it accrued was under a disability, the action may be brought at any time before the expiration of six years from the date when he ceased to be under a disability or died (whichever first occurred) notwithstanding that the period of limitation has expired.

(2) This section shall not affect any case where the right of action first accrued to some person (not under a disability) through whom the person under a disability claims.

(3) When a right of action which has accrued to a person under a disability accrues, on the death of that person while still under a disability, to another person under a disability, no further extension of time shall be allowed by reason of the disability of the second person.

(4) No action to recover land or money charged on land shall be brought by virtue of this section by any person after the expiration of thirty years from the date on which the right of action accrued to that person or some person through whom he claims.

(4A) If the action is one to which section 4A of this Act applies, subsection (1) above shall have effect as if for the words from "at any time" to "occurred)" there were substituted the words "by him at any time before the expiration of three years from the date when he ceased to be under a disability."

(5) If the action is one to which section 10 of this Act applies, subsection (1) above shall have effect as if for the words "six years" there were substituted the words "two years".

(6) If the action is one to which section 11 or 12(2) of this Act applies, subsection (1) above shall have effect as if for the words "six years" there were substituted the words "three years".

(7) If the action is one to which section 11A of this Act applies or one by virtue of section 6(1) (a) of the Consumer Protection Act 1987 (death caused by defective product), subsection (1) above—

(a) shall not apply to the time limit prescribed by subsection (3) of the said section 11A or to that time limit as applied by virtue of section 2(1) of this Act; and

(b) in relation to any other time limit prescribed by this Act shall have effect as if for the word "six years" there were substituted the words "three years".

Extension for cases where the limitation period is the period under section 14A (4)(b)

28A (1) Subject to subsection (2) below, if in the case of any action for which a period of limitation is prescribed by section 14A of this Act—

(a) the period applicable in accordance with subsection (4) of that section is the period mentioned in paragraph *(b)* of that subsection;

(b) on the date which is for the purposes of that section the starting date for reckoning that period the person by reference to whose knowledge that date fell to be determined under subsection (5) of that section was under a disability; and

(c) section 28 of this Act does not apply to the action;

the action may be brought at any time before the expiration of three years from the date when he ceased to be under a disability or died (whichever first occurred) notwithstanding that the period mentioned above has expired.

(2) An action may not be brought by virtue of subsection (1) above after the end of the period of limitation prescribed by section 14B of this Act.

Postponement of limitation period in case of fraud, concealment and mistake

32 (1) Subject to subections (3) and (4A) below, where in the case of any action for which a period of limitation is prescribed by this Act, either—

(a) the action is based upon the fraud of the defendant; or

(b) any fact relevant to the plaintiff's right of action has been deliberately concealed from him by the defendant; or

(c) the action is for relief from the consequences of a mistake;

the period of limitation shall not begin to run until the plaintiff has discovered the fraud, concealment or mistake (as the case may be) or could with reasonable diligence have discovered it.

References in this subsection to the defendant include references to the defendant's agent and to any person through whom the defendant claims and his agent.

(2) For the purposes of subsection (1) above, deliberate commission of a breach of duty in circumstances in which it is unlikely to be discovered for some time amounts to deliberate concealment of the facts involved in that breach of duty.

(3) Nothing in this section shall enable any action—

(a) to recover, or recover the value of, any property; or

(b) to enforce any charge against, or set aside any transaction affecting, any property;

to be brought against the purchaser of the property or any person claiming through him in any case where the property has been purchased for valuable consideration by an innocent third party since the fraud or concealment or (as the case may be) the transaction in which the mistake was made took place.

(4) A purchaser is an innocent third party for the purposes of this section—

(a) in the case of fraud or concealment of any fact relevant to the plaintiff's right of action, if he was not a party to the fraud or (as the case may be) to the concealment of that fact and did not at the time of the purchase know or have reason to believe that the fraud or concealment had taken place; and

(b) in the case of mistake, if he did not at the time of the purchase know or have reason to believe that the mistake had been made.

(4A) Subsection (1) above shall not apply in relation to the time limit prescribed by section 11A (3) of this Act or in relation to that time limit as applied by virtue of section 12(1) of this Act.

(5) Sections 14A and 14B of this Act shall not apply to any action to which subsection (1)*(b)* above applies (and accordingly the period of limitation referred to in that subsection, in any case to which either of those sections would otherwise apply, is the period applicable under section 2 of this Act).

Discretionary exclusion of time limit for actions in respect of personal injuries or death

33 (1) If it appears to the court that it would be equitable to allow an action to proceed having regard to the degree to which—

    (a)   the provisions of section 11 or 11A or 12 of this Act prejudice the plaintiff or any person whom he represents; and

    (b)   any decision of the court under this subsection would prejudice the defendant or any person whom he represents;

the court may direct that those provisions shall not apply to the action, or shall not apply to any specified cause of action to which the action relates.

(1A) The court shall not under this section disapply—

    (a)   subsection (3) of section 11A; or

    (b)   where the damages claimed by the plaintiff are confined to damages for loss of or damage to any property, any other provision in its application to an action by virtue of Part I of the Consumer Protection Act 1987.

(2) The court shall not under this section disapply section 12(1) except where the reason why the person injured could no longer maintain an action was because of the time limit in section 11 or subsection (4) of section 11A.

If, for example, the person injured could at his death no longer maintain an action under the Fatal Accidents Act 1976 because of the time limit in Article 29 in Schedule 1 to the Carriage by Air Act 1961, the court has no power to direct that section 12(1) shall not apply.

(3) In acting under this section the court shall have regard to all the circumstances of the case and in particular to—

    (a)   the length of, and the reasons for, the delay on the part of the plaintiff;

    (b)   the extent to which, having regard to the delay, the evidence adduced or likely to be adduced by the plaintiff or the defendant is or is likely to be less cogent than if the action had been brought within the time allowed by section 11, by section 11A or (as the case may be) by section 12;

    (c)   the conduct of the defendant after the cause of action arose, including the extent (if any) to which he responded to requests reasonably made by the plaintiff for information or inspection for the purpose of ascertaining facts which were or might be relevant to the plaintiff's cause of action against the defendant;

    (d)   the duration of any disability of the plaintiff arising after the date of the accrual of the cause of action;

    (e)   the extent to which the plaintiff acted promptly and reasonably once he knew whether or not the act or omission of the defendant, to which the injury was attributable, might be capable at that time of giving rise to an action for damages;

    (f)   the steps, if any, taken by the plaintiff to obtain medical, legal or other expert advice and the nature of any such advice he may have received.

(4) In a case where the person injured died when, because of section 11 or subsection (4) of section 11A, he could no longer maintain an action and recover damages in respect of the injury, the court shall have regard in particular to the length of, and the reasons for, the delay on the part of the deceased.

(5) In a case under subsection (4) above, or any other case where the time limit, or one of the time limits, depends on the date of knowledge of a person other than the plaintiff, subsection (3) above shall have effect with appropriate modifications, and shall have effect in particular as if references to the plaintiff included references to any person whose date of knowledge is or was relevant in determining a time limit.

(6) A direction by the court disapplying the provisions of section 12(1) shall operate to disapply the provisions to the same effect in section 1(1) of the Fatal Accidents Act 1976.

(7) In this section "the court" means the court in which the action has been brought.

(8) References in this section to section 11 or 11A include references to that section as extended by any of the preceding provisions of this Part of this Act or by any provision of Part III of this Act.

PART III
MISCELLANEOUS AND GENERAL

New claims in pending actions: rules of court

35.—(1) For the purposes of this Act, any new claim made in the course of any action shall be deemed to be a separate action and to have been commenced—

    (a)   in the case of a new claim made in or by way of third party proceedings, on the date on which those proceedings were commenced; and

    (b)   in the case of any other new claim, on the same date as the original action.

(2) In this section a new claim means any claim by way of set-off or counterclaim, and any claim involving either—

    (a)   the addition or substitution of a new cause of action; or

    (b)   the addition or substitution of a new party;

and "third party proceedings" means any proceedings brought in the course of any action by any party to the action against a person not previously a party to the action, other than proceedings brought by joining any such person as defendant to any claim already made in the original action by the party bringing the proceedings.

(3) Except as provided by section 33 of this Act or by rules of court, neither the High Court nor any county court shall allow a new claim within subsection (1)*(b)*above, other than an original set-off or counterclaim, to be made in the course of any action after the expiry of any time limit under this Act which would affect a new action to enforce that claim.

For the purposes of this subsection, a claim is an original set-off or an original counterclaim if it is a claim made by way of set-off or (as the case may be) by way of counterclaim by a party who has not previously made any claim in the action.

(4) Rules of court may provide for allowing a new claim to which subsection (3) above applies to be made as there mentioned, but only if the conditions specified in subsection (5) below are satisfied, and subject to any further restrictions the rules may impose.

(5) The conditions referred to in subsection (4) above are the following—

    (a)   in the case of a claim involving a new cause of action, if the new cause of action arises out of the same facts or substantially the same facts as are already in issue on any claim previously made in the original action; and

    (b)   in the case of a claim involving a new party, if the addition or substitution of the new party is necessary for the determination of the original action.

(6) The addition or substitution of a new party shall not be regarded for the purposes of subsection (5)*(b)* above as necessary for the determination of the original action unless either—

(a) the new party is substituted for a party whose name was given in any claim made in the original action in mistake for the new party's name; or

(b) any claim already made in the original action cannot be maintained by or against an existing party unless the new party is joined or substituted as plaintiff or defendant in that action.

(7) Subject to subsection (4) above, rules of court may provide for allowing a party to any action to claim relief in a new capacity in respect of a new cause of action notwithstanding that he had no title to make that claim at the date of the commencement of the action.

This subsection shall not be taken as prejudicing the power of rules of court to provide for allowing a party to claim relief in a new capacity without adding or substituting a new cause of action.

(8) Subsections (3) to (7) above shall apply in relation to a new claim made in the course of third party proceedings as if those proceedings were the original action and subject to such other modifications as may be prescribed by rules of court in any case or class of case.

Interpretation

38.—(1) In this Act, unless the context otherwise requires—

"action" includes any proceeding in a court of law, including an ecclesiastical court;

"land" includes corporeal hereditaments, tithes and rent-charges and any legal or equitable estate or interest therein, including an interest in the proceeds of the sale of land held upon trust for sale, but except as provided above in this definition does not include any incorporeal hereditament;

"personal estate" and "personal property" do not include chattels real;

"personal injuries" includes any disease and any impairment of a person's physical or mental condition, and "injury" and cognate expressions shall be construed accordingly;

"rent" includes a rentcharge and a rentservice;

"rentcharge" means any annuity or periodical sum of money charged upon or payable out of land, except a rent service or interest on a mortgage on land;

"settled land", "statutory owner" and "tenant for life" have the same meanings respectively as in the Settled Land Act 1925;

"trust" and "trustee" have the same meanings respectively as in the Trustee Act 1925; and

"trust for sale" has the same meaning as in the Law of Property Act 1925.

(2) For the purposes of this Act a person shall be treated as under a disability while he is an infant, or of unsound mind.

(3) For the purposes of subsection (2) above a person is of unsound mind if he is a person who, by reason of mental disorder within the meaning of the Mental Health Act 1983, is incapable of managing and administering his property and affairs.

(4) Without prejudice to the generality of subsection (3) above, a person shall be conclusively presumed for the purposes of subsection (2) above to be of unsound mind—

(a) while he is liable to be detained or subject to guardianship under [the Mental Health Act 1983 (otherwise than by virtue of section 35 or 89)]; and

    (b)   while he is receiving treatment as an in-patient in any hospital within the meaning of the Mental Health Act 1983 or mental nursing home within the meaning of the Nursing Homes Act 1975 without being liable to be detained under the said Act of 1983 (otherwise than by virtue of section 35 or 89), being treatment which follows without any interval a period during which he was liable to be detained or subject to guardianship under the Mental Health Act 1959, or the said Act of 1983 (otherwise than by virtue of section 35 or 89) or by virtue of any enactment repealed or excluded by the Mental Health Act 1959.

3. Administration of Justice Act 1982
Sections 1–6
(Including amendments of Fatal Accidents Act 1976)

PART I
DAMAGES FOR PERSONAL INJURIES ETC.

Abolition of right to damages for loss of expectation of life

1.—(1) In an action under the law of England and Wales or the law of Northern Ireland for damages for personal injuries—

> (a) no damages shall be recoverable in respect of any loss of expectation of life caused to the injured person by the injuries; but

> (b) if the injured person's expectation of life has been reduced by the injuries, the court, in assessing damages in respect of pain and suffering caused by the injuries, shall take account of any suffering caused or likely to be caused to him by awareness that his expectation of life has been so reduced.

(2) The reference in subsection (1)(*a*) above to damages in respect of loss of expectation of life does not include damages in respect of loss of income.

Abolition of actions for loss of services etc.

2. No person shall be liable in tort under the law of England and Wales or the law of Northern Ireland—

> (a) to a husband on the ground only of his having deprived him of the services or society of his wife;

> (b) to a parent (or person standing in the place of a parent) on the ground only of his having deprived him of the services of a child; or

> (c) on the ground only—

>> (i) of having deprived another of the services of his menial servant;

>> (ii) of having deprived another of the services of his female servant by raping or seducing her; or

>> (iii) of enticement of a servant or harbouring a servant.

Fatal Accidents Act 1976

3.—(1) The following sections shall be substituted for sections 1 to 4 of the Fatal Accidents Act 1976—

"**1.**—(1) If death is caused by any wrongful act, neglect or default which is such as would (if death had not ensued) have entitled the person injured to maintain an action and recover damages in respect thereof, the person who would have been liable if death had not ensued shall be liable to an action for damages, nowithstanding the death of the person injured.

(2) Subject to section 1A(2) below, every such action shall be for the benefit of the dependants of the person ("the deceased") whose death has been so caused.

(3) In this Act "dependant" means—

> (a) the wife or husband or former wife or husband of the deceased;

> (b) any person who—

>> (i) was living with the deceased in the same household immediately before the date of the death; and

>> (ii) had been living with the deceased in the same household for at least two years before that date; and

      (iii) was living during the whole of that period as the husband or wife of the deceased;

(c)   any parent or other ascendant of the deceased;

(d)   any person who was treated by the deceased as his parent;

(e)   any child or other descendant of the deceased;

(f)   any person (not being a child of the deceased) who, in the case of any marriage to which the deceased was at any time a party, was treated by the deceased as a child of the family in relation to that marriage;

(g)   any person who is, or is the issue of, a brother, sister, uncle or aunt of the deceased.

(4) The reference to the former wife or husband of the deceased in subsection (3)*(a)* above includes a reference to a person whose marriage to the deceased has been annulled or declared void as well as a person whose marriage to the deceased has been dissolved.

(5) In deducing any relationship for the purposes of subsection (3) above—

(a)   any relationship by affinity shall be treated as a relationship by consanguinity, any relationship of the half blood as a relationship of the whole blood, and the stepchild of any person as his child, and

(b)   an illegitimate person shall be treated as the legitimate child of his mother and reputed father.

(6) Any reference in this Act to injury includes any disease and any impairment of a person's physical or mental condition.

Bereavement

1A.—(1) An action under this Act may consist of or include a claim for damages for bereavement.

(2) A claim for damages for bereavement shall only be for the benefit—

(a)   of the wife or husband of the deceased; and

(b)   where the deceased was a minor who was never married—

      (i) of his parents, if he was legitimate; and

      (ii) of his mother, if he was illegitimate.

(3) Subject to subsection (5) below, the sum to be awarded as damages under this section shall be £3,500.

(4) Where there is a claim for damages under this section for the benefit of both the parents of the deceased, the sum awarded shall be divided equally between them (subject to any deduction falling to be made in respect of costs not recovered from the defendant).

(5) The Lord Chancellor may by order made by statutory instrument, subject to annulment in pursuance of a resolution of either House of Parliament, amend this section by varying the sum for the time being specified in subsection (3) above.

Persons entitled to bring the action

2..—(1) The action shall be brought by and in the name of the executor or administrator of the deceased.

(2) If—

(a)   there is no executor or administrator of the deceased, or

(b)   no action is brought within six months after the death by and in the name of an executor or administrator of the deceased,

the action may be brought by and in the name of all or any of the persons for whose benefit an executor or administrator could have brought it.

(3) Not more than one action shall lie for and in respect of the same subject matter of complaint.

(4) The plaintiff in the action shall be required to deliver to the defendant or his solicitor full particulars of the persons for whom and on whose behalf the action is brought and of the nature of the claim in respect of which damages are sought to be recovered.

Assessment of damages

3.—(1) In the action such damages, other than damages for bereavement may be awarded as are proportioned to the injury resulting from the death to the dependants respectively.

(2) After deducting the costs not recovered from the defendant any amount recovered otherwise than as damages for bereavement shall be divided among the dependants in such shares as may be directed.

(3) In an action under this Act where there fall to be assessed damages payable to a widow in respect of the death of her husband there shall not be taken account the re-marriage of the widow or her prospects of re-marriage.

(4) In an action under this Act where there fall to be assessed damages payable to a person who is a dependant by virtue of section 1(3)*(b)* above in respect of the death of the person with whom the dependant was living as husband or wife there shall be taken into account (together with any other matter that appears to the court to be relevant to the action) the fact that the dependant had no enforceable right to financial support by the deceased as a result of their living together.

(5) If the dependants have incurred funeral expenses in respect of the deceased, damages may be awarded in respect of those expenses.

(6) Money paid into court in satisfaction of a cause of action under this Act may be in one sum without specifying any person's share.

Assessment of damages: disregard of benefits

4. In assessing damages in respect of a person's death in an action under this Act, benefits which have accrued or will or may accrue to any person from his estate or otherwise as a result of his death shall be disregarded."

(2) In section 5 of the Fatal Accidents Act 1976 the words "brought for the benefit of the dependants of that person" shall be omitted.

Claims not surviving death

4.—(1) The following subsection shall be inserted after section 1(1) of the Law Reform (Miscellaneous Provisions) Act 1934 (actions to survive death)—

"(1A) The right of a person to claim under section 1A of the Fatal Accidents Act 1976 (bereavement) shall not survive for the benefit of his estate on his death.".

(2) The following paragraph shall be substituted for subsection (2)*(a)*—

"*(a)* shall not include—
    (i) any exemplary damages;
    (ii) any damages for loss of income in respect of any period after that person's death;".

Maintenance at public expense

5. In an action under the law of England and Wales or the law of Northern Ireland for damages for personal injuries (including any such action arising out of a contract) any saving to the injured person which is attributable to his maintenance wholly or partly at public expense in a hospital, nursing home or other institution shall be set off against any income lost by him as a result of his injuries.

Provisional damages for personal injuries

6.—(1) The following section shall be inserted after section 32 of the Supreme Court Act 1981—

"**32A.**—(1) This section applies to an action for damages for personal injuries in which there is proved or admitted to be a chance that at some definite or indefinite time in the future the injured person will, as a result of the act or omission which gave rise to the cause of action, develop some serious disease or suffer some serious deterioration in his physical or mental condition.

(2) Subject to subsection (4) below, as regards any action for damages to which this section applies in which a judgment is given in the High Court, provision may be made by rules of court for enabling the court, in such circumstances as may be prescribed, to award the injured person—

(a) damages assessed on the assumption that the injured person will not develop the disease or suffer the deterioration in his condition; and

(b) further damages at a future date if he develops the disease or suffers the deterioration.

(3) Any rules made by virtue of this section may include such incidental, supplementary and consequential provisions as the rule-making authority may consider necessary or expedient.

(4) Nothing in this section shall be construed—

(a) as affecting the exercise of any power relating to costs, including any power to make rules of court relating to costs; or

(b) as prejudicing any duty of the court under any enactment or rule of law to reduce or limit the total damages which would have been recoverable apart from any such duty."

(2) In section 35 of that Act (supplementary) "32A," shall be inserted before "33" in subsection (5).

(3) The section inserted as section 32A of the Supreme Court Act 1981 by subsection (1) above shall have effect in relation to county courts as it has effect in relation to the High Court, as if references in it to rules of court included references to county court rules.

4. Supreme Court Act 1981
Sections 32–35
(Corresponding to ss 50–54 County Courts Act 1984)

Orders for interim payment

32.—(1) As regards proceedings pending in the High Court provision may be made by rules of court for enabling the court in such circumstances as may be prescribed, to make an order requiring a party to the proceedings to make an interim payment of such amount as may be specified in the order, with provisions for the payment to be made to such other party to the proceedings as may be so specified or, if the order so provides, by paying into court.

(2) Any rules of court which make provisions in accordance with subsection (1) may include provision for enabling a party to any proceedings who, in pursuance of such an order, has made an interim payment to recover the whole or part of the amount of the payment in such circumstances, and from such other party to the proceedings, as may be determined in accordance with the rules.

(3) Any rules made by virtue of this section may include such incidental, supplementary and consequential provisions as the rule – making authority may consider necessary or expedient.

(4) Nothing in this section shall be construed as affecting the exercise of any power relating to costs, including any power to make rules of court relating to costs.

(5) In this section "interim payment", in relation to a party to any proceedings, means a payment on account of any damages, debt or other sum (excluding any costs) which that party may be held liable to pay to or for the benefit of another party to the proceedings if a final judgment or order of the court in the proceedings is given or made in favour of that other party.

N.B. The corresponding county court section is s 50 of the County Courts Act 1984.

Orders for provisional damages for personal injuries

32A.—(1) This section applies to an action for damages for personal injuries in which there is proved or admitted to be a chance that at some definite or indefinite time in the future the injured person will, as a result of the act or omission which gave rise to the cause of action, develop some serious disease or suffer some serious deterioration in his physical or mental condition.

(2) Subject to subsection (4) below, as regards any action for damages to which this section applies in which a judgment is given in the High Court, provision may be made by rules of court for enabling the court, in such circumstances as may be prescribed, to award the injured person—

(a) damages assessed on the assumption that the injured person will not develop the disease or suffer the deterioration in his condition; and

(b) further damages at a future date if he develops the disease or suffers the deterioration.

(3) Any rules made by virtue of this section may include such incidental, supplementary and consequential provisions as the rule-making authority may consider necessary or expedient.

(4) Nothing in this section shall be construed—

(a) as affecting the exercise of any power relating to costs, including any power to make rules of court relating to costs; or

(b) as prejudicing any duty of the court under any enactment or rule of law to reduce or limit the total damages which would have been recoverable apart from any such duty.

N.B. The corresponding county court section is s 51 of the County Courts Act 1984.

Powers of High Court exercisable before commencement of action

33.—(1) On the application of any person in accordance with rules of court, the High Court shall, in such circumstances as may be specified in the rules, have power to make an order providing for any one or more of the following matters, that is to say—

(a) the inspection, photographing, preservation, custody and detention of property which appears to the court to be property which may become the subject-matter of subsequent proceedings in the High Court, or as to which any question may arise in any such proceedings; and

(b) the taking of samples of any such property as is mentioned in paragraph (a), and the carrying out of any experiment on or with any such property.

(2) On the application, in accordance with rules of court, of a person who appears to the High Court to be likely to be a party to subsequent proceedings in that court in which a claim in respect of personal injuries to a person, or in respect of a person's death, is likely to be made, the High Court shall, in such circumstances as may be specified in the rules, have power to order a person who appears to the court to be likely to be a party to the proceedings and to be likely to have or to have had in his possession, custody or power any documents which are relevant to an issue arising or likely to arise out of that claim—

(a) to disclose whether those documents are in his possession, custody or power; and

(b) to produce such of those documents as are in his possession, custody or power to the applicant or, on such conditions as may be specified in the order—

(i) to the applicant's legal advisers; or

(ii) to the applicant's legal advisers and any medical or other professional adviser of the applicant; or

(iii) if the applicant has no legal adviser, to any medical or other professional adviser of the applicant.

N.B. The corresponding county court section is s 52 of the County Courts Act 1984.

Power of High Court to order disclosure of documents, inspection of property etc. in proceedings for personal injuries or death

34.—(1) This section applies to any proceedings in the High Court in which a claim is made in respect of personal injuries to a person, or in respect of a person's death.

(2) On the application, in accordance with rules of court, of a party to any proceedings to which this section applies, the High Court shall, in such circumstances as may be specified in the rules, have power to order a person who is not a party to the proceedings and who appears to the court to be likely to have in his possession, custody or power any documents which are relevant to an issue arising out of the said claim—

(a) to disclose whether those documents are in his possession, custody or power; and

(b) to produce such of those documents as are in his possession, custody or power to the applicant or, on such conditions as may be specified in the order—

(i) to the applicant's legal advisers; or

(ii) to the applicant's legal advisers and any medical or other professional adviser of the applicant; or

(iii) if the applicant has no legal adviser, to any medical or other professional adviser of the applicant.

(3) On the application, in accordance with rules of court, of a party to any proceedings to which this section applies, the High Court shall, in such circumstances as may be specified in the rules, have power to make an order providing for any one or more of the following matters, that is to say—

(a) the inspection, photographing, preservation, custody and detention of property which is not the property of, or in the possession of, any party to the proceedings but which is the subject-matter of the proceedings or as to which any question arises in the proceedings;

(b) the taking of samples of any such property as is mentioned in paragraph (a) and the carrying out of any experiment on or with any such property.

(4) The preceding provisions of this section are without prejudice to the exercise by the High Court of any power to make orders which is exercisable apart from those provisions.

N.B. The corresponding county court section is s 53 of the County Courts Act 1984.

Provisions supplementary to ss 33 and 34

35.—(1) The High Court shall not make an order under section 33 or 34 if it considers that compliance with the order, if made, would be likely to be injurious to the public interest.

(2) Rules of court may make provisions as to the circumstances in which an order under section 33 or 34 can be made; and any rules making such provisions may include such incidental, supplementary and consequential provisions as the rule-making authority may consider necessary or expedient.

(3) Without prejudice to the generality of subsection (2), rules of court shall be made for the purpose of ensuring that the costs of and incidental to proceedings for an order under section 33(2) or 34 incurred by the person against whom the order is sought shall be awarded to that person unless the court otherwise directs.

(4) Sections 33(2) and 34 and this section bind the Crown; and section 33(1) binds the Crown so far as it relates to property as to which it appears to the court that it may become the subject-matter of subsequent proceedings involving a claim in respect of personal injuries to a person or in respect of a person's death.

In this subsection references to the Crown do not include references to Her Majesty in Her private capacity or to Her Majesty in right of Her Duchy of Lancaster or to the Duke of Cornwall.

(5) In sections 32A, 33 and 34 and this section—
"property" includes any land, chattel or other corporeal property of any description;

"personal injuries" includes any disease and any impairment of a person's physical or mental condition.

N.B. The corresponding county court section is s 54 of the County Courts Act 1984.

Power of High Court to award interest on debts and damages

35A.—(1) Subject to rules of court, in proceedings (whenever instituted) before the High Court for the recovery of a debt or damages there may be included in any sum for which judgment is given simple interest, at such rate as the court thinks fit or as rules of court may provide, on all or any part of the debt or damages in respect of which judgment is given, or payment is made before judgment, for all or any part of the period between the date when the cause of action arose and—

(a) in the case of any sum paid before judgment, the date of the payment; and

(b) in the case of the sum for which judgment is given, the date of the judgment.

(2) In relation to a judgment given for damages for personal injuries or death which exceed £200 subsection (1) shall have effect—

(a) with the substitution of "shall be included" for "may be included"; and

(b) with the addition of "unless the court is satisfied that there are special reasons to the contrary" after "given", where first occurring.

(3) Subject to rules of court, where—

(a) there are proceedings (whenever instituted) before the High Court for the recovery of a debt; and

(b) the defendant pays the whole debt to the plaintiff (otherwise than in pursuance of a judgment in the proceedings),

the defendant shall be liable to pay the plaintiff simple interest at such rate as the court thinks fit or as rules of court may provide on all or any part of the debt for all or any part of the period between the date when the cause of action arose and the date of the payment.

(4) Interest in respect of a debt shall not be awarded under this section for a period during which, for whatever reason, interest on the debt already runs.

(5) Without prejudice to the generality of section 84, rules of court may provide for a rate of interest by reference to the rate specified in section 17 of the Judgments Act 1838 as that section has effect from time to time or by reference to a rate for which any other enactment provides.

(6) Interest under this section may be calculated at different rates in respect of different periods.

(7) In this section "plaintiff" means the person seeking the debt or damages and "defendant" means the person from whom the plaintiff seeks the debt or damages and "personal injuries" includes any disease and any impairment of a person's physical or mental condition.

(8) Nothing in this section affects the damages recoverable for the dishonour of a bill of exchange.

5. Mental Health Act 1983
Section 139

Protection for acts done in pursuance of this Act

139.—(1) No person shall be liable, whether on the ground of want of jurisdiction or on any other ground, to any civil or criminal proceedings to which he would have been liable apart from this section in respect of any act purporting to be done in pursuance of this Act or any regulations or rules made under this Act, or in, or in pursuance of anything done in, the discharge of functions conferred by any other enactment on the authority having jurisdiction under Part VII of this Act, unless the act was done in bad faith or without reasonable care.

(2) No civil proceedings shall be brought against any person in any court in respect of any such act without the leave of the High Court; and no criminal proceedings shall be brought against any person in any court in respect of any such act except by or with the consent of the Director of Public Prosecutions.

(3) This section does not apply to proceedings for an offence under this Act, being proceedings which, under any other provision of this Act, can be instituted only by or with the consent of the Director of Public Prosecutions.

(4) This section does not apply to proceedings against the Secretary of State or against a health authority within the meaning of the National Health Service Act 1977.

(5) In relation to Northern Ireland the reference in this section to the Director of Public Prosecutions shall be construed as a reference to the Director of Public Prosecutions for Northern Ireland.

6. Unfair Contract Terms Act 1977
Sections 1 and 2

PART I
AMENDMENT OF LAW FOR ENGLAND AND WALES AND NORTHERN IRELAND

Scope of Part I

1.—(1) For the purposes of this Part of this Act, "negligence" means the breach—

   (a)   of any obligation, arising from the express or implied terms of a contract, to take reasonable care or exercise reasonable skill in the performance of the contract;

   (b)   of any common law duty to take reasonable care or exercise reasonable skill (but not any stricter duty);

   (c)   of the common duty of care imposed by the Occupiers' Liability Act 1957 or the Occupiers' Liability Act (Northern Ireland) 1957.

(2) This Part of this Act is subject to Part III; and in relation to contracts, the operation of sections 2 to 4 and 7 is subject to the exceptions made by Schedule 1.

(3) In the case of both contract and tort, sections 2 to 7 apply (except where the contrary is stated in section 6 (4)) only to business liability, that is liability for breach of obligations or duties arising—

   (a)   from things done or to be done by a person in the course of a business (whether his own business or another's); or

   (b)   from the occupation of premises used for business purposes of the occupier;

and references to liability are to be read accordingly but liability of an occupier of premises for breach of an obligation or duty towards a person obtaining access to the premises for recreational or educational purposes, being liability for loss or damage suffered by reason of the dangerous state of the premises, is not a business liability of the occupier unless granting that person such access for the purposes concerned falls within the business purposes of the occupier.

(4) In relation to any breach of duty or obligation, it is immaterial for any purpose of this Part of this Act whether the breach was inadvertent or intentional, or whether liability for it arises directly or vicariously.

Negligence liability

2.—(1) A person cannot by reference to any contract term or to a notice given to persons generally or to particular persons exclude or restrict his liability for death or personal injury resulting from negligence.

(2) In the case of other loss or damage, a person cannot so exclude or restrict his liability for negligence except in so far as the term or notice satisfies the requirements of reasonableness.

(3) Where a contract term or notice purports to exclude or restrict liability for negligence a person's agreement to or awareness of it is not of itself to be taken as indicating his voluntary acceptance of any risk.

7. Supply of Goods and Services Act 1982
Sections 1, 4, 12 and 13

PART I
SUPPLY OF GOODS

Contracts for the transfer of property in goods – the contracts concerned

1.—(1) In this Act a "contract for the transfer of goods" means a contract under which one person transfers or agrees to transfer to another the property in goods, other than an excepted contract.

(2) For the purposes of this section an excepted contract means any of the following:–

(a)   a contract of sale of goods;

(b)   a hire-purchase agreement;

(c)   a contract under which the property in goods is (or is to be) transferred in exchange for trading stamps on their redemption;

(d)   a transfer or agreement to transfer which is made by deed and for which there is no consideration other than the presumed consideration imported by the deed;

(e)   a contract intended to operate by way of mortgage, pledge, charge or other security.

(3) For the purposes of this Act a contract is a contract for the transfer of goods whether or not services are also provided or to be provided under the contract, and (subject to subsection (2) above) whatever is the nature of the consideration for the transfer or agreement to transfer.

Implied terms about quality or fitness

4.—(1) Except as provided by this section and section 5 below and subject to the provisions of any other enactment, there is no implied condition or warranty about the quality or fitness for any particular purpose of goods supplied under a contract for the transfer of goods.

(2) Where, under such a contract, the transferor transfers the property in goods in the course of a business, there is (subject to subsection (3) below) an implied condition that the goods supplied under the contract are of merchantable quality.

(3) There is no such condition as is mentioned in subsection (2) above—

(a)   as regards defects specifically drawn to the transferee's attention before the contract is made; or

(b)   if the transferee examines the goods before the contract is made, as regards defects which that examination ought to reveal.

(4) Subsection (5) below applies where, under a contract for the transfer of goods, the transferor transfers the property in goods in the course of a business and the transferee, expressly or by implication, makes known—

(a)   to the transferor, or

(b)   where the consideration or part of the consideration for the transfer is a sum payable by instalments and the goods were previously sold by a credit-broker to the transferor, to that credit-broker,

any particular purpose for which the goods are being acquired.

(5) In that case there is (subject to subsection (6) below) an implied condition that the goods supplied under the contract are reasonably fit for that purpose, whether or not that is a purpose for which such goods are commonly supplied.

(6) Subsection (5) above does not apply where the circumstances show that the transferee does not rely, or that it is unreasonable for him to rely, on the skill or judgment of the transferor or credit-broker.

(7) An implied condition or warranty about quality of fitness for a particular purpose may be annexed by usage to a contract for the transfer of goods.

(8) The preceding provisions of this section apply to a transfer by a person who in the course of a business is acting as agent for another as they apply to a transfer by a principal in the course of a business, except where that other is not transferring in the course of a business and either the transferee knows that fact or reasonable steps are taken to bring it to the transferee's notice before the contract concerned is made.

(9) Goods of any kind are of merchantable quality within the meaning of subsection (2) above if they are as fit for the purpose or purposes for which goods of that kind are commonly supplied as it is reasonable to expect having regard to any description applied to them, the price (if relevant) and all the other relevant circumstances.

PART II
SUPPLY OF SERVICES

The contracts concerned

12.—(1) In this Act a "contract for the supply of a service" means, subject to subsection (2) below, a contract under which a person ("the supplier") agrees to carry out a service.

(2) For the purposes of this Act, a contract of service or apprenticeship is not a contract for the supply of a service.

(3) Subject to subsection (2) above, a contract is a contract for the supply of a service for the purposes of this Act whether or not goods are also—

    (a) transferred or to be transferred, or

    (b) bailed or to be bailed by way of hire,

under the contract, and whatever is the nature of the consideration for which the service is to be carried out.

(4) The Secretary of State may by order provide that one or more of sections 13 to 15 below shall not apply to services of a description specified in the order, and such an order may make different provision for different circumstances.

(5) The power to make an order under subsection (4) above shall be exercisable by statutory instrument subject to annulment in pursuance of a resolution of either House of Parliament.

Implied term about care and skill

13. In a contract for the supply of a service where the supplier is acting in the course of a business, there is an implied term that the supplier will carry out the service with reasonable care and skill.

8. Consumer Protection Act 1987
Sections 1–9, 45, 46

PART I
PRODUCT LIABILITY

Purpose and construction of Part I

1.—(1) This Part shall have effect for the purpose of making such provision as is necessary in order to comply with the product liability Directive and shall be construed accordingly.

(2) In this Part, except in so far as the context otherwise requires—
"agricultural produce" means any produce of the soil, of stock-farming or of fisheries;
"dependant" and "relative" have the same meaning as they have in, respectively, the Fatal Accidents Act 1976 and the Damages (Scotland) Act 1976;
"producer", in relation to a product, means—

(a)   the person who manufactured it;

(b)   in the case of a substance which has not been manufactured but has been won or abstracted, the person who won or abstracted it;

(c)   in the case of a product which has not been manufactured, won or abstracted but essential characteristics of which are attributable to an industrial or other process having been carried out (for example, in relation to agricultural produce), the person who carried out that process;

"product" means any goods or electricity and (subject to subsection (3) below) includes a product which is comprised in another product, whether by virtue of being a component part or raw material or otherwise; and

"the product liability Directive" means the Directive of the Council of the European Communities, dated 25th July 1985, (No. 85/374/EEC) on the approximation of the laws, regulations and administrative provisions of the member States concerning liability for defective products.

(3) For the purposes of this Part a person who supplies any product in which products are comprised, whether by virtue of being component parts or raw material or otherwise, shall not be treated by reason only of his supply of that product as supplying any of the products so comprised.

Liability for defecive products

2.—(1) Subject to the following provisions of this Part, where any damage is caused wholly or partly by a defect in a product, every person to whom subsection (2) below applies shall be liable for the damage.

(2) This subsection applies to—

(a)   the producer of the product;

(b)   any person who, by putting his name on the product or using a trade mark or other distinguishing mark in relation to the product, has held himself out to be the producer of the product;

(c)   any person who has imported the product into a member State from a place outside the member States in order, in the course of any business of his, to supply it to another.

(3) Subject as aforesaid, where any damage is caused wholly or partly by a defect in a product, any person who supplied the product (whether to the person who suffered the damage, to the producer of any product in which the product in question is comprised or to any other person) shall be liable for the damage if—

(a) the person who suffered the damage requests the supplier to identify one or more of the persons (whether still in existence or not) to whom subsection (2) above applies in relation to the product;

(b) that request is made within a reasonable period after the damage occurs and at a time when it is not reasonably practicable for the person making the request to identify all those persons; and

(c) the supplier fails, within a reasonable period after receiving the request, either to comply with the request or to identify the person who supplied the product to him.

(4) Neither subsection (2) nor subsection (3) above shall apply to a person in respect of any defect in any game or agricultural produce if the only supply of the game or produce by that person to another was at a time when it had not undergone an industrial process.

(5) Where two or more persons are liable by virtue of this Part for the same damage, their liability shall be joint and several.

(6) This section shall be without prejudice to any liability arising otherwise than by virtue of this Part.

Meaning of "defect"

3.–(1) Subject to the following provisions of this section, there is a defect in a product for the purposes of this Part if the safety of the product is not such as persons generally are entitled to expect; and for those purposes "safety", in relation to a product, shall include safety with respect to products comprised in that product and safety in the context of risks of damage to property, as well as in the context of risks of death or personal injury.

(2) In determining for the purposes of subsection (1) above what persons generally are entitled to expect in relation to a product all the circumstances shall be taken into account, including—

(a) the manner in which, and purposes for which, the product has been marketed, its get-up, the use of any mark in relation to the product and any instructions for, or warnings with respect to, doing or refraining from doing anything with or in relation to the product;

(b) what might reasonably be expected to be done with or in relation to the product; and

(c) the time when the product was supplied by its producer to another;

and nothing in this section shall require a defect to be inferred from the fact alone that the safety of a product which is supplied after that time is greater than the safety of the product in question.

Defences

4.—(1) In any civil proceedings by virtue of this Part against any person ("the person proceeded against") in respect of a defect in a product it shall be a defence for him to show—

(a) that the defect is attributable to compliance with any requirement imposed by or under any enactment or with any Community obligation; or

(b) that the person proceeded against did not at any time supply the product to another; or

(c) that the following conditions are satisfied, that is to say—

(i) that the only supply of the product to another by the person proceeded against was otherwise than in the course of a business of that person's; and

(ii) that section 2(2) above does not apply to that person or applies to him by virtue of things done otherwise than with a view to profit; or

(d) that the defect did not exist in the product at the relevant time; or

(e) that the scientific and technical knowledge at the relevant time was not such that a producer of products of the same description as the product in question might be expected to have discovered the defect if it had existed in his products while they were under his control; or

(f) that the defect—

(i) constituted a defect in a product ("the subsequent product") in which the product in question had been comprised; and

(ii) was wholly attributable to the design of the subsequent product or to compliance by the producer of the product in question with instructions given by the producer of the subsequent product.

(2) In this section "the relevant time", in relation to electricity, means the time at which it was generated, being a time before it was transmitted or distributed, and in relation to any other product, means—

(a) if the person proceeded against is a person to whom subsection (2) of section 2 above applies in relation to the product, the time when he supplied the product to another;

(b) if that subsection does not apply to that person in relation to the product, the time when the product was last supplied by a person to whom that subsection does apply in relation to the product.

Damage giving rise to liability

5.–(1) Subject to the following provisions of this section, in this Part "damage" means death or personal injury or any loss of or damage to any property (including land).

(2) A person shall not be liable under section 2 above in respect of any defect in a product for the loss of or any damage to the product itself or for the loss of or any damage to the whole or any part of any product which has been supplied with the product in question comprised in it.

(3) A person shall not be liable under section 2 above for any loss of or damage to any property which, at the time it is lost or damaged, is not—

(a) of a description of property ordinarily intended for private use, occupation or consumption; and

(b) intended by the person suffering the loss or damage mainly for his own private use, occupation or consumption.

(4) No damages shall be awarded to any person by virtue of this Part in respect of any loss of or damage to any property if the amount which would fall to be so awarded to that person, apart from this subsection and any liability for interest, does not exceed £275.

(5) In determining for the purposes of this Part who has suffered any loss of or damage to property and when any such loss or damage occurred, the loss or damage shall be regarded as having occurred at the earliest time at which a person with an interest in the property had knowledge of the material facts about the loss or damage.

(6) For the purposes of subsection (5) above the material facts about any loss of or damage to any property are such facts about the loss or damages as would lead a reasonable person with an interest in the property to consider the loss or damage sufficiently serious to justify his instituting proceedings for damages against a defendant who did not dispute liability and was able to satisfy a judgment.

(7) For the purposes of subsection (5) above a person's knowledge includes knowledge which he might reasonably have been expected to acquire—

   (a)   from facts observable or ascertainable by him; or

   (b)   from facts ascertainable by him with the help of appropriate expert advice which it is reasonable for him to seek;

but a person shall not be taken by virtue of this subsection to have knowledge of a fact ascertainable by him only with the help of expert advice unless he has failed to take all reasonable steps to obtain (and, where appropriate, to act on) that advice.

(8) Subsections (5) to (7) above shall not extend to Scotland.

Application of certain enactments etc.

6.—(1) Any damage for which a person is liable under section 2 above shall be deemed to have been caused—

   (a)   for the purposes of the Fatal Accidents Act 1976, by that person's wrongful act, neglect or default;

   (b)   for the purposes of section 3 of the Law Reform (Miscellaneous Provisions) (Scotland) Act 1940 (contribution among joint wrongdoers), by that person's wrongful act or negligent act or omission;

   (c)   for the purposes of section 1 of the Damages (Scotland) Act 1976 (rights of relatives of a deceased), by that person's act or omission; and

   (d)   for the purposes of Part II of the Administration of Justice Act 1982 (damages for personal injuries, etc.—Scotland), by an act or omission giving rise to liability in that person to pay damages.

(2) Where—

   (a)   a person's death is caused wholly or partly by a defect in a product, or a person dies after suffering damage which has been so caused;

   (b)   a request such as mentioned in paragraph *(a)* of subsection (3) of section 2 above is made to a supplier of the product by that person's personal representatives or, in the case of a person whose death is caused wholly or partly by the defect, by any dependant or relative of that person; and

   (c)   the conditions specified in paragraphs *(b)* and *(c)* of that subsection are satisfied in relation to that request,

this Part shall have effect for the purposes of the Law Reform (Miscellaneous Provisions) Act 1934, the Fatal Accidents Act 1976 and the Damages (Scotland) Act 1976 as if liability of the supplier to that person under that subsection did not depend on that person having requested the supplier to identify certain persons or on the said conditions having been satisfied in relation to a request made by that person.

(3) Section 1 of the Congenital Disabilities (Civil Liability) Act 1976 shall have effect for the purposes of this Part as if—

   (a)   a person were answerable to a child in respect of an occurrence caused wholly or partly by a defect in a product if he is or has been liable under section 2 above in respect of any effect of the occurrence on a parent of the child, or would be so liable if the occurrence caused a parent of the child to suffer damage;

   (b)   the provisions of this Part relating to liability under section 2 above applied in relation to liability by virtue of paragraph *(a)* above under the said section 1; and

   (c)   subsection (6) of the said section 1 (exclusion of liability) were omitted.

(4) Where any damage is caused partly by a defect in a product and partly by the

fault of the person suffering the damage, the Law Reform (Contributory Negligence) Act 1945 and section 5 of the Fatal Accidents Act 1976 (contributory negligence) shall have effect as if the defect were the fault of every person liable by virtue of this Part for the damage caused by the defect.

(5) In subsection (4) above "fault" has the same meaning as in the said Act of 1945.

(6) Schedule 1 to this Act shall have effect for the purpose of amending the Limitation Act 1980 and the Prescription and Limitation (Scotland) Act 1973 in their application in relation to the bringing of actions by virtue of this Part.

(7) It is hereby declared that liability by virtue of this Part is to be treated as liability in tort for the purposes of any enactment conferring jurisdiction on any court with respect to any matter.

(8) Nothing in this Part shall prejudice the operation of section 12 of the Nuclear Installations Act 1965 (rights to compensation for certain breaches of duties confined to rights under that Act).

Prohibitions on exclusions from liability

7. The liability of a person by virtue of this Part to a person who has suffered damage caused wholly or partly by a defect in a product, or to a dependant or relative of such a person, shall not be limited or excluded by any contract term, by any notice or by any other provision.

Power to modify Part I

8.—(1) Her Majesty may by Order in Council make such modifications of this Part and of any other enactment (including an enactment contained in the following Parts of this Act, or in an Act passed after this Act) as appear to her Majesty in Council to be necessary or expedient in consequence of any modification of the product liability Directive which is made at any time after the passing of this Act.

(2) An Order in Council under subsection (1) above shall not be submitted to Her Majesty in Council unless a draft of the Order has been laid before, and approved by a resolution of, each House of Parliament.

Application of Part I to Crown

9.—(1) Subject to subsection (2) below, this Part shall bind the Crown.

(2) The Crown shall not, as regards the Crown's liability by virtue of this Part, be bound by this Part further than the Crown is made liable in tort or in reparation under the Crown Proceedings Act 1947, as that Act has effect from time to time.

PART V
MISCELLANEOUS AND SUPPLEMENTAL

Interpretation

45.—(1) In this Act, except in so far as the context otherwise requires—

"aircraft" includes gliders, balloons and hovercraft;

"business" includes a trade or profession and the activities of a professional or trade association or of a local authority or other public authority;

"conditional sale agreement", "credit—sale agreement" and "hire-purchase agreement" have the same meanings as in the Consumer Credit Act 1974 but as if in the definitions in that Act "goods" had the same meaning as in this Act;

"contravention" includes a failure to comply and cognate expressions shall be construed accordingly;

"enforcement authority" means the Secretary of State, any other Minister of the Crown in charge of a Government department, any such department and any authority, council or other person on whom functions under this Act are conferred by or under section 27 above;

"gas" has the same meaning as in Part I of the Gas Act 1986;

"goods" includes substances, growing crops and things comprised in land by virtue of being attached to it and any ship, aircraft or vehicle;

"information" includes accounts, estimates and returns;

"magistrates' court", in relation to Northern Ireland, means a court of summary jurisdiction;

"mark" and "trade mark" have the same meanings as in the Trade Marks Act 1938;

"modifications" includes additions, alterations and omissions, and cognate expressions shall be construed accordingly;

"motor vehicle" has the same meaning as in the Road Traffic Act 1988;

"notice" means a notice in writing;

"notice to warn" means a notice under section 13(1)(b) above;

"officer", in relation to an enforcement authority, means a person authorised in writing to assist the authority in carrying out its functions under or for the purposes of the enforcement of any of the safety provisions or of any of the provisions made by or under Part III of this Act;

"personal injury" includes any disease and any other impairment of a person's physical or mental condition;

"premises" includes any place and any ship, aircraft or vehicle;

"prohibition notice" means a notice under section 13(1)(a) above;

"records" includes any books or documents and any records in non-documentary form;

"safety provision" means the general safety requirements in section 10 above or any provision of safety regulations, a prohibition notice or a suspension notice;

"safety regulations" means regulations under section 11 above;

"ship" includes any boat and any other description of vessel used in navigation;

"subordinate legislation" has the same meaning as in the Interpretation Act 1978;

"substance" means any natural or artificial substance, whether in solid, liquid or gaseous form or in the form of a vapour, and includes substances that are comprised in or mixed with other goods;

"supply" and cognate expressions shall be construed in accordance with section 46 below;

"suspension notice" means a notice under section 14 above.

(2) Except in so far as the context otherwise requires, references in this Act to a contravention of a safety provision shall, in relation to any goods, include references to anything which would constitute such a contravention if the goods were supplied to any person.

(3) References in this Act to any goods in relation to which any safety provision has been or may have been contravened shall include references to any goods which it is not reasonably practicable to separate from any such goods.

(4) Section 68(2) of the Trade Marks Act 1938 (construction of references to use of a mark) shall apply for the purposes of this Act as it applies for the purposes of that Act.

(5) In Scotland, any reference in this Act to things comprised in land by virtue of being attached to it is a reference to moveables which have become heritable by accession to heritable property.

Meaning of "supply"

46.—(1) Subject to the following provisions of this section, references in this Act to supplying goods shall be construed as references to doing any of the following, whether as principal or agent, that is to say—

(a) selling, hiring out or lending the goods;

(b) entering into a hire-purchase agreement to furnish the goods;

(c) the performance of any contract for work and materials to furnish the goods;

(d) providing the goods in exchange for any consideration (including trading stamps) other than money;

(e) providing the goods in or in connection with the performance of any statutory function; or

(f) giving the goods as a prize or otherwise making a gift of the goods;

and, in relation to gas or water, those references shall be construed as including references to providing the service by which the gas or water is made available for use.

(2) For the purposes of any reference in this Act to supplying goods, where a person ("the ostensible supplier") supplies goods to another person ("the customer") under a hire-purchase agreement, conditional sale agreement or credit-sale agreement or under an agreement for the hiring of goods (other than a hire-purchase agreement) and the ostensible supplier—

(a) carries on the business of financing the provision of goods for others by means of such agreements; and

(b) in the course of that business acquired his interest in the goods supplied to the customer as a means of financing the provision of them for the customer by a further person ("the effective supplier"),

the effective supplier and not the ostensible supplier shall be treated as supplying the goods to the customer.

(3) Subject to subsection (4) below, the performance of any contract by the erection of any building or structure on any land or by the carrying out of any other building works shall be treated for the purposes of this Act as a supply of goods in so far as, but only in so far as, it involves the provision of any goods to any person by means of their incorporation into the building, structure or works.

(4) Except for the purposes of, and in relation to, notices to warn or any provision made by or under Part III of this Act, references in this Act to supplying goods shall not include references to supplying goods comprised in land where the supply is effected by the creation or disposal of an interest in the land.

(5) Except in Part I of this Act references in this Act to a person's supplying goods shall be confined to references to that person's supplying goods in the course of a business of his, but for the purposes of this subsection it shall be immaterial whether the business is a business of dealing in the goods.

(6) For the purposes of subsection (5) above goods shall not be treated as supplied in the course of a business if they are supplied, in pursuance of an obligation arising under or in connection with the insurance of the goods, to the person with whom they were insured.

(7) Except for the purposes of, and in relation to, prohibition notices or suspension notices, references in Parts II to IV of this Act to supplying goods shall not include—

(a) references to supplying goods where the person supplied carries on a business of buying goods of the same description as those goods and repairing or reconditioning them;

(b) references to supplying goods by a sale of articles as scrap (that is to say, for

383

the value of materials included in the articles rather than for the value of the articles themselves).

(8) Where any goods have at any time been supplied by being hired out or lent to any person, neither a continuation or renewal of the hire or loan (whether on the same or different terms) nor any transaction for the transfer after that time of any interest in the goods to the person to whom they were hired or lent shall be treated for the purposes of this Act as a further supply of the goods to that person.

(9) A ship, aircraft or motor vehicle shall not be treated for the purposes of this Act as supplied to any person by reason only that services consisting in the carriage of goods or passengers in that ship, aircraft or vehicle, or in its use for any other purpose, are provided to that person in pursuance of an agreement relating to the use of the ship, aircraft or vehicle for a particular period or for particular voyages, flights or journeys.

9. Vaccine Damage Payments Act 1979

Payments to persons severely damaged by vaccination

1.—(1) If, on consideration of a claim, the Secretary of State is satisfied—

(a) that a person is, or was immediately before his death, severely disabled as a result of vaccination against any of the diseases to which this Act applies; and

(b) that the conditions of entitlement which are applicable in accordance with section 2 below are fulfilled,

he shall in accordance with this Act make a payment of the relevant statutory sum or for the benefit of that person or to his personal representatives.

(1A) In subsection (1) above "statutory sum" means [£20,000] or such other sum as is specified by the Secretary of State for the purposes of this Act by order made by statutory instrument with the consent of the Treasury; and the relevant statutory sum for the purposes of that subsection is the statutory sum at the time when a claim for payment is first made.

(2) The diseases to which this Act applies are—

(a) diphtheria,

(b) tetanus,

(c) whooping cough,

(d) poliomyelitis,

(e) measles,

(f) rubella,

(g) tuberculosis,

(h) smallpox, and

(i) any other disease which is specified by the Secretary of State for the purposes of this Act by order made by statutory instrument.

(3) Subject to section 2 (3) below, this Act has effect with respect to a person who is severely disabled as a result of a vaccination given to his mother before he was born as if the vaccination had been given directly to him and, in such circumstances as may be prescribed by regulations under this Act, this Act has effect with respect to a person who is severely disabled as a result of contracting a disease through contact with a third person who was vaccinated against it as if the vaccination had been given to him and the disablement resulted from it.

(4) For the purposes of this Act, a person is severely disabled if he suffers disablement to the extent of 80 per cent. or more, assessed as for the purposes of section 57 of the Social Security Act 1975 or the Social Security (Northern Ireland) Act 1975 (disablement gratuity and pension).

(4A) No order shall be made by virtue of subsection (1A) above unless a draft of the order has been laid before Parliament and been approved by a resolution of each House.

(5) A statutory instrument under subsection (2) *(i)* above shall be subject to annulment in pursuance of a resolution of either House of Parliament.

Conditions of entitlement

2.—(1) Subject to the provisions of this section, the conditions of entitlement referred to in section 1 (1) *(b)* above are—

(a) that the vaccination in question was carried out—

(i) in the United Kingdom or the Isle of Man, and

  (ii) on or after 5th July 1948, and

  (iii) in the case of vaccination against smallpox, before 1st August 1971;

 (b) except in the case of vaccination against poliomyelitis or rubella, that the vaccination was carried out either at a time when the person to whom it was given was under the age of eighteen or at the time of an outbreak within the United Kingdom or the Isle of Man of the disease against which the vaccination was given; and

 (c) that the disabled person was over the age of two on the date when the claim was made or, if he died before that date, that he died after 9th May 1978 and was over the age of two when he died.

(2) An order under section 1 (2) (*i*) above specifying a disease for the purposes of this Act may provide that, in relation to vaccination against that disease, the conditions of entitlement specified in subsection (1) above shall have effect subject to such modifications as may be specified in the order.

(3) In a case where this Act has effect by virtue of section 1 (3) above, the reference in subsection (1) *(b)* above to the person to whom a vaccination was given is a reference to the person to whom it was actually given and not to the disabled person.

(4) With respect to claims made after such date as may be specified in the order and relating to vaccination against such disease as may be so specified, the Secretary of State may by order made by statutory instrument—

 (a) provide that, in such circumstances as may be specified in the order, one or more of the conditions of entitlement appropriate to vaccination against that disease need not be fulfilled; or

 (b) add to the conditions of entitlement which are appropriate to vaccination against that disease, either generally or in such circumstances as may be specified in the order.

(5) Regulations under this Act shall specify the cases in which vaccinations given outside the United Kingdom and the Isle of Man to persons defined in the regulations as serving members of Her Majesty's forces or members of their families are to be treated for the purposes of this Act as carried out in England.

(6) The Secretary of State shall not make an order containing any provisions made by virtue of paragraph *(b)* of subsection (4) above unless a draft of the order has been laid before Parliament and approved by a resolution of each House; and a statutory instrument by which any other order is made under that subsection shall be subject to annulment in pursuance of a resolution of either House of Parliament.

Determination of claims

 3.—(1) Any reference in this Act, other than section 7, to a claim is a reference to a claim for a payment under section 1 (1) above which is made—

 (a) by or on behalf of the disabled person concerned or, as the case may be, by his personal representatives; and

 (b) in the manner prescribed by regulations under this Act; and

 (c) within the period of six years beginning on the latest of the following dates, namely, the date of the vaccination to which the claim relates, the date on which the disabled person attained the age of two and 9th May 1978;

and, in relation to a claim, any reference to the claimant is a reference to the person by whom the claim was made and any reference to the disabled person is a reference to the person in respect of whose disablement a payment under subsection (1) above is claimed to be payable.

(2) As soon as practicable after he has received a claim, the Secretary of State shall give notice in writing to the claimant of his determination whether he is satisfied that a

payment is due under section 1 (1) above to or for the benefit of the disabled person or to his personal representatives.

(3) If the Secretary of State is not satisfied that a payment is due as mentioned in subsection (2) above, the notice in writing under that subsection shall state the grounds on which he is not so satisfied.

(4) If, in the case of any claim, the Secretary of State—

(a) is satisfied that the conditions of entitlement which are applicable in accordance with section 2 above are fulfilled, but

(b) is not satisfied that the disabled person is or, where he has died, was immediately before his death severely disabled as a result of vaccination against any of the diseases to which this Act applies,

the notice in writing under subsection (2) above shall inform the claimant that, if an application for review is made to the Secretary of State, the matters referred to in paragraph *(b)* above will be reviewed by an independent medical tribunal in accordance with section 4 below.

(5) If in any case a person is severely disabled, the question whether his severe disablement results from vaccination against any of the diseases to which this Act applies shall be determined for the purposes of this Act on the balance of probability.

Review of extent of disablement and causation by independent tribunals

4.—(1) Regulations under this Act shall make provision for independent medical tribunals to determine matters referred to them under this section, and such regulations may make provision with respect to—

(a) the terms of appointment of the persons who are to serve on the tribunals;

(b) the procedure to be followed for the determination of matters referred to the tribunals;

(c) the summoning of persons to attend to give evidence or produce documents before the tribunals and the administration of oaths to such persons.

(2) Where an application for review is made to the Secretary of State as mentioned in section 3 (4) above, then, subject to subsection (3) below, the Secretary of State shall refer to a tribunal under this section—

(a) the question of the extent of the disablement suffered by the disabled person;

(b) the question whether he is or, as the case may be, was immediately before his death disabled as a result of the vaccination to which the claim relates; and

(c) the question whether, if he is or was so disabled, the extent of his disability is or was such as to amount to severe disablement.

(3) The Secretary of State may refer to differently constituted tribunals the questions in paragraphs *(a)* to *(c)* of subsection (2) above, and the Secretary of State need not refer to a tribunal any of these questions if—

(a) he and the claimant are not in dispute with respect to it; or

(b) the decision of a tribunal on another of those questions is such that the disabled person cannot be or, as the case may be, could not immediately before his death have been severely disabled as a result of the vaccination to which the claim relates.

(4) For the purposes of this Act, the decision of a tribunal on a question referred to them under this section shall be conclusive except in so far as it falls to be reconsidered by virtue of section 5 below.

Reconsideration of determinations and recovery of payments in certain cases

5.—(1) Subject to subsection (2) below, the Secretary of State may reconsider a determination that a payment should not be made under section 1 (1) above on the ground—

(a) that there has been a material change of circumstances since the determination was made, or

(b) that the determination was made in ignorance of, or was based on a mistake as to, some material fact,

and the Secretary of State may, on the ground set out in paragraph *(b)* above, reconsider a determination that such a payment should be made.

(2) Regulations under this Act shall prescribe the manner and the period in which—

(a) an application may be made to the Secretary of State for his reconsideration of a determination; and

(b) the Secretary of State may of his own motion institute such a reconsideration.

(3) The Secretary of State shall give notice in writing of his decision on a reconsideration under this section to the person who was the claimant in relation to the claim which gave rise to the determination which has been reconsidered and also, where the disabled person is alive and was not the claimant, to him; and the provisions of subsections (3) to (5) of section 3 and section 4 above shall apply as if—

(a) the notice under this subsection were a notice under section 3 (2) above; and

(b) any reference in those provisions to the claimant were a reference to the person who was the claimant in relation to the claim which gave rise to the determination which has been reconsidered.

(4) If, whether fraudulently or otherwise, any person misrepresents or fails to disclose any material fact and in consequence of the misrepresentation or failure a payment is made under section 1 (1) above, the person to whom the payment was made shall be liable to repay the amount of that payment to the Secretary of State unless he can show that the misrepresentation or failure occurred without his connivance or consent.

(5) Except as provided by subsection (4) above, no payment under section 1 (1) above shall be recoverable by virtue of a reconsideration of a determination under this section.

Payments to or for the benefit of disabled persons

6.—(1) Where a payment under section 1 (1) above falls to be made in respect of a disabled person who is over eighteen and capable of managing his own affairs, the payment shall be made to him.

(2) Where such a payment falls to be made in respect of a disabled person who has died, the payment shall be made to his personal representatives.

(3) Where such a payment falls to be made in respect of any other disabled person, the payment shall be made for his benefit by paying it to such trustees as the Secretary of State may appoint to be held by them upon such trusts or, in Scotland, for such purposes and upon such conditions as may be declared by the Secretary of State.

(4) The making of a claim for, or the receipt of, a payment under section 1 (1) above does not prejudice the right of any person to institute or carry on proceedings in respect of disablement suffered as a result of vaccination against any disease to which this Act applies; but in any civil proceedings brought in respect of disablement resulting from vaccination against such a disease, the court shall treat a payment made to or in respect of the disabled person concerned under section 1 (1) above as paid on account of any damages which the court awards in respect of such disablement.

Payments, claims etc. made prior to the Act

7.—(1) Any reference in this section to an extra-statutory payment is a reference to a payment of £10,000 made by the Secretary of State to or in respect of a disabled person after 9th May 1978 and before the passing of this Act pursuant to a non-statutory scheme of payments for severe vaccine damage.

(2) No such claim as is referred to in section 3 (1) above shall be entertained if an extra-statutory payment has been made to or for the benefit of the disabled person or his personal representatives.

(3) For the purposes of section 5 above, a determination that an extra-statutory payment should be made shall be treated as a determination that a payment should be made under section 1 (1) above; and in relation to the reconsideration of such a determination references in subsection (3) of section 5 above to the person who was the claimant in relation to the determination which has been reconsidered shall be construed as references to the person who made the claim for the extra-statutory payment.

(4) Subsections (4) and (5) of section 5 above and section 6 (4) above shall apply in relation to an extra-statutory payment as they apply in relation to a payment made under section 1 (1) above.

(5) For the purposes of this Act (other than this section) regulations under this Act may—

(a) treat claims which were made in connection with the scheme referred to in subsection (1) above and which have not been disposed of at the commencement of this Act as claims falling within section 3 (1) above; and

(b) treat information and other evidence furnished and other things done before the commencement of this Act in connection with any such claim as is referred to in paragraph (a) above as furnished or done in connection with a claim falling within section 3 (1) above.

Regulations

8.—(1) Any reference in the preceding provisions of this Act to regulations under this Act is a reference to regulations made by the Secretary of State.

(2) Any power of the Secretary of State under this Act to make regulations—

(a) shall be exercisable by statutory instrument which shall be subject to annulment in pursuance of a resolution of either House of Parliament; and

(b) includes power to make such incidental or supplementary provision as appears to the Secretary of State to be appropriate.

(3) Regulations made by the Secretary of State may contain provision—

(a) with respect to the information and other evidence to be furnished in connection with a claim;

(b) requiring disabled persons to undergo medical examination before their claims are determined or for the purposes of a reconsideration under section 5 above;

(c) restricting the disclosure of medical evidence and advice tendered in connection with a claim or a reconsideration under section 5 above; and

(d) conferring functions on the tribunals constituted under section 4 above with respect to the matters referred to in paragraphs (a) to (c) above.

Fraudulent statements etc.

9.—(1) Any person who, for the purpose of obtaining any payment under this Act, whether for himself or some other person,—

(a) knowingly makes any false statement or representation, or

(b) produces or furnishes or causes or knowingly allows to be produced or furnished any document or information which he knows to be false in a material particular,

shall be liable on summary conviction to a fine not exceeding level 5 on the standard scale.

(2) In the application of subsection (1) above to the Isle of Man, for the words following "liable" there shall be substituted the words "on summary conviction, within the meaning of the Interpretation Act 1976 (an Act of Tynwald), to a fine of £400 and on conviction on information to a fine".

Financial provisions

12.—(1) The Secretary of State shall pay to persons appointed to serve on tribunals under section 4 of this Act such remuneration and such travelling and other allowances as he may, with the consent of the Minister for the Civil Service, determine.

(2) The Secretary of State shall pay such fees as he considers appropriate to medical practitioners, as defined in Schedule 20 to the Social Security Act 1975, who provide information or other evidence in connection with claims.

(3) The Secretary of State shall pay such travelling and other allowances as he may determine—

(a) to persons required under this Act to undergo medical examinations;

(b) to persons required to attend before tribunals under section 4 above; and

(c) in circumstances where he considers it appropriate, to any person who accompanies a disabled person to such a medical examination or tribunal.

(4) There shall be paid out of moneys provided by Parliament—

(a) any expenditure incurred by the Secretary of State in making payments under section 1 (1) above;

(b) any expenditure incurred by the Secretary of State by virtue of subsections (1) to (3) above; and

(c) any increase in the administrative expenses of the Secretary of State attributable to this Act.

(5) Any sums repaid to the Secretary of State by virtue of section 5 (4) above shall be paid into the Consolidated Fund.

Short title and extent

13.—(1) This Act may be cited as the Vaccine Damage Payments Act 1979.

(2) This Act extends to Northern Ireland and the Isle of Man.

10. The Vaccine Damage Payments Act 1979 Statutory Sum Order 1985 (1985 No. 1249)

Whereas a draft of the following Order was laid before Parliament in accordance with section 1(4A) of the Vaccine Damage Payments Act 1979 (a) and was approved by resolution of each House of Parliament:

Now, therefore, the Secretary of State for Social Services, with the consent of the Treasury, in exercise of the powers conferred upon him by section 1(1A) of the Vaccine Damage Payments Act 1979 and of all other powers enabling him in that behalf, hereby makes the following Order:—

Citation and commencement

1. This Order may be cited as the Vaccine Damage Payments Act 1979 Statutory Sum Order 1985 and shall come into operation on 16th August 1985.

Statement of the statutory sum for the purposes of the Vaccine Damage Payments Act 1979

2. For the purposes of the Vaccine Damage Payments Act 1979 the statutory sum is £20,000.

Signed by authority of the Secretary of State for Social Services.

Tony Newton,
Minister of State,
Department of Health and Social Security.

29th July 1985.

11. Access to Medical Reports Act 1988

Right of access

1. It shall be the right of an individual to have access, in accordance with the provisions of this Act, to any medical report relating to the individual which is to be, or has been, supplied by a medical practitioner for employment purposes or insurance purposes.

Interpretation

2.—(1) In this Act—

"the applicant" means the person referred to in section 3(1) below;

"care" includes examination, investigation or diagnosis for the purposes of, or in connection with, any form of medical treatment;

"employment purposes", in the case of any individual, means the purposes in relation to the individual of any person by whom he is or has been, or is seeking to be, employed (whether under a contract of service or otherwise);

"health professional" has the same meaning as in the Data Protection (Subject Access Modification) (Health) Order 1987;

"insurance purposes", in the case of any individual, means the purposes in relation to the individual of any person carrying on an insurance business with whom the individual has entered into, or is seeking to enter into, a contract of insurance, and "insurance business" and "contract of insurance" have the same meaning as in the Insurance Companies Act 1982;

"medical practitioner" means a person registered under the Medical Act 1983;

"medical report", in the case of an individual, means a report relating to the physical or mental health of the individual prepared by a medical practitioner who is or has been responsible for the clinical care of the individual.

(2) Any reference in this Act to the supply of a medical report for employment or insurance purposes shall be construed—

    (a) as a reference to the supply of such a report for employment or insurance purposes which are purposes of the person who is seeking to be supplied with it; or

    (b) (in the case of a report that has already been supplied) as a reference to the supply of such a report for employment or insurance purposes which, at the time of its being supplied, were purposes of the person to whom it was supplied.

Consent to applications for medical reports for employment or insurance purposes

3.—(1) A person shall not apply to a medical practitioner for a medical report relating to any individual to be supplied to him for employment or insurance purposes unless—

    (a) that person ("the applicant") has notified the individual that he proposes to make the application; and

    (b) the individual has notified the applicant that he consents to the making of the application.

(2) Any notification given under subsection (1)(a) above must inform the individual of his right to withhold his consent to the making of the application, and of the following rights under this Act, namely—

    (a) the rights arising under sections 4(1) to (3) and 6(2) below with respect to access to the report before or after it is supplied,

(b) the right to withhold consent under subsection (1) of section 5 below, and

(c) the right to request the amendment of the report under subsection (2) of that section,

as well as of the effect of section 7 below.

Access to reports before they are supplied

4.—(1) An individual who gives his consent under section 3 above to the making of an application shall be entitled, when giving his consent, to state that he wishes to have access to the report to be supplied in response to the application before it is so supplied; and, if he does so, the applicant shall—

(a) notify the medical practitioner of that fact at the time when the application is made, and

(b) at the same time notify the individual of the making of the application;

and each such notification shall contain a statement of the effect of subsection (2) below.

(2) Where a medical practitioner is notified by the applicant under subsection (1) above that the individual in question wishes to have access to the report before it is supplied, the practitioner shall not supply the report unless—

(a) he has given the individual access to it and any requirements of section 5 below have been complied with, or

(b) the period of 21 days beginning with the date of the making of the application has elapsed without his having received any communication from the individual concerning arrangements for the individual to have access to it.

(3) Where a medical practitioner—

(a) receives an application for a medical report to be supplied for employment or insurance purposes without being notified by the applicant as mentioned in subsection (1) above, but

(b) before supplying the report receives a notification from the individual that he wishes to have access to the report before it is supplied,

the practitioner shall not supply the report unless—

(i) he has given the individual access to it and any requirements of section 5 below have been complied with, or

(ii) the period of 21 days beginning with the date of that notification has elapsed without his having received (either with that notification or otherwise) any communication from the individual concerning arrangements for the individual to have access to it.

(4) References in this section and section 5 below to giving an individual access to a medical report are references to—

(a) making the report or a copy of it available for his inspection; or

(b) supplying him with a copy of it;

and where a copy is supplied at the request, or otherwise with the consent, of the individual the practitioner may charge a reasonable fee to cover the costs of supplying it.

Consent to supplying of report and correction of errors

5.—(1) Where an individual has been given access to a report under section 4 above the report shall not be supplied in response to the application in question unless the individual has notified the medical practitioner that he consents to its being so supplied.

393

(2) The individual shall be entitled, before giving his consent under subsection (1) above, to request the medical practitioner to amend any part of the report which the individual considers to be incorrect or misleading; and, if the individual does so, the practitioner—

(a) if he is to any extent prepared to accede to the individual's request, shall amend the report accordingly;

(b) if he is to any extent not prepared to accede to it but the individual requests him to attach to the report a statement of the individual's views in respect of any part of the report which he is declining to amend, shall attach such a statement to the report.

(3) Any request made by an individual under subsection (2) above shall be made in writing.

Retention of reports

6.—(1) A copy of any medical report which a medical practitioner has supplied for employment or insurance purposes shall be retained by him for at least six months from the date on which it was supplied.

(2) A medical practitioner shall, if so requested by an individual, give the individual access to any medical report relating to him which the practitioner has supplied for employment or insurance purposes in the previous six months.

(3) The reference in subsection (2) above to giving an individual access to a medical report is a reference to—

(a) making a copy of the report available for his inspection; or

(b) supplying him with a copy of it;

and where a copy is supplied at the request, or otherwise with the consent, of the individual the practitioner may charge a reasonable fee to cover the costs of supplying it.

Exemptions

7.—(1) A medical practitioner shall not be obliged to give an individual access, in accordance with the provisions of section 4(4) or 6(3) above, to any part of a medical report whose disclosure would in the opinion of the practitioner be likely to cause serious harm to the physical or mental health of the individual or others or would indicate the intentions of the practitioner in respect of the individual.

(2) A medical practitioner shall not be obliged to give an individual access, in accordance with those provisions, to any part of a medical report whose disclosure would be likely to reveal information about another person, or to reveal the identity of another person who has supplied information to the practitioner about the individual, unless—

(a) that person has consented; or

(b) that person is a health professional who has been involved in the care of the individual and the information relates to or has been provided by the professional in that capacity.

(3) Where it appears to a medical practitioner that subsection (1) or (2) above is applicable to any part (but not the whole) of a medical report—

(a) he shall notify the individual of that fact; and

(b) references in the preceding sections of this Act to the individual being given access to the report shall be construed as references to his being given access to the remainder of it;

and other references to the report in sections 4(4), 5(2) and 6(3) above shall similarly be construed as references to the remainder of the report.

(4) Where it appears to a medical practitioner that subsection (1) or (2) above is applicable to the whole of a medical report—

  (a) he shall notify the individual of that fact; but

  (b) he shall not supply the report unless he is notified by the individual that the individual consents to its being supplied;

and accordingly, if he is so notified by the individual, the restrictions imposed by section 4(2) and (3) above on the supply of the report shall not have effect in relation to it.

Application to the court

8.—(1) If a court is satisfied on the application of an individual that any person, in connection with a medical report relating to that individual, has failed or is likely to fail to comply with any requirement of this Act, the court may order that person to comply with that requirement.

(2) The jurisdiction conferred by this section shall be exercisable by a county court or, in Scotland, by the sheriff.

Notifications under this Act

9. Any notification required or authorised to be given under this Act—

  (a) shall be given in writing; and

  (b) may be given by post.

Short title, commencement and extent

10.—(1) This Act may be cited as the Access to Medical Reports Act 1988.

(2) This Act shall come into force on 1st January 1989.

(3) Nothing in this Act applies to a medical report prepared before the coming into force of this Act.

(4) This Act does not extend to Northern Ireland.

12. Rules of the Supreme Court 1965
Duration and renewal of writ: O 6 r 8
Dismissal of actions: O 18 r 19; O 19 r 1; O 24 r 16; O 25 r 1; O 34 r 2
Discovery: O 24 r 2, r 2 (7), r 3, r 7, r 7A
Interrogatories: O 26 r 1
Evidence: O 38 rr 1–4, 36–38

Duration and renewal of writ (O 6 r 8)

8.—(1) For the purpose of service, a writ (other than a concurrent writ) is valid in the first instance for twelve months beginning with the date of its issue and a concurrent writ) is valid in the first instance for the period of validity of the original writ which is unexpired at the date of issue of the concurrent writ.

(2) Where a writ has not been served on a defendant, the Court may by order extend the validity of the writ from time to time for such period, not exceeding twelve months at any one time, beginning with the day next following that on which it would otherwise expire, as may be specified in the order, if an application for extension is made to the Court before that day or such later day (if any) as the Court may allow.

(3) Before a writ, the validity has been extended under this rule, is served, it must be marked with an official stamp showing the period for which the validity of the writ has been so extended.

(4) Where the validity of a writ is extended by order made under this Rule, the order shall operate in relation to any other writ (whether original or concurrent) issued in the same action which has not been served so as to extend the validity of that other writ until the expiration of the period specified in the order.

Striking out pleadings and indorsements (O 18 r 19)

19.—(1) The Court may at any stage of the proceedings order to be struck out or amended any pleading or the indorsement of any writ in the action, or anything in any pleading or in the indorsement, on the ground that—

(a) it discloses no reasonable cause of action or defence, as the case may be; or

(b) it is scandalous, frivolous or vexatious; or

(c) it may prejudice, embarrass or delay the fair trial of the action; or

(d) it is otherwise an abuse of the process of the court;

and may order the action to be stayed or dismissed or judgment to be entered accordingly, as the case may be.

(2) No evidence shall be admissible on an application under paragraph (1) *(a)*.

(3) This rule shall, so far as applicable, apply to an originating summons and a petition as if the summons or petition, as the case may be, were a pleading.

Default in service of statement of claim (O 19 r 1)

1. Where the plaintiff is required by these Rules to serve a statement of claim on a defendant and he fails to serve it on him, the defendant may, after the expiration of the period fixed by or under these Rules for service of the statement of claim, apply to the Court for an order to dismiss the action, and the Court may by order dismiss the action or make such other order on such terms as it thinks just.

Failure to comply with requirement for discovery, etc. (O 24 r 16)

16.—(1) If any party who is required by any of the foregoing rules, or by any order made thereunder, to make discovery of documents or to produce any documents for the purpose of inspection or any other purpose fails to comply with any provision of that rule or with that order, as the case may be, then, without prejudice, in the case of a failure to comply with any such provision, to rules 3(2) and 11(1) the Court may make such order as it thinks just including, in particular, an order that the action be dismissed or, as the case may be, an order that the defence be struck out and judgment be entered accordingly.

(2) If any party against whom an order for discovery or production of documents is made fails to comply with it, then, without prejudice to paragraph (1) he shall be liable to committal.

(3) Service on a party's solicitor of an order for discovery or production of documents made against that party shall be sufficient service to found an application for committal of the party disobeying the order, but the party may show in answer to the application that he had no notice or knowledge of the order.

(4) A solicitor on whom such an order made against his client is served and who fails without reasonable excuse to give notice thereof to his client shall be liable to committal.

Summons for Directions (O 25 r 1(4))

(4) If the plaintiff does not take out a summons for directions in accordance with the foregoing provisions of this rule, the defendant or any defendant may do so or apply for an order to dismiss the action.

Time for setting down action (O 34 r 2)

2.—(1) Every order made in an action which provides for trial before a judge shall, whether the trial is to be with or without a jury and wherever the trial is to take place, fix a period within which the plaintiff is to set down the action for trial.

(2) Where the plaintiff does not, within the period fixed under paragraph (1) set the action down for trial, the defendant may set the action down for trial or may apply to the Court to dismiss the action for want of prosecution and, on the hearing of any such application, the Court may order the action to be dismissed accordingly or may make such order as it thinks just.

(3) Every order made in an action in the Queen's Bench Division which provides for trial before a judge (otherwise than in the commercial list or the special paper or any corresponding list which may be specified for the purpose of this paragraph by directions under rule 4) shall contain an estimate of the length of the trial and, if the action is to be tried at the Royal Courts of Justice, shall, subject to any such directions, specify the list in which the action is to be put.

Discovery by parties without order (O 24 r 2)

2.—(1) Subject to the provisions of this rule and of rule 4, the parties to an action between whom pleadings are closed must make discovery by exchanging lists of documents and, accordingly, each party must within 14 days after the pleadings in the action are deemed to be closed as between him and any other party, make and serve on that other party a list of the documents which are or have been in his possession, custody or power relating to any matter in question between them in the action.

Without prejudice to any directions given by the Court under Order 16, rule 4, this paragraph shall not apply in third party proceedings, including proceedings under that Order involving fourth or subsequent parties.

(7) Any party to whom discovery of documents is required to be made under this rule may, at any time before the summons for directions in the action is taken out, serve on the party required to make such discovery a notice requiring him to make an affidavit verifying the list he is required to make under paragraph (1) and the party on whom such a notice is served must, within 14 days after service of the notice, make and file an affidavit in compliance with the notice and serve a copy of the affidavit on the party to whom the notice was served.

Order for discovery (O 24 r 3)

3.—(1) Subject to the provisions of this rule and of rules 4 and 8, the Court may order any party to a cause or matter (whether begun by writ, originating summons or otherwise) to make and serve on any other party a list of the documents which are or have been in his possession, custody or power relating to any matter in question in the cause or matter, and may at the same time or subsequently also order him to make and file an affidavit verifying such a list and to serve a copy thereof on the other party.

(2) Where a party who is required by rule 2 to make discovery of documents fails to comply with any provision of that rule, the Court, on the application of any party to whom the discovery was required to be made, may make an order against the first-mentioned party under paragraph (1) of this rule or, as the case may be, may order him to make and file an affidavit verifying the list of documents he is required to make under rule 2 and to serve a copy thereof on the applicant.

(3) An order under this rule may be limited to such documents or classes of documents only, or to such only of the matters in question in the cause or matter, as may be specified in the order.

Order for discovery of particular documents (O 24 r 7)

7.—(1) Subject to rule 8, the Court may at any time, on the application of any party to a cause or matter, make an order requiring any other party to make an affidavit stating whether any document specified or described in the application or any class of document so specified or described is, or has at any time been, in his possession, custody or power, and if not then in his possession, custody or power when he parted with it and what has become of it.

(2) An order may be made against a party under this rule notwithstanding that he may already have made or been required to make a list of documents or affidavits under rule 2 or rule 3.

(3) An application for an order under this rule must be supported by an affidavit stating the belief of the deponent that the party from whom discovery is sought under this rule has, or at some time had, in his possession, custody or power the document, or class of document, specified or described in the application and that it relates to one or more of the matters in question in the cause or matter.

Applications under ss.33(2) or 34(2) of the Supreme Court Act 1981 (O 24 r 7A)

7A.—(1) An application for an order under section 33(2) of the Act for the disclosure of documents before the commencement of proceedings shall be made by originating summons and the person against whom the order sought shall be made defendant to the summons.

(2) An application after the commencement of proceedings for an order under section 34(2) of the said Act for the disclosure of documents by a person who is not a party to the proceedings shall be made by summons, which must be served on that person personally and on every party to the proceedings other than the applicant.

(3) A summons under paragraph (1) or (2) shall be supported by an affidavit which must—

    (a) in the case of a summons under paragraph (1) state the grounds on which it is alleged that the applicant and the person against whom the order is sought are likely to be parties to subsequent proceedings in the High Court in which a claim for personal injuries is likely to be made;

    (b) in any case, specify or describe the documents in respect of which the order is sought and show, if practicable by reference to any pleading served or intended to be served in the proceedings, that the documents are relevant to an issue arising or likely to arise out of a claim for personal injuries made or likely to be made in the proceedings and that the person against whom the

order sought is likely to have or have had them in his possession, custody or power.

(4) A copy of the supporting affidavit shall be served with the summons on every person on whom the summons is required to be served.

(5) An order under the said section 33(2) or 34(2) for the disclosure of documents may be made conditional on the applicant's giving security for the costs of the person against whom it is made or on such other terms, if any, as the Court thinks just, and shall require the person against whom the order is made to make an affidavit stating whether any documents specified or described in the order, or at any time have been, in his possession, custody or power and, if not then in his possession, custody or power, when he parted with them and what has become of them.

(6) No person shall be compelled by virtue of such an order to produce any documents which he could not be compelled to produce—

(a)   in the case of a summons under paragraph (1) if the subsequent proceedings had already been begun, or

(b)   in the case of a summons under paragraph (2) if he had been served with a writ of *subpoena duces tecum* to produce the documents at the trial.

(7) In this rule "a claim for personal injuries" means a claim in respect of personal injuries to a person or in respect of a person's death.

(8) For the purposes of rules 10 and 11 an application for an order under the said section 33(2) or 34(2) shall be treated as a cause or matter between the applicant and the person against whom the order is sought.

Discovery by interrogatories (O 26 r 1)

1.—(1) A party to any cause or matter may apply to the Court for an order—

(a)   giving him leave to serve on any other party interrogatories relating to any matter in question between the applicant and that other party in the cause or matter, and

(b)   requiring that other party to answer the interrogatories on affidavit within such period as may be specified in the order.

(2) A copy of the proposed interrogatories must be served with the summons, or the notice under Order 25, rule 7, by which the application for such leave is made.

(3) On the hearing of an application under this rule, the Court shall give leave as to such only of the interrogatories as it considers necessary either for disposing fairly of the cause or matter or for saving costs; and in deciding whether to give leave to the Court shall take into account any offer made by the party to be interrogated to give particulars or to make admissions or to produce documents relating to any matter in question.

(4) A proposed interrogatory which does not relate to such a matter as is mentioned in paragraph (1) shall be disallowed notwithstanding that it might be admissible in oral cross-examination of a witness.

General rule: witnesses to be examined orally (O 38 r 1)

1. Subject to the provisions of these rules and of the Civil Evidence Act 1968 and the Civil Evidence Act 1972, and any other enactment relating to evidence, any fact required to be proved at the trial of any action begun by writ by the evidence of witnesses shall be proved by the examination of the witnesses orally and in open court.

Evidence by affidavit (O 38 r 2)

2.—(1) The Court may, at or before the trial of an action begun by writ, order that the affidavit of any witness may be read at the trial if in the circumstances of the case it thinks it reasonable so to order.

(2) An order under paragraph (1) may be made on such terms as to the filing and giving of copies of the affidavits and as to the production of the deponents for cross-examination as the Court thinks fit but, subject to any such terms and to any subsequent order of the Court, the deponents shall not be subject to cross-examination and need not attend the trial for the purpose.

(3) In any cause or matter begun by originating summons, originating motion or petition, and on any application made by summons or motion, evidence may be given by affidavit unless in the case of any such cause, matter or application any provision of these rules otherwise provides or the Court otherwise directs, but the Court may, on the application of any party, order the attendance for cross-examination of the person making any such affidavit, and where, after such an order has been made, the person in question does not attend, his affidavit shall not be used as evidence without the leave of the Court.

Exchange of witnesses' statements (O 38 r 2A)

(2) At any stage in any cause or matter the Court may, if it thinks fit for the purpose of disposing fairly and expeditiously of the cause or matter and saving costs, direct any party to serve on the other parties, on such terms as the Court shall think just, written statements of the oral evidence which the party intends to lead on any issues of fact to be decided at the trial.

(3) Directions given under paragraph (2) may—

(a) make different provision with regard to different issues of fact or different witnesses;

(b) require any written statement served to be signed by the intended witness;

(c) require that statements be filed with the Court.

(4) Subject to paragraph (6), where the party serving a statement under paragraph (2) does not call the witness to whose evidence it relates no other party may put the statement in evidence at the trial.

(5) Subject to paragraph (6) and unless the Court otherwise orders, where the party serving the statement does call such a witness at the trial—

(a) the party may not without the consent of the other parties or the leave of the Court lead evidence from that witness the substance of which is not included in the statement served, except in relation to new matters which have arisen in the course of the trial;

(b) the Court may, on such terms as it thinks fit, direct that the statement served, or part of it, shall stand as the evidence in chief of the witness or part of such evidence;

(c) whether or not the statement or any part of it is referred to during the evidence in chief of the witness, any party may put the statement or any part of it in cross-examination of that witness.

(6) Where any statement served is one to which the Civil Evidence Acts 1968 and 1972 apply, paragraphs (4) and (5) shall take effect subject to the provisions of those Acts and Parts III and IV of this Order. The service of a statement pursuant to a direction given under paragraph (2) shall not, unless expressly so stated by the party serving the same, be treated as a notice under the said Acts.

(7) Where a party fails to comply with a direction given under paragraph (2) he shall not be entitled to adduce evidence to which such direction related without the leave of the Court.

(8) Nothing in this rule shall deprive any party of his right to treat any communication as privileged or make admissible evidence otherwise inadmissible.

Evidence of particular facts (O 38 r 3)

3.—(1) Without prejudice to rule 2, the Court may, at or before the trial of any action, order that evidence of any particular fact shall be given at the trial in such manner as may be specified by the order.

(2) The power conferred by paragraph (1) extends in particular to ordering that evidence of any particular fact may be given at the trial—

    (a) by statement on oath of information or belief, or

    (b) by the production of documents or entries in books, or

    (c) by copies of documents or entries in books, or

    (d) in the case of a fact which is or was a matter of common knowledge either generally or in a particular district, by the production of a specified newspaper which contains a statement of that fact.

Limitation of expert evidence (O 38 r 4)

4. The Court may, at or before the trial of any action, order that the number of medical or other expert witnesses who may be called at the trial shall be limited as specified by the order.

Restrictions on adducing expert evidence (O 38 r 36)

36.—(1) Except with the leave of the Court or where all parties agree, no expert evidence may be adduced at the trial or hearing of any cause or matter unless the party seeking to adduce the evidence—

    (a) has applied to the Court to determine whether a direction should be given under rule 37, 38 or 41 (whichever is appropriate) and has complied with any direction given on the application, or

    (b) has complied with automatic directions taking effect under Order 25, rule 8 (1) *(b)*.

(2) Nothing in paragraph (1) shall apply in evidence which is permitted to be given by affidavit or shall affect the enforcement under any other provision of these Rules (except Order 45, rule 5) of a direction given under this part of this Order.

Direction that expert report be disclosed (O 38 r 37)

37. Where in any cause or matter an application is made under rule 36(1) in respect of oral expert evidence, then, unless the Court considers that there are special reasons for not doing so, it shall direct that the substance of the evidence be disclosed in the form of a written report or reports to such other parties and within such period as the Court may specify.

Meeting of experts (O 38 r 38)

38. In any cause or matter the Court may, if it thinks fit, direct that there be a meeting "without prejudice" of such experts within such periods before or after the disclosure of their reports as the Court may specify, for the purpose of identifying those parts of their evidence which are in issue. Where such a meeting takes place the experts may prepare a joint statement indicating those parts of their evidence on which they are, and those on which they are not, in agreement.

Bibliography

Brazier, M — Medicine, Patients and the Law, 1987. Penguin.

Capstick, B — Patient Complaints and Litigation, 1985. National Association of Public Health Authorities.

Giesen, D — International Medical Malpractice Law, 1988. Mohr and Martinus Nijhoff.

Jackson, R & Powell, J — Professional Negligence, 2nd edition. Sweet & Maxwell.

Kennedy, I & Grubb, J — Medical Law: Text and Materials, 1989. Butterworth.

Lewis, C — Medical Negligence, a Plaintiff's Guide, 1988. Cass.

Leahy-Taylor, J — The Doctor and Negligence, 1971. Pitman Medical.

McGregor, H — Damages, 15th edition, 1988. Sweet & Maxwell.

Nathan, P C & Barrowclough A R — Medical Negligence, 1957. Butterworths.

Nelson-Jones, R & Stewart, P — Product Liability: The New Law under the Consumer Protection Act 1987, 1987. Fourmat.

Index